American Farmers
and
The Rise of Agribusiness

Seeds of Struggle

American Farmers
and
The Rise of Agribusiness

Seeds of Struggle

Advisory Editors

AGRICULTURAL ORGANIZATION IN THE UNITED STATES

BY

EDWARD WIEST

ARNO PRESS
A New York Times Company
New York – 1975

Reprint Edition 1975 by Arno Press Inc.

Reprinted from a copy in
The University of Illinois Library

AMERICAN FARMERS AND THE RISE OF AGRIBUSINESS:
Seeds of Struggle
ISBN for complete set: 0-405-06760-7
See last pages of this volume for titles.

Manufactured in the United States of America

Library of Congress Cataloging in Publication Data

Wiest, Edward, 1878-
Agricultural organization in the United States.

(American farmers and the rise of agribusiness)
Reprint of the 1923 ed. published by the University of Kentucky, Lexington, which was issued as v. 2 of the University of Kentucky studies in economics and sociology.
1. Agricultural administration--United States. 2. United States. Dept. of Agriculture. 3. Agricultural societies--United States. 4. Agricultural education--United States. I. Title. II. Series. III. Series: Kentucky. University. Studies in economics and sociology ; v. 2.

S21.C9W66 1975 630'.6'073 74-30666
ISBN 0-405-06842-5

Agricultural Organization in the United States

Agricultural Organization in the United States

BY

Edward Wiest, A.M. Ph. D.,

Professor of Economics, University of Kentucky;
author of the "Butter Industry in the
United States"

With an Introduction by

Dwight Sanderson, Ph.D.,

Professor of Rural Social Organization, Cornell University

UNIVERSITY OF KENTUCKY

Lexington, Kentucky

April, 1923

To
M. S. W.

I am confident that no citizen of this country, in private or public life, who has an understanding of the work of the Department, or the handicaps under which our present-day agriculture is laboring, and of the national problems involved in maintaining supplies of food and raw materials sufficient for our constantly increasing population, will fail to give his sympathetic support to measures which promise increased strength to the nation in its most basic industry, the foundation of all other industries, agricultur.—*E. T. Meridith, 1920 Yearbook, p. 84.*

Why not tell the farmer the truth and advise him if he would escape the consequences of another such disaster, he should organize; organize, Mr. President, not to be the plaything or the instrument of designing politicians, but organize for an intelligent investigation and pursuit of economies; organize for a cooperative marketing of his product; organize, if it may seem desirable, for the cooperative purchase of his requirements; organize for an intelligent understanding of the source and volume of demand for farm products.— *Carter Glass in a speech on the floor of the Senate, January 16 and 17, 1922.*

Preface

The purpose of this book is to present a scientific and an unbiased analysis of the forms, functions, causes, and effects of public and private agricultural organization in America. The author believes that a separate course in colleges and universities in the field of agricultural economics should be devoted to this subject. The public is generally ignorant of the work of our agricultural institutions, and even college students majoring in agricultural economics fail to secure a thorough and comprehensive knowledge of our organized facilities erected for the purpose of improving agriculture in all its phases. The organization of federal and state departments of agriculture and their functions, the organization of agricultural colleges with their extension departments, the experiment stations, agricultural education under the Smith-Hughes law, farmers' organizations, breed associations, and the relation of these parts to one another and to the public, constitute a body of knowledge with which the college students should become acquainted. Certainly students majoring in agricultural economics and especially students taking the teacher-training courses in agricultural education should be familiar with the facts of agricultural organization and its underlying principles. The whole field of agricultural economics is still somewhat wanting in body, and it can well afford, therefore, to add to the specialized courses of cooperation, rural credit, etc., one dealing with organized efforts for the control of the destiny of American agriculture. It is a course whose content presupposes considerable economics and political science and should, therefore, be given in junior and senior years.

Where no separate course is given in agricultural organization the study will afford valuable collateral reading for use in other courses. Considerable historical matter showing the development of our present organization is given and this will never lose its value. Life is dynamic and changes are always in progress; but the changes that are being made from year to year are related to what has gone before and are after all not wholly dissimilar from their precedents.

In the preparation of this study the treatment of cooperation in a formal way was intentionally omitted because this subject is extensively developed in separate textbooks usually entitled, "The Marketing of Farm Products." Marketing is only discussed from the point of view of policy on the part of both public and private agricultural organizations. Federal and state departments of agriculture, quite recently, have rapidly developed an extensive machinery which investigates marketing problems, demonstrates correct marketing methods, provides a market news service, and regulates certain commercial evils. The activity of farmers' organizations in the field of cooperative marketing is set forth with a view to point out mistakes and achievements.

Considerable attention could be given to the sociological and psychological aspects of agricultural organization if it were not for the fact that the inclusion of these phases of the subject would make the study too large and probably too extensive for text book purposes. The social aspect has not been wholly neglected, but so far as causes of organization are concerned the emphasis has been laid primarily upon the economic motive.

Much more space has been given to the United States Department of Agriculture than to state departments or boards of agriculture. The reason for this is not only because the federal department is a great organization and performs functions that affect the welfare of every citizen of the country, but because a repetition of the discussion of all the functions of departmental organization under the head of state departments would be useless.

Organizers of farmers' organizations should find in this study a practical handbook. It points out to him the virtues and shortcomings of both previous and existing organizations and shows him how his private association is related to the public at large and to the state and federal agricultural organization.

The legislator may see in it a survey of forms of departments of agriculture and their history as well as a presentation of ideal public organization. It is hoped that suggestions are made that will enable him to formulate positive opinions as to the construction of a state department and as to the character of functions that should be committed to both federal and state departments of agriculture.

The book is also recommended to the public in general, and especially to the farmers. This is an age of organization. Various economic groups are fortifying their respective positions by organized effort. What is the effect of such group action upon the individual? Does it mean class war? Just how will class demands be satisfied? These and other questions are of interest to all economic groups. The progressive farmer must know the objectives of private organization if his efforts are to count for anything. He must also acquaint himself with all facilities of public organization if he would make the best use of his opportunities.

The author wishes to acknowledge the ready assistance given by officials of the United States Department of Agriculture, of state departments, and of farmers' organizations. He is especially indebted to several of his colleagues for reading portions of the manuscript. Professor M. C. James, Professor of Agricultural Education, read the chapters relating to education; Dr. C. A. Shull, Professor of Botany, now at Chicago University, read the part dealing with the Plant Industry Bureau; and Professor O. B. Jesness, formerly of the Bureau of Agricultural Economics of the United States Department of Agriculture, and now Professor of Marketing, read all the chapters dealing with the federal department. Professor S. E. Leland, who is associated with the author in the Department of Economics and Sociology, assisted in the preparation of the appendix which tabulates the character of state agricultural departmental organization. Professor W. S. Anderson, of the Department of Animal Husbandry, assisted in the collection of facts and bibliography necessary for the preparation of the chapter dealing with breed associations. Miss Margaret I. King, Librarian, was untiring in her efforts to make literature available.

The author is indebted in a special way to Dr. Dwight Sanderson, of Cornell University, not only for reading the manuscript and making valuable criticisms, but also for suggesting a number of persons to whom certain parts of the manuscript should be submitted for perusal before printing, and for being interested in the study to the extent of writing an introduction. In compliance with his suggestions certain chapters were sent to a number of men competent to pass upon particular parts of the study, and as a result the author received very helpful criticisms. For assistance of this character special acknowledgment is due Dean Eugene Davenport, of the University of Illinois, for reading the chapter dealing with the Land Grant Colleges; to Dr. A. C. True, of the United States Department of Agriculture, for reading the chapters dealing with States Relation Service, Land Grant Colleges, Experiment Stations and the Extension Service; to Dr. E. W. Allen, also of the Department of Agriculture, for reading the chapter on the Experiment Stations; to Dean Bradford Knapp, of the University of Arkansas, and to Professor M. C. Burritt, of Cornell University, for reading the chapter on the Extension Service; to Dr. Raymond A. Pearson, President of Iowa State College of Agriculture and Mechanic Arts, and to Hon. Fred Rasmussen, Secretary of Agriculture of Pennsylvania, for reading the chapter dealing with State Departments of Agriculture; to Professor G. A. Works, of Cornell University, and Professor A. V. Storm, of the University of Minnesota, for reading the chapter dealing with Agricultural Education under the Smith-Hughes law; to Mr. J. Clyde Marquis, of the U. S. Department of Agriculture, for reading and editing the chapter dealing with the Bureau of Agricultural Economics; to Mr. W. C. Lansdon, national organizer, for reading the chapter dealing with the Farmers' Union; to Mr. John A. McSparran, master of the Pennsylvania State Grange, for reading the chapters dealing with the Grange; and to Prof. M. L. Wilson, of Montana State College, for reading the chapters dealing with the Alliance and miscellaneous farmers' organizations.

EDWARD WIEST.

University of Kentucky,
Lexington, Kentucky,
April, 1923.

Introduction

Agricultural organization in the United States has grown with such rapidity in the last quarter century that but few persons who have not been leaders of the movement have any adequate conception of the multiform functions of our public and private agricultural agencies and their relations to each other. The growth of governmental departments for giving assistance to agriculture, both national and state, has been both a result and a cause of the rapid organization of agricultural interests in local and regional associations.

Primarily the present movement in agricultural organization has been made possible by better means of communication. When farmers were dependent upon horse-drawn vehicles and mud roads, organization was difficult or impossible; but with the automobile, improved roads, rural free delivery, the telephone and now radio-telegraphy, the handicaps of time and distance have been largely removed. During this same period business and industry have been rapidly and thoroughly organized into large corporations and sales agencies, and labor has been compelled to organize so that it might bargain effectively with its employers. With an increasing intimate knowledge of these movements through their reading of the city newspapers and magazines and their more frequent contact with the cities, it was inevitable that farmers should see the advantages of organization. The increasing complexity of the problem of marketing is responsible for the rapid growth of farmers' cooperative selling associations, and although the author has not entered into a discussion of cooperative organizations their development has been one of the primary aims of most of the farmers' organizations which he discusses. Although the above conditions have been the chief stimuli to agricultural organization, it would have proceeded much more slowly had it not been for the rapid growth of the extension service of the agricultural colleges and the U. S. Department of Agriculture which, as the author points out, has had a unique role in the agricultural movement.

The literature on agricultural organization in the United States is widely scattered and is not easily available without considerable research. Dr. Wiest has, therefore, done a very real service in bringing together into one book a concise statement of the history, organization and purposes of public and private agricultural organizations. There is a real need for such a book, particularly for two classes of readers. One of the chief functions of our agricultural colleges is the training of agricultural leaders, but at the present time very few of them offer courses which give their students any adequate understanding of agricultural organization and of its history and purposes. Here and there such courses are being attempted and now that a text book is available it should develop rapidly. The other class who will find the book useful consists of legislators, editors and men in public life who seek a better understanding of this subject. The legislative activities of the American Farm Bureau Federation, its promotion of national cooperative selling associations or federations, the immense losses incurred by American farmers due to a too rapid deflation of credit after the war and the consequent effect on industry in general, as well as the rise and power of the agricultural bloc in Congress, have brought the problems of American agriculture to public attention as never before. In spite of this it is to be regretted that many of our leading city dailies and weekly journals dealing with public affairs seem to have little understanding of agricultural organization. They devote much space and bold headlines to the Non-Partisan League, but they fail to understand the more significant movements in agricultural organization. The labor movement and the relations of capital and labor are widely discussed but as yet we lack any medium for a serious consideration of agricultural policies. This book will, therefore, be of value to those who appreciate the importance of the agricultural industry in our national life, but who from the force of circumstances have not come into contact with it and whose viewpoint has naturally been influenced by their urban environment.

As he has indicated, his consideration of agricultural organization is chiefly from the economic viewpoint, although he has given as much attention as possible to the aims, purposes and methods of the various organizations discussed. But we are to have a real appreciation of farmers' organization if we must know more of their psychology. We need studies of farmers' movements which will give us an understanding of their social attitudes, of how rural opinion is formed and manipulated, similar to the brilliant work of Robert H. Hoxie and Carleton W. Parker, which has done so much to give us a better appreciation of the spirit and motives of trade unions. Here is a field in which important contributions may be made which will be of very great value to agricultural organizations, but for which a knowledge of their mechanism and economic basis, such as Dr. Wiest has given us, is essential.

Whether or not we agree with his position in all cases, Dr. Wiest's evaluation of methods and principles of organization should stimulate thought and discussion. Such questions as whether state commissioners of agriculture should be appointed by a governor or by a non-partisan board or whether they should be subject to some type of civil service and have an indefinite tenure so that they would be chosen and retained in office for their ability and efficiency as is a member of a university faculty; whether the American Farm Bureau Federation is wise in attempting to act as a mouthpiece for the American farmer with regard to national legislation or whether it might better confine its activities to an educational and economic program; these and similar questions of public policy require a broader and more thoroughgoing consideration.

In developing our agricultural policies we should take heed of all that science, economics, history and social organization can teach. Dr. Wiest has given us the first comprehensive treatise on agricultural organization in the United States from this standpoint.

DWIGHT SANDERSON.

Cornell University,
Ithaca, N. Y.,
April, 1923.

Table of Contents

INTRODUCTORY

PART II—PRIVATE ORGANIZATION

CHAPTER I

PUBLIC VERSUS PRIVATE AGRICULTURAL ORGANIZATION

A Fundamental Anglo-Saxon Characteristic.—Students of political science and public finance have often noted that it is a fundamental characteristic of the Teutonic people to conduct many of its social projects through voluntary or private association. Professor Young says, "the Teuton and especially the Anglo-Saxon, is given to tolerance and cooperation with his countrymen in every department of life. Teamwork is almost instinctive with him, he organizes clubs, committees and societies and devotes himself to their purposes with a readiness, skill and persistence that mark him as a special race type. Whether it be in affairs of the church, the shop, or the athletic field, the Saxon has through long centuries developed traditions and habits of joint action."[1] The farm population was somewhat slow to organize and proceeded at first in a desultory way; but it, too, has learned the advantage of teamwork, so that today the principle of private association as an important means of satisfying human wants is well-nigh universal among the Anglo-Saxon people. Roman political philosophy influenced considerably political organization in Germany and most other parts of continental Europe. If the people of Germany suffer from bureaucracy and if their railroads are government owned, they have also given to the world a model rural cooperative credit system. They have also labor organizations and trade associations. The Danes have developed rural cooperation to a greater degree than any other people, while the English excel in cooperation among consumers. According to Professor Young, "in America group action by associations, both business and civic, is more widespread than in any other country of the world."

There are a great variety of associations, all of which may be conceived of as using direct and indirect methods to

[1] *Vide* Young, *the New American Government and its Work,* p. 575.

carry out their objects. The National Association of Manufacturers, the numerous chambers of commerce, the American Bankers' Association, the American Federation of Labor, the Grange, the Farmers' Union and like organizations operate from two angles. In a direct way they bring their influence to bear upon their members, and through appeal to Congress and state legislatures they seek to secure benefits for their respective groups in an indirect way. The same may be said of such associations that have to do primarily with the improvement of social conditions. It should be recognized that such group action lies at the very heart of democracy. The individual can only secure his rights by joining himself to his group and by supporting the demands of the majority of his group. It is a principle that has been recognized as entirely legitimate when used by chambers of commerce, manufacturers' associations, and bankers' associations in an attempt to secure favorable legislation providing no covert and insidious methods are used. Concerted effort for directly improving conditions in these fields, providing no monopolistic advantage is aspired to, has likewise been sanctioned. Group action among the agricultural class in America has only taken form during the last half of the nineteenth century, and its newness is causing alarm in some quarters. But such alarm is wholly without warrant; for group action among the farmers is only balancing the scale. The time was when group action was considerably one-sided. There was concerted effort in urban centers, but none in the country. Now we may speak of an organized agriculture, and the effect of the universal application of the principle of private association will be to give each individual in each group his rights. In addition to the efforts made to benefit members of groups directly, it is the American way of creating public sentiment in favor of various projects. The process will not lead to class war. The Anglo-Saxon people are sportsman-like; they submit to the rule of the majority; and the goal of group action is fairness and justice to all. No particular group can go farther than sanctioned by composite public sentiment. Capital long ago learned this lesson, and only recently organized labor has come to realize that it, too, is kept within reasonable bounds by the overwhelming force of public opinion. Each group, including the farmers, will help henceforth to create public opinion, but all will bow to its commands.

Basic Principles Underlying Public and Private Initiative. —While the American people use a great deal of private association to realize their aims and purposes in life, they also use a great deal of public organization. A study of agricultural organization would be quite incomplete if it were limited to the field of private association. The combined federal and state agricultural organization is a great service agency that constitutes one of the mainstays of present-day American civilization. In the field of agriculture we are making large use of the government, and to leave this mode of action out of a study that deals with organizational methods for improving rural conditions would portray a picture that would cause our habits of private association to appear to be entirely too prominent. Both fields are therefore studied, and it will be well at the outset to examine basic principles underlying wise public and private initiative.

In 1776 Adam Smith in his *Wealth of Nations* laid down general principles concerning the functions that a state should rightfully perform. These have now become clasic and run as follows: "According to the system of natural liberty, the sovereign has only three duties to attend to: first, the duty of protecting the society from the violence and invasion of other independent societies; secondly, the duty of protecting, as far as possible, every member of the society from the injustice or oppression of every other member of it, or the duty of establishing an exact administration of justice; and, thirdly, the duty of erecting and maintaining certain public works and certain public institutions, which it can never be for the advantage of any individual or small number of individuals to erect and maintain; because the profit could never repay the expense to any individual or small number of individuals, though it may frequently do much more than repay it to a great society."[1] We may lay it down then as a general principal that any function of fundamental social importance may prop-

[1] *Vide* Adam Smith, *Wealth of Nations*, end of chapter IX, book IV.

erly be performed by the government. "This is, in fact," says Seligman, "the criterion which distinguishes them from ordinary occupations—the existence of a sufficiently widespread common interest and public importance to warrant their assumption by the government authorities."[1] There are certain wants that can only be satisfied through compulsory collective action. There are others that can only be satisfied by collective action but not necessarily governmental or compulsory. They may be either satisfied through private and voluntary association or through the government. Still others must also be satisfied through collective action, but should be realized only through private and voluntary association. It therefore follows that in the field of practical politics one encounters a twilight zone within which social activities are advocated by some to be undertaken by the government and by others by the people. Certain it is the more voluntary action in the twilight zone the less need for public organization. One may lay down with considerable ease general and abstract principles governing public and private initiative but it is sometimes difficult to decide just which is the better course when a particular activity is under consideration. In the following study reference is made here and there indicating why various objects should be carried out by public or private enterprise. In the field of agricultural organization much light is thrown upon the problem by classifying all activities according to functions. Some of these functions are clearly governmental and others just as clearly private while others fall into the twilight zone. A careful and complete analysis, however, leaves only a few objects in doubt, and enables one to form more definite opinions concerning them.

Functions of Public Agricultural Organization.—In subsequent chapters public agricultural organization is largely discussed from the point of view of functions. The chapter headed State Departments of Agriculture is concluded with a section dealing with ideal state departmental organization. A more or less detailed discussion is there given of the ideal place of existing and well-established types of work. Also in

---

[1] *Vide* his *Principles of Economics*, 6th edition, p. 618.

other chapters there appear statements pointing out why certain projects should be carried on by public enterprise. It will, therefore, only be necessary to make a general statement here. The functions of public agricultural organization include investigational and statistical work, experimentation and research, education and demonstration, service and regulation. To these may be added the function of suggesting needed legislation to Congress and state legislatures.

Probably the most general and insistent demand of agricultural societies during the first half of the nineteenth century was that the government establish a department of agriculture whose chief duty was to be the collection and dissemination of agricultural statistics. Great results were anticipated not only from the point of view of production, but also from the point of view of marketing the crops and other farm products. It is a function that private enterprise does not undertake in a comprehensive way, and one that requires the force of the executive branch of the federal and state governments to perform successfully. The function includes the collection and dissemination of information concerning crops, markets, climatology, various economic and social practices, as well as data related to scientific problems the collection of which, however, is a process more correctly classified as research. Accurate information concerning prospective yields of crops and existing supplies forms the basis for forecasting prices, and is the means through which violent price fluctuations throughout the year are largely eliminated. It has a widespread social interest and should only be entrusted to a public agency. The collection of climatological data is not one that can be made to yield a profit, and yet it is one of great practical and scientific importance. The location of certain manufactories, the use of certain construction materials, the use of certain types of farming, are all dependent upon a knowledge of the climatology of the country. Home seekers, pleasure seekers and health seekers, also find climatological data of practical value. The scientist finds it of great theoretic value. The collection and publication of market information is somewhat new, but a detailed study of what the federal and state departments are doing in this field will convince one that it, too, is vested with a large public interest and should be performed by public agencies. It has only recently become apparent how much economic waste is being caused by lack of proper organization to provide market information.

Experimentation and research in agriculture are also functions from which private initiative holds itself aloof. Nowhere in the world was anything done in agricultural experimentation of any consequence until the middle of the nineteenth century. In Germany, under the influence of the University of Leipsic, an agricultural experiment station was established in 1851, but in America this important activity was postponed until the early '80s, when state and private institutions here and there and in only a limited way began to work on practical agricultural problems. The real beginning was not made until 1887, when federal aid provided for the establishment of at least one experiment station in each state and territory. The reason for the absence of private experimentation in agriculture is that profits are not sufficiently inviting. In the field of industry patents bestowing at least a seventeen-year monopoly covering the invention of mechanical devices and the discovery of chemical processes, are granted, and this is a spur to call forth both individual effort and organized effort on the part of large corporations. Best results on the farm are obtained where operations are carried on in a decentralized and diversified manner, and this absence of concentration so conspicuous in industry is also a factor discouraging the undertaking of any experimentation along with farming conducted for a living.

The function of education and demonstration is varied and includes instruction at the land-grant colleges, farmers' institutes, the movable school, the demonstration train, vocational education under the Smith-Hughes Law and the cooperative agricultural extension work. Private agricultural organization has done a great service to the country in educating the rural population in the art of farming. Clubs and agricultural societies in a scattered way, from the beginning to the middle of the nineteenth century and since then in a more comprehensive way, have existed primarily for educational purposes. The Grange probably stands preeminent among the older farmers' organizations in America as an agency spreading the gospel of practical agricultural education. The Jewish Agricultural and Industrial Aid Society in its limited way is also very definitely committed to an active educational program. The Farmers' Union and others are also doing good work, while the Farm Bureau Federation is positively friendly toward the cooperative extension service. In recent years railroads have entered the field of agricultural extension with a view to building up a prosperous farming population along their lines in the hope that a considerable increase in freight would follow. Banks and chambers of commerce representing the business men of the city have likewise aided boys' and girls' club work and other forms of agricultural extension work with a view to increase the purchasing power of their clientele. All these efforts, however, were limited to restricted areas, and it was not until the state agricultural departments and agricultural colleges, aided by the United States Department of Agriculture, systematically organized county farmers' institutes that an approach toward reaching all parts of the country with scientific agriculture, was effected. While the farmers' institute remains as a useful agency, it has, however, been found wanting. It does not sufficiently reach every spot of the country, and fails to carry to the door of the farmer a scientific truth in a way that will compel him to incorporate it in his scheme of farming. In order that systematic and regular instruction in agriculture based on well-established scientific principles could be offered to every farmer throughout the length and breadth of the land the cooperative extension service was created. An extended discussion giving reasons why this work should be undertaken by public enterprise or why it should be fostered by the federal government instead of leaving it wholly to the respective commonwealths, could be entered upon. Suffice it to say here that it is the duty of the state, and by that is meant the national government, to eradicate all centers of ignorance and to eliminate as far as possible all contributing causes of poverty. Backward centers are breeding places of crime and disease, and a menace to the solidarity of the nation; and because of prevailing poverty and consequent low standards of living such communities are unable to contribute to the support of the government. Private initiative has been dilatory, inconstant, and restricted in its field of operations with respect to agricultural extension work. From the point of view of increased public revenue as well as from that of improved social welfare the work can only be comprehensibly carried on through the means of public organization.

The work of college instruction in scientific agriculture does not differ very materially in the benefit it bestows upon society from those flowing from the more practical agricultural education. While a very much smaller percentage of the country's population can be given a college education than can be provided with a vocational type of education, it is nevertheless of the very highest importance that the higher education be made available to all who may aspire to attain it. Upon it depends not only the continuity of our present civilization, but also very largely its advancement into higher realms of achievement. The one great service performed by higher education is the furnishing of leadership of all kinds to the people in all walks of life. In agricultural college instruction the process of training leaders for agricultural communities is now recognized as a very pressing function of the agricultural college. In order that vocational education may be taught there must be teacher-training departments in universities where the necessary suppy of teachers may be created. Other demands for scientifically trained men must be satisfied by the agricultural college. There is in fact a very direct relationship between college agricultural instruction and the general education known as agricultural extension work. If it be admitted then that it is the duty of the state to provide certain types of vocational education to its citizens it cannot be denied that it is also the duty of the state to provide college education through which must come the leadership for teaching the vocational subjects. Altogether apart from the relationship between college instruction and vocational instruction there are again the great social benefits that come to every community to which is sent the product of the institution of higher learning. The land-grant college was not established with a view to link it up with a system of vocational education or on the theory that it is the duty of the state to prepare each citizen directly to earn a livelihood, but rather on the theory that it is the duty of the state to provide leadership for the development of its agricultural and industrial resources. The original land-grant colleges served as nuclei around which great universities have been built up, the center of which in most cases is the liberal arts college. This is what Morrill, under whose leadership the law establishing them was passed by Congress, wanted them to be. It would take us too far afield to enter upon a discussion as to the merits of plans to have the federal government provide still larger funds for higher education. What has been done by the federal government so far in this field is altogether justified, and from a study of the history of the land-grant colleges it is apparent that they have rendered immeasurable benefits to the various states as well as to the nation as a whole. It is not unlikely that those states that stand at present at the bottom of educational progress would without the land-grant college act have today no institution of higher learning worthy of the name. They would have been left far behind the march of progress. Their agricultural and industrial resources would not have been developed to the same extent not to mention other beneficient influences that would not have been brought to bear upon the people in those states. It is desirable to have as little federal control as possible; but just as it has become plain that it is the part of wisdom to appropriate state funds to counties for educational purposes, it will become more and more evident that it will be to the best interests of the nation as a whole to provide federal funds to the states.

The function of service may be illustrated by reference to weather, hurricane, and river and flood forecasts of the Weather Bureau. Both hurricane and river and flood forecasts are comparable to the lighthouse service from the point of view of service to commerce. Weather forecasts also have their economic value. While there are some private forecasting agencies, it is too large an undertaking for private initiative to establish observing stations all over the country for the purpose of collecting the necessary meteorological data upon which to make reliable forecasts. The people would not subscribe to the service in sufficient numbers to yield profits to the enterprise, and yet like the lighthouse service it is of immense benefit to the country at large. This function then must also be conducted by public organization.

The regulatory function of the state and federal departments of agriculture has grown to be of immense importance. It involves the inspection of dairy products, of animals at packing establishments, of various food products, of cattle and plants for the purpose of eradicating disease, etc.; it involves also the quarantining of sections of the country as well as foreign countries suffering from diseased animal and plant life. In order to bridge the twilight zone of administration existing because of our peculiar division of powers between the states and the federal government it involves joint action based upon agreements entered into between the state and federal agricultural departments. Altogether this function of public agricultural organization is very large, and is sometimes left out of consideration when the United States Department of Agriculture is viewed from the standpoint of a service and educational agency. It is a police duty and touches every citizen of the country. After it has been fully decided that a certain activity should be regulated, it is at once recognized that all private interests must submit to public control. Just how the activity shall be regulated frequently raises difficult problems. The evolution of an efficient administrative system is traced in the subsequent study of public agricultural organization. In connection with state departmental organization the "state board of agriculture" based upon agricultural societies or controlled by them is condemned and the centralized department is recommended as ideal. The time was when the production and marketing of agricultural products required no regulation, and it made little difference to the people at large whether or not the other functions were wholly determined by the agricultural groups. The great industrial changes and the rise of large urban centers have, however, changed also relationships between the agricultural and other classes and necessitated a large degree of regulation. The whole population is now dependent upon the quality of service rendered by the farmers. It is extremely important that adequate steps be taken to prevent the spread of epidemics in cities, and to establish other fair and just relationships between city and country. Thus the demand of organized agriculture that it be exclusively allowed to control state departments of agriculture can no longer be sanctioned. They must take their place alongside of other executive departments of government and be subject to the will of the whole body politic.

The growth of public agricultural organization, especially the United States Department of Agriculture, is remarkable for the development of its manifold activities. Its rapid development is all the more remarkable when it is recalled that its establishment was postponed more than half a century from the time it was first recommended to Congress by Washington. We were for a long time dominated by an extreme *laissez-faire* economic policy and by a "states' rights" political theory. When a real beginning was finally made its growth was rapid. In the study of this development it is interesting to note the particular forces that are responsible for suggesting the various activities that were added from time to time. It is true that a great many came from farmers' organizations, from humane societies, from the railroads and from business, but it is also true that a large number of legislative recommendations are made every year by the department of agriculture to Congress or to the state legislature as the case may be without any suggestion from outside forces. Much legislation is conceived by the personnel of the department. Conferences are often held with groups who are interested. In fact such conferences are sometimes of the nature of developing favorable sentiment concerning proposed projects. Conceiving legislation on its own initiative, drafting legislation in response to demands from the outside, and recommending that it be enacted into law, constitute another important function of the department of agriculture.

The Functions of Private Agricultural Organization.— The earliest private organization consisted of the general agricultural society. Clubs and county and state organizations were formed. Specialization in agriculture caused the general society to undergo a differentiation. As a result the horticultural society made its appearance early and other societies were later organized along special lines. Thus there are the various livestock, field crop, truck, and fair associations. Since the middle of the nineteenth century there have come into being the newer farmers' organizations. They were born amid a veritable social upheaval. Great organizations developed, the largest of which was the Alliance. It gathered unto itself a membership of 3,000,000 within a few years, and abruptly destroyed its usefulness as an agricultural society by adopting partisan politics. The Grange was the first to organize, and its position seems to be secure. Its policy will, however, have to be somewhat more progressive along the lines of cooperation if it would continue to grow steadily and compete with other organizations.

There are four general functions that private organization performs. They may be stated to be the formulation of national agricultural policies, the improvement of the economic status of the agricultural class largely through the development of cooperation, aiding in the popularization of scientific agricultural education, and the creation of an improved social medium for the rural people. In chapters dealing with private organization the social features of farmers' organizations are discussed, and it is there pointed out that to make rural districts attractive, the people of all ages must be allowed to satisfy the social instinct. Varied amusement and entertainment must be furnished; and what is even more important, the people must have the opportunity to express their respective abilities in various roles. Frequently the only activity that satisfies is of an intellectual character. Literary and scientific discussions must be provided. Farmers' organizations through their local meetings have done much in the way of creating a wholesome social medium for the people of the country. The general introduction of the automobile will add considerably to their social life. A study of the various farm organizations will disclose a marked difference as to the emphasis placed upon the social feature; some in fact have not any. The same is true concerning popular agricultural education. The Farmers' Union and the Grange encourage the discussion of standardized topics. Lecture material is made available for all local organizations. Special lecture hours are set aside for the discussion of subjects of practical interest. The specialized agricultural societies also play an important role in educating their members with respect to the particular farm products with which they are concerned. It was stated above that from the point of view of the country as a whole the educational efforts of private agricultural organization were too limited geographically, and lacked also too much in trained local leaders, to entrust the popularization of agricultural science wholly to it. Farmers' organizations are doing a great work especially in progressive sections of the country, but to insure permanency and the dissemination of scientific agriculture in all parts of the country the cooperative agricultural extensive service had to be created.

Considerable difference obtains among farmers' organizations as to the degree of cooperation they respectively foster. The Grange for many years after the '70s almost abandoned the cooperative movement. It is only recently that it has again become a live issue of the order. The Farmers' Union makes cooperation its principal *raison d'etre*, while the Farmers' Equity Union is virtually only a business association inasmuch as it organizes local unions only to establish cooperative exchanges. It is through cooperation that the farmers are planning largely to improve their economic status. The goal is to eliminate unnecessary middlemen and take their profit. Ultimately it is the plan to link up directly with the consumer. In the history of farm organizations considerable improvement in business methods is apparent. Successes are more general and a more thoroughgoing and more extensive system of cooperation among farmers seems imminent. In certain lines it may go to the extent of developing temporary monopolies, but, as explained in the last chapter, it can never become a public menace.

An important function performed by private organization is the formulation of a progressive agricultural policy. As stated before agricultural policies are not conceived by farmers' organizations alone. The most comprehensive effort at popular agricultural education ever attempted in America, for instance, was promoted by Dr. S. A. Knapp of the United

States Department of Agriculture, who introduced the cooperative extension service. There are always impartial and sympathetic reformers associated with agricultural colleges, farm journals, and now and then with other interests, who lend their support to the advancement of agriculture. They help to formulate a national agricultural policy. But the one outstanding fact, that unless farmers are organized many of their demands go unheeded by legislatures and Congress, must be recognized. Leadership from the point of view of urging the enactment of political issues can only come from the farmers themselves. A tariff favorable to the agricultural class can only be secured through organized effort. It is a kind of tug of war in which various economic groups are concerned. The appointment of a secretary of agriculture who is favorable to the farming interests in the administration of the United States Department of Agriculture is likely to be made only when the chief executive is confronted with a display of organized power. Private organized agriculture maintains a definite relationship not only with the federal department of agriculture, but with the state departments as well. In some states this amounts to control. As already stated agriculture is now subject to considerable regulation and concerns all classes of citizens. Complete control over state departments of agriculture by the agricultural group is, therefore, making too large use of its organized power. However, if moderation is exercised, and if no more is done than to exercise the influence so far exerted upon the United States Department of Agriculture, private organization renders a real service to public agricultural organization. There is danger that government bureaus become too far removed from the people. Germany has been suffering from bureaucracy. Powers opposed to the free exercise of the will of the people may develop within bureaus and check progress or start a movement that will cause ultimate trouble. If the general policies of the United States Department of Agriculture are partially controlled by private forces there is no danger of developing bureaucracy in that branch of the executive government. Dr. Hadley in stating his opposition to a bill proposing the establishment of a federal department of education says: "All the great pieces of progress of the last century were done in opposition to the national incubus of a centralized bureau." In the field of agricultural progress it must be recognized that private organization has done much to pull public organization to advanced mileposts, and that it has achieved progress in other ways; but a study of both public and private aspects of agricultural organization surely gives plently of evidence showing "that great pieces of progress" were also initiated by the Department of Agriculture, and that Dr. Hadley's statement is, therefore, entirely too sweeping.

Under the head of private agricultural organization special mention should be made of the function performed by breed associations. These associations have achieved marvelous results in the improvement of livestock. Their organization is a product of the last half of the nineteenth century, and under their direction more rapid progress has been made in the improvement of livestock than during the entire previous history of animal breeding. They receive no public aid and constitute a form of organization that thrives best as a private enterprise. The motive of organization, that of profits to the breeders, guarantees continuity of existence to breed associations; and inasmuch as the interests of their members and society run parallel, the improvement of livestock may well be left to private initiative.

The Field of Public and Private Agricultural Organization.—From what has already been said it is very obvious that in the field of agricultural progress there is a large body of facts and principles that can only be properly comprehended when studied from the point of view of organization. There is a history of agricultural organization running parallel with our political and economic traditions. Our pioneer status from colonial days down to past the middle of the nineteenth century demanded that efforts be made to import animal and plant life. The idea to organize for the purpose of improving agriculture or increasing productivity through the education of the rural people in practical agriculture was conceived and first applied in a very limited way during the latter part of the eighteenth century. The plan to provide public organization to foster this educational process appears to have been initiated by England and transmitted to this country through correspondence with George Washington. Efforts were made by him and also by others later to establish a federal department of agriculture, but our political and economic theories would not permit the adoption of the suggestion. Private organization was, therefore, wholly left to itself, and its attention to secure the aid of public organization or in some cases only public funds was soon diverted to the state government. As early as 1820 state boards of agriculture were organized. From this time to past the middle of the nineteenth century we had a kind of semi-public state department, but after the 70's the centralized department made its appearance mainly in the South at first and gradually finding favor in the East, and now in the majority of the states of the Union. The coming of the regulatory function had much to do with centralizing departments, although in some states where there is even considerable industrial activity and where the regulatory function is therefore important the old state board under the control of agricultural societies remains. During the first half of the nineteenth century considerable progress was made in the development of agriculutral societies primarily for educational purposes. These continued to demand the establishment of a federal department, agricultural colleges, and experiment stations. The first two objects were achieved in 1862 at a time when the strongest "states' rights" element had withdrawn from Congress. Just before the Civil War there began a new movement among the farmers. It was occasioned by industrial changes. The new and improved transportation facilities created new possibilities and greater advantages for the farmers providing, however, they were not asked to pay exorbitant prices to have their products hauled to the eastern markets or were not exploited in any other way. The movement began to show its head before the Civil War, but was quickly cut off by the necessity to concentrate all energies upon the ensuing conflict. Soon after the close of the war the movement was resumed and a series of conventions were held in the West and South, and then the more permanent farmers' organizations came to the surface. These had altogether a new purpose as their main object of organization. The economic status of the farmers as a class was now to be exalted through organized effort. The old private organization continued and stood in close relation to state public organization. The new organization adopted some of the aims and purposes of the older type of societies, but organically stood entirely separate from public organization.

Thus a brief historical statement discloses at once an exceedingly important content to which the student of economics is rarely introduced, even though special attention is devoted to the more narrow field of agricultural economics. The theory of both private and public agricultural organization has been almost wholly neglected by the economist or political scientist, and yet in public finance it was found necessary long ago in order that the whole field of finance might be surveyed and that problems of reform could be discussed in their entirety to study state tax departments and such parts of the United States Treasury as perform fiscal functions. The student of political science in a study of structural government finds that to go into all the movements associated with the creation of state departments and other detailed forms of public organization would carry him too far afield, and yet the whole program of rural economic and social betterment everywhere touches public organization and can only be fully comprehended by a complete survey of all modes of improvement. Such facts as pertain to agricultural organization should therefore be gathered up and treated separately. In the field of labor also a detailed study of types of labor organization and their aims and purposes has been forced upon the student of economics by the great struggle between capital and labor. The farmers for a time thought that their interests were identical with those of labor, and, therefore, during the early history of organized agriculture common cause was made with labor. Organized agriculture is, however, becoming disillusioned, and is rapidly differentiating itself from other economic groups. It is a movement with an interesting history and a great future, and is worthy of separate and intensive study. Only in this way may a sympathetic attitude toward the great agricultural class be required.

The field of public and private agricultural organization is to be differentiated from a study of cooperative marketing. This subject is only touched insofar as organizational efforts have been put forth to improve marketing conditions. Historically the particular marketing principles advanced by various farmers' organizations are presented. Other historic and current aims and purposes are also chronicled and their respective merits briefly discussed.

The Ambition of Organization.—No social institution can long endure unless it aims to satisfy certain fundamental wants. Thus the family, the state, the church, educational systems, employers' associations, commercial associations, labor and farmers' organizations, all have important functions to perform and exist because of benefits bestowed upon their respective members. The fundamental purpose that brings an institution into being sometimes disappears as was the case with the craft and merchant gilds. When this happens, unless a new large purpose is found, the organization will ultimately die. Society is dividing itself into groups not to wage war but to settle differences through the use of courts of arbitration and conciliation. Farmers' organizations fulfill a great need, and unless we adopt state socialism they will have permanent existence.

The very essence or soul of a farmers' organization is its ambition to grow and render real service to its members. There are, however, sometimes misconceived motives that are responsible for initiating a movement and for developing it into a formidable power. Farmers' organizations have made plenty of mistakes, and this must not be understood as unsympathetic criticism. Commercial organizations, employers' associations, and organized labor have all committed blunders and frequently give evidence that they misunderstand fundamental economic questions. Organization sometimes gropes in the dark, and is led on by leaders of influence who have, however, no thorough understanding of the problems they wish to solve. One is impressed that this was a feature of the alliance. It sometimes happens that a leader in organized agriculture, as well as elsewhere, accepts a fallacious economic doctrine and through his dominant position at public meetings secures official endorsement by the organization. In this way a group of farmers of the Northwest have committed themselves to the incongruous position of favoring the single tax. An erroneous or fallacious principle if persistently advocated before public bodies and continually incorporated among aims and purposes is sometimes accepted by a large majority, and is actually made to form the basis for extending the movement. This of course is to be expected inasmuch as progress is made only by sifting the wheat from the chaff. Although it does seem that much time is wasted because of ill-advised leadership. The farmers, like other groups, have good leaders in some quarters. In others their cause suffers because of erroneous doctrines propounded which become an obsession and stand as an obstacle in the way of improvement. Motives of personal prestige and political aggrandizement sometimes cause leaders and their satellites vigorously to support an organization and simulate sincerity of purpose. But this again is a disagreeable aspect of organization in general and must be kept in mind only for the purpose of ridding the organization of undesirable members.

It appears sometimes in public organization that persons in charge of projects or offices become overzealous in championing the work in which they are engaged. It may easily happen that some officials with no ulterior motives press their particular functions to the extent that appropriations are made for such purpose at the expense of other more worthy objects. Sometimes, and probably quite rarely, motives for increasing their work are the desire for greater prestige or larger salaries. These undesirable motives, however, are shortcomings of public organization. They can be reduced to a minimum but not entirely destroyed by efficient administration.

Social Aspects that Organization Must Foster.—In the final analysis agricultural organization must foster a large degree of private property in land, decentralization in farm ownership, honesty and fairness toward all economic groups, and loyalty to the nation. The farming population is relatively a conservative group, and is, therefore, the mainstay of our institutions. The charge that farmers' organizations have a tendency to be disloyal to the nation cannot be fairly made. But it appears that they sometimes have made unfair charges against other groups for propaganda purposes. This is bad policy, for sooner or later the truth will be clearly recognized by a majority of the people and public opinion will condemn the use of such reprehensible methods. The only organizational methods, aims and purposes that society will ultimately sanction must be characterized as rational and fair with respect to the entire social order.

While a study of farmers' organizations discloses the fact that cooperation is fostered by them and that considerable collective ownership in the form of cooperative enterprise is already under way, there is nowhere a hint that the farm, the basic form of property in agriculture, should be collectively owned. Organized agriculture everywhere favors private property in land, operation of the farm by the proprietor, and decentralization of ownership. These conditions lie at the very root of a satisfactory rural life. Without these conditions no permanent agriculture of a high order can be maintained, and no deep and lasting interest can be evoked among the people in schools, in amusements, or in other rural institutions. Private property in land promotes thrift and rewards effort. It insures ample production. Through it meritorious service is rendered and recompensed. It engenders attachment and love for the home and family. It promotes interest in the community, and results in progress. It prevents decreased production, misery, and hardship. It prevents also a flagging of interest in the home and the community and a stagnation of thought and activity in general. It is the only means of bringing happiness to the rural people.

CHAPTER II

THE UNITED STATES DEPARTMENT OF AGRICULTURE

The Movement to Establish a National Department of Agriculture.—Government aid to agriculture with respect to certain products was probably the first suggestion to the American people that the improvement of agriculture could be very substantially fostered through the use of public organization. Already in the early colonial days England under James I. in 1622, encouraged the breeding of silk worms in Virginia probably because of his aversion to tobacco. At a time when sheep were scarce in the colonies and difficult to secure from Europe the General Court of Massachusetts in 1642 offered premiums for sheep-raising, and in 1657 the Virginia legislature passed an act to stimulate the raising of hops. Silk production was also encouraged in Georgia. Lands were granted to settlers on condition that they plant 100 white mulberry trees on every 10 acres when cleared. An Episcopal clergyman was engaged to instruct the people in the art of raising silk worms and winding the silk. Georgia exported silk under this direction to England from 1735 to 1790.[1] England, during the early part of the eighteenth century, was anxious to make herself independent of certain agricultural European imports. She therefore enacted laws fostering the cultivation of hemp, lumber, pitch, tar, silk and indigo. Duties on these products were repealed and in addition there were offered bounties on such goods as would be shipped to England.[2] In the 10 years preceding 1743 Parliament granted $600,000 to promote the cultivation of indigo and other crops in Georgia.[3] In 1766 the South Carolina assembly voted 1,000 pounds in aid of the silk industry in Charleston. Steps to encourage the sheep industry were taken by the South Carolina and Virginia legislatures in 1775 at the time when the Revolutionary war put a stop to all efforts to aid or improve agriculture.

---

[1] *Vide* article in *Agricultural Report* of Department for 1866, p. 507.

[2] *Vide* Coman, *Industrial History of the United States*, p. 62.

[3] Greathouse, *Bulletin No.* 3, *Div. of Publications, U. S. Department of Agriculture.*

Shortly after the close of the Revolutionary war the leading men of the country turned their attention to agriculture. In a number of towns along the coast agricultural societies were organized. The first one to be organized was on March 1, 1785, in Philadelphia, which was then the seat of the National Government. The society had the support of General Washington, Benjamin Franklin and other public men. While these societies were made up of urban members it should be remembered that they came at a time when agriculture was by far the main pursuit in the country, and it was through them that the first organized efforts for the improvement of agriculture were made. Not a few suggestions for public organization came from England before the close of the eighteenth century. Washington was familiar with the writings of Arthur Young who, because of his wide travels and experience, was the foremost writer on agriculture at the time. Washington was also in correspondence with Sir John Sinclair, who was the leading spirit in the establishment of the British board of agriculture in 1793. Sinclair urged upon Washington the adoption of a similar board at Philadelphia, the national capital, as well as local boards at the respective state capitals.[1] In reply to this suggestion Washington expressed the fear that it would be some time before an agricultural society with congressional aid could be established, and that local societies would first have to prepare the way. This was the old problem of the division of public functions between the Federal and State governments. Sinclair, however, continued to urge Washington while he was President to institute some form of public organization. In his last message to Congress on December 7, 1796, Washington met the two houses of Congress, as was his custom, and called attention to the importance of agriculture in the following terms:

> It will not be doubted that, with reference to either individual or national welfare, agriculture is of primary importance. In proportion as nations advance in population and other circumstances of maturity this truth becomes more apparent, and renders the cultivation of soil more and more an object of public patronage. Institutions for promoting it grow up supported by the public purse, and to what object can it be dedicated with greater propriety? Among the means which have

[1] *Vide* chapter on State Departments of Agriculture.

been employed to this end, none have been attended with greater success than the establishment of boards composed of proper characters, charged with collecting and diffusing information, and enabled, by premiums and small pecuniary aids, to encourage and assist a spirit of discovery and improvement. This species of establishment contributes doubly to the increase of improvements by stimulating to enterprise and experiment, and by drawing to a common center the results, everywhere, of individual skill and observation, and spreading them thence over the whole nation. Experience accordingly has shown that they are very cheap instruments of immense national benefits.[1]

Washington made efforts to enlist the support of prominent agriculturists to carry out his plan. He wrote a letter inclosing papers showing outlines of his plan to Judge Peters, who was a prominent member of the Philadelphia Society for the Promotion of Agriculture.

In the Senate, Senator Read of South Carolina made a speech favoring the President's proposal. In the House the subject was referred to a committee which reported favorably. The plan provided for the establishment of a society at the seat of the government embracing the members of Congress, the judges, the Secretary of State, the Secretary of the Treasury, the Secretary of War, the Attorney General, "and such other persons as may choose to become members, according to the rules prescribed." An annual meeting was to be held at which the President and other officers were to be elected. Also a board of not more than 30 persons was to be elected which was to be called the board of agriculture. Annual reports were to be made. The report was twice read and ordered to be referred to a committee of the whole. No action was taken due to several reasons. It was associated with a recommendation to establish a military academy, to which Mr. Jefferson was openly opposed on the ground that "none of the specific powers given by the Constitution to Congress would authorize it." In replying to his friend Sinclair of England, George Washington expressed regret that nothing had been done by Congress, but believed that its failure to act was not so much due to opposition to the proposal as to a lack of time to enact all but the most pressing bills. He thought it highly probable that the following Congress would enact the proposed agricultural bill into law. These hopes, however, remained unful-

[1] From *Report of Department of Agriculture* for 1866, p. 514.

filled for 66 years. In this connection it is interesting to note the influence that this suggestion had upon organizing agriculture in the several States. In the chapter dealing with State departments of agriculture and in which their development is briefly sketched the character of their embryonic organization can very readily be traced to this plan suggested by Sir John Sinclair of England and presented to Congress by the Father of his Country.

The Movement Leading Slowly to Fruition.—The proposal by George Washington did not fall wholly on barren ground. As is explained in the chapter on State Departments of Agriculture attempts to establish State boards of agriculture through actual legislative enactment began as early as 1820. Shortly before this, in 1817, the Berkshire Agricultural Society of Massachusetts, under the enthusiastic leadership of Elkanah Watson, presented a memorial to Congress asking for the establishment of a national board of agriculture. A bill for the purpose was reported in the House but was defeated by an overwhelming vote. It was argued that there was no constitutional authority for such an institution. It was also opposed on the ground of inexpediency and on the ground that the general agricultural public was indifferent to the measure. This was probably true of the masses, but not of the more intelligent and progressive farmers. President Madison was also opposed to the measure.[1]

While Congress did not believe it had authority to subsidize agricultural societies with appropriations usually called bounties, it provided in 1817 for "the allotment of certain lands within what was then known as the Mississippi Territory to French immigrants for the purpose of promoting the cultivation of the vine and the olive. In 1838, in recognition of services in introducing useful tropical plants into the United States," Congress granted to Henry Perrine "and his associates a body of land in the southern extremity of the Peninsula of East Florida, for the propagation and cultivation of such plants."[2]

[1] *Vide* article by Dr. A. C. True in *Report of Department of Agriculture* for 1894, p. 85.

[2] Circular issued by the Office of the Solicitor of the Department, Oct. 23, 1916.

For more than twenty years before the establishment of the Department of Agriculture in 1862 men like Judge Jesse Buel, who was a farmer, New York assemblyman, judge, and writer on agricultural subjects, developed and prescribed plans for a national department and urged their adoption. Isaac Newton, the first Commissioner of the Department of Agriculture, was also very zealous in his efforts to secure the establishment of a department. A progressive farmer in Pennsylvania, Mr. Newton was an enthusiastic member of the agricultural association of his State and was frequently sent as a delegate to the U. S. Agricultural Society, where he introduced resolutions urging Congress to establish a national department. In fact, the United States Agricultural Society, meeting annually in Washington, D. C., served for some years before the Civil War the purpose of a national board of agriculture such as George Washington had in mind. In 1852 delegates from twenty-three States and Territories representing local agricultural societies were present. The society was incorporated by Congress in 1860. Mr. Newton brought the matter to the attention of Presidents Harrison, Taylor, Fillmore, Buchanan and Lincoln. He enjoyed a personal acquaintance with Lincoln and it was probably due to this close friendship that Lincoln became a warm supporter of Newton's proposal.

In the meantime things were happening in Congress showing that it reflected the passing of events throughout the country. The House of Representatives established a committee on agriculture in 1820 and the Senate in 1825. The Botanical Garden was established during John Quincy Adam's administration. American consuls began sending to the United States rare plants and fine grades of livestock. In 1826 Congress authorized the publication of a manual prepared by Richard Rush, Secretary of the Treasury, concerning the growth and manufacture of silk. In 1828 Count Von Haggi's "Treatise on Rearing Silkworms" was published as a Congressional document.

The Work of the Patent Office.—In 1836 the Commissioner of Patents, Mr. Henry L. Ellsworth of Connecticut, without any legal authority assumed the responsibility of receiving new and valuable seeds and plants sent by Government representatives and others from abroad, and of distributing such seeds and plants among enterprising farmers of the country. At this time it became evident that the soil of New England and in the Atlantic coast States was becoming rapidly depleted. "The falling off in the average yield per acre, which commenced upon the borders of the Atlantic, spreading from New England down to Florida, was creeping insiduously toward the west." Judge Buel of New York as one of the means of staying the depletion of the soil urged the establishment of agricultural colleges and the development of agricultural science.[1] With these symptons of agricultural anemia staring us in the face, Congress in 1839 condescended to appropriate $1,000 at the suggestion of the Commissioner of Patents for the "collection of agricultural statistics, investigations for promoting agriculture and rural economy, and the procurement of cuttings and seeds for gratuitous distribution among the farmers." The following two years Congress failed to make the appropriation of even this small sum, but in 1842 it was renewed. For the years 1843 and 1844 the amount appropriated was increased to 2,000, and for 1845 it was raised to $3,000. In 1846, however, Congress made no appropriation, but in 1847 again provided $3,000. From that time on appropriations for agricultural purposes, the work of which was to be prosecuted by the Commissioner of Patents, were regularly made until 1862, when the Commissioner of Agriculture became responsible for the proper expenditure of appropriations made for the Department of Agriculture.

Thus the first official service performed by the Federal Government was done in the Patent Office. This office soon after the organization of the Government began the practice of exhibiting models of the more important agricultural inventions.[2] More than any other office of the executive branch of the Government it seems to have been early interested in agriculture and therefore was the logical office to fall heir to the paltry appropriations first made by Congress in the interest

[1] *Report of Department* for 1866, p. 524.
[2] *Circular* by Solicitor of Department, Oct. 23, 1916.

of agricultural improvement. At this time the Patent Office was in the Department of State and it was for this reason that the commissioner was in close touch with American consuls abroad. When the Department of Interior was established in 1849, the Patent Office with its agricultural work was transferred to it. In 1861 Isaac Newton of Pennsylvania was placed in charge of the agricultural work in the Patent Office and David P. Holloway of Indiana became Commissioner of Patents. In his first annual report the commissioner makes an earnest argument for the establishment of a separate department of agriculture. The department was established the following year at a time when men's minds turned mainly to the settlement of the question of States' rights and to other issues of the Civil War.

The Influence of the War.—Just what influence the war had upon the establishment of the department is difficult to estimate. Not infrequently are wars the means of bringing to fruition ideas that have been long in the making. As has been shown, the matter of establishing a national department of agriculture had long been in the minds of the American people. As is also shown in the historical sections of the chapters dealing with the land-grant colleges and experiment stations, agricultural education during the second quarter of the nineteenth century was taking form and demanding assistance from the Federal Government. Both the establishment of a department and that of agricultural colleges had been subjected to considerable agitation, and public sentiment in the North was ripe for action. One contribution that the war made toward both these projects was that it removed a large part of the conservative element from Congress producing a more favorable condition for the enactment of this type of legislation. It is also quite likely that inasmuch as the North suffered on account of a shortage in the supplies of cotton and sugar, Congress believed that this organization might be able to help the country in its immediate struggle. In his first report[1] the Commissioner of Agriculture states that he "will take early and active measures to induce farmers in Ken-

[1] P. 23.

tucky, Missouri, Southern Illinois, Indiana and Kansas—all of which States will undoubtedly produce cotton—to turn their attention to the culture of this important staple." The act providing for the establishment of the Department of Agriculture was approved by President Lincoln, May 15, 1862, and went into effect July 1 of the same year. The act establishing the land-grant colleges, known as the Morrill Act, was approved July 2, 1862. Thus legislation for a department of agriculture proposed by the first President of the United States sixty-six years before its adoption, was tardily brought to fruition. While the country was slow to adopt the principle of public agricultural organization, since its adoption it has made very rapid strides until today the United States Department of Agriculture, the agricultural colleges and experiment stations, the agricultural cooperative extension service, and State departmental organizations, are agencies that touch every phase of agricultural activities and rural life aiming constantly to work out improvements and to popularize them among the farmers of the country.

The Act of 1862.—The act of 1862 declared its object to be the establishment "at the seat of the Government of the United States a Department of Agriculture, the general designs and duties of which shall be to acquire and to diffuse among the people of the United States useful information on subjects connected with agriculture in the most general and comprehensive sense of that word, and to procure, propagate, and distribute among the people new and valuable seeds and plants."

The two most popular functions that a department of agriculture should perform were thought to be the collection of statistics and the distribution of valuable seeds and plants. These functions are especially stressed by the act. The collection of statistics and useful information, however, was not confined merely to the collection and tabulation of facts already known. It included experimentation. Section 3 of the act runs as follows:

It shall be the duty of the Commissioner of Agriculture to acquire and preserve in this department all information concerning agriculture which he can obtain by means of books and correspondence and by practical and scientific experiments (accurate records of which experiments shall be kept in his office), by the collection of statistics, and by other appropriate means within his power; to collect as he may be able, new and valuable seeds and plants; to test by cultivation the value of such of them as may require such tests; to propagate such as may be worthy of propagation, and to distribute them among agriculturists.

Both the collection of statistics and the distribution of seeds under the act were so broad as to require the aid of scientific experts capable of making experiments necessary to secure "useful information" and to determine whether or not seeds and plants were worthy of distribution. Section 24 provides that the commissioner was to "employ other persons, for such time as their services may be needed, including chemists, botanists, entomologists, and other persons skilled in the natural sciences pertaining to agriculture."

The act also provides for the making of annual reports. The commissioner was to have charge of all property of the agricultural division of the Patent Office in the Department of the Interior including also the fixtures and property of the propagating garden. The commissioner, who was made the chief executive of the department, was to be appointed by the President by and with the advice and consent of the Senate.

The Department's Early Organization.—The commissioner experienced some difficulty in getting the department organized. The organic act provided for a transfer of the property used by the Patent Office for purposes of conducting its agricultural activities to the newly created Department of Agriculture. At the close of the first year of its existence the commissioner complains that this mandate had not been complied with. In his report for 1865 he recommends a new and separate building for the department. This was contracted for and completed for occupancy in 1868.[1] Up to that time the department's quarters remained in the Patent Office building, where the growth of the work of both the Patent Office and the Department of Agriculture hampered its operations on account of crowded conditions. The propagating garden at Sixth street and Missouri avenue, N. W., in Washington, was placed under the supervision of the commissioner as well as

[1] *Vide Reports* of Department.

forty acres of land between Twelfth and Fourteenth streets, S. W., for experimental purposes. This tract of land now forms the department grounds.

The first scientific expert to be appointed by the commissioner was the superintendent of the propagating garden. A little more than a month later, on August 21, 1862, he appointed a department chemist whose first work was making analyses of grapes and sorghum sirup. This work, the collection and distribution of seeds and plants, and the publication of agricultural statistics constituted the chief activities of the department for the first six months.[1] In 1863 a statistician and entomologist were appointed. In 1868 the Division of Botany was organized to arrange and care for botanical specimens collected by exploring expeditions to foreign countries as well as to western portions of the United States. In 1871 a Division of Microscopy was established and the investigation of cranberry rot, mildews on grapes, yellows in peaches, etc., were carried on. During the first decade of the department's existence only the Divisions of Chemistry, Garden and Grounds, Entomology, Statistics, Botany of Microscopy were in operation and constituted its organization and the range of its activities.

From the close of the first decade to 1882 many new activities were undertaken. The subject of forestry received attention for the first time when in 1877 an appropriation for a forestry investigation was made. In 1878 investigations of animal diseases were instituted. Pleuro-pneumonia among cattle was prevalent at the time and received a large share of attention. Investigations also were made of the history and habits of insects injurious to agriculture and horticulture. Other investigations included the manufacture of sugar from sorghum and sugar beets, the cultivation of sugar beets, the introduction of forage plants and grasses suitable for semi-arid regions, methods for determining adulterations of food, collection of statistics relating to oleomargarine, butterine, the supervision of the work of the experiment stations in the agricultural colleges, etc. In fact during this period there

[1] *Vide Bulletin No. 3, Div. of Publications,* by C. H. Greathouse.

was considerable expansion through the addition of new lines of work, and by 1884 the activities of the department had become so varied that it was necessary to create new and distinct units of organization. In 1884 a Bureau of Animal Industry was organized and headed by a veterinary surgeon. This had been asked by the National Grange in 1880. In 1886 the divisions of economic ornithology and mammalogy, and pomology were created. A Division of Forestry had already been put in operation in 1880.

The Period of Rapid Expansion.—Generally speaking the first three decades of the department's existence may be called its formative period, while the period since 1889 may be designated the period of rapid expansion. In 1887 the experiment stations were established and at that time the scientific work of the department had received general recognition because of its practical service to agriculture. Two years later the head of the department was raised to the rank of a Cabinet member.[1] In 1891 the Weather Bureau was transferred from the War Department to the Agricultural Department. This was a logical step because the Agricultural Department could more satisfactorily extend the benefits of the Weather Bureau service to agriculture than the Signal Office of the War Department. Such other needs for weather information arising out of military, commercial and manufacturing activities can also be very well served.

From its establishment to 1884 the department was wholly confined to the functions of investigation, experimentation, and education. In 1884, however, an important innovation was made in the establishment of an inspection service for the purpose of preventing the exportation of diseased cattle and hogs. Our cattle, sheep, and swine were refused admittance

---

[1] The matter had been agitated for a decade by the Grange. The early bills in Congress provided for a department of agriculture to be concerned also with commerce and labor which was condemned by some prominent grangers. Norman J. Coleman, Commissioner of Agriculture, also a granger. said, "If the department of agriculture could be kept for agriculture alone, I would favor the measure of having its head a member of the President's Cabinet, but if the Labor Bureau, the Bureau of Education and several other bureaus be attached to it, I feel we will be better served and better satisfied under existing laws." The bill was characterized by some in Congress as class legislation.

to Great Britain for the purpose of controlling pleuro-pneumonia and other contagious diseases, and our pork was excluded from most of the continental countries on the ground that it was infested with trichinae. The situation was regarded so seriously that the act, providing for this regulatory function, created also a Bureau of Animal Industry which should together with the Treasury Department carry out the inspection provisions. While this inspection service was a precedent, since 1900 Congress has added many regulatory functions until today they form a very large part of the department's work. Among the more important regulatory acts placed under the administration of the Secretary of Agriculture are the meat inspection act, the cattle quarantine act, the diseased animal transportation acts, the twenty-eight hour act, the virus act, the food and drugs act, the insecticide act, the plant quarantine act, the seed importation act, the Lacey act, the migratory bird act, the United States Cotton Futures Act, and the act to control the livestock industry. In the chapters that follow these and other functions of the department are discussed. Their origin and development are usually pointed out and their importance to the agricultural and other economic groups of the country is shown. These regulatory functions touch the welfare and conduct of virtually every citizen. Much of the regulation is based upon scientific discoveries previously made, and it may be said that while science made in many cases possible the establishment of regulatory functions, they in turn brought increased prestige to the department and an enlargement of activities in general. Thus the addition of the regulatory function has been very largely responsible for the marvelous expansion of the Department of Agriculture during the last two decades.

In a discussion of the growth and development of the department special mention should be made of the new Bureau of Markets. Only since 1907 has marketing received special attention from the United States Department of Agriculture, and since then this activity expanded rapidly resulting in the organization of an Office of Markets in 1913, and the establishment of a bureau in 1917 which in 1919 was fourth in size of all the bureaus in the department. The main activity of the department until 1913 was concerned with increasing production, but now it is also interested in providing the least expensive means of getting the agricultural products to the consumer. The problems of marketing since then have also been rapidly taken up by public agricultural organizations under the States as shown in a later chapter.

Another phase of public agricultural organization that has in recent years swept over the entire country and which is centered in the States Relations Service of the department, is the agricultural cooperative extension service. All previous efforts to popularize agricultural science are unimportant compared with the systematic and continuous work of this new organization.

Summary of the Department's Development.—In the succeeding chapters the development of the department will be discussed in detail from the point of view of bureaus and offices. The beginning of the bureau, its gradual expansion, and final organization, together with its present functions are shown. To bring together into one place a chronological development of the branches of the Department of Agriculture it is well to state in this chapter its growth in tabular form as follows:

1862—Establishment of the Department of Agriculture.
Establishment of Land-Grant Colleges.
Disbursing Office.
Superintendent of Propagating Garden.
Division of Chemistry.
Library.
1863—Division of Entomology.
Division of Statistics.
Fibre Investigation.
1865—Analysis of Soils.
1868—Division of Botany.
1871—Division of Microscopy.
1877—Forestry Investigations.
1878—Investigation of Animal Diseases.
1880—Forestry Division.
1883—Veterinary Division.
1884—BUREAU OF ANIMAL INDUSTRY.
1885—Section of Ornithology.
1886—Division of Ornithology and Mammalogy.
Division of Pomology.
1887—Division of Vegetable Physiology and Pathology.
1888—Office of Experiment Stations.
1889—Secretary of Agriculture and Cabinet Member.
Assistant Secretary of Agriculture.

1890—Division of Publications.
1891—WEATHER BUREAU.
Appointments Clerk's Office.
1893—Office of Road Inquiry.
1894—Foreign Market Section.
Agricultural Soils Division.
1895—Division of Agrostology.
1896—Biological Survey.
1901—BUREAU OF CHEMISTRY.
FOREST SERVICE.
BUREAU OF PLANT INDUSTRY.
BUREAU OF SOILS.
1903—BUREAU OF STATISTICS.
1904—BUREAU OF ENTOMOLOGY.
1905—BUREAU OF BIOLOGICAL SURVEY.
Solicitor's Office.
1906—Office of Public Roads and Rural Engineering.
1907—Investigations of Marketing Fruits.
Studies in Farm Management.
1910—Insecticide and Fungicide Board.
1912—Federal Horticultural Board.
1913—Office of Exhibits.
Office of Markets.
1914—Office of Inspection.
Office of Forest Appeals.
1915—STATES RELATIONS SERVICE.
Office of Farm Management.
1917—Smith-Hughes Act.
1919—BUREAU OF PUBLIC ROADS.
BUREAU OF MARKETS.
1921—BUREAU OF MARKETS AND CROP ESTIMATES.
1922—BUREAU OF AGRICULTURAL ECONOMICS.

It will be noted from the above table that the first bureau organized in the department was that of Animal Industry in 1884 brought about by the addition of the first regulatory function as previously stated. The Weather Bureau was transferred to the department in 1891. The rapid development into bureau organization, however, took place during the five years following 1900. In 1901 the Bureaus of Chemistry, Forest Service, Plant Industry, and Soils were organized; and within the next four years the Bureaus of Statistics, Entomology, and Biological Survey were added to the list. A decade passed before another bureau was created. In 1915 the States Relations Service was organized which was followed two years later by the Bureaus of Public Roads and Markets.

Growth of Department by Appropriations.—The growth of the department may also be studied from the point of view of expenditures or cost of maintenance. The table[1] shows

[1] Compiled from the Disbursing Officer's Report.

the amounts disbursed from 1839, when the work was instituted by the Commissioner of Patents, to 1919.

Table Showing Expenditures of the Department of Agriculture:

Fiscal Year	*Amount Disbursed*
1839	$1,000.00
1840	....
1841	....
1842	1,000.00
1843	....
1844	2,000.00
1845	2,000.00
1850	5,500.00
1855	50,000.00
1860	40,000.00
1865	112,196.55
1870	151,596.93
1875	321,079.83
1880	198,361.72
1885	558,934.89
1890	971,823.62
1895	2,021,030.38
1900	2,947,603.42
1905	5,826,365.63
1910	12,647,918.27
1915	19,408,375.18
1919	25,764,662.45
1920	30,226,626.16

It was noted above that the period prior to the 80's may be regarded as the formative period of the department, while the period since that time as one of rapid expansion. This statement is verified by the table of disbursements. When one turns to the Treasury's figures of expenditures for the entire Government it is noted that this rapid expansion in the Department of Agriculture since the 80's was only a phase of what was in progress in other fields of Federal activity. With the coming of the railroads in 1830 and as a result the development of national markets, many regulatory functions were thrust upon the Federal Government because local governments were wholly inadequate to cope with the new situation. In 1887, for instance, we created the Interstate Commerce Commission. It was a period, because of the complex and intricate economic order as well as the inefficiency and often corrupt local governments, when men generally became accustomed to turn more readily to the National Government for the purpose of correcting public evils. Many regulatory functions have been committed to the Secretary of Agriculture because of their close relation to the work of his department. In addition to these regulatory functions many activities tending to improve the economic and social agricultural conditions of the country have been inaugurated usually through the experts of the department themselves, but receiving the sanction of the people generally.

The Character of the Department's Organization.—In 1919 there were 12 bureaus, the two divisions of Accounts and Publications, the Library, two boards, and the Office of the Secretary, which, however, had under its supervision the important offices of the Solicitor and of Farm Management as well as the minor offices of Inspection, Forest Appeals, Appointment Clerk, and Office of Exhibits. The Office of Farm Management has developed to such importance that the secretary asked Congress to give it the designation of a bureau in the appropriation bill for 1920. As indicated by the tabular statement of the department's development and as pointed out in succeeding chapters, as projects were assumed by the department they were frequently associated with offices to which they had little or no relation. As the work grew and became thoroughly differentiated it was placed under a separate division or office. The next step in its development was the organization of a bureau. The administrative or overhead functions always remain more or less close to the secretary's office, while the bureaus, to which are committed the various differentiated projects of the department, are headed by a chief or director and are much farther removed from the supervision of the Secretary or his assistants. Over some bureaus like the Weather Bureau, for instance, the secretary exercises only a nominal control.

The organization within the bureau is similar to the organization of projects of the department before they become ripe for administration by bureaus. The bureau has its necessary administrative offices which stand close to its chief. Considerable variation exists concerning the remaining internal organization of the respective bureaus. The division, headed by a chief of division, is prominent in some, while in others the work is organized by projects in charge of scientific experts.

While each bureau perfoms a set of functions more or less widely different from the functions of other bureaus, there are many places where they come into contact with one another. Many projects are therefore carried on in cooperation with other bureaus. The Chemistry Bureau is a conspicuous example of a bureau cooperating not only with other bureaus of the Department of Agriculture but with other Departments of the Government. The Weather Bureau and the Forest Service cooperate. All demonstration work of the department is now centered in the States Relations Service and carried on by it with the cooperation of other bureaus. In fact cooperation is a very important principle of the department's organization. Without it there would be stiffness in its service, considerable duplication of effort and expense, and from such duplication unnecessary jealousy and animosity would develop among bureau officials. It is a general principle of organization that when a function is once added to an office its head soon becomes its champion and proceeds to develop it. One reason for this is psychological, the other economic. In the first place he becomes interested personally in the development of the project, and in the second place his salary is often conditioned upon the development of an important office. Reorganization at various times has been necessary in the history of the department to bring about a logical adjustment of related elements in its organization. It is altogether likely that even today some duplication of organization exists in the field forces of the various bureaus. The Weather Bureau has its cooperative observers, and the Bureau of Crop Estimates has its township and county crop reporters. Most of these employes are not paid. Where they are not paid and the function they perform is not duplicated, there is no necessity for a more compact organization. The Weather Bureau, however, has its section centers where crop figures are collected and forwarded to the Washington office and there compiled and published independently of more or less similar work performed by the Bureau of Crop Estimates. It is probable that this work could, for instance, be centralized under the Bureau of Crop Estimates with the cooperation of the Weather Bureau.

The establishment of an executive department of the Government requires a special act of Congress. This is not necessarily true concerning the establishment of a bureau. "Many of the bureaus of the Department of Agriculture exist solely by virtue of the annual appropriation acts, and would be completely disestablished by mere failure of Congress to provide funds for their continuance, without the repeal of any existing statute."[1] The bureau, however, cannot be organized by an administrative regulation of the Secretary, and must rest upon some act of Congress, even though such act of Congress is merely an appropriation act[2] Other offices more directly under the supervision of the Secretary are organized merely by a regulation issued by the Secretary, and depend upon Congress for their existence only in a general way because of the necessity of funds for carrying on the various projects.

In the discussion of the various bureaus it will be noted that some of them have an important field force scattered throughout the country. The Washington offices keep in close contact with forces in the field by requiring them to submit regular and special reports. A large part of the force in the field exists mainly for the express purpose of rendering reports to Washington and other centers. The Weather Bureau and crop-field service are examples. Accounts are audited and closely scrutinized at Washington. In addition to the report as an index of the character of work performed, the bureaus having field forces have inspectors who make detailed inspections of their stations and offices and report their findings to the central office.

Administrative Regulations.—The Department of Agriculture like the other executive departments is called upon to formulate many regulations governing the conduct of its per-

[1] Circular by the Solicitor of the Department, October, 1916.

[2] Fairlie in his *National Administration of the United States*, p. 70, states that the Attorney General has held that bureaus can only be established by act of Congress and quotes as evidence, 10 Atty.—Gen. Opinions, 11.

sonnel and providing detailed rules for the purpose of carrying out laws enacted by Congress. While these regulations are not enacted by a legislative body, they are, however, based upon statutory or constitutional law and have the force of law. Concerning these administrative regulations G. N. Lieber says:

> It is difficult to form a true conception of the vastness and importance of all this great body of executive regulation law, controlling, as it does the administration of all the executive departments with its rules of action. And when we consider that these rules of action are in general made, construed and applied by the same authority, thus combining quasi-legislative, quasi-judicial and executive authority, we cannot fail to be impressed with the extent of the jurisdiction covered by them.[1]

In its fiscal regulations for 1917 the Department of Agriculture has a little booklet alone containing 163 pages of closely printed matter. It has a similar booklet covering administrative regulations. Many other orders or memorandums are issued from time to time governing the conduct of the staff and clerks of the department.

Regulatory acts passed by Congress frequently require the formulation of comprehensive rules and regulations by the Secretary of Agriculture. The department's solicitor assists the bureau having charge of the administration of the law to prepare the necessary regulations. Usually the economic interests concerned in the regulations are consulted before they are finally promulgated. Frequently the farmers, carriers, and dealers give important information concerning the manner in which regulatory laws can and should be administered. In 1919 some of the more important regulations prepared concerned the administration of the migratory bird treaty act, the virus, serum, and toxin law, provision for compensation to owners of tuberculous animals destroyed, the administration of the Alaska game law, the meat inspection law, the plant quarantine act, the grain standards act, and many others.[2]

The Relative Size of the Bureaus of the Department.—The relative size of the several bureaus of the department is shown

---

[1] *Remarks on Army Regulations*, p. 47.
[2] *Vide Solicitor's Report.*

in the following statement of the number of employes taken from the Official Register for 1919:

Name of Office	*Employees*
Office of the Secretary	474
*Office of Farm Management	148
Weather Bureau	952
Bureau of Animal Industry	4,763
Bureau of Plant Industry	1,735
Forest Service	2,835
Bureau of Chemistry	683
Bureau of Soils	164
Bureau of Entomology	425
Bureau of Biological Survey	160
Division of Publications	178
*Bureau of Crop Estimates	214
States Relations Service	420
Library	34
Bureau of Public Roads	613
Division of Accounts and Disbursements	36
Insecticide and Fungicide Board	55
Federal Horticultural Board	122
*Bureau of Markets	1.567
Temporary Employees	407
Miscellaneous (includes collaborators, cooperative agents, special meteorological observers, etc., not included in Directory)	6,987
Total	22,972

The larger bureaus are the ones having a considerable force in the field. These include the Bureau of Animal Industry with its large meat inspection force, the Forest Service, the Bureau of Plant Industry, the Bureau of Markets, and the Weather Bureau. The States Relations Service, Weather and Crop Estimates Bureaus have a large force of local employes, but these are included under the head of "Miscellaneous" at the bottom of the statement. Almost 7,000 belong to this group. The other 15,000 are in the classified civil service. This is a vast army of men not all engaged in work pertaining to the improvement of agriculture. The Weather Bureau serves commerce and industry as well as agriculture. All the regulatory functions performed by the department are to the interest usually of the consumer. Nearly all the investigational, educational and demonstrational work, however, is carried on in the interest of agricultural improvement.

*These have been merged in the Bureau of Agricultural Economics.

Tenure of Department Officials.—All of the employes of the Department of Agriculture except the Secretary, Assistant Secretaries, the Chief of the Weather Bureau and the Solicitor are in the classified civil service. The Secretary, who is a Cabinet member, is not only appointed because of his fitness for the headship of the department, but also for the reason that he has a political following and the good-will of the farmers. The choice of the Secretary of Agriculture has about as much political significance as the selection of any other Cabinet member. Although the Chief of the Weather Bureau is appointed by the President by and with the advice and consent of the Senate, politics has very little influence in making the appointment. This is true because the work is mainly scientific and only a properly qualified chief can efficiently direct the activities of the bureau. In 1895 Willis L. Moore was appointed Chief of the Bureau by President Cleveland at the recommendation of the Secretary of Agriculture. The administration in power at the time was democratic, while Mr. Moore declared his party affiliations to be Republican. The appointment of Charles F. Marvin, the present incumbent of the office, was also solely made on the basis of fitness and qualifications.

The tenure of office of the personnel of the department below the Assistant Secretaries rests mainly on competency, proper conduct, and amiable relations between employes and their superiors. All employes below chiefs of divisions and the scientific staff are usually secure in their position so long as they do not take a hostile attitude toward their superiors because of the protection they have under the Civil Service law. They are secure in their position so long as they assume a proper attitude toward their work. Division and bureau chiefs sometimes develop strained relations with their superiors because of a different viewpoint taken concerning departmental policies. Where this happens the official finds it convenient to resign.

There are some notable examples of long office tenure among the officials of the Department of Agriculture. Dr. H. W. Wiley was chief of the Division and Bureau of Chemistry from 1883 to 1912, a period of twenty-nine years. Dr.

L. O. Howard has been associated with the department as entomologist since 1878, a period of forty-four years. Since 1894 he has been chief of the Division and Bureau of Entomology. Dr. A. C. True has served in the department since 1889, a period of thirty-three years, and since 1893 has been in charge of the Office of Experiment Stations, now the States Relations Service. Mr. A. Zappone, the present disbursing officer, has also had a long period of service. In 1906 he became chief of the Division of Accounts, and for many years before that date he was assistant chief of the division. There are other examples, but enough has been said to show that the tenure of the officials of the department below the secretaries in no way depends upon political party affiliation. In at least one case a bureau chief used his position for political aggrandizement, but was rebuffed through failure both to secure the office to which he aspired and to keep the one he had.

The Secretary of Agriculture with other Cabinet members is paid a salary of $12,000 a year. According to the Official Register for 1919 the first assistant secretary receives $5,000, the chief of the Bureau of Public Roads, $6,000; and other bureau chiefs from $4,000 to $5,000. Chiefs of divisions seldom receive more than $4,000 and frequently less than this amount. Members of the technical staff are limited to $4,500.

The Constitutionality of the Department's Operations.—The legal basis of the work of the Department of Agriculture is found in several constitutional provisions. Its investigational, demonstrational and educational functions, including also the service rendered by the Weather Bureau and the Bureau of Markets, rest upon Article I, section 8, clause 1, of the Constitution. This clause is as follows:

> The Congress shall have power to lay and collect taxes, duties, imposts and excises, to pay the debts and provide for the common defense and general welfare of the United States; but all duties, imposts and excises shall be uniform throughout the United States.

"To lay and collect taxes" for the general welfare of the United States, is the specific authority in the Constitution upon which champions of public agricultural organization have based its legality. The solicitor in a circular issued in

1916 states that "there appear to be no cases adjudicating the precise point but the general extent of the authority of Congress under this clause formed an important subject of discussion by our early statesmen and jurists, and has been alluded to by the courts." The solicitor refers to George Washington's effort to establish a national department and to the inaugural addresses of Jefferson and Madison, both of whom expressed themselves in favor of agriculture as an object which ought to receive special care and aid from the National Government. What the Government may do under authority of the phrase "for the general welfare" was variously construed by our early statesmen. Some constructionists have contended that the phrase is meaningless, and others that it confers upon Congress an independent power under which it may enact any legislation conducive to the general welfare of the country. These are the extreme views, and the more generally accepted view holds that it is not a power in itself but limits the exercise of the taxing power to purposes which conduce to the general interests of the United States. While the taxing power of Congress is distinct and independent, it is not absolute. It may be exercised "(1) to pay the debts of the United States, (2) to provide for the common defense of the United States, and (3) to provide for the general welfare of the United States." This is the position of Justice Story, whose opinion is as follows:

> It is, therefore, of necessity left to the discretion of the National Legislature to pronounce upon the objects which concern the general welfare, and for which, under that description, an appropriation of money is requisite and proper. And there seems no room for a doubt that, whatever concerns the general interests of learning, of agriculture, of manufactures, and of commerce, are within the sphere of the national councils, so far as regards an application of money. The only qualification of the generality of the phrase in question, which seems to be admissible, is this, that the object to which an appropriation of money is to be made must be general and not local—its operation extending in fact, or by possibility, throughout the union, and not being confined to a particular spot. No objection ought to arise to this construction from a supposition that it would imply a power to do whatever else should appear to Congress conducive to the general welfare. A power to appropriate money with this latitude, which is granted in express terms, would not carry a power to do any other thing not authorized in the Constitution, either expressly or by fair implication.[1]

[1] Quoted by the Solicitor in his Circular of October 23, 1916, from Story's work on the Constitution, Vol. 1, Sec. 978.

In the opinion of the Solicitor this is the point of view the courts would take if attempts were made to test the constitutionality of appropriations made to promote the general interests of agriculture. It is, however, unlikely that such proceedings will ever be instituted because Congress has made appropriations for the purpose for more than half a century and its action is thoroughly sanctioned by public sentiment.

The authority for the performance of the greater part of the regulatory function is found in the interestate commerce clause of the Constitution, Art. I, Sec. 8, which provides that "Congress shall have power to regulate commerce with foreign nations, and among the several States, and with the Indian tribes." During the last twenty years Congress has taken a liberal view concerning the construction of this clause. When the food and drugs act was passed in 1906 there were, of course, men like Senator Bailey who attacked the measure on the ground that it was unconstitutional. This and other acts, however, have been passed by Congress on the assumption that the United States has the right under the Constitution to exercise its police power over interstate and foreign commerce. The validity of this assumption has been upheld by the Supreme Court of the United States.[1]

The Place of the United States Department of Agriculture.—Considerable attention is given to the question of the place of the respective functions of agriculture, including general education and demonstration, research, college instruction, investigation or the collection of statistics, service and regulation, in the chapter dealing with State Departments of Agriculture in the section entitled, Ideal State Departmental Organization. The domain of the United States Department of Agriculture will therefore, only briefly be outlined here.

It is plain that the weather service, which extends over the entire country and whose basis lies in data collected from not only American territory but also from the West Indies and other outlying points, must be operated by the federal government. Such other service functions as the collection

[1] Hipolite Egg Co. v. United States, 220 U. S. 45, 55 L. Ed. 364, 31 Sup. Ct. Rept. 364.

and publication of market information and the collection of various agricultural statistics must for similar reasons be placed under a federal department. Inasmuch as Congress grants aid to the states for college instruction, experimentation, and for extension work it becomes necessary that a federal department, preferably the Department of Agriculture, supervise the expenditure of funds appropriated.

The regulatory function, associated largely with the pure food problem and the prevention of frauds in the sale of seeds and fertilizers, requires the use of the executive forces of both state and nation inasmuch as these products pass very largely into interstate commerce. It is contended here as well as later in the chapter dealing with the State Department of Agriculture that all regulatory functions should be divorced from the agricultural colleges and experiment stations and lodged with the State and National Departments of Agriculture. It is pointed out in subsequent chapters that in the administration of such acts as the pure food and meat inspection laws that cooperation with state officials is necessary if all fraud is to be weeded out. There is a twilight zone, so to speak, in the execution of law in the United States due to the division of powers between the states and the federal government and unless cooperation by voluntary agreement is entered into between the inspection forces of the state and federal governments many of the fraudulent practices will go unpunished and uncorrected. The control of contagious and infectious diseases of animal and plant life is a national problem and the federal government must necessarily be armed with quarantine powers against the movement of diseased animals and plants into interstate commerce.

In research, as pointed out in a subsequent chapter, the United States Department should be restricted to problems of national importance covering at least several states in extent and to problems too difficult and expensive for local experiment stations to undertake.

In other words, the department should not work on problems distinctly local in character. It should deal with state institutions as entities and not with inferior officials of such institutions, having in mind especially colleges of agriculture with their extension services. In connection with functions that are distinctly national in character, it may deal with the individual, but in all other cases it should deal with state institutions. That the department does not stay within this domain as outlined is complained of by men associated with the colleges and experiment stations.[1]

The National Importance of the Department.—In order to appreciate fully the importance of the Department of Agriculture as an agency of civilization it is necessary to study in detail the functions of its various branches. It may be doubted by those who do not fully grasp the significance of the laws of imitation that the labors of the department during the last half century ever influenced the life of people in remote parts of the United States. There are many people in parts of the country who have never heard of the Department of Agriculture and its work, but there must be very few or none at all who do not know of Paris Green and other common insecticides. While the department cannot in the case of Paris Green nor in many other cases claim credit for having made the discovery of the scientific methods in use, it has played a very large part in introducing them generally. The practice of one enterprising and successful farmer is soon applied by all farmers in the community, and thus the obvious and simple principles of the gospel of agriculture find their way rapidly into methods of cultivation everywhere. The sad comment is that too few of the farmers of the country during the last fifty years have been taught the use of the less obvious and more intricate principles in the cultivation of their farms. The Department of Agriculture as one agency of public agricultural organization has done a great deal through work at farmers' institutes, through the distribution of its literature, through actual demonstration, and through the stimulation and direction of state centers of public and private agricultural organization. In a vast country like the United States and because of the indivualistic character of agricultural life, more strenuous efforts

[1] Note address by Dean Davenport in *Proceedings* of Twenty-Seventh Annual Convention of the Association of Land-Grant Colleges.

than have so long been used by all forms of organization are necessary in order to bring about a substantial improvement in rural conditions. To the entire credit of the Department of Agriculture it must be said such a program has been initiated and during the last decade has virtually spread over the entire country. This organization is known as the agricultural cooperative extension service. It has stability and permanency of organization because of the large measure of local autonomy accorded its members. It will result in progress because the local unit of organization is headed by a scientific expert who proposes the application of the more subtle scientific methods of agriculture. Through it the Department of Agriculture has stretched its tentacles of service into virtually every rural community of the United States, and through it is enabled to serve the farming population as quickly and efficiently as though our Government were organized on an autocratic basis.

To measure the value of the Department of Agriculture as a servant of the people in terms of money is impossible. Without a doubt many projects pursued by its experts have led to "blind alleys." This, however, is the way of science. It is often just as important to disprove a theory as to prove the correctness of another. Only in this way can progress be made in the general acceptation of right ideas. Failures and shortcomings of all kinds have to be paid for by the people. To one who is familiar with the life and atmosphere of civil service it is obvious that there is a lot of lost motion and considerable inefficiency in its organization. Old employes who should have been pensioned and retired have been retained. In the absence of a pension this is the way it should be. The Government should set an example in the fair treatment of labor. On May 22, 1920, a United States retirement act was approved which retires employes of the Department of Agriculture at the age of 70. From the point of view of affecting the efficiency of the organization of the department, this retirement age is in many cases too late in the life of the employes. Discretionary power should be allowed the officials to retire incapacitated individuals as early as 65.

Taking the department in its entirety, however, much greater benefits are returned to the people than is paid for the services performed by its employes. The scientific experts of the department are usually keenly interested in their problems, and whatever is lost elsewhere in the organization, is more than made up by men who serve their country well and for salaries not commensurate with the value of their services. The detailed study of the department that follows this chapter will reveal its importance to the country and point out some of its scientific achievements. The introduction of forage plants suitable for semi-arid regions brought about by the department, alone justifies its existence. The population of large areas of the West depends almost altogether for its maintenance upon the production of these crops. The country is wealthier, stronger, and greater as a result of this achievement.

SELECTED REFERENCES.

Greathouse, *Bulletin No. 3*, Division of Publications, U. S. Dept. of Agriculture; *Agricultural Report* for 1866, pp. 498-527; True in *Agricultural Report* for 1894, pp. 81-116; *Circular* issued by the Solicitor of the U. S. Dept. of Agriculture, October 23, 1916; *Proceedings* of the Twenty-Seventh Annual Convention of the Association of Land-Grant Colleges; various *Reports* of the Solicitor of the U. S. Dept. of Agriculture; L. H. Bailey, *The State and the Farmer*.

CHAPTER III

Miscellaneous Bureaus and Offices of the United States Department of Agriculture

THE BUREAU OF PUBLIC ROADS

Establishment of the Bureau of Public Roads.—It is a truism that the history of transportation is virtually the history of civilization. In the light of this fact it would seem that the establishment of the Office of Road Inquiry in the Department of Agriculture in 1893 was somewhat tardy, especially when it is remembered that this department is a great educational and demonstrational agency, organized in the main to point the way to economic welfare. When, however, the history of American transportation is reviewed and the character of our government is taken into account, satisfactory explanation is found for the belated departmental activity in the field of public roads.

It is not the purpose to give an extended survey of the history of transportation, and therefore only a few of the more leading events will here be enumerated.[1] Unlike the influence for good roads exercised by the Romans upon all their colonies. British colonists were more or less indifferent to good highways. The poor roads to which our early settlers were accustomed in their mother country were merely duplicated in America. The local or town government also had a marked influence upon road construction. Colonial roads were built by the town or local settlement resulting in poor roads generally. Roads under local-government control were poor enough to cause turnpike companies to be organized and operated for profit. This era began during the last quarter of the eighteenth century. Congress, however, took the view that to cover the interior of the country with a network of roads was a task too great for private enterprise, and in 1806 therefore

[1] A concise history of this movement is outlined in the *Yearbook* for 1899, pp. 367-80. For an extensive study of the subject the reader is referred to a text on transportation.

an appropriation was made to begin work on the Cumberland Road. In 1808 Albert Gallatin, Secretary of the Treasury, presented a comprehensive plan of internal improvements to Congress. In 1817 Calhoun introduced a bill in Congress providing for the construction of a system of roads and canals by the federal government, which, in spite of their belief in the States' Rights doctrine, was strongly supported by Henry Clay and others. The bill was vetoed by President Monroe because he thought it was unconstitutional, and Congress had to return to the method of granting to states a certain per cent of the proceeds of the sale of public lands for road-building purposes. The attitude of Congress toward the building of national highways was considerably influenced by the coming of the canal era, in full swing in 1815, and the railroad era in 1830. These were soon destined to furnish more efficient means of transportation, and necessarily caused road-building to be viewed as unimportant. A new movement of far-reaching consequences was initiated by the State of New Jersey in 1891, followed by Massachusetts, Connecticut, and other States. The plan provided State-aid for the construction and maintenance of roads. State highway departments were established, and it was at that time that efforts were made to establish a Federal office which would at least study road-building problems and carry on a propaganda to popularize good roads. This new interest in road-building was probably forced at this time by an increasing congestion in the country's population. The bicycle fad, which was at its height during the 90's, also had its influence; and now the general introduction of the automobile will cause a continued interest in the subject and a revolution in road-building throughout the country.

Thus thirty-one years after the establishment of the Department of Agriculture the Office of Road Inquiry was organized. The appropriation act provided $10,000 "to make inquiries in regard to the systems of road management throughout the United States, to make investigations in regard to the best methods of roadmaking, to prepare publications on this subject suitable for distribution, and to assist the agricultural colleges and experiment stations in disseminating information on this subject.''[1] A few subsequent changes in organization were made and in 1919 the Bureau of Public Roads was created.

Management and Economics.—In the section, Management, the usual administrative functions are performed. In the section, Engineering Economics, are carried on such important projects as economic highway surveys, general economic and statistical work, economic studies of highway systems, utilization of convict labor in road-building, etc.

With the passage of the Federal aid road act in 1916 necessitating a more extensive cooperation with the States, the need for a large amount of systematically arranged material was greatly felt. Much of this material was found available at State highway departments, but lacking in essential details, correlation, and systematization. Only a centralized office like the Bureau of Public Roads would be sufficiently interested to gather the necessary material. An economic highway survey was therefore begun with the cooperation of the Corps of Engineers of the United States Army, and with the Post-office Department. A large amount of the data collected and compiled shows the tonnage of the products of the field, forest, and mine for the various counties in the United States. Not only is this information useful for purposes of developing an efficient system of highways, but during the war it proved to be of great value in the conduct of military operations.

The office collects and publishes important current data relating to highway mileage expenditures, automobile registrations, and the disposition of revenues derived therefrom. All these facts have an important bearing upon the various problems of road building. The investigations include also a study of the organization of various State highway departments, the sources, amounts, and disposition of State funds applied to roads, the use of convict labor, and traffice studies on experimental roads to be used in solving construction and maintenance problems. Considerable educational work is carried on through the lecture method and the exhibition of models and materials at expositions, conferences, conventions

[1] *Yearbook* for 1894, p. 53.

and fairs illustrating the best methods of road, bridge and culvert construction. Organizations desiring the use of these materials pay transportation costs.

Engineering.—The work of the engineering branch of the bureau falls into two general fields, one pertaining to road building and the other to more strictly farm problems such as irrigation, drainage and rural engineering.

In 1917 the bureau found a "general lack of uniformity in specification requirements for all types of road materials" and in order that standard forms of specifications and standard methods of testing and reporting test results on road materials may become established, it called a conference of State highway testing engineers and chemists for the purpose of coming to some agreement. Twenty-one states responded to this call, and as a result recommendations for forty-one standard forms of specifications for materials to be used in various types of road construction, as well as standards for testing materials, were made. Such standardization is basic in efficient highway construction, and should result in more rapid progress. Numerous tests of road materials are annually made by the bureau. In 1918 samples from all but twelve States were subjected to physical tests, numbering altogether 1,009. Besides physical tests, chemical and microscopic tests are also made. Research on dust preventives and road binders are other important fields of investigation.

The object-lesson road has virtually always been a method used by the department since the beginning of its road work to bring before the farmers and communities the importance of good roads and how to construct them. Already in his report of 1895 the Secretary proposed to build object-lesson roads at experiment stations. Such a road was completed by 1897 at Geneva, N. Y., connecting the experiment station with the city. The object-lesson road, however, has not been confined to experiment stations. During the year 1901 object-lesson roads were built in cooperation with railroad companies and the National Association for Good Roads in a number of southern States.[1] In 1919 one was built in Pierce County,

[1] *Yearbook* for 1901, p. 413.

Ga.[1] How to maintain roads is a very important feature of good roads in these days of the automobile truck. The bureau has therefore broadened its object-lessons to include maintenance.

For about twenty years this office was endowed with only educational and demonstrational functions. In 1912, however, the function of building roads within the National Forests was added. Congress provided that 10 per cent of the proceeds of the sale of timber products of the National Forests should be applied to building roads within the forest. The returns were wholly inadequate for the purpose, and, as remarked by the Secretary, so long as the timber remains inaccessible, so long will the sales be small. However, the funds that became available under this 10 per cent provision were consumed in the building of roads where most needed, and the construction was carried on by the Office of Public Roads in cooperation with the Forest Service. Under authority of the Federal Aid Road Act passed in 1916 a more adequate provision for road building in the National Forests is made, the appropriations amounting to $15,000,000 a year for ten years. This work also is being done by the bureau in cooperation with the Forest Service. A function entrusted to the bureau that will result in revolutionary changes in road building and bring great economic benefits to the country is found in the main provision of the Federal Aid Road Act.

The Federal Aid Road Act.—The Federal Aid Road Act was approved July 11, 1916. Besides the provision for the building of National Forest roads the act provided for the construction of rural postroads in cooperation with the States. The act appropriated $75,000,000 to be matched dollar for dollar by the States. The amount was made available for the five-year period, 1916-1921. The act also limited the cost per mile to the Federal Government to $10,000. Owing to the phenomenal increase in the general price level it was soon found that the limitation of $10,000 representing the Government's share of the cost per mile and the total appropriation of $75,000,000 were obstacles that, if not amended, would

[1] Annual Reports of the Department of Agriculture for 1919, p. 412.

make totally void the intent of the act. Another objection was the Post Office's definition of "rural postroads." Roads so designated often followed zigzag routes in many places off the roads upon which traffic was heavy. In the Post Office appropriation act, approved February 28, 1919, the definition of "rural roads" was broadened so as to allow the expenditure of Federal funds on the more important roads of the country. Amendments also provided for an increase of the $10,000 per mile cost to $20,000 and of the total appropriation from $75,-000,000 to $200,000,000.[1]

Some very important results immediately followed the passage of the act. Rules and regulations to carry out its provisions had to be formulated. This was done at a meeting of the heads of State highway officials held in Washington. "At the time the Federal act was passed, the States of Delaware, Georgia, South Carolina, Indiana, Texas, and Nevada had no semblance of a State highway department, and it was ascertained that the States of Florida, Arkansas, Oklahoma, Michigan, Missouri, Kansas, South Dakota, Idaho, and Wyoming would require additional legislation in order that their highway departments could perform the functions contemplated by the Federal aid road act. By the close of 1917 every State in the Union had a State highway department within the meaning of the Federal aid road act."[2] The act also resulted in the adoption of definite State highway systems by the States which in fact was necessary to comply with the provisions of the law. The American Association of State Highway Officials worked with the bureau in determining standard forms of specifications for materials and standards for testing materials, to which reference was made above. There was thus developed a great deal of organization that must necessarily result in efficient road building. By 1918 all the States, except Alabama, whose legislature meets quadrennially, had given legislative assent to the cooperative plan of road construction. Large funds have been raised by tax levies and through the sale of bonds voted for by the people. The war very considerably retarded road building, just as it

[1] *Vide Reports* of the Director of Public Roads for all data.
[2] *Annual Reports* of Department of Agriculture for 1917, p. 360.

interfered with many other industrial pursuits; and the amount expended therefore is not as large as would have been the case had there been no interruption from roadmaking. "On June 30, 1919, there had been approved by the department project statements for a total of 1,316 projects, involving 12,719.98 miles of road estimated to cost $133,774,568, of which $54,714,219 in Federal aid was requested."[1] Out of the total of $200,000,000 Federal aid available during the five-year period only a little more than a fourth of the appropriation had been asked for by the States at the close of the fiscal year of 1919. This, however, must be regarded as rapid progress under the circumstances. A great deal of preliminary legislative work had to be effected by the States, organization and plans of procedure had to be worked out cooperatively between the bureau and the States, and the war very greatly hampered actual construction. Rapid progress was made during the following year, the total amount requested having risen by June 30, 1920, to $109,830,366. Under authority of additional legislation enacted in 1922 the plan of making available Federal aid to roadmaking will be continued.

Just as we saw great stimulation in roadmaking through the participation of the State during the 90's, we now see great stimulation effected through the entry of the Federal Government into this field of activity. It is proof that exclusive local control, at one time more or less satisfactory, is no longer so after the marvelous changes in our economic organization. There should be no difficulty on the part of the States to secure the necessary funds for the construction and maintenance of these improved highway systems throughout the country. The major part of the tax burden should be borne by the automobile. Even now both the pleasure car and the truck are so universally used that it is no longer correct to divide economic groups into automobile owners, farmers, and others.

Irrigation, Drainage, and Rural Engineering.—It is stated that about 30,000,000 acres of land are potentially irrigable in the Western States, and that about this area is now being

[1] *Vide Director's Report* for 1919, p. 399.

irrigated.[1] The cost of development, however, is so great that the supply of irrigated lands exceeds the demand at the price offered which in many cases is only the cost of development. It therefore appears that the remaining more expensive irrigation projects to be developed will have to wait until either the products of the farm are more valuable or capital and labor cost less. The country is hardly ready to accept the policy of building irrigation plants with general revenues and disposing of them at less than cost, or leasing them at rentals insufficient to pay for the capital invested. However, in spite of this status the bureau is called upon for a great deal of assistance in the irrigation districts of the Western States. For the purpose of effecting economy and more expeditious administration the bureau moved its irrigation headquarters in 1918 from Washington, D. C., to Berkeley, California. The recent increase of farm values gave considerable encouragement to the construction of irrigation plants, and in his report for 1919 the director states that in Idaho alone projects including 1,500,000 acres are in various stages of promotion.

Another type of irrigation which the bureau has investigated and upon which it is prepared to give information, is pumping water from underground sources. Advice is given to farmers on engineering features of pumping equipment. High prices also halted the use of pumping apparatus, but cheaper materials are being provided, and in 1918 it is reported that on the Western Plains the prospects are that a considerable portion of the dry-farming will be overcome through the pumping method of irrigation.

Drainage is another subject receiving the attention of the engineering branch of the bureau. The reclamation of our swamp lands is a means of developing great agricultural resources. Problems taxing engineering ingenuity abound in the swamps along the coast. There are swamps that lie close to great urban centers, which, if drained, would yield very profitable returns. Such an instance is the one near New York City in the State of New Jersey. The bureau cooperates with

[1] *Yearbook* for 1918, p. 437.

a number of states in working out their drainage problems. Considerable attention is given to small farm projects where immediate beneficial results follow. In 1918 drainage surveys and plans were prepared for 226 farms in eighteen States. The bureau gives advice on tile drainage, machine trenching, possible organization in the community to purchase equipment, and among other things assists States in framing proper drainage laws.

When one reviews the work of the bureau in the field of Rural Engineering the impression is received that, at least so far as aims and policies are concerned, the Department of Agriculture leaves not a stone unturned in its efforts to make the farm productive and a comfortable place to live. Engineering assistance given farmers includes hydraulic, mechanical, electrical, architectural, and other problems.

STATES RELATIONS SERVICE

The Office of Experiment Stations.—The basis for the Office of Experiment Stations in the Department of Agriculture was laid with the establishment of the Land-grant Colleges in 1862 and the Agricultural Experiment Stations in 1887. The need for such a coordinating office in agricultural education and research was implicit in the establishment of the agricultural colleges. About a decade before the passing of the Hatch Act of 1887 actual experiment stations were being established and in many of the Land-grand Colleges experimental work was being carried on without an express organization or appropriation of funds for the purpose.

The result was that already in 1885 the Commissioner of Agriculture requested that delegates from all agricultural colleges and experiment stations meet in Washington with a view to coming to an understanding concerning the cooperation between experiment stations and the Department of Agriculture on research problems. The convention warmly approved the plan of the establishment of a central agency whereby the duplication of effort could be largely avoided and through which comparisons of experiments could be made and the results of experimentation throughout the country could be collected and published. In view of these circumstances the Commissioner of Agriculture said: "Believing that the Department of Agriculture can, if wisely conducted, become a vitalizing center for a more general cooperative effort for the promotion of agricultural science, and that the various State Experiment Stations should be encouraged by the most cordial cooperation on the part of this branch of the National Government, I have endeavored with my very limited means and force, to organize a branch in this department to take charge of the returns from these colleges and stations, and to collect and distribute the information obtained for the benefit of all interested parties."[1] Thus without any appropriations for this purpose the Commissioner began the work that later led to the organization of an experiment station office and recommended the new undertaking to the "careful consideration of Congress."

The impetus to establish experiment stations gained momentum and finally found favor with Congress in the passing of the Hatch Act of 1887. An act approved July 18, 1888, making appropriations for the department for the fiscal year 1889 provides for the establishment of an office of experiments stations in the following terms:

> Five hundred and ninety-five thousand dollars; ten thousand dollars of which sum shall be payable upon the order of the Commissioner of Agriculture to enable him to carry out the provisions of section three of said act of March second, eighteen hundred and eighty-seven, and to compose, edit and publish such of the results of the experiments made under section two of said act by said experiment stations as he may deem necessary; and for these purposes the Commissioner of Agriculture is authorized to employ such assistants, clerks and other persons as he may deem necessary.

To carry out the provisions of the act the department formally established October 1, 1888, an Office of Experiment Stations with a director in charge.[2]

Early Functions of the Office of Experiment Stations.— The duties of the department with respect to the Experiment Stations are stated in section three of the Hatch Act. This section provides as follows:

---

[1] *Vide Report of Department of Agriculture* for 1885, pp. 6 and 7.
[2] *Report of Department of Agriculture* for 1888, p. 10.

That in order to secure, as far as practicable, uniformity of methods and results in the work of said stations, it shall be the duty of the United States Commissioner of Agriculture to furnish forms, as far as practicable, for the tabulation of results of investigation or experiments; to indicate, from time to time, such lines of inquiry as to him shall seem most important; and, in general, to furnish such advice and assistance as will best promote the purposes of this act. It shall be the duty of each said station, annually, on or before the first day of February, to make to the Governor of the State or Territory in which it is located a full and detailed report of its operations, including a statement of receipts and expenditures, a copy of which report shall be sent to each of said stations, to the said Commissioner of Agriculture, and to the Secretary of the Treasury of the United States.

As stated in his report of 1888 the Commissioner of Agriculture indicated that in its relations with the stations the department was to "exercise not dictatorship, but leadership." This policy has been continued and is illustrated in the formation of the Association of American Agricultural Colleges and Experiment Stations which meets annually and whose purpose it is to discuss in the general assembly as well as in sections questions relating to the management and work of the stations. The name of the association was changed in 1919 to the Association of Land-grant Colleges. The association is composed of delegates from the Land-grant Colleges and Experiment Stations, the Department of Agriculture, and the Bureau of Education of the Department of the Interior.

To carry out the full purpose of the act, the Experiment Stations Office was to give information of a scientific character to the respective stations and to popularize the results of experiments among the people. The former object was accomplished in the publication of the Experiment Station Record, Station Bulletins, and the proceedings of the conventions of the Association of American Agricultural Colleges and Experiment Stations; while the latter purpose was fulfilled by the publication of Farmers' Bulletins and cooperating with Experiment Stations in supporting the Farmers' Institute movement. From time to time Congress provided funds for conducting special investigations in cooperation with the Experiment Stations. With respect to these special investigations Doctor True presents the following significant facts:

For many years the office carried on very important investigations on food and nutrition which did much toward laying a scientific basis for the home economics work of the colleges and schools. This work is still continued along with investigations on clothing and household equipment and management in the Office of Home Economics of the States Relations Service.

Beginning with 1898 the Office undertook irrigation investigations and this proved to be a large enterprise. Out of this also grew drainage investigations which were extensively carried on. The work in irrigation and drainage was turned over to the Office of Public Roads in 1915 when the States Relations Service was formed. A broad foundation had been laid by the Office of Experiment Stations for the work in irrigation and drainage which the Department is now carrying on.

One of the most important lines of work carried on by the Office of Experiment Stations had to do with agricultural education. With respect to this field of endeavor Doctor True comments as follows:

> A considerable part of this work was carried on in cooperation with the Association of Agricultural Colleges through a standing committee on Instruction in Agriculture, of which the Director of the Office of Experiment Stations was for many years chairman. This work dealt with the courses of instruction in agricultural colleges and schools, collection of data regarding the progress of agricultural education at home and abroad, and the publication of this material in annual reports; propaganda for the development of a comprehensive system of education in the colleges and secondary and elementary schools, and the management of a Graduate School of Agriculture held under the auspices of the Association of Agricultural Colleges. For many years no other federal organization, took any special interest in agricultural education. Now the Bureau of Education and the Federal Board for Vocational Education are working largely on the foundation laid by the Office of Experiment Stations. The States Relations Service is continuing the work in cooperation with the other federal organizations, the Land-Grant College Association, and State Departments of Education, but is now confining its attention chiefly to the preparation of subject matter for use in schools where agriculture is taught.

In 1890 the Office of Experiment Stations was made the depository of the financial and statistical reports of the colleges and stations which provided a means for ascertaining the development of agricultural education in the United States. Beginning in 1898 the Office of Experiment Stations from time to time organized stations in Alaska, Hawaii, Porto Rico and Guam. The States Relations Service took over these stations and has also acquired the station in the Virgin Islands, which was originally maintained by the Danish Government. All these stations are in no way connected with agricultural colleges, but are wholly federal institutions, the employes of the stations being a part of the staff of the Office of Experiment Stations.

The States Relations Service.—From its beginning the Experiment Stations Office was connected with various phases of extension work. With the passage of the Smith-Lever Act, approved May 8, 1914, there was to be a more certain and definite relation between the Department of Agriculture and the States with regard to extension work. The act provides that instruction and practical demonstration in agriculture and home economics shall be given to persons not attending agricultural colleges. The work was to be carried on by the Land-grant Colleges in cooperation with the department. As a prerequisite to sharing in the appropriations under this act the States through the extension departments of the Land-grant Colleges must submit plans of work and secure the approval of the Secretary of Agriculture. This supervision including the expenditure of Smith-Lever funds was at first placed by the Secretary in a committee, but at his recommendation the States Relations Service was provided for by Congress in 1915 to take over virtually all of the functions of the Office of the Experiment Stations and to represent him in his various and detailed relations with the States.

The Regulatory Function of the Service.—As already stated the bureau has a limited supervision over the work and expenditures of experiment stations and extension service of agricultural colleges. The Secretary of Agriculture has to certify to the Treasury Department whether funds may properly be paid to the stations and also report to Congress regarding the work and expenditures of these institutions. The facts for this report are secured through personal inspections, made annually, from printed reports of the various stations, in which they outline their work and expenditures, and from bulletins and other station publications. The policy of inspection is broad and is not confined merely to "an examination of accounts and financial reports, but extends to all the activities of the stations and their relations to other agricultural agencies." Whether or not the expenditures are legal is a matter that must be decided on the basis of good judgment and not merely by reference to the terms of the several statutes. The relation of the station to the Agricultural College results in the use of equipment jointly, and men who teach and at the same time carry on experiments divide their time between two institutions. The division of costs of operation between the college and the station is therefore a matter that cannot be definitely determined. However, an adherence to the policy of allowing only expenses incurred in the pursuit of experimental work and the dissemination of results will afford a basis sufficiently narrow to guarantee the proper expenditure of Government funds.

In connection with the supervision of extension work the Secretary of Agriculture is also required under the Smith-Lever Act to approve programs of work initiated by the extension departments of the Land-grant Colleges. In practice the colleges draw up their own projects or plans of work and submit them to the States Relations Service, which approves or disapproves them according as to whether or not they comply with the terms of the act.

Office of Extension Work.—At the time the States Relations Service was organized as a bureau and commissioned to supervise the extension work under the Smith-Lever Act of 1914, the Secretary in memorandum No. 140 indicated to the Director that the policy of the department from that time on would be to center all extension work of the various bureaus in the States Relations Service. This office of the States Relations Service is the medium through which arrangements for extension service are made with the various bureaus. In accordance with this plan of centralization also we find that the extension work carried on in two branches of the Bureau of Plant Industry was transferred in 1915 to the States Relations Service and placed in two offices, one having charge of the work of fifteen Southern States and the other of thirty-three Northern and Western States. In 1921 these offices were combined in a single Office of Extension Work. The extension service organized under the Smith-Lever Act will be discussed in detail in a later chapter. Only the bare outline of the work therefore will here be given. It includes extension and demonstration work through county men and women agents, boys' and girls' clubs, extension specialists, and through special agricultural campaigns. Representatives of the extension office attend state meetings of county agents, home-demonstration agents and other extension workers in each State; and thus the Federal offices serve as a means of coordinating the work among the forty-eight States of the Union.

Division of Farmers' Institutes.—The farmers' institute may be said to have grown out of the more or less irregular meetings held by various agricultural societies from our national beginning well into the middle of the nineteenth century. Its real beginning, however, began with the establishment of the agricultural colleges and experiment stations throughout the country.[1] The function of these institutions as conceived early by the Association of Land-grant Colleges was not merely to experiment and to teach resident students, but to spread the agricultural gospel everywhere. The practice of delivering lectures away from the home of the institution was therefore begun. In many States the institute was held under the auspices of the agricultural college, while in others it was held under the supervision of the State board of agriculture or under the direction of State agricultural societies receiving State recognition and State aid. County organizations were sometimes maintained for the purpose.

At these institutes practical agricultural problems were discussed by specialists usually from the colleges and experiment stations. The meeting, however, was an open forum where the successful and intelligent farmer would give the community the benefit of his experience. The question box was usually a feature of the program, and this served to direct discussion to problems actually before the farmers.

Without question a great deal of good has been accomplished through the numerous farmers' institutes held throughout the country during the last half century. Yet it is also true that the reports of these meetings are more impressive than their actual results. It has been complained that the institutes are often poorly attended, that only the more progressive and intelligent farmers who already appreciate the importance of scientific agriculture, can be induced to take

[1] *Vide Yearbook* for 1899, p. 170.

an active interest in the meetings, and that remote communities are not reached at all. The absence of a follow-up method by which the farmer could receive continued instruction also caused the work of the institute to be void of very fruitful results. Efforts of course have been made to overcome these difficulties. According to the report for the fiscal year 1908, farmers' institutes were held in all the States except Louisiana and Nevada, and in all Territories except Alaska and Porto Rico. "There were 4,643 institutes held, made up of 14,934 sessions, with a total attendance of 2,098,268. The appropriations from all sources for institute purposes for the year were $297,356.89. Sixteen States held independent institutes with an attendance of 81,845. Eleven States held round-up institutes, consisting of 99 sessions, with an attendance of 28,910. Eight States conducted railroad specials. The attendance in seven of these States upon these specials was 218,710. Ten States held movable schools of agriculture, with an attendance of 6,849, and two States held field meetings, continuing through nine days, attended by 4,100 persons."[1] For the fiscal year 1918 there were held 6,941 institutes in 31 States with 14,446 sessions and an attendance of 1,916,706.[2] In 1920 the number of institutes held in 30 States was 4,542. While these efforts to secure close contact with the people have been made and which have been productive of important results, there was nevertheless no organization that systematically and continuously devoted itself to the demonstration of practical agriculture throughout the length and breadth of the land. Such an organization was conceived and established in the Smith-Lever Act of 1914, which will be discussed in a separate chapter. It was believed that after this extension service would be in full operation the demand for the farmers' institute would decrease, but judging from the figures of 1918 and 1920 just quoted such does not seem to be the case. The number of meetings and number in attendance remains about the same as they were immediately prior to the passage of the Smith-Lever Act. It would seem therefore that the farmers' institute

---

[1] Circular by A. C. True, dated June 7, 1909, p. 18.

[2] *Cooperative Extension Work in Agriculture and Home Economics*, 1918, p. 126.

serves a purpose not fulfilled by other features of the extension service. It is to be noted, however, that while numerous farmers' institutes are still held, their character has been considerably changed by a closer connection with the extension services of the agricultural colleges in most of the States.

The Division of Farmers' Institutes in the States Relations Service collects statistics dealing with institutes at home and abroad. It cooperates with institute workers. During the year 1918 the bureau loaned 604 syllabi of lectures each accompanied by a set of fifty lantern slides to institute and other extension workers.

Division of Agriculture Instruction.—As organized in the States Relations Service this division largely confines its work to the preparation of subject-matter material in agriculture in form for immediate use by teachers, and to furnishing to teachers illustrative material and information as to how they can obtain and use the publications of the Department of Agriculture.

This work is carried on in cooperation with the Federal Board for Vocational Education as regards secondary education; and with agricultural colleges and state departments of education as regards elementary education.

There is also cooperation with the Land-grant College Association and with the Bureau of Education in studies of the more general problems of agricultural education.

Office of Home Economics.—This office conducts experiments and other investigations on food and diet, clothing, household equipment and household management.

The results of its studies are reported in numerous technical and popular bulletins, as well as articles published by the press. The information acquired by this office is also widely disseminated through the Extension Service.

MISCELLANEOUS OFFICES

Office of the Secretary.—The duties of the Secretary are the promotion of agriculture in the broadest sense. He exercises general supervision and control over the affairs of the department and formulates its policies. All such work that is more or less closely allied to general administration, is included in the organization of the office of the Secretary, although it is subdivided into various offices headed by responsible persons in charge. These offices include the Chief Clerk, Solicitor, Accounts and Disbursements, Inspection, Appointment Clerk, the Library, Publication and Information and such offices performing regulatory functions as Forest Appeals and those enforcing the insecticide act, Federal plant quarantine act, and the law relating to the packing industry. In the absence of the Secretary the Assistant Secretary is in charge, and if both these officials are absent the Chief of the Weather Bureau becomes acting head of the department. The Secretary, the Assistant Secretary, the Chief of the Weather Bureau and the Solicitor are presidential appointments and require the confirmation of the Senate, while all other employes of the department are in the classified civil service.

The Office of the Solicitor.—The Solicitor performs all legal work of the department and therefore acts as legal adviser to the Secretary and heads of the various bureaus. The office aids in the drafting of legislative bills to be submitted in Congress, examines and reports violations of regulatory laws, prepares contracts for use by the Forest Service and other bureaus, and examines and approves all rules and regulations promulgated by the Secretary of Agriculture. A great deal of legislation passing through Congress originates in the executive departments because the need for such law is first brought to the attention of the administrator. State officials sometimes submit prospective legislation to the Federal Department for investigation. Members of Congress also frequently refer their legislative ideas to the department for approval. The result is that in spite of the constitutional attempt to separate completely the powers of the legislative, judicial and executive branches of the Government, the Department of Agriculture is playing an important part in suggesting and drafting legislation that affects at many points the behavior of the entire citizenry. During the fiscal year of

1916 the Solicitor reports that more than forty bills relating to agricultural matters were drawn or examined and commented upon.

Division of Accounts and Disbursements.—So far as the actual payment of all claims against the Department of Agriculture is concerned its accounting organization may be said to be centralized under one Disbursing Clerk, while the preliminary functions of examination and certification of accounts for payment are scattered among the various bureaus and offices. In each bureau accounts pertaining to it are prepared, approved by the chief of bureau or his representative, and properly audited, after which they are ready for payment. After the Disbursing Clerk is satisfied that the account is altogether regular he makes payment. The fact of the matter is that he assumes that such accounts are regular and merely signs or has signed by his deputies checks written in the respective bureaus. Every quarter the paid vouchers of all the bureaus are submitted together with an account current and an abstract of vouchers through the main Division of Accounts to the Auditor for the State and other departments at the Treasury Department. The Auditor examines the vouchers very carefully, and if he takes exception to an item the matter is referred to the Disbursing Clerk for further explanation. If the explanation is not satisfactory the item is disallowed and the officials responsible for the payment must adjust it within a reasonable time. This careful auditing of all Government expenditures by an independent auditor causes accounting officers to be extremely cautious.

This office also prepares the "estimates" from year to year. Estimates of the amounts of the various appropriations necessary to cover the proposed expenditures are made up in the respective bureau accounting offices and all brought together in the main Division of Accounts whence they are transmitted to the Secretary of the Treasury and made a part of the Book of Estimates submitted to Congress.

SELECTED REFERENCES.

Yearbook for 1899, pp. 367-80; various *Reports* of Director of Public Roads; various *Reports of Cooperative Extension Work in Agriculture and Home Economics.*

CHAPTER IV

The Bureau of Plant Industry and the Forest Service.

BUREAU OF PLANT INDUSTRY

Beginnings of the Collection and Distribution of Seeds.—As early as 1623 King James for ethical reasons was especially anxious to direct the attention of the colonists from tobacco raising to the cultivation of other profitable crops, and the assembly of Virginia accordingly directed the planting of mulberry trees with a view to introducing silk culture. In "1743 the British Parliament granted $600,000 to promote the cultivation of indigo and other crops in the American colonies, and the assemblies in the various colonies appropriated small sums from time to time to encourage the cultivation of plants new to the country, such as hops in Virginia, mulberry trees for silk culture in Georgia, and vineyards for the establishment of an American wine industry."[1]

Franklin while in England as agent of Pennsylvania and Thomas Jefferson during the time he was minister to France, collected rare seeds for distribution in America. Other representatives followed their example, and under John Quincy Adam's administration definite instructions were given to all United States consuls to forward rare plants and seeds to Washington for distribution. Interest in the use of better seeds was also stimulated by the early agricultural societies through the exhibition of farm products at fairs.

The United States Government began the distribution of seeds in a more systematic way in 1836 when H. L. Ellsworth, Commissioner of Patents, began the work without a specific appropriation for the purpose. In 1839 Congress supported the project by an appropriation of $1,000, and from that time to 1865 appropriations were continued to be made for the combined purpose of seed distribution and the collection of statistics. Appropriations steadily increased and for the year 1922 Congress provided $360,000 for the purpose.

---

[1] *Circular 100*, Bureau of Plant Industry.

Amount of Seed Distributed.—The activity and importance of this function may be seen from the following statement of the distribution of seeds compiled from *Agricultural Reports* and *Yearbooks*.

Year	*No. of Packages*	
1865	763,231	all kinds of seeds
1870	358,391	all kinds of seeds
1880	1,581,253	all kinds of seeds
1890	5,605,246	all kinds of seeds
1905	35,977,135	all kinds of seeds
1910	59,992,840	vegetable and flower
[1]1917	79,914,575	vegetable and flower

The statement shows a very rapid increase in the amount of seed distributed. The seeds thus distributed were of many kinds, including vegetable, flower, cotton, tobacco, sugar beet, sorghum, grass, grain, and other seeds, as well as plants and trees. The following statement shows the classes of recipients of these seeds in 1880 and 1890:

	1880	1890
To Senators and members of Congress..	759,659 pkgs.	4,459,778 pkgs.
To Agricultural Societies	17,444 pkgs.	....
To Statistical Correspondents	139,729 pkgs.	348,882 pkgs.
To Granges	355,452 pkgs.	....
To Special Farmers	127,644 pkgs.	....
To Miscellaneous Applicants	181,305 pkgs.	653,616 pkgs.
To Exp. Sta., Agr. Col., and Agr. Societies	....	142,970 pkgs.

This statement shows that by far the larger part of the seeds were being distributed through the members of Congress, which fact throws some light on the politics connected with this work.

The Object of the Distribution.—The act creating the Department of Agriculture provided that it shall "procure, propagate, and distribute among the people new and valuable seeds and plants." Without question it was the purpose of this legislation to distribute only new and improved seeds and plants. Very soon, however, as shown by the table of the number of packages sent out, there developed between the members of Congress and his constituents a relation which gave a new

[1] In order not to vitiate its comparative value the figure for 1917 is put at five times the number of packages sent out because each package contained five packets.

aspect to the work of distributing seeds. Requests for seeds increased enormously and seeds distributed were by no means all new and improved.

In 1894 a change was advocated and Congress was urged to discontinue the customary distribution.[1] Congress, however, was unwilling to relinquish this time-honored privilege, and changed the law so as to give legal sanction to the distribution of seeds that were not necessarily rare seeds. The Secretary of Agriculture was left no discretion in the matter and the expenditure of the minimum sum of $130,000 was made mandatory. For many years department officials and farmers' organizations had regularly protested to this vicious practice; and in 1921 when Congress was determined to pursue a vigorous policy of retrenchment it reduced the department's appropriation by more than $2,000,000, but continued this time-honored political device at the expense of worthy projects for which it decided funds were not available. That year $239,000 was appropriated for the purpose. Again in the face of strong opposition from the Grange and the Farmers' Union the appropriation for the fiscal year, 1922, was increased to $360,000. The opposition of organized agriculture from all sides finally became strong enough to eliminate this unnecessary evil from the appropriation bill for the fiscal year of 1924.

The introduction of rare seeds and plants must be distinguished from the so-called "Congressional seed distribution." There is full justification for supporting by public funds the importation of new plants. In the case of the colonies the introduction of grains, grasses, and livestock was so important that their very existence was virtually dependent upon it, and at all stages of a country's development the effort to increase the national wealth, especially that of foodstuffs, is to be commended. This is, however, wholly different from the vicious "Congressional seed distribution."

Development of the Bureau.—At the time the Patent Office distributed seed it was under the Department of State. In 1849 this office was transferred to the Department of Interior,

---

[1] *Vide Circular 100*, Bureau of Plant Industry, for facts concerning seed distribution.

and in 1862 the agricultural work was transferred to the new Department of Agriculture. A Seed Division, to carry on the distribution of seed, was organized in 1868, and in 1898 the Office of Foreign Seed and Plant Introduction was established. The same year the seed work was transferred to the Botany Division, which in 1901 was merged with the Bureau of Plant Industry. With the establishment of the Department of Agriculture in 1862 a Superintendent of Experimental Garden was appointed. The purposes of the Garden as outlined by the Superintendent in his first report were experimental, such as improvement of plants by hybridizing, pruning and special culture; pathological, including the investigation of plant disease and destructive insects; and aesthetic, including the collection and adaptation of decorative shrubbery for landscape gardening and the display of exotic plants. This work was also merged with the Bureau of Plant Industry in 1901.

An important and authentic American herbarium had its origin in the collections made by such early government expeditions as the expedition to Japan under Commodore Perry in 1853; the North and South Pacific exploring expeditions, Commodore Wilkes' expedition, and the Mexican Survey; and the Pacific Railroad surveys.[1] The Herbarium was cared for by the Smithsonian Institution, but inasmuch as the department employed a botanist of its own almost from the beginning of its establishment, the funds of the institution also being limited, the collections were transferred to the Department of Agriculture. Subsequent additions, however, soon required larger quarters than the department had available and in 1896 the Herbarium was again returned to the Smithsonian Institution and placed in a fireproof building. This Herbarium, like the herbaria of Europe, has provided a laboratory for the study of plant life in both its practical and theoretical aspects and has been used by botanical students from all parts of the world.

As already indicated the group of functions now performed by the Bureau of Plant Industry were at first scattered among a number of separate offices, the most important

[1] *Yearbook*, 1879, p. 18.

of which was the Botany Division. The Botany Division served as a center around which new functions clustered as they developed from time to time. During its separate existence there had been placed under its charge such offices as Fibre Investigation, Seed and Plant Introduction, Mycological Section, the Herbarium, Agrostology, and Vegetable Physiology and Pathology. Some of this work had its origin in the Botany Division and as expansion took place portions of it drifted away into separate offices only to be gathered up again into a bureau in 1901. The history of the elemental parts of the Bureau of Plant Industry affords an interesting phase of governmental organization. There is always a danger when different but closely related work is assigned to different offices each having the same dignity and authority, that the necessary cooperation between them may disappear. There is also the tendency for each office to add functions from time to time and to bring about a duplication of work. Intense rivalry may be occasioned and needless expense incurred. It is not surprising that Secretary Wilson saw that more "harmonious action" could be secured by affiliating all these related parts and placing them under one bureau. Where there is progress organization cannot remain static. During the next decade the experience of the past reenacted itself with the result that when Secretary Houston took office he found it necessary to divorce farm economics from the bureau and place it under a separate office because it pertains to all farm activities, as well as farm demonstration work, which he placed under the States Relations Service. By this time also such misplaced functions as farm credit and farm insurance investigations found lodgment in the bureau and either became conspicuous among plants and weeds or were overrun by them. These and other functions were removed from the bureau and placed in offices where they stood in closer relation to other work performed.

Present Functions of the Bureau.—The work in the bureau is organized along project lines, all of which except two may be said to be scientific in their character. They are concerned with research work in the laboratroy or in the field, and are not conducted primarily in the interest of pure theory but rather with a view to increasing production. This economic achievement is to be accomplished through two lines of endeavor. The first is the investigation looking toward an increased yield of the plant which frequently means a long, drawn-out study. The second is the cure and prevention of disease so that the results of the first step may be realized in full.

Only one of its projects is of a regulatory nature.[1] This project is known as Seed-Testing Laboratories, and has charge of the enforcement of the Seed-Importation Act of 1912 and 1916. Upon examination of samples customs officers are directed to release or refuse delivery of the shipment according to whether or not they conform to the requirements of the act. Under act of 1904 these Laboratories also purchase seeds in the open market and test them with a view to determining their degree of purity. If samples are found to be adulterated or misbranded the names of the dealers are made public.

The Bureau cooperates freely with other Bureaus of the Department as well as with outside agencies. It makes pathological inspections of fruits during marketing in cooperation with the Bureau of Markets, and in cooperation with the Forest Service it makes pathological studies of trees. There are other points of contact with other offices. Cooperation among bureaus is necessary to cause the Department as a whole to function properly.

Some Achievements.—As early as 1874 the Department began to investigate the possibility of introducing grasses and other forage plants into the South and into the semi-arid regions of the Northwest and Southwest. The grasses grown in the East had been brought from England where the climate is quite similar to that of the eastern part of the United States. In the South and semi-arid regions, however, they could not be grown. Experimentation was begun at Garden City in western Kansas, where an experiment station had been established for the purpose, and by 1893 it had been demonstrated that the two forage plants, Hungarian brome and red Kafir corn, and one grain, Jerusalem corn, could be successfully

[1] In cooperation with the Insecticide and Fungicide Board the Bureau aids in the enforcement of the Insecticide Act of 1901.

grown in the semi-arid regions where irrigation was impracticable.[1] This must be recognized as a great service to the country. Since then Kafir corn has become an important crop in western Kansas and western Oklahoma and is being extensively used in fattening livestock, having directly resulted in increasing and sustaining the meat supply of the country.

In 1885 some remedies for fungous diseases of plants were discovered, notably the prevention of black rot of the grape, and the following year the Commissioner decided to prosecute this work more vigorously with the hearty approval of such societies as the American Pomological Society, the Western New York Horticultural Society, and the Botanical Section of the American Association for the Advancement of Science. B. T. Galloway recalls some of the difficulties encountered in working out these problems and introducing them generally. By growing bacilli in various media in the laboratory it was proven that the same disease may affect different plants. By taking the study to the field it was proven that in the case of fire blight of pears and apples, insects such as bees, visiting many different blossoms, are mainly responsible for the rapid infection of large areas. In spite of these investigations Galloway points out that farmers and owners of orchards were so averse to the use of fungicides that had been invented for the purpose of killing the bacilli that they had actually to be paid in order that object lessons to the community and the country might be given. "Five years after the first successful treatment of black rot, however, carefully collected data showed that there were more than fifty thousand grape growers treating their vines in accordance with the directions issued by the Department."[2]

While other achievements could be mentioned, it should be remembered that not all lines of investigation are crowned with success. Not all hypotheses lead to a solution, and it must not be expected that every dollar appropriated can be matched with a corresponding service that is both definite and practical in its results. For this very reason such func-

[1] *Vide Yearbook, 1897*, p. 90.
[2] *Vide* Galloway's statement in *Yearbook*, 1897, pp. 104-11.

tions as are carried on by the Bureau of Plant Industry should be supported by public funds and should not be wholly entrusted to private initiative.

FOREST SERVICE

The Attitude of the Early Settlers Toward the Forest.—At the time the early settlers came to America, forests in their home countries had already become a matter of public concern and nearly all of them were under strict royal control. The game laws and other regulations bred in these European immigrants a respect for forests that probably had much to do with the enactment of laws providing for the care and protection of forests adjacent to the various communities in Massachusetts, and for the provision by William Penn in Pennsylvania that for every five acres of land cleared one acre of forest should be left standing. As a part of its colonial policy the Crown of England also directed that timber suitable for shipbuilding be protected and not ruthlessly destroyed. The preservation of forests, however, under circumstances prevailing at that time was wholly incompatible with the establishment of colonies. The necessaries of life could only be provided after the land was cleared and crops were grown. Moreover the safety of the population along the frontier for many years was in constant danger because of hostile Indians lurking in the forest and fighting from concealed places. Ruthless destruction of forests soon became general among the colonists. Forests were burned to provide space for raising crops. This was the only sane policy that the colonists could pursue, and no condemnation can be pronounced upon them except it be for not leaving more of a stand on each farm and for the total lack of application of principles of forestry to such stands as were allowed to remain. These matters, however, comprise a body of knowledge the full social significance of which was not then generally appreciated by the people.

The Beginnings of the Forest Service.—This ruthless destruction, however, soon brought a change of sentiment in the East, and as is usually the case with all social movements requiring the attention of the federal government, forestry was first fostered and encouraged by individuals, societies and the states. Thus "in the last decade of the eighteenth century the New York Society for the Promotion of Agriculture, Arts, and Manufactures, and in the first years of the nineteenth, the Massachusetts Society for the Promotion of Agriculture, took action, inspired by a desire to protect and promote the growth of forests."[1] In 1799 Congress passed an act providing for the purchase of a tract whose timber would be suitable for the use of the Navy. Supplemental acts between the years 1817 and 1831 led to the purchase and partial protection of "244,000 acres of forest-bearing land in Florida, Alabama, Mississippi, and Louisiana, and in Florida to some partially successful efforts at the culture of the live oak." Massachusetts in 1858 "offered a premium of $1,000 for the best plantation of forest trees planted in 1860, payable in 1870."[2] California, in a law approved March 30, 1868, provided for the planting of shade and fruit trees along public highways by paying the owner of the property four years after the planting $1 for each tree in good condition. The law specified the kind of trees that could be planted and that the minimum distance between the trees was to be 12 feet. Illinois, Missouri and Iowa also early enacted statutes encouraging tree planting. Bounties were offered by states, societies and individuals to encourage the planting of trees. In some cases railroad corporations were interested in the project. Horace Greeley in a book entitled, "What I Know of Farming," first published in 1871 in the New York Tribune, besides frequent incidental references to forestry, devotes four chapters to the subject pointing out various utilities of forest trees. The Civil War was followed by great activity in railroad building and consequent destruction of forests. It was at this time that agitation in the interest of forestry was coming to be feebly felt, in the words of Gifford Pinchot. "In 1867 horticultural and agricultural societies in Wisconsin appointed a committee to report on the results of forest destruction, and two years later the Board of Agriculture of Maine took action toward the formula-

---

[1] *Yearbook*, 1899, p. 294.
[2] *Yearbook*, 1875, p. 334.

tion of a forest policy for the State. Laws for the encouragement of tree planting were passed between 1868 and 1873 in nine Western and two Eastern States."

While meagre attempts were made by Congress in 1831 to protect the public timber lands through the Solicitor of the Treasury and in 1855 through the General Land Office, it was not until 1878 that Congress provided for a more extended effort to suppress depredations. In 1873, 1874, 1876, and 1878 Congress passed and amended the timber culture acts providing for the occupation of public land by homesteaders on condition that a certain number of trees were planted. Proof of such planting depended upon the testimony of two witnesses at the various land offices.[1] The ends of the act in many cases were realized, "but in many more the law afforded only a pretext for occupation for mearly speculative purposes."[2]

Establishment of the Forestry Division.—In 1873 the American Association for the Advancement of Science appointed a committee "to memorialize Congress and the several State legislatures upon the importance of promoting the cultivation of timber and the preservation of forests, and to recommend proper legislation for securing these objects." The House reported a bill looking to the appointment of a commissioner of forestry. No action, however, was taken until August 15, 1876, when in the regular agricultural bill $2,000 was appropriated for the appointment of an expert who was "to ascertain the annual amount of consumption, importation and exportations of timber and other forest products, the probable supply for future wants, the means best adapted to the preservation and renewal of forests, the influence of forests on climate, and the measures that have been successfully applied in foreign countries or that may be deemed applicable in this country for the preservation and restoration or planting of forests, and to report upon the same to the Commissioner of Agriculture, to be by him in a separate report transmitted to Congress." To carry out these provisions the Commissioner of Agriculture appointed Dr. Franklin B. Hough, who submitted

[1] *Vide Yearbook*, 1875, p. 334.
[2] *Yearbook*, 1880, p. 653.

his first report of 650 pages in 1877 and a second in 1878. The reports together with the first attempt on the part of the Department to serve the interests of forestry were favorably commented upon in the press including the *New York Times*.[1]

Provision was made for continuing the special investigation conducted by Dr. Hough to 1880, and in that year Congress appropriated for the work as a regular and continuous function of the Department. Dr. Hough was placed in charge of the office to which the Commissioner refers as the Forestry Division in his report for 1880, and, although coming comparatively late, its functions soon assumed sufficient importance to require the organization of a Bureau which took place in 1901. In 1884 the Division was charged with the duty of making experiments and in 1885 with the collection and distribution of tree seeds, to which "plants" was also added in 1886. Insufficient funds made it impossible for the Division to do effective work from the start. But back of it all, the real cause for the Division's early inactivity was the fact that its creation was the result of the agitation of scientific bodies and was in fact in advance of a well developed public sentiment. Compare conditions in the United States at that time with those of European countries where the need for a rigorous forest policy had become thoroughly socialized. In 1885 "the Bohemian Forest Department and forestry associations distributed 4,600,000 seedlings, of which nearly 4,000,000 were coniferous. Double the amount was prepared for distribution [in 1887]. The same was done in Styria. The Hungarian Department of Commerce distributes plant material free on board cars. In 1884 the Prussian Forest Department distributed over 25,000,000 seedlings. The large subventions in material and in money granted by the French Government for reforestation have been often pointed out in former reports."[2] In view of the circumstances prevailing at the time the Division was established its main functions were confined to missionary work and the prosecution of such scientific work that the small appropriations permitted. The propaganda carried on by the Division consisted of lectures before farmers' insti-

[1] *Vide Yearbook*, 1878, p. 31.
[2] From Report of Chief of Forestry Division, 1886.

tues and elsewhere, the writing of articles in newspapers and technical journals, and the preparation of official circulars setting forth the social importance of the movement, and in the interests of lumbermen, among other things, the method of securing their property against loss by fire. The agitation of the Division, aided largely by the American Forestry Association and other scientific bodies soon resulted in the development of the present forest policy of the United States.

The Development of the Forest Policy.—The disadvantages, contributing to the slow development of a definite policy of forestry, were the absence in 1886 of forest schools in the United States and forest journals in the English language. Dr. Hough's *American Forestry Journal* issued for one year was abandoned in 1883 for lack of support. The English journal, *The Indian Forester,* concerned chiefly with tropical conditions, was the only journal at the time published in the English language.[1] However, during the next decade state agricultural colleges generally and to some extent other institutions began the teaching of forestry. Such associations as the American Forestry Association and the Pennsylvania Forestry Association also became active in forestry propaganda and played an important part in the evolution of a sane forest policy through the issue of their publications.

One of the most effective ways of popularizing the forestry movement was the general observance of Arbor Day, instituted in Nebraska in 1872 by the Honorable J. Sterling Morton, Secretary of Agriculture from 1893 to 1897. By 1900 provision for its observance had been made in every state and territory of the Union. Its central idea is the planting of trees by school children with appropriate exercises with a view to impressing the young generation with the beauty and usefulness of shade and forest trees and with the need of preserving them for future use.

Complaint was made by B. E. Fernone in his report for 1886, then Chief of the Division, that the central idea of forestry was conceived to be by writers merely the planting of trees and the creation of new forests by artificial means, while

[1] *Vide Yearbook,* 1886, p. 182.

our vast natural forests were permitted to be slaughtered with entire disregard to the dictates of forestry. The application of forest management was entirely overlooked. The movement of tree planting has found its widest application on the treeless plains of the Middle West. It is in Nebraska that Arbor Day was instituted. This is a very important phase of forestry and is becoming more important as the timber supply of the country is being consumed. Four-fifths of the supply of timber is under private ownership, and it is the farmer over the country, having a few acres here and there good for nothing else but for timber reserves, who can by planting trees or tree seeds maintain the necessary supply.

Correct principles of forestry aim at the use of the existing forests in ways that will bring the greatest benefit to the whole country and at the same time keep them in a continuous state of reproduction. To this of course should be added the creation of new forests and scattered tree planting. It will be seen at once that this is a tremendous problem. It involves propaganda to secure a proper use of the ordinary farm wood lot without its extermination. A similar sort of propaganda is necessary with the private owners of large tracts of timber land. It requires the evolution of sound methods of protection against fire and a propaganda to introduce them generally where forests are privately owned. It involves the protection of water flow in order to supply cities and towns with water and maintain the navigability of streams. It involves wise action with regard to the national forests and discrimination between timber land and arable land. Economy in the administration of the national forests demands that a definite amount of grazing be allowed in the interest of the meat supply of the country, and in the interest of the forest it is important that reproduction of the forest is not impeded by too much grazing, or what is worse, that the forest is not destroyed. The preservation of the forests includes scientific investigation as to plant diseases and injury done to trees by insects and animals. Provision for amusement must be borne in mind as a phase of the forest policy. It is to be sure not as important as the main aim of the policy, that of providing a limited supply of timber for the future; yet as the country becomes more and more congested the welfare of the people will depend more largely upon recreation in the forests and city parks. The formulation of these principles and their general recognition in and out of Congress had to be realized before an enlightened forestry policy could be put into practice.

The Creation of Our National Forests.—In an article by the Chief of the Division of Forestry in the *Yearbook*[1] for 1897 credit is given the Division for initial steps leading finally to the reservation of forests on public land. The Division published a bulletin concerning the condition of the forests in the Rocky Mountain States in 1887 and the same year formulated a bill which was introduced in Congress but failed to become a law. Its educational effect, however, the Division claims had much to do with the passage of a law shortly afterward. Gifford Pinchot as Chief of the Division credits[2] the American Forestry Association with efforts to secure the reservation of forests. The facts merely illustrate the character of the Department of Agriculture and show it to be largely an educational institution attacking nearly all of its problems from the point of view of the propagandist and linking itself up with private educational agencies in order that progress may be made both in scientific discoveries and their general introduction.

Because of their unsatisfactory results the timber acts, already referred to, were repealed, in 1891. This repealing act contained a clause authorizing the President to set aside "any part of the public lands wholly or in part covered with timber or undergrowth, whether of commercial value or not, as public reservations, and the President shall, by public proclamation, declare the establishment of such reservations and the limits thereof." Under the provisions of the act the President set aside 18,000,000 acres. This meant that this portion of the public domain was withdrawn from entry by homesteaders. The step indicates the beginning of a definite national forest system. The supervision of the national forests was then under the Department of the Interior, which also had charge of the public land. The Secretary of Interior,

[1] P. 159.
[2] *Yearbook*, 1889, p. 294.

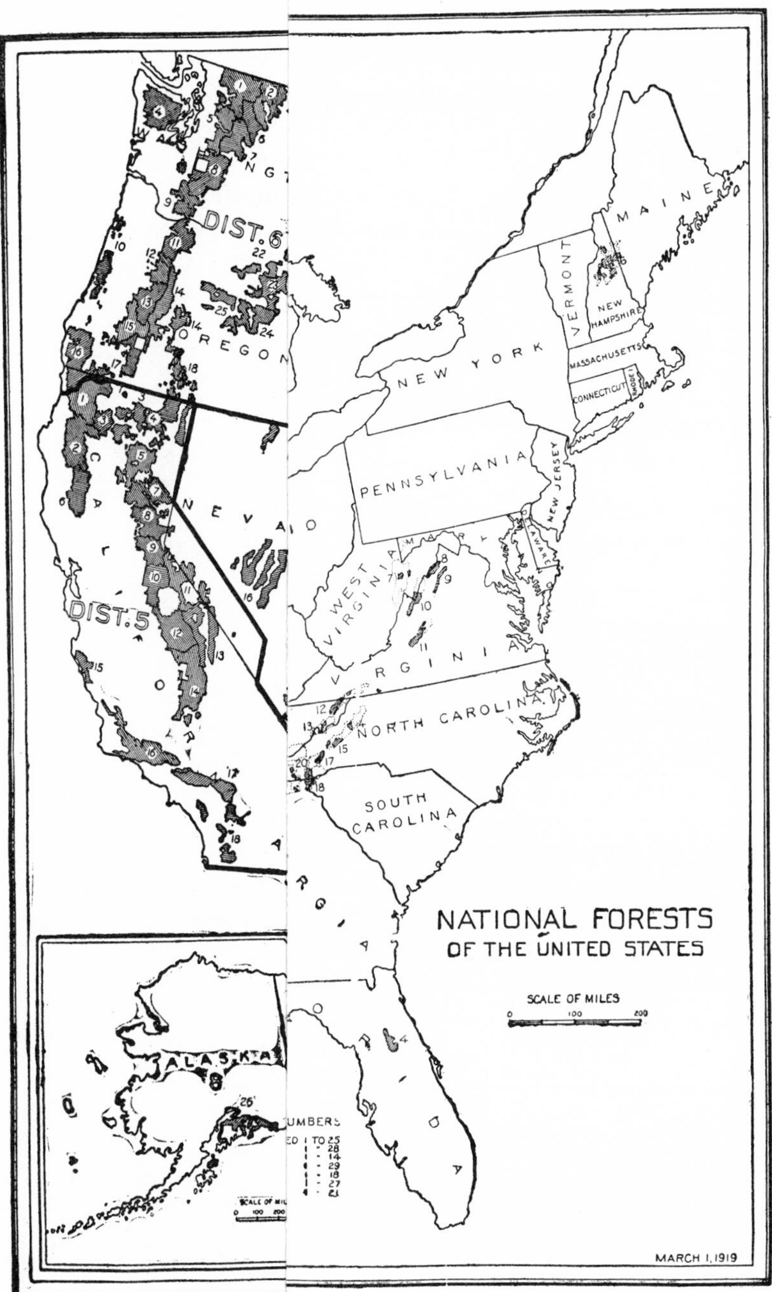
NATIONAL FORESTS
OF THE UNITED STATES
SCALE OF MILES
MARCH 1, 1919
DIST. 6
DIST. 5
OREGON
NEVADA
NEW YORK
PENNSYLVANIA
MAINE
VERMONT
NEW HAMPSHIRE
MASSACHUSETTS
CONNECTICUT
NEW JERSEY
WEST VIRGINIA
VIRGINIA
NORTH CAROLINA
SOUTH CAROLINA
ALASKA

concerned about the safety of the national forests which were "wholly without care or management," addressed to the president of the National Academy of Sciences a request for an investigation and report upon the "inauguration of a national forest policy for the forested lands of the United States." In response to the Secretary's request a committee was appointed which traveled extensively and served without pay. Traveling expenses, however, were provided by Congress in an appropriation of $25,000. The committee recommended as a preliminary step the segregation of eleven new reserves with a total area of more than 21,000,000 acres. These reserves were set aside by the President on February 22, 1897. In the absence of a well-defined national forest policy even at this late date much misunderstanding prevailed both in and out of Congress concerning these reservations. The committee's report clarified many of the issues when it appeared in May. It was not generally understood that the reservations were to be used for various purposes, and the result was that President McKinley and members of the committee were subjected to violent attacks by members of Congress. Action of the proclamation except its application to California, was suspended by Congress until March of the succeeding year, 1898. By that time the issues were well cleared up and a complete change in sentiment had taken place. Congress was now willing to more than double the amount asked for by the Secretary of the Interior for the care and preservation of the national forests. This episode in the evolution of our national forest policy caused vigorous discussion of forest matters by the press and may be regarded as a period during which the nation definitely and permanently decided in favor of Government forest reserves. Since the first reservation of forest land gradual increases have been made both through reserving forests on public land and through the purchase of forest land under private ownership, so that on June 30, 1917, the total net National Forest area included 155,166,619 acres. A glance at the map dated March 1, 1919, published by the Forest Service, shows the distribution of the National Forests.

Acquisition of Appalachian Forests.—The Weeks Act on March 1, 1911, made available $2,000,000 for the purchase of forest land necessary to control or protect the water flow of the navigable streams of the Appalachian system. Approval of purchase was vested in a commission of seven, and the Geological Survey had to establish the fact that control of the lands would promote or protect the navigation of streams. The examination of titles of lands selected for purchase was in many cases difficult because in some of the states the early land records were in a deplorable condition. It was necessary to go back to patents issued by the Crown before the organization of the states. Where acquisition of land was only possible through condemnation the Department of Agriculture assisted the Department of Justice in the preparation and presentation of cases.

In 1916 Congress appropriated $3,000,000 more for the purchase of lands in the Appalachian and White Mountains, recognizing in a definite way the permanence of our National Forest Policy. Up to June 30, 1918, 1,650,790 acres had been authorized for purchase in this section of the country. The map shows where forests in the east are being acquired. The average cost of these tracts was $5.22 per acre. There is great demand for the timber on these lands which is cut in accordance with sound forestry practice.

The Present Organization of the Forest Service.—In 1901 the Forestry Division was converted into a Bureau in order that it might better discharge its manifold duties and relieve the Secretary of needless responsibilities. In 1905 the management of the National Forests, heretofore under the Department of Interior, was transferred to the Department of Agriculture and placed under the Forestry Bureau whose name the same year was changed to Forest Service, which is more indicative of its functions. The transfer of the administration of the National Forests had been recommended by the Chief of the Forestry Division as far back as 1897 inasmuch as the science of forestry, and therefore the information necessary to care for the forests, was centered in the Forestry Division of the Department of Agriculture.

Besides the usual overhead administrative offices and those incidental to operation, the organization of the Service consists of the five Branches of Lands, Grazing, Engineering,

Silviculture, and Research, and the Office of Acquisition. In the interest of better local supervision over the National Forests the United States has been divided into seven districts, each of which is in charge of a District Forester who is given the necessary discretionary power and responsibility to secure the desired administrative results. It has been the policy to call these District Foresters into the central office at Washington and allow them to become familiar with the larger administrative aspects of the Forest Service. The geographic distribution of the Disrticts may be ascertained by reference to the map. It will be noted that Alaska and Porto Rico are included in the Districts.

The Office of Acquisition "designates the areas where lands are to be purchased, receives proposals, appraises lands, conducts tentative negotiations, prepares recommendations to the Secretary of Agriculture and the National Forest Reservation Commission, and makes surveys of lands to be acquired under the act of March 1, 1911, for the protection of the watersheds and navigable streams."[1]

Management of the National Forests.—For a long time it was not generally understood that the National Forests were to be turned to various uses, and much opposition due to this misunderstanding has since disappeared by reason of the fact that the Service is allowing the cutting and sale of timber in such a way as not to injure the immature trees or in any way hinder the reproduction of the forests, as well as the use of wood for domestic purposes, the rental of water power, the grazing of livestock, the preservation of game, and the use of forests for amusement purposes. Some of these forest uses are administered by separate offices both in Washington and in the field.

The Branch of Engineering has general supervision over "road-development plans in connection with national forest administration," waterpower uses, and the surveying and mapping of forest land. The building of roads is important to provide speedy means for the fighting of fires. Lookout places must be built for the purpose of making frequent

[1] *List of Workers, U. S. Department of Agriculture.*

observations. Telephone lines connecting lookout places with headquarters are also necessary to communicate the discovery of fires in order that fire-fighters may be dispatched at the earliest possible moment.

The initial function of the field service was the protection of the forests against fires and depredations by trespassers. The number of fires and therefore the amount expended for fire protection varies considerably from year to year, depending primarily upon the amount of rainfall during the spring, summer and fall. The table shows the extent and causes of fire during the calendar years 1915 and 1916. By far the larger number of fires is caused by lightning. For these years the next largest source is traced to campers, while incendiaries are responsible for the third largest number. Railroads also come in for a large share of the causes of fire. The damage caused in both 1915 and 1916 is slight as compared with that of 1910, during which a long continued drought prevailed throughout the western forest areas.

Table Showing Fires on National Forests.

Extent and Causes of Fire.	1916		1915	
	No. of Fires.	Percentage of Total	No. of Fires.	Percentage of Total
Area burned over:				
Under 0.25 acre	2,634	46.58	2,762	43.67
Between 0.25 and 10 acres	1,499	26.51	1,788	28.27
10 acres and over; damage under $100	1,272	22.49	1,428	22.58
10 acres and over; damage $100 to $1,000	193	3.41	278	4.40
10 acres and over; damage over $1,000	57	1.01	68	1.08
Total	5,655	100.00	6,324	100.00
Causes of fire:				
Railroads	541	9.57	560	8.86
Lightning	1,337	23.64	1,799	28.45
Incendiaries	708	12.52	682	10.78
Brush burning	481	8.51	704	11.13
Campers	990	17.50	1,141	18.04
Lumbering	358	6.33	169	2.67
Unknown	1,019	18.02	988	15.62
Miscellaneous	221	3.91	281	4.45
Total	5,655	100.00	6,324	100.00

Data taken from reports of the Forester.

The Branch of Silviculture has charge of timber sales, "reforestation on the national forests, and of working plans for their better administration. It cooperates with the States and private owners in fire protection and the practice of forestry." Timber is sold to settlers and farmers at cost rates under authority of an act of Congress, and at the market rate to lumbermen. The cutting is done in accordance with sound forestry principles, and precautions against fire are taken. Certain free-use privileges are granted to settlers. In 1916 as many as 42,055 individuals availed themselves of this privilege. During the fiscal year 1917 the total timber receipts amounted to $1,692,520.21.

The Branch of Grazing determines the number of livestock that may graze advantageously on forest lands, determines the fees to be charged, and conducts investigations concerning the best use of the forage resources of the national forests. In 1917 over 1,900,000 cattle, 98,880 horses, 2,306 swine, 7,586,034 sheep and 49,939 goats grazed on these forest lands, the demand for which is continually increasing. The total receipts from grazing in 1917 amounted to $1,549,794.76. This use of the forest is of immediate economic importance in that it contributes very substantially to the meat supply of the country.

Other Activities.—In order that the National Forests may not remain a total wilderness and also that they may be used as fully as possible community development is encouraged. Land within the forest area is examined with a view to determining its agricultural value and if found to be satisfactory, is opened to homesteaders. Patents are also issued for stone, coal and miscellaneous entries. Under the law of July 11, 1916, commonly known as the Federal aid road act, $1,000,000 was made available in 1917 for the building of roads and trails within or partly within the National Forests, and an equal amount is made available for the nine succeeding years. This project is in the interest of community development because it provides means of communication, the opening of schools, the sale of produce, and in general everything that goes with the development of a wholesome citizenry.

The research activities of the Service are also very much worth while. Only through research has it been possible to make the progress in our forestry policy thus far achieved. Progress is desirable. Therefore research is indispensable.

SELECTED REFERENCES.

Circular 100, Bureau of Plant Industry; Galloway in *Yearbook* for 1897, pp. 99-111; Pinchot, in *Yearbook* for 1899, pp. 292-306; various *Reports of the Forester*; John Ise, *Forest Policy of the United States.*

CHAPTER V

BUREAU OF ANIMAL INDUSTRY

Not including the cooperative observers and voluntary crop reporters most of whom are non-salaried employes, the personnel of the Bureau of Animal Industry is larger than that of any other bureau of the Department. In 1917 the number[1] of employes in the Forest Service, which is the second largest branch of the Department, was 2,608; while in the Bureau of Animal Industry it was 4,028. Both of these branches of the Department have large field forces, that of the Animal Industry Bureau numbering more than 2,700. The functions of this Bureau are concerned with the livestock of the country, and may be classified as administrative, investigational, regulatory, and educational. On the basis of the number of employes assigned to these different functions, the regulatory function is by far the most important. In some projects, such as the Tick Eradication, the investigational, educational and regulatory functions are very closely related. The results of the Bureau's efforts have been so beneficial to the farmer, stockman, and consumer that it is well worth while to study its organization, its relations to the public, and the character of its services.

Establishment of the Veterinary Division.—The only funds available for use in connection with diseases of animals before 1877 were appropriations made from time to time for the purpose of collecting various agricultural statistics. With only a meagre sum available from this source, the Commissioner of Agriculture in 1868 commissioned Professor John Gamgee of the Albert Veterinary College of London to investigate the Texas fever which was causing serious losses at the time. The Boards of Health of New York and Chicago conducted similar investigations which show that there was a widespread interest in animal diseases. In the face of all this disease there was a dearth of medical skill in America. Veter-

[1] *Official Register*, 1917.

inary schools were only beginning to be established in Europe by the middle of the eighteenth century and only by the beginning of the nineteenth were they in operation in the principal countries of Europe.[1] The Commissioner in his report for 1868 expresses regret that our domestic animals "have all suffered from the local prevalence of malignant forms of disease, against which little veterinary skill is opposed, and little more than empiricism and superstitious folly is practiced." This situation was very substantially changed by 1897 largely through the efforts of the Bureau of Animal Industry according to the claims of Dr. Salmon, then Chief of Bureau. In 1868 the Commissioner also recommended to Congress the establishment of a veterinary division. Similar recommendations were made in subsequent reports, but no action was taken by Congress whatever until 1877 when $10,000 was appropriated for the investigation of diseases of animals, the action having been impelled by the prevalence of diseases among swine and cattle. Following the year 1877 the Commissioner regularly refers to the work of the Veterinary Commission; while Dr. Salmon in an article in the Yearbook for 1897 states that the Veterinary Division was not established until 1883, which probably means that before that date the organization of the veterinary work of the Department was too small to be regarded as a separate Division.

The Establishment of the Bureau of Animal Industry.—On May 29, 1884, "an act for the establishment of a Bureau of Animal Industry, to prevent the importation of diseased cattle, and to provide means for the suppression and extirpation of pleuro-pneumonia and other contagious diseases among domestic animals" was approved.

In all probability the most important reason why Congress took action at this time to establish a Bureau of Animal Industry with power to extirpate pleuro-pneumonia and other contagious diseases, was because Great Britain had refused to admit cattle, sheep or swine from the United States except for immediate slaughter at the landing places, and because in 1881 our pork was altogether excluded from most of the

[1] Dr. D. E. Salmon, *Yearbook*, 1899, p. 96.

continental countries for the alleged reason that it was infested with trichinae which, unless destroyed by cooking, are dangerous to the health and lives of consumers. It is hinted that the competition of the foreign livestock producer had much to do with the creation of a sentiment unfavorable to the admission of American livestock. The effect of these restrictions was to cause only the fat cattle to be shipped to Europe and sold at from $10 to $15 per head below the market price, and so far as pork was concerned to reduce our sales to France and Germany from 70,000,000 and 43,000,000 pounds [1] respectively to zero after 1880. Microscopic inspection begun in 1891 proved that American hogs were probably healthier than those raised in European countries and led to the removal of the restrictions, but the long exclusion of our pork products from Europe made it difficult to regain the trade. However, six years after the institution of the practice of inspecting pork for export microscopically the amount so inspected rose to more than 43,500,000 pounds. These disabilities suffered by our stockmen were probably the principal reasons for the establishment of the Bureau. In this connection it may be said that American consumers for a long time made the charge that Congress in making provision for the inspection of meats protected the foreign consumer, but left the domestic consumer wholly at the mercy of infectious diseases of animals which necessarily followed from the inadequacy of appropriations for the purpose.

Besides the extirpation of animal diseases, the act also provided for the inspection and quarantining of imported livestock. This function, formerly performed by the Treasury Department, was taken over by the Bureau July 1, 1884. Stations for this purpose are being maintained at the principal ports of entry.

The Eradication of Pleuro-Pneumonia.—As stated above the act creating the Bureau of Animal Industry specifically mentioned the eradication of pleuro-pneumonia among other diseases as one of the functions of the Bureau. The prompt eradication of this disease and the discovery of the method

[1] *Yearbook*, 1897, p. 247.

of transmission of Texas cattle fever together with the rapid progress of the eradication of the cattle tick, are achievements of such great importance that the Bureau of Animal Industry and the Department of Agriculture may justly regard its service to the people with a good deal of pride. It is not always true that definite and concrete results follow all investigations undertaken by the Department, and the solution of these problems, so elusive to the layman, evokes therefore all the more felicitation.

Contagious pleuro-pneumonia had become established in several states east of the Allegheny Mountains, in Ohio and Kentucky and in most of the cattle states of the Mississippi Valley. The Chicago district was also affected. The measures that the veterinary profession generally agreed should be adopted to secure the eradication of the disease were, quarantine, restriction upon the movement of cattle, slaughter of affected animals, and disinfection. The Secretary of Agriculture accordingly issued regulations providing for all of these measures including the destruction of affected animals. The Attorney General of the United States, however, rendered an opinion basing his decision upon the act creating the Bureau, that there were "no provisions for purchasing the diseased and exposed animals." The Secretary's regulations concerning the slaughter of the affected animals were therefore rendered void, and necessitated securing additional authority from Congress providing for the purchase and slaughter of the diseased animals. This authority was granted in 1887 in the appropriation act which allowed the Secretary "to expend any part of this sum in the purchase and destruction of diseased animals wherever in his judgment it is essential to prevent the spread of pleuro-pneumonia from one State to another." [1]

The limitations of Federal authority made it necessary to cooperate with the State authorities in carrying out the provisions of the act. Agreements between the Department and State Governors were entered into whereby Bureau inspectors were to make the inspections and render reports to both State and Bureau. The inspector was to put into effect

[1] *Yearbook*, 1899, p. 443.

the quarantine regulations of the particular State in which the infected herd was found. All affected and exposed animals were to be slaughtered as soon as possible after discovery. The value of cattle so slaughtered was to be appraised, and such portion of the appraised value provided as compensation under the law of the State was paid to the owner by the Department of Agriculture. Where States inoculated herds the Bureau inspectors were given complete supervision.

The activities of the Bureau in cooperation with the State authorities resulted in a complete eradication of this contagious disease by 1892. Already in 1888 was the disease eradicated from the Chicago district. The Secretary in his report for that year says the following:

> The prompt eradication of pleuro-pneumonia from Chicago and vicinity is worthy of more than a simple narration of fact. It may well be considered one of the most important results ever accomplished by the Department of Agriculture. History gives few if any cases where the dairies of a city of the size of Chicago have once been infected with pleuro-pneumonia and where the disease has been eradicated without years of constant work and the expenditure of vast sums of money. Paris was infected more than one hundred years ago, and in spite of the large number of veterinarians in that district, and of the stringent laws and regulations promulgated for its suppression, the disease still exists, and the ravages continue from year to year apparently undiminished.

On March 25, 1892, the last case of the disease disappeared from the United States and six months later the Secretary issued a proclamation raising the quarantine from the last affected areas. The amount expended by the Bureau for the purpose of eradicating the disease was $1,500,000, which is about 1 1000 of the total value of milch cows, oxen, and other cattle in the United States in 1892; and of course the value of the cattle saved by the suppression of the disease cannot be estimated, but in the light of the experience of other countries it may be said that it was many times the amount expended.

Texas Fever.—An achievement of perhaps even greater importance than the eradication of pleuro-pneumonia was the discovery of the cause of Texas fever and a treatment leading rapidly to its complete extirpation. Texas fever, known also as Southern fever, Splenetic fever, Spanish fever, acclimation fever, etc., came to be definitely associated with southern cattle before the Civil War. From 1856 to 1860 many Texas cattle were driven into the States of Kansas, Missouri, Kentucky, Iowa and Illinois, causing the infection of northern cattle with Texas fever along the way. Similar results followed the movement of cattle from the Carolinas into Virginia, Maryland and Pennsylvania. The coming of the Civil War stopped the movement of southern cattle, and by the time they began again to swarm into the northern States in droves the peculiarities of the disease had been generally forgotten. By 1868 the ravages caused by Texas fever were so great that the Commissioner of Agriculture instituted an investigation with a view to determining the manner of its dissemination and methods of prevention. No progress was made until after 1879 when Doctor Salmon, later Chief of Bureau, took up the study of the disease.

The strange facts of the phenomenon gathered from observation and study made it truly appear to be a "romance in pathology." Texas cattle, perfectly healthy, when driven into northern States would cause the infection of northern cattle resulting in the death of entire herds. So violent was this poison that northern cattle allowed to graze in the paths of southern cattle sixty and ninety days after they had passed suddenly developed the disease. Not always did the pastures yield the poison immediately after the southern cattle had passed, which added all the more mystery to the disease. When purebred sires to be used in breeding up southern stock were shipped South they too contracted the fever. It was evident that healthy animals disseminated the fever, and that diseased animals could not do so, an unusual condition in the light of medical experience.

Experiments, begun in 1889, resulted in proving the following propositions: "(1) That northern cattle pastured in a field with cattle from the infected district which were infested with ticks contracted Texas fever; (2) that northern cattle pastured in a field with cattle from the infested district that were carefully freed from all ticks by hand picking did not contract Texas fever; (3) that northern cattle pastured in a field where no cattle from the infected district had been, but over which had been scattered a large number of ticks, contracted Texas fever." The results of these experiments proved "(1) that the disease was inoculable; (2) that the blood of diseased animals contained a miscroscopic protozoan parasite; (3) that ticks picked from southern cattle and spread upon pastures were a means of communicating the infection."[1]

The next step was to show in what manner the healthy animal became inoculated with the fever. It was at first supposed that the tick moving from the southern to the northern animal carried the infection by biting. This, however, was not the case inasmuch as it was proven that mother ticks dropping from cattle into the grass and depositing their eggs transmit the poison through the eggs to their progeny, and that the young ticks fastening themselves upon cattle have the power of inserting the contagion into the blood of the animal. In order to prove beyond a doubt that the transmission of the protozoa in the blood of southern cattle was causing the infection of northern cattle, a small quantity of blood of a southern cow was injected under the skin of a northern cow, producing an acute attack of Texas fever.

Another peculiarity is that southern cattle are immune. It has been found that very young cattle can be immunized by inoculation without producing acute attacks of the fever, and that cattle once infected carry the contagion in an active condition throughout their lives. The solution of this complex problem had to be achieved before ways and means could be devised to prevent the losses caused by Texas fever. The eradication process will be discussed under a separate head.

The Animal Husbandry Division.—The Animal Husbandry Division is concerned with the improvement through breeding of all farm animals except the dairy cow, which falls under the Dairy Division, issues certificates for purebred animals imported, and carries on considerable extension work with a view to improving farm stock. In cooperation with county farm demonstration agents the Division takes part in organizing pig and poultry clubs, and in various ways assists in their operation.

[1] *Yearbook*, 1899, p. 131.

Extensive experiments have been conducted with a view to establishing abstract principles of heredity. In the Department's *Program of Work* for 1919 it is reported that eighteen generations of guinea pigs were bred and the results of inbreeding noted.[1] Breeding experiments include beef cattle, sheep and goats, swine, horses and mules, and various kinds of poultry. The experiments include investigations of feeding, the aim of the projects being to increase the food supply of the country such as meat and eggs, to improve the production of wool and mohair, and to produce more suitable draft animals to serve as co-laborers with man in the production of economic goods.

One important regulatory function is performed by this Division. Under the provisions of paragraph 397 of the tariff act of October 3, 1913, the Department of Agriculture is charged with certifying as to the importation of purebred animals, whose importation is encouraged by admission duty free. The Division has a list of accredited foreign breeding societies which issue certificates at the time the animal is sold. When the animal arrives at the port of entry it is examined by the inspector of the Bureau as to breed, sex, age, size, and markings. These points are reported to Washington and if they agree with those indicated on the foreign certificate, the Bureau issues a certificate of pure breeding and sends it to the collector of customs at the port of entry. The foreign certificate is stamped by the Bureau and returned to the importer. The tariff act of October 3, 1913 admits free of duty cattle, sheep, and swine, so that the Bureau no longer issues certificates for these animals. Certificates, however, for horses, dogs, and cats are issued, and such certification is a guarantee to record societies and others that the animals are as represented. During the calendar year 1917 certificates for 613 horses, 387 dogs, and 3 cats were issued.[2]

The Dairy Division.—The Dairy Division is concerned with increasing the productivity of dairy cattle, with improving sanitary conditions in the production and transportation of

[1] For a full discussion of these experiments the student is referred to the *Program of Work*, 1919, p. 59.

[2] *Vide Program of Work*, 1919, p. 63.

dairy products, with the inspection of "renovated" or "process" butter, and with educational work in dairying carried on in cooperation with State and local institutions.

The project of increasing the productivity of dairy cattle is a very important one, and is not to be regarded as a forlorn hope. Great possibilities to increase the country's food supply lie dormant in the 23,000,000 milch cows maintained in the United States. According to the 1910 census the production of butter-fat per cow was 150 pounds, while it is not unusual for whole herds to average 300 pounds per cow. For the whole of Denmark the average per cow in 1908 was 224 pounds. If the average productivity of the cows in the United States should only equal that of Denmark's, there would be a very substantial increase in dairy products produced in this country; and if the ideal of 300 pounds should be attained, the supply would be doubled. The Division helps to secure this increased productivity through the study of cow-testing and bull associations. In the interest of improving livestock in general J. R. Mohler, Chief of Bureau, in the *Weekly News Letter*, of August 6, 1919, makes the following appeal:

> With confidence that better live stock will bring satisfaction and many benefits to its owners, I invite the concerted action of farmers, stockmen, and others in banishing scrub sires from the United States. The widespread use of inferior male breeding animals has been for many years a cause of low production per animal and of needlessly poor quality.
>
> The continuance of such conditions is uneconomic and unnecessary. The direct and practical means of improvement is to use breeding animals, especially sires, which are true representatives of breeds developed for a definite, useful purpose.

This Division also performs a regulatory function in the inspection of "renovated" or "process" butter, which Congress in an act approved May 9, 1902, defined as "butter which has been subjected to any process by which it is melted, clarified, or refined, and made to resemble genuine butter, always excepting adulterated butter." Before government inspection was provided for butter spoiled and unfit for human food was collected from the trade and after melting was deodorized with deleterious chemicals. It was then churned with milk and sold for fresh creamery butter. The blowing of air through the melted fat is now being generally used to expel faulty odors.[1]

The Secretary of Agriculture is charged by the Act of 1902 with the inspection of renovating factories and storehouses where "renovated butter is manufactured, packed and prepared for the market and of the products thereof and materials going into the manufacture of the same." If the Secretary finds that the finished product whether for export or for interstate shipment, is deleterious to health he is directed to confiscate it. The Secretary prescribes that the renovated butter must be plainly marked. Unlike adulterated butter and oleomargarine there is no tax on renovated butter itself, but an annual tax of $50 is paid by each manufacturer of the product.

The Field Inspection Division.—The duties of this Division are all of a regulatory character. In cooperation with livestock sanitary organizations it inspects sheep for scabies and where they exist diseased or exposed animals are dipped under State or Federal supervision. The affected areas are quarantined to prevent the spread of the disease. At the close of the fiscal year, 1918, there were 56,284 square miles still under Federal quarantine for this purpose. The elimination of the disease is confidently predicted by the Bureau, and when accomplished will mean greater production of mutton and wool. Eradication of scabies in cattle and horses has progressed so rapidly that all areas were released from quarantine April 15, 1918. Inspections, however, are still made at market centers.[2]

An important duty of the Division is the supervision of interstate transportation of livestock. This work involves the inspection of all livestock unloaded at market centers and public stockyards where Federal inspection is maintained. During the fiscal year 1917, more than 19,000,000 sheep and more than 18,000,000 cattle were inspected. Many of these were dipped in order that they could be allowed to continue in interstate transit. During the same year 61,798 cars were

[1] H. C. Sherman, *Food Products*, p. 377.
[2] *Program of Work*, 1919, p. 35.

cleaned and disinfected to avoid the spread of contagious animal diseases. Inspections for various contagious animal diseases are made. One of the most highly contagious diseases of animals is the foot-and-mouth disease, an epidemic of which began to sweep over a large part of the country in October, 1914. The eradication of this disease illustrates the economic importance of the services of the Division.

The infection first appeared in Michigan, and it is believed, came from abroad. It rapidly spread over twenty-two states and the District of Columbia. Quarantines against the movement of cattle into and out of the affected areas were established by the Secretary of Agriculture immediately after the discovery of the infection. The quarantined areas were so extensive that the restraint to interstate trade was not only a severe shock to the stockmen and dealers, but was also severely felt by the consumer. The Bureau cooperated with the States in stamping out the disease. The plan followed was similar to that used in previous outbreaks. All diseased and exposed animals were slaughtered and either buried or disposed of in a way satisfactory to the Bureau. The premises were well cleaned and disinfected. The animals slaughtered were appraised either at their meat or dairy value, and this amount was paid to the owners, half by the Federal Government and half by the State. During the period of infection, which was about a year and a half, there were slaughtered more than 172,000 animals, including cattle, swine, sheep and goats, with a total appraised value of $5,865,720. This appraised value under the existing law could not make any allowance for special values on account of fine pedigrees which frequently raised the value of animals above several thousand dollars. The above figure does, therefore, not represent the true value of slaughtered animals. By 1916, however, the appropriation act allowed pedigree values to be taken into account in the appraisal of animals to be slaughtered on account of being infected with a contagious disease, and Congress appropriated $1,250,000 as an emergency fund to be available for the eradication of foot-and-mouth disease and other contagious diseases of animals. Under the law, therefore, it is now possible to reimburse the owner in accordance with the real value of the slaughtered animal. The Chief of Bureau estimated that the total cost required to stamp out the 1914 epidemic amounted to $9,000,000. In this estimate the cost to the States is included.[1]

Another important duty of this Division is the enforcement of the 28-hour law, approved June 29, 1906, which provides for the humane treatment of cattle while in transit.

The Origin and Operation of the Twenty-eight Hour Law.—The original statute commonly referred to as the twenty-eight hour law was approved by President Grant on March 3, 1873. This law prohibited the interstate transportation of cattle, sheep, swine, or other animals for a period longer than twenty-eight hours without unloading for food, water and rest for which at least five consecutive hours was to be allowed. When cars and vessels were properly equipped to provide food and water, and when enough space was allotted to allow the animals to rest, the provision as to unloading did not apply. The penalty for a violation of the law was fixed at from $100 to $500 for each offense. In 1891, 1895 and 1897 the Secretary of Agriculture distributed circulars among the carriers, in a special way calling their attention to the statute and warning them of prosecutions if violations continued. During all this time, however, the railroads almost completely ignored the law.[2] A special effort was made on the part of the Bureau inspectors in 1905 to collect sufficient evidence against the carriers to secure their conviction. Nearly 2,000 cases of violations were reported. The railroads agreed to observe the law in the future, and during the fall of the same year, in view of the congestion due to the moving of large numbers of cattle from the West, often unloaded cattle on the open prairies and in crowded and insanitary pens, causing loss to shippers and in many cases as much or more cruelty to animals than if they had not been unloaded.

In view of these circumstances the Secretary of Agriculture conferred with a number of the best informed and heavily

---

[1] For a full discussion of this plague and the eradication campaign of 1914 see the *Reports* of the Chief of Bureau of Animal Industry for 1915 and 1916.

[2] *Vide Report of the Solicitor of the Department of Agriculture* for 1907, pp. 759-766.

interested stockmen and cattle dealers. These men were all of the opinion that it would be advantageous to allow 36 hours instead of 28 as the maximum time during which animals may be transported without unloading. It was thought that the facilities of the railroads could accommodate the traffic under this arrangement and that the roads would obey the law if the change were made. The problem was also debated with the railroads and as a result the Secretary of Agriculture recommended to Congress the enactment of a law increasing the continuous transportation period to 36 hours, providing for the humane loading and unloading, the placing of animals in properly equipped pens, allowing shippers to furnish feed themselves instead of making them subject to exorbitant prices for feeds charged by the carriers allowing exemption from the unloading clause if proper provisions for feeding, watering and rest on cars and vessels are made, providing for the application of the law to a railroad in the hands of a receiver to which the Supreme Court had held the law did not apply, and providing for the application of the law to livestock shipped from a territory to a state or *vice versa*. This the court had also held was not covered under the law of 1873. These provisions were all incorporated in an act passed by Congress June 29, 1906.

"The passage of the act was vigorously fought, in committee and on the floor, by members of the various humane societies throughout the United States." It was warmly supported by the railroads and livestock interests. When the humane societies lost the fight in Congress they appealed to the President to veto the bill. With proper explanation from the Department of Agriculture, however, the President approved the bill.

Following the enactment of the law of 1906 the Solicitor of the Department of Agriculture took occasion to warn the carriers that "it would perhaps be more seemly, and possibly just as good policy, if the railroads were to concentrate their energies upon an attempt to obey the provisions of the statute." While it is claimed the enforcement of this law has secured more humane treatment of animals in interstate transit, the following statement will disclose in a measure the attitude of the carriers toward its observance:

Year	*No. of Cases Reported to Attorney General*	*Penalties Recovered*
1912	631	$28,400
1914	1,608	47,595
1916	465	52,450
1917	1,829	37,948

The Meat Inspection Division.—The system of inspecting meats for export was begun under the authority of an act approved August 30, 1890; and a supplementary act passed March 3, 1891, provided "for the inspection of live cattle, hogs, and the carcasses and products thereof which are the subjects of interstate commerce, and for other purposes." The act of 1891 was amended March 2, 1895. To carry out the provisions of these inspection laws a special technique and a large organization had to be devised by the Bureau of Animal Industry. As indicated by the insufficiency of the appropriation to cover the necessary expenses of inspection, Congress had not contemplated the magnitude of the force of inspectors required to make the law operative. Not until 1897, therefore, was it possible to inspect in accordance with the law all the beef and the greater part of the pork and other meat products, exported to Europe.[1] The inspection of meats for interstate trade and domestic consumption, however, was never fully provided for by Congress until 1906 when the public was thoroughly aroused by a nation-wide movement for pure-food legislation.

Before 1906 ante-mortem inspection was carried on at 154 establishments. Many establishments applied for inspection, but the appropriations were too small to allow the necessary expansion of the field force. Many abbatoirs did not care for the inspection because of the low standards maintained and because it would seriously affect their profits. It was said that the establishments subjected to inspection often complained of the unfair competition emanating from the unsupervised abbatoirs. In the act of June 30, 1906, Congress made avail-

[1] *Yearbook*, 1899, p. 459.

able a permanent annual appropriation of $3,000,000 for the complete inspection of meat for interstate shipment. This allowed a tremendous expansion in the inspection force, and is evidence of the fruition of the pure-food movement. Before the close of the year 1906, the number of establishments at which inspection was maintained, was increased from 154 to 644.[1] The inspection force was increased from 981 on July 1, 1906, to 2,290 on July 1, 1907, and since then has grown to more than 27,000.

Not only were the appropriations for inspection insufficient before 1906, but the law was also inadequate. While the ante-mortem inspection of animals was made mandatory as far as funds permitted, the post-mortem inspection was discretionary and was done at the time of slaughtering. It was doubted that the old law gave authority to follow up meats through the stages of packing, or canning, to the time it was placed on the market. Neither did the old law give any authority to correct insanitary conditions of slaughtering establishments, nor to prevent adulterations and the use of chemicals as preservatives. It was these factors that were made the subject of public agitation and concerning which unsatisfactory conditions were disclosed. The law of 1906 remedied all these defects and enlarged the powers of the Secretary to cope fully with the situation. Inspection is now made both ante-mortem and post-mortem, following the meat through all the stages and processes of preparation. Great improvements in sanitation have resulted, amounting in many cases to a complete reconstruction of the buildings. All interstate shipments of meat must be covered with a certificate showing that it has been inspected and passed or that it is exempt from inspection. Full control is given over labeling, so that fraudulent and misleading labeling is no longer possible. The former withdrawal of rejected animals after ante-mortem inspection for slaughter at places where government inspection was not maintained, is no longer permitted, all animals being slaughtered and properly disposed of where the inspection takes place.

---

[1] *Yearbook*, 1906, p. 494.

The limited constitutional authority of the Federal Government places numerous restrictions upon the activities of the Department of Agriculture. This limitation of authority is perhaps felt as much in this Department as in any other executive department. Unlike the Treasury, War, State, Navy, Justice. and Post Office Departments, whose functions are more or less specifically provided for by the Constitution of the United States, the activities of the Department of Agriculture have from our national beginning been conceived to fall under State control. Lack of constitutional authority giving complete Federal control of the inspection of meat is just one of the many instances in which the division of fundamental powers between the State and Federal Government is encountered in the Department of Agriculture. While a large portion of the meats prepared at places where inspection is maintained is consumed within the state, the Department insists upon inspecting the entire output. The Bureau of Animal Industry has developed a large organization, and in 1917 made ante-mortem inspections of more than 63,000,000 animals and as many post-mortem inspections. More than 265,000 animals were condemned, and more than 7,000,000,000 pounds of various meats and meat products were prepared and processed under inspection. Much good is being accomplished in the interest of public health; but the Federal inspection does not, and cannot reach the numerous small butchers throughout each State of the Union where, the Bureau says, the worst conditions are often found and where certainly often no inspection whatever is made. This is a matter for the States and the municipalities to control, and ultimately it is a problem whose solution depends upon the vigilance of the public. With the passing of the "frontier" in the United States more cattle will have to be raised and slaughtered locally, which will cause the need for State and municipal inspection to be still more urgent.

The Quarantine Division.—This Division inspects animals exported as well as those imported, maintains quarantine stations at ports of entry, inspects ships carrying exported animals, and administers the sanitary regulations governing the importation of hides and skins, glue stock, hair, wool, and other animal by-products, hay, straw, forage, etc.

One of the first steps taken in this country to control contagious diseases of animals was requiring the inspection of animals imported. Inspection and quarantine stations maintained for this purpose were at first under the supervision of the Treasury Department, but were turned over to the Bureau when it was organized. These stations are located along the Canadian and Mexican borders, and at the principal ports of entry along the Atlantic and Pacific coasts. Animals seeking entry at seaports are inspected on the vessel before landing. Upon inspection they may be passed, rejected, or quarantined according to circumstances. The quarantined animals are transferred to the stations for observation to insure their freedom from contagion. Upon request of prospective importers of cattle from Great Britain the Bureau's inspector stationed in England applies the tuberculin test before shipment, which saves transportation charges in case the animal is rejected. During the fiscal year, 1917, a total of 574,303 animals were inspected. Of this number 6,552 were quarantined. The tuberculin test was applied to 1,498 cattle in Great Britain for importation into the United States and to 597 head during the quarantine period in this country.[1] The kinds of animals imported from time to time include cattle, sheep, swine, goats, horses, cats, dogs, and other animals. This function of the Bureau is important, and vigilance on the part of the inspectors is the means of preventing epidemics of contagious diseases that would result in great loss to the country.

The inspection law of 1890 and subsequent amendments provided for the inspection of animals for export. By 1897 all animals exported were inspected in accordance with the law. British inspectors contended that animals infected with pleuropneumonia continued to reach their shores from the United States, and American inspectors were therefore place in England to cooperate with the British inspectors with a view to ascertaining the truth of the charges. After several months

[1] *Program of Work*, 1919, p. 38.

during which time 104,296 head of cattle had been imported the inspectors reported to the Bureau that not a single case of pleuro-pneumonia had been found. Animals for export are inspected according to the requirements of different countries and if they pass the test applied certificates showing freedom from disease are issued. During the fiscal year 1917 there were inspected prior to shipment 3,076 animals. There were also exported to Europe subject to inspection by foreign officials 339,166 horses and mules, mostly for Army purposes.

Before the use of the commodious cattle ships of the present day live cattle were carried mostly on "tramps" with only temporary fittings and without facilities for supplying the necessary quantities of feed and water. Ships often arrived at European ports with cattle suffering from hunger and thirst. "Sometimes during storms it was necessary to batten down the hatches, and then on account of deficient ventilation large numbers of animals would die asphyxiated." Sometimes the heavy seas would cause the animals to "become mixed and jammed together in the greatest confusion." In some cases cattle would be swept into the sea. Those landed were often in a condition to make an unfavorable impression.

Such occurrences could not fail to attract the attention of humane people abroad, particularly when the sentiment of humanity was intensified by the desire to limit American competition. The barbarities of the transatlantic cattle traffic were depicted by the pen of romance, the cruelties were exaggerated and magnified, atrocities were described that never were committed, and illustrated pamphlets were prepared and circulated in order that the full power of sensationalism might be invoked. As a result of this agitation, a bill was presented in the British Parliament to prohibit the importation of live cattle from beyond the seas, and the Queen was strongly urged, in the name of humanity, to use her influence to secure its passage.

This emergency was met by Congress through the passage of the act of March 3, 1891, authorizing the Secretary of Agriculture to enforce necessary regulations, to secure the safe carriage, and humane treatment of cattle exported from the United States. Careful investigations were at once made by the Bureau and regulations formulated which were acceptable to the British Government. The rigid enforcement of such regulations drove the poorer classes of ships out of the trade. Magnificent iron ships were constructed for the cattle traffic, with every convenience, with permanent fittings built into the vessels, and having all the comforts and safety for which human ingenuity could provide. The losses were soon reduced to the minimum of about one-third of one per cent. The cattle were unloaded in as good condition, as vigorous and active, as they were when they went on board. As a result of the improved conditions and the greatly diminished losses, insurance rates were reduced from $8.00 and upward per head of exported cattle to less than $1.00 per head. This saving in insurance alone, with an average exportation of 325,000 head, amounts to $2,275,000 per year, nearly three times the annual cost for maintaining the Bureau.[1]

One other function is performed by this Division and that is the inspection at ports of entry of feedstuffs, and animal by-products imported. Certain certificates are required to accompany hides, skins, hair, wool, etc., from various countries. If these are not provided, the products may be shipped to factories and there disinfected under the supervision of the Bureau inspector. The purpose of the inspection is to exclude from this country contagious diseases and supplements the inspection of animals imported.

Tick Eradication Division.—In a former section was given the story of the discovery of the transmission of Texas fever by the cattle tick. The fact that an insect can spread disease has since then been found to be true in connection with malaria and yellow fever, which are spread by mosquitoes. These discoveries are indeed milestones in the history of progress. Secretary Houston estimates that the annual direct loss alone due to the presence of the cattle tick is $40,000,000.[2] Cattle in the infested area, although immune from Texas fever, are being constantly drained of their blood, so that they weigh less, are often scrawny, and when sold for beef, bring less than animals from tick-free areas. Neither do the hides of these animals sell for as much as those of tick-free animals because of the punctures made by the ticks. Ticky dairy cattle yield a flow of milk, depending upon the degree of infestation, 18 to 40 per cent below what it should be.[3] Compared with these constant losses, the cost of the eradication of the tick is trivial. "In several counties in Alabama which were freed from quarantine on December 1, 1915, it was found that the cost of eradication to the county had ranged from 18 to 50 cents per head of cattle."[4] As is pointed out by the writer to whom references are made, the economic importance of the eradica-

[1] Written in 1897 by Dr. Salmon, then Chief of Bureau, and appears in the *Yearbook* for that year on page 246.

[2] *Yearbook*, 1915, p. 18.

[3] *Yearbook*, 1915, p. 161.

[4] *Yearbook*, 1915, p. 162.

tion of the tick is justified not merely on the ground of greatly increasing the value of the animal freed from ticks, but also on the ground that if the livestock industry is made profitable for the South, diversified farming will be more generally adopted, and added prosperity to the entire country will result.

The process of eradicating the tick is dipping the animals at intervals in arsenical solutions. Vats are constructed for the purpose. States and counties are now making liberal appropriations for the work. The Division gives instruction and demonstrations on methods of dipping and carries on an active propaganda. Infested areas are quarantined by the Bureau. When the ticks have been eradicated, the quarantine is lifted, and animals are allowed to move in interstate commerce without any restrictions. This work was begun in 1906 and at that time there were under quarantine 728,565 square miles. Since then 52 per cent of this area has been freed from ticks and released from quarantine.[1]

Tuberculosis Eradication Division.—The eradication of bovine tuberculosis by the use of the "stamping-out" method was first carried on by some of the States, and the only work of the Bureau before 1907 was the condemnation of tuberculous animals provided for under the meat inspection and importation laws. On April 1, 1907, the Secretary of Agriculture directed the Bureau to apply the tuberculin test to the herds of all dairymen who should request such action. A form of agreement was presented for the signature of the owner of cattle under which he obligated himself to allow the slaughter of the cattle that reacted to the tuberculin test and in addition exhibited clinical symptoms of tuberculosis. Animals merely reacting but showing no further evidence of tuberculosis could be slaughtered for food, or segregated from the rest of the herd. If such animals produced milk it could not be used for any purpose unless it was pasteurized. Offspring of such animals had to be separated at once and fed on the milk of healthy animals or the pasteurized milk of affected animals. This method provides for the extirpation of the disease and the

[1] *Program of Work*, 1919, p. 41.

gradual building up of a healthy herd. A system of tagging the ears of cattle receiving the tuberculin test was put in practice. This work, begun by the Pathological Division in the District of Columbia, Maryland, and Virgina, was extended in 1917 when the Tuberculosis Eradication Division was organized.[1]

In the District of Columbia the tuberculin test of cattle was made compulsory in 1909. The first year 18.87 per cent of the cattle reacted, while in 1917 only 0.84 per cent reacted. In other parts of the country the Bureau carries on the eradication process through cooperation with private owners of herds or with State authorities. It also cooperates with the Office of Indian Affairs of the Department of Interior. "In States in which cooperative arrangements are made, owners of tuberculous cattle, when slaughtered, will be indemnified one-third of the difference between the appraised value of the animals and the amount for which they are salvaged."[2] This Division has also charge of the tuberculin testing of cattle for interstate movement.

The Offices of Hog-Cholera Control and Virus-Serum Control.—The Office of Hog-Cholera Control cooperates with State departments and agricultural colleges in the eradication of hog cholera. In 1918, 25 States cooperated with the Bureau where veterinarians apply the preventive serum treatment, or assist in the use of such other methods as quarantine and sanitation, the enforcement of which falls under the combined authority of the Federal and State governments.

The Office of the Virus-Serum Control has charge of the enforcement of the virus-serum-toxin act of 1913, which "regulates the preparation, sale, barter, exchange, shipment, and importation of all viruses, serums, toxins, and analogous products intended for use in the treatment of domestic animals." To assure the elimination of all fraud in the manufacture and importation of these products licenses are issued to manufacturers and permits are issued to importers. Inspections of buildings and processes are made, and the products are tested to insure that they are not "worthless, contaminated, danger-

[1] *Report* of Chief Bureau, 1917, p. 102.
[2] *Program of Work*, 1919, p. 39.

ous, or harmful within the meaning of the act." During 1916 there were 38 cases of violations reported to the Attorney General, but by 1917 general compliance with the provisions of the Act seems to have been secured by previous prosecutions inasmuch as no cases of violations were reported during the latter year.

SELECTED REFERENCES.

Salmon in *Yearbook* for 1897, pp. 236-258; Salmon, *Yearbook* for 1899, pp. 93-134; *Reports* of Chief of Bureau of Animal Industry for 1915 and 1916 and others.

CHAPTER VI

Bureaus of Entomology and Biological Survey

BUREAU OF ENTOMOLOGY

Public Initiative in Economic Entomology.—The first entomologist serving in an official capacity in the United States was Dr. Thaddeus Williams Harris, who, in 1837, "was appointed one of the commissioners for a zoological and botanical survey of Massachusetts."[1] Doctor Harris published a "Systematic Catalogue of the Insects of Massachusetts" and a "Report on Insects Injurious to Vegetation," which was printed by the State legislature. It was enlarged and reprinted in 1852 and again in 1862, the last time under the direction of Charles L. Flint with the collaboration of Professor Agassiz. New York State appropriated "$1,000 for the investigation of insects, especially of those injurious to vegetation, and authorized the appointment of a suitable person to perform the work, the matter being placed in the hands of the New York State Agricultural Society." Dr. Asa Fitch was appointed and served from 1854 to 1870.[2] Illinois entered upon the work of entomology in 1867 and appointed Benjamin D. Walsh, while Missouri joined the list in 1868 with Dr. Charles V. Riley in charge.

So far as the entry of the United States into this field of study is concerned, entomology must be ranked with chemistry and botany and even with agricultural statistics. The law creating the Department specified that the Commissioner shall appoint "chemists, botanists, and entomologists." The first entomologist appointed by the federal government, however, antedates the creation of the Department by eight years. Already in 1854 the Commissioner of Patents appointed Townsend Glover to collect "statistics and other information on seeds, fruits, and insects in the United States under the Division of Agriculture of the Patent Office." His first reports

---

[1] *The American Cyclopaedia. Vide* also *Yearbook, 1899,* p. 136.
[2] *Yearbook,* 1899, p. 138.

dealt with insects injurious to wheat, the cotton plant, and the grapevine; also with the plum curculio, codling moth, peach borer, insects affecting the orange, and beneficial insects. In 1863 Glover was appointed by the Commissioner of Agriculture and placed in charge of the Division of Entomology.

During the years 1874-76 unprecedented damage was done to crops of Western States by the Western grasshopper. This was a period of great activity for the Division of Entomology. In 1877 the situation was regarded so seriously that Congress created a special United States Entomological Commission, placing it in charge of the Secretary of the Interior, for the purpose of investigating the habits of the pest and recommending means of relief. The Commission was attached to the Department of Agriculture in 1881 by act of Congress and in 1890 its work was discontinued. For about fifteen years the Division experienced very little growth. Much of the field work that had been begun before 1888 was rendered unnecessary by reason of the fact that Experiment Stations established that year under the Hatch Act furnished means for the prosecution of the practical investigations in various parts of the country. By 1904, however, the work of entomology assumed sufficient importance to demand the organization of a Bureau. This was the year that Congress made a special appropriation for the investigation of the cotton boll weevil.

Progress in Remedial Discoveries.—The remedial recommendations of the first sixty years of the 19th century made in the United States "were on the whole not very valuable. A few common-sense suggestions were made, based upon the thorough knowledge of the life histories of certain insect pests, due almost entirely to the work of Harris and Fitch and in a lesser degree to the observations of Peck, although in this connection it should also be stated that excellent work was done on the Angoumois grain moth, or so-called fly weevil, of the South by two Southern planters, namely, Landon Carter and Edmund Ruffin. The majority, however, of the recommendations published in the agricultural journals and reports were theoretical and frequently nonsensical, seldom based on any accurate knowledge of the insects' life history."[1] In the *Yearbook* [2] for 1899 a statement by Benjamin D. Walsh is given in which he holds up to ridicule a newspaper article recommending the banding of trees as a remedy against all insects that injure trees. In part it runs as follows:

The worm in fruit trees. As if fruit trees were not afflicted by hundreds of different worms, differing from each other in size, shape, color, and habits of life, time of coming to maturity, etc., as much as a horse differs from a hog. Yet the universal bandage system is warranted to kill them all. Does the apple worm bore your apples? Bandage the butt of the tree and he perisheth forthwith. Does the web worm spin his web in the branches? Bandage the butt and he dieth immediately. Does the Buprestis borer bore into the upper part of the trunk? Still you must bandage the butt with the same universal calico, and in a twinkling he vamoseth the ranch. In obstinate cases it may be necessary to bandage the whole tree, trunk, branches, twigs, and all. Long live King Humbug. He still feeds fools on flapdoodle, and many of them have large and flourishing families, who will perpetuate the breed to the remotest generation.

A new era of remedies, however, was soon ushered in. The rapid spread of the Colorado potato beetle in the East during the period beginning with 1859 and extending into the 70's evoked a great deal of experimental work on insecticides. Paris green was first used early in the 60's, but not generally until about a decade later. This, Doctor Howard, Chief of the Bureau of Entomology, believes, was the first great start for the economic entomologist. The poisoning of the potato bug with Paris green is a discovery of the first importance. Work of this character is a handmaid to such studies as rotation of crops, fertilization, soils, and selection of plants and seeds that are pursued with a view to increasing the yield. Like the latter studies, the effective use of insecticides results directly in improving our economic well-being.

The first recommendation to apply Paris green to fruit trees was made in 1872 when the cankerworm was abundant. By 1878 a number of apple growers in Michigan used it for the same purpose. It soon developed that the spraying of apple trees with Paris green was an effective remedy against the codling moth and the apple worm. Arsenical piosons, rather slowly adopted at first because of the belief that the poisons

[1] *Yearbook*, 1899, p. 144.
[2] P. 146.

would be present in the fruit, are now very extensively used by fruit growers, and are a means of increasing the yield enormously. The effect of spraying is so plain that the most ignorant and most obstinate are convinced of its value by a single demonstration. In his *Report* for 1917 the Chief of the Bureau states that studies are being pursued with a view to determining the effect of the use of arsenicals upon bees at the time apple trees are in bloom and after the falling of most of the petals.

Purposes and Methods of the Bureau.—"The Bureau of Entomology studies insects with special reference to methods of control, experiments with the introduction of beneficial insects, makes tests with insecticides and insecticide machinery, and identifies insects sent in my inquirers."[1] The emphasis of the work, it will be noted, is upon economic rather than upon systematic entomology. This should be the character of the functions of an entomological agency connected with the executive branch of the government. Yet the theoretical aspects of the science cannot be wholly neglected even by a public agency because the practical benefits are very frequently a direct outgrowth of theoretical investigations.

In order that the most satisfactory methods of the extermination of injurious insects may be evolved it is necessary to study the life histories of insects. This will disclose at what particular stage of development their destruction is most likely to be affected. Variation in the habits of different insects has brought about a variety of methods of control as is shown in *Farmers' Bulletin*, No. 835, which summarizes briefly the methods necessary for the detection, elimination, and control of the principal insects, such as the Hessian fly, chinch bug, army worm, cutworms, grasshoppers, white grubs, billbugs, wireworms, and the corn root-aphis, affecting cereal crops. The control of insects infesting fowls and cattle call for the method of dipping or the use of a powder. Orchards, vineyards, and some field crops are sprayed and in other cases specific methods of cultivation are necessary. The problems therefore are many and require the attention of a public body

[1] *List of Workers*, 1917, U. S. Dept. of Agriculture.

working for the benefit of all. When it became known that spraying was efficacious private enterprise soon produced the necessary machinery with which to distribute the insecticides. One of the important functions of the Bureau is to test the efficiency of such machinery.

Besides these various methods used to control injurious insects "the introduction of beneficial insects" has been rather extensively relied upon. These insects feed upon the injurious ones and thus, according to Nature's way, keep down menacing pests. A striking example of this method is the introduction in 1889 of the ladybird *(Novius cardinalis)* from Australia into California under the direction of the Division of Entomology for the purpose of destroying the white or fluted scale, "an insect which had damaged the citron crops of California to the extent of hundreds of thousands of dollars, and which threatened the extinction of the citrus industry on the Pacific Slope." The plan proved so successful that the scale was utterly destroyed and that the international use of such beneficial insects was called "epoch-making."[1]

The Cotton Boll Weevil.—The cotton boll weevil[2] first made its appearance in Mexico, becoming a serious pest by about 1848. About the year 1892 it was carried across the Rio Grande, perhaps in unginned cotton, and gained a foothold at Brownsville, Texas. By 1901 the weevil had traveled 500 miles north of Brownsville. In 1903 it made its appearance in Louisiana, and in 1907 reached Mississippi. Three years later it had traveled two-thirds of that State and entered the southwestern part of Alabama. "In 1914 the weevil-infected territory included the eastern half of Texas, the southeastern part of Oklahoma, the southern half of Arkansas, the whole of Louisiana and Mississippi, and the southwestern half of Alabama. By 1917 the infected territory had increased so as to include also the whole of Alamaba, two-thirds of Georgia, and northern Florida."[3] The boll weevil has been responsible for a very large loss to the cotton growers and the

[1] *Vide* article by Howard, *Yearbook*, 1899, p. 153.
[2] *Vide* article by W. D. Hunter, *Yearbook*, 1901, p. 369
[3] *Yearbook*, 1917, p. 329.

country, and has caused concern in foreign countries, some of which have passed laws prohibiting the importation of American cottonseed.

The spread of the cotton boll weevil has baffled the entomologists. Some progress has been made in discovering ways of reducing the severity of its ravages. Early planting, and other cultural methods have proved of value in combatting its ruinous effects. In 1917 experiments applying arsenicals in a certain way were begun and since then these have been used extensively. The time to apply the poison is late in the evening, at night, or early morning so as to avoid as much breeze as possible and secure the best results.[1] Cotton is so intimately connected with our economic welfare that it is to be hoped some method of control as efficacious as that of the potato beetle may be evolved.

Preventing Spread of Moths.—At various points throughout New England with headquarters at Melrose Highlands, Massachusetts, the Bureau studies the gipsy moth and brown-tail moth with a view to exterminating them. Congress made a special appropriation to prosecute the investigation in 1906 and has since then continued it. The states infested have also liberally appropriated funds to help in the extermination of the moths. The Bureau has cleared highways of all brush, etc., to prevent caterpillars from being carried by vehicles; trees have been banded and sprayed at the proper time, and extensive importations of parasites preying upon these moths have been made. So far as shade trees and city parks are concerned the former methods, it is believed, will bring the desired results, while in the forests the hope for success must depend almost wholly upon the efficiency of the parasites imported from Europe and Japan.

The only regulatory function performed by this Bureau is done in connection with the prevention of the spread of the gipsy and brown-tail moths. All nursery, forest, and quarry products from infested areas in Maine, New Hampshire, Vermont, Massachusetts, Rhode Island, and Connecticut, are

[1] *Vide Weekly News Letter*, August 13, 1919.

inspected before they are allowed to be shipped to points outside the infested areas. The work is carried on in cooperation with State entomologists.

Other Important Activities.—It is not the purpose here to discuss all the activities of the Bureau. The aim is merely to show the relation of the Bureau to the farmer and other classes and to point out the principal beneficial results. A feature of the work carried on by the Bureau has to do with insects affecting the health of man. Thus studies with respect to carriers of malaria have thrown much light upon how the disease is contracted and has made possible the taking of steps to check its ravages upon farm labor and upon people generally. Not only has the mosquito's relation to malaria and yellow fever been ascertained, but the relation of the house fly to typhoid fever and other human problems are being studied. An important study is concerned with the human louse. The Bureau cooperates with charitable institutions and tests various methods of control. This work is a phase of the larger problem of sanitation so important among the ignorant classes in congested districts of our cities. The control of the human louse became a matter of great importance among the armiès of the European War. "Delousing" stations were necessary to maintain the fighting efficiency of the soldier. The "cootie" among the soldiers of all armies became so prevalent that "having them" ceased to be a disgrace. It is thus seen that entomology had a practical place in the conduct of the Great War, and that "military entomology" was a course of considerable content value to those entering the service.

All economic entomological activities, with the exception of bee culture investigations, have to do directly or indirectly with the destruction of injurious insects. Besides making studies of improving results of the domestic species, foreign bees are imported. Demonstrations in beekeeping are made in cooperation with county agricultural agents of the States.

As already stated the work of the Bureau is primarily economic, yet it also names, classifies and establishes systematic relationships of all insects that are being studied in the laboratories or sent in by experiment stations and scientific workers.

With this brief review of the work of the Bureau of Entomology its practical and scientific importance is obvious. The maintenance of the Bureau as a public agency is well worth while.

BUREAU OF BIOLOGICAL SURVEY

Establishment of the Bureau of Biological Survey.—In their economic aspects ornithology and entomology are closely related. To the extent that birds eat injurious insects they are beneficial to the farmer, and it is therefore not surprising to find that the first work undertaken by the Government in the field of ornithology was performed by the Division of Entomology under which a section of ornithology was established on July 1, 1885. Congress appropriated $5,000 for the purpose of studying the relations of birds to agriculture. This work had already been begun a few years before by the American Ornithologists' Union; but inasmuch as the necessarily elaborate investigations required large funds which are usually not available to the private investigator, the Union addressed a memorial to Congress and asked for government aid to continue the work.

A year later, on July 1, 1886, Congress enlarged the scope of the work so as to include mammalogy, and placed it under an independent body designated Division of Ornithology and Mammalogy. The purpose of this appropriation was "for the promotion of economic ornithology and mammalogy, an investigation of food habits, distribution, and migrations of North American birds and mammals in relation to agriculture, horticulture, and forestry."[1]

A still greater scope of the work of the Division was provided for by Congress in 1896 when the name of the Division was changed to that of Biological Survey. Its duties included the study of the geographic distribution of animals and plants, the mapping of the natural life zones of the country, the

[1] *Yearbook*, 1899, p. 264.

investigation of the economic aspects of birds and mammals, and recommending measures for the preservation of beneficial and the destruction of injurious species.

In 1900 the protection of game and the inspection of game imported with a view to preventing the introduction of such pests as the mongoose and the English sparrow, were made additional functions of the Bureau. In 1905 the Division was changed into a Bureau; and while its force of salaried employes is the smallest of all the Bureaus of the Department, it nevertheless performs regulatory functions very valuable to the farmer and the country, as well as services enriching the knowledge of biological science.

The Division of Biological Investigations.—The work of this Division is of special interest to biological science. A large part of it, however, is necessary as a preliminary step in the proper execution of the regulatory functions of the Bureau, and has therefore an immediate and practical application. In order that it may properly protect migratory birds investigations as to the geographic distribution of these birds and as to the time of migrating and other habits must necessarily be made. The data concerning the migration of birds are collected through correspondence with more than 300 voluntary observers located throughout the United States, in many parts of Canada, and in Alaska. Reports of field men also supply information. The information so received is recorded and kept on cards for ready reference. The Bureau also makes bird counts through its force of voluntary observers in certain typical areas of farm, orchard, and forest land with a view to determining the conditions most favorable for the useful species and increasing their numbers.

"To secure and publish definite information concerning the habits and distribution of bird and mammal life of the public domain, particularly in the national forests and Federal preserves, with special reference to the fur-bearers and species classed as game" as well as to the noxious species whose destruction is desirable, the Bureau conducts investigations in the field and laboratory, makes detailed reports, collects information from individuals and institutions, and cooperates with State game commissions, State and other universities, and scientific societies. In this way the Bureau has collected a wealth of data that are drawn upon frequently by the student, and breeders of fur-bearing animals, as well as by administrative authorities who are concerned as to the identity of species in the execution of their duties, one of them being, for instance, the payment of bounties for scalps submitted. The Bureau prepares maps, of the range or distribution of birds and mammals both useful and noxious, which is a service of considerable educational importance and is a necessary precedent to the performance of the Bureau's regulatory functions.

In addition to the investigations of birds and mammals of the public domain the Bureau makes biological surveys of the states and territories. Skilled field naturalists traverse the state, working the mountains, valleys, and plains in sufficient detail to determine the distribution of birds, mammals and principal plants. Specimens needing identification are taken and studied. Field observations as to habits of birds and mammals are recorded. Considerable progress in this work is being made, the surveys of some of the states having been completed and the data published.

The Division of Economic Ornithology and Mammalogy.— The work of this Division is primarily concerned with increasing production and conserving the country's food supply. One of the important functions of the Division is the destruction of predatory animals such as wolves, coyotes, bobcats, mountain lions, and other stock-killing animals on the public domain. The territory infested with these predatory animals is divided into nine districts and is in charge of inspectors. A force of trappers and hunters, varying according to the season from 175 to 300 men, kills these animals and sends their skins to Washington for disposal. Many of the skins are added to the zoological collection of the United States National Museum and the remainder are sold as Government property. In 1917 the net receipts from this source amounted to $36,000. The work is carried on by trapping, poisoning and shooting. During the breeding season den-hunting yields good results, during the year 1917 it is estimated that 75,000 predatory animals were destroyed by poisoning, and 30,512 were taken by trapping or shooting, the latter number including 556 wolves,

22,342 coyotes, 107 mountain lions, 3,053 bobcats, and 60 bears.[1] Bears are considered game and are not molested when encountered except in the case of individuals known to have the habit of killing stock. Stockmen have contributed funds to cooperate with the Bureau in the destruction of predatory animals, and the States of Nevada, Utah, and Washington have also appropriated substantial sums for the purpose and are cooperating with the Bureau. This work results in a very large saving of livestock, and is of very great importance not only to the stockmen and farmers in the infested regions, but to the entire country as well. In the chapter dealing with the Forest Service it is pointed out that an important feature of our forest policy is to utilize the forests at the same time they are being maintained. This idea is carried out in allowing livestock to graze on forest reserves. Agricultural land scattered among forest reserves is thrown open for settlement and stock on these farms is also subject to destruction by predatory animals. In order that our national forests and land adjacent to them may yield the greatest economic services it is necessary to protect livestock, and this campaign of killing predatory animals carried on by the Bureau of Biological Survey supplements therefore in a very important way the services rendered by the Forest Service.

The carnivorous instinct is not the only source of danger in these predatory animals. An epizootic of rabies prevails among coyotes, bobcats, and other wild animals throughout Oregon, Nevada, California, Idaho, and Utah; and the fact that this disease may be communicated by them to human beings, livestock, and other domestic animals, adds another serious menace to the presence of wild animls.

The Bureau's destruction of wild anials is not confined to the stock-killing species, but includes ground squirrels, rabbits, prairie-dogs, pocket gophers, rats and mice, moles and mountain-beavers. Ground squirrels are causing much damage to the crops in the northwestern States, and the Bureau is cooperating with the State extension services in that part of the country in a campaign of poisoning these pests. The squirrels on about 7,500,000 acres were poisoned during 1917,

[1] *Report* of Chief of Bureau, 1917, p. 252.

and as a result crops valued at $1,000,000 were saved.[1] The depredations of jack rabbits upon grain, alfalfa, and other crops cause serious losses in the far western States; and the European hare, introduced into New York some years ago, is increasing rapidly and doing much damage to orchards. Efforts to control these animals are being made by the Bureau. A very active campaign is being waged against the prairie-dogs throughout the western States. This work is so important that, according to the estimate of the Forest Service, the range for livestock improves 50 per cent after the prairie-dogs have been destroyed.

It would seem that a necessary sequence to the progressive destruction of the fur-bearing animals is breeding them in captivity. Experiments of this character are carried on by the Bureau in Essex County, New York. Information is collected concerning breeding, housing, feeding and the preparation of skins and furs for the market. Interests in all these phases of the domestic production of furs is constantly growing, and private enterprise has already become active in this field. The assumption of the risks of experimentation as a proper governmental activity cannot be questioned in this instance because the Bureau possesses a wealth of information concerning these animals which it can apply at little expense to this practical use, and for the further reason that this effort is just another phase of the conservation of our resources which is a policy to which governments have long been committed in more ways than one.

Another important work of this Division is concerned with the study of the economic aspects of birds. The true relation of birds to agriculture can only be determined by an examination of stomach contents. A sufficient number of these must be examined to determine general habits. When the examination shows that a large proportion of grains from the field and virtually no injurious insects have been taken the bird is condemned on economic grounds. The bird's economic status is, however, not the only consideration that determines its destiny. Its aesthetic characteristics have a very important influence in shaping measures either for its destruction or for

[1] Report of Chief of Bureau, 1917, p. 253.

its preservation. When an unfavorable economic status is in conflict with the aesthetic factor, as in the case of the bobolink or rice bird, we find that the bird receives varying treatment in different parts of the country. Under authority of the migratory-bird treaty act the Secretary of Agriculture issues regulations permitting the shooting of the bobolink in the fall in the rice districts and surrounding territory, while in other sections of the country this bird is fully protected. These investigations of the Bureau determine definitely the economic status of birds and provides a sound basis for bird protective laws which in the United States, it is claimed, are the best in the world.

The Division of Migratory Birds.—This Division has charge of the enforcement of the Federal migratory-bird treaty act pased in 1918. In the enforcement of the law the Bureau has divided the country into districts under the supervision of United States game wardens, and cooperates with State authorities, "about 200 State deputy game wardens acting as United States deputy game wardens."[1]

The first attempt at supplementing State game protection laws by the exercise of Federal authority occurred in 1900 with the passage of the Lacey Act. The object of this act was "to aid in the restoration of such [game and other wild] birds in those parts of the United States adapted thereto where the same have become scarce or extinct, and also to regulate the introduction of American or foreign birds or animals in localities where they have not heretofore existed." Under this law it because unlawful to ship dead bodies of wild birds in interstate commerce. Some of the States before 1900 prohibited the sale of game, and in 1917 Louisiana and South Carolina were the only two States that permitted hunting for the market.[2] Hunting for the market is disastrous to the game species, and its prohibition has been demanded by the sportsmen of the country. The passage of the Lacey Act supplementing State control over this practice has therefore been generally welcome. The law is being enforced by collecting evidence from transportation companies, markets, and indi-

[1] List of Workers.

[2] *Report* of Chief of Bureau, 1917, p. 262.

viduals. Violations are reported to the United States Attorney General for prosecution. The vigorous activity of inspectors has caused this illegal traffic to decline very substantially.

A very important step tending to protect migratory birds and increase their numbers was taken by Congress on March 4, 1913, when the Department of Agriculture was empowered to prescribe closed seasons during which it would be unlawful to capture or kill migratory birds. State game commissioners, sportsmen, conservationists and others, were of the opinion that uniformity of laws protecting birds was necessary to prevent their extinction, and that such uniformity could only be attained through the use of Federal authority. Accordingly a bill embodying this idea was introduced in Congress in 1904, but no action could be secured until 1913. The reason for the delay was the questionable constitutionality of the proposed law. The Department issued regulations prohibiting spring shooting, which was generally complied with by sportsmen, and resulted in an increase of birds, it is claimed. The constitutionality of the law, however, was attacked, but appeal to the United States Supreme Court was dismissed because the law in question was repealed. In 1916, at the time the case was pending, the United States Government entered into a treaty with Great Britain providing for the protection of migratory birds in this country and in Canada. After the ratification of the treaty by both countries Congress passed the Migratory Bird Treaty Act, approved July 3, 1918. Under this law "it is unlawful to hunt, capture, kill, possess, sell, purchase, ship, or transport at any time or by any means any migratory bird included in the terms of the treaty except as permitted by regulations which the Secretary of Agriculture is authorized and directed to adopt, and which become effective when approved by the President. The act provides police and other powers necessary for its effective enforcement."[1] That part of the Lacey Act regulating interstate traffic of birds and plumage was covered by the terms of the law of 1918. The passage of this law included a repeal of the migratory law of 1913, whose constitutionality, as was stated, was being tested in the courts. On motion of the Attorney General the appeal

[1] *Yearbook*, 1918, p. 308.

in the case was dismissed and the court's attitude toward the constitutionality of the exercise of Federal authority in the protection of migratory birds therefore remained a moot question until July 2, 1919, when the United States District Court upheld the constitutionality of the act of 1918. It was certain that the treaty entered into, and the statute to enforce the terms of the treaty would give added weight to the constitutional rights of the Federal Government to protect migratory birds. Although it is certainly true that this law involves a very liberal application of the interstate commerce clause of the Constitution of the United States. All State hunting laws in conflict with the Federal statute are void. State laws may, however, supplement the Federal law and lengthen the closed season or limit the amount of game to be taken at one time or during a season; but an open season under a State law falling within a closed season under the Federal law would be void.

In addition to the regulatory functions growing out of the Federal migratory-bird treaty act the Division keeps a record of State game laws. The history of these game laws makes a very interesting study. Legislative measures looking to the destruction of injurious birds and animals have taken the form of bounty and scalp acts. The former type of laws provides for the payment of a small sum for each bird or animal killed, while the latter imposes a tax upon individuals who at their volition may pay the tax or submit a certain number of scalps of birds or animals in lieu of the payment of the tax. In recent years protection laws prescribing closed seasons, have become general.

The Division of Importations of Foreign Birds and Mammals.—This Division issues permits for importations of foreign wild birds and mammals and regulates their entry into this country. The regulation of the importation of wild birds and animals was provided for in 1900 under the Lacey Act, which is a section of the law still in force. The act prohibits "the importation of the English sparrow, mongoose, starling, flying fox, and such other species as may be declared injurious to agriculture." To carry out the provisions of the act six experienced scientific men are employed at the principal ports of entry to make inspections of shipments of imported animals and birds.

Importations of birds and mammals are for various purposes. The rare species go to the zoological gardens, or fur-bearing animals may go to fur farms. States also are making attempts to restock the country with game birds, notably quail and pheasants. The cage birds are in demand for homes. During 1917, 97,993 birds and 4,135 mammals were imported under permits, while 7,007 birds and 339 mammals requiring no permits were admitted to entry. The use of the quarantine at the port of entry is also used to prevent the spread of diseases among birds and animals.

The Division of Mammal and Bird Reservations.—"This Division has supervision over the 74 Federal mammal and bird reservations. The 5 big-game reservations are the Montana National Bison Range; the Winter Elk Refuge in Jackson Hole, Wyoming; the game preserves on the Wind Cave National Park, South Dakota, and Sullys Hill National Park, North Dakota; and the Niobrara Reservation, Nebraska. Birds are also protected on these reservations."[1] In the big-game reservations at the end of the fiscal year, 1917, there were 246 head of buffalo, 184 of elk, and 49 of antelope. During 1918 permanent warden service was maintained on the big-game preserves and on some of the most important bird reservations, while on certain other reservations only temporary warden service was afforded during the nesting season.[2] The work is carried on in cooperation with the Forest Service, War Department, Navy Department, Reclamation Service, United States Coast Guard, Bureau of Fisheries, National Association of Audubon Societies, and other societies, including State game officials and individuals. Obviously the preservation of these species is an enterprise in which private initative is almost entirely lacking. It is therefore fitting that the Federal

[1] List of Workers.
[2] Program of Work, 1919, p. 434.

Government with its extensive forest reserves supplement local governmental efforts in propagating and preserving rare and harmless wild animals.

SELECTED REFERENCES

Howard in *Yearbook* for 1899, pp. 135-156; *Farmers' Bulletin No. 835;* Hunter in *Yearbook* for 1901, pp. 369-380; Palmer in *Yearbook* for 1899, pp. 259-292; various *Reports* of Chiefs of Bureaus of Entomology and Biological Survey.

CHAPTER VII

Bureaus of Chemistry and Soils

THE BUREAU OF CHEMISTRY

Establishment of the Division of Chemistry.—Chemistry, like the distribution of seed and the collection of agricultural statistics, was one of the original considerations for which the Department of Agriculture was established. Judge Buell of New York, twenty years before its establishment, included, among other functions, that a national department of agriculture should perform, "the analysis, by means of a chemical laboratory, of various soils, grains, fruits, plants, vegetables, and manures, and publishing the results for the guidance and benefit of agriculturalists."[1] The Act of 1862 creating the Department also recognized the fundamental character of chemistry in its relation to agriculture inasmuch as it directed the Commissioner of Agriculture "to employ other persons for such time as their services may be needed, including chemists, botanists, entomologists, and other persons skilled in the natural science of agriculture." Under this authority the Commissioner appointed a chemist on August 21, 1862, and a Division of Chemistry was organized the same year. In 1901 its status was changed to a bureau.

Early Investigations.—Unquestionably it was the intent of the framers of the Act that chemical analyses should cover a broad field including the investigation of soils, grains, fruits, plants, vegetables, and fertilizers, with special reference to the needs of the farmer and the public at large. It is interesting to note at this time when there is an overwhelming sentiment throughout the country in favor of prohibiting the manufacture of liquors that the first important work undertaken and energetically prosecuted for some years by the Division of Chemistry, had to do with "the chemical examination of native grapes"[2] with a view to aiding the wine inter-

[1] *Agricultural Report*, 1862, p. 20.
[2] *Ibid*, p. 509.

ests of the country. In his report for 1864, the chemist says: "My attention having been called to the increasing demand of a knowledge of fermentation, its causes, different stages, kinds, etc., I have occupied the time not otherwise employed in a somewhat extended series of experiments upon it, and will preface the account of miscellaneous analyses with some notice of this subject, so interesting to all generally, and in a business way to brewers and wine growers."

However, during its first year the Division also analyzed sorghum and beets for sugar content and pursued the study for many years, being largely responsible ultimately for the establishment of the beet-sugar industry in this country. In the Chemist's report for 1867 the work of the Division is shown to have broadened considerably. During that year examinations included sugar, various kinds of soils, wines, minerals, etc. The complaint is made both in this report and in previous ones that the laboratory was being used too much for the encouragement of private enterprise and not sufficiently in interest of agriculture and the country generally. From the beginning the Division has done excellent work in fertilizers. The analysis of soils and guanos [1] held a prominent place in the work reported in 1864. Says Dr. Wiley: "It was through chemical studies that the farmer was led to import the deposits of guano which had been stored for many thousand years in the arid islands of the Pacific."[2]

Definite Results of More Recent Studies of Sorghum.— Sorghum is closely allied to and resembles broom corn and is cultivated for its saccharine juice and for fodder. Kaffir corn and Jerusalem corn are some of its varieties and have become very important in the semi-arid portions of the country inasmuch as these can be cultivated in these regions when usually all other crops fail. While credit is given to the office of Plant Introduction and the Botany Division as well as to Experiment Stations for the introduction of sorghum and for carrying on certain experiments that led to improvement, the Chemistry Division also played an important part in its development. Analyses were made to test the sugar content and only

[1] *Yearbook*, 1899, p. 237.
[2] *Yearbook*, 1897, p. 78.

in this way could intelligent selection of seed be made. These analyses also pointed out that the juices contained large quantities of starch, gummy matters, and uncrystallizable sugars. It was the object therefore in the selection of seed to propagate the variety that would produce the greatest sugar content with the greatest purity. In eight years, Doctor Wiley says, the sugar content of sorghum was raised from 9 to 14 per cent.[1]

With the increase of competition in sugar production emanating chiefly from the beet-sugar industry which had also been rapidly developed, it was found that production of sugar from sorghum would not be profitable. It is, however, used largely in the manufacture of fine table syrups, and of course for fodder. With these results obtained, therefore, the attempt to develop the extensive manufacture of sugar from sorghum is not lost energy, but is largely responsible for the development of a very valuable fodder, not to mention its value for table sirups, in semi-arid regions where a successful crop is almost a certainty if cultivated properly, making possible the raising of livestock and increasing generally the wealth of the nation.

Comparative Study of Soils.—"A knowledge of the soil is the fundamental structure on which agricultural chemistry is built."[2] This statement becomes forceful when it is remembered that the study of the soil has very substantially increased its productivity. Direct attention to the soil has led to the discovery of increasing the yield of crops while at the same time maintaining, or even increasing, the fertility of the soil. This is of tremendous economic importance. The system of rotating crops, by the use of clover, etc., restores the nitrogen to the soil, so important to plant life. While much progress has been made toward improving the soil without the use of fertilizers, they will probably always be necessary. Just what is necessary, however, in the way of fertilizers, special treatment of the soil due to the presence of alkali, etc., is discovered through a comparative study of native soils under standard meteorological conditions. While the Division of Chemistry by

[1] *Yearbook*, 1897, p. 80.
[2] Wiley, Yearbook, 1899, p. 245.

no means claims credit for the development of agricultural chemistry, it claims credit for having been the first agency in the world to study actually different soils with a view to determine and improve their respective degrees of fertility.

The Division's Collaboration With Other Departments.—As already remarked chemistry is fundamental in agricultural experimentation and inasmuch as it is a study of the elements of nature it is also extensively used as an applied science in the conduct of other Departments. The Bureau of Chemistry of the Department of Agriculture is an agency that not only makes analyses on its own account in the pursuit of its own specific duties, but performs the chemical work for other branches of the Department of Agriculture and also cooperates very largely with other Departments. The development of this phase of the Bureau's work has become so important that it is annually referred to as "collaboration" in the report of the Chief of Bureau.

This collaboration with other Departments began in 1866, and its extension was authorized by Congress from time to time until it includes almost every branch of the Government. The most extensive departmental cooperation has been conducted in connection with the Treasury Department. Up to 1904 the Bureau supervised the polarizations of sugars at the various ports of entry in order that tests at the various points might be in agreement. When this supervisory work was no longer necessary it was discontinued. The Bureau continues its cooperation with the Treasury in making chemical tests of various imported articles whose rate of duty depends upon chemical and physical characteristics.

Many analyses have also been made for the Post Office Department in connection with its attempt to exlude from the mail all uses for fraudulent purposes. Various materials, such as patent medicines, dangerous drugs, etc., have been frequently analyzed; and when it is found that their use is not as represented or tends to be injurious or immoral, "fraud orders" are issued by the Department by which the local postmaster is instructed not to deliver mail to the party being punished. The Drug Division of the Bureau also assists the Post Office Department in the trial of cases. In the case of a drug fraud [1] in 1917 a fine of $30,000 was imposed.

In addition to work performed for the Treasury and Post Office Departments, the Bureau of Chemistry has analyzed many foods for the War and Navy Departments. A large part of the work for other departments has to do with supplies bought under contract, such as inks, and colors used for printing banknotes, bonds, and other Government securities.

It is to be noted that Congress has recognized the feasibility of a central organization for the performance of the major part of the chemical work necessary to carry on the operations of the Government. The growth of this central agency was probably more or less spontaneous. In some of the earlier instances it was the result merely of requests from other department to have analyses made. Soon Congress recognized such collabration by making special apropriations for the work, while the present regulatory work committed to the Bureau bringing it into close touch with other departments was of course a more direct expression of Congress. Centralization in this instance makes unnecessary the investment of a large amount of capital in buildings and equipment that would be required if the chemistry work of the Government were more decentralized.

Association of Official Agricultural Chemists.—This Association has had continuous existence since 1884. Its membership is made up of chemists of the Department, of state departments, experiment stations and colleges as well as those of local governments engaged in agricultural chemistry. The Bureau of Chemistry of the Department of Agriculture has always been the leading spirit of the Association, and has published its proceedings as bulletins of the Division of Chemistry. The Association has steadily gained prestige and is recognized in America and in Europe as the most authoritative body of agricultural chemists in the world.

Among the important things the Association has accomplished is the development of standard methods of research

[1] *Report of the Chemist*, 1917, p. 209.

which have been adopted as official by the courts. It has been active in securing state legislation throughout the Union giving control over fertilizers sold in the market. Their composition must come up to certain standard tests provided for by law. The Association has also worked for the development of standards of purity of foods so that pure food laws could be enacted and effectively executed. In addition to these activities the Association has busied itself with unsolved agricultural problems of a varied character, worked out programs of research, and has in fact assumed the position of an advisory agency to the Department of Agriculture.[1]

Early Efforts to Prevent Food Adulteration.—No activity, however important, has given the Bureau of Chemistry so much prestige and popularity as has its work in preventing the adulteration of foods. The Division deserves a great deal of credit in this connection. It began the analyses of butter early in the history of the pure food movement, and Doctor Wiley, its chief for 29 years, was untiring in his efforts to secure legislation that would protect the consumer and the honest dealer as well as benefit the farmer.

The adulteration of foods is as old as dishonesty, but before the days of the large city and the consequent development of the present market organization it was not a serious social problem. Since the middle of the 19th century the adulteration of foods in the United States has developed into a problem of very large proportions. The commonest form of the earlier adulterations was associated with dairy products, but other food products suffered, among which may be mentioned, flour, tea, coffee, cocoa and chocolate, sirup, honey, confectionery, olive oil, vinegar, pickles, spices, canned gods, etc.[2] The earlier kind of dairy adulteration was the simple form of watering the milk or producing it under very insanitary conditions such as the feeding of distiller's slops to cattle.[3] To prevent this kind of adulteration the State of New

---

[1] *Vide* article by Doctor Wiley in *Yearbook*, 1899, p. 229; also references in other *Yearbooks*.

[2] *Vide Report of U. S. Commissioner of Internal Revenue for* 1888, p. CLXXXVI.

[3] *Vide The Butter Industry in the United States* by the author, p. 213.

York passed a law as early as 1862. Subsequent amendments followed, but the necessary machinery to enforce the law was not provided until 1884, when the office of the Dairy Commissioner was created.

When the first oleomargarine factory in America was established in New York City in 1873 the adulteration of butter took a new turn; and legislation to prevent it was fostered and supported by agricultural societies resulting soon in the enactment of state laws throughout the country. The first laws were passed by New York in 1877 and Maryland in 1878, and during the next decade the movement [1] for legislation spread rapidly, culminating in the enactment of a federal law in 1886.

The Division of Chemistry from the time this menacing evil made its appearance took an active part in studying it through the making of analyses[2] which began in 1883, and relentlessly pursued it through the agitation of effective legislation to the time its eradication became virtually complete.

Examination of Imported and Exported Butters.—The first regulatory functions that the Bureau was concerned with is the inspection of imported foods. This law was enacted March 3, 1903, and requires the cooperation of the Departments of Agriculture and State with the Treasury Department. The Department of State instructs United States Consuls to make special declarations as to foods to be shipped to the United States. The Treasury Department instructs its collectors at the ports of entry to secure samples for analysis of foods upon arival. These are turned over to the chemists of the Bureau which maintains laboratories at various points throughout the country. If the samples are found to be spurious, delivery of the goods is refused. Considerable opposition was at first expressed against this law, but a great majority of importers and the large body of consumers soon heartily supported the efforts of the Department. However, in 1905, one year before the enactment of the popular Food and Drugs Act, the foreign exporter complained that foods imported to this country were subjected, by reason of this inspection law, to

[1] *Butter Industry, op. cit.*, Chapter X.
[2] *Agricultural Report*, 1883, p. 8.

restrictions not placed upon goods produced within the United States which, they pointed out, was discrimination against foreign goods.[1] In this connection the Chemist, Doctor Wiley, makes an appeal for legislation providing for the inspection of foodstuffs entering into interstate commerce.

The Act of 1903 made the inspection of foods exported from the United States purely optional with the exporter. Under the provisions of the Act the Bureau of Chemistry was made available to the exporter for the inspection of foods. In the report of 1905 the Chief of Bureau states that American exporters generally preferred to take chances with the importation laws of foreign countries rather than have their products examined before leaving the United States. As a result, he states further, numerous complaints were made to the State Department concerning foods that were not allowed entry at foreign ports. It would seem that the results of this law, if taken advantage of by all American exporters, would be highly beneficial to both countries concerned and would lead to a phenomenal increase in the export trade of this country by reason of the fact that the genuineness and wholesomeness of American goods would be assured.

Research or Investigational Work.—Most of the investigational work of the Bureau has been concentrated in the laboratories at Washington and "as far as feasible, separated from the routine work of law enforcement. It is believed that the best results cannot be obtained by requiring both kinds of work from the same set of chemists."[2]

The investigational work is of two kinds. One is closely connected with the regulatory function of the Bureau inasmuch as it investigates new forms of sophistication and develops methods for detecting these newly refined and more subtle adulterations. It also seeks the cause and source of contamination in foods which often leads the Bureau to the factory where more sanitary methods are suggested, and in this way this form of investigation indirectly results in constructive work. The other type of investigation is directly constructive and looks to the development of new uses and sources of

[1] *Vide Chemist's Report*, 1905, p. 500.
[2] *Report of Chemist*, 1914, p. 166.

foods as well as proper utilization of by-products and the consequent elimination of wastes. The latter type of investigation illustrates how the Department of Agriculture is branching out into new fields. The emphasis of the work of the Bureau of Chemistry formerly was placed more directly upon efforts tending to increase production in the field, but now its efforts are extended to the factory and the attempt to prevent wastes is even followed through the market to the consumer. This investigation together with the regulatory function has made the Department of Agriculture an agency working truly in the interests of the whole people.[1]

As an example of the results of the newer form of constructive investigation may be cited the Bureau's discovery that citric acid may be successfully extracted from lemon culls.[2] By 1917 manufacturing concerns were utilizing these culls and the manufacture of citric acid was a by-product of considerable importance. Another illustration of this character of investigation is the study concerning the improvement of the durability of leather through tanning processes. The reader may consult recent reports of the Bureau for further details. These processes when worked out are made available for all producers and the monopolistic characteristic so closely associated with industrial progress is eliminated.

While this function of the Bureau of Chemistry is an example of how industrial progress could be initiated by the government, the writer does not want to intimate even that progress in our great complex industrial organization could be solely intrusted to public enterprise. Such investigations that are for the common good and that are too costly to be undertaken by private citizens may well be left to the government.

Office of State Cooperative Food and Drug Control.—This office was organized in 1914 through the effort of Secretary Houston, who called a meeting of the State and Federal food and drug officials at Washington. At this meeting three members each of the Association of American Dairy Food and

[1] For full statement of Bureau's investigational work consult Department's *Program of Work* for 1919.

[2] *Report of Chemist*, 1913, p. 195.

Drug Officials, the Association of Agricultural Chemists, and the Bureau of Chemistry of the Department of Agriculture were selected to constitute a committee for the purpose of fixing working standards for the prosecution of violations of food and drug laws. Anybody who is familiar with the nature of our federal and state governments, not to mention local governments, knows that a "twilight zone" frequently exists in the enforcement of the law, and that only open, frank, and energetic cooperation between executives of the various jurisdictions can bring full and complete observance of the food and drug laws of the country. At this meeting it became apparent that a central organization "for the promotion of cooperation and the exchange of information would lessen the cost and increase the efficiency of administering the food and drug laws by preventing duplication and by encouraging the states and the Federal Government to supplement and assist one another." In accordance with this suggestion the Office of State Cooperative Food and Drug Control was established in the Bureau of Chemistry.

The official in charge of the office visits state dairy and food commissioners and city health departments with a view to establishing cooperative relationships.

The office is made a clearing house for the collection and dissemination of information necessary to prosecute violations of the food and drug laws. The beginning and termination of court cases, court decisions, public hearings, etc., are communicated to all offices concerned. A manual of procedure for use by state officials has been published by this office of the Bureau.

An example of how state and local officials cooperate with the federal authorities is given in the report for 1916. Officials of the Bureau often give information to the Health Department of New York City which frequently leads to the condemnation of adulterated foods not coming under the jurisdiction of the federal act. In turn the Health Department of New York City reciprocates and gives information to the Bureau officials concerning violations of the federal law. Among the most notable instances of violations that have been run down as a result of cooperation "are polluted or watered oysters, watered scallops, adulterated milk or cream, decayed eggs, decomposed canned goods, butter and fish, wood alcohol in liquors, cottonseed meals and other feeds below guarantees, adulterated oats and misbranded nostrums.''

The operations of this office bridging over the ''twilight zone,'' may be said to be extra-legal, and is an example of how the limitations of a detailed written constitution may be overcome by the development of efficient federal administration.

The Food and Drug Act.—This Act was approved June 30, 1906, and was enacted only after similar laws in some of the states had gone into effect. The enactment of the federal law together with its influence upon such states that were slow in enacting pure food legislation may therefore be regarded as the culmination of a movement that was bred by the growth of cities since the 50's and became active in the early 70's. The collection of evidence looking to the enforcement of the Act is committed to the Bureau of Chemistry, and the officials directly in charge of carrying out the provisions of the law are the chiefs of the three Inspection Districts and the Office of State Cooperative Foods and Drug Control. The administrative policy of the Bureau with respect to this Act is not merely to report violations but also to do such constructive work through cooperation with manufacturers' associations that will tend to improve methods of manufacture and decrease the amount of food adulteration and contamination.

In his report for 1917, the tenth anniversary of the enactment of the federal pure food law, the Chief of Bureau attempts to measure the results of the act. Among other things he says: ''The best evidence that many of the abuses formerly occurring in the food industry have ceased, is to be found in the fact that the violations of the Food and Drug Act observed today are hardly comparable with those which obtained during the first few years of the past decade. Most of the staple food products now found in violation are either of a higher grade than formerly or are products of the clever adulterator, that is, of those who have more or less anticipated the ordinary means of detection by so manipulating their products that not infrequently the adulteration can be detected only by the most detailed and painstaking chemical analysis coupled with factory inspection." When the Act went into effect thirty soft drinks containing small amounts of cocaine were being sold. Practically all of them have been suppressed. Baking powder, gelatin and confectionery formerly contaminated with small quantities of lead or arsenic is now sold with these deleterious substances eliminated. More illustrations are cited in the Report of the Chief of Bureau.

The same Report notes some limitations of the law. The prohibition of labeling falsely any package containing food or drugs has been effective, but the method of deception is now practiced through advertising in the newspapers over which the Act exercises no jurisdiction. Other limitations are the inability to inspect warehouses and the lack of any "restriction whatever upon the use of many of the most virulent poisons in drugs." While there are these limitations, some of which are virtually overcome through cooperation with state and local authorities, a great deal of good has been accomplished during the ten years of the Act, and a most notable chapter in the history of progress has been chronicled.

The Sherley Act.—This Act was an outgrowth of an adverse decision to the Government in the case of the *United States vs. Johnson*,[1] in which misbranding was alleged of a so-called "mild combination treatment for cancer," the package bearing statements that the treatment would effect a cure. The court held that "false and misleading statements as to curative or therapeutic effects of medicines did not come within the prohibition of the law." Pursuant to this decision the President addressed a message to Congress asking for remedial legislation. The result was that on August 23, 1912, an amendment to the Food and Drugs Act was approved prohibiting false and misleading statements concerning the therapeutic effects of medicines.

The Bureau exerted itself at once to make the Act rapidly effective. As many chemists as could be spared were transferred to the Laboratories in Washington, New York and Chicago and in a few months analyzed hundreds of preparations. Seizure of several preparations was recommended and

[1] Notice of Judgment, 221 U. S. 488.

the cases were won by default. The Bureau's activity soon resulted in a "vast improvement in the labeling of medicinal preparations." Through cooperation with the Secretary of the Treasury the Sherley Act is also being applied to nearly all importations of drugs.

The facts upon which this kind of legislation rest are that the people are not sufficiently informed to evaluate properly statements concerning the effects of medicines and that a correction of the situation through the process of education would be, if not a hopeless procedure, certainly a very expensive one. It is therefore very proper that false and misleading statements concerning medicines should be prohibited by law.

Net Weight Act.—Another important amendment to the Food and Drugs Act is the Net Weight Act, March 3, 1913, which provides that all packages containing articles of food and shipped in interstate commerce shall be plainly and conspicuously marked to show the quantity of the contents.

The gathering of the information looking to the enforcement of this Act, has also been committed to the Bureau of Chemistry. Simple as the execution of the law seems to be, its enforcement is actually very complex. The moisture contents in the grains, salt, dairy products, etc., varies widely under different conditions of temperature and humidity, and the preliminary work necessary to carry out the provisions of the law, therefore, is to gather data for the purpose of formulating legal standards that may be relied upon in the prosecution of violations of the Act.

Cooperation with the Insecticide and Fungicide Board. The Bureau cooperates with the Insecticide and Fungicide Board in adducing evidence of violations of the Insecticide Act of 1910. Duly authorized collectors of the Board collect samples which are analyzed by the Bureau of Chemistry and the results of these analyses are reported to the Board for its consideration. When adulterations and misbranding appear they are certified to the Department of Justice and prosecutions instituted.

BUREAU OF SOILS

The Department's First Work on Soils.—The first work on soils carried on by the Department of Agriculture was done in the Division of Chemistry. As early as 1865 this Division made analyses of soils, and for many years the Chemist reports analyses of soils from all parts of the country including some even from foreign lands. Analyses for fertilizers and fertilizer materials were also frequently made. Such requests for analyses by 1889 became so numerous and burdensome to the Chemistry Division that the Chief of the Division referred persons making the requests to the respective experiment stations in the States from which the soil was taken. It will be noticed that analyses during this period were made upon request and that there was no systematic effort at making a soil survey of the country such as is now in progress. The popular demand for soil analyses during its early history was very strong and then declined because anticipated results were not realized. In the Yearbook of 1871 the Chemist states the position of soil chemistry in the following terms:

> In the early days of agricultural science much was anticipated from the services which chemistry would be able to render in the way of determining accurately the several substances used in the growth of crops, and the proportion of each of these in the different kinds of crops. Having made these several determinations, nothing more would be necessary than to ascertain what element of plant-food is deficient in the soil, and supply it accordingly. This appears so simple, and, at the same time, so plausible, that it is not surprising that there should arise almost a mania for soil-analysis among progressive farmers. But unforeseen difficulties arose, and these ardent anticipations were doomed to disappointment; and the value of soil analysis is now in danger of being as much undervalued as it was formerly overestimated.

Interest in the work, however, revived and steadily grew, as is shown by the *Chemist's* report in 1885. The investigation by that time had broadened considerably including problems of aeration and climatic conditions. Later with the institution of systematic soil-surveys, soil investigations generally served very important practical uses, and the popularity of the work of this Bureau is attested by the fact that in 1919 there were printed 10,500 copies of the reports of soil-surveys in one volume and in addition a separate report with maps and illustrations of "each area surveyed, in the form of advance sheets, bound in paper covers, of which five hundred copies shall be for the use of each Senator from the State, two thousand copies for the use of each Representative for the congressional district or districts in which the survey is made, and one thousand copies for the use of the Department of Agriculture.''[1]

Establishment of the Agricultural Soils Division.—As already indicated, in order that soil investigations might really be of some practical use to the farmer the influences of texture, aeration, temperature and moisture upon crops had to be investigated. In fact attention for a time seems to have been mainly upon the meteorological aspect of the problem. In 1894 the Agricultural Soils Division was established under the Weather Bureau. The Division was placed in charge of Professor Milton Whitney, who had previously been in the service of the Department as a special agent engaged upon this phase of the soil problem. The work was, however, not sufficiently related to meteorological observations and weather forecasts to warrant its affiliation with the Weather Bureau, and it is therefore not surprising that a year later the Agricultural Soils Division became an independent division in the Department with an appropriation of $15,000.[2]

Establishment of the Bureau of Soils.—The functions of the Division in 1899 were ''enlarged to include the mapping of tobacco soils and other necessary tobacco investigations, with a total appropriation of $26,300.'' It was then that the work of the soil survey was actively and systematically begun with express provision by Congress. In 1900 the appropriation was increased to $31,300, and in the act approved March 2, 1901, the Division was reorganized into a bureau, with an appropriation of $109,140. In his report for 1901 the Secretary of Agriculture says that ''this remarkably rapid evolution of the soil work of the Department from a subordinate division of the Weather Bureau to a bureau organization of its own, within a period of six years from its inception, is based wholly upon the economic importance and value of the work, the careful and conscientious administration of its affairs, and a thor-

[1] *Field Operations* of the Bureau of Soils, 17th Report, p. 2.
[2] *Yearbook*, 1901, p. 39.

ough understanding and appreciation of its aims by the people upon which liberal support accorded by Congress has been granted."

The entire work of the Bureau of Soils aims at increased agricultural productivity. The Bureau has none of the regulative functions so important in some of the other Bureaus. The Bureau's reports of *Field Operations* and published results of researches have a very important educational value inasmuch as they disseminate scientific knowledge of the soil.

Chemical and Physical Investigations.—"The laboratories of the Bureau of Soils are maintained mainly for the support and aid of the field parties," but at the same time they are engaged in the study of fundamental problems concerning the "relation of the soil to plant growth."[1] So far as economic gains are concerned physical investigations have probably yielded greater results than chemical investigations. In the *Yearbook* for 1912 the Secretary says: "The relative amount of sand, silt, clay and the way these are combined or held together has an important influence on the drainage and aeration and on the mechanical work of cultivation, and with the organic content of soils has a very important influence on the retentive power of the soil for moisture and the supply of moisture available for crops. The extent to which these physical properties can be influenced by cultivation, fertilization, and by crops themselves is being investigated as a basis for improved and efficient methods of maintaining the soil in suitable physical condition for those proper functions that are adapted to the needs of our staple or special crops."[2]

The chemical analysis of soils has demonstrated that by ascertaining what soil foods are lacking the yield per acre of a given plot of ground can be increased many times by applying the foods thus found to be absent. In a given demonstration field in Illinois and under the direction of Dr. Hopkins chemical analyses showed the soil to be lacking in phosphate, and with the application of $1.50 of phosphate per acre

---

[1] *Yearbook*, 1908, p. 94.
[2] P. 73.

it was demonstrated that the yield could be increased from a previous yield of 12 or 13 bushels to 50 or 60 bushels.[1]

Besides these investigations that have to do directly with the problem of increased yield, an investigation of great economic importance seeks to discover means to prevent erosion and to reclaim lands already badly washed. In all parts of the country where the topography is mountainous or rolling, erosion is responsible for the destruction of large portions of agricultural land, and to save such land is well worth the attention of a scientific body. One of the methods of prevention suggested by the Bureau is deep ploughing with a heavy mixture of organic matter so as to provide a deep porous reservoir for the storage of water during rainstorms. Another method provides for the construction of terraces across the hillside so as to check the accumulation of flowing water. Where the mischief has been done and reclamation is necessary, filling in and the planting of trees and shrubbery so as to bind the soil through root formation, is recommended.

Investigations of Fertilizer Reserves.—This subject in its broadest sense is so fundamental in the history of mankind that it may well be said that the destiny of the human race largely depends upon the degree of success attained in the fertilization of its land. Unless the fertility of the soil be increased or even maintained, the population of the world faces the alternatives of having its number reduced through famine or through the application of checks, which in fact are already very generally practiced in the western world. The pressure of population upon means of subsistence troubled Malthus and others in the opening days of the nineteenth century. These fears, however, were wholly unwarranted. People are not only learning to regulate their number, but through scientific investigation they have increased the fertility of the soil very substantially; and now that we have our scientists at work supported and maintained by public funds there is every reason to believe that as time goes on continued progress will be made in soil fertility.

During the last 50 years the use of commercial fertilizers has developed to large proportions. The Bureau is engaged in

[1] *Senate Doc. No. 845*, p. 38.

the analysis of materials that gives promise of value for fertilizing purposes, and investigates sources of supply of fertilizer materials whose value has been definitely established. Of these materials the three important ingredients are phosphoric acid and potash and nitrogen compounds. Germany's supply of potash normally precludes attempts to secure the material elsewhere, but during the war, while the German supply was not available, it became commercially profitable to recover potash from the giant kelps of the Pacific coast and Alaska. The Bureau believes that if the potash volatilized in blast furnaces and in the burning of cement can be saved, these sources alone are ample to satisfy the country's demand. So far as phosphate rock is concerned, the Secretary of Agriculture says that the country's supply is sufficient to supply three times the present demand for 12 centuries or more.[1] An important study has to do with the fixation of atmospheric nitrogen and in this connection the Secretary says that "with many sources of nitrogen carriers yet to be utilized to their fullest extent and with practicable methods of 'fixing' atmospheric nitrogen already finding a home in this country, the future may be faced with equanimity so far as problems of supply are concerned."

Soil Survey Investigations.—A complete and systematic soil survey of agricultural land of the United States, like many other services performed by the Department of Agriculture, must be made by the Government for the reason that the project yields insufficient profits to attract private enterprise. In order also that the survey may be made in all parts of the country it is important that the work be conducted by the Federal Government rather than by the States. The States, however, play an important part inasmuch as virutally all projects are carried on through the cooperation of Experiment Stations and State Agricultural Departments, special appropriations being made for the purpose. It has been the policy of the Bureau from the beginning to make surveys of areas in many different parts of the country and not to complete the work in one State before beginning elsewhere. For

[1] *Yearbook*, 1912. p. 153.

instance, according to the *Program of Work* for 1919,[1] areas lying in 24 different States were to be surveyed. "Omitting the sparsely settled Rocky Mountain region, the Northwest Intermountain region, the arid Southwest, and the Great Basin," by 1912 the Bureau had made a detailed survey of 29.2% of the land surface of the United States.[2]

Two classes of surveys are made by the Bureau—one, in the better sections of agricultural land, is detailed; while the other, in sparsely settled sections of the country, is carried out in less detail, and is known as a reconnoissance survey. The latter is used very largely in making surveys of land located within our National Forest Reserves and suitable for agricultural purposes. This is done in cooperation with the Forest Service with a view to eliminating such tracts from the Reserves and making them available for purposes of cultivation. A soil survey determines the exact character of the various soils, their location and extent. It also ascertains from all available sources their best uses, and wherever possible, "forecasts and advises additional and more profitable occupation for each soil·"[3] The work thus aims to raise the yield of land generally to the highest possible point and to disseminate knowledge that may be used by the agricultural investor and enterprisor to the best of his advantage.

SELECTED REFERENCES.

Wiley in *Yearbook* for 1897, pp. 76-84; Wiley in *Yearbook* for 1899, pp. 201-258; various *Reports* of Chemists; various *Reports* of Commissioner of Internal Revenue; *Yearbook* for 1908, pp. 88-102; various *Reports* of Chief of Bureau of Soils.

[1] P. 370.
[2] *Yearbook*, 1912, p. 151.
[3] *Yearbook*, 1908, p. 89.

CHAPTER VIII

WEATHER BUREAU

Early Meteorological Observations.[1]—Almost from the beginning of colonial history, it is said, various individuals began the recording of meteorological data in America. Among some of these early notable meteorologists were John Winthrop of Harvard College, who began the collection of data in 1742; Thomas Jefferson, who made a series of observations from 1772 to 1778; and James Madison, who in cooperation with Jefferson instituted at William and Mary College observations made simultaneously with those at Monticello. These observations, it is believed, were the first simultaneous observations made in this country. At this time the science of meteorology was not understood because no simultaneous observations had ever been made over any extended area. The whole subject was shrouded in mystery and clothed with superstition. Even today, it is probably safe to say, more superstition prevails among the people concerning the weather than with regard to any other natural phenomenon. Scientists held theories concerning the nature of storms, but these lacked proof because sufficient data had never been collected. Franklin believed that the storms traveled in a northwesterly direction; and others, during the first half of the 19th century, advanced the theories of the circular movement of the storms, that their existence depended upon convectional indrafts, and that their form was oblong or otherwise. In view of this scientific interest in meteorology, which before the middle of the century was probably greater than the interest associated with its practical uses, it is not surprising that the development of the science as well as the system for the collection of meteorological data and the distribution of forecasts, was centered in the Smithsonian Institution.

---

[1] All facts concerning the development of meteorological organization before the commitment of the work to the Signal Service of the U. S. Army are taken from an article by Marcus Benjamin in *The Smithsonian Institution, 1846-1896*, pp. 647-678.

Meteorological Organization Before 1870.—The first systematic effort to collect meteorological data was begun by the Army Medical Department in 1814, which was continued to the Civil War. In 1817 the Commissioner of the General Land Office, whose organization scattered over the country was somewhat favorable, also began the collection of data. This in time became the parent of the work carried forward by the Patent Office under annual appropriations made by Congress from 1854 to 1860 for "the collection of agricultural statistics, investigations for promoting agriculture and rural economy, etc." A portion of this appropriation was devoted to assist ing the Smithsonian Institution in collecting and reducing meteorological observations.

In 1846 Alfred J. Henry was elected Secretary of the Smithsonian Institution and almost immediately recommended "a system of extended meteorological observations for solving the problem of American storms." Henry asked the aid of the most prominent meteorologists in the country in maturing his plans which in brief were the placing of compared instruments in the hands of observers, and the coordination of all existing observers into a unified system. In response to Henry's request the Board of Regents of the Smithsonian Institution appropriated for the purpose $1,000 which was, to be sure, a small sum with which to purchase instruments and pay the clerk hire necessary to carry on the correspondence with the observers and reduce the data reported.

Under the leadership of Henry the next step taken was to secure the cooperation of all observers then making observations. There were at that time scientists including Professor James H. Coffin of Lafayette College and Professor James P. Espy, a noted meteorologist, who were in correspondence with individuals taking daily observations. To such persons and other reliable parties a document giving instructions as to the taking and recording of observations, was distributed in 1848 through Members of Congress and others. This list of names of observers includes those of prominent scientists. The systems previously organized by the Army Medical Department and the Patent Office were also utilized and all observations were reported to a central office at the Smithsonian Institution. Mention is made of a Congressional appropriation for meteorological purposes to the Navy Department whose cooperation Henry was anxious to secure. When, however, he speaks of the organization operating between 1854 and 1859 the Navy Department is not included. In fact the Navy observations were "confined exclusively to the sea and had no reference to those made at the same time on land." His words are as follows: "The primary object of the Smithsonian Institution is the advancement of the science of meteorology, and the elucidation of the laws of atmospheric phenomena; that of the Patent Office, to collect facts and to deduce therefrom laws which have immediate reference to agriculture; while the system of the Medical Department is intended to be primarily subservient to the health of the troops and the advancement of medical science. These three Institutions are now in harmonious cooperation, and it is believed that it is no exaggeration to say that under their auspices more is now being done to advance meteorology than has ever before been attempted under any government."[1] Already in 1849 Henry reports that there were 150 regular observers reporting, and that a fair start had been made toward establishing a meteorological organization extending over the greater part of the United States.

Operation of the System.—Blanks were prepared by the Patent Office and distributed under its franking privilege to the various observers who recorded the data and at the end of the month sent the record, known as "registers," also under frank, to Washington. The Smithsonian Institution forwarded the registers to Professor James H. Coffin of Lafayette College, who with a clerical force at his disposal reduced the data. The reduction of data was later done by the Patent Office. In 1860 the appropriation from the Commissioner of Patents was suddenly discontinued so that reductions could no longer be made. This was the period of the Civil War and all things, it seems, conspired to put a stop to meteorological work which, at that time, had not yet found any important practical applications, such as were made during the recent European War

[1] Benjamin, *op. cit.*, p. 661.

in the administering of deadly gases and in the bombing and scouting operations of airplanes.

It must be remembered that the daily observations made by the observers were at first reported monthly and that this was more or less satisfactory from the scientific point of view, but wholly useless for forecasting purposes. The use of the "magnetic telegraph" for reporting daily weather observations early suggested itself to Henry. His funds, however, were limited and he was compelled to ask permission of the telegraph companies for the free use of their wires at a certain period of the day. This request was granted, and made possible the charting of the data on a skeleton map of the United States which showed at a glance the location of the storm, high and low pressure, precipitation, cloudiness, and the likely direction in which the storm would move. Thus it is seen that forecasting is dependent upon rapid communication, and in the history of progress it must be noted that the telegraph was the precursor of the system of forecasting weather, hurricanes, and floods.

The first practical application of the telegraphic reports and charting them on the weather map was made in 1856 when the information was exhibited daily by hanging the map in public places in Washington and displaying the indications of the weather by means of signals from the tower of the Smithsonian Institution. The information was also given to newspapers.

These operations were also interrupted during the Civil War for the lack of reports from the South and because most of the lines of the North and West were too busy with other public business. Also at this time, 1863, Congress passed a law which prevented the observers to send in each month their registers by mail unless postage was prepaid. Inasmuch as these observers were not paid for their services, they could ill afford to pay postage for the forwarding of their monthly reports. The Commissioner of Agriculture was interested in weather reports in connection with the publication of his monthly crop bulletins, and for a time forwarded the necessary postage to the observers. In the meantime he petitioned Congress to extend the franking privilege to the observers for the purpose of forwarding the registers, and soon secured favorable action.

Movement to Establish a Meteorological Department.—To the lack of funds and the interference of the Civil War must be added the fire of the Institution's building destroying many records and instruments in 1865, in summing up the handicap under which the Smithsonian Institution labored in its endeavor to develop a meteorological organization. Attempts were again made in 1867 to secure the free service of the telegraph companies, but without success. At this time agitation was in progress looking to the establishment of a meteorological department with sufficient funds to carry on its operations. Henry at once supported the movement and asked Congress for an appropriation of $50,000. No action was taken until 1869 when a joint resolution was introduced which was approved February 9, 1870, and appropriated $25,000 for the establishment of a weather service under the Signal Service of the United States Army. The joint resolution reads as follows:

> Be it resolved by the Senate and House of Representatives of the United States of America in Congress assembled, that the Secretary of War be, and he hereby is, authorized and required to provide for taking meteorological observations at the military stations in the interior of the continent and at other points in the States and Territories of the United States, and for giving notice on the northern lakes and on the seacoast, by magnetic telegraph and marine signals, of the approach and force of storms.

Expansion Under Signal Service.—In 1871 Congress provided for reporting stages of water in rivers. This function of the Weather Bureau is known as the River and Flood Service, and is one of the most valuable services performed by the Bureau. Stages along all important streams are reported to offices located on them and in this way river rises can be very accurately forecast. It is a service that has very great economic value to people along these streams inasmuch as sufficient time is usually given in the forecast of floods to allow the removal of families and property, or the taking of the necessary steps that will avoid disaster in various ways.

Further expansion followed in 1872 when Congress provided "for the benefit of commerce and agriculture" a system of observations and reports that would give notice of the approach of storms throughout the United States instead of only along the Great Lakes and seacoast as provided for in 1870. The first act obviously was a service to shipping alone, while the second extended the benefits also to agriculture. This action of Congress was enthusiastically commended by the Commissioner of Agriculture in his report [1] for 1873.

It is very plain that even the purely practical phases of a weather service should not be committed to the War Department. Even during times of peace the organization of the Army is not conducive to best results. It does not follow that the Army posts are always favorably located for meteorological purposes or that the Army posts are located where observations should be made. During times of war the meteorological interest, especially its more scientific aspects, would be quite incompatible with the main function of the Army. There is also a more important and more fundamental reason why the weather service should not be conducted by the Army. The weather service is a civil function and promotes the peaceful pursuits of agriculture and commerce. It is not in accord with American traditions to allow the power of the Army or the Navy in any way to engraft itself upon the ordinary walks of life and direct their destiny.

The Establishment of the Weather Bureau.—The various economic interests of the country had their hopes gratified on October 1, 1890, when Congress transferred the weather service from the Army to the Department of Agriculture. The work was placed under a separate Bureau and its chief, unlike chiefs of other bureaus of the Department, was to be appointed by the President, by and with the advice of the Senate. A section of the Act creating the Bureau follows:

> The Chief of the Weather Bureau under the direction of the Secretary of Agriculture, shall have charge of forecasting the weather; the issue of storm warnings; the display of weather and flood signals for the benefit of Agriculture, commerce, and navigation; the gauging and reporting of rivers; the maintenance and operation of seacoast telegraph lines and the collection and transmission of marine intelligence for the benefit of commerce and navigation; the reporting of temperature and rainfall conditions for the cotton interests; the dis-

[1] P. 7.

play of frost, cold wave, and other signals; the distribution of meteorological information in the interest of agriculture and commerce; and the taking of such meteorological observations as may be necessary to establish and record the climatic conditions of the United States, or are essential for the proper execution of the foregoing duties.

It will be observed that the Act extends the service of the Weather Bureau to agriculture, navigation, and commerce. Temperature and rainfall conditions are to be reported for the benefit of the cotton interests. Special observers are located throughout the cotton belt and these report daily temperature and rainfall data during the growing season. At all important cotton exchanges, the largest of which is in New York, meteorological data is daily placed on large glass weather maps, portraying at a glance the weather during the preceding twenty-four hours and the possibility of its continuation, or of a change, either of which may very seriously affect the bulls and bears of the Exchange. Cotton is very sensitive to droughts or excessive rainfall at certain stages of its growth, and its price estimated by speculators during the growing season is therefore also very responsive to weather conditions. While similar maps are prepared for the exchanges dealing with grains, their interest in meteorological data is not as keen.

Navigation is to be cared for under the provisions of the Act, and the benefits accruing to this activity are really very important. The hurricanes originating mostly in the West Indies are very destructive and, inasmuch as their direction can be forecast with a high degree of accuracy, this feature of the Weather Bureau service is well worth while.

The Act also contemplates that agriculture in general shall receive the attention of the Bureau. Forecasts of weather are disseminated broadcast throughout the country and the effort is made to reach a large class of farmers through the press, the display of maps and cards, and the use of local telephones. Farmers having access to maps would do well to familiarize themselves with the art of forecasting; because then they could distinguish "probabilities" from certainties, and arrange their farm operations accordingly.

Finally the Act provides for recording and determining the climatic conditions of the United States. This is a service that has great scientific value and is eagerly desired by meteorologists, physicists, geographers, and educational institutions throughout the world. Inasmuch as the climatology of the country can only be determined by making observations at numerous points and averaging or reducing the data, all of which requiring an organization involving the expenditure of a considerable sum; and for the further reason that the product turned out would, if offered to the market, command only a small price, the project is wholly unsuited for private enterprise and can only be satisfactorily undertaken by the Government.

The Present Organization of the Weather Bureau.—The accompanying chart [1] presents at a glance the present organiza-

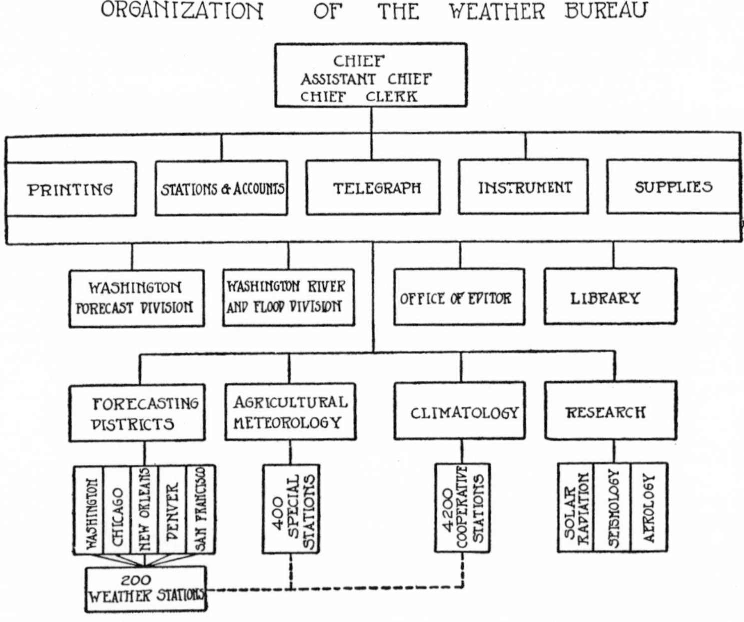

tion of the Bureau. The Divisions directly concerned with administration or operating functions are Stations and Accounts, Printing, Telegraph, Instrument, and Supplies. These are somewhat of a varied character and indicates that efficiency

[1] Chart drawn according to data in *List of Workers and Program of Work*, both published by the Department of Agriculture.

in one or the other of the administration offices, does not necessarily fit the employe for service in the more scientific branches of the Bureau. A good deal of printing is necessary because the Bureau issues regular publications. A Telegraph Division is necessary because the Bureau has some mileage of its own to supervise, and also the relation of the Bureau with private lines requires considerable attention. The Instrument Division compares instruments and is concerned with perfecting them. It also installs instruments in the field and makes adjustments of those in use where necessary with a view to securing accurate meteorological records. Numerous supplies are required by the stations throughout the country, many of them being purchased by the Supplies Division at Washington and shipped to the stations in the field.

The Forecast Division at Washington issues forecasts for all parts of the country and performs very much the same functions as the stations in the field except that its activities are not limited to a local territory like that of the station. The River and Flood Division at Washington is concerned with improving methods of forecasting floods, and to this end studies the effects of precipitation and evaporation throughout the river basins of the country. At Wagon Wheel Gap, Colorado, the Bureau in cooperation with the Forest Service makes observations to ascertain the relation of forest cover to stream flow. The problem is studied on two adjacent watersheds, one of which is to be denuded after ten years of record, and the other left under forest cover. This work was begun in 1910.[1] The Forecast and River and Flood Divisions are engaged in rendering service and should be associated with the other branches of the Bureau including the Forecasting Districts, the Division of Agricultural Meteorology, the Climatological, and the fields of Research. There is, however, another sharp distinction to be made concerning the nature of the activities of all the offices of the Bureau, and altogether, the Bureau's activities may be said to partake of the nature of administration, service, and investigation. The work of the Divisions of River and Flood, Agricultural Meteorology, and Climatological, is largely investigational, while that of the fields of research is

[1] Program of Work, 1919, p. 272.

wholly so. The organization rendering direct service consists of the Forecast Division at Washington and the Forecasting Districts with their 200 stations scattered throughout the country. Through this organization meteorological data for forecasting purposes are collected and all forecasts including weather, hurricanes, and floods, are distributed.

Weather Stations.—As shown by the chart these stations, about 200 of them,[1] are divided into districts. So far as forecasting is concerned stations are under the supervision of the District center whence forecasts to stations within the District are daily telegraphed more as a guide for the local forecaster than as a forecast, from which the local observer in charge may vary, unless, of course, the local observer has no authority to forecast in which case the district forecast alone is issued at the local station.

There is a close relation between the stations and the Agricultural Meteorology and Climatological Divisions inasmuch as the work of these two Divisions is directed through stations. The cooperative and special observers scattered throughout cotton, rice, and truck districts as well as through all agricultural territory, are selected by the men in charge of the regular weather stations and their work is directly supervised by them. One station in the state is designated as the section center and reports from cooperative observers are there received, reviewed, and prepared for publication in the form of state monthly summaries. The stations having supervision over the substations provide the Climatological Division at Washington with the necessary information to establish the history of the climate of various portions of the United States and the data so provided makes possible also the publishing of a weekly snow and ice bulletin during the winter months.

This organization also provides the Agricultural Meteorology Division with the necessary data to supervise the special warnings, such as frost, during the growing seasons. Frost warnings are quite successfully forecast and this service of the Bureau is of very great economic importance to fruit and truck interests and to the country at large. Orchards and vineyards

[1] *Vide List of Workers, and Program of Work,* both publications of the Department.

may be protected by smudge fires and truck may be covered; so that if growers are warned and if they take proper action, they are not altogether left to the mercy of the elements. Data collected from the substations through the section centers enables the Division of Agricultural Meteorology to issue during the growing season its weekly weather and crop bulletin showing the effects of weather upon crops.

Research.—The Bureau conducts three main lines of research, namely, Solar Radiation, Seismological, and Aerological. These investigations may never be productive of such practical results as will enable the Bureau ultimately to improve its service. It is, however, not certain as to the outcome, and it is the business of the Government through the Bureau, in this instance, to search for the hidden laws of natural phenomena. Certainly, valuable scientific principles are discovered through research and made available for the student of pure science. This alone justifies the effort. Perhaps the most promising of these three lines of research is the seismological investigation. The object of this work is "to map the United States according to seismological activity and locate geological faults; to study in detail earthquake vibrations and draw inferences therefrom in regard, on the one hand, to the scientifically important problem of the structure of the earth and, on the other, to the practical question of types of building best adapted to withstand seismic shocks."

Investigations that have to do with the air will no doubt develop important scientific information, but it is questionable whether the accuracy of weather forecasting can ever be very much improved as a result of it. The difficulty is that the medium with which the forecaster deals is so unstable that none of the numerous possibilities of its behavior can probably ever with absolute certainty be foretold.

Forecasting.—Mention has already been made of forecasting weather, hurricanes, and floods. The latter two forecasts are very much more accurate than the every-day weather forecasts. Especially in this true of floods which approaches 100 per cent. The degree of accuracy of weather forecasts is claimed to be about 85 per cent, and with this degree of accuracy purely on the basis of the law of averages these forecasts are a decided advantage to the country. If, however, one is familiar with the art of forecasting, probabilities

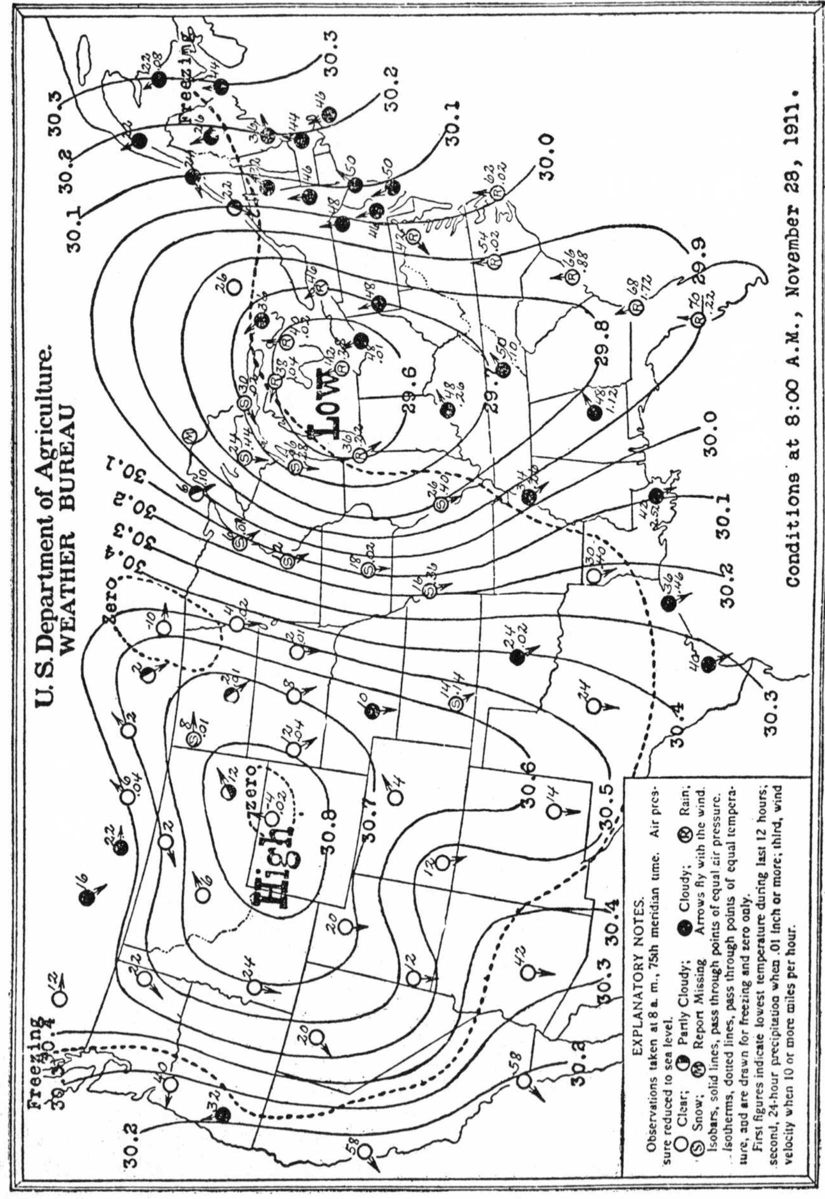

FIG. 1.—Daily weather map Nov. 28, 1911

can quite readily be distinguished from certainties, and for this reason to one who has access to the weather map and can make his own forecasts the value of the Weather Bureau service is very much greater than is indicated by the 85 per cent degree of accuracy. It is very obvious that when the conditions present probabilities certain work will be postponed until little or no risk is assumed, and in this way much property can be saved. With such pronounced high and low pressure areas as are shown on the accompanying map [1] forecasting is virtually 100 per cent certain, and under such conditions the farmer or any other enterpriser the success of whose operations is largely dependent upon the weather, may proceed with confidence. It is not the purpose here to discuss the principles of forecasting. For a full discussion the reader is referred to the Bulletin from which this map is taken or to texts on meteorology. It may be merely noted here that low pressure areas move in a general direction from west to east across the continent and are followed by high pressure. The specific direction that these will take is dependent upon the relative position of various high and low pressure areas and their respective intensities. The air about the "low" revolves spirally inward and upward, causing cloudiness and precipitation in advance of its center; while around the "high" the air piles up and revolves downward and outward, bringing fair and colder weather. Inasmuch as these "highs" bring clear skies and allow the sun to generate heat they are often hotter in the summer than the "lows," but during the winter they are usually associated with cold waves.

SELECTED REFERENCES.

Benjamin, *The Smithsonian Institution*, pp. 647-678; various *Reports* of Chief of Weather Bureau.

[1] From Weather Bureau Bulletin No. 42.

CHAPTER IX

BUREAU OF AGRICULTURAL ECONOMICS

Introductory Statement.—In 1921 the Bureaus of Crop Estimates and Markets were consolidated into one, designated in the appropriation Act for the fiscal year 1922 as the Bureau of Markets and Crop Estimates. In 1922 this combined Bureau and the Office of Farm Management and Farm Economics were merged to form the Bureau of Agricultural Economics. This was a logical step inasmuch as the work of the three bureaus is very closely related. As is shown in this chapter the work formerly performed in the Bureau of Crop Estimates has to do with the collection and publication of crop statistics which was one of the original functions of the Department of Agriculture. It has, therefore, a long history, and before the coming of the Bureau of Markets its organiaztion came nowhere into close contact with any other bureau of the Department except the Weather Bureau, which has its own organization for the collection of data pertaining to the effect of weather upon crops.

However, after the Bureau of Markets was organized in 1913 and vigorously effected an organization, it became manifest that crop statistics and market information were so closely related that, unless a consolidation of the two bureaus collecting and publishing these data were effected, a great waste would result because of the duplication of organization and a lowering of the standards of efficiency of the Department. A reading of the chapter will show that crop statistics fundamentally influence the movement of the price of farm products and must necessarily form a part of a complete market news service.

Inasmuch as farm organization can be intelligently determined only after the prices and marketing conditions of the various crops have been studied, it is evident that the next logical step was the merging of the work regarding farm organization with the two lines of work just described. Dr. Henry C. Taylor, Chief of the new Bureau of Agricultural Economics, states that "one of the economies of the new organization is the establishment of a large division of statistics which will absorb a number of small lines of work." It is to "deal with both production and distribution."[1] Considerable saving can be effected through a correlation of field forces. It will take some time for the new organization to find itself. This is always the case when a new function develops rapidly and encroaches upon old and well-established branches of the Department. It will in the end probably include all activities that fall under the head of agricultural economics.

DEVELOPMENT OF THE CROP-ESTIMATING ORGANIZATION

Origin of the Crop-Reporting Service.—The collection and distribuiton of seeds and the collection and publication of agricultural statistics were the two main roots from which sprang the Department of Agriculture, and from which developed the branches of its present organization. Soon after the first appropriation in 1839, which was for the distribution of seeds, the agricultural appropriations were made for the combined purpose of collecting agricultural statistics and distributing seeds.[2] From that time on the work grew, so that by 1849 a collector of agricultural statistics had been appointed and by 1857 in the section of agriculture of the Patent Office, Department of Interior, a small force of clerks was engaged in the collection of agricultural statistics. It was not until after 1862, however, when the Department was established, that any real progress was made and that a systematic plan for the collection of statistics was developed. This was destined to come because provision for the work was a fundamental and primary part of the Act creating the Department of Agriculture.

Before the Act of 1862 the states of Ohio, Iowa, Kansas, and California collected agricultural statistics, and agricultural societies in some states also attempted the annual collec-

---

[1] From a letter dated August 3, 1921.

[2] *Circular 17, Revised, 1915*, of Bureau of Crop Estimates. The United States Census also for the first time collected agricultural statistics in 1840.

tion of statistics.[1] A circular letter, signed by the president of the Maryland State Agricultural Society, dated July 16, 1855, and addressed to other state agricultural societies, proposes such a plan. Extracts from this letter run as follows:

> For the promotion of the farming interest of the country we are anxious to procure the earliest reliable information possible of the crops, that the same may be laid before the farmer to guide him in the selection of the best time to dispose of the fruits of his labors. The duty should properly be imposed upon an agricultural department of the general government; but in the absence of such provision, and in view of the artful practices of speculators and others, operating most disastrously through the base venality of the press, upon this leading interest, the obligation is devolved upon us.
>
> We will invite your attention to the organization of our Maryland Agricultural Society as well adapted to promote the object contemplated, and for your information ask your perusal of a circular, which we enclose herewith, and which we had the honor of addressing to our sister societies at the time of its date.
>
> We hope to lay before you a statement of the wheat, grass, and oat crops of Maryland by the first of September, and of the corn crop by the first of or middle of November.[2]

A more definite plan was adopted in 1862 by Orange Judd, editor of the *American Agriculturalist*.[3] The number 10 was made to represent an average crop instead of 100 as in the plan used by Prussia at the time. The first Statistician of the Department, Lewis Bollman, gives credit to Mr. Judd for originating a method of collecting statistics, virtually similar to that of Prussia, and later adopted by the United States Department of Agriculture with some modifications.

These facts would seem to indicate that farmers and other groups of the population of the country with one accord supported the movement to establish the process of collecting annually agricultural statistics. This is, however, not the case. Isaac Newton, Commissioner of Agriculture, in his fourth annual report complains that their publication was at first opposed by agricultural papers, "under the erroneous impression that it might conflict with private interests." In the same sentence, however, he also says that such opposition soon disappeared because it was seen that only data national in character were disclosed. Although among the farmers generally, as complained by the Department's Statistician as late as 1874,

---

[1] *Vide Report of Department* for 1863, p. 581.

[2] From *Report of Department* for 1863, p. 586.

[3] *Ibid*, p. 587.

considerable indifference prevailed; and in some cases there was an unwillingness to give information to the Government's reporter because of rivalry on the part of some agricultural societies also collecting statistics. Such obstacles have by now very generally disappeared.

The Growth of Statistical Functions.—The Division of Statistics, organized in 1863, began at once the collection of statistics and the publication of regular statistical reports. The Division was also given charge of "fibre investigation." The Civil War very greatly reduced the supply of cotton, causing capital invested in the New England mills to suffer very seriously. A movement, centering in the Rhode Island Society for the Encouragement of Domestic Industry, was started having for its object the "cottonizing of flax" or the preparation of flax for cotton machinery. Congress made available an appropriation of $20,000 for this purpose, but broadened the project so as to include the study of the cultivation of flax and hemp. No progress was made in "cottonizing" flax or in preparing flax and hemp as substitutes for cotton, but the investigation marks the beginning of the Department's interest in the cultivation of flax and hemp in the United States and led to the successful introduction of ramie and jute. The nature of the investigation was more botanical than statistical, but was not separated from the Division of Statistics until 1890.

The need for information concerning crops produced in foreign countries was early felt in the development of statistical organization. This need was expressed in the Commissioner's second report as "the second special duty" of the Statistical Division. Only by taking account of supplies produced abroad could all the elements of demand be presented to the farmer. By the 70's statistical reciprocity among the countries of the world became exceedingly urgent because by that time ocean steamship and internal railway transportation had advanced to a high stage of development. In his report for 1873 the Commissioner states that the Statistician was sent to Europe to investigate statistical methods and to establish statistical relations with countries abroad.[1] This was, how-

[1] P. 11.

ever, only following the lead of European countries which, largely through the influence of M. Quetelet, organized the International Congress of Statistics at Brussels in 1853. This Congress met at various places throughout Europe up to 1876, but because of its unwieldiness and loose organization ceased to exist.[1] It should be said that at that time the economic relations among the countries of Europe called for statistical cooperation to a very much greater degree than the relations between the United States and countries of Europe. At the instigation of the London Statistical Society a new organization was effected in 1885 known as the International Statistical Institute which met at Rome and was attended by J. R. Dodge, the Statistician of the United States Department of Agriculture. The method by which the Department secured foreign data was at first by exchange of agricultural reports and general documents with agricultural departments of the governments or private statistical agencies of foreign countries which was done both by correspondence direct and through special agents, usually consuls of the Department of State cooperating with the Department of Agriculture. At London the services of the agent were so important that an expert of the Department was stationed there sending reports both by mail and cable. It was not until 1905 that the idea of an international statistical institute was put permanently into concrete form.[2] Representatives of the United States Department of Agriculture now regularly participate in the International Institute of Agriculture at Rome.

Thus the need for world agricultural statistics, which by the 70's had become especially important, made its impression upon the Department of Agriculture. In 1894 a Foreign Market Section was established, and in 1902 a Division of Foreign Markets was organized, which in the following year was

---

[1] *Vide Report of Department* for 1887, p. 589.

[2] The International Institute of Agriculture was established under the patronage and through the efforts of the King of Italy in 1905. By international treaties fifty-three countries were represented in the Institute in 1913, all contributing toward its maintenance. Under the provisions of the treaty the quota for the United States at first was $4,800, but as the work expanded the larger amount allowed, which was $8,000 was called for in 1914. *Vide Senate Document No. 196 63rd Congress, 1st Session.*

merged with the Division of Statistics. In 1903 the Division was changed to a Bureau of Statistics which in 1921 was designated as the Bureau of Markets and Crop Estimates. In 1922 this Bureau was merged with two other branches of the Department to form the Bureau of Agricultural Eonomics.

Relation Between Field and Washington Activities.—In the collection of statistics of livestock and general crops complete independence between Washington and field activities is maintained for the special purpose of providing a statistical check upon data used for crop-forecasting. The field force collects its data through its own corps of reporters, reduces them to state averages, and reports directly to the Crop Reporting Board. The Washington force also has its corps of reporters scattered throughout the producing districts and through them collects data, tabulates and reduces them to averages, making them available to the Crop Reporting Board for crop-forecasting purposes.

With respect to the collection of statistics that concern truck crops and fruit crops, however, a close relation between Washington and field activities exists. In fact there is no organization in the field independent of that in Washington. The list of voluntary truck and fruit reporters is maintained exclusively in the Washington office, and data from reporters are received and digested by it alone. Also the traveling of the truck-crop specialists and the fruit-crop specialists is directed from Washington. However, cooperation between the general-crop field agents and the fruit and truck-crop specialists is maintained. "These specialists have very large territories, being concerned solely with the commercial production of certain crops, must depend to a certain extent upon the field agents, and the policy of the Bureau is working around to the point where eventually the field agents will not only report on the total agricultural production of all crops, but will also be the point of contact between the truck and fruit sections of the Bureau and the growers of specialized crops, each agent for his own territory. Under this plan the Washington offices of these two sections, fruit and truck, will be the points at which the field agents' reports on those crops will be assembled and analyzed on a country-wide basis just as their reports on general crops are now assembled by the Crop Reporting Board.''[1]

Organization and Duties of the Field Service.—At the head of Field Activities there is the Chief of Field Service who has general supervision of the Field Agents as to technical methods. Next there is a field specialist ''working toward the refinement of field methods and the development of cooperation of crop-reporting work between this Bureau and various state departments or boards of agriculture,'' and also ''one officer in charge of field records working toward better office methods.'' Following these three officers, whose work extends over the entire country, there are next in order ''forty-two field agents, one for each state or group of small states, assisted by clerks, collaborators,'' and a large number of crop reporters, aggregating about 35,000 in 1919.

The Field Agent has offices and headquarters in the state to which he is assigned and reports ''to the Crop Reporting Board or to the general offices of the field work, *i. e.*, the Chief of Field Service, the Field Specialist, or officer in charge of field records or to the Chief of Bureau," who is a permanent member of the Crop Reporting Board.[2] The Field Agent is appointed on the basis of a broad experience especially qualifying him and a rigid civil service examination in statistics. He must be familiar with local conditions, and travels systematically over the state, personally inspects crops, and interviews farmers, representatives of commercial houses, mills, elevators, transportation companies, and buying and selling associations of various kinds. Each agent, enlisting the services of from 250 to 1,500 selected crop correspondents, each month makes a detailed estimate on the crops in his territory and forwards it to Washinton for use by the Crop Reporting Board, the report giving full explanatory notes showing causes which have resulted in changes from the estimates for the previous month.

---

[1] A portion of a letter to the author by Leon M. Estabrook, Chief of former Bureau of Crop Estimates, dated July 12, 1919.

[2] Quotation from Estabrook letter.

Field Activities also include "one tobacco-crop specialist and one rice-crop specialist who travel most of the time but publish no reports and maintain only small lists." Two truck-crop specialists and two fruit-crop specialists also travel throughout producing districts, but officially these are closely related to the Washington Activities.

Crop and Livestock Reports.—Two sets of independent reports on general crops, one set coming from township correspondents and another from county correspondents, are sent to Washington. These sets of data form the basis for two separate reports and together with the reports from the Field Agents make available to the Crop Reporting Board three separate reports, independently prepared, for comparative or checking purposes at the close of each month when the final estimate of acreage, condition, yield, or production, is made and given to the public.

"Every possible precaution is taken to prevent the totals from any of the so-called speculative crops, such as corn, wheat, oats, barley, rye, and cotton, from becoming known to any individual prior to the date fixed in advance by the Secretary of Agriculture for the issuance of the crop report. Even the tabulators and computers who make up the totals do not know the states to which they pertain, and the final telegraphic reports and comments of the Field Agents relating to the speculative crops are kept locked in the office of the Secretary until reporting day, when they are turned over to the Crop Reporting Board, and the entire Board is immediately locked in until the minute that the report is issued, guards being stationed at the doors and all telephones disconnected."[1]

Voluntary Reporters.—As already pointed out there are about 35,000 reporters reporting to Field Agents; while under the Washington Activities there is a large number of various township, county, livestock and other reporters, making a total under both activities of about 200,000 voluntary crop reporters in 1919.[2]

---

[1] *Vide Circular 17, Revised, January, 1918,* U. S. Department of Agriculture.

[2] *List of Workers*, U. S. Department of Agriculture, 1919.

The county crop correspondent is a non-salaried employe, receiving, however, usually a package of seeds, a copy of the *Yearbook*, and other publications of the Department as recognition of his services. He reports for his entire county each month on printed schedules directly to the Bureau, basing his estimates upon personal observation and written and telephonic reports. There were 2,900 county reporters in 1919.

The township crop correspondents in 1919 numbered about 33,000. Each agricultural township of the United States is represented by a reporter and, like the county correspondent, receives no compensation other than seeds and Departmental publications, and also reports directly to the Bureau at Washington.

The special list of growers, buyers, and others also report directly to Washington on such crops as potatoes, apples, cotton, beans, cranberries, peanuts, broom corn, maple syrup, honey, special truck crops, and livestock. Special facts are also gleaned from those who handle the crops on their way from producer to consumer.

The early reports of the Statistician compared with later ones issued by the Bureau of Crop Estimates, or with reports now issued by the Bureau of Agricultural Economics, show that there has been an enormous growth in this statistical field. Numbering at first only a few thousand, there were by 1880 as many as 4,000 voluntary reporters; and in 1897 there were 56,700 regular correspondents and 140,000 special correspondents; while in 1919 there were approximately 200,000. When this service was organized it was confined to the North and Middle West. The Civil War excluded the southern states, and the Far West, except the Pacific coast states, was not yet well open to cultivation. Communication with the Pacific coast states was too unsatisfactory before the 70's to establish a field service and receive reports. With the completion of the Pacific Railroad, however, in 1879, the fertile stretches of land farther west were open to cultivation and enlarged the field from which statistics had to be collected.

The Crop Reporting Board.—The data supplied at the close of each month by the Field Agents together with those furnished by the Washington force, "are considered by the

Crop Reporting Board, which is composed of the Associate Chief of Bureau, the Chief Statistician, three statistical scientists from the Washington staff, and one or more field statisticians called in from different states each month, all of whom are expert judges of crops and have had many years of experience in analyzing, interpreting and summarizing crop data. In addition to the special data sent in each month by the field force the Crop Reporting Board has all other data which are available, such as the Weather Bureau reports, and such crop reports as are issued by state authorities, private crop-estimating agencies, associations, and others. From all these data each member of the Board prepares his own individual and independent estimate for each crop and state. These are compared, discrepancies are discussed and explained, and a final figure is adopted by the Board. It is quite certain, therefore, that the Crop Reporting Board has before it more complete, detailed, and accurate data upon which to base its report than any other crop-estimating agency in the world. The members of the Crop Reporting Board are unbiased, because they, as well as all other employes of the Department who have anything to do with the crop estimates, are prohibited by law, under very severe penalties, from speculating in any product of the soil, from giving out any information in advance of the official crop report, and from knowingly compiling or issuing any false statistics."[1]

Method of Issuing Crop Reports.—After the crop reports are prepared by the Crop Reporting Board and approved by the Secretary of Agriculture they are given to the public at a time previously announced. The cotton reports are issued usually on or about the first day of the month during the growing season and reports on other crops and livestock about the seventh or eighth day of each month. The hours at which these reports are issued are usually 11 a. m. or 2:15 p. m., the hour as well as the day having been previously announced so as to give simultaneously to all parts of the country the benefits accruing from a knowledge of the condition of the crops. Telegraph companies reserve their lines at the appointed hour

[1] *Circular 17* of Department.

for the transmission of the data which includes in addition to facts of the current crop, the same facts of previous years for comparative purposes.

The Statistical Basis for Crop Reports.[1]—The Bureau of Agricultural Economics uses two elemental facts to arrive at a conclusion as to production or total yield. One is the acreage of the crop planted and the other is the condition of the crop during the growing season. In 1880 the Census Bureau began enumerating the acreage of each crop and since that time the United States Department of Agriculture has taken the Census report as a standard with which to compare the acreage of each crop during years intervening between census years. At every new census a new standard of acreage is provided for estimating the acreage of crops planted.

The condition of the current crop is compared with a "full crop" or normal crop as the standard. It is not an arithmetic average of the production over a series of years but is the quantity that the farmer expects to harvest under favorable conditions.[2] The standard does not include the extremes of crop failures or of bumper crops, but is supposed to represent the mode, the usual, or normal crop. This normal crop equals 100, and the condition of the crop considered is reported as being a certain per cent of the normal. As previously stated, these facts as to acreage and condition are reported by the field service to the Bureau at Washington. The Bureau converts the condition reports into quantitative estimates of yields per acre, and, multiplying these by the acreage to which the different crops have been planted, obtains a forecast of the total production from time to time during the growing season.

The Accuracy of the Crop Reports.—In addition to the independent sources of data compiled by the Bureau itself it has available information collected by state departments including assessors, private agencies and trade journals. While none of these are very accurate they are helpful in checking against the Bureau's figures. The assessors' reports, for instance, are

---

[1] *Vide Circular 17, Revised 1915 and 1918*, of the Department.

[2] Canada, Great Britain, France, and the International Institute of Agriculture use the ten-year average as the basis for condition reports.

always too low. The student of taxation knows that it is everywhere the tendency not to declare property. The fact, however, that the assessors' reports are always too low does not render them altogether useless; for they are nevertheless valuable in showing the trend of property, such as numbers of farm animals from year to year; and on the basis of the trend the assessors' reports may be advantageously used as a check.

The estimate of the cotton crop can be checked against the ginning report of the United States Census taken every year which is in fact an actual count. During seventeen years, 1900-1916, the highest overestimate made by the Bureau of the cotton crop was 5.1 per cent, the lowest, 0.2 per cent; while the highest under-estimate was 5.5 per cent, the lowest 0.3 per cent. It should be added that the greater variations occurred infrequently, the seventeen-year average being an under-estimate of 1.2 per cent and the average for the last five years of the period being 0.8 per cent.

Forecasts for wheat and rice crops are also probably quite satisfactory, but the estimates for livestock and some of the other crops, the author having in mind hay, are not sufficiently accurate to show such economic relations as hay and rainfall, hay and number of milch cows, milch cows in the vicinity of Chicago and receipts of butter at that point, etc. After all they are estimates and tend to be too regular. The livestock figures do not exhibit the sharp changes that actual counts would show for limited areas. It is the plan of the Bureau, however, to make twelve livestock estimates instead of one and for 3,000 agricultural counties instead of by states. This will probably give much more satisfactory results than the method now in use.

The estimates of the speculative crops are, however, sufficiently accurate to make possible a gradual adjustment of prices during the growing season, and are the means of preventing wide fluctuations between seed time and harvest. They inform the farmer of the prospective yields, and save him from losses due to wide fluctuations in prices because an authoritative government crop report enables the buying public to judge supply more or less accurately from time to time.

MARKET FUNCTIONS AND ORGANIZATION

Marketing and the Department of Agriculture.—In looking over the history of the Department of Agriculture one is impressed with the fact that its efforts have continually emphasized productivity. How to increase the yield and the variety of agricultural products has been its main concern. It should be remembered, of course, that it was largely owing to the need of agricultural statistics that the Department was established; and this activity certainly has ever since been a prominent one. A knowledge of the supply is a very vital part of the elements of information necessary to arrive at a conclusion as to price. For this reason it may be said that this early function of collecting and publishing agricultural statistics is related to the subject of marketing. In 1873 the Statistician was sent to Europe to establish statistical relations with foreign countries; and in 1894 a foreign markets section was established whose function it was to secure and make available international agricultural statistics. However, the problems of marketing as we understand them today have to do essentially with an improvement in the market organization and the prevention of losses during the time the product passes from producer to consumer. From this point of view the field of marketing was almost wholly neglected by the Department from its beginning to 1913.

A step leading into the heart of the problem was taken in 1906 and 1907 when investigations concerning the marketing of fruits, mainly produced on the Pacific Coast, were carried on by the Department.[1] These investigations included studies in harvesting, packing, transporting, and storing fresh fruits of various kinds. The general price level had for some years shown an upward trend; and, probably because we had a cost-of-living problem at the time, the attention of the Department was directed in a special way to the field of marketing. Economists began a vigorous discussion of the problem and as general interest in the subject gained momentum the Department rapidly developed its marketing activities, resulting in the organization of a separate Office of Markets in 1913.

[1] *Yearbook*, 1906, p. 48.

The Office of Markets.—The Office of Markets was authorized by an Act of Congress approved March 4, 1913. In keeping with the early and primary functions of the Department, that of research, rendering service, and carrying on educational campaigns, the Office of Markets was at first confined to investigation and demonstration. This is indicated by the following clause of the Act:

> To enable the Secretary of Agriculture to acquire and diffuse among the people of the United States useful information on subjects connected with the marketing and distribution of farm products.[1]

The Secretary of Agriculture took occasion at this time to call attention to the fact that the organization of the Office of Markets was virtually a new venture and one of great significance. He outlined the scope of the Office as follows:

> First. Marketing surveys, methods, and costs, including especially available market supplies in given production areas, demand at consuming centers, cold and other storages, marketing systems and prices, and costs of wholesale and retail distribution of farm products.
>
> Second. Transportation and storage problems, having in mind the elimination of waste and the study of problems connected with surplus market supplies; terminal and transfer facilities, including freight congestion, car supply, deterioration in transit, extension of the practice of precooling of perishable products, and other special services.
>
> Third. City marketing and distribution investigations, involving a study of the uses and limitations of farmers', municipal, wholesale and retail market houses; systems of city distribution; the promotion of direct dealing between producers and consumers by parcel post, express and freight.
>
> Fourth. Study and promulgation of market grades and standards. A consideration of sizes and suitability of packages and containers, methods of preparation of perishable products, and the ultimate establishment, as far as practicable, of official market grades and standards for farm products.
>
> Finally, cooperative production and marketing investigation.

In addition to the functions of investigation and demonstration with which the Office of Markets began in 1914 it was required to perform a regulatory function with the passage of the Cotton Futures Act. In 1915 the name was expanded to Office of Markets and Rural Organization. During the same year another new function was added, that of news service, in the establishment of the experimental news service for the benefit of producers, shippers and distributors of fruits and vegetables. All of these four functions, investigation,

---

[1]*Yearbook*, 1913, p. 27.

demonstration, regulation, and market news service, expanded rapidly. In the *Yearbook*[1] for 1916 the Secretary of Agriculture says: "Beginning with a modest sum ($50,000), the appropriations for this office, including those for enforcing new laws to promote better marketing, have increased to $1,242,000. Quickly an effective organization was developed and today the Nation possesses in the Department the largest and best trained and supported staff of experts dealing with the distribution of agricultural commodities and rural organization to be found anywhere in the world. It is engaged in investigating all the larger and more difficult problems confronting the farmers in this new field." In view of this very rapid expansion the Office of Markets and Rural Organization was organized as a bureau in 1917 and designated as the Bureau of Markets. No bureau in the Department has had such rapid development as this one. The nucleus of the Bureau was organized in 1913, and by 1919 it was fourth in size. It then had 1,567 employes, and only the Bureaus of Animal Industry, Forest Service, and Plant Industry were larger than the Bureau of Markets.[2] In 1921 and 1922 it was merged with the Bureau of Crop Estimates and the Office of Farm Management and Farm Economics, and its name was changed to Bureau of Agricultural Economics, as already stated. The regulatory work of the Bureau includes administration of the Warehouse Act, the Grain Standards Act, the Standard Container Act, the Cotton Futures Act, etc. The inevstigational and demonstrational work includes a study of the whole range of marketing problems.

Investigational and Demonstrational Work.—This activity of the Bureau is large, and it will be impossible to discuss all its efforts along this line because it would virtually mean a complete study of marketing itself. Enough should be said, however, to show that the Department of Agriculture has begun a vigorous investigation of the problems that have to do with securing a favorable price for the farmers' products. The Department has widened its constructive leadership among the agricultural people of the country and today is guiding the

[1] P. 9.

[2] *Vide Official Register*, p. 11.

farmer with his products through devious paths to the consumer. It is not fair to say, however, that all this research in the field of marketing, demonstration of improved methods, and the news service, are for the farmers' benefit alone. The consumer, dealer, carrier, and farmer are all benefited. If these efforts have, by encouraging cooperative organization among the farmers, or by giving them a reliable market news service, or by demonstrating correct methods of packing and grading, secured for the farmers higher prices, the margin of profits to the dealers has been correspondingly reduced, they being paid merely for the service they render.

An important field of research of the Bureau has had to do with rural organization including rural credit, insurance, and communication. The aim has been to find out what are the farmers' needs along these lines and to provide the necessary assistance. Articles of incorporation for mutual fire insurance companies together with proper accounting systems have been worked out and made available.

A very extensive field of investigation is covered by the activity, marketing and distributing farm products. It studies cooperative purchasing and marketing associations with a view to discover the forms and organizations and methods best suited for their use.[1] Personal visits are made to cooperative associations throughout the country and after studying their methods, improvements in organization and for transacting business are suggested. It may be said at this point that the cooperative movement among farmers is receiving aid from both public and private agricultural organization. In addition to the Department's efforts in this field the Farmers' Union, the Grange, the Farm Bureau, and other associations are very active in organizing and aiding cooperative enterprises. The Bureau proposed a state cooperative law for the purpose of encouraging states to provide for the incorporation of cooperative associations in harmony with the Federal Clayton Act which exempts labor unions and cooperative agricultural associations from the operation of the anti-trust law. The purpose of such legislation is to give the farmers

[1] For detail the reader is referred to the Department's *Program of Work* for 1919, p. 499.

some of the benefits of concerted efforts enjoyed by business through the corporation. The Bureau also studies transportation problems looking to good packing, loading and storing so as to prevent losses. Proper construction for cold storage houses is encouraged. City marketing problems are studied and proper designs for market houses and freight terminals are suggested, and in many places such improvements have been carried out. Market business practice is studied and some special accounting systems have been worked out for particular businesses, such as canneries, milk-distributing plants, etc. The student of business organization recognizes the importance of instituting scientific methods of accounting. This is the first requisite if losses in a business enterprise would be prevented. Investigations are made of "foreign markets for American farm and non-manufactured food products, from the handling at the American seaboard to the distribution in foreign countries." Special attention is given to foreign customs and preferences which is a policy so consistently followed by Germany in the development of her international trade. This study is carried on by special agents going abroad and through cooperation with the consular service and trade advisers of the Department of State, the Bureau of Foreign and Domestic Commerce, growers' associations, trade organizations and other agencies. In addition to all of these more or less general problems the Bureau investigates methods of marketing peculiar to specific farm products, such as cotton, cottonseed and its products, livestock and meats, grain and hay, dairy products, etc.

A service of far-reaching importance also falling under the investigational function of the Bureau is the development "of fixed grades and standards for universal use, with a view to the ultimate national standardization of market grades and packages or containers." Already satisfactory grades for apples, onions, sweet potatoes, Irish potatoes, and tomatoes have been worked out which have been widely adopted by growers. The apple grades have been enacted into law by several states, and the onion grades have been adopted by the state of Texas. A list of cotton standards has also been worked out and promulgated. Space will not permit a discussion of the virtues of the use of satisfactory grades and containers in the marketing of commodities. The matter may be summed up by saying that they make possible satisfying different classes of consumers demanding different qualities of the product, selling expeditiously and reducing substantially the costs and losses of marketing goods. These benefits accrue not only to the farming and distributing classes, but must necessarily extend to consumers in the form of lower prices and better services.

From this very brief review of the Bureau's investigations of marketing problems, the student is impressed with the sudden and extensive initiative taken by the Department of Agriculture in improving the national distributing system.

The Service Function.—Two important functions under this head developed by the Bureau of Markets and continued by the Bureau of Agricultural Economics, are the market news service and the inspection of produce at large distributing centers. The latter service is performed for farmers consigning produce to commission dealers and for the dealers when the shipment appears to be off in quality. Shippers or dealers engage government inspectors to inspect the shipment immediately upon the arrival at points of destination. A small charge is made for the service. Official inspection certificates are issued certifying to the quality of the produce, and in case of dispute between dealer and shipper these certificates of inspection become the legal basis for settlement. The government inspector thus stands as an arbiter, in a way, between dealer and shipper, and many of the old, historic evils perpetrated by unscrupulous dealers upon the farmer are by him eliminated.[1] The history of marketing farm products discloses numerous complaints against commission men including unfair deductions from the selling price for alleged short weight, false grading, poor packing, damage by weather, etc. In many cases, of course, the farmer has himself been to blame, and the Bureau through its demonstration work is now attempting to correct these shortcomings. Whatever the facts and conditions may be, an impartial inspection service will place the

---

[1] *Yearbook*, 1918, p. 284.

blame where it belongs and bring justice to both parties of the exchange.

The Market News Service.—This service was organized by the Bureau for the purpose of giving both farmer and dealer information concerning prices of farm products and the movement of supplies from and to points of shipments. The products concerning which information is given include virtually the whole list of fruits and vegetables and livestock and meats. Information concerning supplies at distributing centers has significance because minor price fluctuations of considerable importance are due to irregularity in the movement of goods to such points. This detail information tends to distribute the products over the country in a way as to bring supply and demand into a nice adjustment.

To secure the information both as to prices and supplies a more or less extensive organization had to be built up. This organization in 1918 included 91 temporary farmers' service offices in producing sections and 34 permanent market stations or branch offices of the Bureau. The number has been reduced since the close of the war.[1] Taking the service in connection with fruits and vegetables as an example, the field offices collect information and telegraph it to Washington as of 9 a. m., where reports are constructed and forwarded to the stations from which they are issued at noon. Local dealers, dealers in other towns, and growers can all secure market news. If they wish telegraphic reports they need only pay the rate to the nearest market station. The market station in addition to issuing regular reports serves as a clearing house for information of a varied and general character. Growers may be advised as to methods of marketing, or they may be given a list of dealers taking a certain group of farm products, or a manufacturer of fruit juice may be given a list of shippers of fruits, or various other questions may be answered.

A government market news service yields very large benefits to all economic groups, and it would, therefore, seem that little need be said to justify the use of public funds for the support of such an organization. Private market reporters

[1] *Yearbook*, 1919, p. 96.

have frequently been charged with favoring the merchants. The wholesale prices are alleged to be often low, so as to induce the producer to sell at a price which will net the merchant a large profit. With respect to many products the farmer often is not informed and the merchant is able to take advantage of him. A market news service reaching far and wide into the producing field and linking it with the receiver has perhaps an element of "paternalism" in it, but it seems to be of a good kind inasmuch as it tends to secure to each party an income in accordance with what he produces. It would make our organized markets more useful because these would operate more nearly in accordance with the law of supply and demand. A complete market service should not be restricted to the movement of supplies and the listing of prices. It should include the reporting of crop conditions and crop production. This is a fundamental factor that affects prices, while the reporting of the movement of supplies to various centers is only a minor one. The latter factor is, of course, of considerable importance inasmuch as it aims to avoid local congestion and tends to secure a more even price for all parts of the country. The necessary information pertaining to crop production was formerly collected in a separate bureau, the Bureau of Crop Estimates, but as the marketing function developed it soon became evident that it and the statistical function must of necessity be placed in the same bureau. In this way much duplication of effort, and friction between the personel of two separate bureaus, is avoided, and much is gained in the efficiency and simplification of the Department's news service. In the interest of economic progress the country can well afford to develop an impartial, regular, complete, and reliable public news service.[1]

Regulatory Work.—This function of the Bureau includes the administration of the Warehouse Act, the Grain Standards Act, the Standard Container Act, and the Cotton Futures Act.

Under the warehouse act passed in 1916 the Department is authorized to license bonded warehouses which handle certain agricultural products including cotton, grains, flaxseed,

[1] The reader is referred to two articles in *Yearbook*, 1918, p. 277, and *Yearbook*, 1919, p. 94.

wool, and tobacco. When a warehouseman applies for a license he agrees to carry out all the provisions of the law including proper grading, weighing and the issuing of a correct warehouse receipt as evidence of the deposit of the product. The purpose of the plan is to develop a warehouse receipt that will actually represent a specific quantity of goods having a definite quality, and that will as a result be regarded by the banks as first-class security. General adoption of the system would mean that the farmer could use his crops with which to secure credit; and as credit is frequently necessary to carry on further productive operations the general introduction of this warehouse system is of vital importance to agriculture. The farmers could probably speed the establishment of the system by organizing cooperative warehouse associations subject to the terms of the act.

The appropriation bill of 1916 contained a part known as the United States grain standards act which provides for the establishment of official grain standards in the United States for corn, wheat and other grains entering interstate commerce. A system of licensed inspection is also provided for by this act.[1] The statute aimed at the elimination of the various grain standards and systems of grading in use at the grain markets throughout the United States and substituting therefor a uniform system of grading based upon scientific principles. The general use of a single set of grain standards takes out of the grain trade the confusion due to lack of uniformity of grading which makes difficult a comparison of values of specific quantities of grain bought and sold in different markets. This legislation also tends to correct abuses that it is alleged have frequently been perpetrated by grain dealers upon the farmers through improper grading, that is the grading of grain low so as to benefit the dealer. While some objections have been voiced to the standards in their present form, much fraudulent grading is eliminated through the use of an official set of standards carried into effect by a licensed inspection force supervised by employes of the Department of Agriculture.

---

[1] *Vide Report* of the Department for 1917, p. 389.

Under the standard container act, which became effective in 1917, the manufacture of various containers for fruits and vegetables entering interstate commerce must be of uniform and specific sizes. The lack of uniformity has long been a source of confusion in commerce, and the only way that this matter can be effectively dealt with is through the Federal government. The enforcement of the act is secured through visits to factories, markets, and producing sections.

The cotton futures act, passed in 1914 and amended in 1917, imposes a tax of two cents a pound on all sales of cotton for future delivery made at organized markets, but provides for exemption from this tax if such contracts are made in accordance with certain provisions of the act which aim to correct evils in future dealing. Future cotton sales must be made on the basis of cotton grades or standards promulgated by the Department of Agriculture the result of which has been that also in all the more important spot markets the government's grades have been adopted as a basis for sales. They have been even adopted by the Rotterdam Cotton Exchange, showing that the act has resulted in general uniformity of cotton grades. It is also the opinion of the Secretary of Agriculture that future dealings now serve as a more correct basis of the value of cotton than was formerly the case.

Farm Management.—In addition to statistical and market functions the Bureau also carries on research and demonstration work that has to do with business operations of the farm, emphasizing especially cost records, with a view to securing to the farmer sure and fair profits. It is also interested in farm-life studies. This latter project includes the consideration of such subjects as schools, roads, health, and general social life as they are affected by the agricultural environment.

The investigations that pertain more directly to farm management are concerned with costs of production, farm bookkeeping, farm finance, and the proper utilization of the factors of production, including labor, capital, and land itself. With respect to the keeping of records and the financing of farm operations the farmers generally have much to learn, and anything that the Bureau can do to educate them in these and other problems will not only benefit the agricultural class but will also serve to stabilize public opinion and place it on a sound basis and ultimately benefit the entire social fabric.

SELECTED REFERENCES.

Circular 17, Revised, of former Bureau of Crop Estimates; U. S. Agricultural Report for 1863, p. 581; *Senate Document No. 196,* 63rd Congress, 1st Session; article in *Yearbook* for 1918, p. 277; article in *Yearbook* for 1919, p. 94.

CHAPTER X

THE LAND-GRANT COLLEGES

Development of Agricultural Education.—Agricultural education in the United States was first fostered through agricultural societies, the organization of which was begun during the last quarter of the 18th century. The first agricultural society was established in 1785 at Philadelphia, then the national capital, and had among its members some of the leading statesmen of the country, including George Washington, Benjamin Franklin and Timothy Pickering.[1] The first effort to teach agricultural science, it is believed, was made at Columbia College in New York in 1792. Dr. Samuel L. Mitchell was appointed "professor of natural history, chemistry, agriculture and the other arts depending thereon." Records do not actually show to what extent Dr. Mitchell developed and taught agricultural courses, but it is almost certain that he gave systematic atention to the application of chemistry to agriculture. He inspired students who studied under him to take a leading part in the movement of agricultural education, and he wrote essays on the chemistry of manures.

In 1794 a committee was appointed by the Philadelphia Society "to prepare outlines of a plan for establishing a State Society for the promotion of agriculture, connecting with it the education of youth in the knowledge of that most important art while they are acquiring other useful knowledge suitable for the agricultural citizens of the state." The committee proposed that agricultural professorships be endowed at the University of Pennsylvania and the College of Carlisle and elsewhere and that the funds of the Society be increased to propagate agricultural knowledge through various ways. The plan proposed the use of the common-school system of the state as a means of carrying technical education to the home

---

[1] The reader is referred to two excellent articles on the history of agricultural education by Dr. A. C. True, for many years Director of the Office of Experiment Stations and States Relations Service, in the *Yearbook*, 1894, pp. 81-116, and *Yearbook*, 1899 pp. 157-190, from which the author has drawn heavily in the presentation of the historical aspects of this chapter.

of the farmer. This comprehensive plan was suggested in the following language:

> The country schoolmasters may be secretaries of the county societies, and the schoolhouses the places of meeting and the repositories of their transactions, models, etc. The legislatures may enjoin on these schoolhouses the combination of the subject of agriculture with the other parts of education. This may be easily effected by introducing as school books, those on this subject and thereby making it familiar to their pupils. These will be giving a knowledge of the business they are destined to follow, while they are taught the elementary parts of their education. Books thus profitable to them in common affairs of life may be substituted for some of those now used, and they can easily be obtained. Selections from the best writers in husbandry may be made by the Society. The essays of our own experimentalists or theorists and the proceedings of the Society will also afford information.

Dr. True says, "this report seems to have been the first formal attempt made in the United States to urge the claims of agricultural education and experimentation upon the attention of a lawmaking body."

On December 7, 1796, George Washington in his annual message to Congress said that, "it will not be doubted that, with reference either to individual or national welfare, agriculture is of primary importance." Speaking further of the efforts of agricultural boards to encourage and assist agricultural improvement, he said: "This species of establishment contributes doubly to the increase of improvements, by stimulating to enterprise and experiment, and by drawing to a common center the results everywhere of individual skill and observation, and spreading them thence over the whole nation. Experience accordingly has shown that they are very cheap instruments of immense national importance. I have heretofore proposed to the consideration of Congress the expediency of establishing a national university, and also a military academy." The recommendation concerning the establishment of a military academy was soon acted upon, but the improvement of agriculture, which largely determines the strength and welfare of the American nation, was passed over as having no significance.

In 1797 the Massachusetts society began the publication of pamphlets dealing with agriculture, and these later developed into a regularly issued journal. In 1801 the society suggested the permanent endowment of a professorship of natural history and the establishment of a botanic garden at Harvard College, which was realized in 1804.

As a means of stimulating interest in agriculture, fairs sprung into prominence in 1804 in Washington, followed by Massachusetts a few years later, and in 1809 in other centers through the organization of the Columbian Agricultural Society which became actively engaged in the work of educating the farmer through the agency of exhibition.

Establishment of Agricultural Schools and Colleges.—The war with England in 1812 undoubtedly put a damper upon interest in agricultural education; and the great industrial development including the canal, the steamship and the railroad, as well as the extensive movement of settlers upon the new and fertile lands of the west had probably much to do with further retarding this interest. While Congress was petitioned in 1817 by the Berkshire Agricultural Society of Massachusetts to establish a national board of agriculture, there was nevertheless a lagging of interest in agriculture for three decades running from 1810 to 1840. Toward the close of this period attention was being drawn to the rapid exhaustion of the soil in the Atlantic seaboard States. The crop failures during 1837 and 1838 turned the balance of trade heavily against us and caused the importation of large quantities of breadstuffs.[1] These conditions revived interest in agricultural education and probably the status of our international trade especially influenced Congress in 1839 to follow the suggestion of Henry L. Ellsworth, to appropriate $1,000 for the "collection of agricultural statistics, investigations for promoting agricultural and rural economy, and the procurement of cuttings and seeds for gratuitous distribution among the farmers."

By 1838 agitation for agricultural education had become so general in New York that a petition with 6,000 signatures was submitted to the State legislature asking for State aid. The New York State Agricultural Society adopted a resolution in 1844 stating that it "regards the establishment of an agricultural institute and pattern farm in this State, where

[1] *Vide* Article by Dr. True, *Yearbook*, 1894, p. 86.

shall be taught thoroughly and alike the science, the practice and the profits of good husbandry, as an object of great importance to the productive agriculture of New York." The chairman of the committee, Professor Potter of Union College, appointed to investigate and report on the resolution, stated that in their opinion "the time has arrived when the elements and scientific principles of agriculture should be taught in all our schools, especially to the older class of pupils." Between 1823 and 1850 a considerable number of agricultural schools of secondary grade were established in New York, Connecticut and Maine.

Yale College in 1846 appointed John P. Norton, professor of agricultural chemistry and vegetable and animal physiology. The demand of teachers of agricultural chemistry became so great that Yale offered a teachers' training course in this subject in 1848.

The first agricultural college was organized in Michigan. The State constitution, adopted in 1850, required that the legislature shall provide for the establishment of an agricultural school for agriculture and the natural sciences connected therewith." The legislature carried into effect this constitutional provision and in 1857, just outside the city of Lansing, the college was formally opened with 61 students and five professors. To Michigan is given the honor for the establishment of a college of agriculture where the science was to be taught on a broad and sound educational basis.

In Pennsylvania the Farmers' High School of Pennsylvania, later organized as Pennsylvania State College, was opened in 1859. Funds for the site, erection of buildings, and equipment were provided by the State legislature, the State Agricultural Society, and private subscription. The first president of this institution had studied in England and Germany and was thought to have been well prepared for the work he was called upon to perform.

The legislature of Maryland incorporated the Maryland Agricultural College in 1856. The act provided for a minimum subscription of stock and nearly 500 "philanthropic and patriotic" citizens took stock in the corporation. The opening of the college in 1859 was made an imposing event, Professor

Henry of the Smithsonian Institution having been selected as the orator of the day.

Public Sentiment Favorable to Agricultural Education.—Professor Brewer states that at this time there was a great clamor for State agricultural colleges. "Many were planned, a few were chartered, and three or four actually opened before 1862." By 1840 chemistry and geology, "scarcely fifty years old," had already "revolutionized some of the arts and produced great changes in agriculture." The benefits of science were beginning to be highly appreciated and there was a widespread demand for an education that would help solve our immediate industrial and agricultural problems. The basic sciences had been developed and the movement for practical agricultural education owed much to this fact, but it must not be forgotten that the movement including the demand for engineering colleges of which there was but one, the Rensselaer Polytechnic Institute at Troy, N. Y., in 1840.[1] The whole movement has its roots back in the dying days of the medieval period and in the dawn of the modern era when men turned their attention more generally from things that pertain to the future world to things earthly. The Industrial Revolution came in 1760 and proceeded rapidly to 1830, and this explains very well why there was this strong appeal from all parts of the country for a more practical education, first manifesting itself in the opening of trade schools, but finally in the establishment of colleges where applied sciences were to be taught. The science taught before the middle of the nineteenth century was a minor part of the work offered by our educational institutions, and little effort was made to use it for practical purposes. There was therefore a demand for institutions in which science and its application to industries should have a leading part.

From this early period down to the present day the fight between the champions of practical and classical education has continued, resulting, however, in the elimination of extreme points of view on both sides and in actually causing the two forces to reach common ground with respect to a large range

[1] Prof. Brewer in the *Agricultural Report* for 1894, p. 93.

of subjects. Gradually certain contested parts of proposed practical education have become reconciled with its opponents and the demand for more of the practical and less of the ancient languages and philosophy is steadily maintained. Many of the so-called practical subjects, it is now admitted, have a large cultural content, and much of the basis for the old hostility has therefore disappeared. It would seem that an educational policy, considered from the point of view of long periods, should be so comprehensive as to provide the roots of civilization but to lay the emphasis on the practical. It looks as though this were the trend of our colleges and universities. However, our emphasis on the practical has perhaps gone too far; perhaps we have gotten too far from the cultural and philosophical studies which serve as a balance wheel and play so large a part in directing the destiny of human thought and endeavor. For the sake of the nation and the world it would be well if our agricultural and engineering colleges would hold on to this type of education. Of course the discussion to be definite must state the degree of cultural training to be associated with the practical. With the progressive specialization of agricultural and engineering colleges into departments there should be an adherence to the courses that train for citizenship which include political science, economics, philosophy, and history. The need for a broader education for all students was never so greatly felt as it was prior to and during our participation in the European war. Sufficient language training should be included to furnish a masterful use of at least the English language and a reading knowledge of the modern languages.

Taking into account the whole structure of the American educational system as at present organized sufficient training may always be secured in enough institutions to provide for the development of the scholar to do research work in the ancient past, and bring to us anew and afresh the ancient history of the world. Intensified training of this type, while it should be a part of a nation's system, cannot be included in the curricula of the practical colleges.

Professor Turner, Father of the Land-Grant Colleges.—Professor William H. Brewer of the Sheffield Scientific School of Yale University gave credit to Justin S. Morrill of Vermont for originating the plan of the Land-Grant colleges. This claim, however, is proven to be erroneous in a thesis [1] written in 1910 by Dr. Edmund J. James, then president of the University of Illinois.

President James gives credit to Professor Johnathan Baldwin Turner for conceiving the plan of the Land-Grant college. Professor Turner was associated with Illinois College at Jacksonville, Illinois, from 1833 to 1848. He had studied at Yale College. He was a lecturer and farmer. He died in 1898 at the ripe age of 93.

In 1851 in order to head off a movement to divide a fund, amounting to about $150,000 and known as the college and seminary fund, among the private colleges in the state of Illinois, the farmers by public notice at county fairs and in the press were called to meet in convention to consider "such measures as might be deemed most expedient to further the interests of the agricultural community, and particularly to take steps toward the establishment of an agricultural university." Professor Turner was the leading spirit of the convention and drew up resolutions asking that an industrial university be established in each state of the Union and especially in the State of Illinois. The plan received wide attention in the daily press and was given support by public agricultural bodies. A second convention was held in 1852 at the time the legislature was in session. This convention addressed a memorial to the Illinois legislature which runs in part as follows:

> We desire that some beginning should be made as soon as our statesmen may seem prudent so to do, to realize the high and noble ends for the people of the state proposed in each and all of the documents above alluded to, and if possible on a sufficiently extensive scale to honorably justify a successful appeal to Congress in conjunction with eminent citizens and statesmen in other states who have expressed their readiness to cooperate with us for *an appropriation of public lands for each state in the Union for the appropriate endowment of universities for the liberal education of the industrial classes in their several pursuits in each state in the union.*

A third convention met in the fall of 1852, where it was decided to organize "The Industrial League of the State of

[1] *Vide The Land Grant Act of 1862* published by the University of Illinois.

Illinois'' to serve as an agency of propaganda for the cause of industrial education. Professor Turner's plan for an industrial university was taken up again and discussed section by section. On the 4th day of January, 1853, a fourth convention met where it was announced that its former proposals to memorialize Congress ''*for the purpose of obtaining a grant of public lands to establish and endow industrial institutions in each and every state in the Union,*'' had been carried out and that a petition had been sent to Congress to that effect. In response to a memorial to the Illinois legislature the General Assembly unanimously adopted, on February 8, 1853, the following resolutions which were also sent to Congress:

> WHEREAS, the spirit and progress of this age and country demand the culture of the highest order of intellectual attainment in theoretic and industrial service; and
>
> WHEREAS, it is impossible that our commerce and our prosperity will continue to increase without calling into requisition all the elements of internal thrift arising from the labors of the farmer, the mechanic, and the manufacturer, by every fostering effort within the reach of the government; and
>
> WHEREAS, a system of Industrial Universities, liberally endowed in each state of the Union, cooperative with each other, and with the Smithsonian Institute at Washington, would develop a more liberal and practical education among the people, tend to more intellectualize the rising generation and eminently conduce to the virtue, intelligence and true glory of our country; therefore be it
>
> RESOLVED, by the House of Representatives, and our Senate concurring herein, That our Senators in Congress be instructed, and our Representatives be requested, to use their best exertions to procure the passage of a law of Congress donating to each state in the Union an amount of public lands not less in value than five hundred thousand dollars, for the liberal endowment of a system of Industrial Universities, one in each state in the Union, to cooperate with each other, and with the Smithsonian Institute at Washington, for the more liberal and practical education of our industrial classes and their teachers; a liberal and varied education, adapted to the manifold wants of a practical and enterprising people, and a provision for such educational facilities being in manifest concurrence with the intimations of the popular will, it urgently demands the united efforts of our strength.
>
> RESOLVED, That the Governor is hereby authorized to forward a copy of the foregoing resolutions to our Senators and Representatives in Congress, and to the Executive and Legislature of each of our sister states, inviting them to cooperate with us in this meritorious enterprise.

These resolutions as well as the documents of the conventions and of the Industrial League, most of which were the product of Professor Turner, were given wide publicity. Professor Turner as director of the Industrial League vigorously pushed the movement. President James gives evidence that he presented the plan by letters to members of Congress, and that Honorable Morrill of Vermont was selected by Turner and his friends to champion the measure in Congress because he was from an older State which had not yet benefitted from grants of land made by the federal government. By 1855, the time when Justin S. Morrill first appeared in Congress, this proposition had, therefore, been discussed generally throughout the country. The plan was conceived in the mind of Professor Turner. Great honor is due him for his unselfish service in promoting the movement that finally led to the establishment of the Land-Grant colleges.

Other Leaders and Other Centers of Activity.—Besides Professor Turner there were men in other parts of the country who were deeply interested in the establishment of agricultural and industrial colleges as already indicated in the discussion showing the development of agricultural schools and colleges, and as to the originality of the idea of a national agricultural college there may be some doubt as to whether or not sole credit should be given to Professor Turner. It is pointed out for instance that the patent office report for 1851 contains several discussions of specific plans for the organization of an industrial university. One of these is by Professor Turner, another by Milton P. Braman of Essex County, Massachusetts, and another by Harvey Dodge of Worcester County, Massachusetts.[1] President Thompson says that in running through agricultural reports of Ohio he finds "that from practically every part of the state there came enthusiastic commendation in 1862 of the Morrill act and the unanimous sentiment that something ought to be done to take advantage of these provisions."[2] He says further that "the discussions as to the methods are not so enlighting" but the fact is established that the movement was supported by the most progressive and prosperous farmers of Ohio and elsewhere. Senator Wade,

[1] From an address delivered by President W. O. Thompson and published in the *Proceedings* of the Twenty-sixth Annual Convention of the Association of American Agricultural Colleges and Experiment Stations.

[2] Thompson *op. cit.*

who introduced the Morrill bill in the Senate, was from Ohio, and President Thompson points out that he was greatly influenced by the sentiment prevailing among Ohio farmers.

With respect to California and the wide extent over which this sentiment prevailed President Thompson says the following:

> This sentiment, amounting practically to public clamor, produced a marked influence upon legislative sentiment. One man from California declared that he had set aside his own judgment and would vote for the measure because the agricultural sentiment expressed through the legislature of California demanded it. The point I wish to insist upon, therefore, is that this new educational reform sprang, not from the educational philosophers or the professional teachers, but from the rank and file of the people themselves. Professor Townsend in Ohio and Professor Turner in Illinois were prophets who had a vision of the needs of the plain people and they were endowed with the intelligence and the courage to express it. They are types of the same kind of leadership in other commonwealths. The fact that Michigan in its constitution had provided for an agricultural college was due, like these other movements, to a proper regard for the sentiment of the agricultural population.

Considerable activity to organize agricultural colleges was in progress in New York state prior to the passage of the Morrill act. Under the leadership of John Delafield, at the time a retired banker and a graduate of Columbia College, the state passed an act in 1853 establishing an agricultural college, creating a board of trustees but making no appropriation. The college was to be located on Mr. Delafield's farm in the town of Fayette, but as he died the same year this enterprise came to naught.

At Ovid, 15 miles south of Fayette, plans for a college actually matured to the extent that buildings were erected and the college was formally opened in 1860 as the New York State Agricultural College. But the opening of the Civil War brought a halt to this effort, the buildings reverted to the state, and were used for an insane asylum,—a rather dismal conclusion of the attempt to establish an agricultural college. Reverend Amos Brown, who was then principal of Ovid Academy, conceived the idea of transferring the state college charter for an agricultural college to the Ovid school and the agitation that followed resulted in the appropriation of $40,000 for twenty-one years without interest and also the private subscription of $50,000 by citizens of the vicinity.

At the same time there was a movement in progress to establish another industrial institution, known as The People's College, at Havana, New York, the incorporation act for which was passed also in 1853.[1] Amos Brown later became the president of this institution and as such took an active part in the discussion of the Morrill bill, and was largely instrumental in securing its passage. Mr. Morrill in a letter gives Reverend Brown credit as follows:

> The Reverend Amos Brown took such active part in securing the passage of the bill referred to whenever it was before Congress, both by his earnest and intelligent advocacy of the measure through personal interviews and by sufficient urging the attendance of members on all questions of any test of votes, his services continuing for months that it is due to him and the institution of which he is the head, whenever an official disposition of the funds shall be made that his merit shall not go unacknowledged by the State of New York. From an early moment after the first bill was introduced he has been unflagging in his efforts to promote the success of this great measure in behalf of agriculture, and it is a pleasure to me to acknowledge the value of his aid and cooperation.[2]

Judging from this letter, Reverend Brown must have been very close to Mr. Morrill, and he must have had considerable influence upon the scope and character of the subject matter to be taught in the land-grant colleges as provided for in the Morrill bill. The New York movement, Dr. True points out, was an agitation for a broad institution, and as such it certainly must have had considerable influence in finally establishing the land-grant college on a sane and sound basis.

After all the available evidence has been reviewed it is clear that progressive farmers everywhere favored the establishment of agricultural colleges supported in part by funds provided by the federal government, but a definite plan, worked out with considerable detail, was in all probability the product of Professor Turner. Dean Davenport writes that he personally met both Professor Turner and Mr. Morrill when

[1] People's College was given New York's share of the land grant, but the institution failed to comply with the conditions of the law, resulting in giving the grant to Cornell University. In connection with People's College it should be noted that the first agricultural college established in the United States, where agricultural subjects were really taught on a broad basis, was in Michigan in 1857, as stated previously.

[2] From an article by Dr. True in the *Report* of the U. S. Department of Agriculture for 1894, p. 91. For other facts concerning the New York movement consult the same source.

both were old men on the occasion of a convention of the Association of Land-Grant Colleges at which time Professor Turner laid positive claims to the scheme as being his own, but Mr. Morrill failed to give any information as to the origin of the plan for establishing the land-grant colleges.[1]

Justin S. Morrill.—While Justin S. Morrill may not be called the father of the American agricultural and mechanical colleges, it is certainly true that to him, more than to any other legislator, belongs largely the credit for their establishment and their subsequent development into institutions that will always be useful to the American people.

Mr. Morrill's life and career are very interesting and suggest the guiding hand of Providence leading and directing him from early manhood to his death. He was born in Strafford, Vermont, April 14, 1810, and was the oldest in a family of ten children. His father was a blacksmith. As a boy Justin attended two terms at Thetford Academy. Because his support for the growing family was needed, he was forced to end his school days at the age of 14 and began work in a store at a salary of $30 for the first year and $40 for the second. At the close of the second year he went to Portland, Maine, where he engaged in a similar service. He returned after four years to his native village, where his former employer made him a partner, Judge Harris furnishing the capital and young Morrill managing the business.[2] After about 15 years of successful business he had accumulated a modest fortune, bought a farm, married, and settled down to all appearances "as a quiet, unostentatious, retired business man." His career, however, only began in a larger sense at this time. In 1854 he was suggested by his friends as a candidate for a representative to Congress. He was practically unknown in the district, but won by a small majority; so that in December, 1855, he began what was destined to be a long legislative career. For 12 years he served in the House, and in 1867 he was elected to the Senate where he served continuously for 32 years, making an

---

[1] From a personal communication to the author.

[2] These data are taken from an address made by George W. Atherton, in 1900 before the American Association of Agricultural Colleges and Experiment Stations.

unbroken legislative record of 44 years. During this period of service he took a wide interest in all national problems including the tariff, reconstruction and many others. He is said to have made 100 set speeches besides numerous extemperaneous remarks. Whatever the worth of his other labors in the halls of Congress, the work that has given him everlasting fame is the support that he gave to the bill proposing the establishment of the land-grant colleges.

While Mr. Morrill probably played an important rôle in framing the bill and consistently supported efforts to improve these institutions through the whole of his career, it must be remembered that he was a child of the environment of that day and stood as an honest and far-visioned interpreter of the trend of the times. From the brief review of the development of agricultural education given above it is apparent that the complete conception of the land-grant college did not appear first in the mind of this great American. There had been clamors for State agricultural colleges and few had actually been established by the States; so that the whole movement may be said only to have crystallized in the mind of Morrill where it produced such deep convictions that the realization of the great project was through him accomplished. This, however, in no way detracts from the importance of his work. The greatness of his vision is clear when compared with the narrow, ignorant, and bitter opposition brought to bear upon the proposal by his colleagues in Congress, and the work of few United States Senators will be so loudly proclaimed through the annals of time as that of Justin S. Morrill.

The Land-Grant Act of 1862.—Mr. Morrill introduced his bill in 1857 at the beginning of his second term in Congress. After four months it was reported to the House by two reports from the committee, the majority report being unfavorable to the bill. Mr. Morrill took the floor in the support of the bill and secured its passage by a margin of five votes in the spring of 1858. Not until 1859 could the bill be brought up in the Senate, where it was championed by Senator Wade of Ohio, but bitterly opposed by southern Senators as well as by some from northern States. The States Rights doctrine, which before the Civil War had a larger meaning than it has now, featured in the debate. Senator Clay of Alabama said:

> The Federal Government is the creature of the States and is dependent upon them for its organization and operation. All its powers are subordinate to the States from which they are derived. The States are in no wise dependent on the Federal Government for their operation, organization, support or maintenance. I stand as an ambassador from a sovereign State, no more subject to the control of the Federal Government, except in a few instances provided in the Constitution, than any foreign and independent State. This bill treats the States as agents instead of principals as creatures instead of creators, and proposes to give them their own property and direct them how to use it.

Senator Rice, of Minnesota, said that he "looked upon the success of this measure as bringing a slow, lingering death to Minnesota." The bill finally passed the Senate by the small majority of 3 votes, only to be vetoed by President Buchanan on the twofold ground that the Government was too poor to carry out the provisions of the bill and that it was unconstitutional.

At the next session the bill was again introduced in the Senate by Senator Wade in 1862 and passed by a vote of 32 to 7. Meanwhile Mr. Morrill had unsuccessfully asked leave to introduce the bill again in the House. When the Senate bill was transmitted to the House for action he gave it his support, and the measure passed by a vote of 90 to 25. The bill was approved by President Lincoln on July 2, 1862, at a time when the nation was in the throes of the Civil War. Because of the southern senators out of Congress a large part of the constitutional opposition had been eliminated at this time; it is also probable that the bill may have been regarded as a reconstruction measure that would yield great benefits at the close of the war, and that the military training provision appealed to Congress.

Section 1 of the act granted to each State 30,000 acres of land, for each Senator and Representative in the respective States, excluding mineral lands from the grant.

Section 2 directed the Secretary of Interior to apportion public land in areas not less than a quarter section in extent, and to select the land for the States in which public land was still available. To States in which there was no public land, scrip was to be issued representing claims to public land lying elsewhere. This scrip was to be sold and the proceeds were to be properly invested.

Section 3 provided that expenses incurred in connection with the management and sale of the land were to be paid by the State and not deducted from the proceeds of the sale of the land.

Section 4 required that all the proceeds from the sale of land or land scrip were to be invested "in stocks of the United States, or of the States, or some other safe stocks, yielding not less than five per centum upon the par value of said stocks." The proceeds so invested were to constitute a perpetual fund, the interest of which was to be appropriated by each State, "*which may take and claim the benefit of this act, to the endowment, support, and maintenance of at least one college where the leading object shall be, without excluding other scientific and classical studies and including military tactics, to teach such branches of learning as are related to agriculture and the mechanic arts, in such manner as the legislatures of the States may respectively prescribe, in order to promote the liberal and practical education of the industrial classes in the several pursuits and professions in life.*"

Section 5 makes the State responsible for maintaining intact the fund invested, allows the expenditure, however, of 10% of this fund for the purchase of college sites and experimental farms, prohibits the use of either the fund or the interest thereon for the construction of buildings or their maintenance, requires States taking advantage of the benefits of the act to provide at least one college within the meaning of the act within five years, provides that annual reports of progress were to be sent by each college to all others and to the Secretary of the Interior, excludes States while in a condition of rebellion against the United States Government from the benefits of the act, and finally stipulates that all these conditions must be agreed upon and the tender of the Government accepted by the State legislatures within two years from the date of its approval by the President in order that States may be entitled to the benefits of the act. The time for acceptance was, however, extended in a subsequent amendment passed in 1866.

Minor provisions are contained in Sections 6, 7, and 8.

The Second Morrill Act.—Mr. Morrill's interest in the development of the land-grant colleges never ceased, and in 1890 he secured the passage of an act known as the second Morrill act which gave further aid to the colleges established under the act of 1862.

Section 1 of this act, which is now practically a dead letter, provides for the appropriation of money arising out of the sale of public lands to the respective institutions at the rate of $15,000 for the year ending June 30, 1890, followed by an annual increase of $1,000 for ten years, making available a total of $25,000 to each institution under this act by 1900. The section also states that this fund shall "be applied only to instruction in agriculture, the mechanic arts, the English language, and the various branches of mathematical, physical, natural, and economic science, with special reference to their applications in the industries of life, and to the facilities for such instruction." This provision clearly shows the type of institutions that Congress intended to subsidize. The section also makes mandatory on the part of the States to provide such education to colored students as well as to white students, allowing, however, the establishment of separate schools for the two classes of student.

Sections 3 and 4 of the act provides that each institution shall make annual reports to the Secretary of the Interior and to the Secretary of Agriculture. The administration of the act is placed in the Department of the Interior, whose Secretary is directed to certify to the Secretary of the Treasury whether or not the provisions of the act are being complied with and whether or not the institutions are legally entitled to Federal aid.

The Nelson Amendment.—The act of March 4, 1907, increasing the annual appropriation to $50,000 per year to each State, is known as the Nelson Amendment. In addition to the $25,000 appropriated under the act of 1890 the act appropriated $5,000 for the year ending June 30, 1907, and for four years thereafter an annual increase of $5,000 over the previous year, so that the total amount of Federal aid appropriated to each State and Territory for instructional purposes now equals $50,000.

As already stated the Second Morrill Act provides that the States must extend the benefits of the law to colored students. This means that in the southern States the Federal aid is divided between schools for white and colored students. Seventeen schools having courses in agriculture are maintained for the colored race. The State of North Carolina, for instance, assigns $33,500 to the fund to the North Carolina College of Agriculture and Mechanic Arts and $16,500 to the Negro Agricultural and Technical College, North Carolina. The law also allows that the State may allot the fund among several instituitons, and we therefore find that in a few States where there is no colored population to speak of, and consequently no separate colored school, this division is being made. Massachusetts, for example, divides the fund between the Agricultural College and the Massachusetts Institute of Technology.

Funds for Instructional Purposes.—Under these three Federal acts the Government makes appropriations to the agricultural and mechanical colleges for instructional purposes. For experimental and extension purposes funds are also appropriated, but the authority for the aid is found in other acts. So far as the instructional work of these institutions is concerned it may be interesting at this point to note that while the Federal appropriation is only $50,000 plus the small income from the land-grant fund, the States and private individuals have in many cases raised the total income available for instruction purposes alone to over a million dollars. Unlike the private institutions these State colleges seldom receive large gifts from private benefactors. In 1915-16 there were only 20 institutions for white students and 3 for colored students credited with contributions from private sources and 47 of them had no private endowment fund. There were at that time 68 of these institutions altogether.[1] However, private gifts to some institutions are made and the total amount so available for 1915-16

[1] *Vide Report of the Commissioner of Education* for 1917, pp. 396-7.

amounted to $6,135,505, which is almost twice as much as the total amount appropriated for instructional purposes by the Federal Government, the total amount under the three acts for the same year being only $3,578,087. The larger part of the income for instructional purposes is provided by the States. The total amount appropriated by the States for this purpose for all schools was for that year $19,269,460, which was about half of the total income available for the instruction purpose. A plan that a number of the States use to raise revenue and one that assures a steady and permanent income is known as the mill tax provision. It provides that a certain number of mills or cents shall be levied upon every $100 of assessable property in the State and that the income from this source shall be paid over to the State university.

The Character of the Land-Grant College.—The whole question as to the character of the land-grant college was in confusion for many years. It was the intention of Congress under the Morrill act to establish colleges "for the benefit of agriculture and the mechanic arts." While it appears that agriculture and the mechanic arts were to be the leading features of the kind of education to be given, the institutions were also to provide "liberal and practical education of the industrial classes in the several pursuits and professions of life." Doctor True reminds us that "liberal" meant classical education while the "professions" were medicine, theology and law. Most any kind of interpretation as to the character of education that should be provided under the terms of the act was possible. Mr. Morrill himself said that the institutions were inadvertently called "agricultural colleges" because the indexing clerk so referred to them. The prominence given in the act to "mechanic arts" would have been sufficient basis to call them industrial or engineering colleges. In a report of the United States Bureau of Education for 1886-87 the following statement is made with respect to the character of the institutions at that time:

> Certain of the schools have developed particularly in the direction of the mechanical arts; others are agricultural colleges, pure and simple; a few combined both departments, with large provision for theoretic instruction; while some differ in no essential particular from the ordinary classical college.

According to the Bureau's report for 1917 the Federal funds under the Morrill-Nelson acts in 1915-16 were expended for instruction in the following subjects: agriculture, 24.4%; mechanic arts, 27.5%; English language, 8.4%; mathematical science, 7.8%; natural and physical science, 23.1%; economic science, 7.4%; training of teachers in special subjects, 1.4%. The fact is that under the law the States may allot income under the land-grant fund and under the acts of 1890 and 1907 for educational purposes, the leading object of which shall be "branches of learning as are related to agriculture and the mechanic arts." The same section of the Morrill act of 1862, however, also says that this leading object shall be carried out without "excluding other scientific and classical studies." In the opinion of the Commissioner of Education the Morrill Nelson funds may be used by the arts and sciences colleges of these institutions for instructional cost not chargeable to students enrolled in the colleges of agriculture and engineering. In a letter from Commissioner P. P. Claxton the following statement is made: "The Morrill Act of 1890 limits the expenditure of the Federal funds to the teaching of certain subjects and for certain facilities. But the law connot be construed to limit the expenditure of the Morrill-Nelson funds merely for instruction of students in agriculture and engineering." In the Federal Rulings and Regulations of the Bureau of Education the character of the work for which the Federal funds may be available seems to be somewhat narrowed. There is no foreign language, for instance, included in this list of studies. The treasurers of the respective institutions are to make their annual reports in accordance with the following classification of subjects:

SCHEDULE A.—*Instruction in Agriculture.*

1. Agriculture.
2. Horticulture.
3. Forestry.
4. Agronomy.
5. Animal Husbandry.
6. Dairying.
7. Veterinary Science.
8. Poultry Industry.
9. Apiculture.

SCHEDULE B.—*Instruction in Mechanic Arts.*

1. Mechanical Engineering.
2. Civil Engineering.
3. Electrical Engineering.
4. Irrigation Engineering.
5. Mining Engineering.
6. Marine Engineering
7. Railway Engineering.
8. Experimental Engineering.
9. Textile Industry.
10. Architecture.
11. Machine design.
12. Mechanical Drawing.
13. Ceramics.
14. Stenography.
15. Typewriting.
16. Telegraphy.
17. Printing.
18. Shopwork.

SCHEDULE C.—*Instruction in English Language.*

1. English Language.
2. English Literature.
3. Composition.
4. Rhetoric.
5. Oratory

SCHEDULE D.—*Instruction in Mathematical Sciences.*

1. Mathematics.
2. Bookkeeping.
3. Astronomy.

SCHEDULE E.—*Instruction in Natural and Physical Sciences.*

1. Chemistry.
2. Physics.
3. Biology.
4. Botany.
5. Zoology
6. Geology.
7. Mineralogy.
8. Metallurgy.
9. Entomology.
10. Physiology.
11. Bacteriology.
12. Pharmacy.
13. Physical Geography.
14. Meteorology.

SCHEDULE F.—*Instruction in Economic Sciences.*

1. Political Economy.
2. Home Economics.
3. Commercial Geography.
4. Sociology.

SCHEDULE G.—*Special Preparation of Teachers.*

1. History of industrial education (with special reference to agriculture, mechanic arts, and home economics).
2. Methods of teaching agriculture, mechanic arts, and home economics.
3. Special instruction to persons teaching agriculture, mechanic arts, and home economics.

Early Struggle for Expression.—For almost a half century the agricultural colleges failed to fulfill the mission for which they were established. Those responsible for their establishment had fond hopes that the new education would "evangelize the modern world." But even moderate success was not to be realized until the close of the nineteenth century. Dean Davenport says in this connection that "after a generation of commonly acknowledged failure it must be confessed that the American agricultural college is an institution of the twentieth century."[1] The causes for the absence of success in the beginning and for the slow development are very admirably set forth in the Proceedings of the Association of the Land-Grant Colleges above referred to by Dean Davenport. These obstacles to early success are quoted in full and are as follows:

1. It was a new departure as to purpose, matter and method, and, like all new enterprises, it was destined to endure many trials, tribulations, and mistakes, even from its friends, not to mention its enemies, who were both numerous and influential.

2. The public had become crystallized in its conviction that any great admixture of indusrty and education is impossible, and they were inclined to look upon the attempt as absurd, if not even undesirable.

3. The special opposition of the classicist who habitually regarded anything like a general use of education as a species of desecration; who in particular deplored both the matter and the method of the new order as a lowering of standards and a "commercializing of education" a proceeding that was assumed without discussion to compass both the heights and the depths of educational transgression—the unpardonable sin of the schoolmaster.

4. The opposition of the farmer himself, who instinctively resented what he regarded as an interference with his business on the part of the bookman in assuming to teach him or his son how to farm the land they had inherited from the grandfather, who was popularly supposed in those days to pass down with the title to the land a full measure of ability for its management. This was reason enough for the opposition of the farmer; besides he had always looked upon education as an avenue of escape from farming into some more favored calling where his son should not be obliged to "work as hard as he had worked." Thus had the hardships of the pioneer pressed like iron into the soul of the farmer, who, like his neighbor, the writer and cartoonist of the day, was unable to separate pioneering from real farming.

5. There existed no body of teachable knowledge. Agriculture in the sixties and seventies was essentially a handicraft. Land had no value because it could be had anywhere for the occupancy. Fertility was disregarded; indeed, it was a common saying that most land was too rich for farming, and it was a universal conviction that the soil would never wear out. Under circumstances like these the best farmer was the most ambitious man with the strongest body and the best "knack" of doing things. Most of these accomplishments were relatively unteachable; besides, the farmer did not feel the need of any help which he could not himself secure by the simple method of "changing works."

6. The greatest of all obstacles to the success of the agricultural college, however, lay in the fact that science was as yet undeveloped and had not begun to shed its flood of light upon agricultural practice. Indeed, science itself had not yet made a respectable place in the colleges. When the land grant act was passed, even Harvard, the pioneer in science in this country, taught less botany than is now taught in

[1] From address published in *Proceedings* of the Twenty-sixth Annual Convention of the Association of American Agricultural Colleges and Experiment Stations.

almost any good high school. The early relation between agriculture and science is further illustrated by the fact that in the seventies the Michigan Agricultural College maintained the largest chemical laboratory and gave the most instruction in chemistry of any institution west of Harvard.

Under these conditions the agricultural college found itself obliged to direct its attention almost entirely along new lines quite counter to the old; and it is not strange that in those days when one spoke of the "new education," it was uncertain whether he meant agriculture or science. Science in those days, like agriculture, was a byword, and where it had been "introduced," it was tolerated like a poor relation. Thus it was that the two illegitimates grew up together and like two cripples tended mightily to prop each other up. For these reasons the future historian will accord to the agricultural college a large share in the early development of science in this country.

This mutual relation abided, and the fundamental need of science in a teachable agriculture grew in the minds of men until it took form in the establishment of the national system of agricultural experiment stations paralleling the system of colleges. In that day was laid the foundation for success, and from that time forward the agricultural college began to succeed.

7. No trained teachers existed. Most institutions vacillated for their professors of agriculture (there was only one in those days) between the successful farmer who could not teach and the so-called scientist of the day who knew little or no farming. Technical studies were postponed until the junior and senior years when the "professor of agriculture" was expected to edify a group of students that had been for two years under the tutelage of specialists in chemistry, botany, zoology, etc.; for when once well started, science rapidly outsrtipped its humbler brother in their early development. It is only in very recent years that, through the findings of the experiment stations, it has been possible for teachers really to train themselves; but from now on we may reasonably hope for an increasing proportion of well trained specialists, though it is yet with the greatest difficulty that the young teacher can find suitable graduate work in the direct line of his needs.

8. Not the least of the obstacles to be overcome was the unfortunate report, coming from nowhere but circulated everywhere that these colleges were especially successful in training young men away from the farm. They were represented as attracting students under the guise of instruction in agriculture, but that by example, teaching, and precept, the influence was toward any occupation but farming. The only color of truth for this report lay in the fact that some of these early colleges, functioning both in science and in agriculture, afforded about the only means of securing an adequate training for the practical things of life, and they were for a little time patronized for purposes of a general education.

But it was always true, and is yet, that the great mass of the students of the agricultural colleges return at once to the land and succeed better than their fathers succeeded. Indeed in many a case the family fortunes have been restored by such a student returning in the nick of time as farming was passing from its pioneer stage into that of a finished and permanent agriculture wherein the man who cleared the farm and improved it could not keep up with the times.

9. Last of all obstacles worth mentioning is the fact that really effective agricultural instruction has been found unexpectedly expensive, both as to men and materials. If it had not also become popular

in recent years, so that money in larger amounts than were ever before devoted to education was forthcoming, the enterprise would surely have broken down of its own weight from sheer inability to do the work required. Even yet a few institutions have not learned that a complete parity in salaries throughout all departments is impossible; that teachers in agriculture cost more than do most others.

Dean Davenport points out that the efforts of the agricultural college were opposed alike by the educators of the classical school and a large portion of the farming population. But the most important obstacles were the absence of a body of teachable knowledge and trained teachers. The science of agriculture was in fact not yet developed. More experimentation was necessary to provide the necessary body of knowledge. Hence the establishment of the experiment stations is readily seen to have had a very important relation to the growth and progress of the agricultural college. Dean Davenport says the first experiment stations were established by scientists and public-spirited men, but the experiment stations established under the authority of the Hatch act were the fruition of a movement propagated by teachers of agriculture who felt the dire need of more material.

Organization of the Agricultural Colleges.—The agricultural colleges perform the three functions of resident instruction, research, and extension service. The latter two functions have not yet been discussed, but will be treated in separate chapters. In the discussion of the organization of the agricultural college the reader should bear in mind that the extension service performed by these colleges has come to be a very important function since the passage of the Smith-Lever act of 1914. The research or experiment function is likewise of great importance. How to organize and supervise these three functions in such a way as to create the most smooth-working and efficient machine, has engaged the attention of the Association of Land-Grant Colleges whose committee on college organization and policy for a number of years studied the problem and also asked the Bureau of Education to make a survey of organization existing among the different colleges of the country. This survey was conducted by C. D. Jarvis, who consulted freely with Dr. True of the Department of Agriculture, and according to its findings there is considerable variation in organization, but, on the whole, it is pointed out that two main types of college organizations exist. One of these types magnifies the subject-matter departments, such as dairy, horticultural, agronomy, soils, animal husbandry, etc., with respect to administration, and gives the head of each department considerable administrative work to perform with respect to the three different functions, but especially with respect to extension. It is pointed out that coordinating agencies are created under this form of organization to secure the desired cooperation. According to the survey of the Bureau of Education the other type of organization creates two or perhaps three administrative headships to supervise the three functions of instruction, research, and extension. This takes away, it is pointed out, considerable of the administrative work from department heads and lodges it under the three administrative officers who are, however, directly responsible to the dean of the college in a university, or president where there is no university organization. The authority for this statement concerning existing organiaztion among the colleges is found in *Circular 8* of the Bureau of Education. As a matter of fact all the larger agricultural colleges have at least an assistant dean who looks after the details of the instructional function and a director of extension who performs the administrative work of the extension service, but both officials act only under the authority of the dean of the college.

In a study of this question Professor Frank A. Waugh states that "the most important unit of college organization is the department, and the most important element in the department is the man who heads it. Everything should be done to maintain the integrity of the departments and to preserve the independence and initiative of department heads. Correlation of departmental work is a problem in every institution, and grows rapidly in difficulty with the growth of the college. Three principal methods are in vogue for serving such correlation. They are: (a) The formation of large departments with specialist assistants; (b) the grouping of related departments into larger divisions, headed by deans or division chiefs; (c) the obliteration of department lines and the organization of the work about men or problems."[1]

There are rumors to the effect that the United States Department of Agriculture has at various times attempted to influence the character of the organization of the colleges. For instance it has been said that the extension director, who represents both the college and the Department, has in some places attempted to deal directly with the Department instead of through the Dean of the College. Rumors also have it that such action was encouraged by the Department. This meant that the relationship between the Department and the extension service would cause the extension policies to be formulated by the Department rather than jointly by the college and the Department. It may be said that the colleges through their chief executives have refused to play the part of "rubber-stamp" agencies and have vigorously asserted themselves in all matters that deal with the formulation of agricultural policies in general with which the colleges and experiment stations are concerned.

The committee of the Association of Land-Grant Colleges studying the problems of organization, at the 1917 meeting, made a number of recommendations the most important of which are that the organization should make it possible for the administration to make direct contact with specialists as individuals; that specialists should devote their time mainly to one kind of service, but provision should be made for exchanges for the mutual advantage of each; that large liberties be given the department in the determination of its subject matter; that the members of the department should have some voice in the choice of its administrative head, and that incoming correspondence, except that of an administrative character, should be referred to the subject-matter departments concerned and there referred to the individual best qualified to supply the desired information; and that the three kinds of service including instruction, research, and extension be each headed by a single administrative officer and coordinated under a chief executive who, in the case of a university, should

[1] *Vide* his *Agricultural College*, p. 44.

be an officer other than the president. It is also recommended "that the leaders in charge of the various phases of the extension service should be regarded as administrative officers and should not usurp the duties of the specialists in the various subjects. Where an individual serves both as specialist and administrative leader a dual responsibility should be recognized."[1]

A splendid presentation of ideal college organization is contained in the following statement:

> The general principle of organization we advocate is, we believe, what is contemplated in the Smith-Lever law, in the Kentucky Statutes accepting its provisions, and in the articles of agreement between the University of Kentucky and the United States Department of Agriculture relative to extension. It is that followed in the organization of the colleges of agriculture in the majority of the state universities in the United States, including some we class among the best. The college of agriculture, in the large sense not only works out information in its research division, which is the experiment station, and imparts the same to students in its division of resident instruction, and to the farming community through its extension division, but it is the collecting, adapting and distributing medium for information developed by other agencies, such as practical farmers themselves, the United States Department of Agriculture, and other institutions in all parts of the world. Each subject matter department should be the chief center and authority for information upon its particular subject, and it is of the greatest importance that this store of information be systematically transmitted to the student in residence, the farmer on the farm and to the housewife in the home practically at first hand. This implies a close organic connection among the three divisions, research, resident instruction and extension. In short each subject matter department should be connected closely and definitely with research, teaching, and extension, and should be held responsible for the finding out of knowledge, its proper organization and its interpretation. Let us repeat that this requires an officer at the head with full power to exact such work of each department.
>
> Again the men who are engaged in research and experiment will often derive their best inspiration from contact with those who make practical application of their results, and this affords another strong reason why the subject matter departments should be brought into the closest possible relation with the farmer and the student. It is apparent, therefore, that those who impart information to the farming community, as well as those who conduct research and resident teaching should be closely identified with the subject matter departments.
>
> This does not mean that the men doing research work and experiments should be distracted from their duties by excess of teaching and extension service, but rather that such men shall do enough teaching and extension work to keep themselves alive to the needs of the student and the farmer, that they may be better prepared to

[1] For these recommendations see Proceedings of the Thirty-first Annual Convention of the Association of Land-Grant Colleges, p. 35.

give general direction of what is to be taught and its interpretation by those who may be giving most of their time to teaching or extension.[1]

In brief it may be said that the unit of contact with the United States Department of Agriculture should be the college through its chief executive and not through an inferior administrative officer such as the extension director. Whether or not the college should perform any regulatory functions is indirectly discussed in the chapter dealing with the state department of agriculture. The position there is taken that all regulatory functions should be performed by the department of agriculture.

So far as the internal organization of the college is concerned differences of opinion prevail as to whether the unit of organization should be the specialist capable of doing independent work or the department. It would seem that the best results are obtained where the department is considered the unit of organization, but where the personnel in the department are given the usual professorial freedom in the conduct of all their duties including research and where they have some voice in the selection of the administrative head. Coordination of the three activities must be effected by administrative officers at the head of instruction, research, and extension who are directly responsible to the chief executive of the college. That there be an administrative officer other than the chief executive at the head of the research function is not so important as in the case of the other two functions. The reason for this is that research or experimentation in its very nature is very largely an individual problem. Inspirations come from various stimuli to the mind of the individual when he is free from unnecessary administrative restraints. It lies outside of the capacity of any one man to assign problems of research to all the specialists. Hypotheses come to the minds of all creative thinkers and it is therefore plain that even the discovery of a problem is usually born within the particular department. The prosecution of such problems must be carried on by men who are specially fitted for the purpose in a

[1] This statement was prepared by Professor George Roberts and appears in the *Report of the Survey Commission* published in a bulletin of the University of Kentucky.

cooperative way. That is, best results are often obtained when a number of men unite their efforts on a single problem. The development or prosecution of problems must have the approval of the administrative head of the college who is responsible to the United States Department of Agriculture as to whether or not Federal funds may be used for their solution. Thus it is readily seen that the administrative aspect of research work is in no way comparable to the discovery and solution of problems, and it is for this reason that a separate administrative officer for this function is less needed than for the other two functions.

The Association of Land-Grant Colleges.—This organization coordinates, unifies and harmonizes the activities of the agricultural colleges. As early as 1883 a convention of delegates from the colleges met at Washington, D. C., "for the special purpose of promoting the establishment of experiment stations." Another convention met in 1885, and at a third meeting in 1887 a permanent organization was effected under the name of Association of American Agricultural Colleges and Experiment Stations. In 1919 its name was changed to the Association of Land-Grant Colleges. While the Association was at first mainly interested in the establishment of experiment stations it was from the beginning interested in general problems as well. The Proceedings of the 33rd annual convention held at Chicago in 1919 show the Association to be subdivided into the sections of agriculture, engineering, and home economics, and as having standing committees for instruction in agriculture, home economics, mechanic arts, graduate study, college organization and policy, experiment station organization and policy, and extension organization and policy. In cooperation with the Department of Agriculture there are joint-standing committees on relations, on projects and correlation of research, and on publication of research. This organization shows a wide and general interest in all problems confronting the agricultural colleges.

Membership of this Association is made up of delegates from the agricultural colleges and experiment stations receiving Federal aid. Delegates from other institutions may be admitted to the conventions of the Association by a majority vote with full privileges except the right to vote.

The Association is supported through contributions from the institutions that make up its respective members.

The Results of the Morrill-Nelson Acts.—The land apportioned to the several States under the act of 1862 ranged from 24,000 acres for Alabama to 990,000 acres for New York. The policy of the Government to dispose of the public land under the homestead act to thousands of settlers and the extensive gifts or grants of land to railroads tended to depress the price of public lands so that States selling their quota early realized but little.[1] In some instances the income from the fund thus established was not sufficient to maintain properly a single department. In a few States, "like New York and Michigan, where the number of acres received was large and the sale of the land was skilfully made, large funds were obtained." The total area of land allotted to the States amounted to 10,-929,215 acres of which 1,149,867 acres remained unsold in 1917. From the sale of these lands permanent funds have been created amounting to $15,105,925, and yielding an income of $916,151. Regardless of the amount of the funds established under the act, the important result was that States complied with its provisions and that agricultural colleges scattered throughout the country were established. State and municipal governments and in some cases private individuals gave liberally to the support of the institutions initiated under the land-grant act.

The result then is that the original Morrill or land-grant act, reinforced by subsequent acts, established agricultural and engineering colleges, and this has resulted in a number of cases in the development of strong universities having large liberal arts colleges. A few of these institutions maintain no agricultural courses, being wholly engineering, and yet receive Federal aid. An example is the Massachusetts Institute of Technology which in 1915-16 received $3,650 of the original land-grant fund and $16,667 of Federal aid under authority of the acts of 1890 and 1907. The experiment station funds made

[1] *Vide Agricultural Report*, 1867, pp. 317-331.

available under the Hatch and Adams acts are, of course, only available for agricultural experiment work. In 1919 there were 69 institutions partially maintained by Federal funds. Of these 67 maintain courses in agriculture.

Looking back and noting how the Land-Grant Colleges have sprung up in every state of the Union and how they have developed into state universities furnishing educational facilities to a large number of the youth of the nation, one may well ask the question whether every state would have established a university without Federal aid. It is indeed very probable, in fact quite certain, that it would not have been done by the less progressive states. The country would do well to rely even further upon Federal aid and if necessary to submit to some Feedral control of our educational system in order that uniformity of educational opportunities may be provided for the American youth throughout the length and breadth of the land. Very little Federal control is being exercised under the Morrill-Nelson acts, which is as it should be. The ideal arrangement would be to receive Federal aid and leave the matter of determining educational policies virtually wholly to the discretion of the educational authorities, and have only general control over expenditures exercised by the Federal government. The time was when state aid to the county for school purposes was thought improper. Now it is recognized that a backward county is a menace to the state, and that granting aid to it is therefore a proper object of expenditure of the state's funds. Similarly the time has come when we must recognize the necessity of granting Federal aid to the state for the purpose of providing uniform educational facilities throughout the nation in order that centers of ignorance and crime may be wiped out, that poverty may be lessened, and that a state of full and complete national solidarity may prevail. With respect to the importance of the establishment of the Land-Grant Colleges, President James says, that "it is not too much to claim, then, that the Federal land grant of 1862 marks the beginning of one of the most comprehensive, far-reaching, and one might almost say, grandiose schemes for the endowment of higher education ever adopted by any civilized nation."[1]

SELECTED REFERENCES.

True in *Yearbook* for 1894, pp. 81-116; True in *Yearbook* for 1899, pp. 157-190; James, *The Land-Grant Act of 1862,* published by the University of Illinois; *Proceedings* of the Twenty-Sixth and Thirty-First Annual Conventions of the Association of Land-Grant Colleges; *Report* of Commissioner of Education for 1917, pp. 396-7; Waugh, *The Agricultural College; Agricultural Report* for 1867 pp. 317-331.

---

[1] *Vide the Land Grant Act of* 1862.

CHAPTER XI

EXPERIMENT STATIONS

The Evolution of Agricultural Experiment Stations.—The beginning of the movement to establish experiment stations in America must be traced to Europe. Liebig in Germany and Boussingault in France demonstrated the importance of applying science to agriculture. "Liebig's theory of fertilizers aroused extravagant expectations in the popular mind, and it was hoped that chemical analysis of soil and plant would be an infallible guide to show what manuring of the crop would produce the most abundant harvests." In 1843 Lawes and Gilbert in England began an important series of field and laboratory experiments. An actual experiment station was organized in Germany in 1851 by a company of Saxon farmers under the influence of the University of Leipsic, and later with some help from the "Government organized the first agricultural experiment station."[1]

In America the State of Maryland was a pioneer in this movement. Section 6 of the act to establish and endow an agricultural college, passed by the legislature in 1856, provides as follows:

> It shall be the duty of the said board of trustees to order and direct to be made and instituted on said model farm, annually, a series of experiments upon the cultivation of cereal and other plants adapted to the latitude and climate of the State of Maryland, and cause to be carefully noticed upon the records of said institution the character of said experiments, the kind of soil upon which they were undertaken, the system of cultivation adopted, the state of the atmosphere and all other particulars which may be necessary to a fair and a complete understanding of the result of said experiments.

Immediately after the college was located and before the erection of buildings began, field experiments concerning the values of different manures were begun and continued until interrupted by lack of financial support incident to the political disturbance brought on by the Civil War.

In the early 70's Harvard conducted field experiments in fertilizers, and at Yale, during the 60's, agricultural experi-

---

[1] Dr. True in *Yearbook* for 1894, p. 103.

ments were carried on which it is said resulted in the development of a young group of advocates demanding the establishment of experiment stations first in Connecticut and later throughout the country. During this period European experiments were attracting attention and in 1872 the United States Commissioner of Agriculture called a convention of representatives of the land-grant colleges at which time the question of establishing experiment stations was discussed and approved. In 1873 the State Board of Agriculture of Connecticut appointed a committee to bring the matter of establishing an experiment station to the attention of the public. The Committee found many enthusiastic friends of the cause, but farmers generally were indifferent. To prevent the failure of the movement Mr. Orange Judd, editor of the *American Agriculturist,* offered $1,000 and the Wesleyan University of Middletown offered the free use of its laboratory. The offers were made on the condition that the legislature should appropriate $2,800 per annum for two years for the project. The appropriation was made, Professor W. O. Atwater was appointed Director, experiments were begun in 1875, "and thus the first agricultural experiment station in America was an accomplished fact." The University of California organized a station the same year. Similar steps were soon taken by other institutions. In 1877 the State of North Carolina established an experiment and fertilizer control station at the University of North Carolina located at Chapel Hill. Cornell University organized a station in 1879 under the initiative of the faculty who, until the Federal act of 1887, performed most of the work without compensation. New Jersey established a station in 1880 by an act of legislature in connection with Rutgers College.

The Hatch Act of 1887.—The movement for the establishment of experiment stations steadily grew, and in 1886 the Committee on Agriculture of the House, in reporting the Hatch bill, made the following statement:

> Since 1881 the legislatures of the several states have either recognized or reorganized the departments of agriculture in the land-grant colleges as "experiment stations," thus following substantially the course adopted by New Jersey. Such stations have been established

in Maine, Massachusetts, Ohio, Tennessee, and Wisconsin. In three other states (possibly more), without legislative action, the college authorities have organized their agricultural work as experiment stations. This has been done in California, Missouri, and New York. But in addition to the twelve experiment stations specifically designated by that name a very large number of the colleges established under the act of 1862 are doing important work of a precisely similar kind. Many of them began such work immediately upon their establishment and have since maintained it continuously. Others have entered upon it more recently. The colleges in Colorado, Indiana, Kansas, Michigan, and Pennsylvania are carrying on what is strictly experiment station work as a part of their ordinary duty.

The agitation necessary to bring the legislation to a favorable conclusion was carried on by representatives from the agricultural colleges. At their convention in 1885 there was appointed a special legislative committee which was largely instrumental in securing the passage of the Hatch act in 1887. As stated in the previous chapter, the movement for establishing experiment stations under the Hatch act received its impetus chiefly from the undeveloped status of agricultural science as a handicap to teaching. The instructional staff in the agricultural colleges lacked the body of knowledge necessary to construct the theory of agriculture. Dean Davenport says "Just as surely as the first experiment stations were the result of the desire of public spirited men and scientists to know more about agriculture, so the Hatch Act was the result of the determination of teachers to secure more material."

Section one of the act provides aid for the establishment of an agricultural experiment station as a department in the land-grant college.

Section 2 of the act provides as follows:

That it shall be the object and duty of said experiment stations to conduct original researches or verify experiments on the physiology of plants and animals; the diseases to which they are severally subject, with the remedies for the same; the chemical composition of useful plants at their different stages of growth; the comparative advantages of rotative cropping as pursued under a varying series of crops; the capacity of new plants or trees for acclimation; the analysis of soils and water; the chemical composition of manures, natural or artificial, with experiments designed to test their comparative effects on crops of different kinds; the adaptation and value of grasses and forage plants; the composition and digestibility of the different kinds of food for domestic animals; the scientific and economic questions involved in the production of butter and cheese; and such other researches or experiments bearing directly on the agricultural industry of the United States as may in each case be deemed advisable, having due regard to the varying conditions and needs of the respective States or Territories.

Section 5 provides for the payment of $15,000 per annum to each State and Territory to perform the experiments and print and distribute the results among the farmers of the country. Administrative provisions already discussed in the chapter dealing with the States Relations Service are outlined in other sections. The franking privilege is extended to the Station for mailing its publications. In order to assure the application of the major part of the Federal appropriation to experimentation only one-fifth of the first year's amount was made available for buildings and thereafter only 5% of the sum may be so expended. The act places the experiment stations under the administration of the Secretary of Agriculture. Section 3 in this connection says that it is the duty of the Department of Agriculture to indicate lines of inquiry "and in general to furnish such advice and assistance as may best promote the purpose of this act." From what was said in the previous chapter on college organization, especially with respect to research, it is very evident that the Department can do very little in the way of indicating lines of inquiry. In the very nature of the case these lines of inquiry must originate very largely with the local stations and in the minds of the research workers themselves. However, under this provision "very close relations have existed and the Department early established an abstract journal, known as Experiment Station Record, to review the investigation in agriculture, now covering the world, as an aid to American investigators."[1] Reports were to be made to the Secretaries of Agriculture and the Treasury. In the appropriation act for the fiscal year 1894 for the Department of Agriculture, the Secretary is directed to ascertain whether the stations' expenditures have been properly made.[2] A larger measure of authority including supervision was given the Department, and this supervision was broadened by the Adams act.

---

[1] Dr. E. W. Allen, Chief Officer of Experiment Stations in a personal communication.

[2] *Yearbook* for 1894, p. 109.

The Adams Act.—The Adams Act was approved March 16, 1906, and had for its object the extension and strengthening of the experiment stations. Section one of the act provided that in addition to the $15,000 appropriated under the Hatch Act of 1887, $5,000 more was to be appropriated for the year ending June 30, 1906, and thereafter an annual increase of $2,000 for 5 years, making a total appropriation of $15,000 under the Adams act since 1911, or under both Hatch and Adams acts a total of $30,000 of Federal aid given to the experiment stations. The act provides further that the amount appropriated shall "be applied only to paying the necessary expenses of conducting original researches or experiments bearing directly on the agricultural industry of the United States, having due regard to the varying conditions and needs of the respective States or Territories."

The total amount appropriated by the United States to all institutions for agricultural experiment purposes under these acts during the year 1915-16 was $1,362,000. During the same year the States appropriated for the use of the stations $1,362,018. In 1920 the support from the Federal Government amounted to $1,440,000 and that of the States to $3,594,441.

Relation to the Department of Agriculture.—In the above discussion it was pointed out that the control of the experiment station by the Department of Agriculture amounts to supervision. Expenditures for types of research must have the approval of the Department. It is only natural that when the Federal Government grants aid to the States that it will demand a measure of control over the expenditure of funds. There is probably little objection to this aspect of the situation. Administration officers may well gracefully submit to this aspect of their relation to the Department inasmuch as it was largely through Federal funds that experiment stations have been established and developed in every state of the Union.

There is, however, a point of contact or a clash in the field of research between the experiment station and the United States Department of Agriculture. Men associated with the colleges and stations think that there are separate domains in research that each of these institutions may rightfully cultivate and that these domains are clearly defined and marked out. The Department has its place even in research. It should not only confine its attention to regulatory functions. It may rightfully interest itself in the educational, service, and research functions. But the research enterprises that should be performed by the Department are of such a nature that they are either too expensive for the state institutions to undertake or else they are big problems or services that extend over a number of States or over the entire country. It is hinted in addresses delivered before conventions of the Association of the Land-Grant Colleges that considerable "irritation and difficulty" have grown out of the Department's attempts to solve local problems. In other words, it has been pointed out that the Department has at various times, with respect to research, gone out of its sphere and entered the domain of the state experiment stations. Purely local problems should be left to these institutions, while such problems that are "of a general character, international, national, or at least interstate in their applications" should be left for the Department.[1]

The Growth of Experiment Station Work.—Much as was the service of the experiment station needed by the college of agriculture in the development of its course of study or its body of teaching knowledge, its growth at first was more or less slow. On the occasion of celebrating the completion of the twenty-fifth year of the history of the American Agricultural Experiment Station, Dr. H. C. White, before the convention of the Association of Land-Grant Colleges, made the following statement:

> The first fifteen or twenty years of the existence of the stations was a period of novitiate. A sufficient number of workers had not yet been trained to man efficiently the large number of stations simultaneously established. The lines of possibly useful experimentation that were offered were so numerous that, lacking experience it was difficult to make wise selection. The true nature and functions of the station were unknown, unappreciated or misinterpreted by many of the communities in which they were established and, sometimes, even by those charged with their administration and control. It was inevitable, therefore, that there should have been more or less of grop-

[1] *Vide* address by Dean Davenport in *Proceedings* of the Twenty-Seventh Convention of the Association of Land-Grant Colleges.

ing after stability and accurate consciousness of purpose. There was undoubtedly much effort that was unwise, much labor that was useless, much duplication that was unnecessary, much wastefulness, if you please, of both energy and means. But, notwithstanding this, the results which were achieved by the stations in this early period of their history abundantly justified the wisdom of their establishment. Investigation and experiment were prosecuted along numerous lines. Ability, earnestness and energy were manifested on every hand. Errors innumerable in agricultural practices were exposed; truths in great numbers were demonstrated; a vast number of useful publications were added to agricultural literature; and the foundations may be truthfully said to have been thereby firmly laid for a really intelligent and scientific agriculture.[1]

After the passage of the Adams Act, which meant larger support, and benefiting by the experience and organization of their early history, the work of the stations made rapid progress. To describe this period of the history of the experiment stations Doctor White said the following:

Desultory and inconsequent experimentation has been largely discontinued; definiteness in experiment work has been more clearly established; and genuine scientific research along all the lines of the natural sciences related to agriculture has begun. A large and able body of competent investigators has been developed and the quality and value of their work challenges admiring comparison with the output of the laboratories of the world devoted to pure research in all the branches of biology, chemistry and physics. Through the station publications and otherwise a body of new truth, demonstrated or suspected, has been given immediately to the workers in the fields for adoption, scrutiny or test, and, as a result, it is probably true that, in America, scientific agriculture—and that means intelligent agriculture, economic agriculture—has made greater progress in the last ten years than in all the years which went before.

Results of the Experiment Stations.—In a country as extensive as that of the United States, where a great variety of topography, soil and climate are to be found, and where in consequence a great variety of crops is produced, there must be a geographic distribution of experiment stations to meet these many varied needs. Congress, therefore, wisely provided that there shall be at least one station in each State. The principle of concentration of effort in agricultural experimentation would result in the neglect of the improvement of agriculture in remote areas. From the Atlantic to the Pacific and from the Gulf to Canada, experiment stations everywhere are engaged upon problems found in their immediate locality, or hav-

[1] From *Proceedings* of the Twenty-sixth Annual Convention of the Association of Land-Grant Colleges.

ing general application. During the year 1918 the Department reports that the investigations followed "various lines of agronomy, animal husbandry, dairying, horticulture, plant pathology, entomology, and veterinary science, modified somewhat by the demands of different sections of the country."

The Alabama station for that year ascertained the most productive variety of cotton and secured its general adoption by the farmers. The proper fertilizers for certain soils were determined as well as the proper proportion needed. The West Virginia station reports the more general adoption of proper methods of spraying for the control of potato diseases. The Louisiana Station reports that the planting of legumes for decreasing the need of nitrogenous commercial fertilizers is becoming more general. In North Carolina the station found the soy bean one of the best summer-growing legumes for the State. The Wyoming station, following the principle of feeding more roughage to stock and saving concentrates, advocated the use of such silage crops as oats, peas, or sunflower where corn cannot be grown, and as a result silos have become common in the State. The Pennsylvania station showed that cattle fed on silage and cottonseed meal can be readily fattened for the market. These are just a few suggestive efforts of the stations and for a detailed and comprehensive review of their work the reader must consult the reports of the Department, *"Work and Expenditures of the Agricultural Experiment Stations."*

Every year the report of the Department records a large number of findings that are of practical value to agriculture. The few illustrations given are only a suggestion of what the experiment stations are doing. Inasmuch as this chapter is not expanded by the inclusion of the history of the achievements of the experiment stations, it must not be taken to mean that they are incomparable in importance with other public agricultural institutions. Much has been said of the United States Department of Agriculture. With reference to some bureaus the more attractive phases of their scientific work were developed at some length. Much more could be said of the experiment stations associated with the Land-Grant Colleges, but space does not permit.

Agricultural Experimentation a Public Enterprise.—It is very obvious that experimentation in agriculture must for the most part be conducted under public enterprise. The spirit of competition is a great motivating power in the field of industry in bringing about inventions and promoting industrial progress, but in agriculture this force is almost altogether lacking. There are various reasons for this. Perhaps the most important is the fact that farming of the most profitable kind is a small business unit. It is not a large-scale industry, and can therefore not afford, even if it were so inclined, to employ high-salaried specialists similar to what is being done in large industrial establishments. For the agricultural masses as a whole it is therefore impossible for the spirit of competition to express itself in the way this force makes itself felt in industry. The very nature of agriculture, however, is also responsible for the actual lack of competition among farmers in the same keen sense that it is found in industry. The farmers are scattered and numerous. Their products are dependent upon many uncertain factors, one of which is the weather, therefore, less subject to control than that of industry. The isolated condition of the farmers has resulted frequently in keeping them uninformed, has imbued them with the spirit of independence and self-reliance, and until recently at least has made them unwilling to give ear to improved methods.

Again, agricultural improvement fundamentally is not concerned so much with the construction of mechanical devices, but with the development and application of profound scientific principles. The problem presupposes in many instances a knowledge of science which only the college man has. Agricultural experimentation requires trained specialists, and these should be employed by an institution whose results are made available for all and their salaries should be paid out of the public treasury.

Finally another obstacle in the way of individual experimentation is the loss to the return of capital and labor that it occasions. The operator is naturally concerned with profits and his greatest opportunity lies in making use of the very best methods in the cultivation of his land, and leaving to others the discovery of new methods. For various reasons, therefore, agricultural experimentation, so important to the future welfare of mankind, must be conducted under public enterprise.

SELECTED REFERENCES.

True in *Yearbook* for 1894, pp. 81-116; Davenport in *Proceedings* of the Twenty-Seventh Convention of the Association of Land-Grant Colleges; White in *Proceedings* of the Twenty-Sixth Annual Convention of the Association of Land-Grant Colleges; various *Reports of Work and Expenditures of the Agricultural Experiment Stations;* various *Experiment Station Records.*

CHAPTER XII

COOPERATIVE AGRICULTURAL EXTENSION WORK

Early Agricultural Extension Work.—The word "extension" in education is used to refer to all work of colleges and universities not included under resident instruction or to all educational activities "extending" beyond the halls of the institution. Agricultural extension aims to make scientific and practical agricultural information and instruction available to farmers generally. Farmers' institutes, lectures, movable schools, correspondence courses, and demonstration work, are various forms of extension activities that have been carried on by the state agricultural colleges. Like all important elements of social organization the present cooperative agricultural extension system is a product of evolution. The early attempts to spread the gospel of good agriculture among the people of the United States resulted in great good, but it soon became apparent to leaders that a more efficient and more far-reaching system had to be devised. In tracing the development of agricultural extension work from its beginnings to the adoption of the present system it is necessary to refer to several precedent movements. Farmers' institutes, cooperative experiments, and the early extension departments of agricultural colleges constitute a series of movements that logically led to the use of the principle of cooperative demonstration which is the essence of the present system.[1]

In a former chapter in connection with the discussion of the States Relations Service something was said concerning the history of the farmers' institutes. It may be stated here that the farmers' institutes grew out of farmers' meetings held more or less irregularly by agricultural societies during the first half of the 19th century, but that their real beginning dates from the establishment of the agricultural colleges in 1862. These institutions from their beginning felt the call of the people on the farms. They furnished speakers, and in

[1] The author is indebted to Professor Dwight Sanderson for some of these historical facts and for pointing out their relation to the present cooperative extension service.

many instances took the initiative in organizing institutes. The close relationship that existed between agricultural societies and the state board of agriculture in the early days, as explained in subsequent chapters, resulted frequently in the placing of the administrative work of farmers' institutes under the state board of agriculture. As early as 1875 the Michigan Board of Agriculture made an appropriation for this work. The United States Department of Agriculture also contributed to the movement by providing speakers and lecture material. By 1908 all states except Louisiana and Nevada held farmers' institutes. There are still fifteen states in which the institutes are managed by the state departments of agriculture, but as this small number indicates, the tendency now is to place the function of holding institutes under the extension service of the agricultural colleges. The number of institutes held remain about the same as formerly, but their character has changed considerably, being now usually a feature of the general extension program carried out in the county. Much good must have resulted from the holding of farmers' institutes, but it was early observed that too frequently only vague impressions were made, and that the backward rural population and those living in remote places were never reached.

Agricultural extension work was given a new mode of attack in some parts of the country through the activities of the experiment stations in connection with attempts to introduce their discoveries among the farmers generally. Cooperative experiments were arranged for, and these really embodied the demonstration principle. Professor Dwight Sanderson has the following to say with respect to the kind of extension activities that grew out of the activities of the experiment stations:

As the work of the agricultural experiment stations developed they found that from the very nature of the problems involved much of their work had to be carried on under actual farm conditions. This involved cooperation with farmers and such investigations were often termed cooperative experiments. As soon as the stations commenced to secure conclusive results from their investigations the problem arose of how to secure their general adoption by farmers. Bulletins reporting the investigations were widely distributed and all farmers' institutes gave a large place to the discussion of experiment station vork; but although much improvement resulted, the utilization of the esults of experimental work was by no means as general as its imortance warranted. It was found, however, that where the experiments were conducted on farms and the farmer became convinced of he practicableness of the better methods discovered that his neighors became interested and would try out the new methods. It beame apparent, therefor, that one of the best means of spreading the eaching of the experiment stations was through an extension of soalled cooperative experiments among considerable numbers of farmers. uch trials were really experiments from the farmer's standpoint alhough really they might be merely demonstrations of results secured y the station investigators. However, in many cases they served to urnish a most desirable means of determining the practicability of he methods recommended under various conditions and so were a ecessary step in the completion of the station's work. Cooperative exeriments were found of value in all lines, but particularly in the inroduction of seeds of new varieties, of testing fertilizers and means f soil improvement of spraying, feeding, etc. The Ohio Agricultural 'xperiment Station developed a very elaborate system of cooperative xperiments with many hundreds of farmers and Ontario and Wisconin organized state experimental associations of those undertaking uch work.[1]

Cooperative experiments must be recognized as a step n the development of extension work. They served to make lear the importance of the use of the demonstration method, nd as a consequence when the county agricultural agent was bout to be introduced the plan found more or less ready cceptance.

From the point of view of administration or organization third step in the evolution of extension work in the United tates is the establishment of departments by the colleges o carry on such work. The Nixon Act passed by the New ork legislature in 1894 appropriated $8,000 to the College f Agriculture at Cornell University for the purpose of conucting "agricultural extension" work. This, Professor Sanerson says, "was the first state appropriation for such work, nd the results so commended themselves to the farmers and o the legislature that in 1900 the appropriation was increased o $40,000 and has been constantly maintained and increased ince then. This work attracted the attention of other states nd several of the agricultural colleges established agriculural extension departments either with or without specific ppropriations for the work, during the years 1905 to 1910.

[1] Taken from Professor Sanderson's class notes.

The work in Iowa was particularly successful and attracted wide attention."

Few men in the United States comprehended the significance of the demonstration method as fully as did the late Dr. Seaman A. Knapp. He it was who fully understood what could be achieved if this principle were made the object of an efficient organization.[1] As is explained later Doctor Knapp must be given large credit for originating the present cooperative extension service. Its basic principle of demonstration had already been worked out, but the creation of an organization that was to be workable, coextensive with the whole range of farm activities, and localized through the employment of county agents, was very largely the result of Doctor Knapp's efforts to improve agricultural conditions in Texas under the authority of the United States Department of Agriculture. By November, 1906, these efforts had progressed to the extent of having secured the appointment of at least one county agricultural agent. In subsequent pages the progress of the extension service will be traced.

At the time Doctor Knapp was promoting the extension system in the South, public sentiment became more favorable to the establishment of a national extension system. This is reflected, it would seem, by the report of President Roosevelt's Country Life Commission, published in 1908. In part this Commission reported as follows:

> The arousing of the people must be accomplished in terms of their daily lives, or of their welfare. For the country people this means that it must be largely in terms of agriculture. Some of the colleges of agriculture are now doing this kind of work effectively, although on a pitiably small scale as compared with the needs. This is extension work, by which is meant all kinds of educational effort directly with the people, both old and young, at their homes and on their farms; it comprises all educational work that is conducted away from the institution and for those who cannot go to schools and colleges. The best extension work now proceeding in this country—if measured by the effort to reach the people in their homes and on their own ground—is that coming from the United States Department of Agriculture. Within the last five or ten years, the colleges of agriculture have been

[1] Doctor Knapp had for some time been associated with Secretary of Agriculture, James Wilson, as professor of agriculture at the Iowa Agricultural College and at his request had investigated rice culture in Japan. Later Secretary Wilson commissioned him to study the agricultural situation in Texas and then appointed him to organize and carry on the extension work there.

able to attack the problem of rural life in a new way. This extension work includes such efforts as local agricultural surveys, demonstrations on farms, nature study and other work in schools boy's and girls' clubs of many kinds, crop organizations, redirection of rural societies, reading clubs, library extension, lectures, traveling schools, farmers' nstitutes, inspections of herds, barns, crops, orchards and farms, publications of many kinds, and similar educational effort directly in the ield.

To accomplish these ends, we suggest the establishment of a naion wide extension work. The first or original work of the agricultural branches of the land-grant colleges was academic in the old sense; later there was added the great field of experiment and reearch; there now should be added the third coordinate branch, comprising extension work, without which no college of agriculture can adequately serve its state. It is to the extension department of these olleges, if properly conducted, that we must now look for the most effective rousing of the people on the land.

Principles Underlying the Cooperative Agricultural Extension Work.—The essence of the system is demonstration; but this demonstration is not done by a specialist without the ull and active interest and cooperation of the farmers themelves. That is to say, it is a new kind of demonstration and nlists the actual cooperation of the farmer to the extent that he himself usually makes the demonstration, instead of having he specialist perform it as is the case on model farms. In agriculture a demonstration in this sense would be the planting and cultivating of a field or portion of a field according to explicit instructions given the farmer by an extension speialist, or the raising of livestock according to instructions. This is essentially different from the older methods of merely alking or even demonstrating to some extent before groups of farmers who were after all not an actual part of the effort of the speaker. Neither does the work of the model farm ttract the farmer, even though it were accessible to all, sufciently to cause him to accept advanced methods of agriculure. Only by actually doing the work himself can the farmrs learn to incorporate generally into agricultural practice he scientific principles worked out by the experiment stations, he United States Department of Agriculture and progressive armers. The fundamental principle embodied in this method f education is expressed by Dr. Knapp in the following tatement:

It is noteworthy that the sciences adopted the demonstration method of instruction long since. The chemist and physicist require

> their students to work out their problems in the laboratory, the docto and surgeon must practice in the hospital, and the mechanical enginee must show efficiency in the shop to complete his education. Th Farmers' Cooperative Demonstration Work seeks to apply the sam scientific methods to farmers by requiring them to work out thei problems in the soil and obtain the answer in the crib. The soil i the farmers' laboratory.
>
> The demonstration method of reaching and influencing the me on the farms is destined ultimately to be adopted by most civilize nations as a part of a great system of rural education.[1]

Dr. Knapp's system of extension was not limited to agri culture and livestock or the work of the men. His schem included the enlistment of the interests of the boys and girl not only for the reason that these will be the men and wome in the next generation and the educative process should begi early, but also for the reason that through the boys and girls and especially the girls, the parents are readily interested. Th same fundamental principle, that is demonstration, was to b used in educating the boys and girls. With respect to th work among the girls the term "home demonstration" wa chosen advisedly as pointed out by Dr. Bradford Knapp, so of the founder of the cooperative extension system and th man who actively continued the work begun in the South afte the death of Dr. S. A. Knapp in 1911. The system of educa tion included the work of the household and it was wisel planned, as stated, to reach the women through the girls. Th interest of the mothers was very readily enlisted through th demonstrations conducted by the daughters. All this wor is referred to as "home demonstration work" and include not only the activities that are directly concerned with th rural home, such as, home-building, home beautification, foo clothing, shelter, etc., but also such occupations of agricultur over which the housewife usually presides, including garden ing, poultry-raising, etc., and the marketing of these product at a profit.[2]

It should be stated that the idea of extension work itsel that is the cooperative demonstration plan and the use of

---

[1] From an article by Dr. Seaman A. Knapp in the *Yearbook* fo 1909 p. 160.

[2] *Vide* paper by Dr. Bradford Knapp in *Proceedings* of Thirty-thir Annual Convention of the Association of Land-Grant Colleges.

county agent, was for some time quite generally opposed not only by his co-workers and associates in the Department, but also by some agricultural specialists outside. All of the early organization was effected in spite of opposition, and the support from the Department was at first not what it could have been if everybody had fully realized from the beginning the efficiency of the system. Also it should be stated that the favorable action on the part of the General Education Board was largely due to the efforts of Dr. Knapp.

The Development of Extension Organization.—These principles of popular agricultural education were first tried out in Texas and Louisiana. The program was a broad one and included the encouragement of better agricultural practice and more diversification as well as the use of practical methods to diminish the ravages of the cotton boll weevil. Dr. Knapp represented the Department of Agriculture and secured the cooperation of business men and several thousand farmers in Texas and Louisiana and extended into Arkansas and Oklahoma. At this time the General Education Board of New York, in view of benefits accruing from the demonstration plan, offered funds for its extension beyond the cotton boll weevil territory.[1] This offer was accepted by the Secretary of Agriculture and the work was extended into Mississippi, Alabama, and Virginia. Extension agents in non-boll weevil territory were paid out of funds provided by the General Education Board,[2] only $1 being paid them by the Department so as to make them Government employes. The Board increased its appropriations from time to time. Starting with $7,000 in 1907 the fund from this source rose to $187,500 in 1914. The appropriations from Congress also grew rapidly as the effectiveness of the cooperative extension idea was more and more appreciated.

During this formative period the demonstration agents covered as much territory as 10 to 15 counties. It was soon felt that much more effective work could be accomplished if the agent's territory were reduced. The first agent to work exclusively in one county was W. C. Stallings of Smith County,

---

[1] *Vide Report on Cooperative Agricultural Extension Work in the United States* for 1915, p. 16.

[2] This board is supported by Rockfeller funds.

Texas, who was appointed November 12, 1906,[1] and this method was destined to become the plan of organization for the entire country. In his report to the Department in 1908, Doctor Knapp made the following significant statement:

> A few demonstration farms scattered throughout the county, say five or six, such as would be the case where one agent had charge of seven or eight counties—do not create sufficient public sentiment and moral force to change the long established usages of the masses. There must be at least five or six demonstration farms and quite a number of cooperators in each township so that practically we reach every neighborhood, arouse interest and competition everywhere, and arouse the whole community. To do this requires at least one agent in each county.

The work thus initiated by the Department and generously supported from 1907 to 1914 by the General Education Board received State recognition for the first time in 1909. That year the State of Mississippi enacted a law under which the county might pay part of the salary of the county agent. From 1909 to 1915 all southern States having constitutional power to grant such authority to the county passed laws permitting their cooperation with the Department of Agriculture in financing the farmers' cooperative demonstration work. These payments to county agents were made out of county revenues. As early as 1911, States began making appropriations direct for the purpose. Alabama made such an appropriation that year.

The organization grew rapidly over the entire South and after 1911 also in the North and West. In the North the cooperative extension plan was first introduced in Broome County, New York, March 11, 1911. On that date the Bureau of Plant Industry of the United States Department of Agriculture appointed John Barron agent for the county, the cooperative parties in the plan being the New York State College of Agriculture, the Binghamton Chamber of Commerce, and the Delaware, Lackawanna and Western Railroad. Commercial organizations and railways have come to recognize the importance of the relation of improved agriculture to business. The first work done by the agent in Broome County was to attend Grange and other local meetings of farmers with a view to get acquainted with their problems.

---

[1] O. B. Martin, *The Demonstration Work*, p. 6.

About the same time that Broome County started its work the Grain Improvement Committee of Chicago offered $1,000 to each of 100 counties that should first organize county agent work. Under this stimulus together with the encouragement coming from the Department to which was given increased funds by Congress for this type of work, many States passed laws permitting counties to give cooperative support, and the county agent movement spread rapidly throughout the North and West. In this part of the United States by June 30, 1912, there were three county agents; at the end of the fiscal year 1913 there were 113; at the end of 1914 there were 203; and by June 30, 1915, there were 340.

In the South the work in the meantime continued to expand both east and west from its point of origin, and its activities were broadened and extended into all lines of agriculture. The boys and girls were included in the movement and already in 1907, boys' corn clubs were organized in Texas and Mississippi. The growth of the movement in the South is shown in the following table taken from the Report on Extension Work, 1915:

Number of agents engaged in farmers' cooperative demonstration work since its beginning in 1904 to 1915, inclusive, in cooperation with colleges, counties and local organizations.

State	1904[1]	1905[1]	1906[1]	1907	1908	1909	1910	1911[2]	1912[2]	1913[2]	1914[2]	1915[2]
Texas	......	......	......	20	28	55	65	71	134	116	133	128
Oklahoma	......	......	......	......	8	16	30	34	54	54	67	83
Louisiana	......	......	......	9	13	44	46	49	60	54	68	58
Arkansas	......	......	......	6	12	28	50	54	68	71	80	83
Mississippi	......	......	......	7	23	37	40	54	78	68	80	84
Alabama	......	......	......	5	17	32	43	83	95	91	101	95
Georgia	......	......	......	......	7	28	53	57	86	99	112	118
Florida	......	......	......	......	......	2	14	14	40	40	61	66
South Carolina	......	......	......	......	15	27	43	56	69	68	84	84
North Carolina	......	......	......	......	13	24	51	51	73	91	108	116
Virginia	......	......	......	2	17	24	28	50	65	79	92	99
Maryland	......	......	......	......	......	......	......	......	6	7	18	23
Tennessee	......	......	......	......	......	......	1	10	23	40	49	67
Kentucky	......	......	......	......	......	......	......	......	......	......	43	69
West Virginia	......	......	......	......	......	......	......	......	......	......	42	56
Total	15	20	25	49	153	317	464	583	851	878	1,138	1,229

[1] Estimate. No records available to show the actual number in each State.

[2] Includes women agents.

Causes for Success.—The underlying principles of the agricultural cooperative extension service responsible for its phenomenal growth are no doubt (1) trained leadership, (2) the demonstration method which tests out ideas and which is the very essence of extension work, (3) the actual participation of farmers in demonstration work and the degree of interest aroused in the improvement of agriculture, and (4) a measure of local control in the management of the affairs of the organization. In the South local control was at first not so conspicuous, but at least a large number of people participated in actual demonstration work. In the end it is always true that while a movement must be initiated by leaders and must be largely directed by them, it can never gain much momentum or have any permanency unless the people are given a measure of control or at least an active participation in the application of its aims and purposes. The initiative taken by outside parties in giving funds to the community in support of the project had, of course, a good deal to do with getting it started. On the question of development, Doctor True has the following to say:

The relation of the people in the farming communities to the extension work is somewhat difficult to define. Historically it has passed through different stages of development. Doctor Knapp's idea apparently was that the demonstration agents should be located permanetly in close contact with the farming people and in full sympathy with them. The agents sought the advice of representative leaders in the community, but the program of work was quite definitely determined by the extension authorities. It is only recently that anything like farm bureaus have been attempted in the South. Doctor Knapp's organization was originally independent of the colleges, and largely continued to be so until the passage of the Smith-Lever Act. In the North the county agent work from the outset was associated with the agricultural colleges, but was at first largely promoted by business organizations and this had some unfortunate results. When it became apparent that to be successful it must have the larger interest of the farmers they were brought into active participation but have never had full measure of control. It was soon evident that the county agents would not do their best work by simply rendering personal service to individual farmers but should work through groups of farmers. This was the main reason for the organization of the farm bureaus. The relationships of the different parties connected with the extension work are most nearly ideal when there is a real partnership and the whole enterprise is truly cooperative. The cooperating parties are usually the Department of Agriculture, the state agricultural colleges, the county governments and the farm bureau or other farm organization. Under good conditions the question of control of the county agent by any one of the parties does not arise. As far as he is supported by public funds he is, necessarily, a public official and should work in the interest of all the people rather than as an agent of any private organization.[1]

When the United States entered the war the extension service had already been well organized throughout the country, and it was a machinery that stood us in good stead. The gospel of increased production and of selective consumption was through it brought home in a systematic and persistent way throughout the length and breadth of the land.

The Smith-Lever Act.—This act was approved May 8, 1914, and had for its purpose the taking over of the cooperative agricultural extension work so generously supported up to this time by the General Education Board of New York and to combine it with the other kinds of extension work which had been carried on by the agricultural colleges and the United States Department of Agriculture. The act provided for cooperative extension work between the agricultural colleges in the several States and the Department of Agriculture. Cooperative agricultural extension work is defined in the act as consisting "of the giving of instruction and practical demonstration in agriculture and home economics to persons not attending or resident in said colleges in the several communities, and imparting to such persons information on said subjects through field demonstrations, publications, and otherwise."

Section 3 of the act provides for the permanent annual appropriation of $480,000, of which $10,000 is to be paid annually to each of the 48 States. In addition to this sum it also provides for an appropriation of $600,000 for the year following the above appropriation, "and for each year thereafter for seven years a sum exceeding by $500,000 the sum appropriated for each preceding year, and for each year thereafter there is permanently appropriated for each year the sum of $4,100,000 in addition to the sum of $480,000." These additional funds shall be allotted to each State by the Secretary of Agriculture in the proportion which the rural population of each State

[1] From a personal communication received from Dr. A. C. True, under date of May 22, 1922.

bears to the total rural population of all the States. It also provides that no payment out of the additional appropriations shall be made to any State unless "an equal sum has been appropriated for that year by the legislature of such State, or provided by State, county, college, local authority, or individual contributions from within the States, for the maintenance of the cooperative agricultural extension work provided for in this act." According to the terms of the act the sum of $480,000 or $10,000 for each state is appropriated without requiring that the sum be matched with an equal contribution by the State, county or other local agency. The additional sum of $4,100,000 ultimately available under the act, however, must be so matched by the state or local agency.

Legislative assent must be given by the states to secure the benefits of the act, or until this is done the Governor of the State may enter into an agreement with the Department of Agriculture concerning the provisions of the act. It devolves upon the Secretary of Agriculture to ascertain whether or not states have complied with the provisions and whether or not they are entitled to receive their share of the appropriation. To carry out this provision the Secretary of Agriculture and the chief executive of the college sign a memorandum setting forth the project agreements or the plan of cooperative work to be carried out during the year. In practice the colleges draw up their own projects and plans of work and propose them to the Department, which approves or disapproves them according as to whether or not they comply with the law.

General Organization.—In previous chapters the various bureaus and offices of the Department of Agriculture have been discussed. The organization of the State Agricultural Colleges has likewise been discussed. It is well now at this point to show all this extensive organization created during the last half century in the interest of agricultural improvement. The organization is splendidly presented in the accompanying chart, which is taken from a circular of the States Relations Service, *Doc. 90.*

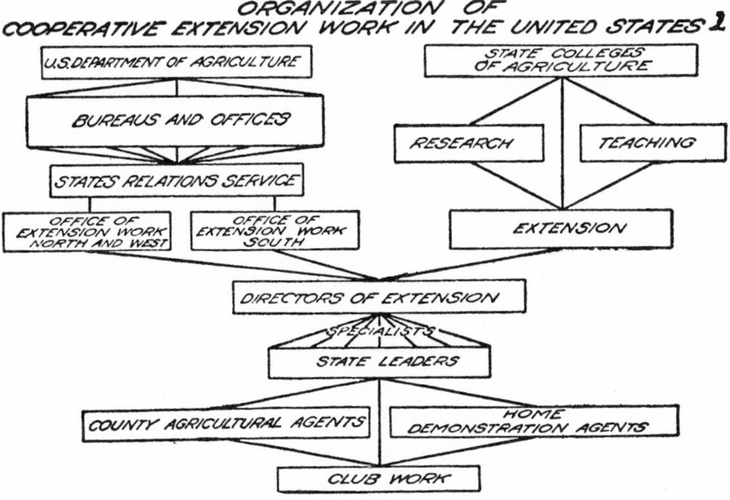

In previous chapters numerous references were made to extension or demonstration activities of the various bureaus and offices. In the discussion of the States Relations Service it was pointed out that all such activities are expected to function through this bureau. By a glance at the chart it is seen that all extension work performed by specialists of other bureaus is centered in the States Relations Service, which performs the administrative duties incident to such work. The chart shows the connection between this office and the directors of extension who are appointed by the State Agricultural Colleges with the approval of the United States Department of Agriculture. The organization of agricultural colleges has also been discussed. It was shown that all extension service emanating from the colleges is centered in the director of extension, and that he appoints state leaders who supervise and supplement the work of county men and women agents and specialists who assist county agents and give instruction to farmers direct where there are no county agents. The specialists have a thorough knowledge of some particular subject and are not confined in their operations to the limits

[1] The two offices of extension work shown under the States Relations Service have been combined into one under the name of Office of Extension Work.

of a county, but may be called to do service anywhere in the State, or if Department specialists, anywhere in the country. The extension director frequently calls upon members of the teaching staff of the agricultural college and sometimes upon those of the liberal arts college to do the work of specialists.

Thus there are three main parts in the cooperative agriculture extension service: the United States Department of Agriculture, the state agricultural colleges, and some form of organization among the farmers in the county. The county organization consists of farm bureaus, county councils, or county boards of agriculture. Wherever possible the county agents establish helpful relations with various farmers' and welfare organizations. There is a cooperative agreement between the colleges and the Department which provides that each college shall maintain an administrative division for the management and conduct of extension work, and as already stated, there is also cooperation between these two parts with respect to the kind of extension work that is to be carried on from year to year. There is likewise cooperation between the county organization and the other two parts concerning the character of the extension program. The employment of the county agents is also done cooperatively, the extension director through the state leaders usually suggesting parties who are qualified for the position.

State Leaders.—In each state the extension director has administrative charge of the whole system and the state leaders of county agricultural work, home demonstration work, and boys' and girls' club work are coordinate officials under the extension director. These leaders supervise the three classes of work. They travel about the state considerably and have their headquarters at the college of agriculture. There are also assistant state leaders and district agents who assist in supervising the work of the county officials. They serve to supplement the work of the county men and women agents. They see to it that the objects of the extension service as agreed to between the college of agriculture and the Secretary of Agriculture are properly carried out.

In the early stages of the cooperative agricultural extension service the leaders having charge of the county agricultural agents also functioned in the capacity of organizers of farm bureaus. The farm bureaus at first were organized exclusively for the purpose of cooperating with the extension forces and carrying out the objects of the extension service in the community. As such it was deemed proper for the county agents and their leaders to organize farm bureaus. This was particularly true after we entered the European war when the government desired to have organization in the farming communities through which it could know what the farmers were doing and communicate to them its wishes regarding agricultural production. During the war therefore an important function of the leaders was to organize farm bureaus. The extension forces during this period took a very active part in organizing farm bureaus especially in the North and West. After the war considerable opposition on the part of farmers' organizations developed to the initiative taken by the extension forces to organize the farmers locally due to the fact that the farm bureaus of the counties in the various states federated into state and national organizations and began to function in exactly the same way as the Grange, the Farmers' Union, the Equity, and other farmers' organizations. That is to say, they effected an organization whose chief aims and purposes are the promotion of specific legislation and the improvement of their economic status as a class. When this federation took form it became at once apparent that it would not be proper for the United States Government to help organize farm bureaus. Hence leaders and county agents are no longer permitted to serve as organizers.

The County Agricultural Agent.—"The county agricultural agent is a local extension representative of the state agricultural college, the United States Department of Agriculture, and the people of the county." The county agent to be successful must possess the qualities of leadership. He must have an education in agriculture and be thoroughly familiar with farm practices. He must be in sympathy with rural life and deeply interested in its problems. He must be tactful, enthusiastic and optimistic. A liberal education including public speaking and music often stand him in good stead. In other words a good county agent first of all should be well grounded in scientific agriculture, but he should be ready to take the initiative in a social way in public gatherings and in a general way he must take an active part as a citizen in the life of the community in order to enjoy the full confidence of the people. An important principle that he must observe is to work with groups of farmers in the capacity of an adviser. He should assist rather than direct. This attitude will secure the greatest degree of cooperation and participation on the part of individuals or local organizations of whatever form they may be.

The duties of the county agricultural agent as stated by Doctor True are as follows: "It is the duty of the county agent to bring to the farmers of his county on their own farms the results of scientific investigations in agriculture and the experience of successful farmers, and through demonstrations to influence the farmers to put these into practice. He assists in reorganizing and redirecting the agriculture of the community and assists all economic and social forces working for the improvement of agriculture and country life. He gives instruction not only in those subjects which are generally recognized under the head of improved agricultural practices but also in farm management, marketing, and purchasing supplies. He carries on a great part of this instruction through farm demonstrations. In these demonstrations the farmer undertakes with his own labor and entirely at his own expense, to grow some particular crop of livestock under the agent's supervision and direction, or to form and conduct organizations for standardizing his animals or crops, marketing, community welfare, etc." [1]

The County Home Demonstration Agent.—The qualifications of a home demonstration agent should be similar to those of the agricultural agent. Like him she is a local representative of the extension service. Her duties are to give instruction and information to farm women and girls. "The annual programs of work in the several communities are made up after consultation with the local people and with a view to meet their immediate needs. Only a few subjects are stressed

[1] From a pamphlet issued by the States Relations Service.

in the individual programs." The range of work includes: income-yielding industries for farm women, such as gardening, poultry, butter and cheese making, canning, etc., the various processes of preserving food; the problems of nutrition or the selection and preparation of food for the family including children and invalids; garment making including dyeing, dry cleaning and remodeling; personal hygiene and home sanitation including the proper disposal of sewage; the selection of a good water supply; the rudiments of home nursing; house planning and furnishing including the beautification of home grounds; household management including the rearrangement of kitchens, running water, bathing equipment, etc., the family budget; and community enterprises such as cooperative buying and selling associations, eggs circles, community markets, food centers, canning kitchens, rest rooms, and recreation centers.

"The work is generally conducted through organized groups of women. The organization and method of conducting the work vary somewhat in the different states. In some of the States the home demonstration agent operates through the same organization as the county agent, while in other states the women of the communities have been organized into separate voluntary organizations or clubs for the purpose of receiving instruction. The women instructed are expected to test out or 'demonstrate' in their own homes the instructions received."[1] Thus the idea of agricultural extension has been broadened to include the work and life of the entire farm. The home is so essentially a part of the business of farming that the success of one is dependent upon the other, and it was therefore wise that the extension service conceived the plan of employing a woman county agent, trained in home economics and commonly known as a home demonstration agent, along with the county agricultural agent, commonly known as the county agent, who devotes his attention to the work of the fields and farming generally. Whether or not a county employs more persons than the agricultural agent may be dependent upon its wealth and economic resources or upon the

[1] From a pamphlet by the State Relations Service.

progressive and cooperative sentiment prevailing among its population.

Boys' and Girls' Club Work.—The first boys' and girls' club work was begun in a few of the northern states by county school superintendents here and there on an independent basis. These efforts were more or less intermittent and failed to make any headway because continuous leadership was lacking. In 1904, 1905 and 1906 the extension departments of the State colleges of agriculture in Iowa, Indiana and Ohio, in some cases cooperating with the department of education, "took up extension work along the lines of corn clubs or contests, home-garden projects, poultry, milk-testing work, and made them State-wide activities."[1] In 1907 the Department of Agriculture took its first steps concerning club work when it organized a boys' club in Holmes County, Mississippi. This was followed up in 1909 by a systematic effort by the farmers' cooperative demonstration agents to organize a few counties in every southern State. In 1912 Congress appropriated some funds for use by the Department of Agriculture in organizing boys' clubs. Two cooperative leaders were employed to start the work in Iowa and Indiana. In 1913 the organization efforts were carried into Massachusetts, Nebraska, Utah and Michigan. As seen by Doctor S. A. Knapp, to whom much credit is given for the rapid advancement of the movement, there are large educational possibilities as well as other advantages resident in boys' and girls' club work. In 1907 he said, the club work trains the boys "to do something and to know something." Three years before the organization of girls' club work he said: "A country home, be it ever so plain, with a father and mother of sense and gentle culture, is nature's university, and is more richly endowed for the training of youth than Yale or Harvard." The girls' club work was begun in 1910 in Virginia and in South Carolina.

Through boys' and girls' club work the extension service brings agricultural education or vocational training to the rural youth of the land. In 1921 the membership in these clubs was 500,000. Much could be said of the educational

[1] Report on Extension Work, 1915, p. 160.

value of the projects to the boy and girl performing them as well as of the social and economic benefits that flow from the system as these young generations rise into manhood and womanhood, serving as efficient producers and steadily improving the standard of living. It is certainly the means of enlisting the interest of the youth in agriculture and of more rapidly introducing scientific methods and improved practices. It helps to provide an intellectual medium for the exercise of the minds of the young people and make them more content with the rural environment.

The clubs are supervised by state agents or club leaders having headquarters at the agricultural colleges. In the county the work is directed by the county agricultural agent, the home demonstration agent, or local club leader.

The local boys' clubs elect officers and hold regular meetings. They choose any line of work offered by the club organization. The program of work usually decided upon concerns some important phase of agriculture carried on in the community. It is for this reason that there are so many pig clubs and corn clubs. Besides these there are peanut, potato, wheat, bean, cotton, poultry, beef cattle, and sheep clubs. Similar work is being done among the negro boys in the South. The requirements in club work are that the boy or girl shall be between 10 and 18 years of age; that each member undertake a definite task, which in crop work must be not less than one acre in extent; and that instructions be followed, that a record be kept, and that a report of the results be made. The boys and girls do not always belong to exclusive clubs. They are often found mixed in garden and pig clubs. A favorite project for the girls is canning. At a club meeting instruction on the projects undertaken is given and the occasion also affords opportunity for recreation, practice in organization work, and the formation of the cooperative spirit. The results of these demonstrations which are thus brought home to a very large part of the agricultural population of the United States have a very far-reaching stimulating effect upon the community in general. It affords many examples that the county agent may use to good effect in the proposal of a program of work to the community committee or other local organization.

Interest in club work is stimulated through the exhibition of products at fairs at the close of the season, through the awarding of prizes to winners, through the giving of short courses to winners at the State agricultural colleges, and in other ways. The boys' and girls' club certificate given by the agricultural colleges doubtless solicits the interest of the members and impresses them with the importance of the undertaking.

Extension Schools and Meetings.—In addition to the regular contract that the county agricultural and home demonstration agents make with the local farming groups at regular meetings, special meetings and extension schools are held at which extension specialists from the colleges of agriculture and the United States Department of Agriculture give instruction along special lines of work. These extension specialists are to be distinguished from the local county agents by the fact that their field of operation is the state if employed by the colleges and the entire country if employed by the Department. They also differ from the county agents in their training, inasmuch as they have specialized in their education and experience in some one subject, such a dairying, horticulture, poultry-raising, or food and nutrition, and are therefore qualified to speak with authority along these lines. In addition to the specialists who devote all their time to aiding county agents or instructing farmers direct where there are no county agents, members of the teaching staff of the colleges are often called upon by the extension director to address farmers' meetings.

The extension school is a more or less serious attempt to instruct the farmers in some phase of agriculture. Local arrangements are usually made by the county agent and the program of study is frequently planned with a view to assist the development of extension projects undertaken in the county. Practical courses of instruction, accompanied by demonstrations, illustrated lectures, and exhibits are organized and conducted by specialists attached to the agricultural colleges. In most instances these schools last during the greater part of a week.

There are also a very large number of other farmers' meetings lasting for a day or two. Many are conducted under the name of farmers' institutes. Others are designated general neighborhood meetings, conferences, etc. At such meetings specialists from the colleges and the Department, experiment station workers, county agents, practical farmers and others give addresses and demonstrations.

The Necessity for Local Organization.—In order that the extension spirit, that is the spirit of demonstration, education, and progress may be thoroughly aroused among the farming people in all communities, it is highly essential that the extension service operate through organized groups instead of through individuals. It is altogether impossible to do extension work with the same degree of expeditiousness through the individual alone as through the group. Contact is readily made, between the extension forces and the officials of a local organization. A large number of people can be instructed at one time. Of fundamental importance, however, is the participation, self-help, spread of interest, and permanency of effort that comes from group action. Local organization of the farmers with whom the extension forces might cooperate was therefore from the beginning conceived to be a necessary feature of the extension system. Leading men in the community had to be interested in the demonstration idea. A number of them had to be made willing to carry out a project according to specific instructions. These demonstrators had to have the moral and financial support of other prominent citizens, such as preachers, bankers, physicians, school superintendents, and general business men. This combination would comprise a council or local agency to cooperate with the county agent.

The Development of Local Organization.—In the South the agricultural or farm council was for some time the common medium through which the county agent worked. *The Progressive Farmer,* a prominent southern agricultural journal, under date of November 1, 1919, described the organization of the farm council and its operation as follows:

The council has appointed five subcommittees, each one charged with a clearly defined share of the agricultural work of the county, and each one representative in that it includes a leading citizen from every district or beat.

The subcommittees and their duties are, roughly as follows: The executive committee advises directly with the agent on general matters and when the council cannot meet, acts in its stand. The marketing committee lists live stock or other farm produce to be shipped and sends the list to the county agent. This group also assists the agent in all details of handling shipments, such as weighing, grading, and loading. The crop and soil improvement committee studies the cropping system and makes recommendations concerning it; studies methods of improving the soil; and is now working on a somewhat flexible system of farming for the county as a whole. The finance committee handles all general funds, as those resulting from shipping, and the publicity committee disseminates information of general value, such as outbreaks of disease, shipping dates, agricultural "drives," and the like.[1]

In most cases the farm council was a loose and more or less inefficient form of local organization. Recently the farm bureau has been very generally organized in the South.

Several forms of farm bureau organizations sprang up throughout the country as stated by the States Relations Service in *Document 65*. One form is a county-wide association having a representative membership of farmers scattered generally through the county and usually paying a small annual membership fee. The organization meets annually and elects a board of directors or executive committee. Sometimes an additional body known as an advisory council is appointed to make recommendations to the executive committee. The executive committee usually meets monthly and the advisory council meets at the call of the president in a body or in community groups. This form of organization was used in 1917 by a number of States including Connecticut, Idaho, Kansas, New York and Vermont.

A second form of organization is one that has a central association made up of delegates from local associations covering townships or other local districts. The fee is often divided, part going to the support of the county organization and part to the support of the local. The locals are sometimes called farm-bureau centers. Monthly meetings are usually held by the locals, while the county association meets at the call of the president. This was a type of farm bureau

[1] Quoted from O. B. Martin's *Demonstration Work*, p. 123.

that was used in 1917 in California and Utah, and in a few counties in Colorado.

In Colorado, Michigan, and Minnesota the agricultural societies in the county including farmers' clubs, granges, farmers' unions, gleaners' equities, etc., appoint a federation committee made up of delegations from the respective societies. The societies comprise the local organization. The central association or federation committee has only advisory power.

A plan developed in Oregon consists of a county agricultural council made up also of delegates from societies in the county, but including one member of the county board of commissioners and three or more representatives of the unorganized farming population.

Another plan consists of non-federated agricultural clubs having no central organization. In some cases, however, coordination is brought about through a board of control which may be the county commissioners or board of education, or a committee of the chamber of commerce. In 1917 agents in Wisconsin and Delaware worked through such dissociated clubs.

As already stated the local organization cooperating with the home demonstration agent in some places is the same as the one through which the agricultural agent works. In some states, notably New York and Illinois, a separate organization has been formed known as the "home bureau." In the opinion of some officials of the United States Department of Agriculture this is a mistake. Doctor True for instance prefers a single organization in which all the activities of the farm household are represented. Others believe that the home bureau as a county organization concerned only with the problems of the home proper and comprising only women among its members will of necessity emphasize home demonstration work and give it more attention than it receives if it is associated with agricultural work.

Whatever the status of the local organization for agricultural and home demonstration work there should be a degree of cooperation. With respect to boys' and girls' club work cooperation between the workers in the two fields is highly essential.

A Suggested Farm-Bureau Organization.—It is to be borne

in mind that the extension forces no longer give any encouragement to the organization of farm bureaus. The States Relations Service of the United States Department of Agriculture as well as the agricultural colleges by reason of recent developments in farm-bureau organization now look upon the local farm bureau as they would upon the local unit of any farmers' organization. So long as the farm bureau remained what it was originally, that is merely an educational agency to cooperate with the extension forces, and kept its hands off commercial enterprises, such as cooperative producing, buying and selling associations which have always been more or less vigorously fostered by the old farmers' organizations and therefore jealously guarded by them as their own field of activity, the States Relations Service and other extension officials could organize farm bureaus without arousing hostility anywhere. During the early history of the agricultural cooperative extension service the States Relations Service of the United States Department of Agriculture took an active interest in the organization of farm bureaus and after studying the various types of organization suggested in its *Document 65* a county organization of which the chief features are the following:

A representative membership, made up largely of farmers scattered generally over the county, each paying a nominal membership fee.

An executive committee of not more than nine or ten members.

(1) Representation may be given on this committee to the strong, active, existing county agricultural organizations, such as the county federation of farmers' clubs, Pomona Grange, the county organization of the farmers' union, and of the society of equity, also to the public schools, usually through the county superintendent.

(2) So far as possible the executive committeemen selected should be well distributed over the county, but in large counties committeemen may be selected with regard to their accessibility to the county seat, or to such other central place where the executive committee conferences may be held.

(3) Only those who can and will devote the necessary time to the work and who are able to attend the meetings of the committee should be selected.

(4) Each member should be selected because of special qualifications to head some important project or important line of work of the bureau.

A Community Committee, consisting of a chairman and two to four members in each district or community in the county with:

(1) Representation given to the strong, active, existing agricu

tural organizations of the community as subordinate granges, cow-testing associations, etc.

(2) Members well distributed over the community.

(3) Each member selected because of special fitness to direct some important part of the community program of work.

A county agricultural council, consisting of the chairman of the the various community committees.

While *Document 65* of the States Relations Service as well as its activity in organizing farm bureaus must now be regarded as mere historical indicents, it still remains true that the type of farm bureau that was suggested is a good form of local organization and one that can bring good results to any community. Inasmuch as farm bureaus are now federated the organization of new local units has now been taken over by the State and national organizations, but this fact does not seem sufficient reason why the extension forces should not exert themselves to organize farmers locally along the above lines where there is no organization or where there is no concerted action among existing organizations for the sole purpose of carrying out the spirit of the extension service. It would seem that the very type of organization suggested in *Document 65*, could be advocated by the extension forces providing extension work be kept entirely separate and distinct from commercial and other class activities as provided for in the memorandum of understanding signed by the representatives of the States Relations Service and the American Farm Bureau Federation, which, of course, admittedly is very difficult. The point is, that the extension service must cooperate through groups of farmers to bring to the county the greatest benefits, for the money expended, and the logic of the situation demands that some kind of initiative be taken by the extension forces to organize the farmers into groups of some sort.

The Local Organization at Work.—Whatever the form of the local organization, it should be of sufficient extent to include a large proportion of the farmers in the county in its membership. Officers including an executive committee should be elected whose duty it is to make up financial budgets, to raise the necessary funds, to authorize the expenditure of money, to determine the policy of the local organization and to cooperate with the state agricultural college in the employment of a county agricultural agent, a home demonstration agent, boys' and girls' club leaders, and other local extension workers nominated or approved by the extension director.

The States Relations Service gives specific examples of the division of projects among members of the executive committee of a farm bureau. In a grain and livestock county in one of the central states the division is as follows: The president is charged with the administration of the bureau; the first vice-president with the project of orchard demonstrations; the second vice-president with farm accounting, farm management, summer and winter meetings; the secretary and treasurer with farm bureau news and advertising; the member representing the county commissioners with finance; the member representing the county fair with demonstrations and exhibition; the member representing the farmers' cooperative elevators with crop improvement and building plans; the member representing the livestock cooperative shipping association with livestock improvement; the county superintendent also a member, is charged with boys' and girls' club work; the member representing the farmers' clubs is charged with cooperation between farmers' clubs, and the development of better marketing facilities; there is one woman on the committee who has charge of home demonstration work. In other parts of the country the respective duties of the committeemen vary in accordance with the type of agriculture and special needs of the community there prevailing. The county agent should aid and direct each committee-man in the development of his project and in time these men become trained local county leaders.

In each community there should be a community committee made up of from three to five local leaders in agriculture. These are appointed by the president of the county organization subject to the approval of the executive committee. If an agricultural society is strong and popular in the community the matter of appointment of members of the community committee should be taken up with its officers so as to avoid jealousy and hostility on the part of the society. The selection should also be made with reference to specialized farming interests. Dairying, poultry raising, hog raising, etc., should be represented by men who have wide experience in these fields. Definite duties are assigned to each member of the committee. It is the duty of this committee to develop a local agricultural program. It will have the assistance of the president and especially the county agent who is expected to meet with the community committee as frequently as time permits. The committee brings assistance to the community through arranging for field demonstrations and winter meetings. It advertises such meetings and demonstrations in the community and tries to develop a general interest in extension work.

The Relationship Between the Extension Service and Farm Bureaus.—The farm bureau has been for some time the principal organization through which the county agent operates, and yet this organization has broadened its scope of work in various ways including the publishing of a paper in places, or the carrying on of a business of considerable proportions. It conducts membership campaigns, distributes literature, and performs functions that are not directly related to objects for which the Extension Service was created. If the county agent, who is paid partly by federal funds, devotes his time in part to these newer functions of the farm bureau the expenditure of Federal funds is not legal under the terms of the act. In order that there may be a clear understanding as to the type of work that the county agent may perform a *memorandum of understanding* was drawn up by the States Relations Service of the Department of Agriculture and signed by Doctor True representing the Department and J. R. Howard, president of the American Farm Bureau Federation, under date of April 22, 1921. An extract of this memorandum sets forth the relationship between the Extension Service and the farm bureaus as follows:

Since these county extension agents are part of a public service defined in the Smith Lever Act, and receive some part of their salary from public funds, they are to perform service for the benefit of all the farming people of the county whether members of the farm bureaus or not, and are to confine their activities to such as are appropriate for public officials to perform under the terms of the Smith-Lever Act. The county agents will aid the farming people in a broad way with reference to problems of production, marketing, and formation of farm bureaus and other cooperative organizations, but will not themselves organize farm bureaus or similar organizations, conduct membership campaigns, solicit membership, receive dues, handle farm bureau funds, edit and manage the farm bureau publications, manage the business of the farm bureau, engage in commercial activities or take part in other farm bureau activities which are outside their duties as extension agents.

In order that the farm bureau as an organization may continue to carry on the functions not included in the Smith- Lever Act the memorandum suggests that the farm bureau organize itself into departments, one of which is to be called the extension department which is to make its contact with the county agent. The other departments would carry on the business and other functions of the bureau and would not be managed by the county agent. Other clerks or employes would have to be appointed to manage these departments. There is no reason why this plan cannot be carried out if all parties concerned have a clear understanding of the limits of their functions and at the same time are conscientious in the performance of their duties. It is not at all unlikely that many county agents, because they must please the people with whom they work, readily incline to perform services that fall outside of extension services. In other words, to keep the extension service at the point of contact with the people wholly divorced from farmers' organizations is not always an easy task.

Growth of the Cooperative Agricultural Extension Work.—There are some good things that come out of war, and one of these good things attributable to the European war is its stimulus to the organization of the agricultural forces of the country. While the extension movement was in no way initiated by the war as was shown in the discussion of its development, the movement of organizing counties was, however, greatly accelerated because of the need of more concerted action. The growth in the number of county agents from 1915 to 1918 is as follows:

Year	*County Agents*
1918	2,435
1917	1,434
1916	1,225
1915	1,136

During this same period the number of home demonstration agents grew as follows:

Year	*Home Demonstration Agents*
1918	1,715
1917	537
1916	430
1915	350

While the employment of a home demonstration agent is essential in extension work, she is usually the second county agent to be employed, the agricultural agent being usually the first worker in the county. In many counties funds are insufficient to employ more than one agent. This accounts for the smaller number of home demonstration agents. Professor Burritt suggests that another reason for the small number is the failure to develop an adequate organization for the support of these agents in most States. In New York and Illinois "home bureaus" have been developed to cooperate with the home demonstration agents, and this he thinks is largely due to the fact that women agents in these states have steadily increased. The county agent work had its origin in the South, as previously stated, which accounts for its very general adoption in nearly all parts of the southern States.

Statistics of extension workers exclusive of extension specialists from May, 1918, to May, 1922, are shown in the following list of employes furnished by Doctor True:

			May		
County Agent Work (Men)	1918	1919	1920	1921	1922
Directors and State Leaders	62	65	60	59	56
Asst. State Leaders and District Agents	295	163	130	126	126
County Agents and Assistants	2563	2451	1993	2031	2097
Local Agents (colored)	129	174	159	153	155
Total	3049	2853	2342	2369	2434
Home Demonstration Work (Women)					
State Leaders	57	48	43	45	46
Asst. State Leaders and District Agents	107	126	102	95	94
County Agents and Assistants	1198	1183	818	718	745
Local Agents (colored)	145	214	67	76	91
City Agents	169	159	10	10	4
City Agents (colored)	14	10	....	....	....
Total	1690	1740	1040	944	980

Boys' and Girls' Club Work (Men and Women)					
State Leaders	45	68	61	60	56
Asst. State Leaders	104	83	61	58	53
County Leaders	763	421	290	227	197
Total	912	572	412	345	306
Grand Total	5651	5165	3794	3658	3720

In addition to this list there are about 700 extension specialists in the various branches of agriculture and home economics.

It is to be noted that in the above list of extension workers the number fell from 5651 in May, 1918, to 3720 in May, 1922, which is a falling off of more than one-third in the number of workers. The reason for this decline is the fact that after the war Congress withdrew emergency appropriations which had been granted for extension purposes from 1917 to 1919. With these emergency funds the number of county workers was rapidly increased until there were agricultural agents in more than 2400 counties and home demonstration agents in about 1700 counties. With the withdrawal of these special funds the number of counties having agricultural agents fell to about 2000, and the number having home demonstration agents to about 800. In addition there were at one time 1000 counties which had leaders of boys' and girls' club work. Now only about 200 counties have such leaders.

In addition to the effect of the withdrawal of special funds upon the extension service, the industrial depression which swept the country in 1920 caused a further decline in the number of agents employed by counties. Farm products were the first to fall in price, and this made it very difficult for the farmers to meet the expenses incident to the maintenance of extension work. Probably the newness of the system has somewhat worn off, and a setback is to be expected for this reason.

It is to be noted, however, that an increase in the number of workers in May of 1922 is registered over that of 1921 as well as an increase in funds as stated below, which, in the face of the economic depression, seems to indicate that the system is again expanding and that it has so far commended itself to our farming people.

Expenditures.—As previously stated, the Smith-Lever Act allows $480,000 or $10,000 to each State for extension purposes without requiring the states to contribute an equal amount. In addition to the $480,000, the Federal Government will pay to the States by 1923 the sum of $4,100,000 which, however, they must duplicate to be entitled to it. The entire federal sum available under the act will be $4,580,000. For the fiscal year ending June 30, 1922, the Department allotted $4,080,000 of the Smith-Lever fund for use in extension work. The total amount expended for extension purposes from the fiscal year, 1915, to that of 1922, including appropriations by the Federal Government, the states, counties and contributions from other sources is as follows:

Fiscal Year	*Total Amount Available*
1915	$3,597,235.85
1916	4,864,180.94
1917	6,149,619.63
1918	11,302,764.75
1919	14,661,560.50
1920	14,658.079.92
1921	16,836,742.05*
1922	18,497,360.00*

(*These amounts are allotments.)

The statement shows that, the amounts contributed to the cause of agricultural extension from other sources are considerable. The initiative taken by the Federal Government has resulted in organizing the movement and enlisting the necessary financial support from the people. When the American people can afford to pay as much as $18,000,000 for a single battleship, it would seem that we can pay that sum annually for the purpose of improving agriculture through the extension or demonstration plan thereby bestowing benefits upon the rural people who live under considerable disabilities because of their environment.

Relations Between the Extension Service, the Public School System and Smith-Hughes Work.—The Smith-Lever Act in the creation of the agricultural cooperative extension service has greatly unified the various forms of extension work in agriculture and has placed it under a definite administrative authority. Subsequently, in 1917, the Smith-Hughes act provided for vocational education in agriculture, home economics and in industry and placed the national administration of this system under a separate authority known as the Federal Board for Vocational Education. This Board is independent of the Federal Bureau of Education and the Department of Agriculture, but is related to them through the fact that the heads of these branches of the Government are members and have the right to vote. In the state its administration may according to the act be placed either under the regular state board of education or under a special board. In these two fields of agricultural extension and vocational education there is some chance for duplication of effort and funds. The activities in which these two systems may overlap are "(1) the junior project work of the schools and the junior extension (boys' and girls' club) work of the college, both in agriculture and home economics, (2) the part-time and evening home-making courses of the state board for vocational education and the home economics extension work of the college, and (3) the short-unit courses in agriculture and home economics, in the public schools, and the extension classes conducted by the land-grant colleges."[1] In view of these points of contact it is necessary that the two systems of administration operate under some plan to which mutual agreement has been given. A memorandum of understanding for the purpose was drawn up and signed by representatives of the two interests as early as February 21, 1918. At their annual meetings in 1920 the Department of Rural Education of the National Education Association and the agricultural section of the National Society for Vocational Education voted independently to create committees to prepare working programs for Smith-Lever extension and Smith-Hughes vocational forces in the various states. The following year joint committees were created by these two organizations and the Association of Land-Grant Colleges for the further study of the problem. The Association of Agricultural Teaching had also appointed a committee and this was in-

[1] From the Report of the Joint Committee on Relationships between Extension and Vocational Forces in the various states, furnished the author by Dean A. R. Mann and to be published in the Proceedings of the Association of Land Grant Colleges for 1921.

vited to work with the joint committees. This report suggests specific lines of cleavage between the extension and vocational forces. It is only the purpose in this chapter to point out the points of contact. In the following chapter, which deals with the Smith-Hughes work, the plan proposed to avoid duplication will be presented.

The question of agricultural education is further related to the public school system on the side of administration. Vocational education supported by Smith-Hughes funds very largely operates through the public school system. In connection with boys' and girls' club work it has been suggested that the schools take over this phase of extension work. The students, it is said, are a part of the public school system and the persons in closest touch with them are the teachers of the common schools. Just because vocational education, including boys' and girls' club work, is a new type of education does not necessarily mean that it can only be satisfactorily administered through independent organizations, the argument runs. From the point of view of organization the argument appears to be valid, but from the point of view of results it would be a colossal blunder. The public school teachers as a rule are wholly unprepared to teach agriculture and in the main are not in sympathy with this specialized or practical kind of education. Furthermore the matter of demonstration which is really the essence of extension work would be sorely neglected among the boys and girls of the country. Cooperation between the Smith-Hughes and Smith-Lever agencies so far as the boys' and girls' club work is concerned is the ideal arrangement. This is the plan worked out in New York state [1] and is approved in the memorandum of understanding drawn up by the Joint Committees.

SELECTED REFERENCES

S. A. Knapp in *Yearbook* for 1909, pp. 153-160; Bradford Knapp in *Proceedings* of Thirty-Third Annual Convention of the Association of Land-Grant Colleges; various *Reports on Cooperative Agricultural Extension Work in the United States; Circular, Doc. 90,* States Relations Service; Martin, *Demonstration Work; Report of Joint Committees,* in *Proceedings* of the Association of the Land-Grant Colleges for 1921.

[1] From a communication to the author by Professor M. C. Burritt, Vice-Director of Extension of New York.

CHAPTER XIII

AGRICULTURAL EDUCATION UNDER THE SMITH-HUGHES LAW

Early Status of Vocational Education.—Vocational education may be defined as the type of education that prepares for the earning of a livelihood. Writers on education generally think of this field of education as preparing for the professions as well as for manual occupations and as consisting of "other than liberal education." The vocational education provided for under the Smith-Hughes act must be of less than college grade and aims to fit the youth for employment in agriculture, the household arts and the trades. The work in agriculture and home economics is broad and includes also preparation for the proper conduct of the home.

Using the term of vocational education in the latter sense, we may say that before the passage of the Smith-Hughes act in 1917 there were a number of states including Pennsylvania, Massachusetts, New York, Wisconsin, Indiana, Minnesota, and some others that provided for vocational education by law. Under these state laws a number of vocational schools were in operation. Private vocational schools were also being conducted here and there. In agriculture it should also be noted that virtually all agricultural colleges offered short courses fitting students for a vocation. All these efforts, however, were more or less scattered and were wholly insufficient to offer vocational training to all who desired it. The explanation for this general inadequacy of vocational education is found in the revolutionary changes that took place in the development of industry. Before the close of the 18th century in Europe generally and to a lesser extent in America the system of learning a trade by serving the usual term of seven years of apprenticeship, prevailed. The system was early fostered by the craft and merchant guilds, and the relationships between master and apprenticeship were regulated by law. In some parts of Europe, especially in England, it was virtually a national system of vocational education. The advent of the factory system, however, did away with much of the hand labor, and the laborer as a consequence is now required to perform highly specialized services. The apprenticeship method so common under the domestic system of manufacture can only be used to a limited extent under the factory system, and this explains the general abandonment of this form of vocational training.

The causes for the development of the movement for a vocational training system have therefore been said to be the decay of apprenticeship; the disappearance of industries from the home and their transfer to the factory where the youth is never admitted and is therefore unable to learn its processes; the unpracticality of the public school system which in the grades has been supplying the bare fundamentals and in the high schools a cultural education, thus really not preparing the boy or girl to earn a living; and the effect of the untrained and inefficient man upon economic and social problems. Without question much of our poverty is due to unpreparedness for some kind of a job on the part of a large number of young men and women. They have not been made producers. They cannot do anything and therefore do not fit in anywhere. Eighty per cent of all children leaving our public and parochial schools do so at the age of 14 or earlier and enter the army of "permit workers." After the age of 16 and approaching full manhood and womanhood they are unprepared to earn a respectable living. The situation develops a large number of idlers, paupers, criminals, and other discontented and menacing citizens.

During the last half of the 19th century the manual training schools came into vogue. These began with an emphasis upon aesthetic drawing, but later took the direction of providing practical training for industry. By the 70's high schools over the country began to offer such work. For the girls cooking and sewing were offered. It was soon found, however, that such training was too narrow and insufficiently correlated with general industry to meet the needs of the prospective worker.

Objections to the Proposed Plan.—There were objections

to the movement for the establishment of public vocational training schools, and these came from two main sources. It was feared on the part of some educators that a public system of vocational training would direct many boys and girls into the trades and industries who would in the absence of such a system continue their study in the field of liberal education. The plan, it was argued, would actually deprive many boys and girls of a liberal education, and the institutions of higher learning would suffer because of a decreased proportion of the boys and girls in the public schools seeking entrance to colleges and universities. This argument is met with the statement that 89 per cent of boys and girls in the public and parochial schools do not go to high school and that 90 per cent of those in the high schools do not seek admission to the university. The provision for vocational training was to be made for the benefit of these two streams of youths who are stepping regularly into the ranks of producers and assume the duties of American citizenship. It would seem that a public system of vocational training made available to all those who wanted it would in fact encourage and greatly stimulate higher education. Many boys and girls even though they are in manual occupations aspire, as they always have, to a liberal education. A wider industrial education in the trades and industries as well as in agriculture and home economics would certainly, it would seem, inspire a general and wholesome respect for advanced learning. A diagram[1] showing how the workers issue from the schools into the field of production is shown on the following page. Individuals of the lower stream, it is proposed through vocational training, are to be made efficient producers. Opportunities to meet the varying conditions are to be made available so that all of this group who wish may receive training for the work they wish to undertake. Full-time, part-time, and evening schools accompanied with practice are to be conducted, so that all young men and women not going by way of the upper route may enter industry trained for some particular job.

[1] From a pamphlet by H. E. Miles, Chairman, Wisconsin State Board of Industrial Education.

A CHOICE OF ROUTES TO EFFICIENCY

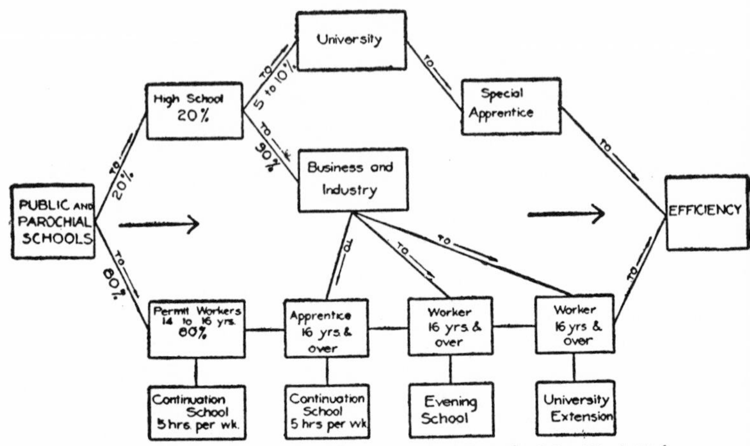

The Lower Route is the Workingman's Opportunity; His High School & College.
Until Recently it has been almost wholly neglected educationally in America.

Another source of opposition to vocational training was organized labor. It was feared that these schools would be controlled by capital and used expressly for the exploitation of labor. Poorly prepared skilled workmen would flood the ranks of labor and reduce wages. It was pointed out, however, that labor could be given a voice on the boards of control and in the management of the system representatives of labor could so direct its policy that the large body of laborers would be especially benefitted. Mr. Gompers, President of the American Federation of Labor, agreed in 1912 that "the prosperity of a nation depends upon its industrial and commercial success, and, in respect to these, success depends upon the training and intelligence of its citizens." He also said that this large flow of boys into the ranks of unskilled labor is attracting attention and "demanding solution."[1]

Objection to the Smith-Hughes act or to a national system of vocational education has also been made on the ground of giving the Federal government too much control over education. It is a hindrance and a nuisance, it is claimed, to have a coterie at Washington dictate the educational policies of the

[1] *Senate Doc. 845*, p. 45.

country. Too much Federal supervision in a comprehensive, national educational system is of course bad, but the degree of supervision exercised under the Smith-Hughes act has so far not become burdensome; and if it should later develop that the government assumes autocratic powers with respect to education the people can at any time exercise their sovereign rights and reduce the degree of supervision. Naturally when the Federal Government subventions the states for educational purposes it must at least have some supervision over the expenditure of funds.

The method of financing, that of making a grant by the Federal government, and requiring the state to match it, is also objected to by some for the reason, it is alleged, that it hampers the internal development of the state. It is claimed that the legislatures will readily appropriate available funds for objects supported concurrently by the Federal and state governments, and that when it comes to making provision for such local objects as eleemosynary institutions revenues are insufficient and many of the hitherto well-supported causes are forced to suffer. This may be temporarily true, but it is the author's strong belief, and experience in the several states seems to support the contention, that education alone is the means through which people will be made willing to support all forms of progressive legislation. The more education the greater willingness to pay taxes for proper objects. History has fully justified Federal aid to education. Without it some states at this late date would probably still be without an agricultural college. The time is fast approaching when it will be just as necessary for the Federal government to aid the state as it has for many years been necessary for the state to aid the county. In the interest of national solidarity and in the interest of equality of educational opportunities among the youth of the country it is essential that educational inequalities be wiped out among the states of the Union.

Recent Development of the Movement.—As early as 1878 the National Grange adopted a resolution demanding the teaching of agriculture in the elementary schools. Rapid progress was made after 1906. A number of societies promoting industrial education have sprung up. Massachusetts appointed a Commission on Industrial Education. The National Society for the Promotion of Industrial Education was especially active in developing sentiment in favor of the establishment of a public system of vocational training. A special tribute was paid to this society for the part it played in the movement by James P. Monroe, former Vice-Chairman, Federal Board for Vocational Education. Other societies interested in the movement are the National Vocational Guidance Association, the Vocational Education Association of the Middle West, and the National Association of Corporation Schools as well as the National Association of Manufacturers which has had a committee working on the subject. These associations gathered information which, supplemented by surveys made of Richmond, Virginia, in 1914 and of Minneapolis, New Orleans, Philadelphia, Seattle, and other places in 1915, threw a good deal of light on the subject, and helped to bring the movement to a successful fruition.

The development in Congress was gradual. The subject of vocational education more or less seriously engaged the attention of our Federal lawmakers for almost a decade before the enactment of the Smith-Hughes law. Mention should be made of the Davis bill, which was followed by the Davis-Dolliver bill. Credit must be given to these men for bringing the question to the attention of Congressmen and for making the passing of a law possible. In 1912 Senator Carroll S. Page of Vermont, to whom accrued the benefits of the previous bills, introduced a bill to provide the necessary funds and organization for the intitution of a vocational training system. By the terms of this bill it was proposed for the United States "to cooperate with the States in encouraging instruction in agriculture, the trades and industries, and home economics in secondary schools; in maintaining instruction in these vocational subject in state normal schools; in maintaining extension department in State colleges of agriculture and the mechanic arts; and to appropriate money and to regulate its expenditure." It will be noted that this bill included in the plan to establish vocational training, a system of extension service. The extension feature, subjected of course to considerable revision, was taken up by Congress in the Smith-Lever bill and enacted into law in 1914, while the part that relates to vocational training in agriculture, home economics, and the trades and industries, was embodied in a revised form in another bill known as the Smith-Hughes bill, which was passed by Congress in 1917.

In the speech supporting his bill for vocational training Senator Page showed that sentiment was generally favorable to the plan. Seven States—Massachusetts, Connecticut, New York, New Jersey, Maryland, Michigan, and Wisconsin—had already enacted laws relating to vocational education and the State of Massachuetts had a commission on industrial education. The Grange and other like organizations representing the farmer passed resolutions favoring the bill. Similar action was taken by the National Educational Association and the Southern Educational Association as well as by the American Manufacturers' Association. The American Federation of Labor was also in accord provided organized labor was given a share of control so as to avoid exploitation of labor by capital. *The Daily Iron Trade Review* said: "It must be made almost impossible for there to be such an anomaly as an untrained man before our country can claim rightfully to have afforded every man an equal chance."

The Smith-Hughes Act.—This act was approved February 23, 1917. Its objects are succinctly stated in the title which reads as follows: "An act to provide for the promotion of vocational education; to provide for cooperation with the States in the promotion of such education in agriculture and the trades and industries; to provide for cooperation with the States in the preparation of teachers of vocational subjects; and to appropriate money and regulate its expenditure." Sections 2, 3 and 4 of the act provide for the appropriation of funds for three different purposes. In cooperation with the States it provides for the payment of salaries of teachers, supervisors, and the directors of agricultural subjects. The same provision is made for teachers of trade, home economics, and industrial subjects; and finally the funds are to be available for the training of teachers of agricultural, trade, industrial and home economics subjects. The whole plan of the act would be of no avail if it did not provide for the training of teachers in these subjects. The practical and the theoretical aspects must have been mastered by the prospective teacher of these subjects to accomplish the purpoes of the act. In agriculture and home economics as well as in some fields of the trades and industry the universities and colleges turn out young men and women who have the foundational training necessary to teach these subjects, but who must take work in the theory and practice of teaching before they can hope to be successful as teachers. In many specialized lines of the trades and industries teachers have to be developed before complete training in these fields can be made available for the boys and girls of the United States. The provision of funds for teacher training is therefore a wise one.

For the purposes of paying salaries of teachers, supervisors, or directors of agricultual subjects, section 2 provides for the appropriation of the following amounts:

Fiscal Year	*Amounts*
1918	$500,000
1919	750,000
1920	1,000,000
1921	1,250,000
1922	1,500,000
1923	1,750,000
1924	2,000,000
1925	2,500,000
1926	3,000,000
Annually thereafter	3,000,000

These sums are to "be alloted to the States in the proportion which their rural population bears to the total rural population of the United States, not including outlying possessions." No State, however, was to receive less than $5,000 during the first 6 years, nor less than $10,000 thereafter.

For the purpose of paying salaries of teachers of trade, home economics, and industrial subjects section 3 provides for the appropriation of the same amounts and for the same years as provided for agriculture. For the fiscal year 1926 and annually thereafter the sum of $3,000,000 is therefore made available for this purpose. The amounts, however, are to be allotted to the States in proportion which their urban population bears to the total urban population of the United States. Of the $3,000,000 appropriated for this purpose not more than 20 per cent shall be expended for the payment of the salaries of teachers of home economic subjects.

For the purpose of preparing teachers, supervisors, and directors of agricultural subjects and teachers of trade and industrial and home economic subjects section 4 provides for the appropriation of the following amounts:

Fiscal Year	*Amounts*
1918	$500,000
1919	700,000
1920	900,000
1921	1,000,000
Annually thereafter	1,000,000

The amounts are to be allotted to the States in the proportion which their population bears to the total population of the United States.

Section 5 provides that in order to secure the benefits of the act each State must accept its provisions by legislative assent, and must designate or create a State board consisting of not less than three members which shall have full power to cooperate with the Federal Board for Vocational Education in the administration of the provisions of the act.

Section 6 provides for a Federal Board for Vocational Education made up of members as follows: The Secretary of Agriculture, the Secretary of Commerce, the Secretary of Labor, the United States Commissioner of Education, and three citizens,—one representing manufacturing and commercial interests; one, agriculture; and one, the interests of labor.

Section 8 gives supervision of the work to be carried on in the respective states to the Federal Boards. Plans must be submitted to the Federal Board for its approval in order to secure the Federal appropriations.

Section 9 provides that only the salaries for the teaching of the specific subjects above named can be paid out of Federal funds. Salaries of teachers necessary to give the students a well-rounded course must be borne wholly by the States. The section also makes the important provision that for every dollar of Federal funds expended the State or local community must expend an equal amount. This then is similar to the Federal aid for extension service and the building of roads.

Section 10 stipulates that the agricultural educational training provided for by the act shall be to fit for useful employment, that the education shall be of less than college grade, and that it is intended for persons over 14 years of age who have entered upon or are preparing to enter upon the work of the farm or of the farm home. The state or community is required to furnish the necessary plant and equipment, and practice in agriculture must be supervised for at least 6 months of the year.

Section 11 makes somewhat similar provisions for trade, home economics, and industrial education. Persons who have not yet entered upon employment shall receive instruction on practical work for at least half of the time. At least one-third of the amount appropriated for this particular group shall be expended for the use of part-time schools where instruction is given to those already employed. Subjects to be taught may include those intended to "enlarge the civic or vocational intelligence of such workers over fourteen and less than eighteen years of age." To attend evening schools the student must have attained the age of 16. Minor provisions are contained in other sections of the act.

Rehabilitation Education.—In 1918 rehabilitation education was provided for disabled soldiers and sailors, the administration of which was also for a time placed under the Federal Board for Vocational Education. In 1921, however, this function was transferred to the Veterans' Bureau. At this time more than 113,300 men were beneficiaries under the act.

Of much more far-reaching economic and social consequences is the education that provides for the vocational rehabilitation of the civilian disabled. In 1920 Congress passed an act providing for the "promotion of vocational rehabilitation of persons disabled in industry or otherwise and their return to civil employment." The legislation is based on the principle that it costs more to maintain the disabled than to cure the disability. This is an undertaking certainly worth while. Under normal conditions "the number of workers disabled each year exceeded the number of our soldiers and sailors disabled in the whole course of the World War."[1] This function is administered by the Federal Board for Vocational Education. Already in 1921 as many as 35 states had accepted the provisions of the federal act, agreeing to cooperate with the Federal Government to rehabilitate persons disabled in industry.

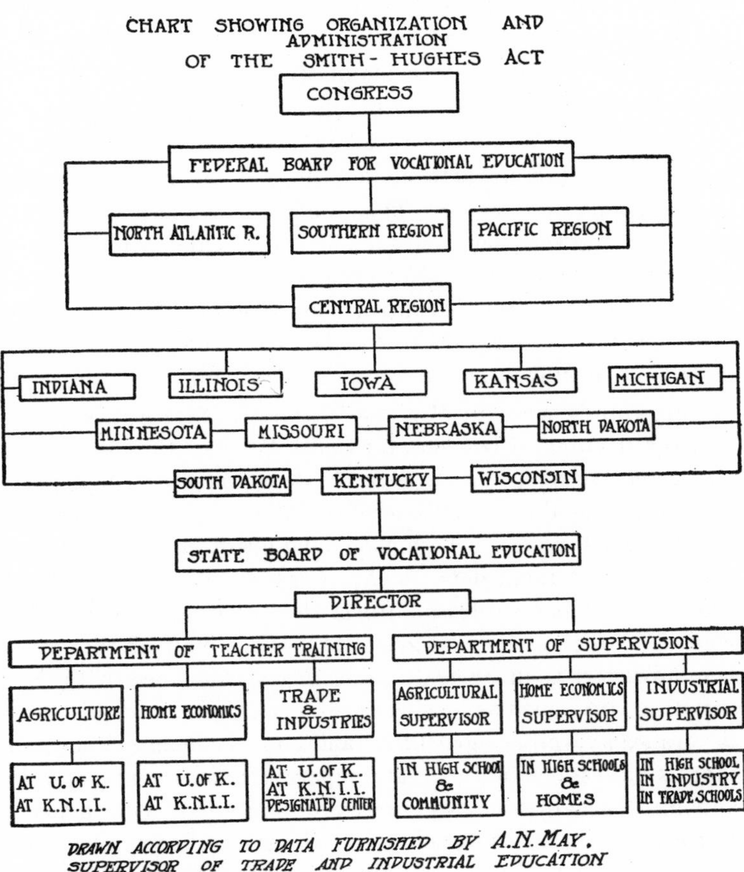

Organization and Administration.—The accompanying chart shows the organization of the vocational educational system established under the Smith-Hughes act. At the head of the

[1] Federal Board for Vocational Education in report for 1921, p. 26.

system is the Federal Board for Vocational Education which, for purposes of convenient administration, first divided the United States into five regions and later into four. The chart shows the States included in the Central region, and the organization in the State of Kentucky. At the head of the State organization is the State Board of Vocational Education, which appoints a director. The director has full charge of the department of supervision and acts in an advisory capacity with respect to the department of teacher training. The university appoints instructors for this department subject to the approval of the director. Just how much supervision he will exercise over this department will depend somewhat upon his qualifications as a leader. This is a point of contact between the Federal government and the university which could become somewhat disagreeable. However, the department is a part of the university and its control must remain under the president of the institution; if this fact is recognized by the director no trouble should grow out of the relationship.

In a study made by Professor Ashley V. Storm it is shown that the training of teachers for Smith-Hughes work is done in a large majority of cases in separate departments. The department head usually has authority to determine the curriculum. The tendency seems to be among land-grant colleges to place this teacher-training department in the college of agriculture. Out of 36 replies Professor Storm shows 24 cases where it is located in the college of agriculture. Only half of this number, however, is in agricultural colleges connected with universities.[1] Inasmuch as teachers are to be prepared for teaching the trades as well as agriculture and home economics about all that is necessary is to create separate departments and to appoint teachers who are thoroughly familiar with general educational theory and who are at the same time sympathetic to these three forms of vocational education and well trained in the sciences underlying the vocations. The department, it would seem under these conditions, need not be in the college of agriculture to bring about satisfactory results.

[1] Vide a pamphlet by A. V. Storm, entitled *How the Land-Grant Colleges Are Preparing Special Teachers of Agriculture.*

Composition of the Federal Board for Vocational Education.—Much discussion has centered around the composition of both the Federal and State administrative boards. It will be remembered that the American Federation of Labor wanted representation on the boards so as to prevent capital from using the system for the purpose of exploiting labor. The manufacturing interests also, as stated by Honorable I. L. Lenroot in debate on the floor of the House, desired representation on the administrative boards. In response to this general demand the law specifically states that the Federal administrative board shall be composed of representatives from the three interests of manufacturing, labor, and agriculture. To these are added as members the Secretary of Agriculture, the Secretary of Commerce, the Secretary of Labor, and the Commissioner of Education. The Federal board is therefore a separate or independent board related no more to the Bureau of Education than to the Departments of Commerce, Labor, or Agriculture. It is, however, related to the Bureau of Education through the fact that the Commissioner is a member and has a vote along with the other members of the Board.

The State Boards of Administration.—Concerning the composition of the State boards the law only requires that each State "designate or create a State board, consisting of not less than three members." The law further states that "the State Board of Education, or other boards having charge of the administration of public education in the State, or any State board having charge of the administration of any kind of vocational education in the State may, if the State so elect, be designated as the State board, for the purposes of this Act." The law could have stipulated that in order that States may receive the benefits of the act they shall set up separate administrative boards composed of representatives of agriculture, manufacturing, and labor. Obviously this requirement would have indicated too close an encroachment on the part of the Federal Government upon the rights of the States. In sections of the country where remnants of the States' Rights doctrine are still held sacred considerable opposition to such a provision would probably have been manifested. It is therefore readily understood why the States were left a free hand in designating their administrative boards.

It is indicated, however, from the discussion of those who supported the bill that the character of the composition of the Federal board should be carried out in the organization of the State boards. The American Federation of Labor said that "if we permit the present academic educational group of the nation to dominate, the whole force and virtue of genuine vocational training will be in danger of being lost sight of and the nation's appropriations will probably be misdirected along minor lines of endeavor, such as manual training, amateur mechanics, and other trifling, unpractical, valueless schemes." Efforts have been made since the passage of the Federal act to secure in the State law accepting the terms of the Federal act a State board of administration patterned after the Federal board. What has actually happened with respect to this matter as announced in the report of the Federal Board for Vocational Education for 1918, is that as many as 32 States designated the general State board of education as the State board for vocational education.

It has been urged by some that a separate board to administer vocational training is even more important than to select its personnel from the respective interests of agriculture, manufacturing, and labor, however important the latter feature may be. These boards, it is argued, should be separate from other general education boards so that their members may take a rightful attitude toward this type of education and truly champion its promotion. It is proposed that the vocational board should be related to the general board by making the chief executive officer of the general board of education also a member of the vocational board.

Of course much is gained in securing a board with the proper attitude and the desired degree of enthusiasm for this type of education when its personnel is selected from the environments of manufacturing and commerce, agriculture, and labor, and it is also true that unless a special state administrative board is created there is some danger in placing the administration of vocational training in a body whose personnel is wholly unsympathetic to this type of education. On the other hand, if a separate board is created a dual administrative system is set up, one having jurisdiction over the academic education and the other over vocational education. Inasmuch as there is but one public school organization it is necessary for the separate board to work through the existing schools in order to reach the youth of school ages. While the general education board may lack in sympathy toward vocational education, its administration through county school superintendents would be much more direct and expeditious than the administration of the separate board, which is more or less dissociated from the whole public school organization. It is a choice then of the lesser of two evils. In the interest of both administrative efficiency and the reduction of overhead charges, it would seem that the most satisfactory results are obtained when the vocational education is administered by the general state board of education.

At this writing it is, however, not at all certain that the wisest procedure is the placing of the administration of vocational education under the general state board. Those who favor the creation of a special board predict that in twenty years from now all states which accomplish much in vocational education will have separate boards. They point out that the unsympathetic attitude of the general board will thwart the intent and purpose of the Smith-Hughes law. In Wisconsin a vigorous fight was waged between the academic and vocational forces in connection with the creation of a separate board. It now looks as though the matter were permanently settled in favor of the vocational group. Vocational education in Wisconsin finds a strong stimulus in the initiative of the vocational board. Important results are achieved in this state under the dual organization, and it may be that the lack of sympathy on the part of the school men of the "old guard" will require elsewhere a dual organization if the system is to function in a thorough and comprehensive manner.

The Department of Teacher Training.—The chart shows how the department of teacher training is organized in Kentucky. The greater part of teacher training in agriculture and home economics is being done at the University of Kentucky. For the colored race teachers in the subjects are trained at the Kentucky Normal and Industrial Institute for Colored Persons. Probably a good deal of teacher-training for the trades and industries will be done at designated centers. The training of teachers in agriculture in some of the States was carried on before the passage of the act, and where it was not done it was a simple step at the agricultural colleges to institute professional educational courses in agriculture and home economics. Instructors preparing teachers in these subjects should have a technical knowledge of agriculture and home economics as well as be proficient in the theory and practice of teaching.

To secure adequate teacher training in the trades and industries is not as readily accomplished as in the other subjects. The person to be trained as a teacher is a skilled mechanic who is receiving a large wage and is loth to enter the public schools at the same or even slightly increased earnings. Much less is he willing to suspend his wage-earning career and go to a distant place to receive the necessary training. The policy of the States has therefore been to bring the professional training in the trades and industries to the place of the workers and give such courses at certain "designated centers."

The Department of Supervision.—In addition to serving in an advisory capacity with respect to teacher-training work the director also heads the department of supervision which oversees the actual teaching of the vocational subjects of agriculture, home economics, and trades and industries. The director in his supervisory work is assisted by three supervisors who are in direct charge of agricultural, home economics, and industrial vocational education. One of the chief duties of these supervisors is to inspect the character of the work given in the local schools throughout the State in order to ascertain whether or not they are living up to the terms of the agreement entered into between the State and the Federal board, and also whether they are keeping faith with the agreement entered into with the State board. However, together with inspection goes the important duty of rendering assistance to the local teachers and communities in getting the work properly started. A large part of the supervisors' work has to do at the present time and for some years to come with promoting vocational education in all communities throughout the State. A supervisor must actually be a "drummer." A system of vocational training that prepares the young man to earn a living is good, but the people are often slow to recognize good things and agitation to bring about a favorable public sentiment is therefore necessary. The Federal board reports that in some instances the importance of supervision is not fully realized due to this fact as well as to the scarcity of qualified persons supervisors have been borrowed from the teacher-training department.

A complete system of State administration of vocational education involves the following duties:[1]

1. Directional:
   (a) Outlining policies to present to the State board.
   (b) Preparing State plans (with assistance of specialists).
   (c) Directing the promotion of vocational education.
   (d) Medium between State and Federal boards.
   (e) Directing work of vocational staff.
   (f) Preparing forms for reports of vocational schools and teacher-training classes.
   (g) Recommendations to State boards regarding schools and classes for approval and reimbursement.
   (h) Bringing together all parties interested in vocational education to the support of a State program.
   (i) Educating the State as to the meaning of vocational education.

2. Supervisory:
   A. Fields of supervision.
      (a) Agriculture.
      (b) Home economics.
      (c) Trades and industries.
      (d) Teacher training.
   B. Duties within each field.
      (a) Assist the directive officer in special field.
      (b) Inspect schools.
      (c) Assist teachers in improving work.
      (d) Studying conditions of State in special line with a view to recommending establishment of schools or classes.
      (e) Assisting in establishment of schools or classes.
      (f) Preparing bulletins and other special literature.

Agricultural Vocational Education.—Secondary agricultural education grew rapidly in the United States in spite of chaotic opinion as to the character of education that should be given in high schools. It was first provided in special

[1] From the *Report* of the Federal Board for Vocational Education for 1918, p. 18.

schools equipped with a farm, herds, flocks, and such working materials as were necessary to secure practice in farming. They were costly and few States took steps to maintain them. The special secondary agricultural school required the boy to leave the home, thus losing the advantages of home life and depriving his parents of his labor during hours out of school. For the agricultural population as a whole it could not serve the purpose of training all prospective farmers in practical and scientific agriculture.

The special agricultural school, however, had a stimulating effect upon high schools. The report of the Federal board for 1918 states that figures collected indicate that by 1900 only 19 public high schools had introduced agriculture as a subject of instruction. By 1910, 413 schools had such courses, and in 1916, 2,981. Of this number only 2,166 gave agricultural instruction in a serious way, and only about 25 per cent of the latter number gave courses that were vocational in purpose. It is further stated that only 676 schools combined classroom instruction with laboratory work, either on school land or at the homes of pupils through the project method. In only 261 schools were the home projects supervised by the agricultural instructor.

Thus it is seen how necessary it was for the Federal Government to stimulate vocational agricultural instruction in the public high schools of the country. Agricultural instruction in high schools must be vocationalized. This requires adherence to standards that actually train the boy to farm, not along traditional lines, but in accordance with the best methods evolved by the agricultural experiment stations. The plan aims at the application of improved methods and not at experimentation. Supervised practical work is therefore necessary, which is usually in the form of home projects. By a home project in agriculture is meant a carefully planned farm enterprise including at least one complete cycle of operation and involving considerable study on the part of the student along the line of such enterprise. For instance, to complete the cycle with respect to a corn project the student would select the seed from the field, would prepare the ground, do the planting, cultivating, harvesting, and marketing. The instruction may be based on a day-school program or on a part-time plan similar to what is being done in the trades and industries. In most cases two, three, or four-year courses of 36 weeks each are offered, which the high school student may take while taking other courses of the curriculum, and thus upon graduation at the end of four years he is enabled to receive both the certificate of agriculture and the high school diploma. The agricultural student while taking his classroom work must carry on his projects on the farm, and these projects must be supervised by the agricultural instructor. The schools recognize that they cannot cover all fields of agriculture, and therefore largely turn their attention to the type of agriculture prevailing in the community. This makes such vocational training directly valuable to the localities everywhere throughout the country. In some cases short courses, lasting for a few weeks, have been introducd by high schools.

A forward step included in the content of the vocational work given in the high schools is farm accounting in connection with home projects conducted by the boy. Records show profits and losses, and this is after all the goal of all this work not only for the boy or prospective farmer himself but for the country at large.

The agricultural work of the high schools necessitates some revision of the curricula in the colleges. Standards must be set by the higher institutions of learning, so as to secure proper preparation for college entrance. Some students taking the vocational ocurses are bound to present themselves for admission at the colleges. All difficulty can be avoided by allowing only a portion of entrance credits to consist of agriculture. Agricultural colleges must make provision to admit such students into more advanced work.[1]

Vocational Training in Home Economics.—The family is the foundation of society, and an educational system that provides training for the performance of the economic and social functions of the home is well conceived. The act provides for vocational training in home economics which is interpreted to

[1] For more detailed information the reader is referred to *Bulletin No. 13* issued by the Federal Board.

mean not so much a preparation for the earning of a living outside of the home as a preparation in the actual art of home-making. In the report of the Federal Board for 1919 it is stated that "the aim underlying the development of vocational home-economics education is to reach all groups of girls and women with a type of home-making training which will function immediately in the solution of the daily problems of home-making." From a national standpoint home-making has many important aspects. One aspect of the home is that it is a business enterprise, and the degree of economy practiced by all the homes of the nation determines to a large extent the quantity and quality of conomic goods enjoyed by all. It has its social and moral aspects which are fundamental in the control of society, and which are most satifactorily maintained where the economic needs of the family are more nearly satisfied. Vocational education in the art of home-making extended to all who share its responsibilities is therefore a worthy undertaking on the part of the State.

Home economics as a part of general education was well established in the curricula of high schools throughout the country before the passage of the Smith-Hughes act. However, in only a few schools was home economics given with a vocational purpose. There is a distinction between offering home economics courses as a part of a general high school course and vocational training in these subjects. From the latter point of view the central feature of the course of study must be a group of technical or home-economics subjects designed to meet the special needs of the special group. Around this special group must be built certain related subjects. In addition subjects tending to enlarge the "civic and vocational intelligence" must be included. The efficient home maker must be skilled in a number of occupations. She is a partner in the management of the home and must be trained to run the enterprise on an economical basis.

Students that may take the work in all-day schools must be more than 14 years of age, so that home-economics instruction may be given in upper elementary grades, in the high schools, or in separate schools. The work in the all-day schools is so arranged as to meet the needs of at least two groups of students. To the group that can stay only a year or two in school a half day is devoted to the more practical subjects in home economics and the other half to related subjects. To the group that stays throughout the four years, both practical subjects in home economics and related subjects are given in a half-day program, necessitating a longer time for the work and allowing the student to take a good deal of non-vocational subjects. The law states that "at least half the time of instruction shall be given to practical work," which the Federal Board interprets to mean practical and related subjects including garment making, foods and cookery, sanitation and home nursing, house planning, and house furnishing, textiles, millinery, dressmaking, and home management. All or a part of the remaining time may be devoted to the non-vocational subjects such as drawing and design, general science, physiology, chemistry, bacteriology, physics, English, civics, history, and elementary economics.[1]

In addition to regular day schools the purpose of the act is only accomplished where all groups of women and girls, whether in homes or in industry, are provided with vocational training. Vocational courses varying in length must therefore be offered in the afternoon and evening. In these classes a more direct touch of the practical must be constantly borne in mind by the instructor. Usually only the more practical features of the common household occupations are taught in these schools held after day-school hours.[2]

Relation of Vocational Training to Extension Work in Agriculture.—In the preceding chapter the organization and work of the agricultural cooperative extension service, including the county and home demonstration agents, the local organization, and the boys' and girls' clubs, were discussed. It was then stated that this extension work is not in the nature of school exercises or systematic intruction such as contemplated by the Smith-Hughes act. The extension service rather deals with specific problems on the farm, in the home, and

[1] *Bulletin No. 1* of the Federal Board for Vocational Education.

[2] For more detailed information the reader is referred to *Bulletin No. 28* issued by the Federal Board.

in the community which are taken up for discussion and solution by those associated with the extension organization. Demonstrations are a very large part of the work of the extension service. Projects such as corn-raising or pig-raising run through the season, and these are directed by the agents of the extension sevice. It is here where a plan of cooperation may be worked out between the extension service and the vocational agricultural instructor. The practice work required by the vocational training courses could be carried out in cooperation with the county agent in charge of extension work. The determination of the character of the practical work as well as its supervision must of course remain under the authority of the state board for vocational education, but unless arrangements are made by the extension and Smith-Hughes forces to avoid overlapping and duplication of effort considerable sums of money will be needlessly spent.

As stated in the previous chapter, after the passage of the Smith-Hughes act a joint committee of the Department of Agriculture and the Federal Board for Vocational Education studied the question of local cooperation with a view to avoiding the duplication of effort. This joint committee came to an understanding and on February 21, 1918, the substance of this agreement was sent out to the state vocational boards and extension directors in the form of a "Memorandum on Instruction in Vocational Schools and Extension Work in Agriculture." Among other points stated in this memorandum the following paragraph sets forth the relation between the extension and Smith-Hughes forces concerning work carried on among children:

> That in counties having vocational schools of agriculture the extension service will conduct its extension work in agriculture with children chiefly through the organization of clubs for the carrying on of definite pieces of work for the improvement of agricultural practice. The practical agricultural work of the schools will chiefly consist of home project work by the students as a part of the systematic practical instruction provided by the Smith-Hughes act. It is advised that in such counties a cooperative agreement be made between the extension authorities and the school authorities whereby it will be arranged for the teachers of agriculture to take part in the extension activities with the children within the territory of the school and that such territory be set forth in the agreement.

In the light of subsequent experience the above memorandum of understanding was found to be inadequate. Joint committees to study the question of relationship further were appointed by the Association of Land-Grant Colleges, the National Association for Vocational Education, the Department of Rural Education of the National Education Association, and the American Association for the Advancement of Agricultural Teaching. This report, concluded on May 10, 1921, suggests the ollowing in the way of relationships to be maintained between the extension and Smith-Hughes forces:

1. It is the function, duty, and responsibility of the public school to provide education for all children, and to provide such adult education as is authorized.

2. Under the law, it is the function and duty of the Land-Grant College of Agriculture to maintain extension service. The theory underlying extension service is that it is, first, to provide suplemental education for persons engaged in agriculture and homemaking, and, second, to enable the college and the Federal department of agriculture to bring their advances in knowledge to farmers and their families who can make the applications. Furthermore, by virtue of its staff of technical specialists and its responsibility for training vocational teachers. the Land-Grant College is in a position to furnish technical information and advice in the fields of agriculture and home economics to vocational work in the schools.

3. It is clearly recognized and affirmed that the college of agriculture is the source of authority, in the state, in technical subject matter in agriculture and home economics. The principle should be clearly observed that neither the state nor any lesser administrative unit charged with the supervision of vocational education, should employ any itinerant subject matter specialists for the purpose of giving technical instruction in any phase of agriculture or home economics. In so far as the vocational schools may have need for the assistance of technical specialists other than the regular vocational teacher or teachers in the local schools, they should look to the college of agriculture to supply such specialists. If, by reason of limitation of funds, the college is unable to meet all demands for aid on technical matters, the remedy is to be found in strengthening the resources of the college to fully meet the requirements, and not in establishing subject matter specialists as part of the state vocational system.

4. There are three types of situation to be considered: (a) Where agricultural and home economics education is fully developed by the local schools, (b) where such education has not yet been undertaken by the local schools, (c) where such education is in process of development by the local schools.

(a) Where the school provides a comprehensive program of agricultural and home economics education which meets the needs of children and adults, through systematic instruction and supervised practice, the extension forces of the Land-Grant Colleges shall not duplicate such work of the schools, but shall rather cooperate with the schools by providing, on request, subject matter, special lectures, conferences, and other similar services. This shall not be interpreted to limit the freedom of the extension forces to prosecute their extension work through local organizations of farmers.

(b) Where the school does not provide such a program of instruction in agriculture and home economics, the extension service of the college should organize extension work. In such localities, the school should give its fullest support and cooperation to the extension workers.

(c) It is recognized that, in some places, schools will be in the process of developing such educational programs. In these cases, the following principles should apply: Extension workers should confine their work with children to those whom the school does not enroll in systematic vocational or prevocational project work, including supervised home practice, unless requested or authorized by school authorities to enroll them. The school should organize its work with adults to provide systematic vocational instruction as defined herein. The school should offer its facilities to the junior extension worker wherever the school has not, in reasonable operation, vocational or prevocational project work accompanied by supervised home practice.

5. Before undertaking junior extension work in any county, the extension division should submit in writing to the county superintendent of schools, the plans proposed for junior extension work in that county, and should endeavor to arrange for a basis of understanding and cooperation. Copies of plans, when agreed upon, should be filed with the state department of education for consideration, before being put into operation.

6. The state department of education should look to the Land-Grant College to furnish technical subject matter in agriculture and home economics in the form of outlines, leaflets, and bulletins for use in the public schools. It is understood, however, that no such material in agriculture and home economics should be used in the schools until approved by the state department of education.

Vocational Training in Trades and Industries.—Somewhat similar provisions are made to provide training in the trades and industries. All-day school programs are established for those over 14 years of age preparing for some particular trade or industry. This type of school is classified as the unit trade school or class. Under this plan boys in school preparing for instance for the plumber's trade receive instruction in both shop work and related class work based entirely upon this trade. In towns of less than 25,000 population where resources do not permit a high degree of specialization and therefore make impossible the employment of a shop-teacher for each separate trade the standards set for the unit trade school are approximated as nearly as conditions allow. This type is known as the general industrial school or class.

To meet the needs of the thousands of both young men and women in industry who are not sufficiently trained the act provides various part-time schools, known as trade extension, trade preparatory, general continuation, and evening industrial schools or class.[1] Only the young man out of employment and reading the classified want "ads" who finds that he is not prepared to fill any of the jobs advertised, can properly appreciate the importance of industrial vocational training. It has a direct bearing upon the problem of poverty and it is the duty of the state to do all it can to correct this social ill.

Investigational Functions.—It is to be noted that the Smith-Hughes act makes no provision for vocational training in commercial subjects. The reason for this probably is that private schools and high schools have in an elementary way fairly well supplied this need. Subsequent bills in Congress have aimed at securing Federal funds to cooperate with the States in the promotion of business education. The Smith-Hughes act, however, directs the federal board to make studies of vocational schools giving instruction not only in agriculture, trade and industries, and home economics, but also in commerce and commercial pursuits. These studies shall be made for the purpose of aiding the States in establishing vocational schools, and they may be made in cooperation with the Departments of Agriculture, Labor, and Commerce, or the Bureau of Education. Pursuant to this provision of the act the Federal Board is making studies on commercial education. In its report for 1918 the Board says that the needs of only a few of the 600,000 boys and girls pursuing commercial courses, are being met owing to the limited scope of the traditional commercial course.

Progress of Smith-Hughes Work.—In its report for 1921 the Federal Board for Vocational Education gives facts showing the progress that this form of education is making. Following is a statement showing the number of schools in the United States in agriculture, trade or industry and in home economics:

Year	*Total*	*All Agricultural Schools*	*All Trade or Industrial Schools*	*All Home Ecomonics Schools*
1921*	3,859	1,721	836	914
1920	3,150	1,375	753	700
1919	2,039	863	575	463
1918	1,741	609	809	323

*Report for Wisconsin, not included.

[1] *Vide Bulletin No. 17* issued by the Federal Board.

The number of students enrolled for 1921 in agricultural schools was 42,709; in trade or industry, 83,532; and in home economics, 63,806. All vocational students for 1921 numbered 305,224. In 1918 the number was only 164,186, indicating that the system is functioning more satisfactorily today than it did in 1918. A very considerable increase in numbers of schools and students is to be expected as the people become more familiar with the system and as they more fully appreciate the benefits of vocational training.

The Economic and Social Importance of Vocational Education.—In reviewing the history of all attempts in the United States at spreading the gospel of scientific agriculture one is struck with the fact that a great deal is yet to be accomplished in the field of improved agriculture. Unquestionably much has been achieved through the various efforts of organized agriculture. But it must be remembered that this country has a vast domain, that it has over a hundred million people, that the harvests are large, and that the reapers are relatively few. To this should be added the fact that the agricultural population in many sections of America has been hitherto too isolated to acquire the habit of organization and through organization the habit of self-improvement. At the bottom of improved agriculture lies science, and considerable education is therefore necessary. The organization of the extension service provided for by the Smith-Lever act and the vocational training in agriculture authorized by the Smith-Hughes act are by no means redundant. The conditions of agricultural education itself and the conditions of the agricultural environment make it the bounden duty of the Nation and the State to do all they can in the way of initiating programs that tend to improve the economic and social conditions of our rural population.

The economic and social welfare of this class is not without influence upon the whole fabric of society. The special provision of the act providing for home-making will tend to give us more comfortable, more sanitary, and happier homes. The vocational training in the trades and industries provides a long-felt need and is one of the simple things the state may do to lessen the amount of its poverty. The poverty of a nation is decreased to the extent that each able-bodied man and woman is trained for some productive process. The lack of preparation for some gainful employment as one of the causes of poverty is easily removed, and is a public function that every progressive state must perform.

SELECTED REFERENCES

Senate Document. 845; various Reports of the Federal Board for Vocational Education; *Bulletins Nos. 1, 13, 17, 28,* of the Federal Board for Vocational Education; *Report of Joint Committees* in *Proceedings* of the Association of Land-Grant Colleges for 1921; Storm, *How the Land-Grant Colleges Are Preparing Special Teachers of Agriculture.*

CHAPTER XIV

STATE DEPARTMENTS OF AGRICULTURE

Early State Agricultural Organization.—The earliest agricultural organization in the United States was influenced by our political traditions inherited from England. In England voluntary or private organization was common. Washington corresponded with distinguished Englishmen associated with agricultural societies and as a result became much interested in the movement to establish such societies in America. In September, 1786, Sir John Sinclair of England wrote to George Washington the following:

> The people of this country, as well as of America, learn with infinite regret that you propose resigning your situation as President of the United States. I shall not enter into the discussion of a question of which I am incompetent to judge; but if it be so, I hope that you will recommend some agricultural establishment on a great scale before you quit the reins of government. By that I mean a board of agriculture, or some similar institution, at Philadelphia, with societies of agriculture in the capital of each state to correspond with it. Such an establishment would soon enable the farmers of America to acquire agricultural knowledge, and, what is of equal importance, afford them the means of communicating what they have learned to their countrymen.

In reply to a previous letter from Sir John Sinclair, George Washington on July 20, 1794, wrote the following:

> It will be some time, I fear, before an agricultural society, with congressional aid, will be established in this country. We must walk as other countries have, before we can run. Smaller societies must prepare the way for greater; but with the lights before us, I hope we shall not be so slow in maturation as older nations have been. An attempt, as you will perceive by the enclosed outlines of a plan, is making to establish a state society in Pennsylvania for agricultural improvements. If it succeeds it will be a step in the ladder; at present it is too much in embryo to decide upon a result.

Already in the last quarter of the 18th century agricultural societies in America began to organize. The earliest societies were established in urban centers of Pennsylvania, South Carolina, Maine, New York and in other States. The older portions of the country including the Atlantic coast

---

[1] This crorespondence appears in the *Agricultural Report* of the Department for 1866, p. 514.

States, and those of Ohio, Indiana, Illinois, Michigan, and Wisconsin, made considerable progress toward agricultural organization during the first half of the 19th century. The organization, however, was virtually everywhere voluntary or private, and not public. In some cases the first step toward public agricultural organization was taken by States during this period by appropriating funds for the support of private agricultural societies. Thus the extraordinary development of present-day public agricultural organization of the country has its roots running back into voluntary association beginning to take form in the last quarter of the 18th century.

The aims and purposes of these early agricultural societies correspond somewhat closely with the functions now performed by the agricultural departments of the States and the Federal Government. The general purpose of the societies may be said to have been to improve agriculture. The holding of fairs at which the best stock and farm products were exhibited together with the reading of papers and discussion were the principal methods of stimulating interest in agriculture. The introduction of new plants and livestock was undertaken by some societies as well as agricultural experimentation. Both of these projects were conducted by the South Carolina State Agricultural Society. This Society was organized in 1785 and early purchased a tract of land on which experiments were conducted.[1] The collection of statistics was attempted by some societies. While a great deal of credit for initiating a great movement must be given to these societies the work performed by them can in no way be compared with the work carried on by the public organizations of today. Even leaving out of the discussion scientific discoveries made since the middle of the 19th century, public organization today is more effective for the reason that it reaches more completely the whole agricultural population than did private organization in those days, or than it has since then, or probably does now. This fact, however, cannot detract from the importance of the service of these societies. Historically, they fulfilled a great purpose. They came at a time when our poliitcal attitude

[1] *Vide Report* of Department of Agriculture for 1875, p. 463.

was unfavorable to the centralization of government. Our traditions favored local government and voluntary or private organization. Only after the 40's did our State governments begin to increase their expenditures rapidly. At this time they took over new functions that had been formerly carried on, if at all, under private initiative. During the first half of the 19th century the agricultural societies were therefore of necessity compelled to perform as best they could such functions as are now carried on by the State and Federal departments of agriculture and the cooperative extension service.

The Transition from Private to Public Organization.—The transition from private to public organization roughly speaking came considerably before the middle of the 19th century when the States began to subsidize agricultural societies and to construct boards of agriculture made up usually of delegates of county agricultural societies. Precedents of this type of organization can be found as early as 1820. In that year the State of New Hampshire "passed an act providing for the organization of a State board of agriculture, to consist of the presidents of the several county societies and a delegate from each." These county societies received appropriations from the State. The board was organized in 1821 with 12 members. "After a brief period" the societies became disorganized and the board ceased to exist. The law, however, remained unrepealed until 1870, when an act of the legislature established the board on a different basis.[1]

Massachusetts was one of the early States to organize agricultural societies. Its earliest society was the Massachusetts Horticultural Society organized in 1829. In 1851 the Norfolk Agricultural Society took steps to establish a State board of agriculture. At a meeting of this society that year it was determined that the presidents and secretaries of the various agricultural societies of the State meet in convention "the object of which shall be to concert measures for their mutual advantage, and for the promotion of the cause of agricultural education." The State was already paying bounties to agricultural societies. The plan worked out at this convention was

[1] The *Report* of the Department of Agriculture for 1875, pp. 437-468, gives a brief history of the early agricultural societies.

that the societies receiving the State bounty organize a central board of agriculture. The board was to be made up of three delegates from ecah society. The board was organized in 1851. Two years later the legislature provided for a State board constituted, however, very much like the private board. Under the State board the Governor, Lieutenant Governor, Secretary of State, the President of the Massachusetts Agricultural College, and one delegate from each society receiving the State bounty including three other delegates appointed by the Governor constituted its members. Formerly the Secretary of State performed all agricultural duties. This work under the new plan of organization was all centralized in a separate board whose secretary compiled reports of the agricultural societies and prepared the annual volume for publication. In 1908 and even up to 1918 the board was still based on agricultural societies to the extent that they elected members of the board (thirty-two in 1908). The secretary of the board was elected by its members and was the administrative officer with headquarters at the State Capitol. He and his assistants were officials whose salaries were paid out of State appropriations. In the reorganization that took place in 1918 a somewhat more centralized department of agriculture was established. The name of the secretary was changed to commissioner, but this official was to be elected by a board made up of 14 members, one from each county and appointed by the Governor.[1] Still further centralization was effected in 1919.[2]

There are other examples of bounties paid by States to agricultural societies as well as of the organization of boards of agriculture made up for the most part of delegates from local societies. New York State under an act of 1819 organized a board made up wholly of delegates of agricultural societies. Although the law remained in effect the board ceased to exist in any effectual way from 1826 to 1832 and from the latter year to 1841 not at all. In 1841 the law of 1819 was virtually re-enacted stipulating, however, the State Agricultural Society instead of the State board of agriculture as the administrative agency. The society performed the functions of a State board

[1] *Vide Report* of Board of 1918, p. 26.
[2] *Vide General Acts,* Chapter 350.

of agriculture and with the exception of a small appropriation from the State "for the promotion of agriculture" it financed all its operations. The State of New York is thus an historical example of a high degree of private organization. Not until 1884 when it became necessary to create a machinery with regulatory functions in order to enforce the dairy laws was any State agricultural office created. The first office was that of Dairy Commissioner, and not until 1893 was a department of agriculture established.

The method of subsidizing the agricultural movement through the payment of bounties to private societies was quite general. Other States that encouraged agriculture in this way are Georgia, Michigan, Wisconsin, Indiana, Illinois, and others. The practice of creating a State board of agriculture either wholly made up of delegates of societies or of such delegates and State officials combined also was quite common by the middle of the 19th century and continued to be so for a half century longer. Even to this day there are still State boards of agriculture varying, however, greatly in the functions they perform as well as in the way they are constituted; and in the more progressive States the practice of appropriating funds to societies for the purpose of promoting agriculture has actually increased.

The Establishment of State Departments of Agriculture. —In the two previous sections agricultural organization was shown to have been at first entirely private and later to have developed into a semi-public form known as the State board of agriculture. The more centralized form of state agricultural organization began to make its appearance during the last quarter of the 19th century, and it was in the South where this type of organization first spread rapidly. Georgia was the first State to have a State department of agriculture. Its department was organized in 1874 and includes such branches as the State Chemist, State Entomologist, State Geologist, and the Pure Food Department. The Department of Agriculture is a part of the State cabinet. This shows a high degree of centralization. The Commissioner, however, is elected by the people. Tennessee followed in 1875 with an even more centralized Department of Agriculture. The Commissioner was to be appointed by the Governor and the deputies and other officials and assistants of the Department were to be appointed by the Commissioner. North Carolina organized a department of agriculture in 1877, Virginia and Alamaba in 1888, Florida and North Dakota in 1889, Kentucky in 1892, Pennsylvania in 1895, Maine in 1901, and Mississippi in 1907. New York created its Dairy and Food Commissioner in 1884 and its Department of Agriculture in 1893. It will be noticed that all of the States mentioned are southern except Maine, New York, Pennsylvania and North Dakota, and that all of these northern States except New York came late in the movement. By 1908 of the eastern States only Vermont had joined the ranks of the movement toward centralization. At this time virtually all of the States west of New York and Pennsylvania had the State board of agriculture. In 1908 then, the South had centralized public organization; in New England and the Middle Atlantic States, Maine, Vermont, New York and Pennsylvania had it; while the whole West except North Dakota, Washington, and Montana were organized on a semi-public basis.[1]

The reason for the dissimilarity between the northern and southern organization is quite clear. The southern States have never been accustomed to the degree of local government that the northern States have. They have no town or township, their smallest governmental unit being the county. Neither has private agricultural organization ever been as intensively and persistently developed as it has in the northern States. For these reasons it is not surprising that the South first turned to the State government to solve its problems in agriculture.

The similarity between the western and the early eastern organization can also be very readily explained. The student of political organization in America finds that many of the political and social customs of the East have been bodily carried westward by the tide of eastern emigration. It is true of constitutional peculiarities, of tax organization, and it is

[1] For this history consult Bailey's *Cyclopedia of American Agriculture*, Vol. 4, pp. 328-339, and the Department *Report* for 1875 and recent *Yearbooks*.

true of agricultural organization. Thus the West largely inherited its institutions from the East.

During the decade following 1908 many States changed the State board for the department of agriculture. According to a list published in the Yearbook of the United States Department of Agriculture only Connecticut, Delaware, Rhode Island and Maryland in the East and five other States in the Union retained the board organization in 1919. In this list of departments there are, however, some in which the State board is still a coordinate part among the usual regulatory divisions. The department in these cases is merely nominal and submits reports of the State board and other divisions to the Governor. With respect to the present status of state departmental organization in the United States, the reader is referred to Appendix 1 showing the varied state organizations in tabular form. The year 1918 saw changes made by Minnesota, Massachusetts, Idaho, and California. Illinois and some other States just recently adopted a highly centralized plan.

Reasons for the Change of Organization.—The reason for the change in the East from the board to the department organization followed freely by western States is largely due to the assumption of agricultural functions by the States that could not be readily performed by a semi-public organization. It should be noted that the aims and purposes of organized agriculture, whether public or private, are to carry on the functions of investigation, education and demonstration, experimentation, and regulation. Experimentation and research have been left largely to the experiment stations. The problem of investigation is so large as to extend beyond the confines of the State or even to foreign lands, and its prosecution is more efficiently and thoroughly carried out by a centralized government. Much of the investigational work is therefore more satisfactorily performed by the Federal Government. There are of course a large number of local problems which can best be investigated by centralized State departments. In the collection of data not only is expense an important phase, but force such as possessed by centralized public organization is often necessary to secure the desired information. The educational and demonstrational function is fairly well administered by even private organization. Compared, however, with the systematic, persistent, and regular efforts applied by public organization behind which there is frequently a large appropriation for the purpose, even the function of demonstration is more satisfactorily performed by public organization. The new extension service centered in the agricultural colleges performs this function admirably, and it should be placed under the college rather than under the State department. The work of farmers' institutes should logically be associated with the extension service.

The function, however, that has been more directly responsible for the growth of centralized State departments of agriculture is the regulatory function. The regulation of agricultural activities is only a phase of the regulation of industry and commerce beginning to take form in the early 70's in the United States. This principle of regulation was the result of a flare-back of the industrial *laissez-faire* policy adopted largely because of the changes occasioned by the Industrial Revolution. The policy of non-interference in industry and commerce soon began to threaten our very existence. It became necessary to regulate not only the railroads, manufacturing and commerce, but agricultural activities as well. Thus, following the rapid growth of urban centers in the United States after the 30's, the adulteration of milk for fresh consumption assumed the proportions of a social problem in New York City in 1840 and elsewhere in the country.[1] Butter and cheese as well as other food products were freely adulterated. The first oleomargarine factory in the United States was established in New York City in 1873, and the product disguised as butter and sold for butter soon appeared upon the market in large quantities. This has been a great error in the history of the oleomargarine industry, and is a policy that has been very generally abandoned because it is recognized that the principle of fraud in the manufacture and sale of oleomargarine leads to the destruction of the industry. New York, Pennsylvania and other States began to legislate against this form of adulteration in the late 70's. It is to be remembered that the adultera-

[1] *Vide, the Butter Industry in the United States by the Author,* Chapter 9.

tion of the dairy products is only one phase of the adulteration of foods which resulted in the passage of pure food laws in the States and in 1906 by the Federal Government.

The Development in New York.—In the State of New York as well as in a number of other States the movement toward centralization in State agricultural organization can be traced directly to the adulteration of foods, especially the dairy products, and the need of regulation. The first laws dealing with the manufacture and sale of oleomargarine passed in New York in 1877, and subsequent laws in 1880 and in 1882 treated the subject in only a general way, leaving the enforcement of the law to the regular prosecuting attorney. It was soon discovered that this officer is concerned with the enforcement of the law in general, and has no time to inspect dairy products and collect the necessary evidence to prosecute the offender of the oleomargarine law. To prevent the sale of oleomargarine as butter, very generally done at this time, an administrative machinery had to be created. Almost the entire menace of food adulteration is an administrative problem. State and Federal officers such as dairy and food commissioners had to be appointed whose special duty it was to administer the laws against adulteration. This officer had to be given a large corps of specially or scientifically trained inspectors whose duty it was to collect the evidence necessary to prosecute offenders of the law. New York made no progress in the prevention of the adulteration of foods until the legislature in an act passed in 1884 created the office of Dairy Commissioner. Wisconsin, Michigan, and other States soon followed with this type of organization, recognizing the principle of regulation as the only means of dealing successfully with the problem of adulteration. In 1893 New York established its State Department of Agriculture. The work formerly carried on by the office of Dairy Commissioner is now performed in a bureau of the Department of Agriculture. In this Department other regulatory functions such as the prevention of adulteration of feedstuffs, fertilizers, the quarantining of districts against diseases of animals such as the rabies, and the administration of the bovine-tuberculosis law, are located. In addition to these regulatory functions it carries on a number of demonstrational functions. History then seems to indicate that the assumption of the State of the investigational, demonstrational, educational, and regulatory functions, but more the latter than any other, has been responsible for the general adoption of greater centralization in public agricultural organization. It is true that some States still adhere to a board form of organization centered in the agricultural college, while some States still have the board organization that is made up of representatives from agricultural societies or from local districts. These boards can quite admirably perform the function of investigation. It is also true, however, that the former Michigan Board, for instance, had charge of only such minor phases of regulation as the inspection of apiaries, and that most of the regulatory work was committed to more highly centralized departments. Furthermore the days of the administrative board seem to be numbered as indicated by the drift during the last decade toward the State department of agriculture. The movement of the short ballot and the demands for greater simplification in departmental organization, and greater efficiency in public accounting and in political machinery all probably played a part in bringing greater centralization into State agricultural organization.

Present Forms of State Organization.—Necessarily among 48 States whose political and social traditions and customs as well as economic conditions differ widely, considerable variation in agricultural organization may be expected. It would make this chapter too long to present in detail all existing forms of State departmental organizations. Little would be gained by the procedure, and the plan decided upon therefore is to present in detail the organization of Pennsylvania which has a very highly centralized department of agriculture, that of New York which for a few years was governed by a council, now by a commissioner appointed by the council, and that of Connecticut which has a State board of agriculture having a coordinate positon with other administrative offices. A discussion of these three forms of organizations will give the student an idea of the prevailing froms of organization throughout the United States. In Appendix 1 a detailed statement of state organization is given. As pointed out in the previous historical sections the State board has been the center around which public organization took form; and the regulatory functons, and to some extent other functions, which the State was forced to assume, have slowly disintegrated this early organization. In some places the board has a commanding position, in others it is coordinate with the newer administrative offices, and where reorganization has brought about the more centralized form the State board is either non-existent or has merely a nominal official relationship with the State departmental organization. The movement toward greater centralization is thus forcing the board from its executive position to an advisory or cooperative position. This is virtually where the Pennsylvania State Board of Agriculture was prior to its abolition in 1919. Where the board is conspicuous agricultural societies elect virtually all of its members, leaving only a few to be appointed by the governor. In some States membership of the board is now based upon congressional districts. Even though the State board has fallen to a position where it is connected with the department only through *ex-officio* relationship, it is nevertheless an important aspect of agricultural organization. It is a means of binding together all agricultural societies and it provides the necessary channels through which the department may reach the people in its attempts to promote agriculture.

The law of Illinois up to 1917 provided that "the Department of Agriculture, for the promotion of agriculture and horticulture, manufactures and the domestic arts, shall be continued, and shall be managed by a board to be styled the 'State Board of Agriculture,' to consist of a president and one vice president from each congressional district in the State, and of the last ex-president of the State Board of Agriculture, said president and vice president to be elected on the fair grounds on Wednesday of the annual State Fair in 1884, and every two years thereafter on Wednesday of the week of the State Fair, by delegates or alternates or their written proxies, chosen by the several agricultural societies in counties," etc. Under this law the State board appointed a secretary and a treasurer and fixed their salaries. Money appropriated to the Department of Agriculture was expended by the State board "as in the opinion of said board will best advance the interests of agriculture," etc. The board could publish with its report that of the State Entomologist and such other reports as in its judgment the interests of the State may require.

Illinois now has a highly centralized department of agriculture whose director is appointed by the governor. The State board has been shorn of its executive power, and in its stead there is an advisory board of 15 members concerned with general agricultural matters and another advisory board having to do with the State Fair. The development of organization in Illinois is typical of the general movement toward centralization. It, however, emphasizes probably more than most states the importance of the advisory board. The advisory board plan has become a conspicuous part of our political organization wherever regulation is a factor. It is a feature, for instance, of our Federal Reserve System. An advisory board will always serve to keep the regulatory bureau in actual touch with practical situations.

Another type of board organization may be called the Michigan form, which centers in the agricultural college and experiment station, the latter two institutions being under the control of the state board of agriculture. The president of the agricultural college and state superintendent of public instruction are *ex-officio* members of the board. In Michigan up to 1921 this board performed a number of regulatory functions which were that year transferred to a newly created department of agriculture. Duties of other regulatory bureaus were also consolidated and brought under the authority of the department. The reader is referred to the appendix for a more complete statement of the present status of Michigan organization. Sufficient has been said to indicate the points of dissimilarity in state organization. A more detailed study of the organization in Pennsylvania, New York, and Connecticut will now be presented in order to show the main points of difference in organization prevailing throughout the country.

State Organization in Connecticut.—In Connecticut the State Board of Agriculture has a prominent place in public agricultural organization. The statement has already been made that it has a coordinate position with the Dairy and Food Commissioner, Commissioner on Domestic Animals, and the Experiment Station. All of these branches report directly to the governor. The accompanying chart shows the Connecticut organization.

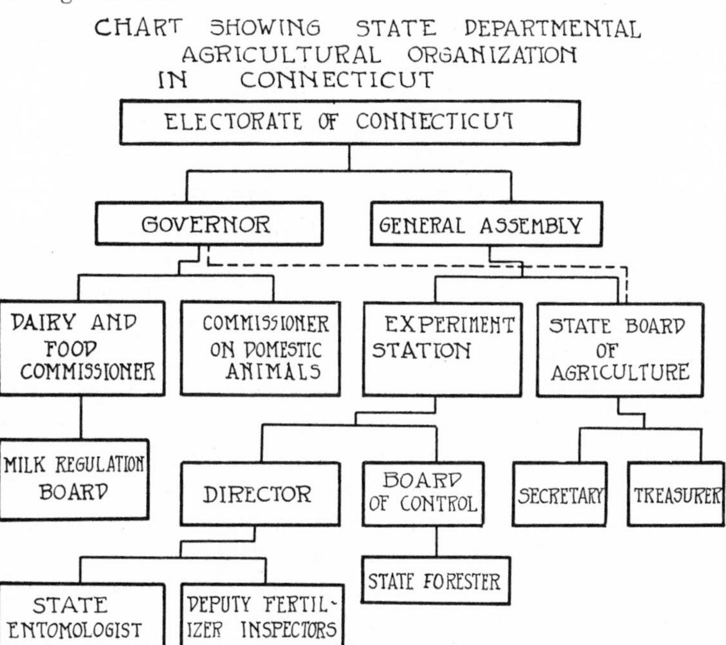

The Connecticut State Board.—The Board consists of 14 persons. The governor is *ex-officio* a member and president. Five of the other 13 members are appointed by the governor with the consent of the senate for a term of 4 years. The governor, however, must select one person from each of the first, second, third, fourth and fifth congressional districts. The other 8 members are elected by the senators and representatives from the respective counties every four years. There are 8 counties in the State so that members of the legislature may select one member for each county.

The Board appoints its secretary and treasurer and such other officers as may be necessary. The duties of both the secretary and the treasurer are prescribed by law. "For the purpose of inquiring into the methods and wants of practical husbandry, ascertaining the adaptation of agricultural products to soil, climate and markets, encouraging the establishment of farmers' clubs, agricultural libraries and reading rooms and disseminating agricultural information by lectures or otherwise, the secretary shall annually visit different sections of the state; and he, or a member or members delegated by the board, shall as far as practicable visit the different agricultural fairs in the state, and annually make a detailed report thereof to the board." The treasurer pays only bills approved by the Board.

The Board is given supervision over the expenditure of funds made by the respective agricultural societies receiving grants from the State. The secretaries of the Connecticut Poultrymen's Association, the Connecticut Beekeepers' Association, the Connecticut Dairymen's Association, the Connecticut Sheep Breeders' Association and the Connecticut Pomological Society all make annual reports to the secretary of the State Board. The Board may prescribe forms and methods of reporting. The poultry association receives $1,000; and the pomological and dairymen's associations each receive $1,500 from the State. The Board makes its report to the governor annually, and this report must contain a special report of fairs held by agricultural societies. The State believes that fairs are an important means of encouraging agriculture.[1]

The Experiment Station.—It should be remembered that the State agricultural colleges and experiment stations perform primarily the three functions of instruction, experimentation and research, and extension, all of which are conditioned by agreements entered into between the States and the Federal Government in order that they may receive the various Federal grants for these respective purposes. All this organization has been discussed in preceding chapters. In Connecticut and in some other States the experiment station, however, is utilized to carry out certain of the regulatory agricultural functions, and it is for this reason that reference is here made to the experiment station. As shown by the chart three im-

[1] The law of public organization is stated in the report of the State Board of Agriculture for 1918.

portant regulatory functions are performed through the agency of the experiment station. The board of control of the experiment station appoints a State forester and the director a State entomologist and deputy fertilizer inspectors.

The director is given charge of the control of injurious insects and is directed to formulate rules of procedure to accomplish their extermination. He may establish quarantines against other States or any areas or district within the State, and may thus regulate the transportation of agricultural prodects for the purpose of destroying plant pests.

It is the duty of the State entomologist to visit and inspect apiaries. If bees are found diseased they must be treated or destroyed. To prevent the spreading of the disease he may establish quarantines against affected areas. All apiaries must be registered with the town clerk. The law gives him also express authority to enter upon property for the purpose of carrying on the campaign against the destruction of the gypsy and the brown-tail moths for which large sums of money have been spent by New England States and the Federal Government. He inspects also all nursery stock coming into the State and not labeled with a certificate of inspection. Notice of such omission is to be given the State entomologist by the express or freight agent. Once a year he or his deputies inspect all the nurseries in the State where stock is grown and sold.

The director of the experiment station has also charge of the control of the fungus disease known as white pine blister rust or currant rust. The director appoints some member or members of the experiment station staff to prosecute this work. Authority is given for the destruction of white pine trees, currant or gooseberry bushes infected with the rust.

The director also appoints deputy fertilizer inspectors whose duty it is to make analyses of all fertilizers registered in the State. Before any such product may be sold a statement on forms prescribed by the director concerning its content must be filed with him. Authority to examine books, enter upon property, and inspect fertilizers is provided. Misbranding, the making of false statements, and interfering with the work of inspectors are punishable by fine.

The State forester appointed by the board of control of

the experiment station is like the preceding officers, a regular member of the staff. He is also *ex-officio* fire warden and as such has supervision of town fire wardens. He instructs them and issues regulations to carry out the provisions of the law.

The Commissioner on Domestic Animals.—On or before July 15, 1921, and quadriennially thereafter the governor is authorized to appoint a Commissioner on Domestic Animals "who shall be a practical farmer and stock breeder of at least ten years' experience." This requirement is just another example of the farmers' ill-advised fear that unless a "dirt-farmer" be placed in public office their interests will not be properly represented. If the requirement were that he shall be a graduate of a creditable veterinary college the agricultural interests of the State would be very much more efficiently protected gainst disease than when the law allows the appointment of a man who has nothing more than a sympathetic attitude toward the business of farming. However, after the creation of a political office at the top the law provides for the appointment by the Commissioner of a deputy commissioner who shall be a graduate of a veterinary college.

The Commissioner is to be notified concerning the importation of all cattle into the State. Such notice shall state the number and their physical condition. He may quarantine all animals infected with a contagious disease. He may order that any diseased animal be killed. The owner is to be paid the value of the animal as determined by him and the Commissioner, or in case no agreement can be reached by these two parties, then as determined by an arbiter. The value paid the owner for animals condemned to prevent the spread of the foot and mouth disease is limited to $125 for any pure-bred bovine or equine animal. For the purpose of eradicating bovine tuberculosis the Commissioner is given authority to cooperate with the Bureau of Animal Industry of the United States Department of Agriculture and is directed to accept financial or other assistance in the condemnation of diseased cattle. Such work, however, can only be undertaken upon the written application of the owner. Where cooperative arrangements are made between the States and the Federal Government the latter will indemnify the owner of the condemned animal for one-third of the difference between the appraised value of the animal and the amount for which it is salvaged.[1] The law also provides for the suppression of hog cholera. The Commissioner is directed to procure a sufficient supply of serum and virus for the vaccination and inoculation of animals. Upon written request of the owner he shall inoculate animals, charging the owner only with the cost of the serum. Quarantines may be established to eradicate the disease.

The Commissioner on Domestic Animals also has supervision over the dogs of the State for the primary purpose of protecting the sheep industry. The law provides that dog tags, to be changed in style each year, are to be furnished by the Commissioner to the town clerk at 5 cents each and by him are to be given to the owners of dogs within the town in which the dogs are registered. As evidence of registration the tag must be placed on the dog collar worn by the dog. The act also provides for the appointment of dog wardens by the select men of the towns. These wardens are indirectly under the supervision of the State Commissioner. Regulations and rues are promulgated by him and sent to the town clerks, who pass them on to the wardens. Owners of dogs are responsible for damage done to sheep and other animals, and wardens as well as any person may kill dogs found to pursue or harass sheep or other domestic animals.

The Dairy and Food Commissioner.—The Dairy and Food Commissioner is appointed by the governor and administers the regulatory functions involved in the inspection of various food products. The inspection of dairy products forms a large part of his duties. His authority concerning the regulation of the sale of milk is somewhat curtailed by the Milk Regulation Board. This Board is made up of the dairy and food commissioner, the attorney-general, the commissioner of health, the secretary of the State board of agriculture, and the secretary of the Connecticut Dairymen's Association. The board, after giving two weeks' notice, may make or suspend rules concerning "the inspection of dairies, the production, care, handling, marketing or sale of milk or cream within the State,

[1] *Vide* the U. S. Department's *Program of Work*, 1919, p. 39.

to protect the public from the use of milk or cream which is insanitary or detrimental to public health."

A Summary of the Connecticut Organization.—Summing up public agricultural organization in Connecticut it may be said that the functions of instruction, experimentation, and extension are performed by its agricultural college and experiment stations. The State board of agriculture is mostly concerned with promoting agriculture and protecting its economic interests from the point of view of the farmer. It is supplemental to the extension service in popularizing scientific principles. Its administrative duties include the making of annual reports covering its own activities as well as those of agricultural societies, and the part played by the secretary as a member of the milk regulation board. The regulatory function is distributed among the experiment station and the two commissioners.

A criticism of the organization would analyze it as both illogical and tinged with two much local government. It is illogical for the reason that regulatory functions are committed to the officers and staff of the experiment station. In a State as populous as Connecticut these functions are burdensome, and to place them in the experiment station is entirely incompatible with both instruction and experimentation. They are administrative duties and as such have no right to disturb either the teaching or research in agriculture.

The attempt to retain a large degree of local influence in agricultural organization through a State board coordinate with other branches hinders directness and efficiency in administration. It should drop out of the administrative field altogether, affiliate itself with the departmental organization only through *ex-officio* membership, and confine its activities to the general promotion of agriculture. This it can do through the holding of fairs and in keeping in close touch with the people throughout the State.

Organization in Pennsylvania.—The States of New York and Pennsylvania are two examples where agricultural organization is highly centralized and where the assumption of new functions has kept pace with the development of agricultural ideas. In both of these States the newly recognized and highly important function of marketing has been undertaken as a public activity.

In General Bulletin No. 332, issued in January, 1920, the Pennsylvania Department of Agriculture sets forth its entire organization in detail by charts. The administrative machinery as thus shown is based on the Act of Assembly of May 8, 1919, at which time a reorganization was effected. The accompanying chart shows the complete agricultural departmental administration. At the head of the department is a Secretary of Agriculture who is assisted by a deputy secretary.

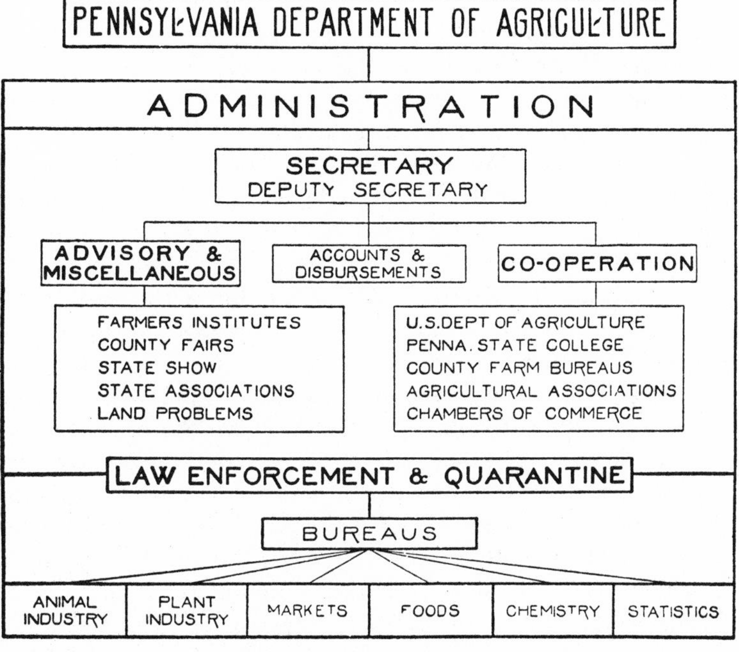

"The function of the Department is to make a study of the agricultural resources of the State and to promote and protect agriculture by dealing primarily with problems which are beyond the control of the individual and the community. In order to carry out this work successfully and economically and in order to avoid duplication, confusion and waste, the Department whenever possible and practical cooperates with other governmental agencies, such as the U. S. Department of

Agriculture, the Pennsylvania State College and the County Farm Bureaus. The Department also works in close cooperation with agricultural associations, Chambers of Commerce and other commercial organizations. Since Bulletin No. 332 was issued, Farmers' Institute work has been discontinued by the Department of Agriculture and all educational work is done by the Pennsylvania State College, except such work as deals directly with the regulatory laws, disease control work and marketing problems.''[1]

In the department are included the six bureaus of animal industry, plant industry, markets, foods, chemistry, and statistics. This bureau organization reminds one of the United States Department of Agriculture with its many bureaus and offices created for the purpose of dealing with the numerous and varied agricultural problems of the country.

The Bureau of Animal Industry.—The work of this bureau is divided into regulatory, disease control and eradication, examinations and investigations, and demonstrations. It should be said that State departments of agriculture supplement and coordinate the activities of the United States Department of Agriculture. It will, therefore, not be necessary to go into a lengthy discussion of the work performed by these respective bureaus. Only some of the more salient features will here be discussed. Under the chapter of the United States Bureau of Animal Industry the Federal meat inspection service was described, and in that connection it was pointed out that unless the States supplement the efforts of the Federal Government, which has inspection powers only over interstate shipments, much of the meat slaughtered and consumed in the United States would fail to receive the necessary surveillance. The State of Pennsylvania is making efforts to meet this situation, but in spite of the fact that the State departmental force has been active in this matter only ''about 50 per cent of the meat consumed in Pennsylvania is slaughtered under Federal, State or Municipal inspection.''[2] During this year 9,997 meat mar-

[1] Statement by Fred Rasmussen, Secretary of Agriculture of Pennsylvania in a personal communication.

[2] *Pennsylvania Report of the Department of Agriculture* for 1916, p. 114.

kets were examined, over 3,000 slaughter houses were examined, and 2,717,783 pounds of meat inspected and passed. Fifty-two meat establishments were closed because of insanitary conditions. The department urges cities, boroughs, and first-class townships to establish their own local inspection. It is pointed out that at establishments where regular inspection service is maintained, proprietors are careful not to present diseased animals for slaughter, and that they sell such animals to dealers or butchers where they may be slaughtered without inspection. This vicious practice renders the law abortive, and should be made impossible through the establishment of local inspection everywhere.

The bureau has power to quarantine against infectious diseases, registers stallions in the State and declares them sound or unsound, publishing the information in bulletin form, aids farmers to eradicate diseases through the use of the tuberculin test for tuberculosis and for other diseases through the use of vaccines.

The Bureau of Plant Industry.—The work of this bureau is divided into regulatory, pest control, investigational, and advisory functions. In its own terms the bureau states that it promotes crop production in the following manner:

1. By advice and aid in controlling destructive plant pests, such as insects, fungous and bacterial diseases, and birds and animals injurious to crops while growing, in storage, or in manufactured form.
2. By inspection of seeds for purity and freedom from weed seeds or other foreign matter.
3. By establishing and enforcing quarantines to prevent the spread of new crop pests.
4. By inspection of over 4,000 acres of nurseries for insects and diseases, thus insuring clean stock for fruit growing and landscape work.
5. By licensing over 500 nurseries, 100 dealers and about 1,200 agents selling nursery stock in Pennsylvania subject to the excellent state law.
6. By inspection of insecticides and fungicides and other chemicals used for spraying, treatment and control of insects and plant diseases.
7. By inspecting apiaries for control of destructive bee diseases, and by encouragement of beekeeping and production of honey and wax.
8. By field surveys and investigations, for control of important pests such as European potato wart disease, white pine blister rust, peach yellows, European corn borer, Oriental fruit moth, cedar-apple rust, Angoumois grain moth in wheat, and insects affecting mills and

milled products, greenhouses, field, garden and truck crops, nurseries, livestock and human beings.

The Bureau of Markets.—In an address at the annual meeting of the Pennsylvania State Board of Agriculture in 1917 Ex-Governor Brumbaugh favored the establishment of a bureau of markets and in this connection made the following statement:[1]

> We do not even market today what we grow, even at a time when we are not growing all that we should, and I am credibly informed by men who have scientifically investigated the matter, that we literally lost millions of dollars of foods in this state during the first season because nobody turned seriously to the problem of marketing that food supply to the people of Pennsylvania. In fact, during the holiday season, I myself passed through an old orchard that was tilled by my own grandfather, and that orchard was literally covered with frozen fruit that had not found its way to the market. Now we cannot be a prosperous Commonwealth unless we make it a point to bring to the market everything that the soil of this Commonwealth produces as a food supply to our people, and the Department of Agriculture here in the past year has given particular study and attention to the importance of establishing a Bureau of Markets to see to it that when a thing does grow upon the soil of Pennsylvania, that that thing will find its best market under competent direction and with immediate returns to the man who grows the food.
>
> I should like to speak particularly of the apple situation in Pennsylvania, in that connection. As we traveled over the state this autumn, we saw literally thousands and thousands and thousands of bushels of apples either hanging upon the trees long after they should have been marketed or lying rotting upon the soil under the trees, just the neglect of somebody or the inability of somebody to sense the importance of gathering all that food and putting it where people needed it and where at this time, by reason of the unusually high cost of food, all of those apples as well as every other product of our soil, would have a ready and a welcome market.

This somewhat lengthy extract is given for the purpose of showing the actual conditions that have existed until recently in many of the States and which still exist in some places, and also for showing the need of public initiative in the field of marketing. Dr. Brumbaugh goes on to say that a friend from Belgium in traveling from New York to Chicago through Pennsylvania and back by way of Washington said to him that the thing that impressed him most concerning America was the wastefulness of the people. In the visitor's country every square yard of ground was made to produce its share of food necessary to sustain the congested population. Dr. Brum-

[1] *Pa. Report* of the Dept. of Agriculture for the fiscal year 1916, p. 457.

baugh also calls attention to a meeting lasting for a whole day called for the purpose of discussing with the farmers of Belgium how to improve the crop of artichokes in that country. As yet minor farm products are not given much attention in this country and the problems of marketing already discussed in a preceding chapter dealing with the United States Bureau of Markets, were, until recently like these minor farm products, wholly ignored in all programs of agricultural improvement. While a Bureau of Markets was established during Governor Brumbaugh's administration, it really did not function until 1919, when a new law was passed and a trained economist was placed in charge.

The work of this bureau is divided into market reports, cooperative organizations, city markets, standardization, and miscellaneous problems. The following statements are taken from General Bulletin No. 332.

The Bureau of Markets assists in improving markets and marketing conditions:

1. By furnishing regular information about prevailing conditions in the larger markets of Pennsylvania concerning prices, supply and special needs as they relate to agricultural products. The marketing of products depends largely on such information.
2. By advising groups of farmers regarding the formation and operation of cooperative buying and selling organizations.
3. By disseminating information regarding the organization and operation of public markets in cities and boroughs of Pennsylvania. Data have been collected on 137 of these markets.
4. By encouraging the adoption of standard grades for farm products and standard containers for fruits and vegetables.
5. By undertaking special studies of problems in transportation, storage, and wholesale and retail distribution; also in the marketing of grain, live stock and other farm products.
6. By cooperating with the United States Bureau of Markets and the Bureaus of Markets of neighboring states in order that marketing matters may be dealt with in a more uniform manner than has been common in the past.
7. By co-operating with Pennsylvania State College through its extension service and county agents to avoid duplications.
8. The greatest markets in the world are at the very doors of the farmers of Pennsylvania. Approximately one-fourth of the entire consuming population of the United States is located within easy reach of producers of Pennsylvania.

The Bureau of Foods.—The bureau of foods, prior to the present organization was known as the Dairy and Food Bureau, and as already pointed out on several previous occasions this work has had a very important place in the history and evolution of public food control as well as in the development of centralized public organization in agriculture. It will be unnecessary here to dwell upon the character of the work performed by this bureau. Enough has been said in the chapter dealing with the United States Bureau of Chemistry as well as in this chapter to give the reader an idea of the historic and present-day importance of this field of public activity. Following is the bureau's own statement concerning its functions:

1. The Bureau of Foods is established for the important purpose of protecting the health of the people of the Commonwealth by controlling the purity and standards of their food supplies.

2. The protection of the food supply of eight million people, who must eat to live is essential and requires constant supervision. Every law enacted for this purpose is for the immediate good of every citizen.

3. Has supervision over the sanitary condition of cold storage plants, as well as the wholesomeness of products offered for storage. Pennsylvania cold storage industry approximates an investment of $75,000,000.

4. Supervises the places licensed for the sale of oleomargarine in order to prevent fraud and deception in the sale of the product.

5. Issues fifty-seven hundred oleomargarine licenses annually, together with eighty licenses to operate cold stroage warehouses, and twenty-five licenses to conduct egg opening establishments.

6. Analyzes approximately six thousand samples of food and drinks annually.

7. Has supervision over the egg-opening establishments.

8. When the first food laws were enacted in 1895, forty per cent of the staple groceries were adulterated or misbranded. Today, the percentage of staple groceries which are unlawfully sold is less than one per cent.

9. The Legislature of 1919 has, by several specific acts relative to the sale of food for human consumption, strengthened the food laws of the Commonwealth, and it is safe to say that Pennsylvania today has the best food laws of any state in the Union.

The Bureau of Chemistry.—The Bureau of Chemistry explains its activities in the following terms:

1. The Bureau of Chemistry registers annauuly all brands of Fertilizers, Lime Products and Feeding Stuffs, and issues licenses permitting their sale.

2. Enforces the laws regulating the manufacture and sale of Feeding Stuffs, Fertilizers, Lime Products, Linseed Oils, Paints, Putties, Turpentines and Insecticides.

3. Collects samples for analyses from selling agents and dealers of all products under the several control laws and inspects methods of labeling and sales.

4. Analyzes annually approximately 4,000 official samples selected by Special Agents, to determine correctness of guarantees and composition and to detect adulteration, and special samples of Feeding

Stuffs, Lime Products, Linseed Oils and Turpentines, submitted by residents of Pennsylvania.

5. The annual sale of Feeding Stuffs in the state is estimated approximately at 1,250,000 tons, having a commercial value of at least $62,500,000; of Fertilizers, 350,000 tons, valued at $12,000,000; of Agricultural Lime, 300,000 tons, valued at $2,400,000.

6. Cooperates with County Agents and other Agricultural Agencies in supplying aid and information regarding the activities of the Bureau and the enforcement of the control laws.

7. Cooperates with the National and State Associations of Officials in the establishment of uniform methods of analysis, labeling and definitions.

The Bureau of Statistics.—The Bureau of Statistics has over 800 field crop and livestock reports scattered over the State. Monthly crop and livestock reports as well as annual reports are issued. The township correspondents report monthly on various agricultural items. The report issued March 1, 1920, on the basis of these reports estimated the number of purebred stallions, bulls, boars, and rams in the State at the time; the number of steers the farmers were fattening for the spring market; the amount of commercial fertilizers used and its price; the amount of lime used and its price; the condition of wheat and rye; the quantity of potatoes in producers' hands; the number of farmers employing female household help; the number of farmers that stored ice during the winter; the number of flocks of sheep; and the number of farm homes having telephones. This list is varied from month to month the content of the report depending largely upon the season. In another monthly report estimates concerning the use of the farm tractor and the general substitution of the automobile and auto truck for the draft animal, are made. Valuable data having a bearing upon market conditions, the progress of agriculture of the State, and the kind of agricultural education and demonstration work that should be emphasized, are collected by this bureau.

The Former Pennsylvania State Board of Agriculture.—The organization above presented shows no connection with a State board of agriculture. It was noted that in Connecticut the secretary of the State board of agriculture is elected by its members, that he is a State officer and has his salary paid by the State, that the State board has a coordinate position with other branches of public organization, and that the board in fact through its secretary, who is a member of the milk regulation board, participates in the regulatory function committed to the office of the dairy and food commissioner. In Pennsylvania the State board of agriculture was abolished by the Act of 1919 providing for the reorganization of the department; while it existed it had no such commanding position as the board in Connecticut. It was in no way a part of the administrative system in the sense that its members were to be consulted before action could be taken. The relationship between the department and the State board was rather that of father to son or that of pastor to the congregation. The State department was grealy interested in keeping intact an organization through which it may carry on propaganda and reach all people in nearby and remote places. The New York department in its report[1] for 1912 recognized the importance of keeping in close touch with agricultural societies and cooperating with them. It is there stated that "largely by reason of this cooperation the old New York State Agricultural Society, which was dormant for a period of about ten years, was revived in 1909 and has held increasingly successful annual meetings since." This, however, was before the days of the complete organization of the extension service. Since the organization of the extension service the need for any definite relation betwen the agricultural societies and the State department is no longer so important.

The membership of the former State board in Pennsylvania was made up for the most part of members elected by the county agricultural societies which elected one member for each county. In addition the Pennsylvania Bee-Keepers Association and the Pennsylvania State Poultry Society each elected a member. In 1916 the governor appointed three members. Important officers of the State's executive departments were also *ex-officio* members. There were 6 of these including the governor, secretary of internal affairs, superintendent of public instruction, master of the State Grange, auditor general, and the secretary of agriculture. All of these officials probably found it convenient to be associated with the organization

[1] P. 518.

for the purpose of educating the people of the State along lines in which they were officially interested. The total membership in 1916 numbered 78. The State board met annually. It had standing committees on various agricultural problems. It had committees on resolutions and on legislation. A very commendable feature of the organization was that it had a group of consulting specialists on botany, entomology, pomology, forestry, etc. In 1916 these specialists numbered 15. The organization was interested in scientific agriculture and in securing its adoption throughout the State. The extension service in Pennsylvania has been placed under the administration of the Pennsylvania State College, and there is therefore less need for the State board of agriculture. Its abolition in 1919 eliminated useless duplication in the State's organization. But the Board was really not representative of agricultural interests. As early as 1895, when the Department was established, it ceased to function effectively. In the early days county associations represented the progressive interests of agriculture, but many of these have long since turned into fair associations and are holding fairs primarily for profit. Members from such groups do not represent the real interests of agriculture.

The Commission of Agriculture.—The Commission of Agriculture was established in 1915, but was abolished in 1919. This commission consisted of seven members, five of whom were to be farmers and were to be appointed by the Governor with the consent of the Senate. The commissioners received no compensation, but were allowed traveling expenses. The commission performed two important functions: first, the approval of all appointments made by the Secretary of Agriculture; second, the preparation of a budget for the department and its submission to the legislature. Of course such an arrangement cannot succeed very long. With the Secretary appointed by the Governor and the budget prepared by an independent commission, difficulties were bound to develop. "Differences of opinion between the Secretary of Agriculture and the Board made this type of a Commission impractical, and it was somewhat of a relief to everybody to have the Commission abolished in 1919.''[1]

It is interesting to note the reasons that led to the establishment of this commission. It is suggested by Mr. Rasmussen that ''it was probably the lack of close contact of the Board of Agriculture with the activity of the Department which led to the establishment of the Agricultural Commission.'' Irrespective of what forces actually were responsible for enacting this piece of legislation and the motives that actuated them, the principle involved is clearly wrong. It gave the agricultural interest control in the government of the department to the exclusion of other citizens who are so vitally affected by the large regulatory powers committed to this executive branch of the government. The power of this commission, while it lasted, approached that of the Council of Farms and Markets in New York. In the discussion that follows the New York organization is vigorously condemned and this commission must be objected to on similar grounds.

At the time the Department was reorganized the question as to whether or not an advisory board should be created was discussed at some length, and in view of the fact that an appointed board is seldom of real service by reason of its lack of interest or lack of training in technical agriculture it was decided to adopt the policy merely of making provision for cooperation on the part of the department with other agricultural agencies in the state and with the federal department. Attention should be called to the fact that the Secretary of Agriculture is *ex-officio* a member of the Board of Trustees of Pennsylvania State College and this has the effect of coordinating all the agricultural work of the State.[2] This freedom of cooperation and the absence of an advisory board of agriculture is proving to be wholly satisfactory in Pennsylvania.

Organization in New York.—Like that of Pennsylvania the New York State department is highly centralized. From 1917 to 1921 the department was governed by a Council of Farms and Markets, which is elected by the legislature. In 1921 the Commissioner of Agriculture was made the actual

[1] Fred Rasmussen in a presonal communication.
[2] Fred Rasmussen in a personal communication.

head of the department who, however, is appointed by the Council. A notable feature of the New York department is the direction that its organization has taken in recent years with respect to marketing. As previously stated, marketing only in the last decade has received attention from public agricultural organization. New York has not been slow to develop this phase of the work and has in fact emphasized it to such an extent that a State Department of Foods and Markets was created. In the reorganization that took place in 1917 the name chosen for the new department is that of Farms and Markets. The accompanying chart shows the department as organized in 1920 to be divided into the two main divisions of Agriculture, and Foods and Markets. Each of these divisions is then subdivided into a number of bureaus. An examination of the chart and a perusal of its descriptive matter will give the student a very good understanding of New York's organization. It must be remembered that the chart does not show that the Commissioner of Farms and Markets is the executive head of the department.

Attention must be called in a special way to the Council of Farms and Markets created in 1917. This was actually the governing body of the department up to 1921. The law provides for the appointment of the first members by the governor by and with the advice and consent of the senate for terms varying from one to ten years. Their successors, however, are to be elected by the legislature for a term of 10 years. The governor can only recommend to the senate to remove members of the council. It consists of one member from the State at large, the commissioner of public markets of New York City, and one member from each of the judicial districts of the State, aggregating eleven embers in 1920. They serve without salary, but are allowed traveling expenses incurred in the performance of their duties. Regular meetings are provided for as well as special ones. In 1919 the Council held 15 general meetings, and 18 additional meetings in connection with the milk problem in 13 different cities. The law in effect from 1917 to 1921 provided that this council was to appoint a counsel, a secretary, commissioners of the two divisions, as well as directors of bureaus and subordinate officers and clerks upon the recommendation of the commissioners. The law enacted in 1921 confined the appointive power of the Council to the selection of the Commissioner of Farms and Markets, while all other employes are appointed by him and hold office at his pleasure. Not even is the appointment of the chief executive vested in the governor; and the organization is thus taken entirely out of his control. However, the governor approves the necessary appropriations and to this extent may control the activities of the Council and the Commissioner. Salaries within the limits of the appropriation were formerly fixed by the Council, but under the new law are fixed by the Commissioner. Under the direction of the President of the Council the Secretary formerly had general charge of the offices of the department, superintended its clerical business and performed such other duties as the council might prescribe. The new law has shorn the Council of its actual governing functions and the Secretary, as well as all other employes, are therefore made amenable to the Commissioner. The Commissioner is amenable to the Council because he is appointed by it and holds office at its pleasure. He is required under the law to submit to it all matters of general policy.

The concentration of the State organization under the Council of Farms and Markets is an outgrowth of the Wicks bill, which was opposed in its original form by all interests concerned in the production and marketing of agricultural products. The supporters of the council plan maintained that it would result in the establishment of a non-partisan board which would serve as an impartial arbiter among all economic groups concerned. This point of view is stated by William E. Dana, President of the Council of Farms and Markets, in a letter as follows: ''The Council was created in response to a demand on the part of the agricultural interests of the State that the Department be removed from political control. Ever since the establishment of the Department of Agriculture it had been used by either political party, when in power, for partisan purposes. The Council was established along the lines of the Board of Regents of the University of the State of New York, under whose wise supervision the entire educational system of the State has been developed and kept free from partisan control." Contrasted with this point of view is that of the *Rural New Yorker,* which consistently opposed the measure on the ground that "the alleged purpose to take the Department out of politics," was evident to those familiar with administrative policies at the time to be a mere pretense. The journal says that the Department is more than ever dominated by politics and to the advantage of the dealers in New York City and other urban centers.[1] The former Department of Foods and Markets, it is claimed, made progress in eliminating market abuses and was looking forward to developing a market system free from all unnecessary middlemen. The new Council of Farms and Markets, it is contended, is being controlled by the dealers and is checking the proposed market reforms.

Criticism of the New York Form of Organization.—It would seem that the Council of Farms and Markets made up of men serving without salary must necessarily consist of a personnel appointed at the urgent request of particular economic interests concerned. These men will surely serve the interests with which they are affiliated. It is stated that the dealers now dominate the situation. In subsequent appointments to be made by the legislature it will be an easy matter for the farmers of the State, if they will exercise their power, to secure control. Whether the farmers or the dealers dominate the board the result for the consumer is unsatisfactory, because extremely important regulatory functions are administered by the Department of Farms and Markets, and the way in which these are carried out is dependent upon policies formulated by the Council.

This Council which controls the Department of Farms and Markets is in no way similar to an educational board. The former has large regulatory functions and is to be compared with such regulatory bodies as State public utility commissions, or the Interstate Commerce Commission, or the Federal Trade Commission. In other words, agriculture is becoming more and more complex and already like manufacturing, com-

[1] Issue of December 27, 1919, p. 1885.

merce, and transportation, creates numerous social problems that require State and Federal regulation for their solution.

There is no valid objection to the creation of a non-partisan commission. Members of such a commission, however, must be paid good salaries and must serve for a long term. Although it is a question at this stage of agricultural development whether such a plan is necessary in all States of the Union especially where an effective short-ballot system is in use. The short-ballot plan of political control provides for the election of the governor and the auditor by the people and for the appointment of all minor officials by the executive who will be held responsible for the policies and quality of work of all departments and offices of the State. The principle is predicated upon a sense of civic responsibility felt by the American people. It is true that the people in general in this country feel it necessary to perform their duties of citizenship. But in a number of States this duty to a large extent degenerates into an obligation of showing allegiance to a political party. It is a question whether the short-ballot principle, even though there be coupled with it the recall of the governor, would in all the States result in lessening political corruption. In New England and in some western States it would probably work well. It is quite certain that in some States corruption would even be greater. Whether the short-ballot plan in New York with its strong Tammany organization would result in an improvement in political appointments is by no means certain, and inasmuch as the regulatory function of the New York department of agriculture has become so important it may be well not to entrust its administration to a personnel appointed by the governor either under the present constitution of the State or under a form of government embodying the short-ballot principle. Probably in New York a thoroughly non-partisan board whose members are paid large salaries and are appointed by the governor for a long term would be the best administrative system that could be erected.

Another objection that should be registered against the New York Council as it existed before 1921, is that it is an unwieldly body of eleven members. The fact also that it is not in continuous session is a hindrance to expeditious administration. Inasmuch as the detail administrative functions have now been vested in the Commissioner of Farms and Markets this objection is no longer so important.

Comparison with Massachusetts Organization.—Before leaving the discussion of the New York form of organization reference should be made to the new Massachusetts department created in 1919.[1] This department is under the supervision of a commissioner appointed by the Governor and his Council. An advisory board of six members, three of whom must be farmers, is also appointed in the same way. But as stated this is only an advisory board and has not the appointive power exercised by the New York Council. The plan provides for close cooperation between the administrative department and agricultural interests, and it would seem that the plan is wholly in accord with sound principles of administration. The authority of the governor over the department together with the establishment of an advisory board is a more feasible plan for the solution of all problems than the New York plan.[2]

Organization in North Dakota.—It is not the plan to discuss in detail the organization in North Dakota or to extend the detail discussion of State organization to other States. In North Dakota, however, the State has assumed new functions under the control of the Non-Partisan League to which at least reference should be made. The functions performed either by the Federal or State departments include the educational or demonstrational, investigational, service, and regulatory. In North Dakota a new function has been assumed by the State administration in the management of public utilities mainly for the benefit of the farmer.

Chapter 151 of the State laws of 1919 creates the Industrial Commission of North Dakota. The commission consists of the governor, the attorney general, and the commissioner of agriculture and labor. The statute authorizes this commission of three men to conduct and manage on behalf of the State certain public utilities. Under chapter 147 the commission

[1] *Vide* Chap. 350 of the *Acts* of 1919.

[2] The reader is referred to the appendix for a summary of present-day state agricultural departmental organization.

has established the Bank of North Dakota; under chapter 150 it has authority to establish Home Building Associations through which homes for rural or urban citizens of the State may be provided; and under chapter 152 it is establishing State flour mills, warehouses, and grain elevators. In a decision upholding the constitutionality of these laws Judge Amidon in the Federal District Court said:

> It is hopeless to expect a population consisting of farmers scattered over a vast territory as the people of this state are to create any private business system that will change the system now existing. The only means through which the people of the state have had any experience in joint action in their state government.

From the point of view of State-owned agrarian utilities it may be too early to say just what the outcome will be, although signs are not lacking that the political organization fostering government ownership in various fields is disintegrating. In the words of Doctor Devine in the Survey of March 6, 1920, North Dakota is a laboratory, an experiment station for the Non-Partisan League. The North Dakota farmers had grievances against the Minneapolis grain dealers on account of dockage for alleged shrinkage in the weight of the grain, and on account of low grading. This is the old charge that the agricultural shipper has been making against the commission merchant and organized produce markets since the days of the large urban centers in America. In some States public officials inspect the grain upon arrival at the market. This is true in those States containing the principal grain markets. In Illinois, Minnesota, Wisconsin, Missouri, Kansas, Montana Oklahoma and Washington the inspection of grain has been made a public function.[1] The Federal Government, through the Bureau of Markets, has also an inspection service, consisting of licensed inspectors, of which shipper and receiver may avail themselves through the payment of a small inspection fee. Full use of either State or Federal inspection machinery has the effect of rendering justice to both parties of the sale, and should do away with such complaints as that of the North Dakota farmer against the Minneapolis grain dealer.

[1] Weld's *Marketing of Farm Products*, p. 370.

These grievances have been in the main the starting point of the economic program of the farmers in North Dakota. They have set up State-owned grain elevators, flour mills where a just price for the farmers' wheat is to be paid, a bank to serve as a clearing center and bankers' bank for the State, and an insurance system to protect the farmers' crops. It is to be noted that elsewhere in the country these facilities are secured through State regulation and through cooperation among the farmers themselves. Both Federal and State agricultural departments including also the extension service have been fostering the cooperative movement. Private agricultural organizations, notably the Grange and the Farmers' Union, have been very active in getting the farmers' enterprises organized on a cooperative basis. It would seem that the cooperative method, because of the direct interest of a special economic group in the business and the exclusion of other non-interested political factions, is going to be more successful than operation under public ownership.

Referring directly to the organization of the Industrial Commission having charge of these farmers' enterprises, and made up of the governor, the attorney general, and the commissioner of agriculture and labor, it may be pointed out that unless experts in the several lines of banking, insurance, milling, etc., are appointed and made responsible to this board, the administration of these enterprises is liable to be inefficient. The members of the Industrial Commission have their respective duties and besides running the danger of overburdening them it seems illogical to place these varied functions under one and the same board.

Ideal State Departmental Organization.—In order to determine the character of ideal State agricultural organization the subject must be approached from the point of view of functions. There is no question concerning agricultural college instruction. This function can only be performed by the agricultural colleges.

With respect to research and experimentation it must be pointed out that there are occasions when the state department must of necessity enter this field in order that it may successfully enforce the laws committed to it. Similarly there are educational problems involved in the enforcement of the law. The inspection forces are not primarily trying to discover an offender of the law but rather take the position that the department is a corrective agency and that considerable educational work is necessary to raise the standard of ethics in the production and marketing of food products. In the control of animal and plant diseases the larger part of the work is not regulatory or law enforcement but educational. In connection with the eradication of tuberculosis, for instance, in a number of states a cooperative agreement is entered into between the individual farmer on the one hand and the state and federal governments on the other. To secure the cooperation of the farmer he must be educated to the point where he realizes that the testing of his herd is not only beneficial as far as profits are concerned, but that it is also of tremendous importance to the health and well-being of the community as a whole. With respect to the amount of research and educational work that a state department of agriculture should do, Mr. Fred Rasmussen, Secretary of the State Department of Agriculture, has the following to say:

Although it is not the function of a State Department of Agriculture to do research work, yet there are times when it is necessary for the Department to do so for its own protection. For example, in connection with tuberculin testing three different tests are used. We have carried out extensive studies on the comparison of the three different tests under field conditions and on a large number of herds. We have also made systematic studies of the technique of applying the tuberculin test as well as the interpretation of results.

Again, in connection with our feed inspection work we have carried out studies in microscopic examinations of mixed feeds which have been very valuable in our control work. The fact is that a good many problems in connection with control work do not come to the attention of or confront the purely scientific investigator in the Colleges and Stations, but do come forcibly to the attention of the people who are charged with the control work and in many cases will have to be taken care of by them. I am making this statement because there is, in many instances, a lack of understanding by men working in Colleges and in Stations of the problems which are before the workers in the Department of Agriculture, the former believing that all the Department should do is purely police work and law enforcement. I agree in principle with the general policy that the educational, the research and the experimental work should be done at the Colleges and Stations, with an undrstanding, however, that the Department of Agriculture of course must use educational methods for accomplishing such work as they are charged by law to do, and that it is understood that the Department would not be transgressing in the field of the Experiment Stations by making a systematic study of such problems the solution of which is necessary for the successful carrying out the prescribed duties of the Department.[1]

While the state department must do some research and educational work in connection with the enforcement of the law, there is no question as to the place of research and experimentation in a primary sense as well as popular agricultural education. Research and experimentation, not clearly and definitely related to administration, belong to the experiment station in the main. The United States Department of Agriculture may also rightfully take up problems of a national characted or problems too expensive for local stations to undertake. All of the cooperative agricultural extension work should be centered in the colleges and placed in charge of an extension director who has at his command not only a force devoting its entire time to the extension service but the faculty of the college whose personnel is ready to give the service the benefit of its mature experience and study.

When this extension organization was in process of rapid development officials of the United States Department of Agriculture believed that all the needs of the farmers' institutes would be provided for by the new organization. This point of view was taken issue with by T. B. Parker in an address before the American Association of Farmers' Institute Workers held at the University of California in 1915. Mr. Parker then said that "we should feel encouraged to push forward and continue the work that is meaning so much to the farmers of our country, improve our methods as our experience teaches us and make our institutes continue to grow in strength and efficiency, the opinion of the gentleman from the United States Department of Agriculture, who last year spoke on the relation of farm Bureaus to Farmers' Institute work, to the contrary notwithstanding." In accordance with figures given at the close of the chapter on the United States States Relations Service the number of farmers' institutes held in the last few years has by no means suffered a decline, and in the opinion of Department officials this institution has come to

[1] From a personal communication.

stay inasmuch as it is believed to perform a special service which the extension work does not provide.

It seems to be a settled question then that the farmers' institute work should continue, and according to a memorandum of understanding adopted by the Association of Commissioners of Agriculture it has been agreed that all educational work should be done by the agricultural colleges. In the report of 1916 of the U. S. Relations Service it is stated that in 24 States the State departments and in 24 the agricultural colleges conducted the farmers' institutes. In the report for 1918, the number conducted by State departments or by special State farmers' institute officials had dwindled to 15, while the number conducted by agricultural colleges through the extension service had risen to 33. These figures indicate a decided drift of the farmers' institute work away from the State department and toward the extension service.

From a scientific point of view it is plain that too much organization is almost as undesirable as not enough. If two organizations exist that can carry on the same function there is occasioned the necessity of increasing salaries, mileage, correspondence and other costs. This is a burden that reverts to the people in the form of increased taxes. Moreover two organizations in the same field performing the same functions often are jealous of each other's success, stir up discord in the community, and interfere with general cooperative agricultural endeavor. It would seem, therefore, that the complete and well-supported extension organization should have no rival in the performance of its own duties, and that its organization, everywhere sanctioned as a necessary one, should be utilized for the purpose also of conducting farmers' institutes. There should, however be cooperation between the extension service and the State department officials. In a highly centralized department like that of Pennsylvania the officials performing the regulatory functions have important educational facts to place before the people, and these officials should be drawn upon by the extension director for assistance in the conduct of farmers' institutes. An *ex-officio* State board made up of the leading members of the State department, the agricultural college, and experiment station, could be created for the purpose of securing the fullest cooperation and marshaling all of the State's resources to the best advantage of agricultural improvement.

Investigational work of the kind that is conducted in statistical offices is seldom of the nature of research. Definite facts often provided for by law are collected and tabulated. The work is mostly clerical and performed under the direction of a trained statistician. Correct methods of collection, presentation, and interpretation are important. The collection of data very frequently must have behind it the respect for State officials and the force of the State, otherwise very unsatisfactory results are obtained. The people of the State will have greater respect for this work if the statistician has offices at the capital. Placing this work in the agricultural college or in a semi-public State board is therefore not good from the point of view of collecting data. It is illogical also to place it in the college because it does not fall under the head of research. It should be placed under a centralized State Department.

The regulatory function remains to be discussed. While this function is largely one of inspection, quarantining, etc., and the institution of prosecutions against offenders of the law all of which are purely executive or police duties; correcting, advising and warning the ignorant and unsophisticated offenders are also important aspects. However, the successful performance of this function requires all the power the State can display without resorting to martial law. A study of food adulteration and the efforts to prevent it will convince one of this need. It is therefore very plain that the regulatory function should not be lodged with the agricultural college or experiment station, nor with a semi-public State board of agriculture. It should be placed in a bureau of a centralized State department of agriculture or in a thoroughly non-partisan board whose members are paid large salaries and are appointed for a long term. As already stated the appointment of a commissioner of agriculture with every change of administration, corresponding to the federal practice, will bring good results in some States. Where political traditions would lessen corruption if the short-ballot system were used the centralized department plan can be made wholly satisfactory. In such States where the regulatory function has become very important and where the short-ballot system could not be relied upon to secure an improved political morality—and there are such States—the best solution of the problem seems to be the erection of the right kind of a non-partisan commission.

SELECTED REFERENCES

United States Agricultural Report for 1866, pp. 498-527; *U. S. Agri. Report* for 1875, pp. 437-468; *Bailey's Cyclopedia of American Agriculture, Vol. IV*, pp. 328-339; various *Reports* of state departments of agriculture.

PART II.

PRIVATE AGRICULTURAL ORGANIZATION

CHAPTER XV

STATE AND NATIONAL AGRICULTURAL SOCIETIES

In the preceding chapter it was shown that public State agricultural organization had its beginning in private agricultural societies. It is the plan in the present chapter to give a more detailed account of these societies and to outline briefly their history so far as records will make this possible. It is to be noted that they have had for their purpose the popularization of technical agricultural education, the importation of pure-bred livestock in the early days, the promotion of agriculture in general for common benefit especially through the holding of fairs, and the creation of a desirable social medium for the rural population. These societies have virtually always lacked the spirit of the newer so-called farmers' organizations whose purpose is also largely educational but which exist primarily to promote the economic welfare of the farmers through cooperation and combination. These more recent farmers' organizations developed virtually independently of the earlier agricultural associations, and organically are altogether separate from them; so that today there are two main types of private agricultural organization. The earlier type has largely continued its original policies and in many states is closely affiliated with public organization, in some actually constituting state boards of agriculture; while the more recent type in addition to the educational activity has assumed as its main function the promotion of the economic status of the farmers as a class, and stands separate from public organization. The latter type of private agricultural organization will be discussed under various heads in succeeding chapters.

Early History of Agricultural Societies.—The earliest agricultural organization in America is associated with the history of the States of Pennsylvania, South Carolina, Maine, New York, Massachusetts, New Hampshire, Georgia and Maryland. As stated in the preceding chapter, these early societies were usually initiated by prominent statesmen who resided in urban centers. It was stated that the Philadelphia society had among its members George Washington, Benjamin Franklin, and Timothy Pickering. Of these George Washington at least was personally interested in the practical side of farming. It is said that he supervised operations on his plantation at Mount Vernon by means of maps which he had before him while conducting his military campaigns. In this way directions were given and accounts of crops from his overseer were checked up. The early efforts of these far-sighted and patriotic citizens were, however, not well received by the farmers generally. "At first these societies were ridiculed by the practical farmers; but it was soon discovered that their transactions contained much valuable information."[1] The Society for Promoting Agriculture was organized at Philadelphia in 1785. It should be remembered that this was at a time when "the farmer who ventured to make experiments, to strike out new paths of practice, or to adopt new modes of culture, subjected himself to the ridicule of the whole neighborhood." Crops were planted during full moon. "The rotation of crops was almost unknown; the value of manures was little regarded; labor-saving implements were never thought of, and the undersized horses, cattle, and sheep were so badly cared for during the winter that they cast but faint shadows in the spring." The cast-iron mould board of the plough had not yet been in general use. The farmers were slow to adopt its use and continued to use wooden ploughs plated with wrought iron. They feared that the new iron plough would poison their crops.

What appears to be the oldest permanent horticultural society in the United States is the Pennsylvania Horticultural Society organized in Philadelphia on the 22d of June, 1828. Matthew Carey, who was an editor and an advocate of the protective tariff, was the presiding officer at a previous meeting held in November, 1827, where the first steps toward organization were taken. The first president was Horace Binney, a "distinguished lawyer and horticulturist." The society began its existence with 65 members of the "best citizens" of Philadelphia. It had for its object from the beginning the stimulation of fruit-growing through exhibits. In 1875 its

[1] From article by Ben: Perley Poore, in *Report* of Department for 1866, p. 513.

headquarters with its library were moved to Horticultural Hall on Broad Street.

Early Organization in South Carolina and Georgia.—The South Carolina State Agricultural Society was established in 1785, the same year that the Philadelphia society was organized. It had for its objects the establishment of an experimental farm, the importation and distribution of "foreign articles suitable to the soil and climate of South Carolina," to educate the public in improved agricultural methods, and to reward those who improved the art. After the Civil War the society began to hold fairs. It imported vines and olives. The vines failed from the beginning, while the olives thrived temporarily. In 1808 the society directed its attention to rice cultivation. It offered medals for the best use of water, and for the best hydraulic machine to raise water. It also offered medals for the "best method of preventing injury by the caterpillar to the cotton plant," and for the best method of extracting oils from the ground-nut, benne, cotton, and sunflower seeds.[1] The Civil War and its consequences seriously interrupted the work of the south. It is reported that its membership at one time was very large, but that in 1875 it numbered only 150, the majority of the members living in the vicinity of Charleston.

In the State of Georgia it appears that its State Agricultural Society incorporated December 6, 1810, was less active in its early days than the South Carolina society, and had also a more irregular existence. The act of incorporation set forth the aims and purposes of the Agricultural Society of Georgia as follows: "to collect information as to the different modes of agriculture then practiced in the State; to suggest such improvements as experience had shown to have been beneficial; to excite among their fellow citizens a desire for making experiments in the renovation of exhausted lands, and for the amelioration of such as in their natural state are nonproductive and unfit for cultivation."[1] It is interesting to

[1] *Vide Report* of Department for 1875, p. 464.

note that the incorporators were authorized to use the lottery method for the purpose of raising $10,000.00 to be applied to the objects of the society. The lottery method was formerly used by governments for raising revenue. For moral reasons England abolished it in 1826 and France in 1836.[2] In the United States statutes generally prohibit lotteries and the United States Government prohibits the use of the mail for this purpose which has been responsible for wiping out the large private lotteries. At the time this privilege was granted by the Georgia legislature, however, the method of raising revenue through the use of the lottery had still more or less general sanction but soon fell into disrepute and today would not be tolerated by any of the Governments in the United States. While there are no records available to show the extent of the activity of this society it is reasonable to believe that it met regularly and by concerted effort was responsible for the passage of the act establishing a "Board of Agriculture and Rural Economy of the State of Georgia" in 1837. However, a new start was necessary in 1846 when the Southern Central Agricultural Society was organized with more than 60 members. John W. Graves, proprietor of Stone Mountain Hotel, seems to have been the originator of the movement perhaps for more or less personal reasons. This was at the time when the agricultural fair began to be popular in the North and West and the Georgia society began immediately to hold fairs, the first exhibit, that of 1846, being, however, quite limited. It consisted merely of a jack and jennet, both of which belonged to the proprietor of the hotel.[3] From a small beginning it soon developed important fairs. The society was incorporated in 1854. In 1860 its name was changed to the Georgia Agricultural Society. From 1860 to 1866, the period of the Civil War, it suspended operations, but after this the society was revived and in 1869 had a very important fair, which was attended by the U. S. Commissioner of Agriculture and other prominent

[1] From a brief historical sketch by Hon. Martin V. Colvin in the *Proceedings* of the annual convention of the Georgia State Agricultural Society for 1914.

[2] *Vide* H. C. Adams *Finance*, p. 273.

[3] *Report* of Department of Agriculture for 1875, p. 439.

men. Since then the society held fairs regularly with the aid of various cities. Mason, Atlanta, Augusta, Valdosta, and Savannah have in turn cooperated with the Society in holding a State fair.

Early Organization in New England.—It is reported that in New Hampshire local agricultural societies date back to 1814. Between that year and 1820 several county associations were organized, all of which received State aid. From the records available, however, it does not appear that the organization in New Hampshire was continuous from this early date to the middle of the 19th century.[1]

Among the earliest societies organized in America is the Kennebec Society founded in Maine in 1787. This society was unique in that it was organized by farmers. Its objects were the improvement of agriculture, the importation of pure-bred stock, improved implements, and the best available seeds.[2] It followed the discussional plan of the Philadelphia society, which received its inspiration directly from England through correspondence between Washington and Sinclair. Thus the Kennebec society met regularly for the purpose of reading and discussing papers bearing on agriculture. At first it held no fairs. As will be shown the fair became prominent throughout the United States later in the century.

Massachusetts was one of the very first States to organize a horticultural society. On February 24, 1829, the first meeting with a view to founding the Massachusetts Horticultural Society was held. The constitution was adopted and final organization was effected on March 17 of the same year with more than 160 members. In 1875 its membership numbered more than 1,000. This society has had a very active history from its beginning to the present. In its *Transactions* for the year 1919 the Secretary was able to say that "the year 1919 completes the ninetieth of the Society's history."[3] Immediately after the organization of the society steps were taken for the formation of a horticultural library. In 1875 the library

---

[1] *Vide Report* of Department for 1875, p. 455.

[2] *Vide* Butterfield in Bailey's *Cyclopedia of American Agriculture*, Vol. IV, p. 291.

[3] P. 137.

contained 2,750 volumes and 350 pamphlets which, it is said, was at the time one of the largest horticultural libraries in the world.[1] In 1831 the Society established Mount Auburn Cemetery with a view to combining the cemetery with an experimental garden. These interests, however, conflicted and it became necessary to abandon the plan. The property was sold and "the income from this land and other sources has given the society more ample means for the promotion of horticulture than has been enjoyed by any similar society in this country." While the real object of the enterprise, therefore, was a failure, it was nevertheless a blessing in disguise. In 1844 the Society built a hall which was probably the first building erected by a horticultural society for the accommodation of its exhibitions. The Society, however, soon outgrew the building, necessitating the use of the historic Fanueil Hall for its annual shows after 1848. Its real estate was sold to advantage in 1860 and a more spacious hall was erected and dedicated in 1865.

The object of the society has always been the advancement of horticulture. In 1875 its officials reported to the United States Department of Agriculture that its exhibitions had been regularly held for 47 years. Before and since that year the Society has held regular exhibits. For some years exhibitions were held every Saturday during the summer and autumn months. For some time a special rose show was given in June. A grand annual exhibition was given in September. Exhibits included fruits, flowers, and vegetables and premiums were offered for the best specimens. Premiums were also offered for the best gardens, pleasure grounds, and the best results obtained in greenhouses. According to the report for 1919 continued interest is manifested in the flower exhibits, but it is complained by a committee that these shows are made up mostly of exhibits from florists and that they no longer stimulate a sufficiently large number of individuals in the community to grow flowers and experiment with them. In 1829 the Society offered $93 in prizes. In 1874 the amount appropriated for the purpose was $5,800. By this time it had paid out more

[1] *Vide Report* of Department for 1875, p. 449.

than $80,000. In the statement above referred to the officials believe that these exhibitions" have not only been a source of refined pleasure to the thousands who have beheld them, but have been the means of educating the community" concerning the "choicest productions of horticulture, and of inspring a love for the art." The society has certainly served a very useful purpose. It is a question whether its activities as they have been conducted are as useful now as they were more than a half century ago when agricultural colleges, agricultural experimentation, and horticultural libraries were only in the embryo state. More will be said in a latter section concerning the activities of horticultural societies and their usefulness at the present day.

During the winter months the Society has held meetings where papers were read. In 1875 it is reported that these meetings were held weekly, which was an ambitious program.

Early Organization in New York.—The New York State Agricultural Society was organized in 1791 with Robert R. Livingston, agriculturist and jurist, as president. The Society was very active from 1792 to 1819, during which period it published the transactions of the society, and, as stated in the previous chapter, was instrumental in having a statute placed on the books providing for the establishment of a State board of agriculture. The board published its reports from 1820 to 1826, after which it ceased to exist, and in 1832 a new State society was organized. Jesse Buel, agriculturist, editor, assemblyman, and judge, was its secretary. "Though organized with much enthusiasm, the society accomplished very little until its reorganization in 1841."[1] At this time the fair became a prominent feature of the society's activities, and seemed to have been one of its chief interests. It was, as previously stated, again resolved into a board of agriculture by an act of the legislature, and as such for many years performed the functions of a State department of agriculture. It has had a continuous history from 1832 to the present.

Organization in Maryland and Virginia.—In 1809 a society spreading across State lines and suggesting the organization of a national agricultural society, such as recommended by

[1] *Vide Report* of Department for 1875, p. 457.

George Washington when he was president, was organized at Georgetown by persons residing in Maryland, the District of Columbia, and Virginia. It began at once to hold fairs, which were probably the first important fairs held in the United States. Five years before, the United States Commissioner had suggested to the municipal authorities of Washington to hold fairs on market days after the English fashion of holding fairs on market days. The idea was eagerly followed by the city officials and three such fairs were held. When the Columbia society began its exhibitions it followed the same plan of combining exhibits with the livestock auction. Early in the morning and late in the day opportunity was given to those who wished to avail themselves of a large group of buyers to sell cattle. The work of the society was fostered by the President of the United States and cabinet members who attended the fairs as stated by the *National Intelligencer*.[1] This was the period when American industries were indeed in their infancy and when much interest was manifested in their development. It is stated that "President Madison sported his inauguration suit, the coat made from the merino wool of Colonel Humphreys' flock." Other prominent citizens and "nearly every person present wore clothing of domestic manufacture." Much interest was shown in the specimens of bed-ticking, cotton bagging, and other materials exhibited by home producers. The fifth semi-annual exhibition held on the 20th of May, 1812, was well attended. "The exhibition of domestic manufactures was highly gratifying in point of number of articles, variety, beauty, and quality. There was a greater number of sheep shown than at any former meeting of the society, especially of the fine-wooled breeds." The society gave premiums for the best exhibits. With the meagre knowledge of agriculture available members of this society tried hard, it seems, to do something in the way of improving agricultural methods. A premium of $20, for instance, was offered "for the best written essay on the mode of gearing and working oxen, founded on experiments." The war with England turned the attention of the people away

[1] Quoted by Ben: Perley Poore in the *Report* of the Department for 1866, p. 519.

from peaceful pursuits, and as a result the society was dissolved in 1812. Whlie its influence as an interstate society was not entirely forgotten, a long time elapsed before another effort was made to establish a national organization. In 1852 this effort became a realization in the organization of the United States Agricultural Society.

It should be stated that in the vicinity of the District of Columbia there was another center of interest in agricultural organization and improvement. At the Arlington estate just across the Potomac from Washington, George Washington Parke Custis held "sheep shearings." The practice was begun in 1802 and continued for eight years. Prominent persons were invited, premiums for the best clip and for other purposes were offered. It was customary for Mr. Custis to deliver a speech on these occasions and always to bring forward his plan of a national agricultural society" to be incorporated by the Government and attached to a national university." The proposal was published in pamphlet form and distributed among the guests.[1]

Organization in the Middle of the Nineteenth Century.—In the preceding sketch of early agricultural organization in the United States together with the facts presented in the preceding chapter in which it is shown that agricultural societies through legislation were frequently constituted State boards of agriculture, the point is established that while both Federal and State governments were appealed to for aid, the American attitude throughout this period was very generally in favor of placing the control of these societies in the hands of the people. Toward the middle of the century we were still very largely influenced by English and early colonial political traditions. History shows that American enterprise was more or less intermittent in its attempts to form voluntary associations for the purpose of improving agriculture. Such efforts were always confined to State lines except in the case of the Columbia society, which included the District of Columbia and two States. However, there was a great change effected during the late 30's. This was the time when railways

[1] *Vide Report* of United States Department of Agriculture for 1866, p. 518.

were being built. It was a period of expansion. It was a time when chemistry and the other physical sciences were beginning to yield results in agricultural experiments. Agricultural organization felt the stimulus of this intellectual and industrial development. An event of special significance is that of James Smithson bequeathing his fortune in 1826 to the United States to found an institution for the "increase and diffusion of knowledge among men." The fund thus made available was eagerly sought by the leading agriculturists of the country. In 1841 a convention was held at Washington whose object it was to organize a national agricultural society and use the Smithson fund in the interest of agricultural improvement. Congress, however, established the Smithsonian Institution in 1846 and the newly organized national agricultural society remained inactive for the want of funds and because of the dampening of the ardor of its leaders until 1852.

That year another convention was called to meet at Washington in which twelve State agricultural associations were concerned. Great interest was manifested in the project and when the convention met it was found that 152 delegates were present representing 23 States and Territories. The delegates organized the United States Agricultural Society whose objects are stated in the preamble to its constitution to have been to "improve the agriculture of the country, by attracting attention, eliciting the views, and confirming the efforts of that great class composing the agricultural community, and to secure the advantages of a better organization and more extended usefulness among all State, county, and other agricultural societies." This was a return to the idea of George Washington. A central organization coordinating all State and county associations was to be established. It was to be a center for the collection of agricultural information and its dissemination among local societies. The society was incorporated in 1860 by an act of Congress.[1]

This national society became at once very active and as stated in the chapter entitled, The United States Department

[1] *Vide* account in *Report* of the Department for 1866, p. 525.

of Agriculture, it served for some years the purposes of a national board of agriculture. It met annually and drew delegates from all parts of the Union. Practical and scientific lectures on agriculture were delivered. Committees were appointed to inquire into the validity of agricultural theories and the practicability of farming implements. National exhibitions and field trials were held in various States including Springfield and Boston, Massachusetts; Springfield, Ohio; Philadelphia, Louisville, Richmond, Chicago, and Cincinnati. These exhibitions were self-supporting. It was at the beginning of the "golden age of the agricultural fair," which is said to have prevailed throughout the United States between 1850 and 1870.[1] Large crowds gathered and the receipts equalled the disbursements of more than $100,000 for premiums and expenses. It stimulated State and local societies and especially helped to develop the fair still further in all parts of the country. It was a gala day which was then, and is now, characteristic of all fairs. "At the banquets with which these national jubilees were concluded eminent gentlemen met upon the broad platform of good citizenship, merging all sectional jealousies and party distinctions in a general desire to improve and elevate that great calling which gives independence and strength to our nation." The Society published for several years its annual transactions. Its operations were interrupted by the Civil War, and when the Department of Agriculture was established in 1862 the need for this type of a national society was no longer felt.

While the establishment of a national department of agriculture was urged at every annual meeting of the United States Agricultural Society, the political leaders of the country, espepecially in the South, were still strongly in favor of private or voluntary association as opposed to public organization. Even Daniel Webster at one of the Society's conventions said that, "the great practical truth and characteristic of the present generation is that public improvements are brought about by voluntary association and combination. The principle of asso-

[1] Butterfield in Bailey's Cyclopedia of American Agriculture, Vol. IV, p. 292.

ciation—the practice of bringing men together for the same general object, pursuing the same general end, and uniting their intellectual and physical efforts to that purpose—is a great improvement in our age.'' This expression was the sentiment of the old school of publicists and of the champions of the doctrine of States' rights, which doctrine, however, was so thoroughly mutilated by the results of the Civil War and subsequently by the great industrial development that it no longer stands as an important obstacle to public organization for the performance of those social, political and, economic functions that cannot be as well performed by private initiative.

The important aspects of organization during the middle of the 19th century were, the beginning of the emphasis upon the holding of fairs and the growth of agricultural associations and clubs for the purpose all over the country, and the organization of the United States Agriculutral Society, leading finally to the establishment of a national department. In the States societies were being constituted State boards of agriculture.

Early Organization in the West.—Organization in the western States necessarily came later than in the East because of the delay in the development of their resources. Relatively, however, they began early to organize in the interest of agricultural improvement and at once manifested a progressive attitude. The State of Indiana as early as 1842 organized a State horticultural society which had only a temporary existence, but which was very active during the time its organization remained intact. Its short life is attributed to the difficulties of transportation and communication then existing. The moving spirit of this center of activity appears to have been the Reverend Henry Ward Beecher, who was at the time a resident in Indianapolis, and who edited and published a monthly journal devoted to agriculture and horticulture, called the *Western Farmer and Gardener,* in which the discussions and proceedings of this pioneer society were published. This is just another example of the numerous characters of America's best men devoting much of their time to the improvement of agriculture and rural life. Because of the economic conditions of the United States no man interested in the welfare of the country could not in the past, and cannot now, neglect agriculture and its environment in a program looking to a fair balancing of the social and economic advantages of the various classes of society. In 1860 the Indiana Pomological Society was organized whose name in 1863 was again given the original title of the society organized in 1841. Transactions in bound volumes were begun to be published in 1866 under State appropriations. The Society began also the exhibition of fruits and flowers at its annual meetings.

Illinois organized the Northwestern Fruit Growers' Association in 1851 and held regular meetings, except in 1854, "for discussion and the making and correcting of lists of fruits, for lectures and essays upon pomology and general horticulture, until the year 1857. In 1856 the Illinois Horticultural Society was organized and the following year the two societies merged. It has been active ever since. Its transactions have been published regularly, and in 1867 the State began to appropriate $2,000 a year for the Society's use. In 1917 its State aid amounted to $11,000.

Wisconsin also organized in 1851 when the Wisconsin State Agricultural Society was founded by "members of the legislature, leading farmers and stock-raisers, and other prominent citizens of the State." It started with 5 life-members, but by 1875 this class of members numbered more than 700. The society was one of the most active in the United States. It published from the beginning its transactions in large volumes and at once began the holding of fairs which, at that time, served a useful purpose in the spreading of agricultural knowledge. In 1865 the Wisconsin State Horticultural Society was organized, but already in 1853 the Western Fruit Growers' Association had been organized and succumbed after a brief existence. The reports of these two organizations as well as such later ones as the Wisconsin State Dairyman's Association show that the State of Wisconsin has always been progressive and energetic in the development of its agricultural interests both with regard to its educational and economic aspects.

Ohio organized a temporary pomological association in 1847, and in 1852 a permanent society was established whose name in 1867 was changed to the State Horticultural Society. Ohio also in 1863 organized a State wool-growers' association. This was at the time when differentation or specialization in agricultural organization according to the particular types of farming prevailing in the State began to manifest itself. Other western States also organized during this period. Kansas organized a society in 1862, Oregon in 1861, and Michigan, which has always been a banner State as far as agricultural organization is concerned, organized its first society in 1830. In 1849 a permanent organization was effected. It received State aid, and the very first year a successful fair was held which stimulated the organization of county associations. A State board of agriculture was established in 1861 affiliated with the State agricultural college. Probably one of the reasons why Michigan has been so active in the form of voluntary or private agricultural organization is that until 1921 it has always had a State board instead of a State department of agriculture. Reasons for this form of public organization must of course be found in the sentiment and character of the people.

The History of the Minnesota State Agricultural Society.—The Minnesota State Agricultural Society has written its history from its beginning to 1910 and has thus made accessible its entire record. Inasmuch as the history of this society presents the functions, aims, and purposes which are more or less common to this type of agricultural society, it will be well to give a somewhat more extended account of its activities.[1]

The first attempts at organization in Minnesota were made in 1852 in Benton County. By an act of the Territorial Legislature the society was incorporated on March 5 of the same year. On the following day a charter was granted to the Ramsey County Agricultural Society. This society had for its object "the collection and dissemination of agricultural knowledge and the encouragement and advancement of agricultural pursuits." Both of these societies never moved beyond the point of organization. They merely prepared the way for a permanent State-wide organization established two years after the incorporation of the first two county associa-

[1] For the account that follows the reader is referred to the Society's history.

tions. A fact that is met with everywhere in the early history of agricultural organization is that its first promoters are usually not themselves engaged in farming, but are public spirited men in the professions, editors, statesmen, and business men. The politician found in these societies a medium for advancing his own interests, and some of the encouragement given had probably a selfish motive, but which, like the economic motive, usually redounded to the benefit of all. "Of the Benton County organization a majority of the members were Indian traders. Of the Ramsey County members, Ramsey was the Territorial Governor; Hoyt was a preacher; Rice, a town builder and politician; Goodhue, Robertson, and Owens were editors; Borup was a banker, and nearly all of the others were land speculators." These men believed that the existence of agricultural societies would constitute a splendid advertisement of Minnesota's natural resources.

In 1853 leading men of Hennepin County secured from the Legislature a charter for the Hennepin County Agricultural Society one of whose objects also appears to have been to advertise the County and the Territory. At the first meeting of this society steps were taken to hold a convention at St. Paul for the purpose of organizing a Territorial society. The following year delegates from a number of counties met and organized the Minnesota Territorial Agricultural Society, which has had a continuous active life from that time to the present.

The people of Minnesota in these early Territroial days were enterprising and aggressive in their efforts to bring the high qualities of its natural resources to the attention of the world. In the summer of 1853 New York City held a "World's Fair," and Minnesota, in spite of the difficulties of transportation to the seaboard and undaunted because of its youth, determined to make a display of her products at this fair. An appropriation of $300 to defray at least part of the expenses was made for the purpose, and Wm. G. LeDuc, then a bookseller at St. Paul and later appointed United States Agricultural Commissioner by President Hayes, was named Commissioner to take charge of Minnesota's exhibit. His journey "was by steamboat to St. Louis and Cincinnati, thence by rail, via Buffalo and Albany, to New York City." Mr. LeDuc's eagerness to call attention to his State led to the idea of including a buffalo bull yearling in the exhibit. After several exciting experiences en route the animal was finally placed in the exhibition building only to give so much trouble and endangering life and property to such an extent that the authorities of the fair threatened him with arrest if he did not remove the buffalo immediately from the fair grounds. The request was complied with, but the Commissioner got the desired advertising. The New York Herald said in part of Minnesota's exhibits that it consists "chiefly of Indian curiosities and furs. Minnesota is the great fur-producing country of the continent. The corn, wheat, rye, oats, and barley of Minnesota compare favorably with any exhibit; and, although specimens are few yet they prove the fallacy of the notion which seems to have possessed the public mind" that neither corn nor wheat can be grown in that latitude. Mr. LeDuc afterward admitted that additions had been made to the collection along the way, but declared that there was no deception because he had seen just as good specimens grown in Minnesota.

The first fair in Minnesota was held by the Hennepin County Society in 1854 and was a decided success. After this the Territorial Society began to hold fairs which speedily developed into great enterprises. Because of the business depression in 1858 no fair was held that year. During the Civil War the fair was also abandoned in 1863. The word Territorial was exchanged for State in 1860 which was, however, two years after Minnesota secured its Statehood.

In its early history the law provided that any number of citizens in the respective counties could organize a county agricultural society and send two delegates together with its president to the State society. Changes were made in 1887, admitting three delegates from county and district societies and the presidents of other prominent State associations, such as the dairy, horticultural, poultry, bee-keepers, etc., providing such associations held fairs. Slight subsequent changes were made concerning the membership of the State society. In 1903 the Society was placed under the control of the State. Section

7 of the act provides that the title to all moneys and other property of the State Agricultural Society "shall be and rest in the State of Minnesota, and there shall be no dividends or division of its assets among its members." Section 9 provides that "the care, custody, and control of said premises, together with any adjoining property which may hereafter be added thereto, is hereby vested in the said State Agricultural Society, as a department of the State government, and the general offices of said society shall be located and maintained upon said premises."

The main function of the Minnesota society has been the holding of fairs from its beginning to the present and as such it has always been one of the most active in the United States. At its annual meetings, however, it served as an agency for the formulation of desirable agricultural legislation. At various times it advocated effective dog laws, a state policy to insure the construction of railroads in the State, the establishment of an agricultural college, the importation of fruit trees from Europe, and other noteworthy projects. In this sense, however, it has only been an agency of propaganda and the object for which it really organized and which it has since consistently carried out is the holding of fairs.

Early Differentiation of Agricultural Societies.—As noted in the preceding historical sketches nearly all of the early private organization was of a general character, the State or county society usually being designated an "agricultural" society. The first differentiation from this general organization came with the formation of horticultural societies. In a few places this division came early. This was true of Massachusetts and Pennsylvania. Horticulture as a separate object of agricultural organization also made its appearance early in the history of the western States. Indiana organized a temporary society in 1842. In other western States reports of societies show that both their discussions in meetings and exhibits at the fairs were from the beginning of a general character and in time horticultural, dairy, and other specialized farm activities were dignified with the establishment of separate organizations representing these special interests. In the Report[1] of the Iowa State Horticultural Society for 1895 the following statement appears:

> Prior to 1866, horticulture was treated in Iowa as a branch of agriculture and its promotion was encouraged by the Iowa State Agricultural Society. During the Civil War fruit growing (more particularly apple growing) was extremely profitable by reason of the high prices prevailing during that era, and under the influences of these prices the planting of fruit trees was largely increased. It was discovered, however, that our people had insufficient knowledge of the conditions affecting successful fruit growing and to the end that horticultural knowledge might be more widely disseminated and the true principles affecting the same become more widely known, Mr. Mark Miller, editor of the *Iowa Homestead*, of Des Moines, Iowa, a man of enterprise and an enthusiast in agricultural science, published in May, 1866, a call for a meeting of all citizens, interested in horticulture for the purpose of effecting an organization for the promotion of horticultural interests.

The reason for the organization of horticultural societies was usually in the interest of fruit- growing. In Massachusetts the aesthetic motive, which included the development of fine flowers and the socialization of a taste or appreciation for them, played an important role.

After horticultural societies the next manifestation of differentation in agricultural organization is the establishment of an association to represent the production of wool. The Ohio State Wool-Growers' Association was organized at Cleveland in 1863. Its objects were educational and the promotion of legislation favorable to the industry. At its meetings papers on sheep-breeding and wool-growing were discussed. In 1864 the National Wool-Growers' Association was organized at the instigation of the Ohio society. "The principal object of this national organization was to prevent unfavorable legislation by Congress touching the wool interests of the United States."[2] The Ohio association was active from the beginning. It exhibited its best sheep at the fairs. At the Centennial Exposition in Philadelphia in 1876 it had an important exhibit. Organization among the woolgrowers spread to Missouri and Kansas where an organization was effected in 1874, having the same objects as the Ohio society. The western people were desirous of cooperating with the national association for the

[1] P. 115.
[2] *Vide Report* of Department for 1875, p. 461.

purpose of preventing a reduction in the tariff on wool from the rates then in effect.

A further disintegration of general organization came with the establishment of dairy associations. Dairying, like other specialized agricultural activities, was at first fostered by State agricultural societies. Already in its first report, published in 1852, the Wisconsin agricultural society gave considerable space to dairying. A separate society, however, representing this industry in Wisconsin was not organized until 1872. The first State dairy association was organized in Vermont in 1869.[1] New York followed with an organization in 1871, effecting a permanent organization in 1877. Illinois organized in 1874, Minnesota in 1877, and from this time forward organization throughout the country proceeded rapidly. Dairying, probably more than any other agricultural activity, is thoroughly organized. The National Dairy Union was organized in 1891, and in addition there were in 1912 eleven other national or international associations concerned with the promotion of the dairy interests.[2] Organization among dairymen was at first wholly for educational purposes. In the more highly specialized dairy sections of the country these societies have been exceedingly active in this regard. At their conventions some of the best dairy specialists of the country have given scientific lectures. While they sometimes have had exhibits and contests for the best butter and cheese products at their annual meetings, their educational program has been carried out mainly through lectures. They themselves have not held fairs, but often exhibit their stock at county and State fairs. In New York under the leadership of X. A. Willard it was the plan to organize boards of trade under the control of the farmer at which the dealers of cities were to buy their butter and cheese. The plan was also tried out in Elgin, Illinois, and in parts of Wisconsin. It was only temporarily successful because of the insufficiency of organization to control the supply which began in spite of the efforts of the farmers to find its way to the big dairy exchanges in New

[1] An American Dairymen's Association having a temporary existence was addressed by X. A. Willard in 1866. *Vide Report* of Department for 1875, p. 409.

[2] *Vide Circular 204*, Bureau of Animal Industry.

York, Boston, Philadelphia, Chicago, and elsewhere. Late in the 70's came the oleomargarine incubus and efforts to stop fraudulent practices in the production and sale of this product gave a great impetus to dairy organization.

Further Differentation and Its Effects.—Since these earlier inroads upon the original simple form of organization there have been a number of other societies forming and pressing themselves to the fore. Corn, rice, fruit, nut, forage, and cotton associations have been organized. Livestock associations have become numerous. These consist of swine, cattle, sheep, goat, horse, poultry, rabbit, and bee associations. Many of these societies have subdivided so as to represent the interests of particular breeds. The degree of differentiation is shown in a list of livestock associations published in Agricultural Yearbooks.[1] A list of agricultural organizations, public and private, and representing the interests of livestock and other agricultural activities for 1912 appears in Senate Document No. 1109, 62nd Congress, 3rd Session. These lists of associations are probably accurate enough to indicate the relative number of State agricultural organizations and the geographic distribution of such State-wide associations throughout the country. However, as an indication of the total amount of organization within the States it is misleading, because in some States there are a large number of unaffiliated local societies. The State of Connecticut is such an example. With this fact in mind a statement based on these lists and consisting of the 20 States having the greatest number of State-wide organizations is presented below.[2]

Name of State	*All Associations in 1912*	*Live Stock Associations in 1919*
Texas	35	9
New York	32	9
Nebraska	30	10
Minnesota	25	13
Wisconsin	23	16
North Carolina	23	4
Pennsylvania	22	4
Massachusetts	22	2
Missouri	22	12

[1] *Vide Yearbook* for 1919, p. 502.

[2] A more authentic and a more recent list has been published by the Department of Agriculture.

Name of State	*All Associations* in *1912*	*Live Stock Associations in 1919*
Oregon	21	7
Iowa	17	9
Oklahoma	17	3
Kentucky	16	7
Illinois	15	11
Kansas	15	9
South Carolina	15	1
Michigan	14	22
South Dakota	14	4
Washington	13	2

Following this list come the remaining States with associations numbering in 1912 from 13 for California to no private organization for Utah. In 1919 this State is credited with one livestock association, the Utah State Dairymen's Association. The State of Utah at present has no public agricultural organization other than its agricultural college including the experiment station and extension service. In addition, however, the State fair is supported by State appropriations. It is difficult to secure complete information as to the number and kind of agricultural associations in the various States, but the statement above indicates probably quite correctly which States in the Union have the greatest number of State associations. As stated, it does not indicate the total organization because of local organizations which are likely to be more numerous where the town or township form of government prevails than where the smallest governmental unit is the county. Nevertheless, the statement, it is believed, may be taken roughly as an index of activity in organization throughout the country.

It is to be noted at this point that the effect of the differentiation of organization upon the old State agricultural societies was to disintegrate them. Many of them have ceased to exist. The Connecticut State Agricultural Society organized in 1852 was constituted the State board of agriculture in 1866, but as pointed out in the previous chapter the basis for the State board had to be changed in 1897, and at subsequent times, from members of agricultural societies to representatives of counties. The reason for this is the fact that the county associations did not remain sufficiently active to perform the function of electing delegates and representing the country on the board of agriculture. As a consequence of the development in Connecticut the State society does not even receive an appropriation, but in its stead the law provides for an appropriation of $1,500 to each of the Connecticut Dairymen's Associations and the Connecticut Pomological Society, and $1,000 to the Connecticut Poultry Association. The Sheep Breeders' Association and the Bee-Keepers' Association also received appropriations in 1918.[1] In Indiana the State Society is constituted the State Board of Agriculture, but the operations of the State department are centered in Purdue University. This is an example where the State society no longer performs any other function except the holding of fairs. For 1920 the State appropriated $10,000 for this purpose. In Minnesota and a number of other States the State society is nothing more than a "fair association." The State of Maryland should be mentioned as an example where the differentiated societies have been reunited into a State society. In an act of 1916 the Maryland State Agricultural Society was incorporated, and its members consist of members of subsidiary societies. In the report for 1919 there were six such societies. A similar movement of federating all special societies is in progress in New York.[2]

As further evidence of the disintegration of the State society and the development of strong specalized societies, a statement showing the State societies receiving State aid could be constructed. However, inasmuch as this type of private organization is so intimately related to the whole movement of public organization, such information would be of little value. In general it may be said that State aid to agricultural societies is for the purpose of conducting fairs and to carry on educational work in the interest of agriculture. In general it may be said also that the appropriation of public funds for the holding of State and county fairs is quite common among the States of the Union; and that in those States where public organization has become highly centralized in a State department as in Pennsylvania and New York little or nothing is appropriated to societies for general educational purposes,

[1] *Vide* financial statements in *Report* of State Board of Agriculture.

[2] *Vide* resolution in *Proceedings* of N. Y. State Agricultural Society for 1918, p. 139.

while in those States where the State board form exists and where as a consequence important educational functions including the publishing of reports are left to be performed by private organizations, more or less substantial sums are appropriated to State societies. Another fact elicited from reports received from all the States is that where exceptions occur to the above statement the horticultural and dairy associations are likely to be the societies receiving State aid. These agricultural interests are usually favored above all others.

Causes for the Differentiation of Agricultural Societies.— The fundamental cause determining the organization of specialized societies must be found in the economic changes that brought about specialization in agriculture. Production for national and international markets instead of for home consumption is a necessary precedent to specialization. This is the one fundamental condition that must obtain before the emphasis in farm operations may be placed upon dairying, wool-growing, hog and cattle raising, wheat growing, etc. The development and extension of the railroads together with the rapid growth of the urban population about the middle of the 19th century established our large national markets. The international markets were made more accessible to us somewhat later with the development of ocean steamship transportation. Proximity to the market has been a potent factor in determing the location of crop and livestock producing areas throughout the United States. For perishable commodities like milk for fresh consumption, there is a nice adjustment according to distance, and for all commodities there is a nice adjustment according to costs of transportation and the particular adaptability of the soils of various sections of the country to certain farm activities. Hay for the urban centers in the east is grown in New England and other eastern States and this fact together with the demand for fresh milk has forced the center of butter production to Wisconsin and other western States. The soil, topography, climate, and skill of the people in this industry also were factors in determin ng the location of the center of butter and cheese production in Wisconsin. Level and fertile stretches of land are often more profitable for the growing of grains and this fact forces out other products. Similar conditions prevail in tobacco and cotton regions. Enough has been said to show that there are a group of objective forces determining specialization in agriculture. In addition there are social forces such as the skill and intelligence of the people, their attitude toward labor and toward progress, that have much to do with bringing about specialization. All natural resources and market conditions may be ever so favorable, if there is no enterprising spirit among the people production will be of a common-place order.

Upon this specialization in farming operations rests differentation in agricultural organizations. Special organizations spring up to promote special interests. They will foster these interests and cause still further specialization. Specialization as a basis for an active association is important because it centers attention upon one object in which all members have a common interest. Another fact of considerable importance is the need for information to carry on the operation successfully. This seems to be verified in the many horticultural and dairy associations. Demand for products of this type depends very largely upon the ability to satisfy the delicate tastes of the consumer. How to produce the product having the desirable quality becomes a technical matter and a subject for discussion in meetings of associations. How to avoid pests and how to conquer diseases in these special fields are problems that also require careful study. Inasmuch as the whole group is interested in the same problems there is provided a binding force that serves to hold the society intact.

Another important social cause of organization is the desire of the community to advertise its products. The first step naturally, is to improve the product, but when this has been done the problem confronting the society is how to bring it to the attention of the people and create a demand so strong and constant as to insure prosperity to the producers. With reference to such products as butter and cheese, apples and oranges, as well as livestock, it is especially important to build up a good will for the community. After this has been established customers need only be told where the commodity was produced to insure its sale. Many examples may be found in the United States where the reputation of the community is a valuable asset in the marketing of its product. New York and Wisconsin cheese and Florida and California oranges are products noted for their quality. The best example is the reputation of Denmark with regard to its butter, which, through its thorough organization and inspection system, has built up a uniform system for the manufacture of butter, resulting in a uniform good quality that sells readily in England and elsewhere. It is the business of the agricultural societies to advertise its products. Fair associations play a large role. As was shown in the history of the Minnesota society, the desire to advertise the Territory through the holding of fairs was the primary motive for organizing it. Agricultural societies stand in somewhat the same relation to the rural community as the commercial organizations occupy in the city. The latter are "boosters" for the cities, while the former are "boosters" for the rural communities throughout the State.

Present-Day Functions of These Societies.—Virtually all of the functions of these societies have already been indicated at various points throughout the chapter. They may be summed up here under four different heads. Generally speaking, the foremost function of these societies is the education of their members in the particular pursuits for which they are organized. This is done through the reading of papers and their discussion at the meetings. Scientific experts are often asked to deliver addresses. In some instances committees are appointed to study particular problems and report on them. Demonstrations are sometimes made. At annual meetings the sum total result is sometimes of an inspirational sort of benefit that finds concrete expression only in scattered places. The fair, the holding of which is their main present-day function, is a means of stimulating the use of improved methods. While some societies do not themselves hold fairs, they are often contributors of speciens at fairs held under the auspices of fair association or other societies. This activity will be discussed under a separate head.

A second function, above discussed, is the advertising of the products of the community and building up a good will.

A third function may be said to be the crystallization of public opinion concerning the activities of the rural community. It has often been noted that no legislative action can be secured without an organization. With a strong organization behind a movement legislative action is always certain because in a republic the lawmakers really represent the people. Examples have been referred to where societies have been instrumental in causing the enactment of desirable legislation. Many examples can be cited. Horticultural societies serve as agencies for organizing sentiment in favor of flower gardens at schools, and to stimulate an aesthetic appreciation of nature. These societies have for many years been used as channels through which the cooperative movement is promoted. It is only in late years, however, that they have taken a very active interest in the subject. However, the actual promotion of cooperative enterprises and organization among farmers for the purposes of controlling costs of marketing and, in a measure, prices of the product, is more generally left to other farmers' organizations to be discussed in succeeding chapters.

Finally the societies help to create a desirable social medium for members of the rural community. Attendance upon meetings, the election of officers which is usually an occasion for some campaigning, the rendering of several entertaining lectures, the holding of banquets, all conspire to give to the rural community a social and intellectual sphere of life so attractive to the normal human being.

The Agricultural Fair.—As already stated the character of the first fairs of the country were more English than American. The first fair believed to have been held in the United States was an exhibition given in Washington in 1804. Three such fairs were held. They were resumed in 1810 and continued for five years by the Columbia agricultural society. The great advocate of the fair, however, and one who has been called the "father of the agricultural fair" as an American institution was Elkanah Watson,[1] who in 1807 exhibited two merino sheep in Pittsfield, Massachusetts, and who in 1810 organized the farmers in his community into the Berkshire Agricultural Society for the purpose of holding fairs. He was also active in assisting in the organization of fair associations

[1] Butterfield, in *Bailey's Cyclopedia of American Agriculture,* Vol. IV, p. 292.

in ten other States. During the first half of the 19th century farmers' clubs and agricultural societies, organized for the purpose of holding fairs and also for educational purposes, prepared the way for the "golden age of the agricultural fair"[1] which is said to have reigned from 1850 to 1870. The designation may be altogether correct from the point of view of relative usefulness of that day as compared with the present. So far as is concerned, however, the indication that this institution is on the decline the designation is at fault, according to a recent study made by S. G. Rubinow of the extension service of North Carolina.[2] He says the following:

> Fairs and expositions have multiplied so rapidly that it is not feasible to try to chronicle the actual number in the United States. More than 3,000 fairs, including State, district, county, community, township, school and street types are held every year at various seasons. And every year sees an increase and a redirection toward better purposes. In North Carolina there were 227 fairs in the fall of 1917. There are strong indications that this number will be widely increased in 1918.
>
> The fall of 1917 was a record breaking season for fairs everywhere. Reports from the West and North present the greatest attendance and the largest number of competitors and entries in the history of fairs. In North Carolina, more than three-quarters of a million people attended the fairs, while the number of entries exceeded 45,000.

State and county fairs are usually conducted by corporations known as fair associations or agricultural societies. They are usually incorporated and as a rule receive State aid. Gate receipts are usually insufficient to meet expenses. State aid is, therefore, necessary. Private subscriptions from merchants, of the town where the fair is held, are sometimes received. The community fair is usually fostered and managed by some rural organization varying in character according to locality. Where there is no organization of any kind merely a loose, unincorporated association is effected for the purpose. The community fair has been more a southern institution than a northern or western one, and has recently come into prominence because it has been encouraged by the new extension service which has rapidly spread over the country in recent years. To the extension service must be given credit in many

[1] *Ibid.*

[2] *Vide Circular* No. 69, North Carolina Agricultural Extension Service.

parts of the country also for the greatly increased vigor that the fair has assumed and with giving it better aims and purposes. The conduct of the State and county fairs is made amenable to the State authorities through the auditing of books of record and through the inspection of exhibitions by duly authorized agents. The most successful fairs cooperate with all public and private agricultural organizations. The support of the State department, the agricultural college, experiment station, and extension service with all its local organization, as well as that of cooperative societies, and all private agricultural societies, is appealed to by the successful fair secretary. Team work or cooperation is in fact the essence of success in fairs.

Like other corporations, the county and State fair associations have their usual executive officers and a board of directors. Inasmuch as cooperation is an important aspect of the association it has been urged that voting should be restricted to the principle of "one member, one vote" regardless of the amount of stock held. The State fairs employ usually a permanent secretary, while county associations can get along with one serving only part of the year. This officer, who may also be the treasurer, is a paid official and is the life and spirit of the organization. Upon him depends largely the success of the fair. He must be a capable executive; he must know agricultural life and social organization in general; he must be genial; and he must be fair and honest in his dealings. To secure the active cooperation of a large number of members it is important to appoint a number of comittees. A desirable classification of such comittees has been suggested as follows: premium, finance, program, grounds, reception, school, entertainent, contest, young people's exhibits, concessions, entries and exhibits, and membership.

The features of the fair should be such as to carry out its fundamental purposes of educating the public and providing wholesome amusement. The 3,000 fairs annually held throughout the United States, and the number seems to be increasing steadily, without a doubt have an important educational value both because their exhibits demonstrate what can be done and because they stimulate people, in a friendly rivalry, to out-do one another. While the institution has this important educational value, the fact should not be overlooked that fair day is rather the realization or culmination of agricultural organization and agricultural education than a medium for the education of the public. It is more truly a show day, a gala day, a time of enjoyment of the fruits of one's labor, and a time for general wholesome amusement, rather than a time for intensive instruction in scientific agriculture. It does not follow from this that demonstration work and all lecture work must be excluded. However, addresses have to be of the popular kind in order to attract and hold the crowd. Demonstrations can be so arranged as to yield educational results and furnish at the same time considerable entertainment. All immoral shows should be excluded from the premises. Races and other contests if properly conducted provide entertainment and encourage the breeding of good horses.

Thus the fair serves the dual purpose of educating the public and allowing in a very broad way the expression of the results of agricultural organization. The fair in a measure may be regarded as the goal of agricultural progress. Those who fail to recognize the relation between the fair and other agricultural organization fail to comprehend the usefulness and the stabilizing elements of all rural organization.[1]

Horticultural Exhibitions and Contests.—These exhibitions have much the same values as the fairs. They are more specialized in their exhibits, however, and have less amusement. They aim to stimulate the cultivation of fruits, vegetables, and flowers. The latter feature is one that enlists the support of urbanites, and has been the means of giving strength to societies whose membership is largely made up of city residents. A committee appointed by the Massachusetts Horticultural Society to report on its future policy doubts the educational value of exhibitions of vegetables that may be bought any day in the city markets. The committee favored fewer and larger exhibitions, and was not ready to abandon the practice of granting prizes for fruit and vegetables. The committee felt

[1] For a study of the fair the reader is referred to circulars published by the North Carolina Extension Service, *Farmers' Bulletin 822* of the United States Department of Agriculture, Bulletins of the Missouri State Board of Agriculture, and reports of fair associations.

the need of coming into closer contact with the people of the community. For some time floral exhibits, it is stated, have been displayed by florists who desire to secure prizes as advertisements to help the sale of their stock. Floral exhibits have thus become commercialized and fail to stimulate effort among a large number of citizens. In order that a society may accomplish its purposes it has become necessary to extend its activities to the home in the form of lawn and garden competitions. This is a kind of work that has only recently been taken up by these societies. The contests naturally have to continue through the year. Bases have to be determined in order that proper comparisons may be made in the awarding of prizes. Some suggested classes are: grounds as a whole, front yards, back yards, lawns, flower gardens vegetable gardens, and the greatest improvement in a single year.[1]

The Place of State and National Agricultural Societies.— What now is the relation of these agricultural and livestock associations to public agricultural organization and to the class of farmers' organizations concerned more particularly with the improvement of the economic status of the farmers as a class through the principle of cooperation and combiantion? Have they a special place that they should continue to fill? Obviously the holding of the fairs, the primary *raison d'etre* of general agricultural societies or fair associations, must be managed by special organizations because of the magnitude of their business operations. The institution is a worthy civilizing agency and should continue. The specialized societies have also a place that is in no way occupied by any other organization. They promote and represent specialized agricultural interests. The fact that each is concerned with a single purpose enables them to popularize scientific knowledge concerning their respective fields; moreover because of their single interest they are enabled to serve as centers for the crystallization of public opinion and the formulation of desirable legislation. They should not violate the principle of representative government. As only one of the economic groups of society, the agricultural class should be satisfied to elect favorable representatives and to press their legislative pro-

[1] *Vide Circular* 62, United States Bureau of Plant Industry.

gram to the attention of its representatives. Organized agriculture, like labor, industry, and commerce, should therefore not be constituted as part of the executive machinery of the State. So far as the educational function is concerned, the extension service supplements or in a measure takes the place of these special societies. The extension service, however, deals with all problems; while these differentiated societies unite and instruct those engaged in like industries, which is sufficient reason for their continued existence. In Maryland it has been noted that the specialized societies have been federated. The same movement is in progress in New York. If this movement should continue throughout the Union this type of societies could readily assume the more economic and business aspects of organizing cooperative societies and promoting the economic status of the farmers as a class. In fact in recent years considerable attention has been given by them to this aspect of agricultural organization. There is, however, room for a separate organization like the Grange or the Farmers' Union, whose main emphasis is upon the economic welfare of the farmers themselves and whose field of action is national in scope.

SELECTED REFERENCES

United States Agricultural Report for 1866, pp. 498-527; *U. S. Agri. Report* for 1875, pp. 437-468; Butterfield in *Bailey's Cyclopedia of American Agriculture, Vol. IV*, pp. 291-297; *Circular 204*, U. S. Bureau of Animal Industry; Rubinow, *Circular 69*, North Carolina Agricultural Extension Service; *Circular 62*, U. S. Bureau of Plant Industry.

CHAPTER XVI

THE FORMATION AND ORGANIZATION OF THE GRANGE

Conditions Favorable to Organization.—In the previous chapter it was noted that agricultural societies having for their primary object the education of their members through the discussion of problems at their meetings and the holding of fairs, were being organized during the first half of the 19th century and that by the time the Civil War came they had become general throughout most portions of the country then opened to cultivation, but were virtually everywhere limited to state lines. In the South during the Civil War many of these societies abandoned all activities, and in the North and West fairs were not held every year. The war brought about a great rise in the general price level due partly to the scarcity of economic goods, but primarily to the issue of greenbacks; and their rapid recovery in value after the Civil War together with the increased production soon caused a decline in the general price level and therefore in the prices of the farmers' products. This probably was the first fundamental fact that prepared the farmers generally to turn a willing ear to the proposal of organizing for the purpose of protecting their class interests. It was noted that the societies then existing had no such purpose and that their organization was not national in scope. It is therefore not surprising that a new organization, announcing as its main purpose the protection of the farmers as a class among other economic groups of society, should take root and develop into a powerful national organization. While some of the important purposes of the Grange first in the mind of Kelley were the education of its members in the art and science of agriculture, the creation of a social medium for the rural population, and the dissipation of sectional differences between the North and South; the real and large purpose of the organization, as stated in its charter and as tacitly recognized by all, was to secure to the farmers "the advantages of cooperation in all things affecting their interests, and of mutual improvement.''[1] In the Declaration of Purposes adopted by the National Grange in 1874 the following comprehensive statement appears: "We propose meeting together, talking together, working together, buying together, selling together, and, in general acting together for our mutual protection, and advancement, as occasion may require.'' Concerning the aims and purposes of the Grange more will be said in the following chapter.

The Falling Price Level, the Most Fundamental Cause of Discontent Among the Farmers.—The accompanying diagram

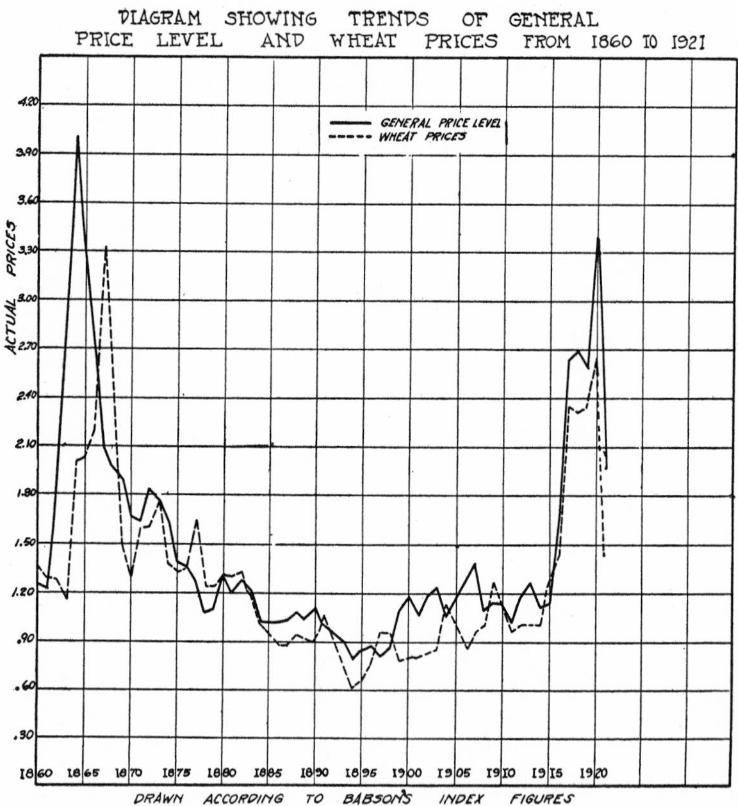

shows the trends of the general price level and of wheat prices from 1860 to 1920. The general trends of both these price

[1] *Vide* Atkeson, *Semi-Centennial History of the Patrons of Husbandry.*

curves are the same indicating that there were fundamental conditions affecting the price of all commodities. The price of corn, not shown on the diagram, follows the same general trend further indicating that the price of farm products together with that of manufactured goods rose rapidly and as rapidly declined, then gradually seeking a lower level, all of which happened in response to fundamental economic conditions. As already stated the one important factor responsible for the rapid rise in prices during the Civil War was the issuance of United States Notes or greenbacks in large quantities, the maximum amount being $431,000,000, behind which there was no reserve to prevent their depreciation. In terms of gold these greenbacks depreciated rapidly, falling as low as 35 cents in 1864. This meant that at this rate a gold dollar was worth $2.85 in greenbacks. Inasmuch as gold was very scarce the country was virtually on a paper basis, and all domestic prices except on the Pacific coast, where the greenbacks found no ready acceptance, were in terms of greenbacks instead of gold. This explains the very rapid rise of the general price level during the darkest days of the Civil War. When the war was ended resulting in the preservation of the Union and as a consequence in the ultimate redemption of all greenbacks at par, their depreciation soon decreased in anticipation of such redemption. However, due to an unwise fiscal policy these greenbacks remained generally at a gold value of less than 80 cents for five years after the war, and for almost a decade following the year 1870 they were worth less than 90 cents. The specie resumption act was passed in 1875 to go into effect in 1879, the main feature of which was the creation of a gold reserve to redeem greenbacks on demand made possible through the provision of selling bonds for gold to maintain this reserve at $100,000,000. The provisions of this act together with the fact that our balance of trade was in our favor, bringing gold into the country, resulted in the disappearance of the depreciation of the greenbacks on December 17, 1878. Thus the primary cause of the tremendous price disturbance of the Civil War period is found in an ill-advised fiscal policy. The issue of greenbacks could have been avoided if the Secretary of the Treasury had been equal to the task of formulating a sound policy and providing also Congress had been sufficiently enlightened to grapple properly with the financial problems of the day. The chart allows a comparison of price changes occasioned by the Civil War and the European War. As is shown the peak rose very much higher in the Civil War than it did in the recent war. In the latter period we held closely to a wise fiscal policy. We also had much more extensive and efficient financial organization, including the Federal Reserve system, through which we could sell and distribute our bonds. Our fiscal policy during this period was an adherence to the principle of heavy taxation and the sale of bonds, and excluded the use of fiat money to meet our war expenditures. However, we were not free from credit inflation and this fact together with the scarcity in consumption goods caused prices to rise very high.

The price situation is the core or the essence of industrial discontent. The steady decline of prices after the close of the Civil War produced a condition favorable to organization. It was hoped through united effort to stem the downward trend of the prices of farm products. In various ways it was contended that the farmers were being exploited. Thus "they fastened the blame upon the bankers, the railways, the legislatures, the tariff, and monopolies, and their grievances along these lines were legion and some of them well founded."[1]

Geographic Readjustments After the Civil War.—The portion of the United States east of the Alleghany mountains up to the middle of the 19th century was devoted to diversified farming. Hay and the grains constituted the main crops of the farmers. After the Civil War with the opening of railroad transportation to the western States the wheat of the West came into competition with the wheat of the East. In the West wheat was grown on virgin soil while in the East it was cultivated on a more or less intensive basis but on an impoverished soil. As a result the cost of producing a bushel of wheat in the East was greater than in the West, necessitating a change in the type of farming in the East. Diversified farming including the production of grains had to give way to specialized farming. The specialty open to the farmers in New York and

[1] Buck, *The Granger Movement*, p. 8.

New England generally including also other eastern States, was dairying, the production of hay for draft animals in urban centers, and the raising of garden vegetables. New York rapidly increased its production of butter between 1850 and 1860, and between 1860 and 1870 it increased its production of cheese by more than 50 per cent.[1] The fundamental difference between the eastern and western agricultural portions of the United States created during the period of readjustment a feeling more or less inimical between the people of these two sections. It is therefore readily understood why the East was at first slow in developing the Grange and why the order made such rapid progress in the western States. Of course it must be remembered that the East was less inclined to establish this type of organization because of its older traditions and that as a result of which it was somewhat more conservative.

The readjustment that became necessary in the East journeyed westward and wrought havoc in Ohio and other States. In a number of these States also changes in the type of farming became necessary. In the South the one-crop system was continued, and as the price of cotton rapidly declined the southern atmosphere also became charged with discontent and created a condition favorable to organization.

The Railroad Situation.—The readjustment in the production of agricultural products brought into the fore the railroad problem. At first in order to secure transportation facilities for the purpose of marketing their grain and other products farmers were in accord with other classes in urging that assistance be given construction companies in the building of railroads. Thus, local governments, States and the federal government, provided capital for the construction of roads or gave grants of land for the purpose. Farmers also subscribed to railroad stock and in many cases mortgaged their farms to pay for it. They expected fat dividends which, however, failed to materialize due to the fact that in some instances roads were pushed into pioneer regions insufficiently populated to produce any revenue for distribution among stock-

[1] *Vide* the author's *Butter Industry in the United States*, pp. 78-80.

holders, while in other cases earnings were dissipated through gross mismanagement and stock-watering. The early mismanagement of the railroads led to reorganizations in which a rearrangement of stocks and bonds took place resulting frequently in a loss of the capital invested. This disastrous result of early railroad finance left many farmers along with other investors heavily in debt because of the mortgages placed on property to pay for railroad stock.

Many complaints were made in the western States, where the so-called "Granger" legislation was enacted, against the "absentee ownership" of the railroads. It was complained that the capital of railroads was largely held in the East or in Europe, and that as a consequence their management instead of centering in the West, which was especially interested in cheap rates to the seaboard, was under the control of men interested not so much in the success of the western farmers as in securing a large return upon their investment. This led to exorbitant rates and the exploitation of the farmers. The one dominant complaint was the high rates charged on products from the West to the seaboard. It was at a time when railroad corporations defied the public everywhere and denied that the State had the right to regulate the business of the carriers. A characteristic expression concerning the public interest in railroads was that of Commodore Vanderbilt who said "The public be damned." Shortly before the 70's the railroads began to take a throttling hold upon the public. Discrimination in rates in favor of large cities and big shippers was begun. Members of legislatures and other men of influence were given passes. As a consequence of the railroad situation States began the establishment of State railroad commissions. In the western States the "granger" legislation frequently gave such commissions the power to prescribe rates for the carriers. In other cases the law passed by the legislature fixed the rate. This was the case of the Potter law passed in Wisconsin in 1874. The roads depended upon the courts for relief from these restrictive measures, but the main principles for which the "granger" legislation contended were upheld, the

Supreme Court of the United States holding in 1877 that States had the right to regulate railway services and charge.[1]

Other Fundamental Conditions.—In addition to the railroad situation there were other grievances that served to permeate the farmers with the idea of class consciousness and prepare them for organization. The complaint against middlemen is as old as the system of producing for the market. The complaint is found in the study of the history of all marketable farm products. There are charges that middlemen make deductions on account of alleged short weights and poor quality, and worst of all that they combine to depress the price paid the farmer. These charges were made against the commission men or the class of middlemen that buy directly from the farmers. In the purchase of their supplies the farmers charged that they were compelled to pay unduly high prices due to monopolistic control in the manufacture of farm implements and other commodities consumed by them. This situation soon led to the policy of encouraging the establishment of cooperative enterprises.

One other serious complaint that the farmers made was the high interest rates they had to pay. It was in the West and Southwest where interest rates to the farmers were the highest. They ran as high as 15 to 20 per cent. Certainly until the establishment of the Federal Land Banks the rural sections of the country especially the West have had just cause to complain that the credit system of the country was fashioned to discriminate against the farmers. The problem was not always fully understood, and as a result erroneous doctrines were sometimes propounded. The grievances, however, were there, and these served to unite the farmers. The farmers also opposed the high tariff rates enacted during the Civil War made possible by the withdrawal of the Southern representatives from Congress.[2]

The Development of the Farmers' Movement.—The result of the fundamental economic conditions prevailing after the Civil War was the development of a great movement among the

[1] For a full account of the early history of railroad construction in the West and the susequent regulation of railroads see a text on transportation.

[2] These fundamental conditions favorable to agricultural organization are all summed up by Buck in his *Granger Movement*, pp. 3-39.

farmers for their economic, social and political improvement. It was merely started or suggested, so to speak, by O. H. Kelley, the chief founder of the Grange, who with a few associates organized the first Grange in 1867 in Washington, D. C. When the movement once took hold it spread so rapidly that the order soon became overgrown. The real benefits that were to come from organization were greatly overestimated. Mistakes in aims and purposes, and especially in the disposition of treasury funds, were made in the early days of Grange organization. Between 1875 and 1880 a reaction, therefore, set in causing a decline in the membership of the Grange, the disorganization of a number of Subordinate Granges, and the loss of some State Granges. The fundamental conditions, however, were still ripe for discontent among the farmers. The price level was still falling. Real and alleged grievances were still complained of as menacing the progress and success of the agricultural class. From this soil of discontent other farmers' organizations sprang up. The Agricultural Wheel was organized in 1882; the Farmers' National Alliance, in 1880; the Farmers' Mutual Benefit Association, in 1887. There were other organizations that came into being during this period. Already in 1875, at the time when the Grange was at its height, the Texas Alliance was organized.[1] Beginning in 1858, nine years before the organization of the Grange, a series of conventions were held in the West and South, protesting against high freight rates and other abuses.[2] Virtually all these assocaitions except the Grange became welded into the Farmers' Alliance which drifted into politics and there met with disaster and complete destruction. The development of all these associations is mentioned at this point to show that a real farmers' movement was in progress, and that the organization of the Grange was not merely the result of one man's whim, but a manifestation of a struggle of a great economic class.

However, initiative, suggestion, and innovation are always necessary factors in the development of a social movement. The conditions may be ever so ripe for its propagation, if there

---

[1] *Vide McVey's Populist Movement*, p. 196.

[2] *Vide* subsequent chapter on Farmers' Alliance.

is no leader the movement will not take form. Much credit is, therefore, due O. H. Kelley for conceiving the plan of a farmers' organization and for his heroic and tenacious efforts to put the Grange on a firm foundation and make it national in scope. The Grange was organized by a lead of more than five years in advance of other permanent farmers' organizations, and as an organization, therefore, it stands pre-eminently in the history of the farmers' movement as an influence toward organizing the rural population for its economic, social and political improvement.

The Founders of the Grange.—In an account by Mrs. Eva McDowell in the Proceedings of the Golden Jubilee of the National Grange held in Washington, D. C., in 1916 seven men are eulogized as the founders of the Patrons of Husbandry. These men were Oliver Hudson Kelley, William Saunders, John R. Thompson, William M. Ireland, Aaron B. Grosh, John Trimble, and Francis M. McDowell. In an amendment to the constitution proposed in 1873 and later adopted these men were named as founders.[1] Mr. Atkeson, the present legislative representative of tne Grange at Washington and author of the *Semi-Centennial History of the Patrons of Husbandry,* is at a loss to understand why Miss Caroline A. Hall was excluded from those officially recognized as founders. Miss Hall was Mr. Kelley's niece and made the very valuable suggestion that women be admitted into the Order on an equality with men. Somewhat tardily the National Grange adopted a resolution in 1892 recognizing Miss Hall "as equal to a Founder of the Order of the Patrons of Husbandry." Later, at the same session, a resolution giving full recognition as a founder was adopted.[2] As late as 1916, however, Mrs. McDowell fails to include Miss Hall's name among those of the founders of the Order. She advances the number seven as the "perfect" number and accords to it a reverence that borders on sacredness because it represents the number of founders as well as the number of the degrees of the Order.

It would seem that the name of Carrie A. Hall should be

---

[1] *Vide* Atkeson, *Semi-Centennial History of the Patrons of Husbandry,* p. 65.

[2] *Vide* Atkeson, *op. cit.*

rightfully recognized as one of the founders, raising the number to eight. Her suggestion that women be admitted into the Order on an equality with men was an important one. Business on the farm depends for its success more equally upon husband and wife than in the city. Both play their parts in the operation of the farm. In the city the woman of the household seldom knows the details of her husband's business, and seldom takes part in directing it. The admission of women into the Order of the Patrons of Husbandry on an equality with the men called to its support the full cooperation of the household. Moreover, the presence of the women in the meetings of the Grange has added a social attraction without which many a local Grange would probably have long since disbanded. Without question the admission of women has greatly helped the Order to endure.

Miss Hall was born and reared in Boston. It was there that she made her suggestion to O. H. Kelley, who accepted it promptly. She prepared herself to teach and followed her uncle to Minnesota, where she became associated with him as secretary. She collected addresses of those interested in agriculture from agricultural journals and elsewhere and carried on an active correspondence in the interest of getting the Order under way. When the Order finally became a fact she accompanied Kelley, who was the first Secretary of the National Grange, to Washington and took charge of his office. The record, therefore, shows that Miss Hall added an important principle to the fundamental character of the Order and took an active and zealous part in establishing the organization.

Oliver Hudson Kelley.—The seven founders above referred to were all but one in the Government service at Washington, D. C. F. M. McDowell alone was at the time engaged in agriculture. It is said, however, that all but one of them were born on the farm and had both a practical knowledge of farming and a sympathetic attitude toward its interests. According to Mrs. McDowell these seven men all had essentially different characteristics and as a group made a competent body for the work of perfecting the details of organization.

The originator of the idea of organization, as stated, was

Oliver Hudson Kelley. He was born in New England but went west, where he served as telegraph operator, clerk and reporter, and later settled upon a farm near Itasca, Minnesota. In 1864 he secured a position in the Department of Agriculture, and in 1866 he was sent through the South to collect information for the Department.[1] Mr. Kelley was impressed with the backwardness of the rural population and believed that a fraternal order organized among them would help to improve their economic and social status as well as go far toward destroying the feeling of sectionalism between the North and South. In 1867 he received an appointment in the Post Office Department at Washington. He was a Mason and, therefore, a believer in the "secret order" feature. Grange writers state that he was unable, however, to formulate a ritual and a constitution for a farmers' organization and was of necessity compelled to call upon other men who became his associates in the original work of organization. Mr. Kelley was a man who liked a change of scenes, but at the same time he manifested considerable determination in the execution of a formulated program. This characteristic he sometimes allowed to govern his relationships with the councils of the Grange to the extent that he appears to have become at times unyielding. He had the enthusiasm of youth, and altogether he was an admirable propagandist. It is stated that he left Washington, headed first for New York and thence for Minnesota, supplied with dispensations to be sold at $15 each, and with but $2.50 in his pocket to cover personal expenses.

Kelley very persistently carried on the work of organization which at first was discouraging enough to dampen the ardor of most men. He was the first National Secretary of the Order and remained in this office until November, 1878. He resigned his position stating that on account of the demands on his time by private business he could no longer serve. Kelley was at this time engaged in a large development enterprise in Florida and desired according to the record to locate the office of Secretary at any place convenient to him. This was opposed by the executive committee, and the incident

[1] In Atkeson's *Semi-Centennial History* biographical sketches of all the founders are given.

appears to have estranged him for many years. Both he and Miss Hall were absent from the sessions of the National Grange from 1878 to 1895.[1] At the thirty-ninth session, which met in 1905, it was reported that all but one of the seven founders had passed to their reward, the surviving member being Kelley. He was then almost 80 years of age. The Grange at this session unanimously adopted a resolution expressing its gratitude for the part he played in founding the Order, and voted him a monthly sum of $100 to be paid him the remainder of his life. He died in 1913, in his 87th year.

Saunders, et al.—William Saunders was born in Scotland, where his forbears for at least three generations had been noted gardeners. His early education prepared him for the ministry, but because of his strong liking for gardening he later took a course in horticulture at the College of Edinburgh. He came to America in 1848, became "assistant editor" of the Horticulturist and formed a partnership at Germantown, Pennsylvania, in the business of landscape gardening and horticulture. In 1862 he was appointed Superintendent of the Propagating Garden in the United States Department of Agriculture. He was the first scientific expert appointed by the Commissioner of Agriculture. One of his many achievements was the planning of the National Cemetery at Gettysburg. He remained with the United States Department of Agriculture to the end of his life, that is until 1900.

Mr. Saunders also conceived the idea of a farmers' organization similar to the kind proposed by Mr. Kelley. Already in 1855 he had outlined such a plan in the *American Farmer*. To him is given credit for the general plan of the organization. He advocated the establishment of township, county, state and national bodies which was carried out as far as practicable. He is also credited with first suggesting the name "Grange" for the meeting place. The word means farmhouse, including all the necessary farm buildings. The title of the Order, Patrons of Husbandry, is also his suggestion. A large portion of the first four degrees was written by him as well as the preamble to the constitution. During August of 1867 Mr. Saunders attended a meeting of the Pomological Society held

[1] *Vide* Atkeson, *op. cit.*, p. 187.

at St. Louis, where he distributed a circular by Mr. Kelley setting forth the insufficiencies of the agricultural societies then existing, and proposing to establish a "secret order of farmers, modeled on the Masonic order, with the usual equipment of degrees, signs, and pass-words, the object being to advance agriculture and bind the farmers together."[1] Mr. Saunders served as Master of the Grange for the first six years and later as a member of the Executive Committee.

John R. Thompson was from New Hampshire, but at the time Kelley took the initiative to organize the farmers he was a clerk in the Treasury Department at Washington. He was a high-degree Mason, and was well informed concerning "rituals and laws of fraternities." He assisted in the preparation of the lower degrees and is virtually given full credit for writing the sixth and seventh degrees. In the first days of the Order he was a Lecturer, and later was made Treasurer.

William M. Ireland, a clerk in the Post Office Department, was also a high-degree Mason. Mrs. McDowell credits him with being an expert in parliamentary law and journalism and with framing the constitution and by-laws of the Order. He also prepared the proceedings of the early meetings for the printer.

Reverend Aaron B. Grosh, employed in the Department of Agriculture at the time of organizing the Order, also contributed to the ritual. His chief work was furnishing all the prayers for the lower degrees. He also collected the first group of Grange melodies. The work of Reverend Grosh brought into the Order a religious reverence, and through the collection of songs he helped to build up traditions that tend to cause an organization to endure.

Reverend John Trimble, employed in the Treasury Department, is characterized as a "critic and adviser." His criticism of proposals was usually found to be correct, and his constant vigilance and power of analysis won for him the title of "the wet blanket of the Order." For some years he refused to accept an office in the Order, but he was already willing to give his best efforts to the constructive work necessary in its early days. Later he became a member of the Executive Com-

[1] Buck, *The Granger Movement*, p. 41.

mittee and served to the time of his death, a term of eighteen years.

Francis M. McDowell was the only one of the seven who was not a Government clerk. He was a pomologist of Wayne, New York, and is credited with setting the finance of the Order on a firm basis. Its first surplus funds were at his suggestion invested in Government bonds, which was the means of providing a reserve for the future of the Order. There came a time when its income fell below its disbursements, and at that time the reserve served the purpose of a steadying influence of considerable importance.

Mrs. McDowell sums up the work and character of the founders as follows: "We have here a propagandist, an organizer, a ritualist, a parliamentarian and journalist, a man of God, a critic, and a financier."

Preliminary Stages of Organization.—Upon his return from St. Louis, where he had distributed circulars concerning the proposed order among members of the United States Pomological Society. Mr. Saunders reported to Mr. Kelley that he had mentioned the "Order to a good many, and all agree in considering the thing a grand idea." Ireland frequently spent the evening with Kelley in the latter's room at the hotel, where the prospects of the Order were discussed. Any little encouragement gave these two founders great enthusiasm. Trimable also often joined these meetings and served as a balance wheel in the group. Atkeson says that Kelley never admitted any difficulties. In answer to a letter from Anson Bartlett of North Madison, Ohio, he stated that in twelve months the number of the members of the Order was to be counted by the million. "I long," he says, "to see the great army of producers in our country turn their eyes up from their work; stir up those brains, now mere machines; get them in motion in the right direction; make them discard their old almanacs and signs of the moon; and just imagine what a volcanic eruption we can produce in this age! Everything is progressing. Why not the farmers?"[1]

In order to interest the farmers throughout the country

[1] Atkeson, *op. cit.*, p. 16.

a rough circular letter was now drawn up and sent out broadcast. This circular read in part as follows:

> A number of gentlemen engaged in agriculture and its kindred branches in different states are now perfecting a Ritual for an Order, to be composed wholly of persons, male and female, directly interested in agricultural pursuits.
>
> The whole, it is believed, will do much toward elevating our occupation as well as establishing a unity of sentiment among the farmers of the country and materially increase the circulation of publications devoted to the interests of agriculture, and consequent increase of knowledge.
>
> Should such an organization meet with your approval and you see fit to offer any suggestions to enable the originators to make further improvements before it is introduced to the public, the same will be most cordially received and duly considered.

A problem of considerable importance was the selection of an attractive and significant name. Among the names suggested by various people for the organization were: Independent Farmers, Independent Order of Progressive Farmers, Knights of the Plow, Knights of the Flail, Knights of the Sickle, Lords of the Soil, Sons of the Soil, Brethren of the Vine, Yeoman of Columbia, Order of Jacob, Rustics, Mushrooms, Fungi, etc.[1] As previously stated, both the name of the Order and that of the subordinate bodies were first suggested by Mr. Saunders. At a meeting held in the latter's office on November 15, 1867, "for the purpose of organizing an Order of Agriculture in the United States," the names as suggested by Mr. Saunders were finally officially adopted. By common consent the word, Grange, has been accepted as designating the entire Order.

The question of dues concerned the organizers quite a little. Calculations were made as to the income of the National Grange on the basis of 10 cents from every member. Because of the difference between the wages for men and women it was decided to make the entrance fees for women only half as large as those for men.[2] Later this ratio was changed.

At a second formal session held December 4, 1867, later fixed as the birthday of the Order, the motto, *Esto Perpetua,*

---

[1] *Vide* Atkeson, *op. cit.*, p. 17.

[2] *Vide* Atkeson, *op. cit.*, p. 20.

Let it endure forever, was adopted, and the following organization was effected:

Master—William Saunders.
Overseer—Anson Bartlett.
Lecturer—J. R. Thompson.
Steward—William Muir.
Assistant Steward—A. S. Moss.
Treasurer—W. M. Ireland.
Secretary—O. H. Kelley.

On January 8, 1868, a subordinate grange was organized among clerks of the Post Office Department for the purpose of trying out the ritual. In a later section the development of the organization from its beginning to the present will be traced.

The General Plan of Organization.—The constitution provides that a Subordinate Grange, corresponding to the township organization suggested by Mr. Saunders, is to be the unit of organization. The Subordinate Grange must have at least thirteen members of which there must be at least four of either sex. In a state where no State Grange exists application for authority of organization is made directly to the National Grange, which issues a dispensation as evidence of such authority and receives dues directly from the Subordinate Granges. In the chart showing the organization of the Patrons of Husbandry the relationship between the Subordinate and the National Grange is shown by a dotted line inasmuch as membership in the National Grange can only be secured through the organization of a State Grange. When this is effected application for the organization of Subordinate Granges is made to State Granges and charters showing authority for such organization are passed through the state bodies for the signature of state officials. All charters authorizing the organization of Subordinate Granges are issued by the National Grange, but passed through the State Grange for record. Four degrees for the Subordinate Grange are provided, and must have been conferred upon the 13 applicants before the dispensation or charter may be issued. Admission into the Order was at first at the age of 16 for females and 18 for males, but in 1874 it was placed at 16 for both sexes. Fifteen Subordinate Granges are required to organize a State Grange.

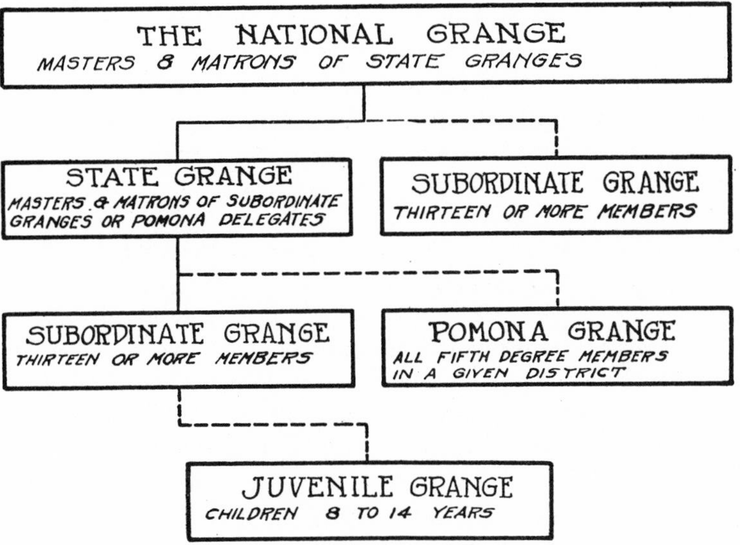

As shown by the accompanying chart, Masters and Matrons of Subordinate Granges, or in some states Pomona delegates, constitute the State Granges and Masters and Matrons of State Granges constitute the National Grange. The constitution provides that State Granges may reduce their membership by the election of delegates. A State Grange is also allowed to give Pomona Granges representation in its own body, so that some states follow the practice of basing their representation upon a certain number of delegates from each Pomona according to membership.

While Saunders had suggested the establishment of county granges in his scheme of a farmers' organization the constitution actually adopted by the founders and used as the fundamental law of the Order to 1873 omitted this step for the reason, it is said, that its use was found impracticable. There was, however, soon a demand for such an organization for the purpose of carrying on cooperative enterprises and for unifying in a general way the interests of local organizations over a territory corresponding to that of the county. The State

Grange of Missouri made provision for a union of Subordinate Granges into Councils before 1873, when the National Grange proposed an amendment to make such action regular. The Missouri provision, however, allowed only the formation of unions among Subordinate Granges for business purposes, which seems not to have been a violation of the National Grange constitution.[1] When the National Grange authorized the organization of county granges it chose the word Pomona to designate it. Pomona is the name of the fifth degree and was from the beginning conferred by the State Grange and therefore associated with that branch of the Order. Up to 1873 degrees and branches of the Order ran parallel, but in that year the degrees above the first four were dissociated from the State and National Granges to the extent that the higher degrees could be conferred upon all who desired them, the pre-equisite of passing through all the chairs of the Subordinate and State Granges being no longer necessary. The relation between the degrees and the structural parts of the Order would probably have been less confusing if another name had been selected to designate the county grange. The Pomona Grange then was the result of a growing demand for facilities to carry on cooperative enterprises and educational activities within limited areas. Because of these developments it is a structural part tacked on to the Order as it were. In 1887 this branch was allowed representation in the State Grange at the discretion of the state body. It is composed of all fifth degree Patrons in good standing within a given district. The Pomona Grange is therefore not a delegate body made up of officials of Subordinate Granges.

The Grange makes full provision for all ages of society. At the 24th annual session of the National Grange a ritual was provided for the Juvenile Grange, which has been used ever since. In this Grange children between eight and fourteen are taken care of, and those below eight may be taken into the meetings of either the Juvenile or subordinate bodies. In this way all members of the family are provided for.

At the 1919 convention of the National Grange there were

---

[1] *Vide* Periam, *History of the Farmers' Movement*, p. 180, for the Missouri constitution.

S AND M

products, and
e State weights an
of food products.

o).

COUNSEL (Div. of Fo
To advise Commissioner and
evidence of violations, prepa
General, represent Division
quires at formal hearing
rules and needed legisl
Counsel (Same as
of Farms

BUREAU OF
INDUST

To carry out provis
cultural Laws on
insect pests and
eases among trees
and on grading of
horticultural in

Director
Assistant
Inspectors (2
Stenographer a

KETS
E

law, to
d furnish
ket prices
ods of
arketing

reau
ectors(4)

BUREAU
ASSO

To aid in organ
ation of produ
cooperative

Director or
Agent (Acti
Inspector (Act
Organizer (
Stenograph

of Division in New
ssue daily and week
nts, and correct
thods of marketi

nt (Acting as supervisor

58 voting members present representing 30 different States. There were also 12 honorary members in attendance. The honorary members consist of past-masters and past-delegates. The Proceedings for that year state the total regular membership of the National Grange to be 64, representing 33 states. The National Grange is often largely attended. In 1913, according to Atkeson, there were probably 10,000 members in attendance. The seventh degree that year was conferred upon a class of 5,459 persons.[1] The meetings usually last 10 days. The 32d session, convening in 1898, lasted for 16 days. There has been a demand for shorter sessions, but the time seldom falls below 10 days.

The Relation of Degrees to Organization.—As already stated, up to 1873 degrees and branches of the Order ran parallel. To each structural part certain degrees were assigned. The government of the organization was carried on by persons who were both high officials and had taken the higher degrees. In fact the upper chamber, designated the Senate and composed of seventh-degree members had joint legislative powers with the lower house known as the Council and composed of sixth-degree members. The lower house was the national Grange or masters and matrons of State Granges meeting in convention. It had the exclusive privilege under the first constitution to originate all legislation. All members joining the Order have always taken the first four degrees conferred by the Subordinate Grange. It is still necessary in order to secure an election to the higher offices to take the higher degrees, but the reverse is no longer true. The sixth and seventh degrees, for instance, are successively conferred upon fifth degree members without the prerequisite that such members first pass through the chairs of the National Grange. In other words, the degrees of the Order have been virtually separated from official position making it possible for others than masters and past-masters of the National Grange to be admitted into the rank of the seventh-degree. As a matter of fact, according to a letter from a Grange official, "any fourth-degree member may take the higher degrees of the Order." There was at one time considerable opposition to the higher

[1] *Vide Semi-Centennial History*, p. 287.

degrees, but when they were thrown open to anybody desiring them the opposition disappeared. Unquestionably this was a wise procedure inasmuch as it had the effect of making the Order more popular. From the viewpoint of Grange leaders the secret work of the Order is influential in securing the loyalty of its members, providing considerable social interest, and maintaining the stability of the entire organization. The accompanying table shows the relation between the degrees of the Order and its several organic parts.

It is to be noted that the Senate was lopped off from the Order in 1873. This was a step of considerable importance

Table Showing the Relation of Degrees to the Several Branches of the Patrons of Husbandry as at First Organized.

Branch of Order	Degrees 1867		1873	1874	1887
	(Man)	(Woman)			
Subordinate Granges	1st—Laborer, 2nd—Cultivator, 3rd—Harvester, 4th—Husbandman,	Maid Shepherdess Gleaner Matron	1st 2nd 3rd 4th	1st 2nd 3rd 4th	1st 2nd 3rd 4th
Pomona	....		....	5th	5th
State Grange	5th—Pomona (Hope). Composed of officers and Past Masters of Subordinate Granges who were entitled *ex-officio* to the 5th degree.		5th	5th	5th 6th
National Grange	6th—Flora (Charity). Members of the 6th degree constituted the National Council which was composed of masters and past masters of State Granges, who were entitled *ex-officio* to the 6th degree.		6th 7th	6th 7th	6th 7th
Senate	7th—Ceres (Faith). Composed of members of the Council who served one year therein, and who were entitled *ex-officio* to the 7th degree. All acts and resolutions were to originate in the Council (6th degree) and were subject to the approval or rejection of the Senate (7th degree).		....	....	....

(The names of the higher degree have been slightly rearranged since the adoption of the first constitution.)

inasmuch as this body, consisting of seventh degree members, had joint control of the organization. Under the present arrangement control is wholly lodged with the members of the National Grange. The seventh degree body is now known as the Assembly of Demeter and has charge of the secret work. Its highest officer is titled High Priest. The constitution adopted in 1873 also constituted this body as a court of impeachment of all officers of the National Grange, and made seventh-degree persons members of the National body, allowing them to hold office therein but denying them the right to vote.

In 1887 an amendment was ratified allowing the State Grange also to confer the sixth degree. When the degree is conferred by the National Grange the full fee of one dollar is paid into the National treasury. When it is conferred by the State Grange the fee is equally divided between the state and national bodies. The national body always provides the certificates. The practice of allowing State Granges to confer the sixth degree made it possible to prepare a very much larger group of members to be eligible for the seventh degree. It is a great convenience for Grange members to receive the sixth degree in their home state, and inasmuch as the National Grange follows the itinerant plan of holding its meetings, the new plan has been the means of feeding the ranks of the seventh degree with a large number of new recruits every year. In 1913 the number was 5,459 and in more recent years it has kept close to 1,500. The change has also been the means of adding considerable income to the National Grange, and came at a time when its treasury faced the condition of ultimate depletion.

The Officers of the Grange.—The officers of the four Granges are as follows: Master, Overseer, Lecturer, Steward, Assistant Steward, Chaplain, Treasurer, Secretary, Gatekeeper, Ceres, Pomona, Flora, and Lady Assistant Steward. The National and State Granges may also appoint Deputies to organize Subordinate Granges. Where a State Grange exists the Deputies are appointed by it. In addition to organizing Granges it is the duty of the Deputy to keep a vigilance over weak ones and endeavor to establish them on a sound and permanent basis. The executive committee, made up of some additional members, should also be mentioned in the list of officers. The constitution of 1873 provides that officers of Subordinate Granges are to be elected annually; those of State Granges, every two years, and those of the National Grange every three years. In 1875 the latter term was reduced to two years.

It is the duty of the Master of the several bodies to preside at the Grange meetings. He is a member of the executive committee and is the administrative head of the Grange. The Master of the National Grange prepares and delivers an annual address which represents virtually the opinion of the Grange concerning various public questions.

The Overseer assists the Master in the conduct of meetings and presides during his absence. He has little else to do except to assist at the annual meeting.

The founders of the Order provided for a feature in the Subordinate Grange known as the "Lecture Hour," which has been characterized as the "heart of the Grange." It is the means of bringing before the members of each community important ideas on technical agriculture and such other problems that affect the social, political, and economic life of society. Each Grange has its Lecturer. In the local organization his duties are largely confined to his own Grange. In the State Grange his duties spread over the entire state and may be said to be of a two-fold character. His duties are first to instruct the Granges within the borders of his state. The methods used in the various states vary somewhat. In all states it is necessary that he travel over his territory and everywhere there is the tendency to standardize throughout the state ideas and objects of instruction. In a number of states this is done through the preparation of materials for local use. In the second place it is the duty of the Lecturer to instruct and educate the people outside of the Order with reference to Grange policies and standards. This is done through lectures delivered before commercial organizations and through the press. The work of the National Lecturer covers the entire country. He visits state and local Granges as much as he can, and consults with State Lecturers concerning the content of lecture work. An interchange of lecture material is encouraged.[1] During the war the lecture hour served to disseminate among the members of the Grange the attitude of the Government and the ideals necessary to bring the war to a successful conclusion. It is always the means through which rural thought and action may be mobilized for the best interests of the country. The lecture work is one of the best features to establish unity of purpose and tends to prevent defections within the Order.

The Steward presides in the absence of the Master, Overseer, or Past-Masters. His main duties, however, are to take charge of the paraphernalia and other property of the Grange used in the secret-order work, to conduct the ballot and to arrange the work incidental to the admission of candidates. The assistant steward takes part in escorting candidates during initiation and gives general assistance to the Steward. At a time when several thousand are initiated the incumbent of this office performs more or less arduous or exacting duties.

The National Treasurer keeps a record of all receipts of dues, fees for degrees conferred, and fees for charters or dispensations, as well as of all expenditures. Receipts are deposited with a fiscal agent. The Treasurer of a Subordinate Grange reports at regular intervals to the State Treasurer, and pays over to him the amount due the State Grange. Similarly the State Grange Treasurer reports to the National Treasurer and pays him the amount due the National Grange. The Treasurer of the National Grange reports to the Master regularly and to the National Grange at the annual meeting.

The National Secretary keeps a record of all proceedings of the meetings and of receipts that come into his hands through issuing charters and dispensations, conferring sixth and seventh degrees, and sales of stock such as manuals, gavels, copies of ceremoneis, etc. All charters are issued by the Secretary of the National Grange and those for the Subordinate Granges must pass through the State Secretary for record. The Secretary's office keeps a record of the membership and of all Granges.

While it is the duty of the Gatekeeper to guard the door

[1] *Vide 1919 Proceedings* of the National Grange, p. 17.

of the lodge room, the office stands as a reminder that only those having a professional interest in agriculture are to be admitted into the Order. At the National Grange meeting of 1897 the Gatekeeper in his report said the following: "As Gatekeeper permit me to ask whether we are confining our membership strictly to those who have a direct, personal and professional interest in farming or cultivating the soil? Are any admitted within our gates who have not a sufficient direct interest in tilling the soil, or may have some interest in conflict with our purposes?"[1] The admission of persons into the Order was at first not everywhere strictly confined to those directly interested in agriculture, and at one time leaders feared the disintegration of Grange policies and the exploitation of the Order for other than agricultural purposes.

The duties of Ceres, Pomona, and Flora, are mainly ceremonial. They represent respectively grains, fruits, and flowers. Flora encourages the use of flowers and the beautification of the home.

Other Organization Details.—The constitution may be amended by the adoption of a resolution in the National Grange supported by a two-thirds vote and the ratification of the proposed amendment by two-thirds of the State Granges.

Any subject pertaining to constitutional revision is submitted from the lower organizations to the National Grange through the regular official channels and passed upon, or it may be introduced at the national meeting by any member of the National Grange on his own initiative.

By-laws may be amended by a two-thirds vote of the members present.

The constitution provides for annual meetings for the State and National Granges, and monthly meetings for the Subordinate Granges. Between annual meetings the executive committee performs important work. The annual words used in the Granges are communicated to the National Master by the High Priest every year at the annual meetings.

The important work of the State and National Granges is done by committees whose reports are presented to the entire

[1] *Vide Atkeson, Semi-Centennial History,* p. 199.

body for adoption. Many of the committees are regularly appointed. In 1919 there were committees on agriculture, auditing, claims and grievances, constitution and by-laws, cooperation, credentials, digest, education, finance, foreign relations, forestry and conservation, good of the Order, home economics, insurance, Master's address, production and distribution, taxation, woman suffrage, and others, numbering 28 in all. There is even a committee on the Master's address which aims to bring before the Grange the salient features of the address and have the entire body pass upon them so as to give all its members an opportunity to play a part in the formulation of Grange policies.

Another important feature of the National Grange is the report of the State Master. The State Masters' reports give general atmosphere as to the status of the Order throughout the country. These reports, together with reports of committees and the National Master's address show annually the work that the Grange is doing and the position it takes on economic, social and political questions.

Salaries.—The salaried officers are the Master, Treasurer, Secretary and Washington representatives. The executive committee including also delegates to the National Grange are paid on a *per diem* basis and are allowed traveling and other expenses. Considerable changes in salaries have been made from time to time. In 1873 the Treasurer was paid $1,000 and the Secretary $3,500. In 1875 the Master was paid $1,200; the Treasurer, $600 and expenses; the Secretary, $2,000 and expenses; and the Lecturer $5 a day and expenses. After that year a vigorous retrenchment policy was necessary because the receipts for some time remained below the disbursements. The Grange had built up a large reserve during the period previous to 1875 and was criticized from the outside as an organization with great wealth and powerful influence. There was also criticism from the inside and demands were made for the donation of a large part of these resources to State Granges. A sum, amounting to about $100,000, was donated. In 1879 the Grange's reserve was less than $50,000. The membership dues to the National Grange had been reduced from 10 cents to 5 cents in 1875 and this fact together with the donation policy made it necessary to reduce salaries so as to keep expenditures within receipts. A gradual reduction of salaries was, therefore, made reaching as low as $500 and expenses for the Master, $300 and expenses for the Treasurer, and $600 for the Secretary in 1879. By 1911 they had again risen to $2,000 for the Master, $500 and $4 a day for the Treasurer, and $1,200 and $4 a day for the Secretary. In 1921 the Secretary's annual salary was increased to $1,500, and the Lecturer was given an annual salary of $500 in addition to the $4 a day and traveling expenses formerly paid him.

The record shows that the administration of Grange funds has on the whole been wise. The only exception is the handling of the reserve, which leaders think should have been invested in a Washington building instead of dissipated in the making of donations from which no good resulted, it is claimed.

It would seem that the National Grange would do well to pay out somewhat more in the way of salaries. Its experts at Washington and those engaged in extension should be well paid. The Grange is a farm organization representing the interests of an economic class, and if it would meet successfully the opposition of other organized groups it must hire experts that have the ability to shape public sentiment in favor of the agricultural group. Men of this caliber are high-priced men, and to secure their services they must be paid attractive salaries. This is the plan that capital in industry and commerce has used for many years, and labor also is beginning to see its advantages.

Receipts and Expenditures.—The financial support of the Granges comes from three main sources,—membership dues and fees paid for degrees and charters. During the formation period the latter was an important source of income. The National Grange receives fees for charters and dispensations at the time Subordinate Granges are organized. For every authority of organization issued the National Grange receives $15. Initiation fees or fees charged for entrance into the Subordinate Grange, are also sources of income of considerable importance to the lower branches of the Order, and were placed at $5 for men and $2 for women in the constitution of 1873. In 1877 they were changed to $3 and $1 respectively. Another amendment granting State Granges the privilege of reducing the fee to $1 and $0.50 respectively was passed in 1885 and in some states the reduction has been made. Both the charter and initiation fees during the early years of rapid growth were very important sources of income for the various branches of the Order, the charter fee going to the National Grange and the initiation fee being divided between the Subordinate and State Granges. The National Grange also counts among its receipts the proceeds of the sale of stock which consists of various forms, manuals, etc. The amount received from this source, however, only represents the cost of printing, binding, etc., and cannot be regarded as income available for the general support of the organization.

The most important source of income is the dues paid by members. The constitution of 1873 provides for a minimum monthly sum of 10 cents to be paid by each member into the treasury of the Sudordinate Grange. Of this annual sum of $1.20 the State Grange was to be paid 24 cents, leaving 96 cents to be retained by the Subordinate Grange. The State Grange was to pay an annual sum of 10 cents to the National Grange for every member in the state and retain 14 cents for its own use. In 1874, because of the great plethora of funds coming into the treasury of the National Grange, the amount to be paid to it was reduced to 5 cents per member. In 1918 an unsuccessful attempt to increase the national dues was made. It was again brought up in 1919 when a resolution to increase the dues from 5 to 8 cents was adopted. The main arguments for increasing the dues at that time was the added expense occasioned by the establishment of the Washington office representing the interests of the Grange at the seat of the Government and cooperating with other farm organizations in the effort to urge upon Congress legislation favorable to the agricultural class and also to prevent the enactment of laws that are inimical to its interests.

The total receipts of the National Grange for the fiscal year ending September 30, 1919, were as follows:

Dues from State Granges	$25,500.50
Sixth degree fees	2,493.00
Seventh degree fees	1,524.00
Charter fees	4,035.00
Subordinate Grange dues	1.25
Sales of stock	3,525.53
Interest on bank account	281.75
Interest on note	600.00
Interest on bonds	2,727.00
Total	$40,688.03

The total disbursements for the same year were as follows:

Officers' salaries	$4,100.00
Executive committee	723.12
Legislative committee	45.52
Secretary's office, expenses	940.46
Master's office, expenses	425.53
Lecturer's office, expenses	851.43
Washington office, salaries and expenses	4,516.34
Treasurer's office, expenses	74.32
Expenses, 52d annual session	8,415.22
National Grange Monthly	4,380.75
Supplies of Secretary's office	4,066.28
Field Day expenses	105.53
Contingent expenses	394.72
Home economics	53.46
Extension work	6,268.46
Total	$35,361.17

There was an excess of $5,326.86 of receipts over actual disbursements.

The resources of the National Grange on September 30, 1919, were as follows:

Deposit with fiscal agent	$15,709.17
Deposit in savings bank	6,952.84
Railway and municipal bonds	55,654.12
Liberty bonds	15,251.25
Loan on real estate	12,163.28
Unexpended Grange extension fund	731.54
Unexpended Washington headquarters' fund	546.16
Total	$107,008.36

These statements show that the status of the finances of the Grange is good. The large resources swell the receipts with interest income which in 1919 amounted to $3,608.75. The receipts are in excess of expenditures. If this condition can be maintained it will not be long until the leaders of the

Grange will have their wish graitfied with respect to a temple standing as a monument to the Order at Washington. It is always wise to have on hand a reserve which may be drawn upon at times when receipts fall below expenditures. No man can foretell the future, and it may be that from time to time considerable expense must be incurred in order to maintain the Grange in a virile condition throughout the country. The hiring of high-priced experts would probably be of service to the organization. Moreover the existence of a reserve gives the appearance of stability and success and exerts not a little influence in maintaining the organization intact.

Early Struggle of the Grange.—When Kelley left Washington in 1868 with a ticket to Harrisburg, Pennsylvania, and with but $2.50 in his pocket to pay expenses he was of the opinion that little difficulty would be encountered in the organization of farmers throughout the country. These hopes, however, were too radiant to be speedily realized. He had correspondents at Harrisburg and at Penn Yan, New York, but was unable to organize a Grange at either place. He left, however, a dispensation at Harrisburg and received $15 for it, which helped him with his expenses. He then went to Wayne, New York, where he met Mr. McDowell, who helped him financially. He was finally successful in organizing a Grange at Fredonia, New York. This Grange was the first to be organized outside of Washington and has continued without interruption to the present. From Fredonia Kelley went to Ohio, where he found sentiment favorable to organization, but was unable to organize a Grange. He instructed Mr. Bartlett concerning the details of organizing granges. He also instructed persons in Chicago and proceeded to Madison, Wisconsin, where he also failed and where he was forced to borrow $15 from a Mason brother to pay for his way home to Itasca, Minnesota. Soon after his arrival he received word that a Grange had been organized at Newton, Iowa. In the meantime printing bills and other debts were pressing in Washington and needed to be liquidated. Miss Hall now joined Kelley in Minnesota and aided very materially in sending out literature. A number of agricultural journals gave aid by advocating organization and a number of other local papers became friendly to the movement. Signs of life were simulated at Washington by the printing of resolutions authorizing Mr. Kelley anew to organize granges and commending him to friends of the cause of organization. In September of 1868 the first permanent Grange was organized at St. Paul, Minnesota, and two more were organized in the state before the close of the year. Three were organized in January of the following year and three in February. On February 23, 1869, Minnesota organized the first State Grange, which had representatives from eleven Subordinate Granges. The work of extending the Order throughout the state and into other states was at once undertaken. Fredonia Grange had by April 13, 1869, as many as 100 members. Several deputies for organizing granges were secured, and before the close of the year there were Granges in Illinois, Iowa, and Indiana. At a National Grange meeting held in Washington on January 25, 1870, Secretary Kelley reported the following condition of the Order: "Minnesota, 40; Illinois, 3; Iowa, 3; Pennsylvania, 1; New York, 1; Ohio, 1."[1] At the close of the year, 1870, there were 71 Granges in existence, 47 of which were in Minnesota. Missouri, Tennessee and California were added to the list of States having Granges. An active and wide correspondence gave promise for a more rapid extension of the Order. Kelley moved the Secretary's office to Washington in order to add prestige to information sent out from Grange headquarters. Glowing reports as to the progress of the Order were by him fabricated for some time. During the year, 1871, 130 new Granges were organized, and the progress of the Order during the following year is summarized by Buck in The Granger Movement, p. 56, as follows: "State Granges were organized in six states—Indiana, Vermont, South Carolina, Nebraska, Mississippi and Kansas—and reorganized in Illinois and Wisconsin, thus making, in all, ten state granges in operation. In nine states—Nebraska, Oregon, Michigan, Virginia, Louisiana, Kansas, Alabama, Arkansas and Georgia—the order found lodgment during 1872, so that at the close of the year, twenty-five states had active subordiante granges within their limits. Although the strength of the order was, at this time,

[1] *Vide Atkeson, op. cit.*, p. 34.

concentrated mainly in Iowa and Minnesota in the Northwest and South Carolina and Mississippi in the South, still its spread was so general and its centers so far apart, that it must be looked upon even thus early as distinctly national in character. In the North Central group, every state had now been entered, and the territory of Dakota alone remained untouched by the order; while of the Southern states, all had granges except Delaware, Maryland, West Virginia, Florida, and Texas. In the eastern or North Atlantic states, little progress had been made except in Vermont, while on the Pacific coast, the order had been introduced into both California and Oregon, though as yet these States had but one grange apiece.'' There were thus 10 State Granges organized at the opening of the year, 1873. By its close 22 more were added, making a total of 33 State Granges. The story of the early struggle of the Order is full of discouragement. Only men with an ardent zeal that is not subdued by failure would push on with the work of organization under conditions that surrounded the founders of the Grange. To be sure economic and social conditions were ripe for organization, but after all the human element, or initiative, is the factor upon which the origin and propagation of a movement depend.

Subsequent Development of the Order.—The subsequent development of the Patrons of Husbandry can be readily shown by membership statistics. The acompanying table shows changes of membership from 1874 to 1922.

Table Showing Membership of Grange from 1874 to 1922

Year	Members	Year	Members	Year	Members
1874	268,368	1890	135.461	1906	289,580
1875	858,050	1891	139,920	1907	410,622
1876	728,313	1892	145,331	1908	338,180
1877	411,244	1893	205,740	1909	339,470
1878	334,782	1894	127,160	1910	425,033
1879	246,383	1895	179,247	1911	502,322
1880	124,420	1896	131,942	1912	415,143
1881	151,040	1897	167,206	1913	539,426
1882	137,165	1898	178,187	1914	515,280
1883	122,960	1899	179,522	1915	540,085
1884	111,472	1900	187,482	1916	508,094
1885	117,620	1901	196,580	1917	565,061
1886	109,763	1902	218,022	1918	519,264
1887	118,341	1903	250,169	1919	510,010
1888	109,526	1904	260,813	1920	541,158
1889	106,782	1905	284,646	1921	587,091
				1922	676,056

Figures from 1874 to 1915, computed from dues paid to the National Grange, are taken from Atkeson's *Semi-Centennial History*. The figures for the last seven years have been computed in a similar way, the source of information being the Proceedings of the National Grange. Some difficulty is encountered in estimating the membership for 1920 in as much as the change of dues from five to eight cents, adopted by the National Grange in 1919, in all probability caused payments to be made by the state granges during the succeeding year on two different bases. Figures prior to 1874 are not available.

The accompanying diagram is drawn according to figures shown in the table and more readily portrays the changes in the membership of the Order. As this diagram shows there was

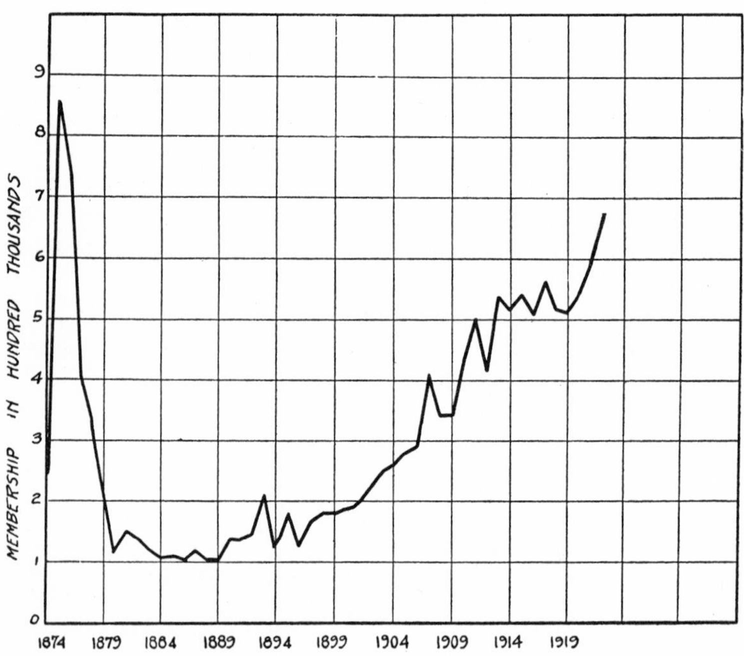

a very rapid extension of the Order during the years of 1874 and 1875. After 1875 there was a very rapid decline constituting almost a debacle. The highest membership reported was 858,050 in 1875 and the lowest point, after some temporary recoveries, was 106,782 in 1889.

The principal cause for the precipitous decline was the

reaction following the rapid growth in 1873 and 1874. During this period the standards of admission were such as to allow many to come into the Order who had no other interest than self-aggrandizement. It is said that "everybody wanted to join the Grange then; lawyers, to get clients; doctors, to get patients; merchants, to get customers; shylocks, to get their pound of flesh; and sharpers, to catch the babes in the woods." Many directly interested in agriculture joined under a misapprehension that organization was a cure-all. Doctor Buck summarizes the causes of the decline to have been a necessary reaction to the overgrown condition of the Order, the partication of local granges here and there in the political movement which was led by various "Independent Farmers,' and Anti-Monopoly parties," the failure to accomplish everything they had hoped for in the way of railroad legislation, and the disastrous failures of cooperative enterprises organized by state granges. Doctor Buck says that this fact "contributed more than anything else to the almost total collapse of the Grange throughout the West."[1]

Since 1889 there has been a gradual upward tendency in the growth of the Order. Some few fluctuations appear along the way; but they are not of a violent nature, and all indications point to the fact that the organization has become a permanent American institution. The larger of these fluctuations seem to have some relation to price changes or business depressions. The above diagram on which the general price level from 1860 to 1921 is charted shows periods of depression, for instance, in 1894, 1908, and 1911; while the diagram showing fluctuations in membership indicates corresponding declines in 1894 and 1908. A decided falling off in membership is indicated in 1912, which is a lag of one year behind the depression of prices in 1911. It is very probable that declining prices have sufficient influence to cause a smaller amount in the form of dues to be paid into the national treasury, and inasmuch as membership figures are computed on the basis of dues similar fluctuations would be indicated in the status of membership. Another reason for these fluctuations is that the dues for a given year are sometimes reported in the succeeding year. At

[1] *Vide the Granger Movement*, p. 73.

any rate the fluctuations are not violent and are not sufficiently strong to hinder a general upward climb in the growth of the Order.

Geographic Distribution of the Grange.—Considerable changes have taken place in the geographic distribution of the strength of the Order since 1876. The following statement shows its present distribution as well as that of 1876.[1]

	1876	*1919*
North Atlantic Division	80,013	281,317
South Atlantic Division	61,302	3,275
North Central Division	276,961	154,663
South Central Division	146,624	3,022
Western	23,625	34,601

The most radical declines have occured in the South Atlantic and South Central Divisions. These are the sections of the country most poorly represented. The South was greatly affected by the Farmers' Alliance; and after its force was spent, as will be shown in a later chapter, it is in this territory where the Farmers' Union was strongest during the first years of its history. The north central section has lost almost half of its former strength, but is still well represented in some states, notably in Ohio, Michigan and Kansas. The Western Division has gained slightly since 1876. It is in the North Atlantic Division where the Grange is the strongest. This is the conservative section of the country and it is not at all surprising that the growth of the Order in New England and in States immediately south of it was at first slow. On the other hand, now that it is well established in this region, its future is well-nigh secure. Its center of strength will probably remain for many years in the East, and from there it may continue to radiate afresh to other sections of the country.

SELECTED REFERENCES

Annual Reports of the National Grange; Buck, *The Granger Movement;* McVey, *The Populist Movement;* Atkeson, *Semi-centennial History of the Patrons of Husbandry;* Kelly, *History of the Patrons of Husbandry;* Periam, *History of the Farmers' Movement;* Marquis in *Country Gentlemen,* May 15, 1920.

[1] The figures for 1876 are from Buck's *Granger Movement* and those of 1919 were computed from the Treasurer's report after reducing dues reported from the various states to an annual basis. The total membership figure for 1919 in this statement is therefore not in agreement with the figure given in the previous membership table.

CHAPTER XVII

AIMS AND PURPOSES OF THE GRANGE

Early Objects of Organization.—Kelley's first ideas as to
he need for organizing the farmers were to foster agricultural
education and social intercourse in every community, and to
obliterate the feeling of sectionalism between the North and
South through the formation of a national organization that
would cause the people of the two sections to mingle in fra-
ternal fellowship and on a common economic basis. These
deas came to him while on his trip through the South as agent
of the Department of Agriculture. The organization was to
nclude only those directly interested in agriculture because
t was this economic group in which he was especially inter-
ested, and because the farmers seemed to be greatly in need
of aid. The agricultural classes seemed to him more ignorant
han other groups; they lacked the social advantages found in
rban centers; and during the reconstruction period following
he Civil War their economic status was wholly unsatisfactory
or reasons stated in the previous chapter. It was very evident
hat an organization to help the farmers had to exclude other
economic groups because the other groups, if admitted, would
work at cross purposes with the agricultural class. Moreover
he objects of organization through which he was going to
mprove the status of the farmers were agricultural education
nd social intercourse. Lecturers from the Department of
Agriculture were to address members of the organization from
ime to time. Also study and discussion were to be conducted
mong themselves. Certainly the function of agricultural edu-
ation would not interest people engaged in economic pur-
uits other than farming. The principle, as later expressed
y Saunders, that the time called for new organizations "based
pon the industrial arts rather than upon political theories"
eems very obvious to us now. Organization along specialized
conomic lines in industry, commerce and finance has always
ad a parallel existence to a greater or less degree. Already
uring the medieval period people in Europe were organized
long craft and trade lines known as gilds, but in agriculture

virtually no organization was effected before 1800, and, as shown in previous chapters, the organization effected in Amer ica before the middle of the nineteenth century was scattered inconstant, and of little consequence even from an educationa point of view.

When Kelley actually began the work of organizing the Grange and met the farmers face to face with his scheme he had to give a very conspicuous place to direct economi aspects among the aims and purposes of the Order. He founc among them the desire to organize for the purpose of fighting monopolies, especially the railroads, as well as for the purpose of conducting cooperative enterprises. Kelley at first seem not to have been interested in these objects. The first direc action aiming at the protection of economic interests of the agricultural class fostered by Kelley was the keeping of a record of reputable and disreputable dealers. In a red book were to be recorded the names of honest dealers, and in a blu book those of dishonest dealers. The plan was to be extende into a national secret and protective association. A plan o recording the wants of customers and the available supplie of farmers was also suggested, and was to be carried ou through the appointment of a business agent by each loca Grange. In 1868 a circular printed in St. Paul stating th benefits seems to have gone somewhat beyond the aims and purposes of the Order as first conceived by Kelley. It read as follows:

> Systematic arrangements for procuring and disseminating i the most expeditious manner, information relative to crops, deman and supply, prices, markets and transportation throughout the countr and for the establishment of depots for the sale of special and genera products in the cities; also for the purchase and exchange of stoc seeds and desired help at home or from abroad, and situations fo persons seeking employment; also for ascertaining and testing th merits of newly invented farm implements, and those not in genera use, and for detecting and exposing those that are unworthy; and fc protecting, by all available means, the farming interests from frau and deception of every kind.[1]

In 1869 at the meeting of the State Grange of Minnesot it was suggested that the various local granges "have flourin

[1] (From Atkeson, *Semi-Centennial History of the Patrons of Hu bandry*, p. 30.

mills, flour their own wheat and keep the bran and shorts for feed, and not send any raw material into the eastern market, but, instead, appoint a business agent at St. Paul, who should receive the flour and ship it to the agent in New York City, who shall sell it on commission." Kelley wrote concerning this matter to McDowell, who disapproved of the plan on the ground that it was fraught with too much danger. The Minnesota Grange, however, persisted in its attitude and threatened to bolt the Order. Kelley, therefore, told them to proceed, advising them at the same time that it was not sanctioned by the National Grange and that it must be considered wholly a local matter. The appointment of a "State Agent for buying supplies and farm implements" in Minnesota followed. This was the first cooperative enterprise connected with the Grange. It was the beginning of a movement which grew rapidly and met with quick disaster because of a failure to recognize the limitations of the field within which cooperative work may be carried on.

Aims and Purposes in the Preamble.—The preamble to the constitution of 1873 written by Saunders places the aims of the organization on a very high plane. "Human happiness," it states, "is the aim of earthly ambition." Happiness is the goal of organization, and this is to be attained principally through a study of agricultural science. The only hint given in the entire preamble that organization is for the purpose of protecting the economic interests of the agricultural class in a direct way is the phrase, "for mutual instruction and protection." These ideas are stated in the following general terms:

> The productions of the earth are subject to the influence of natural laws, invariable and indisputable; the amount produced will consequently be in proportion to the intelligence of the producer, and success will depend upon his knowledge of the action of these laws, and the proper application of their principles.
>
> Hence knowledge is the foundation of happiness.
>
> The ultimate object of this organization is for mutual instruction and protection, to lighten labor by diffusing a knowledge of its aims and purposes, expend the mind by tracing the beautiful laws the Great Creator has established in the Universe, and to enlarge our views of Creative wisdom and power.

In the last paragraph of the preamble reference is made

to the necessity of unity of action to secure the proposed benefits. A ceremony of initiation is to bind the members of the order "in mutual fraternity as with a band of iron." The problem of organizing the farmers is of course fundamental. They are very numerous and widely scattered. They live under few restraints and become accustomed to an independent and individualistic philosophy of life. Hence it was thought that unity of action among the agricultural class could not be acquired without discipline, and discipline could not be enforced without the fraternal feature in the organization.

One of the first paragraphs of the preamble aims to justify the organization of agricultural producers. It reads as follows:

> The soil is the source from which we derive all that constitutes wealth; without it we would have no agriculture, no manufactures, no commerce. Of all the material gifts of the Creator, the various productions of the vegetable world are of the first importance. The art of agriculture is the parent and precursor of all arts, and its products the foundation of all wealth.

The inference is that organization among producers, if anywhere justifiable, is especially so in agriculture because it is the source of all wealth. This reminds one of the old economic theory enunciated during the eighteenth century by a group of French thinkers known as Physiocrats. They believed that agriculture was productive in a special way and characterized manufacturing and commerce as *sterile*, or unproductive. The idea came down through the Middle Ages when agriculture was regarded as highly productive and trading as a parasitic occupation. To this day one is liable to hear the same idea expressed by those who have never carefully analyzed the philosophy of production. Production in its broadest sense is the creation of utilities and making them available for society. It is not only the creation of form utilities, but time, place, and possession utilities as well. In other words, the placing of a bag of flour in the pantry of a New York consumer is just as much a utility as the planting and growing of the wheat in Minnesota. Society as at present organized could simply not exist without its system of transportation, its telegraph and telephone lines, its credit institutions, and its capitalistic industrial establishments. It is useless to say that agriculture comes first in the productive process, and, therefore, is the most important part of the chain. In a complex economic organization, such as ours, society could not long exist with the suspension of any one of the phases of production including the extractive, manufacturing, and commercial processes.

It should be stated that the preamble considered from the point of view of objects of organization is a laudable document. The fundamental philosophy upon which the organization was to be founded was sound. Its aims and purposes included nothing of an extreme or radical nature.

The Declaration of Purposes.—As previously stated the Grange grew by leaps and bounds up to 1875. During the year 1874 there were 11,941 local granges organized. By 1875 there were 858,050, or not far from a million members in the order. It was a time when everybody wanted to join. Master Adams said: "To be a Patron of Husbandry is no longer of doubtful propriety, but the proudest in the land are knocking at our door. The Order has become recognized as one of the great powers in the land, and the gates are being besieged from ocean to ocean by hordes of speculators, demagogues, small politicians, grain buyers, cotton factors and lawyers, who suddenly discovered that they are interested in agricultural pursuits." It was a time when there was a widespread demand for a more definite statement of the aims and purposes. Persons within the order clamored for such a statement as well as those without. Its rapidly growing membership at the time was an undisciplined mass and more or less confused with reference to aims and purposes. From the outside the order was criticized as a secret organization aiming to undermine the economic *status quo*. The Declaration of Purposes is, therefore, begun with the following introductory paragraph:

> Profoundly impressed with the truth that the National Grange of the United States should definitely proclaim to the world its general objects, we hereby unanimously make this Declaration of Purposes of the Patrons of Husbandry.

With respect to the principle of unity of action the Declaration expresses the attitude of the Grange through an endorsement of the following motto: "In essentials, unity; in non-essentials, liberty; in all things, charity." For a short statement that is at the same time comprehensive and definite, this motto very splendidly declares the policy of the order. With respect to matters pertaining to the economic welfare of the agricultural class unity of action would be urged, while in the fields of religion or partisan politics full individual liberty is guaranteed. The last phrase of the motto urges that even in matters on which unity is urged a charitable attitude is to be assumed. A very striking characteristic of the Declaration and of virtually all measures and policies approved by the order is the quality of moderation and the absence of radicalism. The principle of moderation is a necessary foundation stone of any organization that would endure.

The Declaration pledged the labor of members to the good of the order, to their country, and to mankind. Manhood and womanhood is to be raised to a higher plane. The laws of the country are to be "maintained inviolate." With respect to the distribution of wealth and the usurpation of political power the Declaration says the following:

> We desire a proper equality, equity and fairness; protection for the weak, restraint for the strong; in short, justly distributed burdens, and justly distributed power. These are American ideas, the very essence of American independence and to advocate the contrary is unworthy of the sons and daughters of an American republic.

Kelley's idea to extinguish the flames of sectionalism is touched upon in a separate paragraph as follows:

> We cherish the belief that sectionalism is, and of right should be, dead and buried with the past. Our work is for the present and the future. In our agricultural brotherhood and its purposes, we shall recognize no North, no South, no East, no West.

Special attention is called to the "abilities and sphere of woman." She is admitted not only to membership but also to position in the order. The Grange has been one of the pioneer influences looking toward the promotion of woman as counselor in our political and social institutions. Long before woman suffrage became a fact in the United States the National Grange had many times endorsed the principle.[1]

The Declaration comes out strongly for education and

[1] Atkeson, *Semi-Centennial History*, p. 298.

especially advocates the teaching of practical agriculture and domestic science in the agricultural colleges of the country. At the time these Purposes were drafted (1874) domestic science, now known as home economics, was very rarely taught in colleges. In *Teaching Home Economies* by Cooley, Winchell, Spohr, and Marshall, it is stated that "as early as 1872 the State College of Iowa gave lectures on housekeeping. In 1873 the State College of Kansas gave its first instruction in sewing, and in 1875 a course in foods. In 1874 the University of Illinois, then the 'Industrial University,' started to develop home economics instruction and a course of four years leading to the bachelor of science degree in the school of domestic science was planned. Kansas, Iowa, Oregon, and South Dakota had departments in their state colleges by 1890. During the next ten years others were added and the number increased to thirty."[1] The Grange was, therefore, in the very forefront of the movement to develop a sentiment that sought to establish in our higher institutions of learning the kind of education that pertains to the making of the home.

In a very positive way the principle of cooperation is enunciated as one of the important purposes of the Grange A clear-cut statement as to its attitude toward partisan politics is also given. Both these subjects will be discussed in later sections.

Opposition is voiced to large corporate profits, and the declaration made that the order does not accept communism. Railroads are regarded as necessary facilities for the fullest development of agriculture, and the order is, therefore, declared to be friendly to such railroad corporations that endeavor to enhance agricultural interests.

A principle of considerable importance is the acceptance of the plan to avoid litigation and to attempt to settle disputes rising among members by submitting all differences to a committee of arbitration appointed by the Grange.

The document is certainly very sane and conservative. The use of violence to carry its purposes into effect is no where threatened or even hinted. Contrary to the methods used by

[1] P. 47.

the Industrial Workers of the World or here and there by labor unions, the Grange has always respected the rights of property and the sanctity of human lives. The document closes by imploring the "continued assistance of the Divine Master" and with a pledge to return "to the wisdom, justice, fraternity and political purity of our forefathers."[1]

The Relation of the Grange to Politics.—Through its entire history the Grange has declared that it is not a political party, and that it is its confirmed policy as an organization not to participate in partisan politics. The Declaration of Purposes states clearly the position of the Grange with respect to nearly all aspects of the problem. The statement follows:

> We emphatically and sincerely assert the oft-repeated truth taught in our organic laws that the Grange—National, State or Subordinate—is not a political or party organization. No Grange if true to its obligations, can discuss political or religious questions, nor call political conventions, nor nominate candidates, nor even discuss their merits in its meetings.
>
> Yet the principles we teach underlie all true politics, all true statemanship, and if properly carried out, will tend to purify the whole political atmosphere of our country, for we seek the greatest good to the greatest number.
>
> We always bear in mind that no one by becoming a Patron of Husbandry gives up that inalienable right and duty which belongs to every American citizen, to take a proper interest in the politics of his country.
>
> On the contrary it is right for every member to do all in his power legitimately to influence for good the action of any political party to which he belongs. It is his duty to do all he can in his own party to put down bribery, corruption and trickery; to see that none but competent, faithful and honest men, who will unflinchingly stand by our industrial interests, are nominated for all positions of trust; and to have carried out the principle which should charactérize every Patron, that the office should seek the man and not the man the office.
>
> We acknowledge the broad principle that difference of opinion is no crime, and hold that "progress toward truth is made by differences of opinion," while the fault lies in bitterness of controversy.
>
> It is reserved by every Patron, as the right of a freeman, to affiliate with any party that will best carry out his principles.

These Purposes enjoin each member to take an intelligent and honest part in politics. Representatives are to be elected who favor agricultural interests. Absolute freedom is guaranteed every Patron to affiliate with any political party that may best serve his interests. Difference of opinion only when

[1] The Declaration is published in full in Atkeson, *op. cit.*, p. 69.

attended by bitter controversy is condemned. On one point the Declaration was not altogether clear. "Political or religious" questions were debarred from discussion. At a later date these words were supplanted by the words "partisan or sectarian."

The Discussion of Political Questions.—There is an important difference between political problems considered from the standpoint of political science and from that of political expediency. The whole subject of government, including political parties even, is studied in colleges and universities in a purely objective and scientific way with partisan feeling altogether eliminated. In a similar way the Grange, it was later declared, could take a measure like the election of senators by popular vote, a subject clearly in the field of political science, and endorse it on purely scientific grounds. A great many questions, in fact the great majority with which the Grange is concerned, fall into the category of economics. Such questions are transportation facilities, road building, rural credits, free coinage of silver, international trade, and a host of others. Considered abstractly all these problems are economic instead of political. When, however, a political party accepts them as a part of its platform the voters of the country regard them as political issues. As stated the Grange early substituted the words "partisan or sectarian" for those of "political or religious" and thus clarified its position as to both politics and religious or ethical questions. The revision gives indisputably full power to formulate legislative programs to be urged upon Congress and state legislatures. As a matter of fact the Grange almost from the beginning made use of this means of expression in one way or another, and by now has become efficient in the matter of securing favorable legislation.

The Grange has developed a *modus operandi* concerning the formulation of legislative programs that is thoroughly democratic. Subordinate granges are permitted to introduce subjects in the state granges, and the latter in turn may introduce measures in the national grange for its consideration and approval. The master of the national body delivers an annual address and attempts to set forth all problems that concern the interests of agriculture, but only after his address has been considered by one or more committees, reported back to the Grange, and voted upon by its members is it regarded as an expression of the sentiment of the Grange. In addition to matter brought before the national grange in the two ways stated, there are a number of committees that report on various subjects on their own initiative. The national legislative program in 1919 included among others the following subjects: public economy, price fixing, education, marketing, collective bargaining, packers' monopoly, roads, better farm credit, land tenantry, farms for soldiers, fertilizer supply, daylight saving, oleomargarine, control of trusts, tariff, equal suffrage, taxation, militarism, prohibition, postal zone system, league of nations, etc.

A Legislative Representative.—The Grange early urged its members to watch the conduct of legislators and elect men who take a favorable attitude toward agricultural interests. This plan is now supplemented by a more intimate touch with Congress. A national representative of the Grange keeps a close watch upon bills that come up in Congress, and in some instances in cooperation with the National Board of Farm Organizations the initiative to present a farmers' bill to members of Congress is taken. The National Board of Farm Organizations is a board representing a number of farm organizations the most important of which are the Farmers' Union and the National Milk Producers' Federation. It maintains a Washington office to urge upon Congress legislation favorable to agriculture, and while the Grange is not a member of the board it has its own representative at the capital who works with the board in securing the desired legislation. The suggestion that the Grange join the National Board of Farm Organizations has been made but rejected. The feeling is that the Grange is the oldest of all farm organizations and that for the good of the Order it is preferable to stand altogether separate. Instead of officially detailing a representative, therefore, to the board it set up its own headquarters with a view to cooperate with it. The difference is only a matter of sentiment and of little consequence. At first thought it seems to indicate a spirit of self-sufficiency, the manifestation of which, however, if such it be, is excusable because the Grange has weathered the storm of reaction and is the oldest organization of its kind in the country. On the other hand, it must be remembered that the Grange stands ready to cooperate with other agencies and entertains no jealousy toward other organizations. In a number of instances throughout the country it cooperates with farm bureaus.

In his relations with members of Congress the Grange representative is entirely open and does not resort to secret lobbying. In a statement addressed to members of Congress the following expresses the manner in which relations are to be maintained:

> The Grange representatives are not "lobbyists" in the usually accepted meaning of that term and there are no unclean dollars paying us for our service. We are in Washington in a spirit of helpful cooperation in our efforts to place before Congress and the various departments the true farmers' viewpoint of the food production problems which are now receiving so much attention, and upon which the welfare of all our people so largely depends.
>
> In a spirit of helpfulness we hope to go over these rural problems with the members of Congress and with congressional committees who have charge of the measures effecting the interests of agriculture in order that we may, if possible, assist them in arriving at a fair and unbiased understanding of the problems and points of view of the real farmers. With this object in view we will be glad to have the facilities of this office made use of by the members of Congress to the fullest extent. We extend a very cordial invitation to each of you to visit the Grange office at any time.

The plan of bringing pressure to bear upon members of state legislatures while legislation is in the process of enactment is also being followed by some of the State Granges. It is obvious that this method is the sensible one for the farmers to use. It is the one that has been used by large corporations, manufacturing and trade associations for many years, and more recently by organized labor as well. The charge that money was being used by representatives of railroad and industrial corporations used to be freely made. In more recent years the practice of bribing Congress and state legislatures has given way to a more honorable and scientific method of lobbying. Although much of the lobbying going on today is still of the secret and vicious kind. President Wilson in 1913 in order to pry Congress loose from the horde of lobbyists representing various industrial interests at Washington when the Underwood tariff was under consideration had to issue a public statement concerning the real nature of their work. When lobbying is done in a perfectly free and open manner there can be no objection to the plan and in fact much good comes from the practice. The demands made by the various economic groups upon the legislative body with respect to bills in process of enactment should be given to the press and thrashed out fully. In a republican form of government public opinion is ultimately the force that determines the nature of laws, and the press is the medium through which such public opinion is formulated. Bills are digested and criticized from the point of view of various groups concerned. It is not infrequent that in connection with a wholly new issue a legislator when approached with a view to ascertaining his attitude concerning the measure is reported as saying that he has not formulated an opinion. The point is that no one can take intelligent action on an issue without first studying the facts involved. The action that he will finally take will depend largely upon the character of the facts presented to him. In other words, the problem of guiding legislation is not wholly an ethical one. It is primarily a scientific one. It involves the marshalling of the people behind organizations whose representatives go to Congress and the press with their demands where all facts are digested and the best interests of the country as a whole become plainly distinguishable. An important fact, however, is organization. It is the number of "men behind the guns" that will determine whether or not the facts presented will be regarded with a proper degree of seriousness. With a strong organization behind the farmers' representatives the work as to a legislator's attitude can be passed along to his constituents and action consistent with his conduct may be taken at the polls.

Farmers as Lawmakers.—While the Grange has always in one way or another sought to urge favorable legislation upon those elected to lawmaking bodies, it does not appear to have at any time seriously held the doctrine that legislative representation should be based on occupational groups. This is a principle that has been enunciated by the Farmers' Union and will be discussed at greater length in the chapter dealing with that organization. However, statements, pointing out that the farming interests are not well represented in Congress and that the Chairman of the Committee on Agriculture in a certain case has been selected "from the legal profession of a large city where agriculture is not supposed to be extensively practiced or well understood," have been made by Masters of the Grange.[1] The implication is that only a farmer has the necessary sympathetic understanding to represent the interests of the agricultural class in a desirable way. In the main this point of view is correct. Virtually all persons are biased in their viewpoints because of the particular type of education they have received and because of the environment in which they live. For instance, capitalists are unsympathetic to labor because they are not acquainted with facts pertaining to labor, and organized labor is hostile to capital because it is not familiar with correct principles of business. Examples of public men could be cited to illustrate the important principle that the environment has much to do with the formation of opinions that one is liable to hold concerning public questions. In other words, one's interpretation of facts depends upon the amount of detail taken into account. While the fact that an agricultural environment and a detailed knowledge of agriculture are necessary to enable one to act intelligently, it does not follow that one who has studied law cannot retain his relations with the subject of agriculture and remain sympathetic to the wants and needs of the rural people. How a legislator will represent his constituency depends upon the wishes of the people in his district. The most thoroughly organized groups will secure the most favorable attention. That a practical farmer be elected to a legislature in order to secure proper agricultural representation, is not necessary; and in fact it is not to the best interests of any class unless such a representative have at the same time a training in the field of law, economics, and other social sciences.

Farmers as Executives.—The Grange was very active in the movement to make the chief executive of the United States Department of Agriculture a member of the President's Cabi-

[1] *Vide Atkeson Semi-Centennial History*, p. 112.

net. This was accomplished in 1889, and ever since the Order has brought its influence to bear in the selection of the Secretary of Agriculture. Norman J. Colman occupied the position of Secretary of Agriculture only for a few weeks, and because of a change in the administration was followed by Jeremiah M. Rusk of Wisconsin on March 4, 1889. In connection with his appointment the Master of the Grange made the following pertinent remarks at the annual meeting of the national body.

It was sincerely hoped that the known wishes of this large body of law-abiding, industrious citizens would have weight and influence with the President, and that he would seek out from among the millions who till the soil one of its confidential advisers. We thought we had good reason to expect this recognition in the person of the man selected to watch over and advise, in regard to the need of agriculture. It did not seem unreasonable to ask, inasmuch as in no other department was recognition expected. We fully and cheerfully acknowledge the high character and ability of the gentleman selected, and would have been gratified to see him in any of the departments for which his public life has fitted him. But for the Department of Agriculture we wanted a man identified directly with that great interest. And we do not hesitate to say that the selection of one who has never been considerd a farmer was a great disappointment to those who for years labored and waited for this opportunity to secure recognition for their class.

Any pretence of acquiescence in a policy which thus ignores a class representing 50 per cent of our people to serve some personal political purpose is cowardly in the extreme, and unworthy of a true Patron. If we for personal or political reasons hesitate or hold our peace now, let it be *forever* so far as the selection of the head of the Department of Agriculture is concerned.[1]

The next Secretary of Agriculture was J. Sterling Morton of Nebraska, selected by Cleveland at the beginning of his second administration in 1893. Judging from the content of a speech delivered by Morton in October, 1893, before a Congress on Agriculture held at Chicago the President had not consulted the farmers concerning the appointment of a Secretary of Agriculture. Extracts from this speech run as follows:

American farmers have foes to contend with; they are not the natural foes—not the weevil in the wheat, nor the murrain in cattle. nor the cholera in swine, nor the drouth, nor the chinchbug. The most insiduous and destructive foe of the farmer is the professional farmer, the promoter of Granges and Alliances, who for political purposes farms the farmer.

He will not succeed better by farming Granges and Alliances which generally seek to attend to some other business, than farming, and frequently propose to run railroads and banks, and even propose

[1] *Vide* Atkeson, *op. cit.*, p. 152.

to establish new systems of coinage for the government than he will by individual investigation of economic questions.

The one book which I can recommend to the farmers for their perusal is Adam Smith's *Wealth of Nations*. I would also have, if possible, a daily newspaper from a great city at every fireside.[1]

The speech shows that Morton was wholly out of harmony with the interests of agriculture, and that he had no knowledge of the political aspects of the agrarian movement including the Grange and the Farmers' Alliance. Both of these organizations he represented as political organizations which was only true of the latter, and then only in its latter days. The statement that the farmer will not succeed better through the formation of farm organizations than through an individual investigation of economic questions, also shows that he failed to understand, or found it convenient not to admit, that the more important legislation of the present day is brought to fruition through the acitivity of organized groups. The tone of the speech was colored with ridicule which was bitterly resented by the Master of the Grange as well as by the National body through the adoption of a resolution. His recommendation that farmers read Adam Smith's *Wealth of Nations* would have been all right for a student of the history of economic thought, but for a busy man seeking immediately practical knowledge a more modern text on the principles of economics, or political economy more often called at that time, should have been recommended. The Master expressed his feeling with respect to the speech as follows: "Experience has demonstrated the fact that the farmers will endure much neglect, submit to being ignored, but it has not yet been shown that they will not resent ridicule and insult from one who should be their trusted advisor and friend."

When McKinley was about to appoint a new secretary the Grange appointed a committee to wait on him asking "that a practical farmer be honored with a seat in his Cabinet, and that said member be a Patron of Husbandry, in recognition of the wisdom and labor of our Order in the creation of said Department of Agriculture." In a previously suggested resolution nothing more than the appointment of a practical farmer

[1] *Vide* Atkeson, *op. cit.*, p. 172.

having the confidence and esteem of the farming population was urged. This would have been far better than the resolution as finally adopted. The Grange made a blunder when it asked that one of its members be appointed. The large mass of unorganized farmers as well as those affiliated with state and county agricultural and livestock societies had reason to object to the demands made by the Grange. The result was that James Wilson of Iowa was appointed Secretary and J. H. Brigham, Master of the National Grange, Assistant Secretary.

At various times the Grange has enumerated the qualities that the appointee to the office of Secretary of Agriculture should possess. When President Wilson was considering the appointment of his Cabinet officers a Grange committee again called on the President-elect presenting the names of several candidates any one of whose appointment would meet with their approval, and at Wilson's request wrote out a memorandum of conditions under which the appointment should be made. At the last moment the wishes of the Grange were ignored. Following is the memorandum which states the position of the Grange on the appointment of a Secretary of Agriculture:

1. We trust that the office of the Secretary of Agriculture may never be awarded as a political favor, but because of fitness for office only.

2. We believe that the Secretary of Agriculture should have broad scholarship, far-seeing statesmanship, and splendid executive ability, but he must have something more than these.

3. The position of Secretary of Agriculture is a professional one, and he should be a farmer to the same extent and for the same reasons that the attorney general should be a lawyer.

4. He should stand for the American farmer, should not only be in sympathy with farmers, but so identified with them in vocation, ideas and effort that farmers recognize him as one of themselves.

5. A man reared on the farm and whose life has been spent in a study of its problems would be best qualified to deal with them.

6. He should have made a study of the agricultural conditions and possibilities, and know the agricultural resources of the country and the possibilities and probabilities of their development with the material at hand.

7. It is most essential that the head of this department shall be a man identified in the public mind with agricultural matters, around whom agricultural interests and workers will rally with confidence in his leadership.

8. We believe that two or three of the men who have been suggested would have the confidence of the farmers and otherwise measure

up to the requirements of the office, and we trust that after mature deliberation you will select the man who most nearly fills the specifications enumerated above.

9. His location, his training, his early life on the farm, and his known sympathy with the farmer people of the country, as well as his demonstrated executive ability, should indicate his fitness for large usefulness to American agriculture.

The qualifications of the Secretary of Agriculture may be discussed from an ideal point of view as well as from the point of view of practical politics. From an ideal point of view it is necessary that he have a practical and theoretical knowledge of agriculture. In a study of all the functions of the various bureaus of the Department of Agriculture one is impressed with the fact that agriculture has its basis in a complex body of facts, and in order that the head of the Department may best serve the people he must know the theory of agricultural science. In the second place he cannot have a thorough knowledge of the science without at the same time being familiar with its practical aspects. In the third place because of the numerous regulatory functions committed to the Department including also functions of marketing, its head should have a thorough training in economics and the social sciences. A knowledge of the law would also be helpful. In the fourth place the farmers of the country have a right to have their interests represented in the executive branch of the national government, and the Secretary should, therefore, be a man who is sympathetic to the agricultural interests.

From the standpoint of practical politics the controlling motive in the appointment of executive heads is the settlement of political indebtedness. A second consideration is the attempt to please the various social groups of the country. Those engaged in business desire a man satisfactory to them. Organized labor desires a man who is sympathetic to labor. The executive head is, therefore, a political appointee; and his personal qualifications, while they are given weight in the selection of the incumbent, are minor considerations. In most cases the personnel to whom is entrusted the technical aspects of the work of the departments is permanent. With a change of the administration the executive head changes also, while the technical expert below him usually remains. This allows for the continuity of the organization and at the same time makes possible the bringing of the departments into close touch with the moving conditions among the people. In view of the conditions of practical politics under which executive heads in America are appointed, it would seem that the farmers of the country should be given the same consideration that is given to other groups. He should be a man who is sympathetic to the agricultural class. It does not seem that he need actually till the soil. A man who edits an agricultural journal, or who is identified in some way with agricultural education could very satisfactorily fulfill the requirements of the office.

Agricultural Leadership.—The Grange has at various times contended that agricultural leadership can only come through organization among the farmers. This in the main is true although not wholly so. That part of progress which is dependent upon legislation, for instance, is often brought about by the activity of reformers. College professors and others often have a deep human interest in life and frequently head a movement looking toward social improvement. In the study of the United States Department of Agriculture it was noted that in numerous instances proposed legislation aiming at the improvement of agricultural conditions was originated by the executive branch of the government and recommended by it to Congress to be enacted into law. However, as pointed out in the foregoing sections private agricultural organization in a general way aims to keep the Department of Agriculture intimately connected with actual agricultural conditions, and also brings its influence to bear directly upon Congress and state legislatures. In matters pertaining more especially to improving the economic status of the farmers, such as the elimination of middlemen and taking his profits, or the enactment of a tariff that is favorable to the agricultural class, leadership must come virtually altogether from the organized farmers themselves. Certainly the motives or demands must be sustained and pressed to the attention of the people as a whole by the farmers themselves. It should be done through specially trained experts who can be made sympathetic to rural projects by the payment of respectable salaries. The California Fruit Exchange, for instance, has adopted the plan of paying its experts large salaries, in some cases amounting to as much as $25,000. When this is more generally done by organized agriculture its influence and consequent results will be more generally manifest. Atkeson says the following on leadership:

> The only true friends of the farmers must be the farmers themselves. And the Grange seeks to equip them for such leadership as will enable them to demand and secure that equitable deal to which the basic industry of agriculture is entitled. The improvement of the business of farming must come out of its own leadership. In all the efforts made for the betterment of agricultural conditions the farmer has been considered simply as a producer. In other occupations it is different. The manufacturer carefully counts the cost of production and proceeds to control the price by reducing the quantity and also through the means of tariffs and other special legislation. The professional men fix a schedule of remunerative prices. The merchant marks up his wares to a profitable price. The money lender demands his usury, and the transportation companies charge what the traffic will bear. The farmer is told to work harder and raise bigger crops so that others may live more economically, without regard to whether he receives a profit on what he produces or not.[1]

The picture here drawn paints all economic activities other than agriculture as being monopolistic which, of course, is an extreme statement. The statement concerning transportation is also no longer true. However, much of our industry is monopolistic or partially so, and Congress in the past has shown it considerable favor. The writer goes on to say that these conditions have been brought about "because the farmers have largely let other people do their thinking, and the laws of the state and nation are almost wholly made by people opposed to agriculture or controlled by special and selfish interests." So far as the distribution of wealth is concerned it is quite clear that leadership must come from the farmers themselves if they would protect themselves fully against burdens that should be borne by others. In the matter of taxation, for instance, they desire the income tax. In the support of this measure the farmer is associated with the large laboring class and others of small income.

Leadership in Agricultural Education.—In the case of de-

[1] *Vide Semi-Centennial History*, pp. 216, 217.

termining the character of agricultural education and experimentation conducted at land-grant colleges in the various states of the Union the Grange has been quite active. Just what influence it has exerted it is difficult to say. In the study of state departmental agricultural organization in a preceding chapter it was found that public agricultural organization grew out of private organization and that it is to this day in some parts greatly influenced by agricultural societies. The Grange has demanded that the boards of control of the experiment stations "be composed of *progressive, practical farmers.*" It has been said that "no one not thus connected directly with agriculture can thoroughly understand what problems need the most urgent attention. In a majority of the states, men who are not practical farmers have been appointed to control their stations. This is an insult to the farmers and should be resented." The tendency for organized agriculture to desire a close union with colleges and experiment stations is commendable providing actual control is not called for. The fact has often been lamented that contrary to European practice American industry holds itself aloof from engineering colleges and departments of chemistry whence much valuable information could often be secured. In other words, a spirit of cooperation between the colleges and industry has been urged in the interest of national industrial progress. In spite of this aloofness on the part of industry it cannot be said that our industrial institutions have failed to meet the practical needs of industry. About the same kind of reasoning, it would seem, applies to agricultural colleges. They, too, serve the interests of agriculture without any control on the part of the farmers. Although with respect to experiment stations there is some danger that a program of investigation is undertaken which lies too much in the field of pure science and which has little relation to applied agricultural science. However, as was stated in the chapter dealing with experiment stations, the subjects of investigation carried on by the various stations are agreed upon by the United States Secretary of Agriculture, and inasmuch as the Adams act requires that such experiments shall have a "bearing directly on the agricultural industry of the United States, having due regard to the varying conditions and needs of the respective states and territories," the danger that practical agricultural problems will be grossly neglected is quite remote.

It does not seem to require more direct control of the experiment stations in order to give the farmer his due than to have the governor and the state secretary of agriculture *ex-officio* members on the board of trustees of the University. The present law of Oklahoma, which probably was not the result of Grange influence, makes the State Board of Agriculture composed wholly of men who have had five years of practical experience in farming, "regents of all agricultural and mechanical colleges in the state." Whether actually exercised or not, the law gives the board the power to "select the professors, presidents and other employes of each of said schools, fix their salaries and prescribe their respective duties."[1] Such direct and detailed interference with the administration of an agricultural college or experiment station can lead only to confusion, a general lowering of educational standards, and a demoralization of the college *esprit de corps*. The selection of men fitted for responsible positions is acknowledged to be a necessary faculty of the successful executive. To insure the best results in every way the selection of a professorial staff should be virtually wholly entrusted to the president of the university and the deans of the respective colleges.

The Grange has consistently agitated the extension of general educational facilities throughout the rural sections. At various times the establishment of district high schools has been recommended as well as the improvement of elementary schools. As early as 1880 it agitated the teaching of agriculture in the public schools.

Grange Attitude Toward Organized Labor.—In former years the Grange was more sympathetic to organized labor than it appears to be today. In 1894 the national body adopted a resolution which runs in part as follows:

> The farmers are interested in the amicable settlement of the differences between employer and employee. We will sustain with all our influence the right of labor to organize. Capital is thoroughly organized, so is every profession. Labor must respect the rights of

[1] *Vide Oklahoma Acts* of 1920.

the employer and also of the public. They will then be invincible in demanding what is clearly right.

In 1907 the National Grange adopted a resolution condemning "lawlessness and criminality" as means to accomplish the ends of organized labor, and urging the punishment of offenders of the law. In 1909 "agreements between organized capital and organized labor in legislative matters to the detriment of the farmers were opposed.

In 1919 at the convention held at Grand Rapids the Grange declined an invitation from Samuel Gompers, President of the American Federation of Labor, to participate in a conference of representatives of organized labor on the ground that the interests of organized agriculture and organized labor are not identical.[1] The discussion of the resolution, according to the press, brought out the point that attendance at the conference would be a tacit admission that there were mutual interests. The resolution senses correctly the position of the farmer among the economic groups of society. The economic interests of organized labor, constituting as it does industrial labor, and those of organized agriculture are in no way mutual, and in fact are diametrically opposed. In transportation, wages depend upon freight rates, while high freight rates reduce the farmers' profits. Organized labor is fighting a reducation in wages at the same time that organized agriculture is demanding a reduction of freight rates. There are industrial establishments here and there that have established the "shop committee" plan of management and instituted some system of profit-sharing. Where labor and capital are thus in collaboration their interests become merged and are pitched against the consumers under which class the whole population falls with respect to the consumption of manufactured products. Of course, where no monopoly exists no harm can come to the consuming group under the plan. The analysis is only made to point out the fact that the economic interests of organized labor and organized agriculture are not mutual. With respect to agricultural products the two groups of capital and labor constitute the consuming class and the agricultural group has to look to them for its share of the world's income.

[1] *Vide Report* for 1919, p. 121.

The Grange and the Railroads.—The Grange played a very effective role in the establishment of the important principle that the railroads are not private enterprises but public service corporations and therefore subject to state regulation. Before 1870 the West courted the extension of railroad facilities and gave all aid it could including state and local governmental aid and private subscription to capital stock. When the roads proceeded to exploit the farmers by "charging what the traffic will bear" the Grange, which was then in rapid process of formation and whose organization was greatly accelerated by the railroad situation, began to enact the so-called "Granger laws." These laws conceived of the railroads as public service corporations and regulated their rates. The farmers in the newly settled states were remote from the market and it is but natural that they desired cheap transportation. President Grant's message in 1872 gave expression to this demand by asking for "more certain and cheaper transportation of the rapidly increasing western and southern products to the Atlantic seaboard." Congress as a result appointed the Windom Committee, which recommended among other things that not more may be charged for a shorter than for a longer haul and that a general reduction of rates be made. This report was submitted in 1874, but no action was taken by Congress until 1887, when the Interstate Commerce Commission was established. In the meantime the Grange, through state legislatures, succeeded in placing laws on the statute books that were in many instances extreme and which were later repealed. However, the principle that a state may regulate rates became established after cases arising out of this early state legislation had been decided upon by the United States Supreme Court.[1]

The attitude of the Grange toward the railroads was stated in the Declaration of Purposes to be friendly. It recognizes the necessity of having adequate transportation facilities. In its

[1] The establishment of the principle of state regulation may be traced by reference to the cases of *Munn v. Illinois*, 94 U. S. 113; *Peik* v. *Chicago* and *Northwestern Railway Company*, 94 U. S. 164; and the *Wabash, St. Louis* and *Pacific Railway Company* v. *Illinois*, 118, U. S. 557, and by consulting textbooks on transportation.

legislative program of 1919 it favors "the strictest governmental control of the railroads and other public utilities" and adequate "protection from every form of exploitation, discrimination and injustice."

Attitude Toward Cooperative Enterprise.—As stated in the first part of this chapter cooperation was not an accepted policy of the Order at the time of its organization. The principle was forced upon the leaders through the persistent efforts of the Minnesota Grange in 1869. It was sanctioned by Kelley in order to save this State Grange from leaving the national organization. It was made plain, however, that the movement was not fathered by the National Grange. By 1874 the demand for cooperation had become so general among the Patrons of the Order that the principle was expressed in very positive terms in the Declaration of Purposes as being one of the leading objects of the Grange. Thus the Declaration proposes "buying together, selling together, and, in general, acting together for mutual protection, and advancement, as occasion may require." It also proposes "to bring producers and consumers, farmers and manufacturers, into the most direct and friendly relations possible." It is necessary, therefore, to "dispense with a surplus of middlemen," not because there is manifested an unfriendly feeling toward them, but because they are not needed and for the reason that their exactions diminish the profits of the farmers. The statement as it appears in the Declaration of Purposes could be construed to exclude manufacturing cooperative enterprises and to sanction only the simpler aspects of cooperation such as buying and selling together under agreements involving a limited number of ventures. The Granges, however, speedily entered the field of cooperation on an extensive and varied scale. Milling, manufacturing, and merchandising were undertaken. In West Virginia a factory to build reapers and binders was erected Woolen mills, grist mills, and creameries were built. Mutual fire insurance companies and Grange exchanges were organized. Failures soon beset the movement, and by 1880 nearly all ventures except fire insurance, exchanges, and such cooperative methods that merely call for the pooling of orders in the sale and purchase of goods, had closed out, leaving the Order in bad repute especially throughout the West and to a lesser extent elsewhere.[1] This early rapid expansion of the cooperative movement under grange patronage was never heartily sanctioned by the national body. It was fostered by state and local granges. State business agents were appointed. At the ninth annual session of the National Grange when an attempt was made to establish national business agencies the plan was defeated by a vote of 35 to 8.[2]

By 1883 the Grange had learned that there are limitations to cooperative enterprises. That the more technical forms of manufacture and certain mercantile businesses had better not be undertaken by the farmers. The Master of the National Grange then said that "it cannot reasonably be expected that persons who have had no practical experience or special training in mercantile business, milling or manufacturing, can be qualified to successfully manage such enterprises." On the other hand, he recommended that cooperation should have a place in every subordinate Grange, however small the beginning and limited the means. If well managed and patronized, it cannot fail to prosper.

After the panic of 1893 the principle of cooperation again became a more vital doctrine of the Granges. In 1906 cooperative creamories, elevators, savings banks, building and loan associations, warehouses, and cooperative marketing systems were recommended. In 1910 a resolution was adopted reading as follows:

> The Grange must work out the great principle of cooperation and present it to the farmers in some workable form by which they may secure for themselves and their families a larger share of what the harvest yields.

The spirit of cooperation has been steadily gaining momentum. In 1919 a committee gave the subject considerable attention. It recommended that every subordinate Grange have "its business agent, alive and alert, studying conditions and cooperating with the other agents of the county, making a strong unit of the county, and the county units uniting in

---

[1] *Vide* article by J. Clyde Marquis in the *Country Gentleman*, May 15, 1920, p. 17.

[2] *Vide* Atkeson, *Semi-Centennial History*, p. 120.

making the state the great clearing house for furnishing supplies and marketing produce; the state uniting through the national Grange or men chosen by it, until the vast and greatest industry of all should act as one man." The report said further that "the possibilities are great" and urged the appointment of a committee to study in detail the amount of cooperation carried on by local granges with a view to establishing a national system. This report confined itself to joint-selling of farm produce and joint-buying of materials consumed by the farmers. The belief was expressed that the farmer should "have a voice in making the price of the products of his labor."

At the annual convention of the National Grange held in November, 1920, the Master is reported by the press to have predicted the formation of nation-wide selling organizations which shall fix the price of farm products. He said: "We are willing to have a fair understanding of values, the farmers receiving the same pay for the same hours of work that others receive, no more, no less, but we feel that this is the last call. If no attention is paid to this now by bankers, manufacturers, railroads and labor organizations, and if the government continues to use its great power to import raw material free of duty to reduce costs, then the Grange will be the first to help organize nation-wide selling organizations which shall fix the price of farm products." Since then, according to press reports, under the leadership of American Farm Bureau officials, the United States Grain Growers, Inc., has been organized, and is being joined by the Northwest Wheat Growers' Association in the marketing of the wheat crop of the country. Since the early days of Grange cooperation much has happened in the field of cooperation. The California and other fruit exchanges have been wholly successful, and show that farmers producing other crops can adopt a similar plan of marketing their products.

The Grange on Taxation.—It is to be expected that land owners would oppose the "single tax" which is a tax to be levied on land values alone. The single tax, according to Henry George, is to take the full economic rent or, in other words, the entire yield of land above the cost of operation. The

Master of the National Grange in 1896 said in connection with this tax that occasionally we find a farmer who has become a convert to the theory of the single tax, "but the masses of farmers will be slow to accept this theory."

In 1909 the Grange favored the taxation of all "real or personal property for local purposes except such as is exempt under the Constitution." The student of taxation would criticize the stand taken on the taxation of personal property. This object of taxation is very generally not declared by tax payers, and the situation results in inflicting great injustice upon the few who are pious enough to declare their personal property at full value. It is a part of the general property tax that is being abandoned by the states for the reason that it is no longer productive of revenue and because of the injustice that it occasions. The other part of the general property tax, that of real estate, is not being abandoned but is being given over for local use in order to avoid the injustice occasioned by the inequalities of assessments among counties when used for state purposes.

Exemption from taxation account indebtedness on real estate was favored where an exemption was allowed because of indebtedness on personal property. Mortgages were to be taxed at the situs of the property and the mortgagor was to be taxed minus the indebtedness on the property as evidenced by the mortgage. The more recent development of thought concerning the mortgage tax favors the imposition of a low mortgage-recording tax and omitting the tax on the mortgage itself for the reason that such a tax is only shifted to the mortgagor in the form of higher interest rates that he has to pay on money that he borrows. The mortgagor should be taxed on the full value of the property without a deduction on account of the mortgage. The equitable taxation of all forms of property is favored including all bank property Equality of assessment is demanded.

As early as 1880 the Grange favored the income tax. In its legislative program of 1919 "equitable income and inheritance taxes" are recommended. "All property shall be taxed equally according to its true and actual value." Both from the point of view of the science of public finance and the economic interest of the agricultural class the income and inheritance taxes are proper forms of taxation. There is no more just tax than the inheritance and income taxes because both are ased on the principle of "ability to pay." From the point of view of the agricultural class they are proper forms of taxation to advocate for the reason that large numbers in the class have incomes that do not rise above the amount of the exemption. And inasmuch as we have maldistribution of wealth it is only fair to exempt farmers, laborers, teachers, or anybody else whose income does not rise much above the means of subsistence.

Maintenance of the Institution of Private Property.—The members of the Grange are virtually all land owners and as such strongly believe in private property except as to certain enterprises. In 1906 the Master of the National Grange made the following statement:

> With the law-ignoring rich on one side of us, and the government-destroying anarchists on the other, it is manifest that the perpetuity of American liberty depends largely upon the sober thinking, loyalty and patriotism of our rural people, for whom and to whom the Grange speaks in its effort to create a wholesome public sentiment. The responsibility upon this body of farmers is greater than many good people seem to appreciate.

At first blush the opening sentence seems extreme. The author probably had in mind, however, the corrupt practices of trusts in by-gone days and discrimination and other wrongs committed by the railroads. The whole paragraph expresses the idea that the great body of rural people are conservative and serve as a balance wheel in a progressive movement.

Only in certain fields of activity does the Grange desire governmental ownership and operation. With regard to trusts and railroads it wants only strict control. In such tried fields where there is no doubt but that efficient management can be secured by public operation it has taken the position in favor of public enterprise. Such activities include the parcels post, postal savings banks, and the telegraph. All of these activities are beneficial to country life if made generally available, and are therefore proper objects for organized agriculture to advocate. The government telegraph has yet to be tried in this country, but because of its simplicity it can probably be operated as efficiently as the post office, and like it can be made to serve civilization in various ways including the spread of education and general intelligence and the formation of business and national solidarity. The great host of farm proprietors know the joys and comforts that flow from land ownership. They know that production succeeds best where the proprietor of the land is also its operator. They know that the making of sterling character in manhood and womanhood, and the stability of the family depend upon the institution of private property. They stand for the correction of abuses, the elimination of special privilege, and for a greater equality in the distribution of wealth; but they would be the last among other economic groups to accept a complete system of collective ownership of property.

Grange Attitude Toward International Arbitration.—The agricultural class are a peace-loving people, and it is not surprising that the Grange has always favored international arbitration. In 1903 it went on record as follows:

> From the earlist history of the Order the Grange has advocated arbitration, and we believe that in the enlightenment of this the twentieth century all international differences should be settled by arbitration instead of resorting to arms and the shedding of blood.

In 1904 when the Russo-Japanese war was in progress Overseer Atkeson in expressing the sentiment of the Grange said that "agriculture is an occupation of peace and thrives only under peaceful conditions." The true Grange spirit, he said, "can but deprecate everything that tends to develop the war spirit in our own country."

When the European war broke out in 1914 the Grange opposed the movement of "preparedness" on the ground that the wide ocean separating us from Europe guaranteed us against attack and against being injured in any way by the several belligerents. In this they were of course mistaken. Under the present complex economic organization with its branches and roots extending to all parts of the world a policy of exclusion can no longer be maintained. There is, therefore, all the more need for a system of international arbitration. When America entered the war the National Grange at its meeting in 1917 hastened to send a telegram to President Wilson pledging its support to the full limit of its energies and its resources to help win the world victory for democracy.[1] Consistent with its earlier position on international arbitration the Grange in its legislative program of 1919 favored a league of nations, "the covenant of which adequately upholds and protects the sovereignty and interests of the United States."

Miscellaneous Measures.—The Grange has at various times expressed itself on a large range of subjects. With the omission of the silver dollar from our monetary system in 1873 thereby giving the country a single gold standard, and with the subsequent demonetization of silver throughout Europe and the simultaneous opening of new silver mines in the West, the price of silver fell very rapidly; and a campaign for the return to a bimetallic standard which would create a market for silver was demanded by the western people as well as by others who desired higher prices for the products they had to sell. The result of agitation that began during the 70's and waned only after the defeat of Bryan in his 16 to 1 campaign in 1896 was the enactment of compromise laws in 1878 and 1890 which required the United States Treasury to purchase a certain amount of silver and issue certificates therefore. The repeal of this provision was effected in 1893. In 1889 the Grange adopted a resolution favoring the free coinage of silver and placing in circulation a sufficient volume of paper money that would "prevent any further contraction and consequent embarrassment to our prosperity." The student of monetary history knows that paper money if not properly secured and if not redeemable in specie on demand depreciates in value and causes great disruptions not only in prices but in the shares of income of all the groups of society. It is economically wrong to have either a bimetallic standard or to place the country on a paper basis. The monetary subject is probably the most difficult of all economic subjects and many people do not understand it for the reason that they have never studied the theory of prices. The Grange in its resolution together with the whole free-silver movement was wrong. In

[1] *Vide Report* for 1917, p. 8.

1894 the Master, while not attempting to speak for everybody, made an argument against the free coinage of silver.

Rural credit is another subject that the Grange has favored strongly. Resolutions to this effect were adopted in 1913. It has opposed the speculation in food supplies. It has favored the building of roads, the adoption of pure-food laws, the conservation of forests, the prohibition of the production and sale of liquor and cigarettes, the adoption of woman suffrage, the repeal of daylight saving laws, etc. With a change of conditions and the rising of new problems the Grange revises its legislative program, dropping the things that have been achieved and attacking those that have yet to be realized.

The Grange as a Social Agency.—One of the important reasons why the sons and daughters of the farming population drift to the city in such large numbers is because there is a great lack in the country in the way of an attractive social and intellectual medium in which the individual may express himself. The Grange through its local bodies has helped to provide such a medium. All efforts of organized agriculture provide social advantages that could in no way be secured by the individual acting singly. The addition of the automobile to the farmers' means of transportation is going to make a very general improvement in the social life of the country because it will make possible the coming together of a larger number of people to a central place. In his address delivered before the National Grange in 1895 the Master said the following concerning the social features of the Order which very well expresses its splendid advantages:

Farmers, with their wives and children, have come together in the Grange, cultivated sociability, friendship and confidence in each other, submitted to useful discipline, learned parliamentary usage, accustomed themselves to read and recite in public, write and read essays, and speak in debate and on the rostrum. Coming together as a band of brothers and sisters, under pledges of fidelity to each other, and a firm resolve to cultivate a higher manhood and womanhood for themselves, they have been inspired to labor with diligence in their efforts to excel, to emulate worthy examples and conduct themselves with circumspection. By cultivating respect and esteem for each other the ties of fraternity have been strengthened. By taking an active part in the literary work of the Grange a greater desire for useful knowledge has been created, and the shelves and center tables better supplied with books and journals. Under the direct influence and teachings of the Grange thousands of rural homes have been beautified and their surroundings made more cheerful and attractive; and many sad and despondent hearts have been made to rejoice in happier homes and more endearing family ties. The early care and training of children have received attention, and many parents have been made happier in realizing its solitary influence upon the lives of their sons and daughters and their growing attachment for home, and in being able to keep the loved ones on the farm.[1]

In reading the history of the Grange one is impressed with the genuine friendship that it fosters. Of course, at times factions arise which show themselves in the election of officers, but in latter days they have not been pronounced. Atkeson in his history of the Grange records a speech made by Secretary Trimble on the occasion of presenting a gold-headed cane to J. J. Woodman whom the Grange honored for his long labors in the national body. The strong ties of friendship between these two men are manifest in the opening paragraph which reads as follows:

Dear and esteemed brother Woodman, when I gave it a second thought I saw that it was right and seemly that you and I should meet face to face here tonight in the presence of the National Grange, the true spirit of our fraternity. Many, many years have we labored together in the interests of the dear old Grange, which no one loves nor can love more sincerely than you have loved and will love it.

The social function of the Grange is well told by a woman member in the *Country Gentleman* under the heading, "What the Grange has Meant *to Me*."[2] The writer relates the story of her early life when she was sent to a Boston private school, and how after her return to her home in the country she was out of harmony with her former environment. At the boarding school she had been accustomed to musicales, literary treats, artistic furnishings, and other attractions, all of which she missed in the country. Upon an invitation to attend a Grange entertainment a new vision came to her which she tells in the following words:

That the farm people about me were having most enjoyable and profitable times, and that, too, without my help; that a number of the women and girls exhibited a grace and ease in hospitable entertaining which I was uncomfortably conscious of lacking; that there was a delightful degree of friendliness in the neighborhood to which I was a stranger; that a number of people whom I had looked upon as exceedingly restricted in their opportunities were capable, well

---

[1] Atkeson, *op cit.*, p. 131.

[2] *Vide* issue of December 1, 1917, p. 37.

poised and singularly at home in a gathering of this kind; and that, moreover, these people had a degree of technical culture of which I knew nothing. Could it be possible that that was why they were interested in farm life and I was not?

In recounting the subsequent events of her life which were closely associated with local grange activities she gives credit to this farm organization for giving her an appreciation of nature, instilling in her a sense of duty to her loved ones, taking a constructive interest in the beautification of her home, educating her in the principles of scientific housekeeping, for gaining tact, poise, and self-control, and among other things for influencing her own children to remain in the country. In summing up she says the Grange has meant to her "blessing and honor and riches untold." The same could be said of any farm organization that provides social and educational advantages to its members.

SELECTED REFERENCES

Vide list at the close of the preceding chapter.

CHAPTER XVIII

THE FARMERS' ALLIANCE

The Beginning of a Farmers' Movement.—In the two preceding chapters the origin and development of the Grange were set forth, and it was then stated that its rapid development was part of the expression of a larger farmers' movement. Already in 1858, which was nine years before the organization of the Grange, a convention consisting of independent farmers met at Centralia, Illinois, to protest primarily against high freight rates. General interest in the Civil War and the high prices occasioned by it caused a cessation in organization activities until 1869, when high freight rates became greatly accentuated by a steadily falling price level. The movement was general, and was not initiated by only a few men, nor confined to narrow limits. The literature of the day refers to it as a "groundswell," and that is what it was. Throughout the South, and at two different centers in the West the movement was virtually simultaneously originated, and from these points it spread to all parts of the country. In its early stages, rejecting the use of partisan politics, the movement advanced the Grange from a mere nominal secret order to a mighty national organization within a few years; but later, accepting the principle of political action or partisan politics, it resulted in causing the newly formed Farmers' Alliance to become the basis for a political party known as the Populist Party, and in destroying finally the Alliance as well as probably also checking for a time the recovery of the Grange.

Before the formation of the Farmers' Alliance in 1875 a number of scattered and desultory attempts to effect organization among the farmers were made. These preliminary efforts appear to have been spontaneous. Contrary to the carefully prepared plans of the Grange, they were merely a protest against certain existing abuses and did not include the idea of building an institution for all time. As stated, work was begun at three different centers and at about the same time. In the

Illinois district the following events must be considered in the study of the early phases of the movement:

September, 1858, a general convention was held at Centralia, Illinois, where a declaration of principles was drawn up urging the formation of local farmers' clubs, the establishment of cooperative buying and selling associations, the establishment of a national agricultural bureau, and the election of "producers" rather than "non-producers" to positions of public trust.

April, 1869, a convention of farmers, called by H. C. Wheeler, met at Bloomington, Illinois, to make an organized protest against high freight rates and to bring its influence to bear upon Congress and the Illinois Constitutional Convention. The convention discussed other subjects.

October, 1872, a convention of farmers' clubs, called at the suggestion of the Farmers' Club of Avon, met at Kewanee, Illinois, to discuss ways and means of accomplishing "a saving to their members in purchasing, selling, and in transportation."

January, 1873, a convention of farmers' clubs, members of Granges, horticultural and other agricultural societies, met at Bloomington, Illinois, to organize the Illinois State Farmers' Association and to discuss railway abuses and those associated with the sale of agricultural implements and the exactions of commission merchants in connection with the sale of farm products.

April, 1873, the Illinois State Farmers' Association met at Springfield, Illinois, and vigorously began the work of reorganizing local societies in the State as well as establishing new ones. The transportation problem was the main subject of discussion.

October, 1873, at the call of the Illinois State Farmers' Association a convention composed of 300 delegates from Illinois, Wisconsin, Iowa, New York, Indiana, Nebraska, Minnesota and Canada, met at Chicago. The subject of discussion was transportation.

A second center of organization was the South, the work originating in Alabama and Tennessee and later becoming consolidated. The movement was carried as far west as St. Louis and as far north as Indianapolis, and finally in 1888 even to Chicago. The events to be taken into account in connection with this district are as follows:

Probably in 1870, the Agricultural Congress was formed. It was a general association uniting local agricultural societies in the South.

October, 1871, at the instance of the Tennessee Agricultural and Mechanics' Association, an Agricultural Congress was held at Nashville, Tennessee. At a meeting to be held in St. Louis the subject of consolidating the Congress and the Tennessee Association was to be considered.

December, 1871, the Agricultural Congress met at Selma, Alabama having for its object the organization of all agricultural societies into one body, especially those in the South and West.

May, 1872, the Tennessee Agricultural and Mechanics' Association and the Agricultural Congress met in joint session at St. Louis and effected a consolidation of the two societies under the name of the National Agricultural Congress. More extended local organization was encouraged. A partisan paper was read but generally condemned Technical agricultural subjects were discussed.

May, 1873, the National Agricultural Congress met at Indianapolis. Transportation was the chief subject of discussion. Other evils were to be fought. The Congress voted to meet in Atlanta in May, 1874.

After 1879 more rapid progress was made. Meetings were held at Louisville, Nashville, New Orleans, Washington, D. C., and Chicago. The meeting at Chicago was held in 1888. The name appears to have been changed to the Farmers' Congress in 1879. The present Farmers' National Congress probably grew out of this organization.[1]

The third center was Kansas. In March of 1873 at Topeka a convention, called by the Manhattan Farmers' Club, met and organized the Farmers' Cooperative Association of the State of Kansas. Further local organization was urged, and the subjects of transportation and taxation were discussed after which the convention adjourned *sine die*.

Parallel to this organization in the West and South the Grain Growers' Transportation and Loan Association was organized in New York for the purpose of financing cheap transportation facilities between the West and Eastern Seaboard. It was promoted by the men prominent in the western agricultural movement and was to have a capital stock of $10,000,000. The stock was never subscribed, but the plan interested New York City because it was concerned in retaining its large receipts of grain for export and local distribution. A second meeting was decided upon which also met in New York in May, 1873, and was known as the Farmers' and Producers' Convention. Josiah Quincy of Boston was made President. The demands of the Convention were to secure cheaper railroad rates, and to increase water transportation facilities so as to escape as much as possible the exorbitant charges of the railroads. A third convention was called by Quincy which met in Washington in January, 1874. At this meeting the organization of the American Cheap Transportation Association was effected which asked Congress to enact "certain laws for the regulation of railroads, in order to meet such wrongs and avert such dangers as an investigation may bring to light."[2]

The Character of the Illinois Organization.—By the middle

---

[1] For data prior to 1875 see Periam's *Authoritative History of the Farmers' Movement*. For developments since that time see Dunning's *Farmers' Alliance History*, p. 298-302.

[2] The data contained in this section are virtually all taken from Periam's *Authoritative History of the Farmers' Movement*.

of the nineteenth century farmers' clubs had become more or less numerous in all parts of the country. These clubs constituted the centers of agitation which resulted in county meetings and later in state-wide and almost nation-wide conventions. The declaration of principles drawn up by the first of these conventions, which was held at Centralia, Illinois, in 1858, urged "the formation of Farmers' Clubs wherever practical, the object of which shall be to produce concert of action on all matters connected with their interests." The number of farmers' clubs seems to have increased rapidly immediately after the Civil War in the West and somewhat later in the South. Local meetings were held in the West urging the formation of "a general association similar to the Trades' Unions, which, in England, and to a smaller degree in the United States, were obtaining great power."[1] The Civil War naturally turned the attention of the farmers away from agriculture. It was eleven years from the Centralia convention to the meeting held at Bloomington which met in 1869. Considerable more systematic effort at organization appears to have been made at Centralia than at Bloomington. The farmers' plans included the organization of local clubs and the building of a general association upon these. Its interests were of a general economic character, outlined with some care. The Bloomington convention was called by Mr. Wheeler and seemed to be primarily interested in the transportation problem which was taken to be the most serious trouble menacing the farmers' welfare, but other problems were also discussed. So far as launching a permanent association is concerned, the Bloomington convention was a failure; but from the standpoint of creating sentiment that led to further organized efforts, it must be regarded, together with the Centralia convention, as the harbinger of the Illinois State Farmers' Association organized in 1873.

In the spring of 1872 the work of organization in Illinois was carried forward by members of the Farmers' Club of Avon. By correspondence with other clubs they found a sentiment favorable to calling a convention "for the purpose of

[1] From Periam, *op cit.*, p. 224.

comparing views, and consulting together on the best means of organizing a general union of farmers for their mutual benefit and protection against the monopolizing tendencies of the age.'' The convention met at Kewanee in October, 1872. Fifty delegates were in attendance, nearly all of whom were strangers to one another. All of them were farmers. Some were engaged in farming or stock-raising on a large scale and some were prominent in politics. One of the organizers of the Illinois Grange as well as other members of the order were present. The subject of advancing local organization was given some attention A State Central Committee was appointed which was to record the names of all clubs, protective associations, and granges together with their officers in the state. An executive committee was also appointed. Jealousy between the Grange and this new organization was thought to exist, but the meeting is reported to have been altogether harmonious.

The executive committee elected at the Kewanee Convention had been instructed to issue a call for a convention to be held at Bloomington. The second Bloomington convention met in January, 1873. Delegates from various agricultural organizations were present including grange members who, it is said, attended these conventions as individuals and not as delegates. It was urged that every county organize with clubs in every school district. The committee on State Organization presented its report which recommended the organization of the Illinois State Farmers' Association. The article on membership reads as follows:

> Its members shall consist of delegates from the various Farmers' Clubs, Granges, and Agricultural and Horticultural Societies of the State, each of which shall be entitled to at least one delegate, and where the number of its members exceeds fifty, to one delegate for every one hundred members or fraction exceeding half that number. The members of the State Board of Agriculture shall be, *ex-officio*, members of this association, and from counties or parts of counties in which Clubs, Granges, or other Agriculture or Horticultural Societies are not organized, persons, not delegates, may be admitted by vote of this association. All members shall pay an annual fee of $1.

Immediately after the organization of the Illinois State Farmers' Association vigorous efforts were made to reorganize existing local societies and establish new ones. It is reported that "within three months over a thousand organizations had been perfected in the State."[1]

The Illinois legislature was to be in session early in the spring of 1873 and it was, therefore, decided to call a convention in April in order to impress it with the earnestness of the movement and call attention again to the need for railroad legislation. The Association met in Springfield "with more than 300 delegates present, representing Farmers' Associations in 72 counties." The convention had a strong debate on the tariff, being about equally divided on the question of free trade or protective tariff, and prabably because of this and other disagreements the number of delegates in attendance the second day dwindled to 75. Contrary to the previous harmonious meetings, this one was a stormy one and tended to halt the progress toward organization rather than promote it. Yet, the officers of the Association were persistent and called a convention in October of the same year to meet in Chicago and to be known as the North-Western Farmers' Convention.

The convention was attended by "about 300 delegates from lllinois, Wisconsin, Iowa, New York, Indiana, Nebraska, Minnesota, and Canada." It was virtually a north-western convention inasmuch as all delegates hailed from that section except three from the State of New York. "Thorough organization of the farmers of the country in local, county, and state organizations was recommended. It was moved that the convention adjourn *sine die*, but this was objected to because of the gravity of the situation. It was said that "the producing classes sustain the same relations in modern society as serfs did in the days of history." A resolution to meet at the call of the president of the Illinois State Farmers' Association was finally proposed and adopted.

The Aims and Purposes of the Illinois Movement.—The Centralia convention, meeting in 1858, drew up a "declaration of principles" which is a practice that must of necessity be followed by all large organizations. Among farmers' organizations the Centralia declaration was a precedent and was followed by the Grange and others only because aims and pur-

[1] *Vide Periam, op. cit.* p. 280.

poses must be declared in order to bring together into one association people whose interests are common. The Centralia convention made no protest against the railroads. Its protests were chiefly directed against the marketing system. It contended that the merchant "should not have a chief voice in the establishment of prices." Cooperative buying and selling was to be established. There are to be formed "wholesale purchasing and selling agencies in the great centers of commerce, so that producers may, in a great measure, have it in their power to save the profits of retailers." It is to be noted that here was a demand for cooperative enterprise nine years before the Grange was organized and that the founders of the Grange at first omitted this object of organization altogether, admitting it among the purposes only after the pressure from the West became irresistible. It was also urged that a national agricultural bureau be organized. Similar demands had been made in the East for many years as stated in previous chapters, so that the movement finally brought to a successful conclusion in 1862 had become general throughout the country. The main objects of the department as stated by this convention were to be the collection and publication of agricultural statistics and the collection and dissemination of valuable seeds and plants. The only note that could be interpreted as being of a political character was that they favored the election of "producers"—by which they probably meant farmers, miners, and manufacturers—to positions of public trust, and the exclusion from such places of "non-producers" by which they seem to have referred chiefly to merchants.

Beginning with 1869 the transportation problem in the face of declining prices became the one dominant object of organization. Taxation was also declared to be oppressive in 1869. Cooperative buying and selling practiced by local farmers' clubs by which means "large savings were effected," received considerable attention in 1873 at the second Bloomington convention. It was also urged at this time that farmers boycott such manufacturers of agricultural implements who refuse to sell to farmers' associations. At the North-Western convention transportation was again the dominant note. A new and aggressive object of organization agreed upon at this convention was the recommendation that "in order to carry out in a practical manner the spirit and letter of cooperation, they will withhold from the market their livestock products until the price shall reach such a figure that the producer shall receive the legitimate fruits of his labor." The resolution named a price at which pork ought to be sold.

It is not the plan to review here the demands of transportation except to point out some of the more striking proposals. The particular method of dealing with the railroads was a matter of much confusion. At the Bloomington convention it was said that it may be "direct regulation by act of our General Assembly; it may be national legislation, under the constitutional power to regulate commerce among the several states; it may be the building of national highways that shall traverse the continent, north and south, east and west, and running with fixed rates, compel the private companies to reasonable rates."[1] A resolution adopted by this convention recommended that "a commission be appointed to take charge of roads and run them in compliance with the law." The State of Illinois had already created a commission in 1871 and had also enacted a law naming maximum freight rates and passenger fares. The commission lacked the necessary power, and in response to a demand for a stronger one a law enacted in 1873 provided that the commission shall prescribe "a schedule of reasonable maximum rates of charges for the transportation of passengers and freight."[2] One of the difficulties in the way to regulate railway rates was the legal principle established in the Dartmouth College case, decided in 1818, which held that a corporate charter was a contract entered into between the corporation and the state and that such contract was irrevocable. Inasmuch as no powers had been reserved by the states to regulate rates, the railways contended that all legislation looking to the regulation of rates was inviolation of the contract. Of course it was also contended that regulation was illegal on the ground that the transportation is a private business, not vested with a public

---

[1] *Vide* Periam, *op. cit.*, p. 252.

[2] *Vide* Johnson and Van Metre, *Principles of Railroad Transportation*, p. 476.

interest, and that interference in rates is, therefore, a violation of the principle of the freedom of contract which is guaranteed to citizens of the United States under the constitution. At the Northwestern convention resolutions were introduced to ask the national government to build ship canals from the Atlantic seaboard by way of the Great Lakes to the West and from the north central states along the Mississippi river to the Gulf. The resolution relating to transportation that was finally adopted recommended the improvement of water routes and the building of railways to be owned and operated by the federal government. It reads as follows:

> We demand the construction of railroads, and the improvement of water communications, between the interior and seaboard, the same to be owned and operated by the General Government, for the purpose of affording cheap transportation, and to protect the people from the exactions of monopolies.

It will be noted that in all this early agitation the control of railroads through the principle of maintaining competitive conditions was one of the leading ideas. Since then we have learned that competition in transportation is not a workable basis in the control of rates, and, as stated before, the principle finally settled upon is that of state and national regulation. As stated in the previous chapter, the farmers of the West through this so-called Granger legislation forced the principle of regulation to be adopted earlier than if left to eastern sentiment.

The Movement in the South.—In the South the movement began to express itself through two associations,—the Agricultural Congress and the Tennessee Agricultural and Mechanics' Associations. Local societies had become more or less numerous in the South by the 70's and both of these general associations were delegate bodies representing local organizations. The Agricultural Congress held a convention at Selma, Ala., in December of 1871, and announced as its plan to "unite every agricultural society throughout the land, but especially those of the southern and western states, into one body, in which there should be a delegation from each of these societies, the basis of representation being one delegate to each fifty members or fraction thereof, and to include representatives from any society, whether state, county, district, or township association.''[1] At the instance of the Tennessee Association the Agricultural Congress met at Nashville, Tennessee, and was attended by delegates from eleven states and representing more than forty different agricultural societies and associations. At this meeting it was decided to call a convention at St. Louis, where the question of consolidating the two associations was to be considered. Accordingly ''on the 27th of May, 1872, the two societies numbering about three hundred delegates'' met in convention and proceeded to form a national body which was effected under the name of the National Agricultural Congress. It was urged at the convention that the farmers organize themselves into clubs and have monthly meetings. The next convention was shifted to Indianapolis, the capital of a middle western state. It met in 1873 ''with a large attendance of highly intelligent delegates from twenty-five states.'' According to the secretary's report the Congress now represented 3,000 socities which, taking into account also the parallel Grange development, is evidence that the farmers' movement was not only widespread, but touched the community and the individual and was, therefore, in a position to develop a strong feeling of ''a consciousness of kind'' among the rural people. The secretary estimated that there were in existence at that time at least 10,000 societies, two-thirds of which had organized during the previous year. Difficulty was experienced in getting societies having membership in the Congress to pay their dues. An excess of expenditures over income, amounting to $350, was reported. It was voted to meet at Atlanta in 1874.

President Butterfield thinks that the Farmers' National Congress grew out of the National Agricultural Congress. The former as at present constituted consists of a voting membership appointed by the governors of the states. They are selected from the various congressional districts and each agricultural college is given representation. Agricultural societies may elect delegates.[2] It is altogether likely that the Farmers' National Congress grew out of the National Agricul-

[1] *Vide* Periam, *op. cit.*, p. 209.
[2] *Vide Cyclopedia* of *American Agriculture*, Vol. IV, p. 296.

tural Congress because the local substructure of the organization broke down in time and delegates had to be provided chiefly through appointment by the governors of the states. This is further indicated by the subsequent history of the early southern movement. By about 1879 the name had been changed to the Farmers' Congress meeting at various points in the South including Louisville, Nashville, Atlanta, New Orleans and Washington, D. C. The New Orleans meeting was held in 1886 and represented by 19 states. In 1888 a meeting was held in Chicago. This continued activity in the South had broken the ground for the Alliance and had prepared the way for rapid progress under the new organizations.

Like the organization having its center in Illinois the National Agricultural Congress as well as its elemental associations rejected partisan politics as a means of attaining the ends of organized effort. From the beginning and including the meeting at St. Louis in 1872 the aims and purposes of organization were primarily to improve agriculture through the process of education. At St. Louis such problems as the conservation of forests, the planting of trees, fertilizers, and the admission of fertilizer materials free of duty, were discussed. Professor C. V. Riley, State Entomologist of Missouri and later associated with the United States Department of Agriculture, gave an address on practical entomology. Professor Turner of Jacksonville, Illinois, who played a prominent role in the establishment of the land-grant colleges to which reference is made in a previous chapter, read a paper on the education of the farmers. Com. Maury read a paper on meteorology and urged the taking of weather observations and the making of forecasts for the benefit of the farmer. It was not until the meeting at Indianapolis in 1873 that the question of transportation was considered. By this time the southern movement was beginning to embrace western societies whose membership was keenly interested in cheap transportation to the seaboard.

The problem of making the land-grant colleges institutions in which the teaching of agriculture was to be a prominent function engaged the attention of the Indianapolis convention. It was stated that the professorial staff of these institutions tried to construe the Morrill act to mean that it provided for classical insead of for agricultural education. Reference in previous chapters is made to the early confusion as to the real meaning of the act and to subsequent acts providing additional funds which were to be used in the teaching of agriculture including other subjects, but establishing the fact that agriculture was to receive a prominent place among the subjects to be taught in the land-grant colleges.

The Movement in Kansas.—The movement in Kansas originated with the Manhattan Farmers' Club, which asked the Secretary of the State Board of Agriculture to call a convention to be composed of delegates of farmers' clubs. The call was enlarged so as to include granges and other argicultural societies. The convention met at Topeka in March, 1873. It prescribed a form of a constitution for local societies whose membership was to be restricted to those interested in farming. The Farmers' Cooperative Association of the State of Kansas was organized with a membership clause as follows:

> Any county, township, or district organization in this state, whether called Union, Grange, Clubs, or other name, which shall forward to the Treasurer the sum of five dollars for each county society, and one dollar for all other local societies, and such assessments as shall be made, from time to time, by the Executive Committee for the benefit of the Association, whose Secretary shall correspond with the Secretary of this Association, and whose members shall cooperate in its general objects, may become auxiliary to this Association and be entitled to all its benefits.

It was urged that a local organization be effected everywhere which was to be affiliated with a national body. It was said that such an organization could follow the example of combination in industry and fix prices at which its products were to be sold. The "law of supply and demand," it was said, "was obsolete" and that "the prices of iron and other commodities from New York to San Francisco" were fixed through combination. A national agricultural body could collect facts concerning prices and itself name the figure at which its products should be sold. Taxation received some attention. A revision of the tariff providing for the admission of salt and lumber free of duty and the reduction of the duty on iron, was asked for. Transportation was given its rightful attention. The state legislature was to regulate rates and fares justly, and the federal government was to assert its power with reference to the regulation of the railroads. After the work of the convention was completed it adjourned *sine die*.

Summary of This Preliminary Organization.—The basis for this organization preliminary to the formation of the Farmers' Alliance was the agricultural clubs existing here and there throughout the country. The purposes for organizing these clubs varied probably considerably. In most places their chief functions seem to have been educational and social. Early in the movement it was reported at the conventions that cooperative buying and selling was practiced by many. Some of these were known as protective associations which probably means that the chief function of some clubs was to protect the members of a community against highwaymen. In Marion County, Illinois, it was reported that 30 farm organizations existed in 1873 and that these clubs "were originally organized as a protection against horse thieves." A similar motive for organization including also the protection of land claims, it is said, actuated the formation of local clubs in Texas out of which the Texas Alliance later grew. It is quite likely that in the newly settled portions of the West the original motives of organization of the agricultural clubs were the protection of land claims, protection against highwaymen and the maintenance of order in general. As the country became more thickly settled the newer functions including cooperative enterprise, social and educational activities, were added. When the regional associations were organized the clubs were not only established in large numbers but their functions were largely directed by the associations with which they were affiliated.

The movement to organize farmers into state and national organizations originated at three different centers at about the same time extending over a period beginning in 1858 and ending in 1873. From this time forward the Farmers' Alliance was beginning to take form, and by the late 80's it was virtually the chief agency through which the farmers of the country stated their demands. However, immediately after 1873 and continuing for about three years, the Grange was the all-absorbing organization. As stated in the chapter dealing with the development of the Grange, it suffered a very precipitous decline after 1876, and this gave opportunity for the Farmers' Alliance to form.

The aims and purposes of the foregoing organization were first to promote agriculture through a popularization of scientific principles and cooperative buying and selling among the farmers. The subjects of taxation and how to control the prices of agricultural products were given attention. Beginning with 1869 cheap transportation to the seaboard became the chief topic of discussion. The South, however, only became interested in this subject when its convention was shifted to Indianapolis.

The Origin of the Farmers' Alliance.—The activity of the farmers in the middle west after 1873 and up to the late 70's or early 80's seems to have been dominated by the Grange. Meanwhile, however, seeds were sown in the southern states including Arkansas, Louisiana, and Texas, and in the state of New York, which took root and developed an organization that entwined itself around the Grange and almost overwhelmed it. There is some doubt as to the origin of the Farmers' Alliance, but an account given by G. Campbell of Kansas, claiming that it originated in his state, is generally thought to be correct. It was noted that Kansas was one of the early centers of organization and the truth of the claim, therefore, seems not unlikely. From 1864 to 1870 settlers took possession of land in Kansas known as the "Osage ceded lands," which was done under the supervision of the Department of the Interior. The railroads, however, contended that this land was covered by a patent granted them and demanded that the settlers pay for the full value of the farms. This the settlers refused to do and in 1872 organized the Settlers' Protective Association, otherwise known as the Settlers' League, or Alliance. At first it was open, but later in order to combat the movements of the railroads and in order to prepare plans without disclosing the details to their enemies the principle of secrecy was adopted. Mr. Campbell states that he sent a plan of organization to New York where an alliance was formed in 1875, but on account of the popularity of the Grange its growth at first was very slow. At about the same time that the dispute as to the title of the Osage land in Kansas was in progress some of the settlers emigrated to Texas, where they organized similar organizations. This, Mr. Campbell asserts, accounts for the claims that the Farmers' Alliance originated simultaneously in Texas and New York. As a matter of fact, it originated in Kansas and was carried from there to both Texas and New York, where it began to spread, the New York organization moving west, it is thought, and forming the Northwestern Alliance, and the Texas Alliance uniting with the Louisiana Farmers' Union to form the National Farmers' Alliance and Cooperative Union moved east and was often referred to as the southern alliance. However, it became national in scope, invading even the territory of the northwestern alliance. In 1889 a working agreement between the Southern Alliance and Knights of Labor was entered into and the name of the former was changed to the National Farmers' Alliance and Industrial Union.

The National Farmers' Alliance of the Northwest.—The New York alliance was organized in 1875 at Rochester. The constitution adopted provided that only farmers were eligible. A state alliance was organized. The principle object of the organization was to watch legislators and elect those favorable to the farmers. In 1880 a call was issued for the formation of a National Farmers' Alliance. The meeting was held at Chicago and the Secretary of the New York state alliance was elected its president. The National Farmers' Alliance, otherwise known as the Northwestern Alliance to distinguish it from the Southern Alliance, is thought to have developed out of the Chicago meeting. However, a local alliance is said to have been organized in the office of the *Western Rural* in Chicago as early as April 15, 1880. Dr. C. W. Macune, the chief leader of the National Farmers' Alliance and Industrial Union of the South, studied the plan of organization of the National Farmers' Alliance of the Northwest through the *Western Rural*, its official organ, with a view to consolidate the northern and southern alliances. He found, however, that while the southern alliance was a secret organization the northwestern was non-secret, admitted colored persons, and was also more loosely organized. These differences were considered too great to make consolidation possible and the southern organization, therefore, decided to send organizers into the northwest territory and gain a foothold through the establishment of local alliances of its own. Strong efforts, however, were made in 1890 in spite of the differences between the two organizations to effect some kind of a combination, but these failed, it is said, because of opposition on the part of a few men.

The northwestern alliance was strongest in Iowa, Nebraska, and Minnesota. Its membership in 1889 was estimated to have been 400,000. The organization was non-secret. Its declaration of principles were as follows:

1. The free and unlimited coinage of silver.
2. The abolition of national banks and the substitution for their notes of legal treasury notes, and the increase of currency to $50 *per capita.*
3. Government ownership of railroads and telegraphs.
4. The prohibition of alien ownership of land, and of gambling in stocks, options, and futures.
5. The adoption of a constitutional amendment requiring the election of President, Vice President, and United States Senators, by direct vote of the people.
6. The Australian ballot system.[1]

The Movement in Texas.—The Texas Alliance had its origin in Lampasas County, where the first organization was effected in 1874 or 1875. As previously stated, Mr. Campbell of Kansas claims that the plan of organization was brought into Texas from Kansas. The motives for organizing were several. Cattle and horse thieves infested the country and committed depredations continually. Land titles also were in constant danger because of the activity of litigation instituted by the so-called landsharks. The settlers decided to defend their homes against all hazards. Immediately after the panic of 1873 the farmers attempted to increase their profits through cooperative buying and selling, which, for a time, it is said, constituted an important function of these clubs. The protective functions necessitated the use of secret work.

[1] *Vide* Dunning's *Farmers' Alliance History* for full statement of the facts pertaining to the Farmers' Alliance.

One of the degrees, it is stated, was based on the method of catching a horse thief. The organization spread in Lampasas County and to two other adjoining counties, after which the Grand County Alliance was organized. This was done in February, 1878, and in the following May the Grand State Alliance was organized. The organization allowed politics to creep in, and active participation in the Greenback campaign was taken resulting in dissensions among the members that caused its immediate destruction.

W. T. Baggett, a member of an alliance in Coryell County, moved to Parker County and took with him the plan of organization. An alliance was formed in Parker County omitting from its declaration of principles the partisan feature which has wrecked more than one farmers' organization as well as labor unions. From the new center in Parker County the movement began to spread, resulting in the formation of the Grand State Alliance in December, 1879.

The Farmers' State Alliance of Texas was for some years a small body, meeting usually in school houses and several times a year. By August, 1882, according to the report of the secretary, the sub-alliances numbered 120. In 1883 the delegates to the State alliance numbered 56, but the following year 180 were in attendance. Because of the tendency of the State organization to become an unwieldly body the delegates from local alliances were reduced to three from each county in 1885. In 1886 the largest meeting that had yet assembled was held with 84 counties represented. At this meeting there was considerable unrest and a feeling was entertained by some of the leaders that the Alliance would launch into partisan politics. To avoid such disaster a secret meeting was held and a new charter was secured with the same vice-president and treasurer as that of the regular alliance. It was at this time that Dr. C. W. Macune, chairman of the executive committee, and for many years the leading spirit of the movement, stepped forward as the one person who could harmonize the discordant elements and secure pledges anew that the Alliance was to avoid altogether the use of partisan politics in the attainment of its ends. The new organization was persuaded to hold back until the State Alliance could be convened, when

Dr. Macune was elected president and succeeded in uniting all factions. By January, 1887, the order had grown to 35,000 sub-alliances. In about a year and a half prior to 1887 it added 28,000 local organizations.[1]

Character of Organization of the Texas Alliance.—The representation of the State Alliance was at first direct from the local clubs or local alliances. In other words, there were no county alliances at first which is also the way the Grange started out. The county organizations were established to afford cooperative buying and selling agencies which is also the reason for the establishment of the Pomona Grange. Women were admitted into the alliance from the beginning and were the means of making its social activity a prominent feature of the organization. Only white persons were eligible for membership. The officers of the organization were as follows: president, vice-president, secretary, assistant secretary, lecturer, treasurer, doorkeeper, assistant doorkeeper, and the executive committee. Members paid 25 cents dues monthly of which 10 cents was given to the sub-alliance, 5 cents to the county alliance and 10 cents to the state alliance.

The alliance started out with three degrees, but in the interest of democracy or the elimination of classes these were consolidated into one in 1886. There was, however, a demand later for a second degree which was in fact given by some county organizations and known as the cooperative degree. Compared with the complex secret-order work of the Grange, which has seven degrees, that of the Texas alliance was very simple.

Aims and Purposes of the Texas Alliance.—The declaration of purposes of the Texas Alliance remind one of the various declarations of the Grange. In 1880 the state alliance adopted the following purposes which with later modifications are as follows:

Profoundly impressed that we as the Farmers' Alliance, united by the strong and faithful ties of financial and home interest, should set forth our declaration of intentions, we therefore *resolve*:

1. To labor for the education of the agricultural classes in the

[1] *Vide* Dunning, *op. cit.*, pp. 20-55.

science of economic government, in a strictly non-partisan spirit, and to bring about a more perfect union of said classes.

2. To endorse the motto, "In things essential, Unity, and in all things Charity."

3. To develop a better state, mentally, morally, socially, and financially.

4. To create a better understanding for sustaining our civil officers in maintaining law and order.

5. To constantly strive to secure entire harmony and good will among all mankind and brotherly love among ourselves.

6. To suppress personal, local, sectional, and national prejudice, all unhealthy rivalry and all selfish ambition.

7. The brightest jewels which it garners are the tears of widows and orphans, and its imperative commands are to visit the homes where lacerated hearts are bleeding; to assuage the sufferings of a brother or sister; bury the dead; care for the widows and educate the orphans; to exercise charity towards offenders; to construe words and deeds in their most favorable light; granting honesty of purpose and good intentions to others; and to protect the National Farmers' Alliance and Cooperative Union until death. Its laws are reason and equity; its cardinal doctrines inspire purity of thought and life; its intention is, "Peace on earth and good will to men."

The first of these objects was amended, so as to read as stated, after the troublous meeting in 1886. Dr. Macune was anxious to have the principle of non-partisan activity firmly and securely re-established. At a special meeting which he called as chairman of the executive committee for the purpose of restoring harmony he pointed out that the basis of the organization is the particular occupation of farming. "All the different classes and occupations of society are engaged in organization for mutual advancement and protection to a greater extent than ever before in the history of the world." The alliance was to organize the farmers for mutual advancement and protection, but was to avoid partisan politics if it would save itself from dissension and final destruction. This was merely a reiteration of the orthodox doctrine of the alliance. Even at the stormy session of 1886 a resolution embodying the same idea was adopted. It says, "that as citizens we have a right to belong to any organization, political party, or church, we may see proper, but as a Farmers' Alliance we will not consider such subjects within our body." In a previous resolution the alliance pledged itself not to nominate any man for office as a distinct political party.

The motto endorsed in the declaration of purposes suggested in a special way the Grange's declaration of 1874. The

Grange used an additional phrase, and its complete motto reads as follows: "In essentials, unity; in non-essentials, liberty; in all things, charity." In 1887 the National Farmers' Alliance and Cooperative Union was organized and this body is referred to in the last object stated. A few other items were added at the time the national body was formed. Inasmuch as stock raising was a prominent industry in Texas it is not surprising to find among the objects of organization a provision for the return of stray stock to its rightful owner without any charge for such services. The brand of the stock found by alliance members was to be reported to the secretary of the state alliance and by him to the county secretary of the sub-alliances. To expedite this service the alliance adopted the Texas statutory county brand as its own, and in addition adopted an alliance brand to be placed on the animal's jaw. Through this means it was possible to identify the animal first as one belonging to an aliance member and second determine the county in which its owner was located. For returning an animal to a non-member through this channel a charge of 50 cents was to be made.

The dominant purpose of the alliance, however, was the promotion of cooperative enterprise among the farmers. Cooperative buying and selling was one of the motives for organizing the first clubs and at every important meeting of the state body the subject was given business-like attention. Members of sub-alliances were to pool their cotton through county alliances, and the state business agent to be appointed by the executive committee was to negotiate for the sale of the entire supply. The state agent was also to buy all the supplies to be handled by all the cooperative stores and lumber yards that each county alliance was asked to establish.[1] The recommendations actually adopted by the Texas Alliance with respect to cooperation were in the main not unsound. Dr. Macune, however, in his enthusiasm went considerably beyond the bounds of wisdom at this time. In order to cope with monopolies he suggested that the farmers of Texas build cotton mills to manufacture what cotton they would use, plant only as much

[1] *Vide* Dunning, *op cit.*, p. 55.

as they would care to manufacture, spend the remainder of their time in raising a diversity of crops for home consumption, and thus make themselves independent. The manufacture of cotton would have been a costly undertaking, and because of the entrepreneurial inefficiency peculiar to cooperative organization it would in all probability have resulted in complete failure. A few years later Dr. Macune struck a more conservative note with respect to cooperation.

High freight rates, a greater charge for a shorter than for a longer haul, and rebates were all condemned, but transportation does not seem to have been such a burning question in Texas as it was in the central west. In addition to the issues mentioned the farmers were concerned in making the railroads bear a just share of taxation.

The Texas Alliance was especially sympathetic toward organized labor. This is significant because the Farmers' Alliance later joined hands with the Knights of Labor. The combination, although a loose one, was a fundamental error in organization and was probably one of the influences that caused the alliance to drift into partisan politics. The Grange and Farmers' Union today recognize that the economic interests of organized agriculture and of organized labor are not common. The Farmers' Alliance tried to help organized labor, but in so doing it destroyed itself. The Texas Alliance recommended the call of a labor conference to be represented by men from all labor unions for the purpose of discussing measures of interest to the laboring classes. In another resolution it recognized "the right of the laboring classes to organize, and condemned any effort on the part of any man, or set of men, who seek to prescribe the right of any man exercising his freedom by joining any labor organization having for its object the bettering of the laboring man's condition." The Texas Alliance probably had in mind the fighting of monopoly through combination with organized labor. This idea is suggested in a resolution whose language expresses the hope that "cooperative stores, and other associations may be organized by the industrial classes to improve their financial condition, or to promote their general welfare." It has been suggested by leaders of the Grange that labor organize itself into cooperative groups to which the farmers could sell their produce direct instead of through middlemen. The same idea seems to have been the basis for the strong sympathy entertained by the Texas Alliance toward organized labor.[1]

The Formation of the National Farmers' Alliance and Cooperative Union of America.—After the meeting of the Texas Alliance in 1886 rapid strides in organization were made. Through the leadership of Dr. Macune much of this progress was for a time accomplished through the process of consolidating with other similar existing associations. Dr. Macune corresponded with the officers of the Louisiana Farmers' Cooperative Union and discovered that their organization was virtually similar to that of the Texas Alliance. He therefore suggested a consolidation of the two state associations, which was effected in 1887 under the name of the National Farmers' Alliance and Cooperative Union of America. The admission of the Louisiana Union made little change in the character of the organization of the alliance or in its policies. The declaration of purposes of the Texas alliance was virtually accepted in its entirety, only a few unimportant items being added.

The national body was to have representation from state associations in the proportion of one delegate for each four counties which, as pointed out by Dr. Macune later, was a very unscientific basis of representation. It ignored both the number of sub-alliances and the total membership in the state. Delegates had to be 25 years of age to be eligible to membership in the national body. The charter gave authority to the national body for the issue of charters to state organizations. Its control over the lower parts of the organization was not as specific as that of the Grange. In the charter of 1890, however, it was given more control over membership. Only persons over sixteen years of age could be admitted to the order. Membership was wholly limited to the country. A farmer, a farm laborer, a country mechanic, a country preacher, a country school teacher, or a country doctor could be admitted. The matter of admitting colored persons was left to the discretion of state bodies, but no colored person could be sent as delegate

[1] The aims and purposes of the Texas Alliance are taken from Dunning, *op. cit.*, pp. 20-55.

to the national body. This was done to encourage combination with western and northern bodies. The national body was to be supported by dues paid by state associations amounting to 5 per cent of their "gross cash receipts."

In Louisiana a temporary open club organized in 1880, but soon began to languish. It was followed by another in 1885, to which the secret feature was added. Clubs sprang up rapidly, resulting in the organization of a state association the same year. When the suggestion came from Dr. Macune that a national association be effected by uniting the two state bodies, the Louisiana Union was prepared to enter the combination as a growing and virile organization.

Consolidation With the Agricultural Wheel.—The Agricultural Wheel was organized in 1882 in Prairie County, Arkansas, by a group of men who were all hard-working farmers. It was made at once a secret order. Only male whites were admitted. Its objects were "the improvement of its members in the theory and practice of agriculture, and the dissemination of knowledge relative to rural and farming affairs," as well as "to ameliorate the condition of the farmers in every possible manner."[1] "God," they said, "created all men free and equal and endowed them with certain inalienable rights such as life, liberty, and the pursuit of happiness, and that these rights are a common inheritance, and should be respected by all mankind." They said further that the fruits of the laboring class, the real producers of wealth, was "absorbed by a class who propose, not only to live on the labor of others, but to speedily amass fortunes at their expense."

In April of 1883 a state organization was effected with more than 500 members. By 1884 there were 114 sub-organizations having a total membership of 5,000. County Wheels were organized the same year. At the meeting of 1885 a combination with the Brothers of Freedom was effected. At the time of this consolidation there were 462 subordinate Wheels and about 650 organizations of the Brothers of Freedom having a joint membership of more than 40,000.[2]

The organization known as the Brothers of Freedom was

[1] *Vide* Dunning, *op. cit.*, p. 199.
[2] *Vide* Dunning, *op cit.*, p. 201.

organized in Arkansas during the same year as that of the Agricultural Wheel. Its declaration of principles is in some cases a verbatim reproduction of those of the Wheel, and its ideas throughout are virtually the same, indicating that one was suggested by the other. The Brothers of Freedom seem to have come after the Agricultural Wheel. The Wheel, as stated, absorbed the former organization in 1885. Both the Agricultural Wheel and the Brothers of Freedom thought the interests of the farmers and those of organized labor to be common. No distinction seems to have been made between tillers of the soil and laborers in manufacturing establishments or on the railroads.

By 1886 the movement had spread to other states and the formation of a national Agricultural Wheel was effected with representation from Arkansas, Kentucky and Tennessee. By November of 1887 the order had grown very rapidly. The Wheel held its first national meeting that year and it was reported then that the states of Missouri, Mississippi, Alabama, Texas and Indian Territory were added to the list of states previously organized. Plans were made to carry the work of organization into other states. Its total membership at that time is stated to have been 500,000. The membership in 1886 is stated to have been 50,000, which shows that the Agricultural Wheel like the Alliance of the south with which it consolidated, experienced a mushroom growth.

The National Farmers' Alliance and Cooperative Union had invited delegates from the National Wheel to attend its meeting held at Shreveport in October, 1887, which was one month before the national meeting of the Wheel. Both the character and the objects of the organization were quite similar and there was, therefore, very little objection voiced to the proposed combination at the national meeting of the Wheel. Final consolidation plans were effected at a meeting of the National Farmers' Alliance and Cooperative Union held at Meridian, Mississippi, in 1888 when the delegates of the two associations met in joint session. The necessary ratification of state associations speedily followed. The name chosen for the new combination was the National Farmers' and Laborers' Union of America. This meant a tremendous addition in scope and membership to the alliance. In 1889 its total membership is stated to have been 3,000,000.[1] This figure probably took into account the membership of all federated associations including the Knights of Labor. Ben Terrell, a lecturer in the Alliance, stated the membership of the organization without its federated parts at more than 2,000,000 in 1890.[2]

There were then two consolidations effected by the southern Alliance. First in 1887 the Louisiana Farmers' Cooperative Union united with the Texas Farmers' Alliance to form the National Farmers' Alliance and Cooperative Union of America, and in 1888 the National Agricultural Wheel, which had previously absorbed the Brothers of Freedom, united with the Alliance under the name of the National Farmers' and Laborers' Union of America. Thus four different societies, organized about the same time, were welded into one gigantic association. This ended the process of consolidation, but not of confederation or the practice of entering into a compact with other associations to carry out policies that were thought to be of common interest. In connection with confederation plans the name of the Alliance was subjected to one more change. With these numerous changes and the admission of elements that were undisciplined in organization and uninformed as to proper objects of organization; is it any wonder that the alliance finally drifted into partisan politics and declared in favor of a third party?

Confederation With Other Associations.—The process of complete consolidation was carried as far as possible. That is to say, this plan of combination proceeded to the point of uniting all associations whose character of organization was virtually similar to that of the alliance. There were other agricultural associations that had to be brought into the movement if the scheme of organizing the farmers was to be complete. Some of these, however, did not have the secret feature, of which the National Farmers' Alliance of the Northwest was an example; and one of them was composed of colored people. The main branch of the Alliance had committed itself

---

[1] *Vide* McVey, *Populist Movement,* p. 196.
[2] *Vide* Dunning, *op. cit.*, p. 294.

to the policy of excluding colored persons for obvious reasons. It was stated before that the Alliance as well as the elemental associations it absorbed were wholly sympathetic to labor, so much so in fact that in the Wheel territory the economic interests of labor and agriculture were in no way distinguished. The friendly feeling toward labor, therefore, led to an agreement for joint action on legislative matters with the Knights of Labor in 1889. In 1890 a provision was adopted for the establishment of a confederation committee to be composed of five members from each association to be federated with the Alliance. At this time, however, no specific arrangement had been made for cooperation with the Knights of Labor through the channel of the confederation committee. But inasmuch as an agreement had been entered into between the two associations at the St. Louis meeting in 1889, and since the Knights of Labor sent fraternal delegates in 1890 to meet the Alliance in convention at Ocala, Florida, it may be presumed that cooperation between the two associations was quite close. The Knights of Labor was at first a secret organization, but in 1881 the principle of secrecy was generally abandoned. So far then as traditions were concerned there was a common feature in the character of the organization of the Knights of Labor and the Alliance. In 1886, the height of the strength of the order, its membership was more than 700,000. It was not limited to a single trade, and women were admitted. Skilled and unskilled workmen were alike eligible to membership, making altogether an unstable organization. One of the important causes for its decline was its entrance into politics.

Definite provision for cooperation with the Farmers' Mutual Benefit Association and the National Colored Farmers' Alliance and Cooperative Union through the confederation committee was provided for by the Ocala convention. All associations that entered the federation agreed to support the St. Louis platform adopted in 1889. Each association pledged itself to assist in "local efforts to better the condition of the people." Fraternal delegates from one to any of the other organizations were never to be excluded. Any plans agreed upon by the committee on confederation were to be fully carried out by all the associations. This virtually superimposed a power above the legislative body of the Alliance.

The Farmers' Mutual Benefit Association was organized in 1883 by a group of farmers in Johnson County, Illinois. Organization, it is said, was suggested to them by an alleged refusal on the part of local dealers to buy the wheat they had brought to town. The farmers telegraphed for wheat prices and found them steadily rising. They also secured a car which they could use to ship their wheat, but to do this they had to have the cooperation of their neighbors. The incident finally led to the formation of local clubs, and in order to accomplish their object it was thought necessary to make the organization secret. The general association coordinating the local lodges was called General Assembly. The growth of the organization reached its height in 1887.[1] At the time it federated with the Alliance its membership is stated to have been 150,000.[2]

The Colored Farmers' National Alliance and Cooperative Union originated in Houston County, Texas, in the organization of a secret club in 1886. The movement at once spread rapidly, resulting in the formation of a state alliance in 1887 and a national alliance the following year. The declaration of principles adopted by the Texas association was virtually the same as those of the white organization. At the time the national body was formed the following were added:

> To elevate the colored people of the United States, by teaching them to love their country and their homes; to care more for their helpless and sick and destitute; to labor more earnestly for the education of themselves and their children, especially in agricultural pursuits.
>
> To become better farmers and laborers, and less wasteful in their methods of living.
>
> To be more obedient to the civil law, and withdraw their attention from political partisanship.
>
> To become better citizens, and truer husbands and wives.

The adoption of these latter principles showed some originality, and also emphasized objects of organization peculiarly important to the colored race. According to General R. M. Humphrey, who was elected superintendent of the order, the alliance was the means of very considerably bettering the

[1] *Vide* Dunning, *op. cit.*, p. 226.
[2] *Vide* McVey, *Populist Movement*, p. 196.

condition of the colored people. It was instrumental in establishing many high schools and academies, in building better churches, and improving generally the character and quality of the work done by colored teachers and preachers. From the start the maintenance of peaceful relations with the white people was one of its foremost objects.[1] At the Ocala convention, as stated, it was agreed to federate the colored and white alliances. In 1891 the colored association is said to have had a membership of 1,250,000. This meant that the National Farmers' Alliance and Industrial Union, not taking into account the Knights of Labor with whom only a joint agreement had been made, could influence the conduct of considerably more than 3,000,000 souls.

The Alliance as a Social Agency.—The social advantages coming to members of an organization flow primarily from its local bodies. The Alliance was the means of creating a social medium for the rural people in a way somewhat similar to that of the Grange; although the latter organization having a more homogeneous membership, and for the reason that it is now well established, probably far exceeds anything the Alliance ever afforded its members in the way of social opportunities. Up to the Ocala convention of 1890 the admission of membership seems to have been quite free, and even under the constitution adopted that year prospective members were not to be wholly limited to persons actually engaged in farming. Any person engaged in any other pursuit, if living in the country, was still eligible to membership. The secret work of the alliance was also early reduced to one degree, and this probably to a great many people served to diminish interest in the meetings of the sub-alliance. In the study of the origin of various farmers' organizations it was not infrequently the case that the adoption of the secret feature served to promote their development. At the present day it seems that the masses of our population still like secret organizations largely because of the peculiar interest that attaches to degree work, paraphernalia, rituals, countersigns, pledges, etc. Thus, while the Alliance secret work lacked the interest of a more com-

[1] *Vide* Dunning, *op. cit.*, p. 288.

plex system, it was the plan of the national organization to foster the development of the social function in all sub-alliances. Lecturers were provided for, and these would encourage the feeling of a democratic attitude toward all members. Educational work was recommended, and religious principles were to be applied to every-day rural life and especially to its economic aspects. Like the Grange, the Alliance admitted women and this aided very materially in giving the meetings a social color.

The Alliance on Sectionalism.—Sectionalism endangers the continuity of the state. Its existence is a menace to our national solidarity, and is a subject, therefore, of fundamental importance. One who reads the history of the early farmers' organizations is impressed with the splendid service rendered by them in the days immediately after the early 70's when the feeling was still intense. The mingling of delegates from all parts of the country, all having the same interests and representing everywhere the citizens of rural districts, must have contributed very largely toward allaying the feeling of bitterness and healing the wounds occasioned by the Civil War.

The Alliance in its declaration of purposes stated that one of the objects was "to suppress personal, local, sectional, and national prejudices, all unhealthy rivalry, and all selfish ambition." L. L. Polk, president of the Alliance in 1890, in his annual address at the convention held in Ocala, Florida, did a great service in the interest of his country when he said the following:

> Must we as Christian parents, entail upon our children the bitter legacy of hate? Hundreds of thousands of noble, aspiring, hopeful, and ardently patriotic young men all over the land are manfully enlisting in the responsible duties of American citizenship. Born since the war —thank God—their infant vision was first greeted by the light of heaven, unobscured by the smoke of battle, and their infant ear first caught the sweet sound of hallowed peace, unmingled with the hoarse thundering of hostile cannon. Shall they be taught to cherish, and foster, and perpetuate that prejudice and animosity, whose fruits are evil, and only evil?
>
> Let us as an organization, with new hope, new aspirations, new zeal, new energy, and new life, turn our faces toward the rising sun of an auspicious and inviting future, and reconsecrate ourselves to the holy purpose of transmititng to our posterity a government 'of the people, by the people, and for the people,' and which shall be unto all generations the citadel of refuge for civil and religious liberty.

As has been pointed out the greatest strength of the National Farmers' Alliance and Industrial Union was in the South and West, extending from the Atlantic coast into the State of Texas and north into the middle western States. There were, however, representatives at the Ocala convention from the middle Atlantic States including New York and Pennsylvania, and from the far northern states including Michigan, North and South Dakota, and Minnesota. The state of California was also represented. In consequence of the wide area from which representatives came, the influence of the National Farmers' Alliance and Industrial Union was truly national in scope. Had the effort to confederate with the National Farmers' Alliance, whose territory was mainly in the Northwest, succeeded, its influence would have been still greater. Serious efforts were made to effect a confederation, and while the admission of colored persons in the northern alliance was at first an obstacle this was removed later by the adoption of a clause at Ocala empowering each state association to prescribe the eligibility of persons for membership with reference to color. The ultimate failure to confederate was not in any way controlled by sectional feeling, but by certain personal objections entertained by a few leaders. The compact entered into with the Knights of Labor, whose headquarters were at Philadelphia, and the reception of its fraternal delegates at the conventions of the southern alliance was also a channel through which the influence to obliterate sectionalism was extended.

The Alliance on the Race Problem.—The exclusion of the colored person from membership in the alliance seems altogether logical to one who has lived or traveled extensively in the South. From beginning to end the Texas and other southern state alliances adhered to the principle of excluding the negro from membership in their own bodies, and for some time this policy was also strictly adhered to by the national association. The program of expansion, however, made it necessary to compromise on the principle. In parts of the territory of the Agricultural Wheel it was customary to admit a few negroes, and in order to legalize such practice full power was given to each state association to control eligibility for membership as to color according to its own pleasure. The national body, however, refused to receive colored representatives from state associations. This greater freedom was also a step toward union with the northern alliance which, as stated, was at one time seriously considered. In the interest of establishing a larger control the alliance agreed to confederate with the colored association. Of course, the contact was to be effected through a confederation committee on which only five negroes were to be represented. This was merely in the nature of a conference and not a dparture from the principle of keeping social activities of the two races entirely separate. The basis on which confederation was effected was unusually liberal. The recommendation of the committee which was adopted by the Ocala convention is as follows: "We recommend and urge that equal facilities, educational, commercial, and political, be demanded for colored and white Alliance men alike, competency considered, and that a free ballot and a fair court will be insisted upon for colored and white alike, by every true Alliance man in America."[1] This is indeed an advanced position, and, with respect to its political aspects, is not in harmony with the so-called "grandfather" legislation enacted by some of the southern states.

Lessons in Cooperative Enterprise.—The Alliance, like the Grange, had to learn by experience that cooperative enterprise was subject to definite limitations. Mistakes were made and these were admitted by Doctor Macune, who declared that in spite of such mistakes the order continued to grow. The organization among farmers of the past should be regarded as experimentation. The lessons of the past should not be forgotten. A new venture into the fields of impossible or doubtful sources should not be made, but rather a look backward should now and then be taken so as to avoid pitfalls in the future. Leaders of farm organization should acquaint themselves with sound principles of cooperative marketing. The subject has been studied by experts and a wealth of material is now available showing the simplest and most successful forms of cooperative enterprise. It is important that farmers' organizations de-

[1] *Vide* Dunning, *Farmers' Alliance History*, p. 163.

velop cooperation for the benefit of the farmers, but while so doing they must adhere to sound principles if they would escape criticism and maintain their strength and influence in their respective territories.

The first effort at cooperation under Alliance tutelage was the establishment of Trade Committees whose territory corresponded with the county. The best five men from various sections of the county were appointed to serve as a committee whose duty it was to approach a merchant and offer to buy supplies only from him providing he was willing to sell to them at a discount. If such an agreement was entered into between the merchant and the trade committee the information was then given to all the members of the sub-alliances and all were expected to purchase from the particular merchant designated. Complaints as to prices or quality of service were made to the trade committee, which was to take action in the matter of securing justice to all parties concerned. The contract entered into usually stipulated that the merchant should employ at least one Alliance clerk, who was the farmers' representative and who was to report violations of the agreement. In addition the trade committee fortified itself against fraud by demanding that it be given full liberty to examine invoices, and all costs, as well as be made acquainted with the cost mark used by the merchant.[1] Doctor Macune says that this so-called contract system by which the farmers' trade was centered with certain merchants was for about a year the main purpose of the order. While the plan was being tried the entire energy of the lecturing force was used to extend it to every sub-alliance. After about a year's trial the plan seems to have been generally discarded and the energies of the alliance leaders and lecturers was now directed toward the establishment of the practice of appointing business agents who were to conduct the buying and selling of goods consumed and produced by the farmers without the intervention of the local merchant. A state exchange was created and county business agents dealt with this exchange. It purchased supplies for the farmers and sold their cotton.

Before coordination among the counties through the crea-

[1] *Vide* Dunning, *op. cit.*, chapter XXII and p. 258.

tion of a state exchange was effected, the farmers within each county were advised to cooperate in the sale of their products. The feature was thoroughly discussed at the meeting of the Texas State Alliance held in 1886. It was suggested that the membership bulk their cotton and have sale days on which city buyers were to be invited. It was thought that the scheme would develop competition among the buyers and thus raise the price to the farmers. In this connection one is reminded of similar attempts on the part of farmers to establish trade centers in the country for other farm products. For instance, boards of trade to sell dairy products established in country districts with a view to attract buyers have been tried at a number of points with no success. Wherever practicable the Alliance advised that cotton yards be provided. At these yards the cotton was to be received, weighed, sampled, graded and prepared for shipping. The plan proved unsuccessful because buyers from a distance failed to patronize the sale days. The Alliance cotton yards were converted into warehouses and as such served a useful purpose.

With the failure of the county cotton sale days, which were said to have failed largely because the merchants had combined against the farmers, the Alliance members resolved to organize a state business exchange which was to receive the cotton collected at the county warehouses and sell it direct to the mills, thus ridding themselves entirely of the middlemen. The contract system for the purchase of supplies from certain merchants was also discontinued. "Supply stations" in the county were provided, a business agent was appointed, and orders for goods the farmers were in need of were by him dispatched to the state business agent, who would buy in large lots and distribute goods in small quantities among the counties as required. It is claimed that this practice reduced costs considerably to the farmer. It was, however, not properly appreciated by the farmers generally, it is said, for the reason that competing merchants would in many instances meet the exchange prices and in fact at times sell below them. This made the farmers' organized efforts appear altogether fruitless and unnecessary, resulting also in making the business agent the victim of considerable unpleasant criticism. This, however, is another lesson in cooperation which the farmers of the country here and there are learning all over again. If they would reconstruct the market system, or buy operating materials at reduced costs, organization must not be spasmodic but continuous.

The Lesson of the State Exchange.—In order to sell the cotton held in the county warehouses the state business agent, who happened to be Doctor Macune, made a trip to Boston and Fall River and tried to negotiate a sale direct with the mills. He discovered that the cotton could be sold in this manner, and at the State Alliance meeting of 1887 he proposed the establishment of the Farmers' Alliance Exchange of Texas, which included a plan to raise a capital of $500,000, of which, however, only a small amount was at first to be paid in. Members of sub-alliances were assessed $2 each and the capital was divided into twenty-five shares of $20,000 each and committed to twenty-five trustee stockholders elected from the several congressional districts. The stockholders held the stock in trust and considered the interests of his constituents in the discharge of his duties. The capital was used to erect buildings, purchase farmers' supplies and sell cotton as well as other products that could be collected in bulk. Under wise management it would seem that the plans of the exchange so far were not unsound. In fact, it is reported that large profits were saved to the farmers. It was the next step that brought ruin to the undertaking.

It was found that many of the cotton growers mortgaged their prospective crops to the merchants in the spring in order to secure the necessary funds with which to do the planting. This practice placed the cotton under the control of the merchant and foiled the scheme to sell all alliance cotton through the alliance exchange. Undaunted, Macune now proceeded to extend the necessary credit and virtually carried the Exchange into the field of banking. Notes were taken from farmers and submitted to the state Exchange through the county business agent, who was to see to it that all such notes were properly secured. The Exchange accepted notes aggregating about $400,000. This was an obligation on its part to furnish merchandise to the farmers during the spring and summer so as to allow them to continue their farming operations. Its total paid-in capital was only $56,000, while the building in course of construction was to cost $35,000, leaving a balance of $21,-000 with which to buy the $400,000 worth of merchandise. An attempt was made to borrow the necessary money at the bank, but inasmuch as the security behind the notes was not known to the bankers and also because the Exchange was new and without an established reputation the notes had to be posted at a collateral value of only 40 per cent of their face value. This meant that only 40 per cent of the $400,000 plus a portion of the $21,000 not needed for expenses was available for advancing merchandise to the farmers. The plan therefore necessarily failed. The incident illustrates the importance of cheap credit to the farmer, and reminds us that since that day much has been accomplished toward realizing it. The Federal Land Bank system as constituted in the rural credits act of 1923 will in time provide the necessary credit that the farmers in Texas and elsewhere in the country in 1887 were trying to secure by strictly cooperative effort.

The Sub-Treasury Plan of Extending Credit.—From the state-exchange plan of extending credit to the farmers it was only a step to a plan under which the federal government would establish in each county throughout all states where as much as $500,000 worth of farm products was annually offered for sale a sub-treasury office and all the necessary warehouses to house farm products on which credit would be desired. After the failure of the credit function of the state exchange a monetary committee, headed by Doctor Macune, brought forward the new government plan for extending credit. Altogether apart from the farmers' need of ready and cheap credit it served the purpose of directing the attention of the people away from the failure of the exchange to a new object of organization, and thus served as a stimulus to continued effort.

The plan proposed the establishment of government warehouses for the housing of all farm products including wheat, corn, oats, barley, rye, rice, tobacco, cotton, wool, and sugar. It was to be the duty of the warehouseman to examine and classify all products and to issue certificates of deposit to their owners who were to receive as much as 80 per cent of their value in government currency. The owner could then take advantage of the best price and sell the certificates of deposit, receiving the difference between the sale price and the amount advanced to him; while the latter amount would be a prior lien on the goods and would be paid to the sub-treasury. The plan included charging one pér cent interest for advancing the money and a small fee for handling, storage and insurance. The counties were to donate the land and the government was to provide the buildings which were to be fireproof and in every way satisfactory. The great obstacle in the way of extending a warehouse system at that time to all farm products on which credit could be given, was the absence of well established grades. This obstacle has since been removed inasmuch as virtually all farm products are now graded. It is proper to call attention here to the service rendered by the United States Department of Agriculture in this connection, a full discussion of which is given in the chapter dealing with the Bureau of Agricultural Economics. It should also be said that credit based on the farmer's products and demanded by the alliance in 1889, is now available to him under the Warehouse Act passed in 1917 under which the United States Department of Agriculture licences warehousemen and authorizes them to receive, weigh and grade his products, and issue therefor warehouse receipts which the owner may use as collateral to borrow money. Thus he is able to sell at a time when prices seem to him most satisfactory. The plan provided for under the act requires the full cooperation of the farmers if it is to be generally introduced. The warehouse feature *per se* advocated by the alliance was not unsound, but the ideas of currency associated with it were wrong. One is reminded of the recent monetary proposal of Mr. Edison, which was virtually in all details similar to the Alliance proposal.

The principle of storing goods during the season of plenty and holding them for sale during the season of scarcity is a valuable service to society. Somebody in our economic organization has to do this. The reason that private initiative is willing to perform this service is because an opportunity is seen to buy when prices are low and sell when they are high. It is referred to as speculation and, therefore, often erroneously condemned. The middlemen in the past have seized this opportunity, while the farmer unable to secure either warehouse space or cheap credit had to sell during the season of plenty when prices were low. It would seem that if any group in society has a right to this increment of value of farm products due to holding them from the season of plenty to the season of scarcity, it is the farmer. It must be acknowledged that whoever does it performs a service to society and has a right to demand compensation for his labor and the risk involved. There should be equal privileges for all groups. Our warehouse and credit systems should make it possible for the farmer to hold his crops if he so desires. The farmers have had a real complaint here and only after ample short-term credit facilities are provided will they be in position to take full advantage of the opportunity that should be theirs. But, as is so often the case, they wanted to change the situation by the use of an erroneous monetary system.

The Alliance on Currency.—The alliance theory of prices was wholly based on the quantity of money in circulation throughout the year. The price depression during the season of plenty was the result of a consciously arranged system by the middlemen and bankers, and was caused not by a change in the ratio between supply and demand but wholly by a change in the ratio of goods to money in circulation. Economists recognize that money stringency causes great inconvenience and often assumes the proportions of panics at a time when there is an over-expansion of business. An inflexible currency system in a country whose needs for currency are subject to violent fluctuations is a great evil and should be corrected. That the price can be held exactly level, however, from one season to another by the issue of a large quantity of money during the harvest season and its withdrawal during the season of scarcity is well-nigh impossible, and is so crude a plan as to encourage an unhealthy expansion of business and ultimately result in violent price changes and general business failures. The primary cause for low prices in the season of plenty, accentuated before the days of adequate storage, is a change in the ratio between supply and demand, and this fact was not recognized by the alliance leaders.

In view of the sag of prices during the harvest season the alliance demanded in conection with its warehouse system that the government issue paper money based on silver or the silver itself, during the late summer months, and withdraw it when the crop-moving season has passed. To carry out this scheme the alliance favored "the free and unlimited coinage of silver, or the issue of silver certificates against an unlimited deposit of bullion."[1] This was a part of the so-called St. Louis platform adopted in 1889 and again adopted the following year at Ocala. The St. Louis platform included also "the abolition of the national banks" because these were thought to be especially instrumental in shaping money policies so as to depress prices during harvest time. Fractional paper currency was to be issued by the government so as to provide a means for making exchanges through the mail. As stated in connection with the Grange attitude on the question of the free coinage of silver, a bimetallic standard of curency is impracticable and the stand on the silver issue, therefore, was wrong, not to mention the alliance scheme of equalizing the price of farm products throughout the year by changing the quantity of money in circulation from time to time through governmental initiative.

The Alliance Attitude on Private Property.—The alliance stood clearly for the institution of private property with the exception of "the means of communication and transportation" which according to the St. Louis platform of 1889 were to be "owned and operated in the interest of the people, as is the United States postal system." At the next year's convention its attitude was somewhat moderated. It then favored strict governmental control of railroads as a first remedy; and if regulation fails to correct abuses, then government ownership and operation were to be undertaken.

With respect to land the feeling of the Alliance was that the settler should be given full possession. Lands in the possession of railroads and other corporations were to be made available for the people. Moreover, land owned by foreign syndicates and aliens was to be secured for use of the Ameri-

[1] *Vide* Dunning, *op. cit.*, pp. 122-130.

can settler. Opposition to alien ownership of land was constantly voiced by the Alliance and has also been advocated by the Grange. With respect to private property in general, and especially in farms, it is to be expected that an organization of farmers would strongly favor it.

The Labor Compact.—As already stated, the alliance regarded the status of the farmer very largely as that of a laborer. The economic interests of the two classes were at first not at all distinguished, and in its later history only vaguely. The vision of organized agriculture of today has been clarified by recent developments, and joint action with the American Federation of Labor is now refused on the ground that interests are not mutual. In 1889, however, the alliance, consistent with its traditional sympathy, entered into the following agreement with the Knights of Labor:

> The undersigned committee representing the Knights of Labor, having read the demands of the National Farmers' Alliance and Industrial Union, which are embodied in this agreement, hereby indorse the same on behalf of the Knights of Labor, and for the purpose of giving practical effect to the demands herein set forth, the legislative committees of both organizations will act in concert before Congress for the purpose of securing the enactment of laws in harmony with the demands mutually agreed.[1]

The demands mutually agreed upon were as follows:

1. The abolition of the national banks and the establishment of the sub-treasury system having power to issue government currency as needed.
2. Prohibition of dealing in futures of "all agricultural and mechanical" products.
3. Free coinage of silver.
4. Abolition of alien ownership of land.
5. Making land held by large corporations available to settler.
6. Taxation, national or state, was not to be used to build up one interest or class at the expense of the other.
7. Revenue of state and nation to be limited to expenses.
8. Issue of fractional paper currency to facilitate exchange through the mail.
9. Government ownership of railroads and means of communication.

The Drift Into Politics.—From the beginning to its convention at Ocala, Florida, held in 1890, leaders persistently at-

[1] *Vide* Dunning, *op. cit.*, p. 122.

tempted to steer the Alliance away from partisan politics. At the convention in 1888 Doctor Macune said: "Let the Order be the great school of truth, in which, by a thorough exchange of ideas, all may be truly educated. Let it be agreed that great principles shall be indorsed. Leave partisanship to the individual, but study and discuss political economy as a class and arrive at true conclusions. There need be no apprehension as to what will be the partisan policy of any people who believe and think alike, from enlightened understanding of the same subject." This then was to be the policy of the Alliance, which in theory was similar to that of the Grange. It was, however, less able than the Grange to enforce the principle because of its heterogeneous membership brought together by a series of consolidations.

The particular event that seems to have turned the alliance toward the idea of a third party was its political success in the fall of 1890. The wide area covered by the organization gave it large powers. The application of the principle of supporting the candidate who favored the "St. Louis demands" was so successfully carried out in Kansas and to a lesser degree in other middle western states as well as in the South, that about fifteen independent candidates were elected to Congress. The event strongly suggested the formation of a farmers' party or one that could be supported also by organized labor. This political success came in the fall of 1890 and the Ocala convention met in December of the same year. Doctor Macune, who had steadfastly preached the doctrine of "non-partisan politics" now found himself wavering. He stated that the South favored adherence to the old principle, while the West and Northwest thought the Order would retrograde unless sanction to the third-party plan were given. As a compromise to the western demand he suggested that a convention of organized agriculture and labor be held with a view to adopting joint demands for use under the old method, but if it should be the sense of such a convention that a third party be organized "it need not be feared."

A Complete Disintegration of the Alliance.—The next Alliance convention was held in May, 1891, at Cincinnati. It was a gathering of about 1,500 delegates of which 407 were from Kansas, 317 from Ohio, and 100 from Illinois, showing that the delegates from the South were in the minority.[1] The leaders protested as usual to avoid the formation of a third party, or at least to defer action until a year later. This opposition, however, "was brushed aside and the party was lauched with a platform." The planks of the platform, President McVey says, were as follows: "Free coinage of silver, abolition of national banks, loans on land and real estate, subtreasuries, income tax, plenty of paper money, government control of railroads, election of President, Vice-President and Senators by direct vote, non-ownership of land by foreigners, revenue of the state and nation limited to expenses, eight hours' work, and universal suffrage." The adoption of the eight-hour plank was not accomplished without objection. The farmers objected on the ground that they often work as long as "sixteen hours and never less than twelve." However, the Alliance had now launched upon a third party and if it would secure the support of the labor group the eight-hour plank would have to be adopted as a compromise. This seems to be the first reminder to the Alliance constituency that the economic interests of organized labor and agriculture are not identical.

At the February meeting of 1892, again held in St. Louis, a preliminary national committee, with power to call a national convention for the nomination of candidates for President and Vice-President, was selected. There was a contest between the southern and northern delegates for the control of the convention, which finally ended with victory to the northern faction. A platform was again adopted. The People's Party was now well under way and the alliance organization was being rapidly disintegrated and transformed into a third political party.[2] The measures advocated by the alliance and the People's Party were not all unsound. Some of them have since then been fully accepted. Universal suffrage and popular election of senators are examples. The eight-hour day in many

---

[1] *Vide* McVey, *The Populist Movement*, pp. 138-9, on the Cincinnati convention; also subsequent pages for the development of the People's party.

[2] For a study of the People's Party, the reader is referred to McVey, *Populist Movement*.

industries has been accepted. While the particular method of providing cheap credit for the farmer was unsound, the grievance was a real one and is now being solved in a different and scientific way. While the movement has, therefore, in some cases been ill-advised, and while mistakes could have been avoided to a large extent if expert knowledge had been sought on such matters as finance, it nevertheless resulted in bringing real grievances to the attention of the public and causing a scientific solution for them all to be evolved.

SELECTED REFERENCES

Periam, *Authoritative History of the Farmers' Movement;* Dunning, *Farmers' Alliance History;* Butterfield in *Bailey's Cyclopedia of American Agriculture*, Vol. IV, p. 296; McVey, *The Populist Movement;* Chamberlain, *The Farmers' Alliance and Other Political Parties;* Morgan, *History of the Wheel and Alliance.*

CHAPTER XIX

THE FARMERS' UNION

Origin of the Farmers' Union.—The Grange had made a good beginning in organizing the farmers of the South, but, after 1875 along with the general decline of the order this part of the country lost very heavily, leaving a freer field for a new order, the Farmers' Alliance, to start the process of organization again, extend itself rapidly throughout the whole southern and middle-western territory, and finally exterminate completely the Grange throughout the length and breadth of the Gulf States. The rapid and extensive development of the Alliance was even more marvelous than that of the Grange; and if the decline of the Grange in its reactionary period may be thought of as a debacle, the end of the Alliance must be recorded as a precipitous and thoroughgoing disaster, destroying every vestige of the order and leaving only memories of what it might have been if only correct policies of organization had been adhered to. For the second time, therefore, the southern field, as well as part of the Middle-West, was without a farmers' organization and awaiting a new movement.

The third movement to organize the farmers of the South was begun in 1902 at the little town of Point, Texas, under the leadership of Mr. Newt. Gresham. Mr. Gresham was one of the official relics of the Alliance. He had been an organizer in the old order,[1] and must, therefore, be recognized as the connecting link between the Farmers' Alliance and the Farmers' Union. There were ten men in the original group of organizers, all of whom were farmers. Mr. Gresham was also the editor of a newspaper. The order soon spread rapidly into other communities. Organizers were early sent out to meet the demands for the establishment of local unions. They were sent to Arkansas, Oklahoma, Mississippi, Indian Territory, Louisiana, Alabama, and Georgia. In 1903 the order was established in Louisiana, Georgia, Arkansas, and Oklahoma, and by 1905 a national organization was effected with representation from

[1] *Vide* C. S. Barrett, *The Mission, History, and Times of the Farmers' Union*, p. 180.

state unions in Texas, Arkansas, Oklahoma, Georgia, and Louisana.[1]

The name selected for the organization has never been changed. Its full name is the Farmers' Educational and Cooperative Union of America. Long names are usually abbreviated, and in this case it soon became customary to refer to the organization as the Farmers' Union. It is apparent that the Farmers' Union copied much from the Alliance. Under the circumstances it could not be different. In the preceding chapter it was pointed out that the Farmers' Alliance of Texas consolidated with the Farmers' Union of Louisiana under the name of National Farmers' Alliance and Cooperative Union of America. In the selection of a name for the new organization the use of the word "alliance," an appellation in bad repute and at the time still fresh in the minds of the people, was wisely avoided, but the other terms at one time or other used by the Alliance were heavily drawn upon.

Development of the Farmers' Union.—The average annual membership of the Farmers' Union for the three-year period, 1908-10, was 121,826, while for the three-year period, 1917-19, it was 140,066.[2] This shows a gain in the latter period over the membership of the early days. Compared with the Grange, whose membership in 1919 was more than 500,000, the Farmers' Union is only medium-sized. It is, however, a virile organization in the West to-day and is doing a great deal of good among the farmers.

Rapid growth during the first years of a farmers' organization when "joining" is a novelty and when great hopes for the realization of benefits from organization are anticipated, followed by a reactionary period when people become indifferent and when they learn that even organization can not accomplish the impossible, are always aspects of large organizations. The membership of the Farmers' Union as a whole does not indicate that the order is suffering from such reaction. If, however, an analysis is made with respect to regions or groups of states this dread reaction is clearly portrayed to be gnawing at the vitals of the order in those parts of the country where it was first

[1] *Vide* Fisher's *Farmer's Union*, p. 15.
[2] Computed by Fisher. *Vide* his *Farmers' Union*, p. 15.

organized. It is important that leaders of the Union, or of any organization, inform themselves as to the question of regional status, for it is only through an analysis of the situation that steps may be taken to bolster up the sections that are falling behind and in the end save the entire organization from ruin. Such an analysis of the Farmers' Union has been made by Mr. C. B. Fisher in his *Farmers' Union*.[1] The changing conditions are expressed in terms of dues paid by local unions to the national body. For the South-Central group of states, the section in which the Union originated, the dues paid in 1908 were more than $13,000, but from this time on the amount gradually diminished and fell to a little more than $2,000 in 1919. In the South-Atlantic group, the region that was early invaded by Union organizers, the dues paid to the national body had risen to $7,000 in 1911, but here too was a gradual diminution until the amount fell to just above $2,000 in 1919. The Pacific-Coast states likewise showed great activity in 1909, that year paying more than $3,000, but like the southern groups a gradual decline is registered until only $767 was paid in 1919. In the North-Central group, comprising the states of Illinois, Indiana, Iowa, Minnesota, Missouri, and Ohio, the movement has been somewhat erratic. Almost $2,000 was paid in 1909 after which there was a fall to a little more than $600. Several spasmodic recoveries followed. In 1917 all previous records were exceeded when more than $5,000 was paid in. In 1919 it dropped to a little more than $2,500. It is in the Western group, comprising the states of Colorado, Kansas, Montana, Nebraska, New Mexico, North Dakota, South Dakota, and Wyoming, where the greatest virility of the order at the present time is exhibited. In this section of the country progress of organization was for some years slow, but after 1913 it proceeded very rapidly. In 1908 it paid less than $900 and from this time on the amount increased steadily to more than $4,000 in 1914. In 1915 it jumped to $10,000, and in 1919 to $13,000, or about the same amount that the South-Central group paid in 1908. In the following statement the amounts of dues paid by the various groups of states are shown for four different years; and these

[1] Pages 13 and 14.

in a measure show the rapid growth and subsequent reaction as well as the recent recovery in each district, and, therefore, also the geographic distribution of the present strength of the order:

Year	*South-Atlantic*	*North-Central*	*South-Central*	*Western*	*Pacific*
1909	$4,061.16	$1,608.74	$13,702.38	$885.23	$1,324.69
1912	7,004.84	809.24	8,493.75	1,084.70	1,176.36
1919	2,194.48	2,692.45	2,307.31	13,050.49	767.10
1921	4,517.47	3,847.27	7,933.43	18,944.23	1,145.37

Thus the analysis shows that the South-Atlantic group needs the attention of organizers, although considerable improvement has been effected recently. The North-Central group is about holding its own, but symptoms are not lacking that a revival of activity could effect considerable improvement. The South-Central group very plainly shows the effects of a strong reaction, and this district, more than any other, is in need of encouragement; yet, as is the case with all districts, a very substantial increase in dues is registered for 1921.

The Western group is in its period of prosperity, and if a reaction is to beset this territory it has not yet become visible. In fact there seems to be a very healthy growth in this district. The Pacific group suffered a strong decline, but has recovered nearly all it had lost. For the good of the order it would seem that the efforts of organizers and financial resources of the Union should be concentrated upon the sections of the country showing defection; on the other hand to keep a farmers' organization organized it is necessary to engage in a never-ending program of education even in the most promising sections. Mr. Barrett, President of the Farmers' Union, at various places in his history of the Union refers to the difficulties involved in organizing farmers on a sane and permanent basis. A continuous, vigorous, and sound educational program, devoid of all impossible aspirations and mistakes in economic theory, will without a doubt in time bring the majority of the farmers into one or more farmers' organizations that will keep organized.

General Character of Organization.—The general plan of organization of the Farmers' Union is shown in the accompanying chart. It is very similar to that of the Grange and other farmers' organizations. The national organization is a delegate body made up of representatives from state unions in the proportion of one delegate to each state union having a member-

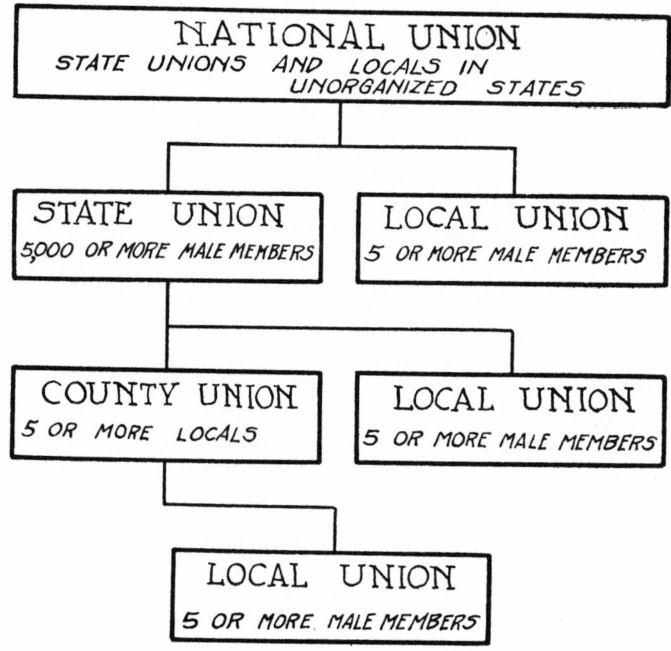

ship of 1,000 to 5,000 and one additional delegate for each additional 5,000 members or major portion thereof. The national officers and members of the board of directors are *ex-officio* members of the national body.

The national constitution provides that before a state union may be organized there must be at least 5,000 male members in the state. Its charter, or authority for organization, is issued by the National body, but rules and regulations as to dues and membership of lower bodies are left to the state union, provided there is no conflict with the provisions of the national constitution.

Local unions must have at least five prospective members before a union may be organized. In a state having a state union, charters to the locals and county bodies are issued by it, otherwise the charter is issued by the national body. The fee for organizing the local union is not less than $15, which is the same as that of the Grange.

Like its two predecessors the Farmers' Union has found it convenient to organize county unions. Five or more locals may form a county union.

The officers of the national body are: President, vice-president, secretary-treasurer and a board of directors.

The Farmers' Union started out with the secret feature which was rigidly controlled and enforced among all local bodies by the national organization from its beginning to 1914. There was, however, dissatisfaction expressed with respect to the secret work prior to that year, and in 1913 a one-hundred dollar prize was offered for a more acceptable ritual. However, in 1914, the national union yielded its authority to prescribe its form, and the states of Nebraska and Kentucky were allowed to devise a ritual to suit their own needs. This meant lack of uniformity throughout the organization, and served as a first step toward a partial abandonment of secret work. It is well known that some religious teachings oppose the use of secret work in organizations. There are also a great many people opposed to it because it fosters aristocracy. A few are opposed to it because they see in it nothing but sham. With all the flourishing secret orders in existence to-day it is a question whether the rank and file can be held as closely in an open farmers' organization as in a secret one. However, the steps toward an open organization had been taken, and in 1917 an amendment to omit the work of the ritual was offered at the national convention. Democratic and religious arguments in favor of such omission were made, and its elimination finally effected by a vote of 24 to 15. A business manual was drafted and adopted in place of the ritual. The Union, however, still allows states to use the ritual where it is desired.[1]

Conditions of Membership.—"Any white person or Indian may be admitted to membership, if of sound mind, over the age of 16 years, of industrious habits, believes in a Supreme Being, is of good moral character, and if a farmer, country mechanic, school teacher, physician or minister of the gospel, and not engaged in any of the following occupations, to-wit: Banking, Merchandising, Practicing Law, or belonging to any trust or combine" engaged in speculating in agricultural products. The mere holding of bank stock does not exclude one from being eligible to membership. In reading these membership qualifications one is reminded of their similarity to those of the Farmers' Alliance adopted at the 1890 convention. The selection of persons is from the country, and may include teachers, preachers, doctors, and editors. The Union admits also city editors providing they pledge themselves to support the order in the columns of their papers. A banker, merchant, and lawyer are construed to have at no time interests in common with the farmer and they must therefore be excluded. Whether the farmers' relationship with respect to the banker and lawyer, and with respect to a large number of merchants as well, is properly contrasted with his relationship to the teacher, preacher, and doctor, is questionable. From the point of view of common interests it would seem much more logical to exclude all persons not directly interested in agriculture. From the point of view of providing social attractions it is of course well to admit the best country talent, but all other activities such as agricultural education and cooperative enterprise do not directly interest those not engaged in agricultural pursuits.

Women are admitted to membership in the local, county, and state unions, and may even be elected delegates to the national body. Women and men are on an absolute equality in the union except that women do not pay dues.

Income and Expenses of the National Body.—Like that of

[1] W. C. Lansdon, Organizer, in a personal communication.

other farmers' organizations, the most important source of income of the National is the dues paid by members of local unions. From 1908 to 1919 the amount of dues varied from $15,500 which was paid in 1913 to $24,500, paid in 1917. For many years the dues per member paid for the support of the National were 16 cents. In 1919, however, the amount was raised to 25 cents. This probably was a wise step, not only because of the rise of the general price level necessitating a greater outlay in the way of expenses, but also because the Union has not yet built up a reserve of any consequence which in times of slumps becomes available for running expenses, or which could be used to put up a headquarters building. The Farmers' Union like the Grange is also anxious to erect a "temple of agriculture" at Washington. Taking the financial statement of the National body for 1917 when the dues amounted to as much as $24,500 the following summary of receipts and disbursements and cash on hand may be shown:[1]

Receipts

Total amount of dues	$24,579.84
Fees from charters issued	662.50
From miscellaneous sources	259.17
Total receipts	$25,501.51

Disbursements

Cost of 1916 meeting:	
Delegates' expenses, etc.	$3,746.05
President's Department:	
Salary ($3,000), transportation, etc.	5,886.40
Secretary-Treasurer's Department:	
Salary ($1,800), transportation, etc.	3,360.59
Board of Directors' Department:	
Per diem, transportation, etc.	2,486.58
Official Organ Department:	
Mailing to National Field Subscribers	401.95
National Business Agent	257.20
Organizing Department:	
Expenses of four organizers	2,639.92
Vice-President's Department	275.55
Cost of mailing constitutional amendment	98.75
Printing and miscellaneous expenses	1,299.72
Total Disbursements	$20,459.71

[1] From annual Report.

Recapitulation

To total receipts	$25,501.51	
To balance in treasury last year	6,231.50	
By total disbursements		$20,452.71
By cash on hand		11,280.30
	$31,733.01	$31,733.01

The statement shows the receipts for 1917 to have amounted to 25,501.51 and the disbursements to $20,459.71. There was, therefore, a gain of over $5,000 for the year and altogether there was a balance on hand amounting to $11,-280.30. By 1920 the balance on hand had increased to more than $20,000. This is of course considerably smaller than the Grange resources whose total reserve in 1919 was $107,008.36. The salaries paid out by the Farmers' Union are not at all exorbitant. The president received only $3,000 and expenses, and the Secretary-Treasurer, $1,800 and expenses in 1917. In 1919 salaries were increased to $4,000 for the President, and $2,500 for the Secretary-Treasurer. Organizers are also only moderately paid. It takes a peculiar fitness to organize farmers' organizations and to serve them successfully in an official capacity. Leaders should be intelligent and well trained with respect to economic, social, and technical agricultural questions. They should have unflagging enthusiasm, be untiring in their efforts and have a deep love and sympathy for the agricultural class Such men are difficult to find and must, therefore, be well paid.

Federation of Farmers' Organizations.—In a study of the Alliance it is noted that consolidation and confederation were important means of expanding that organization. The Farmers' Union, it appears, was going to use similar methods to enlarge itself and extend its influence. Consistent with this policy the convention of 1910 discussed the proposal that a combination with the American Society of Equity be effected. The report of a committee on consolidation favored the union of the two organizations, and the board of directors proposed such combination to the officials of the Society of Equity. For some reason the union was not accomplished.

In 1915 Mr. Barrett, President of the Farmers' Union, appointed Mr. C. H. Gustafson to study the problem of uniting all farmers' organizations with a view to unifying demands of organized agriculture to be made upon Congress. As a result of this initiative, the Master of the Grange and the President of the American Society of Equity met in a conference with the Union official to formulate a rural credits bill and another on federal standardization, inspection and grading of farm products. Out of this original conference grew the plan to federate all societies for legislative or propaganda purposes. The various organizations have not always been in unison on legislative demands made upon Congress, and it is, therefore, well to digest and crystallize thoroughly all legislative projects in which farmers generally are interested. This can only be done through unity of action among organizations. The efficiency of the plan must necessarily have considerable influence upon Congress. As previously stated, the National Grange has not joined the plan of associating itself with the National Board of Farm Organizations, but instead is supporting its own representative at Washington who is cooperating freely in all matters with which the Board is concerned. The Pennsylvania State Grange, however, is a member of the Board. Under this plan of federation, developed largely through the efforts of the Farmers' Union, organized agriculture can stand united in legislative demands, and with respect to organization policies each association can follow its own traditional customs and strictly maintain its own identity.

General Objects of Organization.—In the preamble to the first constitution the general objects of the Farmers' Union are stated as follows: "Speculators and those engaged in the distribution of farm products have organized and operate to the great detriment of the farming class." Organization among the farmers, it is stated, is therefore necessary to protect their interests. This was later revised and the preamble as it stands today reads as follows:

> In the course of modern industrial development we find it necessary that the farmer not only apply the principles of scientific agriculture, but that he systematize his business by cooperation and apply the principles of scientific commerce.
>
> Expensive and wasteful methods of exchange have been a constant drain on the farming class, and speculation has been allowed

to demoralize markets and prevent the normal operation of the law of supply and demand.

It will be noticed that the revision discloses a more intelligent understanding of market conditions. The first statement seemed to lay the blame for all evils growing out of the present market organization upon the shoulders of the urban speculator and merchant, while the latter suggests that a remedy for the situation may be found through a reorganization of the market undertaken by the farmers themselves. Following the preamble there are a number of "purposes" as follows:

1. To secure equity, establish justice and apply the Golden Rule.
2. To discourage the credit and mortgage system.
3. To assist our members in buying and selling.
4. To educate the agricultural classes in scientific farming.
5. To teach farmers the classification of crops, domestic economy and the process of marketing.
6. To systematize methods of production and distribution.
7. To eliminate gambling in farm products by Boards of Trade, Cotton Exchanges and other speculators.
8. To bring farming up to the standard of other industries and business enterprises.
9. To secure and maintain profitable and uniform prices for cotton, grain, live stock and other products of the farm.
10. To strive for harmony and good will among all mankind and brotherly love among ourselves.
11. To garner the tears of the distressed, the blood of martyrs, the laugh of innocent childhood, the sweat of honest labor, and the virtue of a happy home as the brightest jewels known.

It is clearly recognized that these "purposes" are an offspring of those of the Farmers' Alliance. Number 10, for instance is copied virtually verbatim from the "purposes" of the Union's predecessor. Number 1, embodies the idea of "equal rights to all and special favors to none" adopted also by the Alliance. The most striking relation to the Alliance's "purposes," however, appears in number 11. To express this sentiment the Alliance said: "The brightest jewels which it garners are the tears of the windows and orphans," etc.

To sum up in a fundamental way these objects of organization it may be said that the Union recognizes happiness and self-respect as the chief goal of organized effort. The importance of scientific agricultural education is duly acknowledged but a scientific study of market organization with a view to reconstruct it in such a way as to give greater advantage to the farmer is considered equally important. Happiness, self-respect, and social standing are to come through the two-fold means of agricultural education and control of the market organization, the former lightening the burden of production, the latter increasing the farmers' share of the distribution of wealth.

Educational and Social Activities.—The Farmers' Union has been active in creating a favorable educational sentiment throughout the country. This is an important function. In many rural districts it is still possible to find families with good intellects who are indifferent to education. It is not uncommon to hear that this or that family does not believe in education. Most states have compulsory education laws, and the children of such families are compelled to attend school a certain percentage of the school year. This fact will in time operate to create a favorable sentiment for progress in education. In the immediate present, however, the educational training and, therefore, the future welfare of the children who are now of school age, depend upon the attitude of adult citizens of the community, county and state. The shaping of this attitude toward education is, therefore, of vital importance, and the Farmers' Union proposes to play its role in the movement.

The Union favors the construction of better school houses, the consolidation of schools, the building of rural high schools, and the extension of the time of attending school beyond the age of 14 years. They demand also a right to determine the course of study that the famrers' children shall take. Such a course is to include agriculture. For agricultural colleges they demand that marketing and rural economics be taught.

In the annual report of 1917[1] there is a strong arraignment against present-day influences that control our public school system. The report says that "we permit teachers' associations to direct the course of our school system and propose school laws, even as commercial clubs and chambers of commerce have in the past managed our business and manipulated our legislation. Our children have sought more learn-

[1] *Vide*, p. 32.

ing and others have fixed the course they should study. Commercialism has dominated all. Our homes have been broken up, our children scattered, our plans disorganized, and our occupation has become a drudgery." There is a good deal of truth in the statement that the course of study in rural districts has not been formulated to meet the needs of the farmer. The same year (1917) that this report of the committee of education was adopted by the Farmers' Union the Smith-Hughes act was passed by Congress providing for the teaching of agricultural education in the rural high school and community. Certainly up to 1917 the course of study provided for the boys and girls who for various reasons do not enter college, failed to meet the needs of our agricultural population.

As was stated in the chapters dealing with the Smith-Hughes act and the Land-Grant colleges, considerable opposition against the introduction of agricultural education has been manifested on the part of that group of educators concerned only with cultural education. Of course it is the duty of the state to provide an educational system that will prepare every citizen for some gainful occupation or profession. This much can and must be done toward the removal of poverty. There is some warrant for the criticism directed at "teachers' associations" by the Farmers' Union. Their vision concerning present-day needs of agricultural and industrial life has been befogged by too much medieval atmosphere. On the other hand there are always progressive elements in all groups of society and it is to progressive educators that farmers should look to solve their problems instead of making the condemnation general. The educator who specializes in the principles of education, if he has at the same time a sympathetic attitude toward practical education, should be consulted by the farmers instead of brushing all this expert knowledge and experience aside under the guise of a general accusation that all are opposed to the introduction of practical courses of study and that the entire system is thoroughly and completely dominated by commercialism. As a matter of fact a strong arraignment can be made against the farmer for not taking greater interest in educational problems. For many years the consolidation movement, now well under way, for instance, has been preached to the farmers, and the response was at first very niggardly. The accusation, therefore, that "teachers' associations" and "commercialism" are the enemies of the agricultural community and are to be wholly blamed for the lack of educational advantages in rural districts is altogether too sweeping and not fair. The farmer's lack of interest, his indifference, in many instances his opposition, are probably as much to blame as anything for the inequalities of educational advantages between city and country. Physical conditions of the rural environment have always been a handicap; but with the general use of the automobile truck the consolidation school can be made very successful, and the physical disabilities can therefore be largely overcome. For the permanent good of the organization it would seem that sensational charges had better not be made. Hard, honest and never-ceasing propaganda in the long run accomplishes both the objects sought and at the same time promotes the growth of the order.

The high schools of the country should provide all types of education, the practical as well as the cultural, so that the country boys and girls may prepare themselves for that field of endeavor for which nature has especially endowed them. Such opportunity should be opened to youth everywhere and the Farmers' Union according to its program is in accord with a plan that provides these advantages.

In 1911 the board of directors called attention to the loss of membership experienced in some states, and at this convention efforts were made to devise ways and means of stimulating greater intellectual and social interest in local Union meetings. As a means of accomplishing this end it was decided to appoint a committee to draw up a set of topics suitable for discussion and which were to be made available for the use of all local Unions. The practice has since been continued, and is serving a useful purpose in as much as the Union under the plan gives opportunity to the community to express itself in a profitable and entertaining manner.

The Union and Political Representation.—Like the Grange, the Farmers' Alliance while it lasted, and the American Federation of Labor, the Farmers' Union does not believe in going into partisian politics. It believes in supporting a candidate who is favorable to agricultural interests, and at various times it has expressed itself in favor of constituting legislatures and Congress on the basis of proportional representation of occupational groups. Mr. Barrett says: "Every corporation and big business of every description is today in politics. You cannot point me to a single industry in this country, save that of the farmer, which has not accredited representatives in Congress and in the large conventions that meet to determine party nominees every two or every four years."[1] Among the items of a legislative program formulated and adopted by the convention of 1919, there is the definite statement that the Farmers' Union favors "proportional representation based on occupational groups.[2] In the report for the same year an analysis of members of Congress according to occupation together with a proposed proportion of representation is shown.

Table Showing Occupational Representation in Congress as Constituted in 1919, and Occupational Representation, Proportionate to the Number Engaged in the Occupation, as Proposed by the Farmers' Union.

Occupation of Members	*Constitution of 1919 Congress*	*The Union's Proposed Constitution*
Agriculture	18	165
Mechanical		140
Transportation	5	33
Professional	454	

[1] *Vide* his *History of the Farmers' Union*, p. 45.

[2] It is denied by some that this principle has ever been really an organization policy.

Occupation of Members	*Constitution of 1919 Congress*	*The Union's Proposed Constitution*
Law	323	
Business	44	
Journalists	28	
Educators	17	
Manufacturers	17	
Bankers	15	20
Medical	5	
Labor Organizers	2	
Hatters	2	
Iron Moulder	1	
Trade		50
Domestic Service		50
Clerical		25
Mining		15
Politicians	54	

This proposal is unsound for several reasons. In the first place it is well-nigh impossible to erect a system of electing candidates by occupational groups. It would cause all manner of confusion on election day. In the second place it is wholly undesirable. In order that representatives may successfully perform the function of enacting into law the voice of the people they must have a certain type of education. In connection with the discussion of the Grange it was stated that the educational content most important for the legislator is law, economics, and social science. It is, therefore, not surprising that law is most largely represented in Congress. The lawyer has a knowledge of our political institutions and usually has the ability to present public questions to the people and his colleagues in legislative halls. On the other hand the educational preparation of men in the trades, of farmers, and businessmen is usually altogether too limited and not of the right sort. Such men can fit themselves to serve as representatives, but their occupation has a tendency to make this impossible. As Fisher points out "no trust nor corporation wants to be represented by an 'oil man,' a 'meat man,' an 'implement man,' a 'steel man,' etc."[1]

There is a great lack of social vision on the part of many of our representatives. They do not recognize the needs of the agricultural class as they should. Many of them are grossly ignorant as to the specific needs of all economic groups of our social structure. Their isolated environment and one-sided educational training are responsible for this viewpoint, but it is a matter that can only be remedied through an intelligent and vigilant use of the ballot.

The only way that any economic group may secure the desired representation in legislative assemblies is through the election of leaders who have both the necessary training and class sympathy required to make themselves felt as important factors among their colleagues. If they fail to exert their influence for the cause for which they were elected, the only remedy is a removal from office through the exercise of the ballot. This is sound doctrine, and the one upon which the Farmers' Union should concentrate its efforts. The efforts of influencing legislation while it is in the making, now undertaken by the National Board of Farm Organizations of which the Union is a conspicuous member, is effective and is a method that is to be commended; but representation based on occupational groups is impracticable, wrong in principle, and should be dropped from the legislative demands of the Farmers' Union.

The Farmers' Union on Credit.—The Farmers' Union was one of the strong advocates of a rural credits bill, and in 1916 when the Federal Land Bank act was under consideration by Congress representatives were on hand to press the demands of the Union. They wanted loans to run as high as 80 per cent. of the purchase price of land, and the interest was not to be more than 4 per cent. The law as enacted allows loans equal to 50 per cent. of the value of the land and equal to 20 per cent.

[1] *Vide* his *Farmers' Union*, p. 57.

of the value of permanent insured improvements. The law also provides that the interest rate charged the farmer may not be more than 6 per cent. In normal times 80 per cent. would leave a safe margin, but during the violent price changes of the European war it would have probably involved the credit system in considerable loss if it had been in full operation. The interest rate of 4 per cent. for agricultural long-term credit in normal times is not at all impossible and should be aimed at by organized agriculture. The cooperative credit associations in Europe do even better than this, and in the United States the Jewish Agricultural and Industrial Aid Society has been for years making loans to Jewish farmers at 4 per cent on a ten-year basis. A reduction of the interest rate, however, requires cooperation and local supervision of the expenditure of the sum borrowed. A local committee must pass upon whether or not the applicant for a loan should engage in the proposed enterprise, for instance, if the demand is for short term credit, the purchase of steers to be fattened for the market; and the supervision must extend to the fattening process to see that no loss is likely to come to the credit association. As Henry Wallace points out lower interest rates for credit requires local supervision and supervision will take away the farmers' independence with respect to the operation of his farm.[1] It is a question whether the farmer is willing to surrender his independence for lower interest rates.

When times are normal and under circumstances that do not contemplate the creation of an artificial demand such as the use of bonds as security for note issue the United States Government can issue bonds at par at a rate of about 4 per cent. This means that under favorable economic conditions the Federal Land Banks may sell bonds with the guaranty of the Government and extend long-term credit to the farmer at a fraction above 4 per cent. The excess above 4 per cent would have to be sufficiently large to pay expenses of operation. An excess of ½ per cent. might be large enough so that the loan to the farmer would have to be at least 4½ per cent. But even if it were 5 per cent. the farmer would be getting funds at rates

[1] *Vide* article in Moulton's *Money and Banking*, Part II, p. 392.

far below those he has been compelled to pay in some sections of the United States up to the present. It appears therefore that the demand of the Farmers' Union, that the rural credit act provide "4 per cent. money with easy payments to encourage home ownership," was slightly beyond what may be accomplished in the near future with this kind of a rural credit system.

The Farmers' Union was opposed to loaning money through associations and stood for loaning direct to the farmer. In the interest of safety, which means also lower interest rates, the association plan is a good one. Greater supervision over the objects for which money is borrowed and over the borrowers themselves may in this way be exercised. This, however, means less independence, and the preference of the Farmers' Union should be given some weight with respect to this matter in the framing of a rural credits bill. In the report of the Federal Farm Loan Board for 1921 it is recommended that the Federal Land Banks be allowed to make loans direct to individuals when the interests of the community are not properly served by a Farm Loan Association or when there is no association. Thus it appears that the Union's demand as tested by experience was entirely proper.

With respect to short-term credit the Union in 1919 demanded that the "Federal Reserve Banks make loans on insured farm products in bonded warehouses on the same basis as to member banks." This would be asking a much greater advantage than is accorded to manufacturing and commerce, and, therefore, falls into the class of special privilege. It can not be allowed unless it be conceded that agriculture operates under sufficient handicap, as compared with industry and commerce, to be entitled to such advantage. That it does operate at a considerable disadvantage, especially with respect to credit, is pointed out more fully in the final chapter.

At a meeting of the Farmers' Union held at Washington in April, 1921, a report on comparative credit extension was drawn up by a committee of which Mr. E. L. Harrison, President of the Kentucky State Union, was chairman, and which was printed in the Congressional Record at the request of Representative J. Campbell Cantrill. In this report the charge is made that of the total Federal Reserve rediscounts for the year, agriculture received 14 per cent; manufacturing, 21 per cent; merchandising, 26 per cent; and speculation and miscellaneous, 39 per cent. The report recommends that speculation be denied any credit whatever. As stated in previous chapters, the economist does not agree with this point of view for the reason that it can never be wholly separated from the usual necessary buying and at the same time maintain a free and open market. In the absence of price regulation it is everywhere recognized that dealing in future socializes prices and forecasts them for a considerable time in advance, a function which is of great service to society. There are other good services rendered society through the free operation of organized markets. However, it is unquestionably true that too much of the available credit of the country has been allowed to flow into speculative channels. Banks could curtail the amount so used, and make more of it available for use in agriculture. Assuming that the above figures expressing the ratio of credit received by the various economic groups are substantially correct, agriculture should have fared much better. It is a tremendous advantage in the matter of acquiring wealth to be able to secure credit at the right time and in proper amounts. Fortunes are made buying and selling real estate, agricultural and other commodities, and corporate securities with credit received from banks. The practice of speculating, it does not seem, can be wholly controlled so as to make such profits impossible and yet not injure business. When, however, a group of individuals are given undue advantage to make such profits and others are denied the privilege there exist gross inequalities of opportunity, and this again is certainly not in accord with our fundamental principles of democracy. The thing to do then is to make credit available for all classes alike; and if any favoritism should be shown, it should be on the side of the farmer because of the natural disabilities, such as weather, isolation, etc., under which he is forced to operate.

Of course the particular way in which this is accomplished is exceedingly important. The very best currency that any nation has yet provided is associated with the commercial bank having a specie reserve sufficiently large to maintain specie payments on demand, but basing its note issue and check currency very largely on short-term paper whose liquidation is virtually guaranteed. The Federal Reserve system was founded on this principle, and while paper originating in industrial and commercial transactions is limited to 90 days—and no hardship is occasioned thereby because in these fields there are frequent turnovers—notes drawn by persons engaged in agriculture or in the live stock industry may run for six months.[1] This was in the nature of a concession made to agriculture at the time the bill was drafted and was said not to be in accord with the principle that a bank furnishing currency to the country should have only short-term and self-liquidating assets such as a draft that comes into being at the time of the purchase of a bill of goods and is paid at the time of sale. The latter form of bank asset is regarded as *par excellence* and should make up a large part of a commercial bank's assets upon which the country's currency is to be based. This is correct theory underlying an elastic note issue. On the other hand the farmer must have credit and it is well known that in actual practice numerous extensions of credit are made whose character differs in no way from the note and its security offered by the farmer. If it is found that the allotment of a larger percentage of credit available under the Federal Reserve system to the farmers endangers the currency system and the ability of the banks to maintain specie payments, then it is necessary to organize a banking system for the special purpose of financing short-term agricultural paper. The Farmers' Union has favored "a cooperative banking code, both state and national, which enables the farmers to deposit their money under their own control and themselves decide how their surplus shall be allotted to other lines of business."

After the crop is grown, graded, and placed in warehouses it becomes considerably easier to secure credit. Full support given the Federal Warehouse act would secure cheaper credit to the farmer after the crop is grown and enable him to sell at the most advantageous price. The rural credit act passed by Congress in the Spring of 1923 in response to the

[1] In 1923 the time was increased to nine months.

demands of organized agriculture will provide further facilities and will probably remove in large part the disabilities under which the farmers as a class secured credit in the past.

In its report of 1921, above referred to, the Union charges that deflation caused great losses to farmers. This is true, but the Federal Reserve Board should not be blamed for such losses. The decline in prices was inevitable and the policy of restricting loans which the Board especially applied to speculative enterprises prevented a still higher rise and started the downward trend under conditions that avoided a disastrous panic. The policy of restricting loans was inaugurated none too soon, for some of the Federal Reserve banks were for a considerable length of time below the legal reserve minimum.

The Union and Organized Labor.—The Farmers' Union seems to have inherited its viewpoint with respect to organized labor from the Farmers' Alliance. It was stated in a previous chapter that the Grange refused an invitation from Mr. Gompers to participate in a conference with the American Federation of Labor on the ground that such participation would be a tacit admission that the interests of organized agriculture and organized labor were mutual. The Grange in recent years has taken the attitude that the interests of the two groups are not mutual. The Farmers' Alliance, it was stated, was always extremely sympathetic toward labor. It received fraternal labor delegates at its conventions, entered into an agreement to support jointly certain legislative measures, and finally together organized a third party which proved to be the undoing of both the Farmers' Alliance and the Knights of Labor. The Farmers' Union has in part followed the practice of its predecessor. It has for years received labor representatives at its annual conventions, and has at times wired greetings to the conventions of the American Federation of Labor.

At the annual convention of 1910 a "Committee on Closer Relations with Organized Labor" pointed out alleged common ground between labor and agriculture, and in order to improve the conditions of each the farmers were urged to buy whenever possible only such goods that bear the "union label." This would be evidence that goods were made by unionized labor and, therefore, by labor receiving satisfactory wages and working under proper conditions. If carried far enough it would, it was hoped, unionize all labor and improve labor conditions everywhere. In the report of 1921 the Farmers' Union states the relation of organized agriculture to organized labor as follows: "The farmer is both a producer and a consumer. The laborer is both a producer and a consumer. Each is the principal customer of the products of the other." Society is a complex organism and it is true that the welfare of the laborer means also the welfare of the farmer. The chain of causation, however, runs the other way. Large crops and the welfare of the farmers causes greater manufacturing activity, the movement of a larger freight tonnage, greater commercial and financial activity, and an increase in business generally, resulting in better wages for organized labor. Large crops place the farmers in position to buy the products of labor and capital, and this sets the wheels of industry in motion, puts men to work, and ultimately raises the wages of organized labor. The completion of the cycle means a stronger demand for all agricultural products and therefore better prices. It must not be forgotten that the products purchased by the farmers, including transportation service, farm implements, automobiles, etc., are the joint product of capital and labor. Both must be paid for their services, and both will produce only when there is a market and an opportunity to make all expenses of production, including at least some profit. As pointed out previously, the relationship is closer between capital and labor than between labor and agriculture. Signs are not lacking that all groups are beginning to adopt a compromising attitude toward one another; but before cooperation between the groups will have proceeded to the point where no strife or discord will be heard, labor will have aligned itself with capital and they together will negotiate with agriculture.

The Farmers' Union and Private Property.—In 1919 the Union favored "government ownership or control of all natural resources, including minerals, oil, coal, phosphate, lime, building stone, timber and water power, to the end that both the public and the workers be protected." The Union took quite an advanced position in this instance concerning private property. There is no inconsistency in advocating government ownership in these natural resources and not in land. Conditions of production surrounding the two fields are wholly different. As to land there is so much greater productivity under conditions of private property, while with respect to natural resources the amount produced annually is a matter subordinate to the problem of exploitation or conservation. The future generations must be protected. The conditions of labor may also demand a different status in the field of natural resources, and it is not unlikely that its close relationship with labor influenced the Union to take this advanced position concerning private property.

In 1917 the State Union of Colorado asked the state legislature to declare sugar factories, coal mines, and stockyards to be public utilities so as to be enabled to regulate them. As time goes on and more and more industries become centralized the field of public utilities steadily grows larger. For some time we have regarded the railroads, street railways, municipal gas and electric light plants, and water works to fall in this class and, therefore, as vested with a large public interest. Only this year has Congress passed the "packers' bill" which aims to regulate the packing industry under the assumption that it too is virtually a public utility. The addition of coal mines and sugar factories to the list is again an advanced position, but no one may say at this time that some day they will not be so classified.

With respect to land the Union wants "an absolute limitation of ownership." It is opposed to large holdings. "Co-operate ownership of land, not necessary for the conduct of business," is to be prohibited, and the country is to be rid of its tenancy problem through the imposition of a progressive tax on absentee landlordism. These are all very good reforms and tend to increase production as well as maintain a social order in the country that is stable and interested in rural and other progressive movements. The Union would do well to urge strongly the adoption of these reforms, and is to be commended for its efforts to bring them about. They are so important that it is virtually proper to say that their general introduction lies at the bottom of all social improvements throughout rural districts. A shifting tenant class and a landlord continually absent from the community can not be counted upon to join farmers' organizations or to back any progressive undertaking such as cooperative marketing, better schools, better roads, etc.

Taxation has a definite relation to property and it may be stated here that the Union has declared itself in favor of the principle of "ability to pay as the only just basis of taxation." This is of course a broad statement. It would, however, certainly include the income tax and exclude the "single tax." This basis of taxation is altogether proper. In 1921 it favored the placing of a heavier tax on profits made during the war. This is unwise because such profits have either by now found their way into investments or else they have been spent for consumption goods.

The Union and Cooperative Enterprise.—The Farmers' Union has probably fostered cooperation more and it may have actually established more cooperative enterprises than any other farmers' organization in America. This is the chief function of the Union and the one upon which it relies most to keep its organization alive. In the words of W. C. Lansdon, lecturer of the National Union, "wherever cooperative business is firmly established there our Farmers' Union is strong; wherever cooperation has been neglected or has failed through lack of knowledge, sense, or courage, the Farmers' Union is dead."[1] The Board of Directors declared in 1919 that the future success of the Union depends very largely upon the development of cooperative enterprise. This is a motive that appeals to the farmer in a special way because of expected profits. If he were more patient and willing to make personal sacrifices at times, he would patronize farmers' organizations for the purpose also of shaping legislation, the development of particular phases of agriculture, and other more distant, but important, objects. In the hope of brightening the economic status of the farmer the Union from its beginning made co-

[1] Quoted by Fisher in his *Farmers' Union*, p. 33.

operation its chief *raison d'etre,* and it is this function that has brought its greatest support.

The Farmers' Union took up cooperation where the Farmers' Alliance dropped it. The Alliance under the initiative of Dr. Macune organized a state exchange in Texas, but failed because he attempted to purchase merchandise on notes given by the farmers. He was unable to secure the necessary funds because bankers regarded these notes too poorly secured. Before the close of the Alliance's career efforts were made to establish a national business agent. The Farmers' Union recognizes the necessity of beginning the work of cooperation in a small way at first. The community is to organize itself with a view to federating with other cooperative enterprises in the county, and the county is to federate with other counties and form the state exchange. In a number of states the Union has made a real success of cooperative enterprise, showing that the failure of the past and those of the present in many sections of the country could have been successes if only proper business methods had been applied and the right kind of leadership had been available. After all is said and done successful cooperation depends upon the particular field of endeavor, upon intelligent and willing leadership, and upon the intelligence of the farmers themselves. It virtually resolves itself then into a problem of education.

The Union recommends the Rochdale principles as the basis of cooperative enterprise. The most important of these principles are a small per capita investment, one vote per member regardless of amount of stock held, the payment of the prevailing interest rate on capital invested, and the division of profits on the basis of transactions entered into by each member of the cooperative association. The plan is in accord with the usual practice of paying interest for the use of capital, and provides for buying and selling at virtually the same prices at which competitive dealers buy and sell. In this way the least possible friction is generated among dealers, and the profits of the middlemen are saved for the farmers.

The Union's plan to federate local enterprises was first definitely formulated in 1908 by C. T. Ladson of Atlanta,

Georgia, and counsel for the Union. President Barrett thought the 1,500 Farmers' Union warehouses scattered mainly throughout the South were not as successful as they ought to have been, and, therefore, took up the matter with his counsel. Mr. Ladson advised the formation of state and interstate companies to receive and house cotton for two principal reasons.[1] Warehouses operated by large responsible companies could issue warehouse receipts on which credit could be secured. This would enable the farmer to hold his cotton and sell at the most reasonable price. Of course the farmer of the South, as is well known, frequently pledges his cotton before it is grown, and if he has done this, it can not be placed in the possession of such a state company except under proper guarantees to his creditor and with his consent. Mr. Ladson's second advantage associated with state warehouse companies is closely related to the advantage of securing credit. The cotton may be sold gradually throughout the year instead of "dumping" it in the fall and thus secure better prices for the grower.

The cooperative activities fostered by the Union at various local points at one time or another include cooperative buying and selling, manufacturing, and fire, live stock and hail insurance. The undertaking in the field of manufacturing has been limited to simple processes with the exception of a few instances. They include pickle factories, flouring mills, phosphate plants, packing plants, creameries, implement factories, tobacco factories, etc. Some of these, such as the implement factories, should never have been undertaken because of their technical character. These enterprises have not always been wholly cooperative, being sometimes in the nature of a joint stock company.

Cooperative fire insurance was initiated by the officials of the Colorado State Union. On a five-year policy the premium in 1920 was $6 per $1,000 with the right reserved to assess policyholders for any large and unforeseen losses. No such assessments were ever made according to a report rendered in 1920. The total cost for the state was reported at $75,000, and it is claimed that if the insurance had been written by an

[1] *Vide* Barrett's *History*, p. 131.

old-line company it would have cost $625,000. On the basis of these figures this form of cooperation appears to be very successful. The movement is spreading to Kansas, Nebraska and other states.

The states of Kansas, Iowa, Nebraska, and also some other states are doing a very large business through state exchanges. Kansas has organized the Farmers' Union Jobbing Association. It does business with "Some 325 Farmers' Union elevators, 265 Farmers' Union stores, approximately 500 produce stations, 300 shipping associations, and 310 active organizations in the states of Kansas and western Missouri. Last year's volume of business totaled $3,000,000. This amount was more than doubled in the first ten months of 1920, in the selling of hay, grain, machinery, binding twine, coal, flour, feed, wheat, salt, vegetables, fruit, ropes, fertilizer, and general merchandise."[1]

Thus the Farmers' Union stands today among other farmers' organizations of America as one of the greatest agencies for propagating the movement of cooperative enterprise. It looks as though the permanent and substantial success of the cooperative enterprise conducted by the California Fruit Growers' Exchange is to be duplicated in the grain, tobacco, and cotton states of the country. This can be accomplished through a persistent and rational educational campaign conducted by organized agriculture. In this campaign the Farmers' Union is playing a conspicuous role.

SELECTED REFERENCES

Annual Reports of the Farmers' Union; Barrett, *The Mission, History and Times of the Farmers' Union;* Fisher, *The Farmers' Union.*

[1] *Vide Minutes of National Union* for 1920, p. 8.

CHAPTER XX

THE AMERICAN FARM BUREAU FEDERATION.

Origin of the Farm Bureau.—The first farm bureau in the United States was organized in Broome County, New York, through the initiative of the Binghamton Chamber of Commerce which was interested in developing and maintaining a wholesome agricultural status in the territory contiguous to its own city. It was recognized that the trade of the city was very largely dependent upon the farming population surrounding the city and that the economic welfare of the nearby country districts meant also in a measure prosperity to the urban population. The man who realized this relationship between city and country sufficiently to bring about definite action on the part of the Binghamton Chamber of Commerce was Byers H. Gitchell, then secretary of that organization.[1] The Chamber of Commerce appointed a committee on agriculture which made a tour of Broome and other counties. The Committee was accompanied by representatives from the New York State College of Agriculture, the New York State Department of Agriculture and the United States Department of Agriculture. Later when the development of agriculture was discussed at a meeting of the Chamber of Commerce George A. Cullen, who was traffic manager of the Lackawanna Railroad, showed great interest in the plan and pledged the aid of his road to the undertaking. The railroads have for years taken a keen interest in "keeping people in business," for the amount of freight hauled and therefore the amount of the revenue is directly dependent upon production and trade. It was therefore natural that the Lackawanna Railroad should be willing to become an active partner in the rejuvenation of the declining agriculture.

When the discussion proceeded to the point where definite plans had to be devised expert aid was sought. The committee of the Chamber of Commerce favored the demonstration farm and this idea was proposed to Doctor Spillman, then of

[1] *Vide The Farm Bureau Movement* by O. M. Kile, p. 94.

the United States Department of Agriculture. But Doctor Spillman explained to them that a demonstration farm serving as an object lesson in a community did not take hold of the people, and instead recommended the county demonstration plan which Dr. Knapp had introduced and which was working out very satisfactorily in the southern states. The Committee believed that Doctor Spillman's suggestion was the one to adopt and proceeded to raise funds for the employment of a county agent and to start the work. The Binghamton Chamber of Commerce, the Lackawanna Railroad, and the Department of Agriculture jointly contributed to the enterprise. "John H. Barron, a graduate of the state agricultural college, was engaged as county agent, who began his work on March 20, 1911."[1] A few days previously, he had received his appointment from the United States Department of Agriculture and was, therefore, acting in the capacity of its representative.

Mr. Barron soon made close contact with the people in the various communities. He selected community chairmen as the first step in the development of local organization. He also enlisted the aid of existing organizations such as the Grange. While this first farm bureau was different from the character of the organization of the present-day farm bureau, it must be regarded as the first organization of its kind in as much as it had a regularly appointed county agent and a "local governing, consulting, and cooperating body."

At this stage of the development the farm-bureau movement was still potential or unborn. That is to say, the aims and purposes of those interested in helping agriculture were all educational. The objective of these early efforts was to organize in every community a group of farmers who would with great precision "demonstrate" on their own farms principles which had for years been known to those familiar with the literature of scientific agriculture. In other words the farm bureau movement as it is known today had to wait until the agricultural cooperative extension service, discussed in a previous chapter, had become widely established. The organizing of the extension service was done by public officials rep-

[1] Kile, *The Farm Bureau Movement*, p. 96.

resenting the United States Department of Agriculture and the State College of Agriculture. As explained Doctor Knapp, representing the Department of Agriculture, may be regarded as the promoter of the new form of extension service. Before the passage of the Smith-Lever Act in 1914 the United States Department of Agriculture laid the foundations of the work, and after the passage of the act all the colleges began active campaigns to propagate the extension service throughout the States. What was done in Broome County, New York, therefore was merely the planting of a seed that bore fruit later in a way wholly unexpected by the officials of the Department or by any of the other parties who took part in preparing the soil for its growth.

Among the first states to seek the support of the farmers locally, says Mr. Kile, was West Virginia. The farmers were asked to take a membership in a farm bureau and pay a fee of one dollar. Officers were elected, and the bureau after it was launched was to extend itself by soliciting more members. In this way funds were provided for the employment of the county agent. New York state organized about the same time in a similar manner. Some states passed laws allowing county courts or county boards to appropriate sums of money for the use of farm-bureau work. New York passed such a law in 1912 and the Broome County Board made an appropriation of $1,000 for this purpose. The plan of having the farm bureau made up of a large and widely scattered membership proved so successful in New York and elsewhere that the Broome County bureau changed its form of organization to the membership basis in 1914.

Rapid Development Under Public Initiative.—Most of the states in the East and Middle West as well as a few of the far western states rapidly adopted the farm-bureau form of organization for the purpose of cooperating with the extension forces. In this development of farm bureaus the colleges and the federal Department took an active part. Document 65 explaining the organization of a model farm bureau was published by the States Relations Service. The European War added great fury to the efforts of the extension forces. Referring to the part these two institutions played, C. E. Gunnels in a speech delivered in 1920, at which time he was still connected with the Department, made the following statement:

Why did the Federal and State Governments develop such an organization? Why didn't they cooperate in extension work directly with the Grange in counties where the Grange is strong, or with the Farmers' Union in counties where the Union is strong, or with the Equity, where the Equity is strong? The reason is simple enough. Practically all of these are secret organizations, or class organizations, or commercial organizations. In a considerable degree they are exclusive organizations, and since the work of the Federal and State Governments is financed by all the people, these institutions felt the necessity of developing a non-class, non-secret, non-commercial, and permanent institution open to all the farmers in the county and through which all could find expression, and could deal directly and in an organized way with the State colleges and the Federal Department of Agriculture.

Besides, none of the farmers' organizations with which the Department was acquainted had been developed with the idea of extension work in mind, and the agents of the Government hesitated to take up work with them, or propose work to them which would necessarily involve a redirection of their organization, to say nothing of their jealousies which might have been created by apparent favoritism in the selection of one organization in preference to another.

Types of Farm Bureaus.—As explained in the chapter dealing with the cooperative extension service the farm bureau varied considerably in the character of its organization in the various states. Reference was made to Document 65 of the States Relations Service which suggested a desirable form of organization.[1] There were four principal types. (1) One of the most successful forms of organization has a widely scattered and representative membership paying a fee of from one to ten dollars, an executive committee, and an advisory council elected or appointed meeting usually monthly to consult with the county agent. One frequently finds these forms incorporated. (2) Another form of organization has a central body made up of delegates from local groups of farmers. (3) Another form has its central body made up of delegates elected by more or less well established farmers' organizations, such as Granges, Farmers' Unions, Gleaners, the Equity and Farmers' Clubs. This amounted to forming a federation committee

[1] The reader is referred to the Chapter dealing with the extension service for a more detailed discussion of the forms of organization and their operation.

which serves more in the capacity of an advisory council than as a body having plenary power. The real power lies with the local associations. (4) Still another form brings together clubs having no affiliation with state or national farmers' organizations. In the South the county council was for some time the common form of organization. It was made up of a select group of men from communities of the county and divided into subcommittees, "each one charged with a clearly defined share of the agricultural work of the county, and each one representative in that it includes a leading citizen from every district or beat."[1] "In a few cases the county board of commissioners or supervisors constituted the central organization, and in a few others an agricultural committee of a local chamber of commerce has been a cooperating body."[2]

The Seat of Control of the Farm Bureau.—The Smith-Lever funds are provided jointly by the federal government and the state, county or local group of people. The county agent's salary and other extension expenses are paid, at least partially, out of these funds. The agent is a public employee, representing both the Department of Agriculture and the state agricultural colleges. Control, according to Doctor Bailey, depends very largely upon the source of the funds. "Administration follows funds," he says; and he has in mind only extension and not commercial activities. "If the Farm Bureaus establish themselves and become more effective, the appropriation of local funds will gradually and prominently increase. This will more and more place the control of the Farm Bureau in the hands of the people, for they will manage it from among themselves."[3] On the other hand Doctor True insists that the system is a tri-party cooperative scheme and the question of control should never arise in extension work. So far as extension operations alone are concerned there is probably little trouble over the question of control. However, it has been found that the most successful local organizations are the ones with a representative membership enjoying the right to determine in a measure the activities that are to be followed.

[1] *Vide The Demonstration Work* by O. B. Martin, p. 123.
[2] *The Farm Bureau Movement* by O. M. Kile, p. 90.
[3] From *The Farm Bureau Movement* by Kile, p. 103.

Objects of Organization.—It has been made plain both in the discussion of this chapter and in the one dealing with the agricultural cooperative extension work that the first object for which the farm bureau was organized was providing ways and means for cooperating with the colleges and the United States Department of Agriculture in making demonstrations directly on the farms throughout the country. The first object then was entirely educational. The Department officials, however, started a movement that was not to be confined to educational activities alone. Farmers are not satisfied with the kind of education that merely looks towards increasing the yield of the product, or that acquaints them with certain conveniences, or beautifies the home and brings to them a measure of culture. These things are appreciated in the main, but they want more than this. One speaker, prominent in the circles of a well established farmers' organization, in referring to the efforts of our public agricultural institutions to improve conditions made the statement that they everlastingly want to give us "doses of education." There are some things to which the farmers as a class have a legitimate right to aspire that education will not bring about. It takes organization for commercial purposes. In other words cooperative organization along commodity lines is necessary to help give the farmer his share of the distribution of wealth. But even commodity organization is not enough to give him his just due. The world's economic and social organization is complex and is very greatly affected by legislation relating to the tariff, railroads, monopolies, roads, schools, etc. To give the farming population a voice in the state and federal councils commensurate with its size it must be organized on a wide scale. This has been the vision of leading farmers in the United States since before the Civil War. Efforts were made that resulted in "groundswells" which soon subdivided. In other cases results were more enduring. In the light of the history of the American farmer it is only natural that he should use the farm bureau for purposes other than as an agency to cooperate with the extension forces.

After the farm bureau was organized and busily engaged

in demonstration projects, the most natural thing for them to do was to talk over the question as to how they could order fertilizers in carload lots so as to reduce freight rates and save the major portion of the middle-man's profits. From fertilizers it was but a step to feed, salt, coal and other supplies that could be bought cooperatively. Likewise the selling of their grain, live stock, dairy and poultry products, etc., cooperatively was in due course given attention in a number of places. It followed therefore that the farmers soon "tacked on" to the farm bureau as an object of organization the policy of buying and selling cooperatively.

Formation of State Federations.—It is suggested by Mr. Kile that the idea of state organization grew out of the practice of inviting county farm-bureau presidents to attend conferences held annually at the state agricultural colleges in a number of states. "The state extension forces," he says, "were quick to realize that a state federation of the county farm bureaus would provide a powerful influence in securing liberal appropriations from the legislatures for further extension work."[1] In New York the county bureaus federated in 1917. Vice-Director of Extension, M. C. Burritt, then State Leader of County Agents, played the leading role in effecting the federation. There were at the time thirty-nine active county farm bureaus, thirty-four of which sent delegates to the state meeting. In January of the same year Mr. N. T. Frame, State Leader of County Agents in West Virginia, called a meeting of delegates from the different county bureaus which appointed an organization committee and instructed it to report the following year. In January 1918, the West Virginia County bureaus also federated and a number of states soon effected similar organizations.

The Formation of a National Federation.—On February 12, 1919, only two years after the organization of the first state federation, representatives of twelve states met at Ithaca at the call of the New York federation for the purpose of discussing the formation of a national farm-bureau federation.[2] Only

[1] *The Farm Bureau Movement*, p. 111.
[2] *Vide The Farm Bureau Movement* by Kile, Chapter IX.

nine states had actually federated associations at this time but the other states represented were engaged in the process of federation.

Up to this stage of organization it appears that the point of view of the educational leaders was still the dominant motive that actuated those interested in the formation of a national farm-bureau federation. President Strivings of the New York State Federation stated the objects of such an organization to be as follows:

(1) To provide the nation with some sane organization thoroughly representative of agriculture throughout the entire United States, which might speak for the farmers of the entire country.

(2) To take advantage of a nation wide organization—the Farm Bureau—which promises great possibilities of usefulness in developing a program which will reach the entire country and which will bring into action the strongest farmers of the nation.

A representative of the States Relations service, Mr. C. B. Smith, was present and urged that efforts be made to get real local associations established in every county in as much as only 800 counties at the most had farm bureaus and not more than 400 of which functioned properly.

It was decided to call a meeting at Chicago on November 12th and 13th of the same year for the purpose of perfecting the national organization. In the meantime campaigns were to be instituted looking toward the federation of unorganized states. Between this and the fall meetings the discussion as to the aims and purposes of the national organization moved toward a business and class-propaganda program. This sentiment came from the Middle West, while other sections of the country still held to the educational idea as the primary function of the organization.

These two ideas clashed when the convention met in Chicago. "Five hundred delegates and visitors were in attendance, 220 of whom were from Illinois." One delegate from each state was finally seated regardless of the farm-bureau membership in the respective states.[1] The business point of

[1] *Vide Farm Bureau Movement, op. cit.*

view was presented by Harvey J. Sconce, president of the Illinois federation. A portion of his remarks follows:

> The great idea should be to keep control of our food products until they get much closer to the ultimate consumer than they do at the present time, thereby not only returning to us a profit on the article produced, but serving humanity in a more efficient manner by giving the consumer an article of quality at no increased cost.

Mr. S. L. Strivings, president of the New York federation, held more nearly to the educational function, while Mr. J. R. Howard, president of the Iowa federation, took a middle ground. There was also great difference on the question of the amount of dues that should be paid to the national organization, because its revenues would necessarily have to be determined with reference to its functions. If its aims and purposes were to be educational primarily then ten-cent dues would be ample; if it were to engage in a national cooperative enterprise, vigorously foster organization and maintain capable legislative representatives at Washington, the dues would have to be considerably larger. There was danger of bolting the convention and in view of the conflicting opinions it was decided to defer final organization until March 3, 1920, when the constitution was to be ratified.

The hopes of the Middle-Western delegates and others from this section of the country who had expected that the organization meeting would speedily result in the establishment of a nation-wide business organization for the sale of farm products and possibly the purchase of supplies as well as for the fostering of favorable legislation, met with sore disappointment.

At the ratification meeting the representation had changed somewhat and the delegates all felt the necessity of getting to work and perfecting the organization. As a consequence a more conciliatory attitude was taken and the feeling that the business function should be one of the dominant policies of the federation prevailed. The name chosen for the national organization is The American Farm Bureau Federation.

Details of Organization.—The membership of the national federation as stated in the constitution consists of "state farm bureau federations and state agricultural associations based on the farm bureau or similar plan when approved by the executive committee of the organization.''

A board of directors is provided for and is composed of members elected by the respective state federations which meet for this purpose once every year. Each qualified state is entitled to one director and one additional for every 20,000, or major portion thereof, of paid-up members of the county organizations which are affiliated with the state organizations. The only qualification of the director provided for by the constitution is that he must be a practical farmer, which means that the formulation of the policies of the federation will be largely determined not so much from the point of view of agricultural education but rather from the point of view of the interest of the farming class itself. Each director has one vote.

The officers, including the president, vice-president and the executive committee, but not the secretary and treasurer, are elected by the directors. The secretary and treasurer are elected by the executive committee. Elections are held every year. Any officer or director of the federation who becomes a candidate for a state or federal office shall at once resign and be automatically dropped from his official position of the American Farm Bureau Federation. This provision makes it difficult for a Farm Bureau official to ''ride'' into a political office on the strength of his popularity as a servant of the farmers.

A ''house of delegates'' is provided for and consists of delegates of the members of the federation. As stated the membership of the federation is made up of state federations or of associated state agricultural societies organized on the farm-bureau plan or in a manner meeting the approval of the executive committee. Membership in the national federation consists then of these organizations and not of individuals. Each such member sends one delegate to the house of delegates and one additional for every 10,000 farmers of the state, or major portion thereof. These delegates sit with the directors and have the same privileges as directors except the right to vote.

Annual meetings are held and special meetings of the board of directors may be called by the president with the approval of the executive committee.

The annual dues, after some changes, have been fixed at fifty cents per local member. That is for every individual who is a member of a local farm bureau, fifty cents is paid into the treasury of the American Farm Bureau Federation. This is about five times the national dues of the Grange and Farmers' Union.

The federation started out with the policy of getting expert servants to perform its functions. High-grade men can only be secured when large salaries are paid. The president's salary was placed at $15,000; and the secretary's and the Washington representative's salaries, at $12,000 each. Members of the executive committee, the vice-president and treasurer are to be paid not more than $10 *per diem* while attending to the business of the organization. Mileage is also paid. J. R. Howard was selected president; J. W. Coverdale, secretary; and Gray Silver, Washington representative.

Aims and Purposes.—At the meeting of March 3, when the national organization was finally effected, Henry C. Wallace, editor of *Wallace's Farmer,* and later appointed Secretary of Agriculture by President Harding, said: "This federation must get to work at once on a real business program if it is to justify its existence."[1] The objects of the federation as stated in the constitution are "to correlate and strengthen the state farm bureaus and similar state organizations of the several states in the national federation, to promote, protect and represent the business, economic, social and educational interests of the farmers of the nation, and to develop agriculture." It is to be noted that the business and economic functions are mentioned first and that education, the purpose for which the local farm bureau was originally organized, is given a secondary position. It is also to be noted that in the declaration of its purposes the Federation broke new ground with re-

[1] From Kile's *Farm Bureau Movement,* p. 123.

spect to phraseology. The terminology used and in part the sentiment expressed in the declarations of the old farmers' organizations were discarded, indicating that new, and probably better trained, leadership, was bestirring itself. The attitude of the Federation toward various current problems is registered in its annual reports and its legislative programs, the latter containing resolutions passed by the executive committee in conference with representatives of State Farm Bureau Federations.

The Federation at Work.—To carry out the aims and purposes of the Federation, departments were created, each performing a special set of functions. The Organization Department was authorized "to assist any and all states" in membership campaigns. Special field men were employed for the purpose. The Information Department engages in publicity work. *The Weekly News Letter* is sent to all county farm bureaus as well as to various officials of the State and national federations. The Department also secures publicity of Farm Bureau activities through the daily press and magazines. A very creditable feature is the Department of Research which aims to study in a scientific way problems of economic interest to the farmers. This is indeed highly commendable. It is the kind of thing that chambers of commerce and manufacturers' associations have done for years. The importance of the employment of expert business statisticians has long been recognized in the fields of industry and commerce. Organized labor has also recently come to recognize the value of the plan. Other departments have been created including the Legislative, which represents the Federation's interests at Washington by bringing to the attention of Congress and individual members the needs of agriculture and requesting favorable legislation; the Legal Department, which draws up contracts and renders various legal services in connection with bills proposed to Congress and the enforcement of laws in which organized agriculture is especially interested, as well as in other ways; the Transportation Department, which aims to improve facilities of transportation and seeks to have freight rates reduced so as to bring them into harmony with other prices; the Department of Cooperative Marketing, which has been very active in establishing state-wide and nation-wide commodity selling associations; and the Finance and Administration Departments which perform administrative functions and take an active part in all matters of importance.[1]

Cooperative Enterprise.—Almost from the start the county organizations began to develop cooperative buying associations to handle the purchase of fertilizers, coal, salt and other supplies. In Franklin County, Ohio, the orders for supplies are pooled and placed with certain merchants who handle them at an agreed commission which is frequently half of what they customarily receive.[2]

Carload lots are ordered and a saving secured on freight charges. Negotiations with manufacturers result in securing special prices. Altogether there is a very considerable saving effected by the members of this farm bureau.

The state federations are primarily interested in the creation of selling associations. A fundamental principle to be observed in cooperative marketing is that selling associations must be organized along commodity lines. The Ohio Farm Bureau Federation follows this principle in detail. Its plan of organization comprises a grain growers' association which owns and operates local elevators and markets the grain for the state. An advisory committee made up of members of this association, the Grange, and the Ohio Farm Bureau Federation, coordinates the marketing efforts of the two farmers' associations. It is also planned to develop similar associations for the sale of wool, live stock, fruit and vegetables, and dairy products. Federations of other states are also planning to organize for the purpose of selling the products of their members.

The largest cooperative scheme that has ever been attempted is the creation of the United States Grain Growers, Inc., organized under the initiative of The American Farm Bureau Federation for the purpose of marketing the major

[1] For further details of organization the reader is referred to annual reports.

[2] *Vide*, Kile, *The Farm Bureau Movement*, pp. 141-146.

portion of the grain produced in the United States. At the time of the organization of the American Farm Bureau Federation there were marketing associations some of which were state-wide while others operated in several states. These were fostered by other farmers' organizations each of which had aspirations of seeing the child of its creation develop into a national selling association. For instance, "the Farmers Union of Nebraska had just claims to preferential treatment because of its broad and successful experience in pure, farmers' cooperative grain handling. The national Wheat Growers Association with headquarters at Wichita laid claim to the control of the bulk of the wheat of Kansas and Oklahoma. The Equity Cooperative Exchange of Minnesota and the Dakotas had developed a big business at St. Paul. The Missouri Farmers' Clubs owned a large percentage of the cooperative elevators in that state and, its officers at least, had very little use for the farm bureau which they considered an active rival. The Farmers National Grain Dealers' Association centering around Chicago, owned through its members a large number of elevators, and had national aspirations. The Non-partisan League also had its own idea as to how grain should be handled."[1] Thus there were already a number of cooperative grain-selling associations doing a big business, but there was no coordination among them. At the call of the American Farm Bureau Federation 500 men representing cooperative grain selling associations, Farmers' Unions, State Granges, Societies of Equity, etc., met at Chicago, July 23 and 24, 1920, to consider the feasibility of organizing a national grain-selling association. This action, it will be recalled, was in line with the sentiment prevailing at the March organization meeting. In view of the existing, rival selling associations and because of the differences of opinion as to the plan to be used by the proposed national selling association it was necessary to study the question before final action could be taken. President Howard of the Federation was instructed to appoint a committee of seventeen to make a thorough investigation and to recommend a form of organization. In the appointment of

[1] *Vide*, Kile, *op. cit.*, p. 149.

this Committee due consideration had to be given to the aspirations of rival farmers' organizations, and the bringing of harmony into the situation was not accomplished without considerable difficulty. The committee studied cooperative associations in California and Canada and consulted grain and financial experts, including Julius Barnes, Bernard M. Baruch, and others. The Committee of Seventeen finally completed its labors and agreed upon a plan which was to be ratified at a convention on April 6, 1921.

As finally ratified the plan proposed that a national sales agency was to be organized under the name of the United States Grain Growers, Inc., and that membership is to be limited to grain growers who pay a ten-dollar entrance fee and sign a contract to sell their grain for a period of five years through certain specified ways which would result in placing it ultimately under the control of the national sales agency. The plan further provides to use local cooperative associations already in operation, and where none exists to organize them and build elevators as speedily as possible. Cooperation between the local elevator companies and the national sales agency is effected by means of a contract. The contract with the individual grower provides that he may sell individually for a cash price offered by the local elevator company or consign through the elevator company to the national sales agency. Under the latter plan the "control of time of delivery, shipment, and sale remain with the grower." Or he may use the pooling method. In this case the local elevator may store the grain or the grain may be shipped to an elevator controlled by the national sales agency. The pool decides when the grain shall be sold. Advances of from fifty to seventy-five per cent of the value of the grain may be paid to the grower. "The national sales association acts, for the most part, like a commission house. It receives grain, sells it, or, on request, stores it. Certain pools are managed by it."[1] The question of compulsory pooling was considered by the convention but the idea was abandoned on the ground that the organization might be

[1] Hibbard, *Marketing Agricultural Products*, p. 324.

construed to be monopolistic and for the further reason that some individuals would prefer to sell their grain separately.

It would make too long a survey to present in detail all the cooperative plans that are now in the making and which have been or are to be undertaken as a result of Farm Bureau initiative. In its annual report for 1921 the Federation gives itself credit for arousing a general cooperative spirit in the following terms:

> The most important single achievement of the Department of Cooperative Marketing, in cooperation with all the other departments of the American Farm Bureau Federation, the state farm bureau federations, the county farm bureaus, and other organizations, has been to develop a cooperative conscience in American agriculture, and in some measure to crystallize the cooperative conscience into a cooperative marketing achievement.

The commodity marketing conference first used with reference to grain has also been used with reference to live stock, dairy products, fruit, and wool. The grain and live-stock committees have reported and as a result national cooperative marketing associations have been established for these two commodities. Other committees are still at work.

The Federation on Finance.—In its legislative program for 1921 the Federation states that "recent experiences demonstrate that the farmer is not being adequately financed through the present financial system. The present short-time commercial credit jeopardizes the farmers' welfare when he avails himself of credits in this form, owing to the needs of the commercial banks in maintaining a liquid asset which is on a much shorter time basis than the production of agricultural crops." The statement shows that the Federation understands the reason why commercial banks, that is, the banks formerly organized under the National Bank Act and now under the Federal Reserve Act, are not in position satisfactorily to finance farm operations. In connection with other farmers' organizations it has been pointed out that banks enjoying the note-issue function must have a large part of their assets in liquid form. Also if the business man is to be provided with credit, there must be a large portion of the bank's assets in the form of short-term paper. In as much as the merchants and manufacturers usually have turnovers within periods running from thirty to ninety days, it follows of necessity that the bank must stand ready to extend loans at all times. The extension of credit for six months and longer is a function that differs considerably from commercial banking. Such a function if performed on a large scale by a commercial bank should either be carried on with resources more or less separated from those supporting commercial credit or be placed in a wholly separate and distinct banking system.

The Federation has sought to improve the credit facilities for the farmer through the enlargement of the powers of the Federal Land Bank System and of the War Finance Corporation.[1]
Efforts were made to establish a "Government corporation which would promulgate export trade in agricultural products and carry agricultural financial relief." These efforts resulted in granting additional powers to the existing War Finance Corporation which issues bonds on Governmental account and with the proceeds may now extend credit to co-operative organizations and to European buyers who have good securities to offer. Financial aid was also to be given banks for the purpose of holding domestic products prior to exportation and for the purpose of extending credit in anticipation of payment. Secretary Hoover gave his support to these features. For some time the Federation attempted to organize a finance corporation to be owned and operated by the farmers of the nation, but after considerable study and investigation the plan was abandoned.

In as much as the Federal Farm Loan Board has found it difficult to float its bonds at five per cent interest Congress was petitioned to allow the Board to sell bonds at a maximum rate of five and one-half per cent. A bill incorporating the idea was introduced by Senator Kenyon and enacted into law. The Federation also urged that a "revolving fund of $25,000,000" be created for the purpose of buying mortgages and use them as a basis of bond issues. This feature was also passed. The Federation also stands for direct loaning to the individual

[1] *Vide Report* of Third Annual Meeting, p. 40.

instead of through local associations. This has been recommended by the Federal Farm Loan Board to be allowed where conditions require it.

The Federation on Taxation.—In the main the Federation takes an intelligent and advanced position on taxation. It stands primarily for taxing net income in accordance with ability to pay which is the basis approved by students of the subject. This attitude is expressed in the following language:

(1) The measure of ability to pay taxes for the support of the National Government is net income, and the bulk of the taxes should be levied and collected on that basis.

(2) The tax should be progressive; that is, the greater the income, the higher the rate.

(3) As this is the country of all the people, all the people should have some part in supporting the government, and a certain part of the revenue may justly be raised by means of tariff and other consumption taxes.[1]

As this last paragraph shows the Federation believes that all citizens should contribute at least a small portion toward the support of the Government. This is a principle that is at variance with that of ability to pay. It must rest on benefit received, and the benefit theory of taxation has been discarded on the ground that benefits received from the Government are indeterminable. The Federation believes that some of the taxes may be in the form of consumption taxes, but it has gone on record as being strenuously opposed to a national sales tax.

Attitude Toward the Tariff.—With respect to the tariff the Federation's position is that for revenue purposes the tariff may in part be resorted to, and that agriculture should be given the same consideration as industry when it comes to the application of the principle of protection. In fact it asks that agriculture be given protection. The following extracts set forth its views on the tariff:

We request further that regard be had to the new economic burdens being imposed upon agriculture by high domestic transportation costs and high cost of money.

We disapprove of any plans to make agriculture the burden bearer in the rehabilitation of our commerce on the seas, by which selling abroad the products of mill, mine or factory our merchant marine may seek to load back to our shores the food products of other lands which come in direct competition with our own.

---

[1] From a pamphlet published by the Federation.

We demand the right to feed our own people at such prices as are just both to producer and consumer, always having in mind the perpetuity of our fundamental industry, the production of food.

We recognize the dangerous competition from the foreign producer, who in many cases can market his product duty free at a price so low as to be destructive to the American farmers, but when translated into money of his own country gives him a good profit. Against such competition there must be some protection.

The Federation on Transportation.—The Federation points out that following the European War prices of agricultural products declined rapidly but transportation rates remained for some time at the war level making it unprofitable to market fruit and vegetables, cattle and hogs, cotton, and grain which in some cases was used for fuel. The position is taken that freight rates must be adjusted so as to be in harmony with other prices. To make this possible wages and other operating costs must be reduced. Labor is censured for resisting the reduction of its wages. "We respectively ask," says the legislative program, "that railroad labor and railroad corporations should both share with other industries in price reductions."

With regard to highway improvement the Federation approves the plan that makes available federal funds for road building, provided these funds are matched by state and local governments. The plan, it is pointed out, has given a great impetus to road building. The Federation, however, is opposed to the building of a few trans-continental roads with such funds so long as local roads connecting the farm with the market need urgent attention.

President Howard gives strong support to the maintenance of an American merchant marine in the *Weekly News Letter* of May 25, 1922, published by the Federation. He contends that in as much as America will for years continue to be an agricultural exporting country and because the farmers are large consumers of a variety of goods, efforts should be made to provide American bottoms so as to make the American farmer independent of foreign vessels and not subject to freight rates determined by shipowners in "conference." Rates should be controlled by the United States Government in the interest of the American shipper. In his opinion there is therefore ample justification for granting ship subsidies.

The improvement and coordination of interior transportation, including rail and water facilities, should be effected so that goods may be moved with the greatest efficiency and at the lowest cost.

The Federation's Attitude Toward Labor.—The Federation properly comprehends the relation of organized agriculture to organized labor as well as to other economic groups. Note the following statements:

> We reiterate our sympathy is with the laboring man and we will do everything in our power to aid him to secure just wages and fair working conditions for efficient services rendered.
>
> We are, however, concerned in assuring orderly and lawful protection to every citizen, and we are unalterably opposed to organized strikes and sympathetic lockouts which interfere with the orderly conduct of business.
>
> We declare that the farmer is entitled to compensation for his services equal to actual cost of efficient production, and a reasonable return upon his capital invested, and we pledge our efforts to bring about these results.[1]

As already stated the Federation understands that freight rates cannot be reduced unless wages also are reduced, and that the interests of the wage-earning class are therefore not common to those of the agricultural class. The attempt to join hands with labor and thus confuse interests of the various economic classes, is an error that organized agriculture has made in the past, but which it probably will never be guilty of committing again. As a doctrine, however, the principle still finds acceptance in a limited way in some farmers' organizations. These errors of organization would tend to disappear more rapidly if throughgoing departments of research, headed by expert economists, were established more generally.

The Federation Approves the Extension Service.—One of the last items in the program to which the Indianapolis convention of 1921 pledged its support was agricultural education including extension work. "We highly commend," the program says, "the good work of the home demonstration and county agricultural agents, junior project leaders, the agricultural extension departments and the experiment stations, and

[1] *Vide Annual Report* for 1921.

we pledge our hearty cooperation to them in the furtherance of their work along practical agricultural lines, and the improvement of home and community.''

It is to be remembered that the local farm bureaus were organized for the purpose of conducting extension work and that the state and national federations grafted themselves on top of the local extension organization. The development of an organization having an extensive economic program was wholly unlooked for by the extension authorities and the necessity to separate the educational and economic functions became apparent. This matter is treated in the chapter dealing with the extension service where extracts from the memorandum of understanding signed by representatives of the Federation and the Department of Agriculture are quoted.

The Federation's Outlook.—The individual membership of the American Farm Bureau Federation in 1921 included 967,279 farmers. This membership is considerably larger than that of any other existing farmers' organization. There were that year also 1,486 county farm bureaus and 46 state farm-bureau federations showing that the organization has a territorial basis which is virtually coextensive with the territory of the entire country. In as much as the national dues per local member are fifty cents, the Federation has large resources. For 1921 its total budget amounted to $323,893. This sum is also considerably larger than the amounts that other national farmers' organizations may spend because their dues are on a ten-cent basis.

In view of these facts will it necessarily follow that the American Farm Bureau Federation will be more stable than other farmers' organizations have been? The primary function of the Federation from the start was economic. It was interested from the beginning in placing the marketing of farm products upon a nation-wide business basis. It has assumed a very generous and charitable attitude toward all farmers' organizations and has been successful in harmonizing agricultural groups with respect to cooperative marketing. If the business experiments of the Federation will succeed the chances are that its general membership will continue to be large, although this does not necessarily follow. The cooperative organizations are now being fostered by all farmers' organizations, and after they have once been properly established, that is along commodity lines, they may continue without the parent's watchful care.

It is believed by some that because it is so closely related to extension work in the local farm bureau its further growth and continued existence is guaranteed. This again in the opinion of the author does not follow. It is probably true that the local organization in the community necessary to carry on extension work fosters organization for economic purposes, but this should help all farmers' organizations. The Farm Bureau as a farmers' organization serving the class interests of the farmers can not depend upon extension funds to carry out its own objects of organization. The public will not tolerate the use of extension funds for American Farm Bureau purposes. These must be supported wholly by private funds. Whether or not the Federation will live depends upon its continued usefulness to the farmers. It must see to it that expert leadership is placed at the helm, and its policy must always be one of moderation. Whatever action it may take in the interest of its members, the influence that such action may have upon other groups of society will have to be given just consideration if the organization is to endure.

SELECTED REFERENCES

Annual Reports of the American Farm Bureau Federation; *Document 65*, U. S. States Relations Service; Kile, *The Farm Bureau Movement;* Hibbard, *Marketing Agricultural Products.*

CHAPTER XXI

MISCELLANEOUS ORGANIZATION

The American Society of Equity as Originally Organized

The Formation of the Society of Equity.—The American Society of Equity was organized on December 24, 1902, in Indiana by Mr. J. A. Everitt who is recognized as its founder. This was only a few months after the organization of the Farmers' Union which is discussed in the preceding chapter. The Farmers' Union, it was stated, followed upon the heels of the Alliance. It was organized in Texas and spread rapidly east through the Gulf states, and later into the middle-western, and north-western states. Its earliest triumph was in the South where the complete disintegration of the Alliance had left the farmers without an organization. A somewhat similar situation existed in the middle-western states at the time. The Grange suffered very seriously in this territory during the decline of the late 70's and early 80's, and its recovery was checked by the coming of the Alliance. When the Alliance broke down the middle-western field offered an opportunity for a new movement. This opportunity was seized by the founder of the American Society of Equity who advanced the idea that the principles fostered by the previous organizations were unsound while those adopted by the Society of Equity would result in a movement that would endure for all time. He said, "You now have for the first time the right plan, and are directed for the right objects. Give this society the same membership that you gave the Grange or Alliance and the work will be done now and forever. Give the members one-tenth of the benefits this society is capable of giving and they will never abandon it."[1]

The movement spread somewhat slowly at first, but by 1906 there were state organizations in Indiana, Illinois, Kentucky, Michigan, Wisconsin, Minnesota, North and South Dakota, Nebraska, Kansas, Oklahoma, Arkansas, and New York. From this spread of territory it is apparent that the

---

[1] *Vide*, Everitt, *The Third Power*, p. 243.

Society of Equity had made substantial progress within four years from the date of its origin. Divisions, however, developed due probably largely to the action of certain leaders. In 1910 the Farmers' Equity Union, said to be stronger now than the parent organization, was organized. Another branch organization is the Farmers' Society of Equity. At the present time the parent organization is strongest in Wisconsin where it has a membership of more than 40,000. It is also strong in the north-eastern part of Iowa. In addition to these two states it is organized in Minnesota, North Dakota, and Montana. It lost its hold altogether in Kentucky. In North Dakota it has suffered seriously from the rise of the Non-Partisan League and in some other states by the support given the Farm Bureau organization. In the opinion of Professor M. L. Wilson the Society of Equity for some years represented the radical thought among the famers of the North-West and "is truly the parent of the Non-Partisan League." It fought the Minneapolis Chamber of Commerce and attempted to substitute a competitive grain market of its own. In 1914 the Society had about 20,000 paid-up members in Montana and probably more than this number in North Dakota. A large part of this membership entered the Non-Partisian League and many of the leaders prominent in the Society of Equity transferred their allegiance to the League and became its most ardent supporters of government ownership in various fields.[1] The Society has undergone considerable changes both in organization and in aims and purposes, as will be explained in a later section.

General Plan of Early Organization.—The general plan of organization of the American Society of Equity has some new ideas not embodied by other farmers' organizations. According to the constitution of 1907 there were to be local, county, state, section, department, and district unions. The National Union was to be a delegate body made up of representatives from local, county and state unions. A local union could be organized by ten persons. If the county and state were organized record of the request for a charter was to be made by

[1] Professor M. L. Wilson in a personal communication.

these bodies and communicated to the National Union which issues all charters. The charter fees for the local and county unions were only $2.00 in 1907. That of the State Union was $5.00. Three local unions were required to organize a county union. In addition to its business functions the county union was expected to look after the general interests of the Society and appoint extension committees with a view to maintain the organization intact. A state union could be organized when five county unions had been organized. The section unions were to be purely business associations.

They were to comprise several states. The plan proposed provided for about six sections for the country. Reporting supply and demand of crops, and directing marketing operations were to be the functions of the section unions. State, county and local unions were to be made use of in performing this function. Parallel to the section union, but independent of it, the department union was to be organized to carry on marketing operations for a particular crop. The district union was to be organized as a subsidiary of the department union in such cases where the crop varies considerably as to type, of which tobacco is an example. It is to be noted that the organization was fashioned to carry on the marketing of farm products. Through the society's marketing plan the price of these products was to be controlled, and, as will be explained in a later section, this was the main object for establishing the organization. The Equity Society has always been non-secret.

Admission of Members.—While the Society of Equity was organized in the main for the purpose of assuming farm-business operations, it was nevertheless founded on broad principles of equity embracing in its aims virtually the whole economic order, and proposed to extend benefits to all classes not receiving their proportionate share of the distribution of wealth. The admission of members was, therefore, not confined to farmers, but was extended to "friends" of farmers or, to all who favored an equitable arrangement of the economic organization of the country. Regular membership was limited to males more than 14 years of age. Wives of regular members and their sons and daughters could become special members. Special members were exempt from all dues and were denied the right of vote in the election of officers. In other matters each local union was given full power to determine whether or not the women were to have a vote at all. This was a discrimination against female farm owners and operators, and compared with the Grange and to a lesser degree with the Farmers' Union, was a reactionary step.

The annual dues paid by each member were to be $1.20. This amount was to be distributed among the several bodies as follows: 20 cents to the local union, 20 cents to the county union, 20 cents to the state union, and 60 cents to the national union. In the absence of a county or state organization $1.00 was sent to the national union. The amount paid by each member to the national body would seem exorbitant were it not for the fact that it included the subscription price of the Society's official organ the *Up-to-Date Farming.* Membership fees and subscription to the official organ were lumped so that the Society's propaganda could be more readily carried out. Other farmers' organizations have their own official organs, but they keep their maintenance separate from dues received from members.

The constitution provided for members at large. In communities where no local could be organized a single person could become a member of the national union by paying a fee of $2.00, which also paid for the Society's journal for one year. This was a bid for the speedy organization of the Society in all parts of the country.

General Aims and Purposes.—The constitution of 1907 stated that "the first and great object of this society is to obtain profitable prices for all products of the farm, garden and orchard." The assumption was that the existing marketing system and monopolistic combination had distorted the law of supply and demand with respect to farm products, reduced their prices, and as a result established a relatively low standard of living for the agricultural class. The Society recognized an unequal distribution of wealth between the farmer on the one hand and the merchant and manufacturer on the other.

It virtually adopted the following motto: "Farmers are under no legal or moral obligation to feed the balance of the world at unprofitably low prices." This statement appeared on all the early literature. "Unprofitably low prices" give the farmer a relatively low standard of living, and this fact is pointed out to be "unequitable." The fundamental mission of the Society is to reestablish "equity" in the economic order, and the appeal for members is, therefore, extended not to the farmer alone but "to all other people who are tired of graft and exploitation and who want equity to prevail. Thus, while it is a farmers' Society of Equity on account of the great number of farmers, the importance of their industry, and the great power that they can exert in an organized condition, it will be a national society, or truly an American Society of Equity, and can be used to secure equity for all Americans, in society, business, and government."[1]

It is to be noted that the word, "equity," was not chosen merely for the want of a name, but that its use embodies the very essence of the doctrine propounded by the Society of Equity. "New conditions must be produced guaranteeing to each man, woman, and child, equal opportunities, promising to each justice, a fair return, a fair reward, a fair wage measured by effort and merit." This justice or equity was to be brought about by an industrial organization without affiliation with any political party. Its great numerical strength would cause any party in power to give ear to its demands, and "quickly accomplish all the reforms that the people of all classes are asking for."

As a social doctrine *per se*, it must be admitted that it was a sublime one. Public opinion will support any economic organization that bases its demands upon justice or equity. These terms, however, are abstract, and their application to concrete situations is not as easy a matter as the enunciation of the doctrine. The Society of Equity's plan was to have the farmers name the prices of their products themselves. Through this control they were to receive higher prices, and a greater income for each farmer of the country would mean a greater

[1] *Vide*, Everitt, *Third Power*, p. 230.

purchasing power among the great rural consuming class and set up a demand for manufactured goods. "This gain will be reflected in the business done by merchants, bankers, professional men, laborers, etc."

An Outline of the Original Plan.—The marketing plan proposed by the Society of Equity called for complete cooperation among the farmers. That is, all farmers had to pledge the sale of their surplus products through the Society's representative. Local unions were to report their supply to the county unions and these to the state unions. At the national convention the total supplies of all farm crops of the country were to be referred to committees which would name a fair price at which they were to be sold. Representatives were to be placed in all important cities and towns of the country who were not to buy and sell but only to receive orders for products from merchants, millers, and other large consumers of raw products. Such orders were to be transferred by the representatives to the state unions which in turn would communicate them to the county unions. The county unions would apportion the orders among the local unions. Shipments would be made to the purchaser who would remit to the members of the local union selling the product. The Society, while it would perform functions of a middleman, would never actually sell the product and, therefore, never assume any risk. The proposed plan differs very materially from the cooperative selling association so general among farmers to-day, and seems to be a move in the wrong direction. Instead of reducing the number of middlemen it increases their number and this tends to increase the cost of the product or reduce the price to the farmer

The American Society of Equity of to-day has broken away from the original idea and carries on marketing operations based on the cooperative principles. In Wisconsin considerable progress is being made in the establishment of various cooperative enterprises.

Other Objects of Organization.—Other objects of organization originally fostered by the American Society of Equity were as follows:

To obtain equitable rates of transportation.

To secure legislation in the interest of agriculture.

To open up new markets and enlarge old ones.

To secure new seeds, grain, fruit, vegetables, etc., from home and from foreign countries, and distribute them with a view of improving present crops and giving a greater diversity.

To report crops in this and foreign countries, so that farmers may operate intelligently in planting and marketing.

To establish institutions of learning, so that farmers and their sons and daughters may be educated in scientific and intensive farming, and for the general advancement of agriculture.

To improve our highways.

To irrigate our land.

To prevent adulteration of food and marketing of same.

To promote social intercourse.

To settle disputes without recourse to law.

To promote farmers' societies in foreign countries

The American Society of Equity of To-day

Character of Organization.—As already stated the parent organization is strongest in Wisconsin where it has a membership of more than 40,000. The general structure of the organization is about the same as at first planned. Some minor changes have been made. According to the present constitution seven persons may organize a local union. Five local unions may organize a county union, and five county unions may organize a state union. State unions are federated into the national body. Where no state bodies exist the lower bodies have direct membership in the national body. In organized states, dues for the national body are sent by the locals to the state unions and by them transmitted to the national union. An admission fee of $2.50 is charged for entrance into the local. In organized states the amount of annual dues paid to the national treasury per member is $0.50. The state union determines the amount of dues paid to lower bodies by each member but the total annual dues may not be less than $5.00. In unorganized states each member pays $4.00 into the national treasury. Where a county union is formed $0.20 is remitted to it. Membership dues include payment for subscription to the official organ, *The Equity News*.

An important change as to conditions of membership has been made. Under the present constitution "females are eligible to membership on the same conditions as males and entitled to all the rights and privileges." This extends the benefits of the Society to female property owners, and also adds considerable social atmosphere to local meetings.

Present Aims and Purposes.—The Society has continued virtually all the objects of organization enumerated in connection with a study of its early organization. It has, however, made radical changes with respect to its marketing policies It now favors the establishment of cooperative enterprises, and the former system of merely creating an organization for holding supplies and reporting demand without actually buying and selling the products has been altogether discarded. In the articles of incorporation filed with the Secretary of State of Illinois in 1911 the following important object was added to the aims and purposes of the Society: "To promote the formation of cooperative trading companies to be organized for the purpose of distributing farm products and the necessities of life as a means of equalizing the distribution of wealth among the people of the United States and to prevent monopolization due to obstructed distribution." Thus it will be seen that the American Society of Equity has also come to the principle of organizing cooperative enterprises among the farmers and of eliminating unnecessary middlemen. Taking the whole history of farm organization there is clearly noticeable an evolution in method for conducting farm business. All farmers' organizations agree to-day on at least the essentials of coopera tion, and while some stress it a good deal more than others, they all foster it to a greater or less degree.

The Farmers' Equity Union

History and Character of the Organization.—The Farmers' Equity Union is a child of the American Society of Equity and has therefore inherited some of the ideas of its ancestor. It has, however, developed a totally different market system from that first proposed by the parent organization. It is organized virtually for the sole purpose of establishing cooperative enterprises among the farmers. In fact the organization of the Farmers' Equity Union and that of the cooperative business concerns are so closely related that the local unions have no separate existence apart from business enterprises. One may say that the Equity Union took the chief aim of its predecessor, that of raising the price of farm products to the farmer, but has adopted a different method for realizing it. It should be noted that while the Equity Union is primarily a business organization, it uses its power to influence Congress and legislatures to secure favorable legislation. It is an active member of the National Board of Farm Organization.

The Equity Union was chartered on the 16th of December, 1910. Mr. C. O. Drayton is recognized as its founder. The organization is found in "Ohio, Indiana, Illinois, Texas, Kansas, Nebraska, Colorado, Idaho, and some other States." Its total membership is in the neighborhood of 65,000.

The Equity Union broke away from the idea of local organization for general purposes. Like its predecessor, it is non-secret, but the plan to organize township, county and state unions was wholly discarded and the organization was wholly fashioned to meet economic needs. A local union and a local exchange are one and the same organization. They have, of course, a dual existence inasmuch as they have representation in the national body and to which each member pays a fee of $10.00 when he is admitted into the local and annual dues of $1.00. The latter amount secures for him the *Equity-Union Exchange,* the official organ of the association, and together with the entrance fee of $10.00 defrays the expenses of the national body which is engaged in extension work and the general maintenance of the organization. The local unions and the national body constitute the Farmers' Equity Union, but the local unions are only organized to conduct cooperative enterprises. It is for this reason that township, county and state lines are disregarded. Locals are established in towns along railroads where business facilities are available, and in the large cities central exchanges are established to serve the needs of the locals. Each local maintains its individual identity so far as its own business enterprise is concerned, and each central exchange is maintained separately from other exchanges. The ultimate goal, however, is national cooperation.[1]

Local and Central Exchanges.—"Local exchanges are organized at local market points. The business of these locals is governed by the needs of each particular locality." Exchanges are organized to carry on the business of grain elevators, stores, creameries and some other lines. The exchange is chartered by the state in which it is organized. Each member subscribes to two shares of stock at $100 each. The first share he is asked to pay for by cash or note. The other share he is sometimes allowed to pay for out of the profits due him. The stockholders elect a board of five directors who employ a manager and place him under bond. Every three months the books are audited. Its business policy is similar to that of any private concern. That is, goods are bought and sold at the market price. The products of a non-member are handled in the same way as any dealer would handle them, the difference being that the non-member would not share in the cooperative profits made by the exchange. Interest on capital invested is paid at the rate of 3%. The rules usually require that the two shares must be fully paid up before any dividends are paid. Out of the profits, then, are first paid the expenses for running the exchange, and second, the 3 per cent dividend on full-paid stock outstanding. The remainder of the profits are distributed among the members in proportion to the amount of the business each transacted with the exchange. If a member sells $500 worth of wheat to the exchange and the net profit happens to be 10 per cent he will be paid in addition to his dividend a profit of $50.00. Large growers have as much as $800 returned to them in the form of profits.

Centralized exchanges, otherwise known as centralized companies, are organized in the large cities and serve both as buying and selling agencies for the local exchanges. The Denver Company, according to a pamphlet issued by the Equity Union, is only a buying agency. It "buys coal, lumber, posts, fencing, fruits, vegetables, automobile tires, etc., for about one

---

[1] *Vide* pamphlet of the Farmers' Equity Union entitled *Plan and Purpose.*

hundred and ten exchanges located on the lines of railways leading into Denver.'' The Kansas City Company is a great grain-marketing concern. The Chicago Company buys farm machinery, binder twine, fertilizer, fencing, wire, posts, books, office supplies, etc. It also acts as a selling agency for the Equity Union creameries. The Ohio Company is primarily a grain-selling agency. It is readily seen that these exchanges may be made to sell the farmers' products as well as to buy his supplies.

The centralized company issues stock, like the local exchange, but its stockholders are the local exchanges instead of individuals. Each local doing business with the Chicago Company subscribes to $400 worth of stock which may be paid all at once, or $100 in cash and the remainder at the rate of $100 a year. This remainder may be satisfied by leaving the profits due the local with the Chicago exchange. In fact no profits are prorated to locals whose stock is not fully paid up. Both the financing of the centralized company and its policy of doing business are similar to those of the local exchanges. Reports indicate that these exchanges are well managed and run on good business principles. The Equity Union is one of the foremost farmers' organizations in the field of cooperative enterprise.

A **National Marketing Program.**—The Equity Union has the aspirations of its ancestor to organize the supply and demand of farm products on a nation-wide basis, but, of course, the plan of accomplishing it is different. The early plan of the American Society of Equity was to create a reporting system and hold the crop for sale at the order of the farmers' representative who was to be an extra middleman. The Equity Union's plan is to create also a reporting system through the establishment of local exchanges placed at points where business facilities are available, and the federation of the locals into county associations, and finally the federation of these into a national association, all of which to be based on the Rochdale principle of cooperative enterprise. In other words, the plan already carried out within given areas is to be extended to cover the entire country. The Equity Union realizes, however, that no single farmers' organization now existing can hope in the near future to make itself master throughout all portions of the country, and the sane plan is, therefore, advanced that all farmers' organizations foster the movement and federate for this particular purpose. A "national clearing house" can be organized and can operate in the same way, it is pointed out, as the centralized exchanges. "When the supply of farm crops, the necessities of life, are controlled by the producers, or by their organization—when they are no longer thrown on the market to blindly seek the demand—then the demand will seek them. It cannot be otherwise, or people will be hungry with nothing to eat."[1] All telephone and other costs for reporting and marketing the products are to be added to the price. There is a feeling that products can always be sold above the cost of production. This can not always be done, especially when violent general price reductions have occurred or are imminent. A national marketing system controlled by the farmers, however, will save to them the middlemen's profits and bring to them a greater share of the distribution of wealth. This has been demonstrated. It will eliminate useless middlemen, and to this extent will benefit the whole country. As previously pointed out, the aim of the Equity Union and other farmers' organizations is in process of accomplishment. The United States Grain Growers has incorporated to provide a national marketing system for the handling of grains. If the right leadership is secured to conduct these business agencies they will be successful and the time is fast approaching when the farmers can be universally persuaded to support them.

The Ancient Order of Gleaners

Origin and Character of Organization.—The Ancient Order of Gleaners is a farmers' fraternal organization very strong in Michigan but being established also in some other states, notably in Indiana. The order was founded in the village of Caro, Michigan, in 1894. This was only a few years after the Alliance as a farmers' association went to pieces, and con-

[1] From a pamphlet, *A National Marketing System.*

siderably in advance of the establishment of the Farmers' Union and the American Society of Equity. From the records available it appears that the Alliance never became well established in Michigan. The Grange, however, had in 1874 secured a good hold in the state and by the following year is reported to have had more than 33,000 members. Grange dues paid by Michigan in 1919 indicate that the state has at present virtually 40,000 Grange members. This is quite a showing for the Grange in Michigan, and the formation of a new organization attracting a membership of more than 80,000, virtually all of which are within the state, is, therefore, quite remarkable.[1] The reason for the formation of the Order of Gleaners and its rapid development is probably due to the conservative tendency of the Grange in the past. The Gleaner organization has fostered cooperation in a very positive way, while the Grange after its ill-fated attempts in the 70's virtually discarded it as a national policy, and has only recently in view of successes attained in many parts of the country again subscribed to the principle.

The Order of Gleaners follows the usual practice of organizing apart from the establishment of cooperative business concerns which, as was noted, is a peculiarity of the Farmers' Equity Union. The general plan of organization includes local organizations, county federations, state federations, and at the top the Supreme body. In 1917 there were 1,360 local organizations. Its membership is confined to farmers "actively engaged in farming and living upon farms." When members cease to be farmers they lose their right to vote. In Detroit the Order owns a building, designated the National Gleaner Temple, which is claimed at this time to be the only home of a farmers' organization in the country.

Objects of Organization.—The Order of Gleaners has two main objects for its *raison d'etre*—one is of a fraternal character, including the payment of death benefits, and the other is the establishment of cooperative enterprises, including mutual fire insurance. The organization also uses its power to influence legislation and for this purpose has joined itself to the

[1] *Vide* pamphlet entitled *The Gleaners.*

Farmers' National Council, which is one of the farmers' representative offices having permanent headquarters at Washington. The Order claims that "the farmers of Michigan have a greater representation in the State Senate and Legislature, and have a greater power in securing just and equitable legislation as affecting the farmers' interests, than any state of the Union."

The insurance feature provides for the payment of annual premiums on certificates of policies ranging from $250 to $2,000. Several plans of insurance are offered. For a twenty-payment-life plan the cost of insurance per $1,000 at the age of 30 is $25.40 per year when the premium is paid semi-annually. Under two plans policies are payable at death and under another at the expiration of 60 years. The Order claims to have paid out more than $5,000,000 in benefits to its members. Its motto, "Each for All, All for Each" embodies this spirit of fraternalism which has been developed in a very practical way.

The Gleaners believe in a farmers' organization apart from cooperation, but they also believe that to foster cooperation is a very essential function of the organization. Organization they say, however, must precede. "Cooperation without organization is impossible." Cooperation with them rests upon democracy, equality and brotherly love. "With the practically applied lessons taught through fraternity and a loyal brotherhood, the Gleaners are in a position to build their cooperative enterprises upon a foundation sure and strong." In a pamphlet issued by the Order its cooperative system is described as follows:

> The National Clearing House is, as the name suggests, a national clearing house for all farm products and farm supplies. Here, with ample facilities, leased wires to market centers, expert salesmen, and representatives at all leading terminal markets, those in charge are able to direct shipments to all parts of the world. Each state is to have its Central Clearing House, each neighborhood its Gleaner Elevator, Shipping Station, Coal Station or Distributing Warehouse. Recognizing the part which the law of "supply and demand" plays in the marketing of all farm products, the Gleaner plan prevents glutted markets, dishonest manipulation and unfair competition. Thus we reach from the heart of the nation's buying center back to the individual Gleaner farmer, through his local association.
>
> And again, through buying in large quantities, the National Association is enabled to enter the markets as one of the world's largest

buyers, and to meet all competition on equal footing. Through this plan it will at once become apparent that the interests of the local clearing houses and elevators are linked up with a more powerful organization, and that instead of the little concerns competing with each other, the entire business is conducted along the line of present day activities, and the farmers' co-operative enterprise is enabled to meet its competitors on a leval.

The usual practice of buying and selling at market prices is followed, and profits are distributed in proportion to "patronage dividends." Profits made by the central clearing house are distributed among the local clearing houses and by them together with the profits made locally are distributed to the individual farmer. The plan has been successfully operated "for more than a decade." It is the aim ultimately to join hands with the consumer.

The Jewish Agricultural and Industrial Aid Society.

Jews as Farmers.—Two opposing views have been advanced with respect to the adaptability of the Jew to the vocation of farming. It is pointed out on the one hand that the Jews were originally and for many centuries engaged in agriculture, and that members of the race would, therefore, do well to return to the economic pursuit of their forefathers. On the other hand attention is called to the fact that the great majority of jews have not been tillers of the soil for nearly 2,000 years, and in view of this almost complete separation from the land they are now ill suited to engage in agriculture. Both these statements throw very little light on the question of the Jew's fitness to become a farmer. The environment has probably changed his mental characteristics very little. The Jews have always been a keen, intelligent, ambitious, philosophical, and vigorous people. There is enough racial adaptitude among them as well as enough individual differentiation to furnish producers for all phases of economic activity. They are successful not alone as traders, but in the professions of law, medicine, teaching, and journalism as well. Their contributions to science, music and literature are a rich heritage to all generations. A more sensible and practical explanation of why the Jew is so rarely found to be engaged in agriculture is because in virtually all countries to which he has immigrated he has been either restricted by law or by custom from holding land, and has been forced to live in the city, in medieval days sometimes in a definite Jews' quarter. Dr. Loeb says: "We might compare the serf who was forcibly tied to the soil, and whose descendants form the body of the agricultural population of present Europe, with the medieval Jew who was not allowed to possess any land outside the ghetto limit, and whose descendants are now seeking to gain a foothold among the farming population of America. There will be in every country that does not impose arbitrary restrictions upon the freedom of motion of its inhabitants, a certain tendency toward the cities and a countervailing trend toward the open country. This freedom of exchange must be recognized as an inherent condition of personal liberty, and if, for economic or sociological reasons, a relative increase of rural population is desired, only such means can be adopted as will make agricultural life permanently attractive."[1] Virtually the same idea is expressed by Leonard G. Robinson when he says that "the only inducement to engage in agriculture or, indeed, in any other occupation, is the individual profit and satisfaction expected therefrom. If a man can improve his condition—not necessarily financial—on a farm, it is good reason for his becoming a farmer; if not, there is good reason for his staying away. As for the Jewish farmer, he is a human being and is actuated by the same motives, and must be judged by the same standards, as the average, human being."[2] As a matter of fact the reports of the Jewish Agricultural and Industrial Aid Society give ample evidence that the Jews of our day make thrifty and entirely successful farmers, although in America according to reports they have shown a special adaptitude to such specialized forms of farming as dairying, poultry-raising, and vegetable-gardening and their success has been probably greatest in these fields.

The only country in which they have engaged in farming to any considerable extent since the taking of Jerusalem and the dispersion of the Jewish people by the Romans is Russia,

[1] *Vide Afterword* by Morris Loeb in Robinson's *Agricultural Activities of the Jews in America*, p. 90.

[2] *Vide* Robinson, *op. cit.*, p. 3.

and even there they have been confined to settlements embracing in 1870 a total area of 269,378 acres and a population of 63,342. In 1897 the farming population of the Russian settlements proper and those of the Polish provinces including also the individuals of scattered holdings numbered 200,000. The total acreage owned by the Jews in the Empire was 6,422,684.[1] In Palestine some few scattered settlements have continued since the Roman dispersion, and recently efforts have been made to reestablish the Jew in the land of his forefathers. In all other countries of the old world he has never become established as a farmer. Because of the pogroms, or riots instituted by the officials under the direction of the central government or with their connivance, leading Jews in Russia and elsewhere sought to provide a refuge for oppressed members of their race in the new world. Argentina and Brazil in South America and the United States and Canada in North America were selected as suitable countries in which to establish Jewish colonies. The first settlement in Canada was made in 1884 and another wave from Russia came in 1892. Settlements in South America were established in the late 80's. In the United States there were two Jewish settlements organized in the first half of the 19th century—Ararat, on Grand Island in the Niagara River, and Shalom, in Ulster County, New York. Both came to a speedy end. "The real beginning of the Jewish agricultural movement in the United States is contemporaneous with the Jewish immigration which was set in motion by the reign of lawlessness and persecution that swept over Eastern Europe in the early eighties of the last century." The Hebrew Emigrant Aid Society of the United States was organized to direct the immigrants to farms and assist them in getting established. Numerous settlements sprang up at various places throughout the country, but virtually all succumbed after a brief struggle.

The Jewish Agricultural and Industrial Aid Society.—In 1889 there was a renewal of persecution of the Jews in Russia and Baron de Hirsch with his millions determined to help his people who were driven from their homes through political and

---

[1] *Vide*, Robinson, *op. cit.*, p. 21.

religious oppression. He, therefore, established a fund of $2,400,000 the income of which was to be used for the purpose. The fund was incorporated by a group of prominent American Jews. Oscar S. Straus who was a close friend and adviser of Baron de Hirsch was made one of the trustees of the Hirsch fund. The aims of the fund were comprehensive and not merely confined to placing families on farms. In order to bring greater efficiency into the agricultural activity with which the fund was concerned, a separate organization was incorporated in 1900 under the name of the Jewish Agricultural and Industrial Aid Society. The general objects of this society, however, were not wholly agricultural and were stated to be as follows:

1. The encouragement and direction of agriculture among jews, residents of the United States, principally immigrants from Russia, Roumania, and Galicia, the removal of such persons dwelling in the crowded sections of cities to agricultural and industrial districts, and provision for their temporary support.
2. The grant of loans to mechanics, artisans, and tradesmen, to enable them to secure larger earnings and accumulate savings for the acquisition of homes in suburban, agricultural, and industrial districts.
3. The removal of industries now pursued in tenements or shops in crowded sections of the cities, by aiding manufacturers and contractors to transfer their shops and business to agricultural and industrial districts where their employees may continue to labor and acquire individual homes.
4. The encouragement of cooperative creameries and factories and of storage houses for canning and preserving fruit and vegetables and making wine.

From these objects it is observed that the functions of the new society at its beginning were not wholly agricultural. That part of its work that had to do with the removal of immigrants from congested cities, however, was soon placed under a separate management, and in 1907 it became completely divorced and was taken over by an independent organization. Since then the work of the Jewish Agricultural and Industrial Aid Society is said to have been virtually wholly confined to the field of agriculture. The objects of the Society as stated by Gabriel Davidson in his report for 1920 are as follows:

To develop a class of farmers from a people to whom farming was for two thousand years a proscribed occupation, to make these farmers a happy, contented and permanent part of our national organism is an effort, lofty in conception, beneficent in results and far-reaching in possibilities. Viewed from a national eminence, it assumes a significance of transcendent import. Our nation's great problem is the Americanization of the immigrant. If Americanization is not confined solely to the teaching of English, of civics, and of the theories of government, but is conceived to be broad enough to embrace all acitivity tending to elevate the standards of living, then the work of our Society in all its manifold phases is Americanization of the highest type.

The resources of the Society are in part contributed by the Baron de Hirsch Fund, which includes a legacy of the Baroness de Hirsch, and by the Jewish Colonization Association. The society at once busied itself with the remnants of the Jewish settlements that had been organized during the 80's, and made efforts to place all Jewish farmers on an independent economic basis. Instead of planting colonies and governing them, it follows the policy of directing individuals to farms, advising them as to the purchase of property, instructing them in the art of agriculture and in subjects that pertain to sanitation and community interests in general, and loaning funds to them on strictly business principles with a view to making them independent of all charitable aid and developing in them the ambition and the ability to play a conspicuous part in the direction of the affairs of the community in which they live.

Departmental Organization.—In order to expedite its work the Jewish Agricultural and Industrial Aid Society has departmentalized itself into its Farm Settlement Bureau, the Extension Department, the Sanitation Bureau, the Farm Labor Bureau, and the Farm Loan Department. It has in addition established a western office with agencies at Cleveland, Detroit, and Cincinnati, a Philadelphia office, and an Ulster-Sullivan office embracing counties in New York State, the main office of the Society being in New York City. The editing of *The Jewish Farmer,* which is claimed to be the only agricultural journal in Yiddish in the world, is also an important activity of the Society. The Council of Jewish Women, an independent organization, cooperates with the Society and sends its workers in the homes of Jewish agricultural settlements.

The Society welcomes the work of the Council because of the difficulty Jewish women experience in adjusting themselves to the "life in sparsley settled sections where neighbors—especially of their own class—are few and far between." Its workers are virtually "home-demonstration agents" for Jewish families They "give instruction in the better management of the home and in the use of devices designed to lighten household duties, in the care of children, etc. In some communities it established traveling branch libraries; in others, hot lunches for school children. In short, it has set before itself the task of helping make life more livable for the women and children of the farm. Upon their happiness depends, to a large extent, the success or failure of a farming enterprise. Many a promising venture fails from no other than these human causes. To remove these causes, or at least to reduce their operation, is to help in a practical way in building up a stable, growing, promising Jewish farming class in this country."[1]

The Work of the Farm Settlement Bureau.—The work of this Bureau has to do with finding suitable farms for Jews desiring to engage in farming. A broad point of view is taken by the Bureau so as to make its advice to applicants truly worth while and its whole work of lasting consequence. The person desiring to engage in agriculture is "enlightened as to what farming actually embraces, that it is not merely an occupation but also a mode of living; that as an occupation it requires capital, experience, physical vigor, a knowledge of business practices; that as a mode of life it requires the capacity of adaptation to new surroundings and changed conditions, especially on the part of his family."[2] The Bureau considers it just as important to dissuade the unfit from entering upon farming as to encourage the fit. For this reason in 1920 out of 1,736 applicants for aid only 171 were actually settled. The applicants are described as belonging to several classes as follows:

There is the workingman or small business man who in times of prosperity saved up a few thousand dollars and who at last sees his opportunity to realize a long cherished hope of becoming a farmer. There is that man who fearing that the wheel of fortune is bound to turn back, wants to invest his savings in a venture which will not only safeguard his money but also to assure him a livelihood. Then there is the idealist who wants to return to the calling of his fathers, and the Zionist whose American experience is merely a preparation

[1] *Vide Annual Report* of the Jewish Agricultural and Industrial Aid Society for 1920, p. 43.
[2] *Vide Annual Report* for 1920, p. 6.

for his eventual settlement in Palestine. There is, too, the man whom the doctor advises to take up outdoor work or whose wife or child needs country air. The passing of the peak of prosperity in the course of the year—industrial depression, closed shops, strikes, etc.—increased the stream of our farm seekers and brought to our office a large number of applicants who looked to farming as a haven of safety.[1]

The problem of farm settlement is conceived of as consisting on three steps: "The instruction of the individual, the selection of the farm, and the fitting of the one to the other." The general situation is presented to the applicant as already stated, and if it is thought that actual experience is important in coming to a definite conclusion he may be advised to take for a time a position as farm laborer. The Farm Labor Bureau accordingly places him with a Jewish farmer, and the reports show that this sometimes speedily results in making up his mind in the negative. In the selection of the farm inspection trips are made. The Bureau is guided by the success of Jewish farmers already established and attempts to place the applicants in their community.

In 1920 it examined 550 farms in 10 states. The Connecticut River Valley has been chosen as one of the fields of activity, and during 1920 there were "almost a score of farmers settled there." Also 22 farmers were settled in recognized poultry sections of New York and New Jersey. The finding of the right sort of farm embraces the third step, and in this connection the applicant's experience, capital, physique, religious requirements and family demands, are taken into account. Specialized farming is a matter that is considered, and as stated, poultry-raising is in high favor; although, in as much as general farming is the safest for beginners, farms suited for this purpose constitute the greatest number purchased. One of the important services performed by the Bureau is the negotiation of the purchase of the farm at a reasonable price. The prospective farmer, in view of his unfamilarity with land values, is often saved large amounts and at times his entire savings.

The Extension Department.—After the Farm Settlement Bureau has completed its work in placing the individual upon

---

[1] *Vide Annual Report* for 1920, p. 7.

his newly purchased farm the Extension Department proceeds to map out a plan of farm management for him. It assists him in the purchase of tools and implements, seeds and fertilizer, horses and dairy stock. Frequent visits are made to the new settlers, and when it is found that their farm management plan is not sufficiently varied a revision is suggested. The department considers individual extension work by far the most effective. In 1920 its field men visited 1,300 Jewish farmers in 64 communities in 5 states.

A second type of work deals with groups instead of directly with individuals. The department, therefore, fosters farmers' organizations through which they arrange for meetings of various kinds. In 1920 there were held 135 farmers' meetings at which agricultural subjects were discussed by means of demonstrations, models and charts. In the summer "Field Days" are arranged where lectures and demonstrations are given and entertainment provided. "Farmers' Institutes" are being held. These are in the nature of schools where elementary agriculture is taught, and are conducted mainly in Yiddish. In its extension work the Department does not neglect the buying and selling phases of farming. It is instrumental in securing cooperation among the Jewish farmers in the purchase of seed, lime, fertilizer, and high-grade dairy stock. Proper shipping relations with railroads are sought by the Department in the interest of the farmers. Because of the clannish characteristic of the Jewish people it would seem that they would cooperate much more readily than the usual American farmers who are bound together only by motives of profit. The one fundamental condition necessary to make cooperative enterprise succeed is willingness on the part of individuals to cooperate with one another. It is sometimes said the way to cooperate is to cooperate.

The Department has provided an agricultural correspondence course which consists of a series of written lessons all in Yiddish and is supplemented by special articles in the *Jewish Farmer*. The course is edited by Dr. J. G. Lipman, Director of the New Jersey Agricultural Experiment Station and Dean of the New Jersey College of Agriculture.

Interest in the short courses of agriculture given by state agricultural colleges, is stimulated by the awarding of scholarships on a competitive basis. In 1920 twenty such scholarships were awarded to persons from New York, Massachusetts, Michigan, and New Jersey. In a statistical study made by the Extension Department, it is found that three times the proportion of the Jewish to the general population of the United States is represented in the enrollment of students at 106 institutions including colleges, universities and professional schools, while in agriculture Jewish students are very few. To change this status in higher education the Society makes students' loans. In 1920 such loans were made to students at the state agricultural colleges in Connecticut, Ohio, Michigan, Minnesota, New Jersey, and New York.

By means of *The Jewish Farmer* an effort is made to create a feeling of unity among the various Jewish agricultural communities of the country. Notes of interest to the various sections are published. Local farmers' associations organized at the various settlements have formed the Federation of Jewish Farmers of America which holds annual conventions and which finds *The Jewish Farmer* useful in disseminating matters that pertain to the interest of all farmers. The journal answers questions and this is regarded as a very helpful means of instructing the practical farmer. The local associations aim to promote the social features of community life through the holding of picnics and various other entertainments. The influence exerted by *The Jewish Farmer* and the Federation of Jewish Farmers of America is a cohesive force that binds together the various Jewish settlements and individual Jewish farmers scattered throughout the country.

The Sanitation Bureau.—The Sanitation Bureau was organized in 1918 and was at first not considered to have an important function to perform, but surveys conducted convinced the Department that its duties were many and of a varied character. The work is essentially an educational process and the results of efforts in this field are, therefore, not so plainly visible as in many other lines of endeavor. However, considerable progress is reported.

The work of the Department covered sewage disposal, water supply, garbage disposal, fly prevention and food protection. The methods used to bring home to the farmers sanitation facts and principles included personal visits, demonstrations of sanitary appliances, health talks, illustrated lectures, and the distribution of pamphlets and posters. Health reels were secured from the New York State Board of Health and shown to communities. At Ellenville, New York the Society built a sanitation exhibit whose features include a well, spring enclosure, a garbage incinerator, a septic tank, double leeching cesspools, a subsoil irrigation system, sanitary outhouses, etc. The elements of this exhibit, illustrated and fully described, are made available in pamphlet form for general distribution. The Department cooperates with local authorities in securing legislation aiming to provide more sanitary conditions in the community. In its report for 1920 the predominant improvement features for the year were shown to have been "in the line of protection of water supply and proper sewage disposal."

The Farm Labor Bureau.—It is during periods of prosperity when the Labor Bureau is most active. At this time manufacturing and commerce absorbs most of the available labor because shorter working hours and other working conditions are more attractive in the city than in the country. In periods of depression there is a temporary back swing of labor from the city to the country, but during its existence of fourteen years the Bureau has found every season that it performed a useful and necessary service in bringing the job and the jobless man together. The employment is mostly seasonal. It is not infrequent that the same young man returns to his former employer. Some of the boys placed wish to spend their summer vacations on the farm. Some are in agricultural schools and desire practical experience. Some want experience with a view to begin farming on an independent basis. Others merely want some form of employment. "Toward the end of each year questionnaires are mailed to employers to learn how long men remained with them and whether they gave satisfaction."

In 1920 the Bureau placed 1,030 men in 19 different states, but the larger number were located in new York, New Jersey, and Connecticut because it is in these states where the greatest number of Jewish farmers are concentrated and also for the reason that these sections of the country are in close proximity to our congested urban centers.

The Farm Loan Department.—"The fundamental activity of the Jewish Agricultural and Industrial Aid Society is the rendering of financial assistance to those desiring to become farmers and to enable those who are already on the farm to maintain their foothold."[1] This statement was made by Leonard G. Robinson in 1912 and is still true, but judging from the extent of the recent growth of the Society's educational activities it will not be long until these functions will be regarded as important as the loaning of funds. The operating resources of the Society are the income from part of the Hirsch fund and that of the Jewish Colonization Association. Loans in 1912 were made at the rate of 4%. The purposes of loans in 1920 included the purchase of farms which constituted 23% of the total number of loans made, the purchase of equipment which constituted 22%, the construction or repair of buildings which constituted 14%, the paying off of mortgages or other debts which constituted 14%, and to provide working capital which constituted 27% of the total number of loans made. The provision of funds for the purchase of farms is steadily growing as an object of loaning funds. The ratio of this object was 7% in 1917, while in 1920 it had risen to .23. The society loans as a rule an amount equal to 75% of the value, although in individual cases it loans much more, going sometimes higher than the total value of the farm.

It is a policy with the Society not to extend loans where credit can be secured at favorable rates elsewhere. Its security, therefore, is more often on second and third mortgages than on first. It even makes loans on fourth and chattel mortgages. In 1920 it made "51 loans on first mortgage, 178 on second mortgage, 85 on third mortgage, 14 on fourth mortgage, 4 on chattel mortgage or other personal security, 9 on

[1] *Vide* Robinson, *op. cit.*, p. 52.

purchase contract on farms bought through the Society. The remaining 103 were on unsecured notes.'' The latter were for seed purposes granted in the spring of the year. The maximum credit so extended was $100 per individual, but the results have been so satisfactory that the Society in 1920 felt justified in raising the maximum to $150.

In 1920 there were 801 applications for loans 444 of which were granted and 243 rejected. The applications came from 24 different states. The amounts of loans outstanding has steadily increased from $7,500 in 1900 to $1,064,179.37 in 1920. Collections have kept pace with the growth of loans. The same year there were 1,906 farm loan accounts outstanding and of this number 7 were charged to profit and loss. It is claimed that if loans are placed with due regard to the character of the borrowers, even though there is no other security than a promise to pay, there is little danger of losing the principal and interest. There are some arrears on interest and principal, but these are not large enough to prevent the rapid increase of loans extended every year.

In addition to granting credit directly to individuals the Jewish Agricultural and Industrial Aid Society has encouraged through *The Jewish Farmer* and otherwise the formation of credit unions through which short-term personal cooperative credit is to be provided. The work of organizing credit unions was actively begun in 1911 when three unions were formed. Five more were organized in 1912, and nine in 1913.[1] The Society furnished two dollars for every dollar subscribed by the union. Each union raised $500 and the Society contributed $1,000. The union's part is raised through the sale of shares at $5 each. Voting follows the Rochdale principle of ''one share, one vote.'' Loans in 1912 were limited to a term of six months and for an amount not exceeding $100. The borrower paid 6 per cent. Dividends on stock were declared from this income after operating expenses and a small amount to go toward building up a reserve fund, were deducted. These Jewish cooperative credit unions are claimed to be the first

[1] From Moulton's *Money and Banking*, Part II. p. 376.

short-term personal cooperative credit associations organized in the United States.

Summary.—In the annual report of the Jewish Agricultural and Industrial Aid Society for 1919 Gabriel Davidson sums up its work as follows:

If our financial feature has been a helpful factor in building up the Jewish agricultural movement, our other activities have wielded a much more powerful influence. Our Information Bureau, intended to give the prospective farmer information by which he can weigh the subject from all angles, to give him an intelligent point of view of what farming is and what it is not; our Farm Employment Bureau, which affords him the opportunity of testing out his fitness on the farm of another—a desirable and inexpensive schooling; our Farm Finding Bureau, which helps him select his farm and saves him from the clutches of the rapacious land shark; our Extension Department, with its several branches—*The Jewish Farmer*, a Yiddish agricultural magazine which comes to him monthly, the lectures and visits of our itinerant instructors, the Credit Unions, the encouragement to organize and cooperate, the aid given toward community undertakings—religious, social, and educational; the competition open to the sons and daughters for free scholarships in the short courses at their State Agricultural Colleges; the student loans; the opportunity to obtain free expert advice on every conceivable farming problem; and our latest activity, the Rural Sanitation Bureau, which aims at the sanitary improvement of farm conditions—these are the things that gave the movement its impetus and that have contributed in greatest measure to place it on its present strong and solid footing. If we have made mistakes, as is inevitable in any human undertaking, we have, nevertheless, the satisfaction of feeling that we have made a substantial and lasting contribution to Jewish farming, and helped to place the Jewish farmers in the vanguard of every forward looking movement in American agriculture.

Concerted Legislative Effort.

Four Offices at Washington.—Reference has already been made in previous chapters to the fact that farmers' organizations have their representatives at Washington to present to Congress the farmers' point of view, with respect to legislative matters of vital interest to them. As stated by the representative of the American Farm Bureau Federation his "duties are to reflect, as best he can, the wishes of the farmers and to report to them the things they are interested in."[1] There are at present (1921) four regularly supported legislative offices at Washington representing farmers' organizations. They are

[1] From the *Hearings* before the Select Committee on Expenditures in the War Department, H. of Rep., 66th Cong., 3rd section.

as follows: The National Board of Farm Organizations, The National Grange, The American Farm Bureau Federation, and the Farmers' National Council.

There is close cooperation between the National Board of Farm Organizations and the National Grange officers. These two agencies represent organizations whose attitude toward public or legislative questions is very much the same; and while the National Grange has chosen to support its own representative, it nevertheless cooperates freely with the National Board of Farm Organizations on all important legislative matters. There does not appear to be such close cooperation between these two agencies and either of the other two. The aversion to the American Farm Bureau Federation seems to be due to its recent rapid growth and to the fact that it endangers the existence of some of the other farmers' organizations. Also its close relation to the extension service caused for some time at least considerable enmity against this farmers' organization among the leaders of the older organizations.

The National Board of Farm Organizations includes the following farmers' organizations: The Farmers' Union, Farmers' National Congress, National Agricultural Organization Society, National Conference on Marketing and Farm Credits, National Dairy Union, National Milk Producers' Federation, Farmers' Society of Equity, Farmers' Equity Union, American Society of Equity of Wisconsin, Pennsylvania State Grange, Federation of Jewish Farmers of America, and a few others.

The Farmers' National Council.—The Farmers' National Council, however, is by virtue of its stand on economic questions excluded from cooperation with the other legislative offices. In testimony given before a House Congressional Committee it was stated that the Council developed out of concerted action on the part of certain state granges. A "Conference of Progressive State Granges" was held for the purpose of pressing legislative demands supported by state granges and including those supported by the National Grange itself. The states taking part in this independent action were referred to in grange circles as the insurgent state granges. In the final alignment that followed the Farmers' National Council was organized with the support of the following groups: The Washington State Grange, The National Gleaner Federation, Michigan Potato Growers' Exchange, and the North Carolina Farmers' Union. The Council also received support from the Plumb Plan League because it stood for government ownership of railroads. A number of individuals contributed to the support of the council. The state grange of Washington very curiously supported the single-tax principle of taxation. It is very difficult to see how a group of farmers owning land can subscribe to this principle. To the student of taxation who recognizes "ability to pay" as the only fair and just basis of taxation the position of a farmer favoring the principle of imposing the whole tax burden solely on the farmer is not only illogical on the general ground of injustice but also entirely incongruous because the farmers as an economic group are desirous of increasing their shares of the distribution of wealth. The exclusive use of the single tax would be a move in the wrong direction. Many business relations affording opportunities to amass fortunes would go untaxed in spite of what single-tax theorists have to say on the subject, while the agricultural group would bear the whole burden of supporting the government. If the farmer understands his position he will favor the income tax. The Council group favors government ownership and operation of the railroads, of natural resources, and of ships. The other parts of their program have to do with packer control, cheap credits, etc., and are not very different from the programs of the other groups.

Other Organizations

The Farmers' National Congress.—In the chapter dealing with the history of the Farmers' Alliance reference was made to the Farmers' National Congress, and it was then pointed out that this organization probably grew out of the Agricultural Congress which was organized in 1870 uniting local agricultural societies of the South. Its name was changed in 1879 to the Farmers' Congress, and in subsequent years it held meetings at various points in the South. In 1888 it held a meeting at Chicago and this is the year, it is said, that marks the birth of the Farmers' National Congress. Since 1888 this association has had no local units. Its annual meetings are composed largely of delegates appointed by Governors of states, prominent agricultural workers, and representatives of other agricultural associations.[1]

The International Farm Congress.—This association has also no local units, its membership being made up entirely of individuals. It dates its beginning to the organization of the International Dry-Farming Congress at Denver in 1906. This association was incorporated in 1915 when it changed its name to the International Farm Congress. In 1917 the International Irrigation Congress was merged into the association. The organization centers in the Middle West, its headquarters being at Kansas City, Mo. Many of the larger farmers' associations send fraternal delegates to the annual meetings. Dues are two dollars a year per member. Other important sources of income are receipts from admissions to the Soil-Products Exposition, and the sale of space to exhibitors, and subscriptions to the *Agricultural Review,* a monthly publication.

Its aims and purposes are concerned wholly with agricultural education and the promotion of agricultural progress in general. As stated by the Congress in its own words: "It is purely a research and educational institution. Its membership is composed of those who believe in education, and in the theory that the development of individual efficiency and self-reliance must precede co-operative effort." In its Year Book it professes to be interested in all phases of agriculture, including educational and co-operative features.

Miscellaneous Organizations.—"The National Agricultural Organization Society was founded in 1915 under the auspices of The National Conference on Marketing and Farm Credits, but had only a short-lived existence. It was created as a service agency to give farmers' organizations an opportunity to make use of true and tried principles and methods of business practice."[2] Attention is called to the fact that such organiza-

[1] *Vide Yearbook* of the International Farm Congress for 1920, p. 146.

[2] From *Circular 2* of the National Agricultural Organization Society by Charles W. Holman.

tions exist in Europe and that in America with its large territory and scattered organization a similar agency would be of great benefit. The purposes of the Society are outlined below and have to do very largely with the establishment of cooperative enterprises on correct principles. It has been pointed out that professional promoters have entered the field of organizing cooperative associations and are taking as their compensation from 15 to 20 per cent of the stock issued by the companies. The result has been in some cases that a large foreign element was paid interest from the start and that even after the promoter's stock was sold to farmers interested in the particular enterprise the company's capital contained water upon which interest had to be paid. The purposes were as follows:

(a) To cooperate with central bodies and local branches of societies or other associations, for the promotion of "Better farming, better business, and better living."

(b) To organize agriculture and other rural industries in the United States on cooperative lines.

(c) To examine into the methods of production and distribution of farm products with a view of evolving systems of greater economy and efficiency in handling and marketing the same.

(d) To encourage and promote the cooperative organization of farmers and of those engaged in allied industries for mutual help in the distribution, storing, and marketing of produce.

(e) To aid in the economical transfer of agricultural produce from the producer to consumer.

(f) To supply instructors and lecturers upon the subject of cooperation among farmers, auditing and accounting experts and legal advice in matters relating to organization.

(g) To issue reports, pamphlets and instructions that will help in spreading knowledge of the best means of rural betterment and organizations.

(h) To encourage and cooperate with educational institutions, federal and state departments, societies, educational centers, etc., in all efforts to solve the questions of rural life, rural betterment and agricultural finance and marketing and distribution of produce and the special application of the facts and methods discovered to the conditions existing among the farmers of America and to the solution of the problem of increasing cost of living.

(i) To investigate the land conditions and land tenure with a view to working out better, more equitable and fairer systems of dealing with this problem so vital to the social and the economic well-being of the country.

(j) To call from time to time such conferences or conventions as will carry out the above mentioned objects.

In addition to the organization already discussed in detail there are some organizations like the National Conference on Marketing and Farm Credits, now also defunct, that are composed largely of college men and others who are familiar with the experimental and theoretic aspects of rural economic problems, and are engaged in issuing pamphlets of a scientific character for the express purpose of placing before the people correct principles of marketing, credits, and of such other subjects upon which technical information may be desired. There are also other organizations existing fundamentally for the purpose of conducting a cooperative enterprise like the Dairymen's League, or the National Milk Producers' Association which are nevertheless using their organized power to influence legislation and in some cases for educational and social purposes. For a complete roster of both public and private agricultural organizations in America the student is referred to the *Directory of American Agricultural Organizations* issued by the United States Department of Agriculture.

SELECTED REFERENCES

Everitt, *The Third Power;* Robinson, *Agricultural Activities of the Jews in America; Year Book* of the International Farm Congress.

CHAPTER XXII

BREED ASSOCIATIONS

In the development of this subject only a few of the associations that have been organized for the improvement of domestic animals used in agriculture, will be discussed. Space would not permit to treat all the associations, nor would such a procedure be necessary to set forth their character and principles of organization, their aims and purposes, and their achievements. The discussion will, therefore, be based mainly on the American Short-Horn Breeders' Association, the American Jersey Cattle Club, the Percheron Society of America, the American Hampshire Sheep Association, and the American Berkshire Association. There are of course other associations organized for the purpose of improving various breeds of live stock. In England there are about sixty different breed associations, while in America there are almost as many.

Early Conditions.—While domestic animals were obtained from the wild animals of the forest and plain long before the dawn of history, as far as is known no individual attempts to establish or improve the character of certain breeds of live stock on a large scale were made until after the beginning of the modern era. It would seem that scattered efforts to improve live stock on the part of owners of large herds during the pastoral and agricultural ages must have been carried on to some extent, although such attempts must have been few and also futile because the character of political and economic organization of the early stages of civilized life rarely permitted experimentation of any kind. Such advances as may have been made during the time when the Roman Empire was in the height of its power and glory were largely lost and failed to be transmitted to the posterity of the western world. Under the manorial organization of the medieval days society was static because of the traditional rules of serfdom and methods of agriculture which were adhered to from generation to generation. Experimentation was only possible on the lord's demesne, but probably rarely consciously carried on because of a lack of knowledge of correct breeding principles or any appreciation of possibilities, and especially because of insufficient feedstuffs to carry cattle through the winter. The development of cattle throughout Europe was really impossible before the general introduction of the improved grasses, including timothy and clover, which provided hay in much greater abundance than the few meadow lands formerly relied upon as the main source of winter feedstuffs. Then too, the chief motive, that of selling pure-bred stock at advanced prices, which actuates breeders to organize and perpetuate breed associations and establish systems of registry, did not exist during the days of the manor when cattle was less freely bought and sold than now and seldom imported from foreign countries. Before the days of individual efforts to improve cattle and before the formation of breed associations the development of breeds and the character of such breeds were dependent upon the environment and the simple discretion exercised by owners of cattle. Such desirable qualities as gentleness and to some degree also productivity were consciously developed by mankind from the time animals were domesticated to the present day. In some parts of the world the environment played an important role in establishing breeds because of its isolation from other parts of the world and because of its equable climate providing sufficient feedstuffs throughout the entire year. This factor, probably more than any other, established the breed of Jersey cattle on the Island of Jersey in the English Channel. But the progress made under all these silent forces of nature during all the years of the ancient past up to fifty years ago, says Professor W. S. Anderson, is in no way comparable to the improvement effected during the last half century under the influence of breed associations.[1] The marvelous result of conscious breeding is, therefore, at once apparent, and breed associations which are the source and fountain head of conscious breeding must be recognized as a very important form of social organization.

The Origin of Breed Associations.—The world owes to

[1] For assistance in the collection of the bibliography and some of the facts the author is indebted to W. S. Anderson, Professor of Genetics at the University of Kentucky.

English breeders a great debt because it was in England where most of the breeds of live stock were originated. The first record of pedigrees of live stock appears to have been made of the race horse. Horse racing was an established practice in England before 1700 because in 1709 the first records of racing were published and from that time on racing records were preserved. In 1786 William Pick published all the pedigrees of English race horses that he could obtain.[1]

The first attempt to publish a herd book of any character or description was made in 1803 when Mr. Weatherby of England published the first volume of the General Stud Book. In one way or another the record of the race horse has been continued in the subsequent publication of the General Stud Book. It must be said, however, that the publication of the English race-horse General Stud Book has been more a venture of a group of individuals than of a regular breed association.

The next attempt to form a breed association was made by Shorthorn cattle breeders. "Authentic history of the Shorthorns begins in the eighteenth century, but tradition carries the origin of the breed back 200 years earlier, when they were owned by the dukes and earls of Northumberland. In the seventeenth century the Aislabies of Studley Park had Shorthorns, and other herds existed in Durham and Yorkshire. Sir Hugh Smithson, who was made a peer with the title of Duke of Northumberland in 1766, was so fond of his Shorthorns that his fellow peers called him the Yorkshire Grazier."[1] A number of breeders early interested themselves in the improvement of Shorthorns because they milked well and fattened quickly, but "the most marked improvement" in the Shorthorns in this period was made by Charles and Robert Colling who carefully studied the scientific methods of Robert Bakewell. This man is given credit for first applying scientific principles in the breeding of cattle and sheep in England. His experiments were carried out with a breed called Longhorns which had only a brief existence. The Colling brothers used the best of his methods and soon developed a breed which

---

[1] *Vide* scattered references in Wallace's *Horse of America.*

From a pamphlet issued by the American Shorthorn Breeders' Association.

attracted wide attention. They advertised their Shorthorns largely by exhibiting them at fairs. In 1796 Charles Colling raised and fattened a steer which at five years old attained a weight of 3,024 pounds. It was bought by Mr. Bulmer for $700 for exhibition purposes and was moved in a wagon from fair to fair. Later Robert Colling raised a pure-bred heifer which was so extensively exhibited that it became known as "The White Heifer that Traveled." In 1810 he sold a herd at auction which brought him an average of $755 per head. One cow sold for $2,050, and the bull, Comet (155), brought $5,000, the first Shorthorn to sell for that sum.

Prominent among the names of breeders of Shorthorn cattle are Bates and Booth of England who bred especially for the development of milking qualities, and Cruickshank of Scotland who developed a heavy and early maturing class of cattle and, therefore, suitable as beef cattle. While both milking and beef strains of Shorthorn cattle have been highly developed in America and abroad "it is now the exception to find a herd of distinct Bates blood, but Bates cattle topped with Scotch bulls are quite numerous."

Out of these individual efforts to improve the Shorthorn breed of cattle there developed the plan of organizing a breed association and the publication of a herd book. As early as 1812 a meeting was called in England at which such distinguished breeders as the Colling brothers, Bates, Booth, Trotter, Wetherell, Baker, Wright, Stephenson, Hustler, Raine, Hutchinson, Rudd and Coates were present. While the cattle of these English breeders were pure-bred, pedigrees were not always carefully kept, and many Shorthorns were imported into the United States between 1820 and 1850, some as early as 1790, without pedigrees, probably for the reason that it was not thought important. The first Shorthorn herd book was published in 1822 by George Coates. At intervals of about seven years other herd books appeared until nineteen volumes were printed down to 1871, when the association had passed through the uncertain and experimental stage and became one of the established institutions of England.

The first American Shorthorn herd book was published

in 1846 by Lewis F. Allen of Buffalo, N. Y., who was later joined by Wm. T. Bailey in its publication. Other volumes appeared at irregular intervals. Several Shorthorn registers were brought out in different states resulting in considerable confusion and finally in the consolidation of all the records into one register published under the authority of the American Shorthorn Breeders' Association. Alvin H. Sanders, editor of the *Breeder's Gazette* in his *Shorthorn Cattle* has the following to say concerning the development of an authoritative Shorthorn herd book in the United States:[1]

> One of the most important events of the period under review was the purchase in the autumn of 1882 by the American Shorthorn Breeders' Association of the Herd Book, which had up to that date been issued as a private enterprise by Lewis F. Allen, Buffalo, N. Y. The price paid was $25,000. More or less confusion in reference to American records had arisen from the fact that a pedigree register, known as the American Shorthorn Record, had been established and published for some years in Kentucky and that a similar book, known as the Ohio Shorthorn Record, was being issued by the breeders of the Buckeye State.
>
> Both of these registers were the manifestation of disapproval of the manner in which Mr. Allen was conducting the herd book which he had established in 1846. The purchase and consolidation of these various records by the national breeders' association was the happy solution of a situation that was becoming fairly intolerable, and since 1883 but one book has been in existence.

The American Jersey Cattle Club was organized in 1868, which is twenty-two years after the formation of the American Shorthorn Association. The Jersey breed, however, was imported into the United States as early as 1817.[1] Importations were more numerous after 1840. That year Henry Clay imported the breed into Kentucky, and later larger numbers were imported into New England and other sections of the country. The purity of the Jersey breed was early fostered by the fact that its home was on the Island of Jersey. The natural or geographic influence was aided by special legislation in 1789 which recognized the Jersey breed of cattle as the only desirable breed and prohibited the importation of cattle into the Island under a penalty of a heavy fine and imprisonment. Only for immediate slaughter may cattle be imported.

Page 742.

[1] *Vide* pamphlet published by the American Jersey Cattle Club.

The Jersey breed of cattle is known for its economical production of butter fat. Its long isolation has fixed this characteristic and is now perpetuated and promoted in the United States by the American Jersey Cattle Club. On the Island of Jersey a herd book is published by the Royal Jersey Agricultural Society in which only prize animals and their offspring are entered.

The Percheron Society of America was organized in 1902 and finds its *raison d'etre* in the promotion of the Percheron horse. This breed of horses has existed since time immemorial in the ancient French province of *le Perche.* Because of its strong and sturdy character it was used in warfare during the feudal days of France and by the Crusaders in their efforts to re-establish the Christian faith in Palestine.[1] His physical strength and gentle nature make him a very satisfactory draft animal and his further improvement fostered by the Percheron Society of America is, therefore, a service rendered to American agriculture that is well worth while.

While the domestic sheep is older than civilization and while wool was for a long time the chief material from which garments were made, a concerted effort to improve this domestic animal, known in history, song and literature for its beauty, docility and usefulness, was, as in the case of other live stock, delayed until a relatively recent period. The American Hampshire Sheep Association was not organized until 1889. Its protege, the Hampshire sheep, is also a product of England. In 1855 John Wilson, Professor of Agriculture in the University of Edinburgh, wrote, "The rapidly increasing breed of Hampshire sheep appears to be the result of a cross or intermingling of the bloods of the pure South Down and the horned sheep of Hampshire and Wiltshire by which the hard working qualities of the former are combined with the superior size and constitution of the latter to the improvement of both."[2] It is stated that the Association made at first slow progress, but that in recent years it grew rapidly, that demand for the Hampshire increased to large proportions, and that importa-

[1] *Vide* the *Percheron Review* of January, 1922.

[2] *Vide* pamphlet by the American Hampshire Sheep Association entitled *Hampshire Sheep Lore.*

tions of pure-bred Hampshires in 1913 according to the Association were three times the number of all other breeds of sheep combined.

The American Berkshire Association was organized February 28, 1875, and is said to be the oldest association organized for the recording of pedigrees of the breeds of smaller live stock.[1]

Other breed associations might be referred to, but enough has been said to show that the movement to establish such associations is of comparatively recent origin, and that the conditions under which they are organized vary somewhat, but that the chief motive for their organization is profit to the breeder. They are primarily a product of the last half of the nineteenth century. The causes for their establishment and their continued growth will be more fully understood after one becomes familiar with their character of organization, their aims and purposes, and their achievements.

Character of Organization.—Breed associations are generally organized as corporations, with or without capital stock. When shares are issued the more usual par value of stock is probably ten dollars. This is the par value of the stock of the Percheron Society of America, while that of the stock of the American Shorthorn Breeders' Association is twenty-five dollars. The American Jersey Cattle Club is an example of a non-stock corporation, membership in the Club being secured through the payment of a fee of one hundred dollars. The American Berkshire Association was formerly a stock corporation which issued its stock first at a par value of one hundred dollars, but in 1903 it reduced it to twenty-five dollars and later to ten dollars. In 1921 a reorganization was effected, and membership is now attained by the payment of a fee of ten dollars.

The stock corporations pay no dividends in as much as profit in this form is not the motive of organization. Certain advantages, however, accrue to members that are not secured by other breeders. It should be stated in this connection that the influence and work of the breed association are not limited

[1] From the *Berkshire Bulletin*, April, 1921.

to benefits bestowed upon its members. There is a large number of non-member breeders who register animals according to the prescribed rules in the herd book and record of merit, and whose product receives the same recognition in the market as that of members. Membership advantages in some associations are of considerable importance, while in others they only amount to receiving a copy of the herd book free, record fees for members and non-members being the same. This plan is followed by the Shorthorn Association. The Jersey Cattle Club and the Percheron Society, however, make an important distinction between members and non-members with respect to the amount of the registration fee. A member pays only half as much as the non-member, five dollars being paid by the member under certain conditions in the case of both of these associations and ten dollars by the non-member, which in the case of five registrations a year is a sufficient inducement to join the association. Besides the pecuniary advantage there is of course the advantage of control. The larger breeders are interested in the formulation of policies and the institution of activities that will popularize the breed and set up a strong and active demand for their product.

Membership in some associations must necessarily be large because of the inducements given to breeders to join. In stock corporation membership is limited to the amount of authorized capital stock. At present the Shorthorn Association has 800 shares which are owned by nearly as many stockholders. The Jersey Cattle Club in 1921 had 974 members. The Percheron Society has an authorized capital stock of $350,000 or 35,000 shares of $10 each. The Berkshire Association in 1921 had nearly 2,000 members which at the time was limited by the amount of stock outstanding. While members are admitted into the association upon the payment of a fee or through the purchase of stock they must have certain qualifications in order to receive the approval of the board of directors. To be eligible for membership the applicant must be a careful and reliable breeder, and in some cases must have the endorsement of several members.

Annual and special meetings are held. The associations

have the usual corps of officers, including the executive committee to which the board of directors entrusts a large part of the management. The secretary is appointed by the board of directors and is a paid official. His main duties are the preparation of the herd book and the record of merit, which are publications containing records of birth of registered animals and performance of registered animals respectively.

Registration fees charged by the different associations vary, and in some cases, as stated, members are charged a smaller sum than non-members. The Shorthorn Association charges $2.00 for calves under twelve months of age and $1.00 for recording a transfer from one owner to another. These amounts are considerably lower than the fees charged by some other associations.

Many of the associations have local and state organizations. The national association encourages this divisional organization in order that the interests of the breed may best be promoted in all parts of the country. The following is taken from a circular letter of the Shorthorn Association:

> A plan was adopted for the organization of states and groups of states into districts, each to have its Shorthorn breeders' association. Each district association will employ a manager or secretary who will be expected to devote his full time to the management of breeders' sales and in other ways help to dispose of cattle either in or out of his own district. If breeders will take hold and help by joining their district associations and by devoting some of their efforts to promote the work of their district manager, the new plan can be expected to stimulate a greater business in Shorthorns than ever previously known.

Local organization enables the national association more readily to aid the breeders in the promotion of their interests. Cooperative advertising schemes may more readily be used; field men can readily ascertain information concerning the dates of farmers' and other meetings where they may do something toward the advancement of the breed, not to mention the more direct service of facilitating sales of registered live stock.

Breed associations are wholly private. They receive no public aid from the state or federal governments.

Rules and Methods of Registration.—Rules of entry in the herd book vary among breed associations according to the history and character of particular breeds of live stock. As previously stated, most of our pure-bred live stock originated in England. It, therefore, follows that American breed associations usually have provisions permitting the registration of imported stock in American herd books, provided such stock is registered in the foreign herd book. The American herd book in fact is in most cases a continuation record of pedigrees started in England. In the case of the Percheron horse an imported animal to be eligible for registration in the Percheron Stud Book of America must have been registered in the Percheron Stud Book of France. Imported stock, however, may not be registered after a certain period has elapsed. The Shorthorn Association does not permit registration after three years from date of importation, and encourages registration earlier by charging larger fees if registration is delayed.

In the registration of an American-bred animal the one important condition is that its sire and dam must have been registered. Only in this way can a breed remain pure. It would of course not do to allow the registration of stock which has only one registered parent. Foreign blood can only be excluded by admitting to entry in the herd book only offspring whose sire and dam are both registered. In this way characteristics of breeds become fixed, and through the use of pure-bred males these characteristics may be transmitted to a large degree to the herds of farmers throughout the country. This is an important service rendered by breed associations. They may be thought of as the custodians of the breed, and it is through them that live stock throughout the country generally may be improved.

The American Shorthorn Association requires that "pedigree applications for animals bred or born in the United States must give sex, name, color, birth-date, breeder's name and address, purchaser's name and address, and date of purchase, name and record numbers of both sire and dam, and signed by the breeder—the breeder being the owner of the dam at the time of service."

It is the practice in America to show pedigrees in herd books usually for ten generations only. That is to say, the names of ten ancestral sires and ten ancestral dams are given with the additional information that the earliest sire and dam "trace" to imported animals. It follows, therefore, that frequently many generations are omitted between the earliest animal and the imported one. The records of past generations can, however, be obtained from former herd books.

The usual form in which pedigrees are shown is known as the columnar form. This method traces the animal back through the maternal side, showing, however, also the sire of each of the ten dams. A more satisfactory method of showing pedigrees is the tabulated form which by means of brackets traces the animal's ancestors on a larger scale and shows a wider degree of relationship. The customary method is the columnar form, but this information in the case of the Shorthorn Association is supplemented by foot-notes which give the data necessary to put the pedigree in tabulated form as far back as the first three sires. The Percheron Society agrees to furnish tabulated pedigrees for the sum of ten dollars. In this information they include eight generations which represent approximately 510 ancestors. Other information, such as color of all ancestors, interesting facts about their show records, etc., is also given.

As already stated, each animal to be registered must be given a name. The association assigns a number to the animal, and this number it should be remembered is more important as a mark of identification than the name. However, the name has its significance and should be selected by the breeder according to a definite plan. If it is desirable to show connection with a famous line of ancestors, the same name with successive numbers could be used, such as, Clara 72nd, Clara 76th, etc. If it is desirable to give the animal a name in no way indicating relationship or succession, its outstanding qualities should be given consideration. Gentility, refinement, and performance in the case of female cattle, or strength and masculinity in the case of males, are qualities that suggest significant names. Associations limit the length of names, in some cases to four words of a certain length.

The Register of Merit.—From what has been said it is obvious that the performance of registered or pure-bred stock is not necessarily better than non-registered stock. It is probably true that the larger breeders are more or less careful in registering animals. The poorest animals are probably not registered, but according to the rules all animals of sires and dams having recorded pedigrees, regardless of their individual worth, are eligible for registration. In other words the breed association through the herd book maintains the purity of the breed, but does not necessarily through each successive generation improve the quality of live stock. This improvement of live stock or the elimination of the animal poor in quality or unsatisfactory from the point of view of performance, is accomplished by means of registers of merit, also called records of merit.

To be eligible for entry in these advanced records the animal must of course first have been registered in the herd book, but it must also be meritorious. Through this means the breed association is enabled to set standards of performance. Progressive breeders are naturally eager to avail themselves of the opportunity of having worthy animals recorded in records of merit, because this means that animals so recorded have had their performance impartially and accurately tested, and that as a consequence their market value is greater than animals only registered in the herd book. In the case of dairy breed associations the standard of performance making the animal eligible for entry in the record of merit requires the production of a certain quantity of milk and butter fat graduated according to the age of the cow. The Shorthorn requirements are as follows:

	Yearly Production in Pounds	
Age at Starting Record	*Milk*	*Butter Fat*
30 mo. or under	5,250	210
36 to 42 mo.	5,790	228
42 to 48 mo.	6,330	246
48 to 54 mo.	6,870	264
54 to 64 mo.	7,410	282
60 mo. or over	8,000	300

These quantities of milk and butter fat must be produced within twelve months. The standard of the Jersey Register of Merit expressed in terms of butter fat is higher than the above standard by 60 pounds if tests are continued for only 305 days; and by 100 pounds, if continued for 365 days. In other words a Jersey cow recorded in the highest class, if five years of age or more, must within 305 days produce 360 pounds of butter fat.

The register of merit records of performance in classes or grades depending, in the case of the Shorthorn cow, upon the character of the supervision of the test. These grades of performance are designated A, B, and C. The value of the test is dependent upon the accuracy and impartiality with which it is conducted. The test recorded as A is supervised by experiment stations; that recorded as B, by cow-testing associations; and that as C, by private parties who report at short intervals and submit sworn affidavits to the association. In the latter case the association may provide supervision. The Jersey Cattle Club allows only one way of supervising tests and that is through the agricultural colleges and experiment stations. This association also has three classes of entries, but its classification is based on the length of the period between calvings and also upon the length of the testing period. The highest class, AAA, for instance, allows only fourteen months between the current and previous calvings, and the testing period is limited to 305 days. The second class, AA, allows sixteen months between calvings and 365 days for the testing period. At the age of five years the productivity of a cow for entry in the second class must be 400 pounds of butter fat. The Jersey association also allows the registration of bulls in the Register of Merit if the animal has three daughters, out of different dams, entered therein.

The use of the record of merit which permits the setting of quality standards is common among breed associations. The basis of these records is usually performance graded in some cases by competent judges according to points scored. In the case of the trotting and race horses, records made on the track are collected and recorded in a year book.

The Self-Propagation of Breed Associations.—Once a breed of live stock is established and is acknowledged generally as the best or one of the best of its kind the future existence of the association fostering the breed is virtually assured. The strength of the association lies in the herd book which records lineage and especially in the register of merit which records performance of pure-bred stock. The older the breed the larger the number of animals registered and the larger the number of breeders interested in the success of the breed. This means that as the breed is improved the number of registrations will steadily increase. The impelling motive to improve the productivity of live stock is competition or rivalry among different breeders within the same breed and especially among different breeds. The breeder most successful in raising animals having high productivity is the one to receive the highest prices for his stock. This necessarily tends to raise the quality of a particular breed. In a number of cases there is strong competition among different breeds. If it can be demonstrated that the Jersey cow produces butter fat more economically than any other breed, the general use of the Jersey for the production of butter and cream is assured. If a particular breed can be made to produce larger quantities of milk with a sufficient quantity of butter fat, the use of such a breed for the production of milk for fresh consumption will become general.

The primary force that causes associations to expand is the productivity of the breed, and this productivity is constantly raised because of competition among breeders within the breed as well as outside the breed. Organization campaigns are, therefore, not so necessary as in the case of farmers' organizations of the type of the Grange, the Farmers' Union, and the Farm Bureau. The cohesive force among breeders resulting in the formation of breed associations and their perpetuation is of much greater intensity than any of the influences that tend to organize farmers in a general way or even to form cooperative associations based upon a single commodity. However, it is important that any commodity be advertised if it would have a sale, and pure-bred live stock is not an exception. Performance records must be made known if a good-will for the breed is to be created. Associations, therefore, do well to advertise their stock widely, and this, in fact, is what they are doing.

The success of the breed association is not merely dependent upon the intrinsic worth of the breed it fosters, but is influenced by economic conditions in general. The power of substitution plays an important role not only with respect to the horse and mule, or such animals that provide power for various purposes including transportation, but also with respect to animals that provide meat. In the case of power for various purposes, mechanical power is to a very considerable extent taking the place of animals or horse power. In transportation a very marked substitution has taken place and is still under way. As time goes on economy of production will determine to a large extent what animals will be most generally called upon to furnish the country's meat supply. This factor will very largely determine whether it will be cattle, sheep, chickens, rabbits, goats, or other animals. Of course the taste of the consumer, whether educated or uneducated, plays its part in the direction of the production of foodstuffs, but difference in costs of production in a congested population in the long run is a great force in determining consumption and, therefore, the general introduction of certain kinds of meat. The extent to which this or that domestic animal will be produced in the future, obviously, rests upon a number of complex factors, and of course the *raison d'etre* of the breed association continues only so long as the demand for the animal it fosters continues to exist.

Association Activities.—The maintenance of the herd book and the register of merit is fundamental to the life of the breed association. Other activities are known as publicity and extension work. These activities are propaganda conducted in the interest of particular breeds fostered. Virtually all associations publish journals setting forth the virtues of their breeds and containing news items more or less closely related to them. The national association in some instances spends large sums for advertising purposes. The American Jersey Cattle Club in its advertising makes two lines of appeals. In selected farm journals it appeals to the farmers to buy Jerseys; through general publications it makes an appeal to the consuming public to demand Jersey products. This two-fold system of advertising finally results in setting up a demand for pure-bred Jersey stock, and in this way benefits the breeders. The club also engages in cooperative advertising. The national association in its own advertisement announces its willingness to send free literature explaining the virtues of its breed, and with this advertisement there are associated those of Jersey breeders. This makes a larger Jersey advertisement than would result from placing single "ads" and, therefore, attracts more attention. Local clubs use this same cooperative plan in advertising their stock and products. In the retailing of Jersey milk the national association suggests cooperative advertising among breeders, and where the retailing is done by middlemen it is suggested that they join the breeders and share a part of the expense. The national association has standard cuts which it stands ready to make available for breeders and breed associations. During the fiscal year ending March 31, 1922, the national organization of the Jersey Cattle Club spent $4,012.10 for advertising in newspapers and magazines, while the Shorthorn association spent $10,240.48 for this purpose during the fiscal year ending October 31, 1921.

The chief form of extension work among breed associations is usually carried on in connection with fairs. The national association usually offers large sums every year as premiums for the best entries at state, district, and county fairs. Attractive displays representing stock and its products are also shown. The Jersey Cattle Club during the above fiscal year paid out $8,277.30 as premiums but had offered as much as $10,450. The Shorthorn association during the fiscal year of 1921 spent nearly $6,000 for the exhibition of stock at shows and $103,652.47 in the form of premium awards, while the Percheron Society paid out $6,085.75 for the latter purpose.

Another important extension activity is field work, which consists of the sending of association representatives to farmers' meetings where problems of agriculture and especially those of live stock are discussed. Field men also consult with breeders and frequently assist in the making of sales.

The national association receives a large number of inquiries from persons who wish information concerning the nearest breeder from whom they may buy stock. Associations generally assist breeders in placing them in touch with prospective buyers. The Percheron Society has a special organization for this purpose which it calls the Service Bureau. The list of buyers provided includes names of persons living in Canada and other foreign countries.

Other activities include the encouragement of the organization of boys' and girls' live-stock clubs, the making of moving pictures and lending them for exhibition at various meetings, the distribution of literature to schools, colleges and individuals, and the suggestion of the use of proper business methods on the part of breeders.

Revenues and Expenditures.—The more important breed associations handle a very considerable sum of money during the course of a year. The total income of the Shorthorn association for the fiscal year of 1921 was $321,422.65, and its total expenditures amounted to $346,120.24 which was more than $24,000 in excess of income. The association at the close of the year, however, still had a surplus of more than $120,000 which was invested in sound and liquid securities. The total income for the Jersey Club during the fiscal year of 1922 was $299,498.26 out of which it spent $216,633.89. This association at this time had a surplus of more than $180,000.

The chief sources of revenue of all breed associations are charges for registrations in the herd book and in the register of merit and fees for the recording of transfers, that is, the recording of the names of purchasers of pure-bred animals. The Jersey Cattle Club for the year under discussion collected herd-book registration fees amounting to $121,603, transfer fees amounting to $69,227, and register-of-merit fees amounting to $28,951.

As already indicated the main object of expenditure has a tendency to be the extension work of which fair and show exhibits, including premium awards and field work, represent the principal outlays. Head-office clerical expenses constitute an important item, while amounts spent for the publication of herd books, registers of merit, and breed journals are also large.

Some Achievements of Breed Associations.—As previously stated, most of the breed associations are less than fifty years old, and yet the work which they have accomplished is indeed marvelous. Greater improvement in the development of live stock has been effected during the last fifty years than was made throughout the entire previous history of animal breeding. This improvement could not have been made without the breed associations. It should be stated, however, that the work of live-stock improvement on the farm has really only begun, and an enormous amount of work is yet ahead of the breed associations to rid the nation of the inferior scrub animals that now very largely hold sway upon the farms of America. In time through the efforts of the breed associations these will disappear and pure-bred animals will be in use everywhere.

This discussion is primarily concerned with breed associations that foster the improvement of farm animals. The principle of scientific breeding has probably nowhere yielded greater results than in the development of trotting and race horses; but farming is little concerned with these animals, nor is the country at large as much dependent upon them today as formerly, now that more efficient means of transportation have been perfected. It is the improvement of dairy and beef cattle, hogs, and sheep, in which farmers generally and also the consuming public are primarily interested. The average production of butter fat per cow per year in the United States is in the neighborhood of 150 pounds, and yet the minimum Shorthorn requirements for entry of cows of five years of age in the register of merit is 300 pounds, while that of the Jersey is 360 or 400 depending upon the conditions of calving and whether or not the test is continued throughout the entire year. But the achievements of pure-bred dairy cattle according to accurate and authoritative tests conducted by officials of experiment stations or otherwise are much greater than these minimum requirements. Following is the record of a few Shorthorn cows in class A:

Name	*Pounds of Milk*	*Pounds of Butter Fat*
Snow-drop	15,550.8	691.59
Doris Clay	17,241.5	653.67
Dairymaid 8th	16,460.3	587.10
Bare Fashion	17,027.9	581.47
Rose of Blackwood 3rd	17,564.0	569.70

The possibilities of productivity of the Jersey cow may be seen from the record of the best five tested cows over five years old as follows:

Name	*Pounds of Milk*	*Pounds of Butter Fat*
Sophie 19th of Hood Farm, 189,748	17,557.8	999.1
Spermfield Owl's Eva, 193,934	16,457.4	993.3
Eminent's Bess, 209,719	18,783.0	962.8
Dosoris Park Lily, 233,783	16,728.1	957.4
Jacoba Irene, 146,443	17,253.2	953.0

While the Shorthorn cow does not produce as much butter fat as the Jersey, it is, however, consistently a good milker; and this fact coupled with her beef producing qualities makes the Shorthorn breed of cattle very profitable under certain conditions of farming and demand for live-stock products. The records shown above indicate that the present low average of productivity of American cows can be very readily more than doubled. The average production of whole herds may readily be raised to 500 pounds of butter fat which of course would mean a tremendous increase in the food supply of the country. What may be accomplished with the dairy cow illustrates the possibilities in the production of beef, pork, and mutton. Much credit is due breed associations for improvements in meat-producing animals.

In noting the character of organization of breed associations and the benefits they bring to society one is reminded of the fundamental dictum enunciated by Adam Smith in his *Wealth of Nations* in 1776. He strongly contended that with respect to economic activities the interests of the individual and society run parallel. The individual actuated by motives of self-interest produces a plethora of economic goods and makes them available for society. He was opposed to minute government regulation and government ownership of most of the instruments of production, believing that private enterprise will result in greater productivity. The breed association, unaided by public funds, and enjoying the elements of cohesion in organization, self-propagation, and continuity of existence, bestows immeasurable benefits upon society, and is an example *par excellence* of a private enterprise thriving best under a *laissez-faire* status.

SELECTED REFERENCES

Wallace, J. H., *The Horse of America;* Lewis F. Allen, *History of Shorthorn Cattle;* Sanders, *Shorthorn Cattle;* P. L. S. Mourant, *The Jersey Cow;* C. L. Hill, *The Guernsey Breed;* British Board of Agriculture and Fisheries, *British Breeds of Livestock;* various pamphlets issued by breed associations.

CHAPTER XXIII

THE FARMER AND THE CLASS STRUGGLE

Historic Conceptions of Class Struggle.—From time immemorial mankind has developed its social classes to a greater or less degree. Primitive society had its weak and strong members. Its leaders were richly rewarded for protecting their own groups from extermination by hostile tribes. Natal differences as to ability have always existed among mankind. This is a biological factor that will forever breed social classes. Jesus said to his disciples, "Ye have the poor always with you."[1] The most that may be hoped for is that the poor class may rise considerably above the level of mere subsistence; but a state of some degree of relativity will always obtain. The economic factor of the division of labor also to a greater or less degree has always been operative in society and played an important role in the creation of classes. As time goes on and inventions increase this factor has a tendency steadily to complicate our social stratification. The division of labor throws people into groups and causes them to have economic interests in common. "In all past ages we find a complicated division of society into ranks and classes. In Rome patricians, knights, plebeians, slaves; in the Middle Ages feudal lords, vassals, guild-masters, journeymen, apprentices, serfs."[2] The breakdown of the manor and the Industrial Revolution did not do away with classes but gave us new ones. A number of classes constituting present-day society could be enumerated. The more prominent groups are the agricultural, manufacturing, merchant, labor, financial, professional, transportation, communication, and public-service classes. Society has always had its classes and has always had its class struggle; but real life is one thing and its interpretation is another. The theory of life is not always rightly conceived. This we find true with respect to the interpretation of the class struggle.

In literature of all times at least the recognition of social

[1] *Bible*, Matthew, XXVI-11.

[2] Simkovitch in his *Marxism Versus Socialism*, p. 192, referring to historical allusions made by Karl Marx.

classes may be found. The idea that classes are engaged in a bitter struggle is also an old one. Karl Marx writing in the first half of the nineteenth century is not the inventor of the idea, but found the conception of class struggle glibly made use of in the writings of Sismondi, Saint-Simon and other French and German socialists. Simkhovitch points out that also Guizot, the great historian and statesman, bewailed the existence of the class struggle as prime minister in 1848 and regarded it as "a scourge, a shame that our age cannot endure."[1] The same author cites references written as early as 1767 in which a similar portrayal of bitter class war is made. The early socialist writers saw only misery in the existence of classes and denounced the capitalistic order. Communistic societies were proposed and in a limited way tried out. Thus the idea of a bitter class struggle had been suggested many times to Karl Marx who embodies it in a deterministic form in his theory of socialism. Marx was a student of history and philosophy and believed with Hegel, the German philosopher, that history must of necessity be continuous. He rejected however, Hegel's idea that a *welt-geist* or world spirit was ever trying to realize itself or to express itself in an improved form among mankind. Karl Marx was one of those who believed that all history is determined by the economic life of man. The one activity that shapes all history, he believed, is the class struggle, and history through all the ages must necessarily lead up to a time when it shall all end in a glorious victory for the oppressed classes. Briefly stated Marx's theory holds that a "division of labor produces a division of classes, with the lower class in constant struggle against the upper class. The concentration of industry leads to a concentration of capital, which, while narrowing the capitalist class to a small circle of financial and industrial magnates, pushes the middle class—artisians, shop-keepers and farmers—into the ranks of wage-earners. The continuous development and frequent revolution of technique make production more and more independent of the workingman's skill and physical strength. Improved machinery displaces labor and makes it possible to

[1] *Vide Simkhovitch, op. cit.*, p. 157, and chapter VIII, *passim.*

substitute unskilled for skilled labor, child labor for adult labor. These changes increase the reserve army of the unemployed and make the living conditions of the employed more and more precarious. The growing misery of the working class increasingly accentuates and embitters the raging class struggle."[1] According to Marx the time finally comes "when the class struggle nears the decisive hour. The process of dissolution going on within the ruling class, in fact, within the whole range of society, assumes such a violent, glaring character, that a small section of the ruling class cuts itself adrift and joins the revolutionary class, the class that holds the future in its hands."[2] The social revolution is now at hand. The proletariat, or the wage-earning and revolutionary class, is now all-powerful and proceeds "to destroy all previous securities for, and insurances of, individual property."[3]

A Rational View of Class Struggle.—Professor Simkhovitch has no difficulty in proving that the revolutionary or Marxian theory of class struggle is wholly a misinterpretation of economic life. To one who studies the demands of the various social classes it seems visionary, fanciful, and far removed from the reality of life. There are social classes and there is a class struggle, but there is no force operative in society leading ultimately to the abolition of all private property, including the farm, and the merging of all classes into one. There are biological differences that will forever tend to cause intellectual stratification in society and aid the economic factor, the division of labor, to establish and maintain social classes. The farmers, the manufacturers, the merchants, the bankers, the professional men, etc., belong to separate classes, and members of each class have certain economic interests in common. The complex economic organization necessarily requires specialization in production. In as much as business does not rest on charity, but is rather based on self-interest, there is a tendency among economic classes to exploit one another. Legislation could be enacted that would benefit one class to the exclusion of other groups and deserve the familiar characterization of

---

[1] Statement from Simkhovitch, *op. cit.*, p. 147.
[2] From the *Communist Manifesto.*
[3] *Ibid.*

"class legislation." Occupational grouping or division of labor does cause members of groups to have certain economic interests in common which if fostered to an extreme degree for one group become detrimental to other groups. Thus protection granted manufacturers and none the farmers is detrimental to the agricultural class.

The physical environment and the sphere of activity of the various classes are themselves responsible for bestowing advantages upon some groups and inflicting disabilities upon others. As a result the social life of the various classes must necessarily be different. Thus the farming population is generally recognized to be laboring under disabilities as compared with the city classes. The farmers' isolation in the past, which, however, is rapidly diminishing, has made it difficult to provide educational facilities equal to that of urban centers. Unlike trading or manufacturing, the very character of farming makes it difficult for the agrciultural class to secure credit as readily as other classes. The short-term operations of the manufacturer and trader and the ease with which they can develop a personal acquaintance with bankers and secure their confidence, are in their very nature advantageous to these classes in the matter of obtaining credit. From the point of view of obtaining credit, therefore, the manufacturer and merchant have preeminently the advantage over the farmer. The nature of the profession of law places the lawyer in a very favorable position to enter the field of public service as legislator or executive. The fact that lawyers predominate in Congress and in our state legislatures is often deplored by the farmers, but in the very nature of the case it can not be otherwise. Illustrations might be continued showing that if the advantages and disadvantages of all classes were balanced against one another there would be a pronounced disability registered against the agricultural class, that the members of each class have certain economic interests in common, and that if such interests were fostered to an extreme degree for one group they would become antagonistic to other groups.

The common economic interests of members of classes including the influences that flow from various types of social life resulting from the existence of classes, are, however, not all-inclusive and do not control the whole range of man's activities. If there are interests that cause people to divide themselves into classes with respect to certain economic and social questions, there are other motives that unite them into national solidarity and still others into a world brotherhood. Patriotism causes all classes to subordinate their differences and to unite their efforts for the glory of their country. In spite of the fact that President Wilson disappointed the Grange in the selection of a secretary of agriculture that did not have its approval, at its very first session after our entry into the war the National Grange wired the President and pledged him the support of the organized farmers to the "full limit of their energies and their resources." Orthodox socialism had for years tried to make internationalism supplant nationalism in the minds of its adherents, and yet when the European War began only a small minority of socialists in Germany refused to take up arms against their brothers in France. Regardless of race, nationality, or language the spirit of religion actuates the missionary to carry the gospel of his faith to all peoples. Regardless also of race, nationality, language, customs, religion, or previous mean and shameful behavior, the spirit of humanity is greater than all class prejudices and saves from starvation the indigent and suffering women and children of foreign lands. From a purely economic point of view there are inter-class interests that necessarily cause groups to compromise with one another. No single class is economically self-sufficient. Each is dependent for its existence upon others. The old theory of a general strike has long been recognized to be fallacious in as much as a complete cessation of work would inflict even greater punishment upon the families of organized labor than upon those of the capitalist group. A food strike on the part of the farmers, if such were successfully instituted, would bring retaliations from other groups. But Bernard M. Baruch in the *Atlantic Monthly* of July, 1921, says: "My contacts with the farmers have filled me with respect for them—for their sanity, their patience, their balance. Within the last year—and particulaly at a meeting called by the Kansas State Board of Agriculture and at another called by the Committee of Seventeen—I have met many of the leaders of the new farm movement, and I testify in all sincerity, that they are endeavoring to deal with their problems, not as promoters of a narrow class interest, not as exploiters of the helpless consumer, not as merciless monopolists, but as honest men bent on the improvement of the common weal." The law of supply and demand ultimately fixes values, and it is the money value of products sold that constitutes the medium through which the amount of wealth is distributed among all classes. The law of supply and demand can only operate and the distribution of wealth can only proceed in a satisfactory manner so long as friendly relations among classes are maintained. The class struggle then that is observed on every hand is primarily a struggle for a more equitable distribution of wealth. The methods used are the election of favorable representatives to legislatures, the employment of qualified representatives who are to influence legislators in a legitimate way, the creation of a favorable public sentiment to sway the whole body politic, and various self-help methods. It does not lead to class war, but rather to a fair and just administration of the nation's economic organization through a sportsmanlike submission to public opinion, the final arbiter of social differences.

Alignment of Economic Groups.—The interdependence of business enterprise rather than class interests or class struggle is the great outstanding characteristic of present-day economic organization. Society in all its aspects is centripetal rather than centrifugal. "Our industries are carried on by sets of nominally independent plants which pass on goods to each other in serial succession. For example, one series embraces wheat-growers, grain-carrying railways, elevators, flour mills, wholesale dealers in provisions, bakeries, and retail distributing agencies. Each set of members in such a series is dependent upon the preceding set for its chief supplies and upon the succeeding set for its chief vent. The wheat, the flour, the loaves flow through the successive sets of enterprises in a ceaseless river, though the volume of the flow is not steady.

Further. no industrial series is self-sufficing, even as a whole. Each set of enterprises in our example, from the farms to the retail agencies, is industrially dependent on other industrial series which equip it with buildings, machines, fuel, office supplies, etc. A peculiar degree of mutual dependence exists between the whole mass of industries on the one hand, and the railways on the other hand. Coal mining and the steel trade also touch practically every industrial establishment in one way or another.''[1] The banks and also largely insurance companies are as directly related to industry and commerce as the railroads; for the turnover process requires a large use of credit in all lines of business activity. In no field can production long be carried on without concurrent production in all fields. From the point of view of the distribution of wealth unless all groups of producers operate a very slackening demand for the products of those who do work will set in. The consequent reduction in the purchasing power of consumers will necessarily reduce the price of products available for sale and thus decrease the income of those who remain at work. A cursory analysis of our economic relations makes it at once apparent that class interdependence is of much larger significance than class interests or class disputes. There are, however, great inequalities of opportunity for acquiring wealth among the several classes; and while the classes suffering disabilities can not improve their condition by resorting to class war—for this only destroys all—they can through group action present their demands to the public at large whence will come relief in proportion as such demands are fair, properly presented, and properly comprehended.

Class interdependence may be shown in a more concrete way by referring to some of the actual measures and principles that various classes mutually favor. The maintenance of the institution of private property is subscribed to by the United States Chamber of Commerce, by all farmers' organizations, and officially by the American Federation of Labor. The *Nation's Business,* the offiicial organ of the United States Chamber of Commerce, in its June, 1921, number declares

[1] Mitchell, *Business Cycles,* p. 23.

among other things for railroads under private management, better country roads, improved foreign trade, and governmental economy. In recent annual reports and other documents of the Grange and the Farmers' Union a substantial agreement is expressed with regard to all these matters. The time was when the farmers were opposed to national aid for road construction. But the very general introduction of both the passenger automobile and auto-truck has caused organized agriculture also to favor the project.

Similarly class interests may be shown by reference to a few measures upon which there is a division among classes. The daylight-saving measure necessitated by the exigencies of the war is a matter of minor consequence, and yet it occasioned great inconvenience to the agricultural class. The farmers were willing to rise in the early dark hours of the morning and get their produce to the city an hour in advance of sun time so long as the war lasted, but when the city classes showed themselves desirous of making the practice permanent they strenuously objected and secured a speedy repeal of the federal law. After the war railroad labor took a very defiant attitude on the question of wage reduction in the face of an inevitable falling general price level. During the war because of rising costs freight rates were raised, but later because of a decline in prices the high freight rates inhibited the free movement of goods and tended to prolong business inactivity. The farmers favored a wage reduction for labor in order that freight rates might be reduced so as to give them a chance to sell their farm products at a greater return to themselves. In other words there are opposing class interests here between the farmers and organized labor that need to be equitably adjusted in the great social court of public opinion. In the early days of organized agriculture it was customary for farmers' organizations to make common cause with organized labor. Recently, however, it has become perfectly plain to them that their class interests are opposed to those of labor. Transportation and public-service strikes are now vigorously condemned. It is complained that a railroad strike may completely destroy the product of the farmers' labor. In a statement issued by

Washington representatives of farmers' organizations the organized strike is recognized to be morally wrong for both farmers and organized labor. The protective tariff on manufactured articles is a measure that has been favored by the manufacturing group and opposed by the farmer. The farmers pay higher prices for their supplies under a protective tariff and to this extent reduce their actual income. On the other hand the general consumer may complain against a protective tariff on sugar in the interest of cane and beet-sugar growers. The farmers have in the past complained against alleged monopolistic prices they had to pay for farm implements and have opposed the renewal of patent rights. In taxation there is shown considerable class interest. Virtually all elements of organized agriculture favor the graduated income tax. There is not always harmony in all details, but the Farmers' Union squarely favors fashioning all taxes after the well-recognized tax canon, "ability to pay." The income tax is favored by them especially for the reason that many farmers have incomes that fall below a reasonable exemption. For the same reason the income tax is generally not in favor, unless it is given a very low exemption, among the manufacturing and commercial groups. The cooperative movement that is assuming large proportions among the farmers seems to have opposition only from a small group of merchants—those handling farmers' supplies used for productive purposes and those handling farm products. In some quarters bitter opposition develops, but a united campaign can easily win over the support of the banks, secure railroads or shipping facilities, and bring about favorable relations with manufacturers and dealers. It will mean of course the elimination of the middlemen handling the products that farmers propose to buy and sell co-operatively. The number to be eliminated is small. Here and there some manufacturing operations such as milling and canning are to be performed cooperatively. The proposed invasion into the manufacturing field is of little consequence and, therefore, raises little criticism from this quarter.

Whether or not one believes that class disputes can only be settled by bloody class wars depends upon the range of facts taken into account. If one centers attention merely upon organized effort on the part of farmers' organizations, organized labor, manufacturers' and commercial organizations, one is liable to drift to the conclusion that even in a democracy flagrant special privileges will become firmly established and that class war will necessarily follow.[1] When, however, all the cohesive forces of society are taken into account, including the intricate relationships of our economic organization, and the various social, religious, and political instincts, the possibility of class war of any consequence in America becomes remote, and one is inclined to regard class interdependence of greater significance than class hatred and class struggle.

The Disabilities of the Agricultural Class.—It should be clearly recognized that the agricultural class not only labors under serious disabilities compared with city classes, but that these disabilities inhere in the physical environment and sphere of activity of the farming population. Farmers sometimes make bitter accusations against the bankers, merchants, and manufacturers as though their disadvantages were consciously inflicted upon them by these classes, when as a matter of fact manufacturing and merchandising operations under our present economic organization inherently afford greater advantages than agriculture. The disabilities suffered by the agricultural class for the most part unfortunately are objective and resident in their sphere of activity. They can be very largely corrected through self-help measures. A vigorous and continued educational campaign is required. The agricultural masses must be marshalled under the leadership of sound and expert opinion.

With respect to credit it has been pointed out before that manufacturing and merchandising operations are begun and completed within a short time, and that for this reason commercial loans form an excellent basis for note issue. A loan based on merchandise already in existence has in it an element of certainty that the loan will be paid. It also runs for a short

[1] *Vide The Menace of New Privilege* by George W. Alger in the *Atlantic Monthly*, February, 1921.

term, 30 to 90 days, and allows a constant rearrangement of bank assets. When a banker pays out notes or extends credit on a draft drawn on goods in transit he is virtually certain that liquidation will follow at the stated time. The very necessary quality of flexibility in currency is provided by loans based on merchandising and manufacturing operations and largely absent in farming. This naturally gives a distinct advantage to the merchant and manufacturer, and explains why economists and bankers were loath to allow loans to be based on agricultural operations to extend to six months at the time the Federal Reserve Act was in process of enactment. It is a matter of great concern for the entire country that we maintain flexibility in our currency. Expansion is a quality that makes possible the easing up of tight money situations and thus avoid panics, and contraction introduces an automatic check against undue inflation and a violent upward tendency of the general price level. In normal times borrowing affords a tremendous advantage for making profits. So long as interest rates are lower than profits made, the more turnovers effected and the larger the year's profits. This is why borrowing is such a necessity in highly competitive businesses. If urban classes have splendid credit facilities and farmers have not there exists a serious disability on the side of agriculture. The Federal Farm Loan system as at first constituted provided long-term credit to the agricultural class, but until recently it was sorely in need of short-term credit facilities.

In the matter of control over economic risks the farmer's occupation is also inherently at a disadvantage. The character of his crops is very largely dependent upon weather over which he has no control whatever. Drouths or excessive rainfall may completely destroy them or greatly reduce their value. As yet also there is much uncertainty that a crop will pan out even though the weather is favorable, due to the many insect pests that infest plant life. But the risk of primary importance to the farmer in the long run has to do with prices. He is in no such favorable position as the manufacturer and merchant who make frequent turnovers and can adopt a "hand to mouth" policy in their business operations and thus avoid loss due to a decline of prices. The farmer at the time of planting must largely trust to luck with reference to the demand for his products. More efficient organization and concentrated marketing could largely direct the efforts of farmers into the more remunerative channels at the beginning of the season and aid in the elimination of loss, but even with efficient organization and a perfect statistical crop and market service the advantage would still lie with the urban classes because of the shorter terms within which their turnovers are made. It is to be expected that the larger the crop the smaller the value that will be realized per unit by the farmer, and if his increased production would always net him as much as decreased yields his troubles would not be so serious. Here is a decided disadvantage in agriculture. Professor Mitchell says that with pig-iron it is the rule that "increased production and high prices go together."[1] The reason for this is of course the fact that in the steel industry supply follows demand and can speedily be adjusted to the needs of business. "In general," says Professor Mitchell, "the opposite holds for crops—reduced yields cause high prices and increased yields cause low prices. Indeed, a deficiency in the yields sometimes causes such a rise of prices as to make the pecuniary value of the short crop greater than that of a large one, and superabundant yields sometimes cause such a drop in prices as to reduce their pecuniary value. Instances of the first kind occurred, for example, with corn in 1901, wheat in 1904, and cotton in 1909; instances of the second kind in 1894 with cotton, 1895 with corn, and 1898 with wheat."[2] This is a disability that makes it exceedingly difficult for the farmer to maintain a definite relation between his costs and his profits, while in the fields of industry and commerce it is relatively simple.

The isolation or scattered status of the farmer is responsible for the lack of social and educational advantages of rural districts. Theaters and some other forms of amusements can not be operated in the country because of insufficient patron-

---

[1] *Vide* his *Business Cycles*, p. 239.

[2] *Ibid.*

age. The automobile will do much to obviate the difficulty. The same physical environment has caused a backward status in educational facilities, although a transformation is now in process because of the consolidation of schools. The farmers are sometimes accused of not favoring education. This in some cases is true, but he is a product of his environment and can not be expected to see beyond the range of facts he assimulates. The agricultural class is at a disadvantage when it comes to organizing and directing reform movements. It is a large, scattered, unwieldy mass, and necessarily responds much more slowly to an appeal for better education or other projects than the compact city folk.

In view of these disabilities it is only right that the government should collect crop and marketing statistics, provide scientific and practical agricultural education, perform experiments for the general improvement of agriculture, forecast weather, which, however, is also for the benefit of other groups, give substantial aid in the matter of constructing a satisfactory rural credit system, and assist agriculture in other ways. The government has done much for industry and commerce through protective tariffs, bounties, the consular service, and other ways; and when all facts are taken into account and the benefits accruing to the entire country through public aid to agriculture are kept in mind, it must be admitted in all fairness that the farmers are not enjoying special privileges.

The Goal of Organized Agriculture.—It is the hope of organized agriculture that the farmer's standard of living may be raised to a higher level. First of all a larger income is desired. If this is accomplished all other things will come as a matter of course. The farmers want more luxuries, including modern improvements in their houses. Running water, a bath room, and electric lights are facilities enjoyed by only a few farmers in the United States. From a few scattered studies that have been made of farm labor income it appears that the farmer's income is relatively lower than that of other classes. Thus in a study made by the Department of Agriculture it is stated that "the average farm income of 25 farmers in Palmer township, Washington County, Ohio, for the seven years, 1912 to 1918, was $610, the labor income $276, and the return on the capital 4.6 per cent.'' This is one of several studies conducted by the Department at the same time.[1] The $610 of farm income includes the labor income, or the farmer's own wages, and the earnings of capital invested which computed at 4.6 per cent amounts to $334. The farm income does not constitute the total family income. There are certain perquisites and a portion of the farm products that are produced for home consumption. ''In the Ohio area the value of the items, food, fuel, and house rent furnished by the farm was estimated at $359 per farm for the seven-year average.''[2] Thus in a case where the farmer owned and operated the farm and had no debt outstanding his total average income for the seven-year period was the sum of $276, his labor income, $334, interest on capital invested at 4.6%, and $359, which was the value of the house rent, fuel, and food furnished directly by the farm. This makes a total average annual income of $969. When the farmer's total return is compared with that of railroad labor it appears very inadequate. For December, 1917, the average monthly compensation per employee for all employees of class one railroads was $89.83, or an annual income of $1,077.96.[3] This was a little more than the farmer's total income for the seven-year average which, however, included capital earnings, the labor income being only $276. For a tenant farmer owning no property to speak of the labor income together with the usual perquisites would have been about $600, which is, considerably less than the railroad employee's income. For the particular year of 1917 the total farmer's income amounted to $1,565 of which $666 constituted labor income. In 1918 his total income fell to $1,341 and his labor income to $333. If figures were available for 1920 and 1921 they would probably show very little for labor income because of the tremendous drop in the prices of farm products. While

[1] *Vide Bulletin No. 920,* U. S. Dept. of Agriculture. Summary appears on p. 5.

[2] In order to make a fair comparison of the farmer's income with that of the urban worker, these perquisites should be valued at the price at which they may be purchased by the city consumer which is considerably higher than the price received by the farmer.

[3] *Vide Monthly Labor Review, for December,* 1919, p. 235.

the study referred to shows that the farmer's income began to register a decline in 1918 the income of the railroad employee had risen to an average monthly wage of $119.38 or to an annual income of $1,432.56 by July 1919. Computing the investment income at 5% the labor income of the farmer is relatively very low. Comparing the investment rate of 5% with the average return of railroads it is somewhat high and if reduced to the level of the average railroad return would raise slightly the labor income; but the increase in labor income would be negligible. In normal times the average return for railroads of class one is less than 3% on stock outstanding and about 4½% on bonds.[1] The assumed capital earnings of 5% for the farm are only half of the average return for the national banks of the country during the period of 1900 to 1919.[2] Of course the average return of banks is normally higher than that of industry and commerce; but even though the capital earnings are computed at 3% it would only mean that the farmer's labor income would have to be slightly increased. It would not in any mysterious way increase the farmer's total income. As wage-earner and capitalist his income appears to be somewhat less than that of the average wage-earner. According to the National Bureau of Economic Research only 2% of the farmers in the United States received an annual income above $2,000 from 1910 to 1914, while in other economic groups as many as 4% received incomes in excess of this amount during the same period.[2] It is to be hoped that figures showing the distribution of wealth according to economic classes will become available shortly on a more extensive scale so that thoroughly reliable conclusions may be drawn. As yet this is not possible, at least so far as farmers are concerned. Farming is not a concentrated industry. There is no great opportunity for individuals to amass fortunes. There are, however, advantages that people hold very dear. Almost complete independence in the way one may work is a characteristic probably more pronounced in farming than in any other mode of earning a

---

[1] *Vide* statistics tabulated by the Bureau of Railway Economics.

[2] *Vide* Friday, *Profits, Wages and Prices*, p. 42.

[3] *Income of the United States*, Vol. I, p. 112.

living. Individual enterprise, skill, initiative, and a scientific education bring their reward on the farm.

Organized agriculture says: Give us a larger income and all other things shall be added unto us. One frequently sees in agricultural literature the desire for greater recognition in the press and to play a greater role in the political and social life of the country. It is due to our present economic organization very largely that these disadvantages inhere in country life. Before the Industrial Revolution the landed interests held the reins of political control. Since the advent of concentrated industry, rapid transportation, and the great cities with their improved water, electric light, heating and trolley systems, their splendid educational facilities, good churches, theaters and other amusements, their first class stores where varied wants may be satisfied, and with their expert medical and other professional services, the center of intellectual activity and influence has shifted to the city. As is pointed out elsewhere, actual farming and political representation do not mix readily. There is, however, hope that as transportation and farm machinery improve, as the educational facilities are extended, as a larger use of business enterprise is applied, mainly through cooperation which allows combination on the farm and according to experience gives the farmer the middleman's profit, and finally as team work through the channels of public and private organization is more generally and constantly engaged in, the rural population shall have a social and intellectual medium that shall rival that of the city, and it shall also largely regain its social standing which, however, is more a fancy than a reality, and exists merely in the minds of the ignorant, and the prejudiced, narrow and aristocratic social classes. Stage jokes concerning him and his relative social standing among the classes need not give the farmer any concern. He should rather be deeply and earnestly interested in the removal of all fundamental conditions that tend to make country life less attractive than city life.

Our Policy of Regulation.—Our policy of governmental interference in business before the 70's was one of an extreme *laissez faire* character. Before that time we relied wholly upon the force of competition to correct evils and adjust prices. In 1887 we began the federal regulation of railroads and since that time several acts have been enacted that give the Interstate Commerce Commission wide powers, including the absolute right of determining railroad rates. States have also their public utility commissions that have jurisdiction over interstate roads, street railways, gas, electric light and water companies. We recognize the fact that these businesses are natural monopolies and that if left to themselves they would engage in cut-throat competition and bring ruin not only to their own stockholders but to the general public as well in as much as these businesses are vested with a large public interest. In the field of transportation and public utilities generally we have applied the policy of regulation. We not only aim to protect the consumer against extortionate prices, but we protect also the concern in this field against the onslaughts of competition. But for strikes this policy provides uninterrupted service at reasonable rates to the public.

In the field of general business we have so far endeavored to maintain the operation of the principle of competition. Wherever monopoly manifests itself we dissolve the business organization under authority of the Sherman anti-trust act of 1890. In the anti-trust act of 1914 we define in a more definite way what actions of big business are to be regarded illegal. The most important abuse of big business corrected by this act is that of price discrimination. No concern may sell at the same time at different prices except as occasioned by differences in transportation costs between different points. The purpose of this is of course to keep competition alive. Thus in all fields of business activity our statutory law reinforces common law and provides that monopoly can nowhere obtain unless it is subjected to regulation.

In the field of agriculture it is contended that a concerted effort is being made, with aims already partially realized, to exempt agriculture from the operation of the anti-trust act.[1] The particular federal statute that is referred to is the anti-

---

[1] *Vide* article by Alger in the *Atlantic Monthly* of February, 1921.

trust act of 1914 and similar state acts. Section 6 of the federal act provides as follows:

> That the labor of a human being is not a commodity or article of commerce. Nothing contained in the Anti-Trust laws shall be construed to forbid the existence and operation of labor, agricultural, or horticultural organizations, instituted for the purpose of mutual help and not having capital stock or conducted for profit or to forbid or restrain individual members of such organizations from lawfully carrying out the legitimate objects thereof; nor shall such organizations, or the members thereof, be held or construed to be illegal combinations or conspiracies in restraint of trade under the Anti-Trust laws.

Since the enactment of this statute a number of states have passed laws legalizing the organization of cooperative agricultural, dairy or horticultural associations, giving such associations the usual privileges of ordinary corporations, and defining their relations to members and non-members. From all this legislation no evil can come to the public. Only beneficial results can come to the farmer with no injury to the consumer of farm products. Leaving out of the question for the time being both the possibility of creating a monopoly in the production and sale of agricultural products and the intent of organized agriculture to establish monopoly, which, however, is a matter of no significance if it can be shown that agricultural monopoly need not be feared, the privilege of mere combination for the conduct of business is one that has been exercised by trade and industry since the medieval days, first through the partnership and the joint stock company and later through the corporation, and to grant the privilege of combination to the merchant, banker, and manufacturer while it is denied to the farmer would be gross injustice and class privilege of the rankest sort. The farmers must be given the legal right to form associations that allow combination not under the old autocratic principle of "one share, one vote," but under the new democratic plan of "one shareholder, one vote, regardless of number of shares held."

If by chance agricultural monopoly could become a fact and assuming for the moment that it may, the courts, regardless of the power of organized agriculture and of the intent of enacted legislation, would never sanction monopoly. They would take the same attitude toward business organizations in agriculture that they have taken toward business organizations elsewhere. Common-law precedent and public sentiment would force the courts to this position. The time was when the manner of attacking the trust problem involved the marking of combination forms of business organization with the stamp of illegality and prohibiting their use. This, for instance, was done with the pool and the combination trust. But when the holding company was evolved and became the usual device for organizing big business, the court changed its tactics and looked upon the purpose and intent of business organization rather than upon its form. Says Judge Taft: "The court will look through the form of the device adopted to evade the effect of the law to the essence, to the intent and to result."[1] Business may organize itself under the cooperative and other forms of business organization except the pool and combination trust which remain on the statute books as illegal, without incurring the danger of being dissolved by the courts unless its conduct is monopolistic. The courts now consider the behavior of the particular concern, and the case of each particular concern is decided upon whether or not it has acted in unreasonable restraint of trade. Deciding the question as to whether or not a combination should be dissolved on the ground of the reasonableness of its restraint of trade, is another important advanced step the courts have taken with respect to the whole problem of regulation. Under this interpretation of the law not all combinations in restraint of trade are illegal. They must be unreasonably in restraint of trade says the Standard Oil case before the United States Supreme Court will declare them illegal.[2] This wise opinion allows business to combine and to effect the economies of production flowing from concerted effort and yet protects the public against the abuses of monopolistic power. Precisely the same attitude would be taken by the courts toward combination in the field of agriculture. Otherwise special privileges would be enjoyed by the agricultural class under the assumption that monopoly in agri-

[1] From an article by William H. Taft, in N. Y. *Times*, June 14, 1914, and quoted by Gerstenberg.

[2] 221 U. S. 1.

culture could obtain. Public opinion in America will never confer special privileges upon any class, and even granting for the sake of argument that monopoly in agriculture may become a fact, public opinion and the courts would speedily come to the rescue of the public.

Monopoly in Agriculture Need not be Feared.—There is, however, no danger that monopoly in agriculture will ever injure the public. And the reason for this is not failure on the part of farmers to organize effective selling associations, for this they are doing already with respect to certain farm products in many sections of the country. The reasons for the absence of monopoly in agriculture are the complete lack of control over production and the power of substitution enjoyed by the consumer. Even though all the farmers pledge to sell their wheat through one selling agency the price for a given year's supply would have to be quite moderate. Otherwise a high price, even one as high as the "monopoly price" or a price fixed at a point that will just barely insure the consumption of the entire year's crop, will cause individual farmers to increase their acreage for the ensuing year and thus necessitate a reduction of the price in order to get rid of the increased supply. Concerted action with reference to acreage or other units of production can never be realized. The number of individuals involved is too large. The farmers may hold their conventions and at the earnest behest of their leaders they may adopt a resolution to hold production at a certain level, but when they return to their respective farms the old story of the railroad pool where members secretely engaged in rate-cutting will be reenacted in another form only on a very much more extensive scale. The temptation on the part of the individual farmer would always be to increase his production in order that he might sell a large output at a high price and thus increase his income while others were expected to abide by the order of the convention. Only by such drastic measures as "night riding" can production be controlled. Few localities have ever resorted to such a practice, and nowhere will it any longer be countenanced.

There are some agricultural products in which a temporary

control over production may inhere by reason of the fact that their supply may not be increased from year to year and also for the reason that their production is confined to narrow limits. The most conspicuous examples of this kind of products are the prunes and raisins which are grown primarily in the vicinity of Fresno, California. It has been the custom for the growers of these products to enter into a contract with the jobbers to sell a certain quantity of certain grades at a price later to be determined on the basis of conditions of supply and demand. This price is obviously adjusted in accordance with the principle of "what the traffic will bear." In other words the growers seek to sell their goods at the "monopoly price." It is that price at which the public is just willing to consume the entire year's supply. It has happened that the price fixed by the prune growers was too high, necessitating the holding over part of the crop into the next year. If the following year's crop is again normal and no new sources of demand are developed, there is necessity under such circumstances to make a reduction in the price in order to "move" all the goods. There is temporary control over production with respect to prunes because all the growers in the prune-growing district are members of the California Prune and Apricot Growers, Incorporated, and because it takes five or six years for new orchards to mature or for the supply to respond to an increased price. A temporary monopoly may then obtain in a few products such as prunes and raisins. It can not readily obtain where products are grown over a widely scattered area such as apples and most other fruits, because the chances are that producers are less subject to control in the sale of the product. But even though a cooperative selling association is able in the case of the prune to determine the price at which the entire supply shall be sold, the public is in no danger of being injured because of the great power of substitution it enjoys in the field of fruits. The so-called monopoly price that may be secured for the prune is probably very close to the competitive price. The grower can reap larger profits because of the elimination of some middlemen, and thus the practice confers benefits upon the growers without injuring the consumer.

The production of milk is sometimes cited as an instance of monopolistic control in as much as producers under co-operation may sell milk for fresh consumption at a higher price than the milk they sell at the same time to creameries and cheese factories. The situation with respect to milk differs in different sections. Around the urban centers of Boston and New York the area from which the supply may be drawn is more restricted than around most other cities. Chicago's milk area, for instance, is large and suffers no disabilities on account of distance in securing fresh milk. If the cooperative agency raises its milk price to a favorable figure, it not only invites expansion within the field itself but encourages an enlargement of the milk-supplying district. The result would be that the monopolistic price could not be obtained.

Assuming that cooperation between the New England Milk Producers' Association and the Dairymen's League, would proceed to the extent of pooling all milk produced in the New England states and in New York, eastern Pennsylvania, New Jersey, and northern Delaware, there would still be no cause for alarm. While this region is more restricted than most other milk-producing areas, it, however, has tremendous possibilities for expansion. In all milk-producing areas in order that there may be an even flow of milk to the city throughout the year there must be a time in the spring when the supply will be too large for absorption as fresh milk, and this surplus must be diverted into butter and cheese. Even dealers in the city find it necessary to run creameries in order that the surplus resulting from the irregularity of supply and demand may be consumed and not be allowed to go to waste. The nature of the industry requires that this be done. The milk that can not be shipped to the city for fresh consumption, even with the general practice of winter dairying, becomes at times a large surplus that must be sold to cheese factories or creameries at a price lower than is received for city milk. If all the producers in the eastern milk district should pool their milk, sell what they could as city milk, divert the surplus to the cheese factory and the creamery, and divide receipts according to the amount of milk produced regardless of whether all, a portion, or none of a particular producer's milk went to the city, can they build up a vicious monopoly in that part of their industry that pertains to supply New York and the other urban centers with milk? There is ample justification for taking less for milk furnished the cheese factory and creamery than for the milk shipped to the city. The latter involves a heavy transportation charge increasing according to distance, requires to be bottled, and necessitates extra equipment and labor costs. Also the price of milk used to manufacture butter and cheese is determined by different conditions of supply and demand from those determining the price of milk for fresh consumption. The center of the production of butter and cheese in the United States is Wisconsin. The price of these products is determined by the supply produced in regions remote from the fresh-milk producing area. When, therefore, the surplus in the fresh-milk district is disposed of it must meet the competition of other parts of the country, while the conditions of supply and demand surrounding the city milk enable the producers to secure a higher price for the latter product solely on a competitive basis. If all the milk in the eastern district is pooled the lower price for the surplus and the higher for the city milk would be averaged and each producer would be given his share of the pool prorated according to production. Under these circumstances the cooperative agency might attempt to secure the monopoly price for the city milk, and for a short time it could be successful. If it does decide to charge the monopoly price, the average income of all producers will increase. This will stimulate production for both surplus and city purposes, resulting in a larger amount of milk to be used in the manufacture of butter, cheese and condensed milk and, therefore, in a reduction of the price received for surplus milk. The final result is a decreased income to the producer. The policy of asking the monopoly price for city milk could not be carried on for a longer period than a season without encouraging an increase in production, for a tremendous increase in the flow of milk can be readily effected by the simple process of better feeding, not to mention the addition of a few cows to each herd. For the country at large there is no menace in a milk monopoly. New York and other urban centers of the East may be inflicted with the monopoly price for fresh milk for a brief space of time, but even there it can never become a public menace or a social problem that demands such drastic measures as price-fixing by the government or by consumers' committees, or even the dissolution of the business organization that the farmers may use for marketing their milk.

The social consequences that flow from rural cooperative enterprise are all good. The farmers are enabled to increase their income and raise their standard of living. There is no danger of monopoly because there is no control over production, and because the consumer can exercise his power of substitution. Vigorous public and private agricultural organization is necessary to bring to the country a full taste of the educational, economic, social and political advantages enjoyed by the city.

SELECTED REFERENCES

Simkhovitch, *Maxism Versus Socialism;* Marx and Engels, *The Communist Manifesto;* Baruch, in *Atlantic Monthly*, July, 1921; Mitchell, *Business Cycles; The Nation's Business*, June, 1921; Alger in *Atlantic Monthly*, February, 1921.

APPENDIX A*

STATE AGRICULTURAL DEPARTMENTAL ORGANIZATION

STATE	DESIGNATION	MANNER OF CHOOSING EXECUTIVE OR MEMBERS OF BOARD	MAIN SUBDIVISIONS OF OFFICE OR ITS DUTIES	CHIEF COORDINATE EXECUTIVE BODIES AND ADVISORY BOARDS
Alabama	Department of Agriculture and Industries.	Commissioner of Agriculture and Industries elected by the people.	Statistics, regulation of fertilizers, regulation of dairy products.	
Arizona	Commission of Agriculture and Horticulture.	Members of Commission appointed by the governor.	Destruction of insects injuring cotton, etc., plant pathology.	Dairy Commissioner, Water Commissioner, Apiary Inspector, Live Stock Sanitary Board, Sheep Sanitary Commission.
Arkansas	Bureau of Mines, Manufactures and Agriculture.	Commissioner appointed by the governor.	Warehouse and Marketing, Plant Board, Crop Estimates, Inspection of Feed and Fertilizer.	
California	Department of Agriculture.	Director appointed by governor.	Plant Industry, Animal Industry.	
Colorado	State Board of Immigration.	Governor is ex-officio member of Board. Three other members appointed by the governor.	Collection of statistics including agricultural.	Dairy Commissioner, State Entomologist, Board of Horticulture. State has a Board of Agriculture, but duties are largely confined to administration of agricultural college.

*This table was constructed from data taken from state agricultural reports and from state laws. The author was assisted by Professor S. E. Leland in the collection of data from state laws. With the exception of a few cases it is up-to-date and on the whole shows great variation in state departmental organization.

STATE AGRICULTURAL DEPARTMENTAL ORGANIZATION—Continued

STATE	DESIGNATION	MANNER OF CHOOSING EXECUTIVE OR MEMBERS OF BOARD	MAIN SUBDIVISIONS OF OFFICE OR ITS DUTIES	CHIEF COORDINATE EXECUTIVE BODIES AND ADVISORY BOARDS
Connecticut	State Board of Agriculture.	Five members appointed by governor, eight members appointed by Assembly, governor is ex-officio member.	Preparation of annual report; board is a member of milk regulation board.	Dairy and Food Commissioner, Commissioner on Domestic Animals, Experiment Station, inspection of fertilizers, etc.
Delaware	State Board of Agriculture.	Board consists of a member from the three counties in the state and are appointed by the governor.	Chemical Department: Enforcement of fertilizer law, seed inspection, feed inspection. Live Stock: Tuberculosis eradication, suppression of hog cholera and other diseases. Bureau of Markets.	
Florida	Department of Agriculture.	Commissioner of agriculture elected by the people every 4 years.	Publication of statistics; analysis of foods, drugs, fertilizers; regulation of feeds; marketing; supervision of shell-fish industry; supervision of prisons.	Board of Commissioners of Everglades Drainage District, State Live Stock Sanitary Board composed of Commissioner of Agriculture, State Treasurer, and Superintendent of Public Instruction.
Georgia	Department of Agriculture.	Commissioner of Agriculture elected by the people every two years.	Publication of reports, analysis of fertilizers, quarantining of cattle, live stock inspection, suppression of diseases among cattle, food regulation including dairy products.	State Board of Entomology composed of Commissioner of Agriculture, President of Georgia State Horticultural Society, and President of Georgia State Agricultural Society.
Idaho	Department of Agriculture.	Commissioner of Agriculture appointed by governor.	Markets, Animal Industry, Plant Industry, Fairs.	

Illinois	Department of Agriculture.	Director of Agriculture appointed by the governor.	Divisions: Game and Fish, Animal Industry, Apiary Inspection, Plant Industry, Food and Dairies, Dairy Extension, Agricultural Statistics, State Fair.	The State has a board of 15 agricultural advisors and also a state fair advisory board composed of 9 persons.
Indiana	State Board of Agriculture.	The governor and dean of the agricultural college are ex-officio members. Thirteen other members are appointed by the governor.	Conducting the Indiana State Fair	Under the Department of Conservation in the Division of Entomology there is carried on the work pertaining to plant diseases, destruction of insect pests, inspection of apiaries and of nursery stock. Under the Board of Public Health, inspection of foods and drugs. Live Stock Sanitary Board.
Iowa	Department of Agriculture. (Management by a board.)	Management of Department by Board of Agriculture which consists of the governor, president of the agricultural college, food and drug commissioner, president of live stock sanitary board and of some elective members, one from each congressional district.	Food and Drugs, Live Stock Sanitary Board, Weather and Crop Service, State Fair and Grounds, preparation of year book.	
Kansas	State Board of Agriculture.	Delegates chosen by agricultural societies, including county farm bureaus, which elect 16 members to the State Board.	Preparation of annual report, preparation of program for annual meeting of delegates of agricultural societies.	Live Stock Sanitary Commissioner.

STATE AGRICULTURAL DEPARTMENTAL ORGANIZATION—Continued

STATE	DESIGNATION	MANNER OF CHOOSING EXECUTIVE OR MEMBERS OF BOARD	MAIN SUBDIVISIONS OF OFFICE OR ITS DUTIES	CHIEF COORDINATE EXECUTIVE BODIES AND ADVISORY BOARDS
Kentucky	Bureau of Agriculture, Labor and Statistics.	Commissioner of Agriculture elected by the people.	Publication of statistics and reports.	State Board of Agriculture: An advisory body consisting of commissioner, director of experiment station, and one citizen from each of the appellate court districts of the State. State Live Stock Sanitary Board composed of commissioner, director of experiment station, head of division of animal husbandry of experiment station and four members of State Board of Agriculture. Ky. Exper. Sta. licenses Babcock milk and cream testers. State Board of Public Health inspects dairies, creameries, etc.
Louisiana	Department of Agriculture and Immigration.	Commissioner of Agriculture and Immigration elected by the people every four years. The new constitution proposes a board headed by the Commissioner which makes rules and regulations but in a concluding section is not given control over the office of the Commissioner.	Statistics, Regulation of sale and the purity of Paris green, feed stuffs, fertilizers; seed inspection and quarantine. Constitution proposes establishment of bureau of marketing.	Live Stock Sanitary Board, Entomological work under direction of Entomologist of Experiment Station.
Maine	Department of Agriculture.	Commissioner of Agriculture.	Animal Industry, Plant Industry, Markets Inspection, Administration.	

Maryland	State Board of Agriculture.	A board of nine members appointed by the governor, constituting also the board of trustees of the agricultural college.	Investigations and publication of reports, regulation of sale of seed, inspection of apiaries.	State Live Stock Sanitary Board with inspection and quarantine powers, State Board of Forestry, State Board of Horticulture made up of certain professors of agricultural college. Agricultural college analyses fertilizers.
Massachusetts	Department of Agriculture.	Commissioner of Agriculture appointed by the governor and his council.	Superintendent of Farm Machinery, Nursery Inspector, Entomologist, Ornithologist, Inspector of Apiaries, General Dairy Agent.	An advisory board of six members appointed by the governor and his council.
Michigan	Department of Agriculture.	Commissioner of Agriculture appointed by the governor with consent of Senate.	Powers and duties formerly vested in the Department of Animal Industry, State Food and Drug Commissioner, State Veterinary Board, Immigration Commission, and Market Director, now vested in the new Department of Agriculture. Other duties are the inspection and regulation of orchards, vineyards and nurseries; inspection of apiaries; testing seeds; examination of fertilizers and insecticides; statistical work; holding fair property.	State Board of Agriculture of six members elected by the people. Board elects a president of the agricultural college who is ex-officio chairman of the board. It controls the agricultural college, but regulatory duties formerly performed by it are now vested in the Department of Agriculture.
Minnesota	Department of Agriculture.	Commissioner of Agriculture appointed by the governor.	Cooperation with Minnesota University in all ways that may be beneficial to agriculture, but all police	

STATE AGRICULTURAL DEPARTMENTAL ORGANIZATION—Continued

STATE	DESIGNATION	MANNER OF CHOOSING EXECUTIVE OR MEMBERS OF BOARD	MAIN SUBDIVISIONS OF OFFICE OR ITS DUTIES	CHIEF COORDINATE EXECUTIVE BODIES AND ADVISORY BOARDS
Minnesota (Continued)			powers to be administered by Department. Licensing of commission merchants, investigation of fraudulent dealing, collection of statistics, etc.	
Missouri	Department of Agriculture.	Commissioner appointed by the governor.	Miscellaneous, Horticulture, Dairying, Poultry, Fairs, Veterinary, Grain and Warehouse, Marketing.	
Mississippi	Department of Agriculture and Commerce.	Commissioner of Agriculture, Statistics and Immigration elected by the people every four years.	Statistics, inspection of fertilizers, regulation of dairy and creamery activities, inspection of feeds.	Live Stock Sanitary Board, Plant Board. Commissioner is a member of both boards. Both boards exercise quarantine and other functions.
Montana	Department of Agriculture, Labor and Industry.	Commissioner appointed by the governor.	Divisions: Farming and Dairying, Grain Standards and Marketing, Horticulture, Labor and Publicity.	
Nebraska	Department of Agriculture	Secretary of Agriculture appointed by the governor with consent of both houses of legislature.	Bureau of Food, Drugs and Oil, Bureau of Animal Industry, Bureau of Markets, Division of Game and Fish.	
Nevada				Governor empowered to employ a veterinary surgeon to investigate contagious diseases among animals.

New Hampshire	Department of Agriculture.	Commissioner appointed by the governor.	Markets, Animal Industry, Insect Suppression, Nursery Inspection.	An advisory board consisting of six practical agriculturists; appointed by the governor; meets every two months.
New Jersey	Department of Agriculture. (Management by a board.)	Management by the State Board of Agriculture consisting of persons elected by various agricultural societies including the State Grange and county granges. Agricultural College and Experiment Station each have a vote in the election of a board. Members of board serve without pay except its secretary.	State Board of Agriculture; Bureau of Animal Industry; Bureau of Lands, Crops and Markets; Bureau of Statistics and Inspection.	
New Mexico				The Board of Regents of the Agricultural College administers the State's agricultural laws.
New York	Department of Farms and Markets.	Commissioner of Farms and Markets is the head of the Department. He is appointed by a non-salaried board, first members appointed by the governor, but successors elected by the legislature. The law of 1921 places the executive functions of the Department under the Commissioner and requires him to submit only general policies to the Council of Farms and Markets.	Division of Agriculture: Plant Industry, Animal Industry, State Institution Farms, Farm Settlement, Dairy Products, Statistics. Division of Foods and Markets: Markets and Storage, Cooperative Associations, Licenses, Weights and Measures, Food Products, Food Standardization.	

STATE AGRICULTURAL DEPARTMENTAL ORGANIZATION—Continued

STATE	DESIGNATION	MANNER OF CHOOSING EXECUTIVE OR MEMBERS OF BOARD	MAIN SUBDIVISIONS OF OFFICE OR ITS DUTIES	CHIEF COORDINATE EXECUTIVE BODIES AND ADVISORY BOARDS
North Carolina	Department of Agriculture.	Commissioner of Agriculture elected by the people. Management of Department with consent and advice of a board of agriculture consisting of commissioner and 10 members appointed by governor from various congressional districts.	Publication of statistics, control of disease of live stock, quarantine, destruction of injurious insects; analyzes fertilizers and publishes results; regulation of foods and drugs.	
North Dakota	Department of Agriculture and Labor.	Commissioner of Agriculture and Labor appointed by the governor.	Publication of statistics, operation of experimental creamery, regulation of dairy industry, live stock brands, etc.	Hail Insurance Commissioner.
Ohio	Board of Agriculture.	Secretary of Agriculture elected by a bi-partisan board of 10 members who are appointed by the governor for five years. Board also acts largely in an advisory capacity and approves all appointments made by the Secretary.	Bureaus: Fair Administration, Live Stock Industry, Horticulture, Feeds and Fertilizer, Markets, Dairy and Food, Fish and Game, Agricultural Statistics.	An advisory board consisting of the Secretary of Agriculture, Dean of the Agricultural College and Director of the Experiment Station, aims to coordinate the work of all the public agricultural institutions in the state.
Oklahoma	State Board of Agriculture.	President of the Board is elected by the people for a term of four years. He is the executive officer but acts under instructions of the Board. Board is made up of President and four other members appointed by the governor.	Appointment of faculty in agricultural college, quarantining, live stock inspection, meat inspection, dairy inspection, statistics, weights and measures, etc.	

Oregon	State Board of Agriculture.	Board of five persons is appointed by the governor. Presidents of agricultural societies are ex-officio members.	Management of fairs and exhibitions.	Dairy and Food Commissioner, State Board of Horticulture with quarantine powers, State Live Stock Sanitary Board, State Lime Board.
Pennsylvania	Department of Agriculture.	Secretary of Agriculture appointed by the governor with the consent of the Senate.	Animal Industry, Plant Industry, Markets, Foods, Chemistry, Statistics.	
Rhode Island	State Board of Agriculture.	Members appointed in part by agricultural societies, agricultural college, and governor.	Insect control, control of cattle disease with quarantine powers. Analysis of fertilizers.	Food and Drug Commissioner, Commissioner of Birds, Commissioner of Forestry.
South Carolina	Department of Agriculture, Commerce and Industry	Commissioner of Agriculture, Commerce and Industry elected by the people every two years.	Chemical Laboratory, Bureau of Statistics, Inspection of Feed, Inspection of Food and Drugs, Inspection of Oils and Gasoline, Inspection of Weights and Measures, Inspection of Manufacturing Establishments.	
South Dakota	Department of Agriculture.	Commissioner of Agriculture appointed by the governor.	Statistics, reports, etc. Complete information not available.	Insurance Department handling hail insurance, Live Stock Sanitary Board, Rural Credits Department, Soldiers' Land Settlement Board, Brand Commission, Pure Food and Drug Commission.
Tennessee	Bureau of Agriculture, Statistics and Mines.	Commissioner of Agriculture, Statistics and Mines appointed by the governor.	Statistics, inspection of greenhouses and nurseries, inspection of apiaries, analysis of fertilizers, and publication of results.	State Board of Entomology.

STATE AGRICULTURAL DEPARTMENTAL ORGANIZATION—Continued

STATE	DESIGNATION	MANNER OF CHOOSING EXECUTIVE OR MEMBERS OF BOARD	MAIN SUBDIVISIONS OF OFFICE OR ITS DUTIES	CHIEF COORDINATE EXECUTIVE BODIES AND ADVISORY BOARDS
Texas	Department of Agriculture.	Commissioner of Agriculture elected by the people.	Collection and publication of statistics, protection of fruit trees, inspection of nurseries.	A board made up of the governor, commissioner and lieutenant governor, having power to designate places for establishment of local experiment stations. Dairy and Food Commissioner.
Utah	State Board of Agriculture.	Commissioner of Agriculture appointed by the governor. He is the executive officer of the Board. The Board, consisting of seven members and also appointed by the governor, appears to have merely advisory powers; although the office is designated as State Board and powers and duties are assigned to it.	Pests, live stock, weights and measures, feeds and fertilizers, diseases, standards, inspection of factories, milk, stores, hotels.	
Vermont	Department of Agriculture.	Commissioner of Agriculture appointed by the governor.	Control of insect pests and fungus diseases; inspection of apiaries and nursery stock; regulation of live stock industry; supervision of forests; collection of statistics, etc.	
Virginia	Department of Agriculture and Immigration.	Commissioner of Agriculture elected by the people for four years. A board made up of a practical farmer appointed by the governor and the president	Collection and publication of agricultural information, administration of dairy and food laws, regulation of sale of agricultural seeds.	Board of Agriculture has power to lease land for experimental purposes, and appoints auditors to audit accounts of Department of Agriculture.

Virginia (Continued)		of the Virginia College of Agriculture and Polytechnic Institute, has a part in the management and control of the Department. Office of Dairy and Food Commissioner created within Department. This official appointed by the governor.		Live Stock Sanitary Board, State Veterinarian.
Washington	Department of Agriculture.	Director of Agriculture appointed by the governor.	Agriculture, Horticulture, Dairy and Live Stock; Foods, Feeds, Drugs, and Oils, Weights and Measures.	
West Virginia	Department of Agriculture.	Commissioner of Agriculture elected by the people every four years.	Publication of biennial report, encouragement of organization of agricultural societies, regulation of commercial feed stuffs, live stock sanitation.	
Wisconsin	Department of Agriculture.	Commissioner of Agriculture appionted by the governor.	Agricultural Statistics, Entomology, Feed and Fertilizer Inspection, Horse Breeding, Immigration and Rural Planning, Live Stock Sanitation, Seed and Weed Control, State Fair, Markets, State Humane Agent.	State Fair Advisory Board, Board of Veterinary Examiners.
Wyoming				Dairy, Food and Oil Commissioner.

Index

American Farmers and The Rise of Agribusiness

Seeds of Struggle

An Arno Press Collection

Allen, Ruth Alice. **The Labor of Women in the Production of Cotton.** 1933

Bailey, L[iberty] H[yde]. **Cyclopedia of American Agriculture.** Vol. II: Crops. 1912

Bankers and Beef. 1975

[Bivins, Frank Jarris]. **The Farmer's Political Economy.** 1913

Blumenthal, Walter Hart. **American Indians Dispossessed.** 1955

Brinton, J. W. **Wheat and Politics.** 1931

Caldwell, Erskine and Margaret Bourke-White. **You Have Seen Their Faces.** 1937

Cannery Captives. 1975

Children in the Fields. 1975

The Commission on Country Life. **Report of the Commission on Country Life.** 1911

The Co-operative Central Exchange. **The Co-operative Pyramid Builder.** three vols. July 1926-January 1931

Dies, Edward Jerome. **The Plunger:** A Tale of the Wheat Pit. 1929

Dunning, N. A. **The Farmers' Alliance History and Agricultural Digest.** 1891

Everitt, J[ames] A. **The Third Power:** Farmers to the Front. 1907

The Farmer-Labor Party—History, Platform and Programs. 1975

Greeley, Horace. **What I Know of Farming.** 1871

Hill, John, Jr. **Gold Bricks of Speculation.** 1904

Howe, Frederic C. **Privilege and Democracy in America.** 1910

James, Will. **Cowboys North and South.** 1924

Kerr, W[illiam] H[enry]. **Farmers' Union and Federation Advocate and Guide.** 1919

King, Clyde L. **Farm Relief.** 1929

Kinney, J. P. **A Continent Lost—A Civilization Won.** 1937

Land Speculation: New England's Old Problem. 1975

Lange, Dorothea and Paul Schuster Taylor. **An American Exodus:** A Record of Human Erosion. 1939

Lord, Russell. **Men of Earth.** 1931

Loucks, H[enry] L. **The Great Conspiracy of the House of Morgan and How to Defeat It.** 1916

Murphy, Jerre C. **The Comical History of Montana.** 1912

The National Nonpartisan League Debate. 1975

Orr, James L. **Grange Melodies.** 1911

Proctor, Thomas H. **The Banker's Dream.** 1895

Rochester, Anna. **Why Farmers Are Poor.** 1940

Russell, Charles Edward. **The Greatest Trust in the World.** 1905

Russell, Charles Edward. **The Story of the Nonpartisan League.** 1920

Simons, A. M. **The American Farmer.** 1902

Simonsen, Sigurd Jay. **The Brush Coyotes.** 1943

Todes, Charlotte. **Labor and Lumber.** 1931

U. S. Department of Labor. **Labor Unionism in American Agriculture.** 1945

U. S. Federal Trade Commission. **Cooperative Marketing.** 1928

U. S. Federal Trade Commission. **Report of the Federal Trade Commission on Agricultural Income Inquiry.** 1938. three vols. in two

U. S. Senate Committee on Education and Labor. **Violations of Free Speech and Rights of Labor.** 1941. three vols. in one

Vincent, Leopold. **The Alliance and Labor Songster.** 1891

Wallace, Henry C. **Our Debt and Duty to the Farmer.** 1925

Watson, Thomas E. **The People's Party Campaign Book.** [1893]

[White, Roland A.]. **Milo Reno, Farmers Union Pioneer.** 1941

Whitney, Caspar. **Hawaiian America.** 1899

Wiest, Edward. **Agricultural Organization in the United States.** 1923